KT-154-668

How to trace
your family
history on the
internet

READER'S DIGEST

How to trace your family history on the internet

Published by The Reader's Digest Association Limited
LONDON • NEW YORK • SYDNEY • MONTREAL

Contents

First steps 10

Before you launch into the adventure of family history, it pays to do some groundwork. This chapter introduces you to the best family history websites, sets out the basics of family history research and then looks in more depth at what's online and where to start. You'll see the types of documents you should collect, and learn how to get the best out of your PC as your research progresses.

Building your family tree 66

Now it's time to turn detective and discover your ancestors – the building blocks for your family tree. You'll see how to work online with the key web resources – indexes to births, marriages and deaths, census returns, parish register indexes and wills. You'll then learn how to identify ancestors from old documents and how to work back through the generations to find those early forebears.

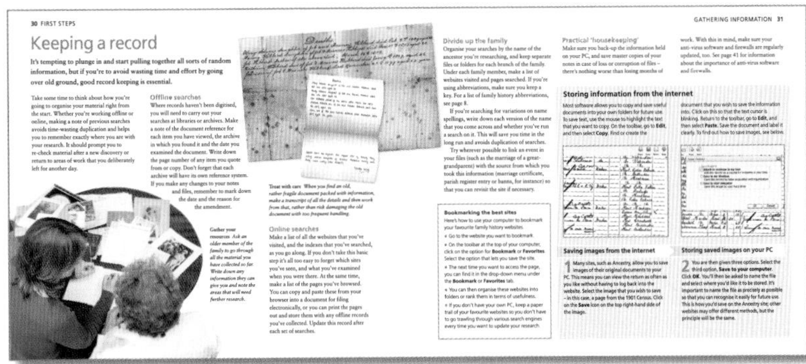

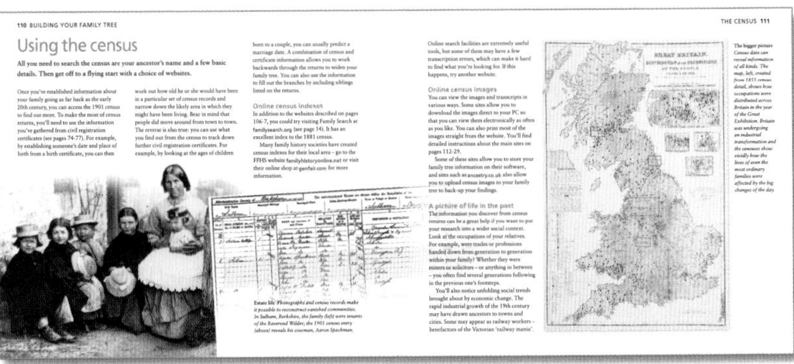

Your family's story 176

Once you've discovered who your ancestors are, you can start to bring them to life. You'll learn about how they lived day-to-day, their homes, work and hobbies, and the society to which they belonged. Using online resources you can find out about your ancestors' occupations, military service and their travels, including immigration and emigration – and even if they broke the law.

Making contact 262

When you've gathered all the information about your family, you'll probably want others to enjoy it as well. This chapter shows you how to use the internet as a tool for sharing discoveries with your immediate and extended families. Case histories will help you to trace living relatives and show you how to put your own discoveries online, including photographs, documents and family trees.

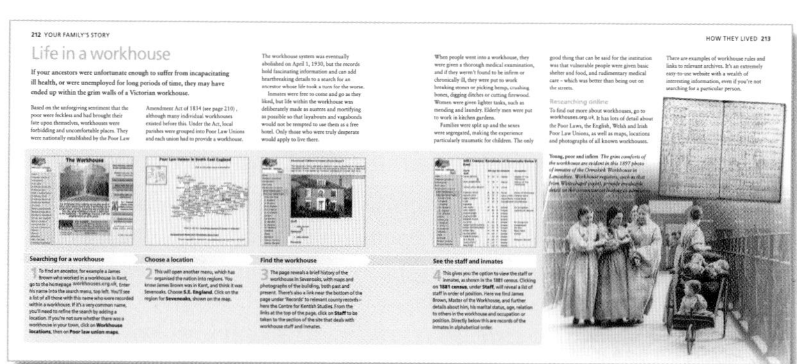
212 YOUR FAMILY'S STORY
HOW THEY LIVED 213
Life in a workhouse

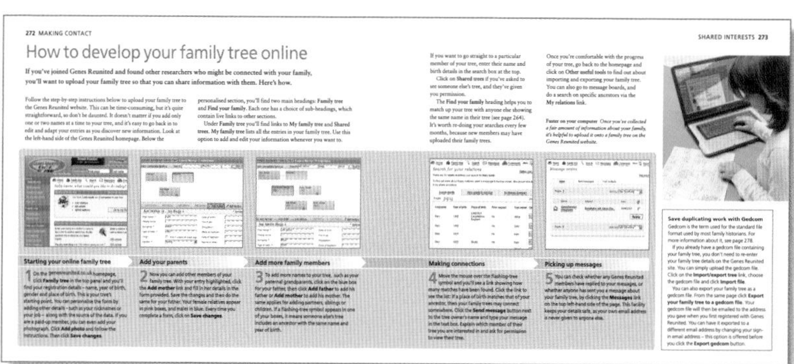
272 MAKING CONTACT
SHARED INTERESTS 273
How to develop your family tree online

About this book

Although you're probably itching to get started on your family history, it's a good idea to browse right through the book first, to get an overall view of what it contains, what the possibilities are and consider how far you want to go in the search for your ancestors.

Once you've decided what area of your family you want to research, you're ready to start making your first steps, guided on your journey by the pages of this book. You may be content simply to create a family tree for you and your immediate family to enjoy. Or maybe you have grander ideas and plan to share your findings with far-flung family members, get involved with family-tree sharing websites or even start your own blog or forum. Be prepared for surprises – you may become so absorbed by your researches that you find your initially modest plans transformed into something more ambitious.

What you'll find in the book

How to Trace Your Family History on the Internet is divided into four chapters – First steps, Building your family tree, Your family's story and Making contact (see pages 4-5 for more detail). They introduce you to family history, show you how to build a family tree, help you to find out what sort of people your ancestors were and suggest ways of making contact with your wider family.

At the back of the book, as well as the index, you'll find a 'Directory' with addresses, phone numbers and websites for all the information sources mentioned in the text, as well as other bodies that may help you to take your research even further.

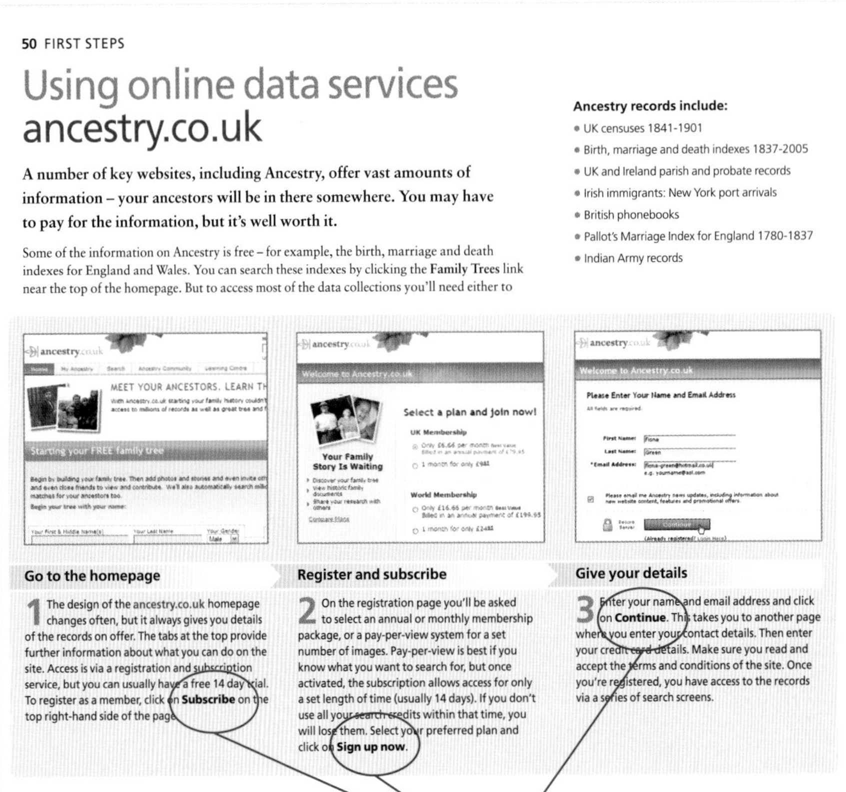

50 FIRST STEPS

Using online data services
ancestry.co.uk

A number of key websites, including Ancestry, offer vast amounts of information – your ancestors will be in there somewhere. You may have to pay for the information, but it's well worth it.

Some of the information on Ancestry is free – for example, the birth, marriage and death indexes for England and Wales. You can search these indexes by clicking the **Family Trees** link near the top of the homepage. But to access most of the data collections you'll need either to

Ancestry records include:
- UK censuses 1841-1901
- Birth, marriage and death indexes 1837-2005
- UK and Ireland parish and probate records
- Irish immigrants: New York port arrivals
- British phonebooks
- Pallot's Marriage Index for England 1780-1837
- Indian Army records

Go to the homepage

1 The design of the ancestry.co.uk homepage changes often, but it always gives you details of the records on offer. The tabs at the top provide further information about what you can do on the site. Access is via a registration and subscription service, but you can usually have a free 14 day trial. To register as a member, click on **Subscribe** on the top right-hand side of the page.

Register and subscribe

2 On the registration page you'll be asked to select an annual or monthly membership package, or a pay-per-view system for a set number of images. Pay-per-view is best if you know what you want to search for, but once activated, the subscription allows access for only a set length of time (usually 14 days). If you don't use all your search credits within that time, you will lose them. Select your preferred plan and click on **Sign up now**.

Give your details

3 Enter your name and email address and click on **Continue**. This takes you to another page where you enter your contact details. Then enter your credit card details. Make sure you read and accept the terms and conditions of the site. Once you're registered, you have access to the records via a series of search screens.

Following the steps Throughout the book, case histories are used to show you how to make the most of websites and family history software. These examples appear in a coloured band running across a page or spread, with each step clearly titled and numbered. The step text includes simple instructions, giving you the links you need to follow (with just a click of your mouse) marked in **bold type**. Above each step is an image of what you'll see on screen during the process – you'll simply need to insert your own family search details or requests at these points. Where the book shows screens from downloaded software, don't worry if the borders and buttons look a little different on your PC – this should not affect any instructions the book gives you.

Websites Wherever a website is mentioned in the text it's indicated in red type – for example, **nationalarchives.gov.uk**. To avoid repetition, the **www.** that precedes the majority of sites has been omitted. See right for more advice on accessing the websites given in this book.

ections of a page. There are also options to ownload higher-quality images – these take onger to download, but you may be able to ead the writing in the image more easily.

The Enhanced Image Viewer is designed o be used with the browser Internet Explorer, ersion 5.5 or later. It doesn't work with ome other browsers, so you may need to witch to Internet Explorer to get the best ut of the Ancestry site. To use the Enhanced nage Viewer, you'll need to install a special iece of browser software, or plug-in, on our computer (see page 40). Usually your omputer will prompt you to install the plug- is you need. If your browser settings or nti-virus software try to prevent installation, ou'll find Ancestry's help pages have the iformation to solve the problem.

Lawful union

There's a double chance that you'll be able to trace your ancestors' wedding because most Anglican marriages generate two records: of the banns and of the marriage itself. In the 19th and early 20th centuries, weddings usually took place in the bride's parish church. Then, as now, the banns would be read by the vicar on three Sundays before the wedding. The banns publicly proclaim the couple's intention so help to avoid a bigamous or unlawful marriage. Records of banns and marriages can be found at **ancestry.co.uk**.

DNA testing service

Ancestry offers a range of DNA tests which allow you to find out if others with the same surname are related to you. You can buy a testing kit through the website and send off a simple mouth swab to get the results.

Box tips Many pages in the book include an information box offering extra research tips and advice relevant to the subject covered on that page. This might give you website addresses in **red type**, as well as actions that you'd need to carry out on your own computer.

Using the case histories

You'll find your research supported by dozens of case histories showing step-by-step instructions on how to use websites to uncover information about your relatives. Many of these sites are free to use; others charge fees, although these will seem well worth it when your ancestors start to emerge.

Other case histories show you how to use national and regional archives, libraries and museums. And there are also step-by-step instructions to help you to create family trees on your computer, upload your results to the web and share your successes with family.

When a website looks different

One of the things that makes the internet so exciting – and occasionally baffling – is that new websites and new information are constantly appearing. This is particularly true of sites concerned with birth, marriage and death records, where big changes in access and archiving are underway (see page 72). Even the established websites change their appearance. Just when you've become used to the look of a homepage, you'll open it up to find it looks quite different. Don't worry: it will still function in much the same way as it did before, as the principles involved in searching for information remain constant. If you find that the information search process has changed, the site will usually prompt you.

When a web address won't work

All internet World Wide Web sites require **http://** and **www.** in front of the site name, but your browser can usually fill this in for you. You should be able to access most web sites without typing **http://** or **www.** if you're using a conventional browser such as Explorer, Firefox or Netscape.

But if a website is designed with **www.** built into the name, some browsers won't automatically fill it in for you. In this case, put in **http://** followed by **www.** and then the website name, and you'll be sure to get to the correct site. If all else fails, use Google or another search engine to find the site you're looking for.

Throughout this book we've deleted the **www.** or **http//:** prefixes, as a matter of style.

best. Taking one step at a time helps you to avoid the common pitfalls that often beset newcomers to family research. Starting slowly and gradually going from success to success works best for most people.

Advice from the experts

Experienced family historians use the following research methods to ensure the best possible results.

present as possible. To get to your great grandparents, you first need to find out as much as you can about your grandparents. Their life stories will contain clues that will make it much easier for you to find relevan documentation about their parents.

DON'T TAKE A GIANT LEAP BACKWARDS

It's tempting to jump back to the 1901 cens and see if you can find anyone who might b

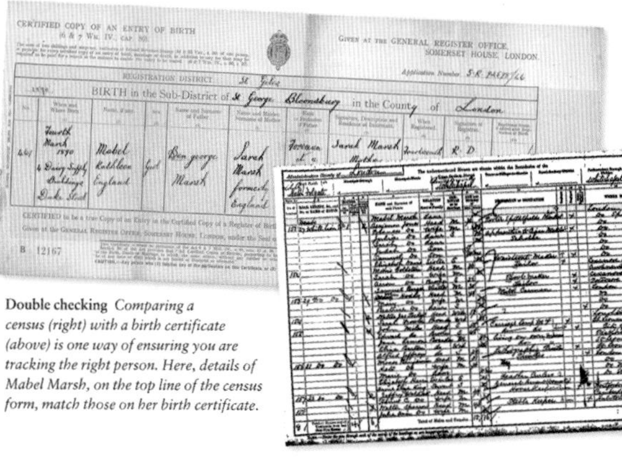

Double checking *Comparing a census (right) with a birth certificate (above) is one way of ensuring you are tracking the right person. Here, details of Mabel Marsh, on the top line of the census form, match those on her birth certificate.*

As it was written Where possible, the book shows you what the original records – such as a census return and birth certificate, above – look like. What you find online is often a transcription of a record, although you can often download and print off a copy of the original.

Family history terms and abbreviations

When you start to research your family's history, it's a good idea to get to know the sometimes unfamiliar words and phrases you'll come across. Some define family relationships and events, others crop up in documents and records.

Being consistent right from the start in your use of terms and abbreviations will help you to avoid confusion farther along the line. It also means that other family historians will understand your notes if you publish your findings online. Using proper terminology when describing family relationships will help you to organise your family tree as you go and see at a glance how people are related.

'False' relatives

Most of us grew up calling all sorts of unrelated family friends and neighbours 'auntie' or 'uncle'. These honorary relatives need to be removed from the family tree to avoid confusion. Until quite recently, 'cousin' was often used as an all-purpose word for someone who is related to you but outside your immediate family. It's also easy to get confused with the terms 'half brother' (a brother through one parent only) and 'stepbrother' (a child of your step parent, unrelated to you).

Describing family relationships

Working out the ways in which members of your family are related to one another isn't always easy. The relationships closest to you are usually fairly straightforward, but the farther back in time you go, the more complex they can become, particularly where there are divorces and remarriage. The chart on the right helps to clarify relationships.

Common family history abbreviations

b.	born	gf.	grandfather	s. and h.	son and heir
bach.	bachelor	gm.	grandmother	spin.	spinster
bapt. or bp.	baptised	ggf.	great grandfather	unm.	unmarried
bur.	buried	ggm.	great grandmother	w.	wife
by lic.	married by licence	inf.	infant	wdr.	widower
c.	christened	m.	married	wid.	widow
d.	died	mar.	married	2.	second marriage
dau.	daughter	otp.	of this parish	=	married
dsp.	died childless	s.	son	?	uncertain or unknown

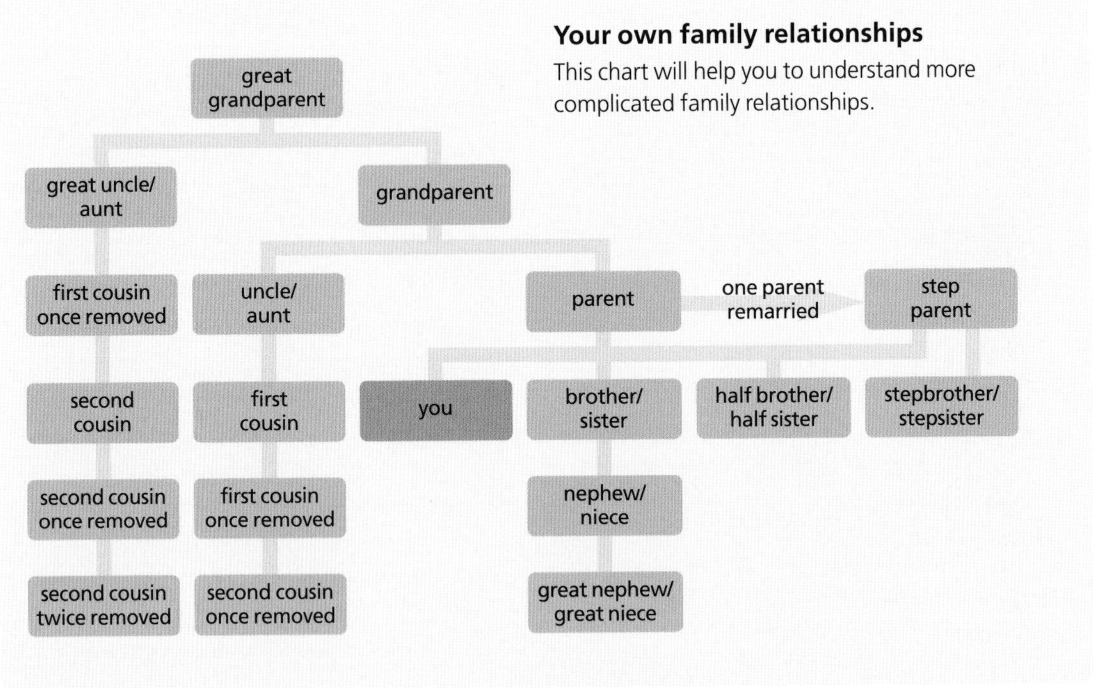

Your own family relationships
This chart will help you to understand more complicated family relationships.

Internet terms you need to know

The introduction of the internet has created a flurry of new terms that you'll need to familiarise yourself with. They'll become a useful form of shorthand for your research.

Like the internet itself, the terms that are used when you start researching your family history online continue to change and develop as people discover new ways of doing things. Keeping up with these new phrases can be challenging, but the words shown in the list here will make sure you start with the basics 'under your belt'. You may want to make a note of new phrases or acronyms that you come across.

A glossary of internet terms

Bandwidth The capacity of your internet connection

Bookmark A facility to save links to favourite websites so that they're easy to find again

Broadband A means of connecting to the internet with a bigger bandwidth, which is faster than a dial-up connection

Browser A program for viewing web pages. In this book, Internet Explorer and Mozilla Firefox are the browsers used

Cache A directory on your computer that stores recently visited web pages so they can be loaded faster the next time you visit

Cd-rom Stands for Compact Disc Read Only Memory. A disc for storing and saving information from your PC

Chat room A website that allows you to take part in real time 'chat' conversations with other website users

Cookie Information sent by a website to be stored on your PC, which allows you to revisit a site and be signed in automatically

Database A structured collection of information that's stored on a computer, or a program to manage this sort of data

Dataset Another word for database, mainly used for digitised records from a single original source

Dial-up connection Connection to the internet using a phone line and a modem

Download Saving and storing information to your computer from the internet or another computer

Email Electronic mail, a method of communicating via the internet

FAQ Stands for Frequently Asked Questions, usually found on website help pages

File Information stored on your computer, created by you, which has been dated, stored and named

Firewall A filter to prevent unauthorised access to your computer from the internet

Forum A place on a website where visitors can post messages and share information

Gateway Usually relates to websites that are a source of information and links to internet resources on a particular topic

Gedcom Stands for GENealogical Data COMmunication. A standard file format for sharing family trees between different computers or programs

Html Stands for Hypertext Mark-up Language, the way in which a web page tells the browser how to display material on the web page

ISP Internet Service Provider – the company that supplies your internet connection

Log off To disconnect from a website

Log on To identify yourself to a website to gain access to its content or to facilities specifically intended for you

Network A series of computers, all connected so people can work together and share files

Online Connected to or located on the internet

Password A secret word that allows only a specific person to access certain internet resources

Portal A site that offers a single entry point for a selection of internet resources

Search engine A website that allows you to search for other websites by using key words; also a similar facility which searches an index of a single website

Service provider The company that supplies your internet service

Software Computer programs that can be installed on your computer to allow you to carry out certain tasks

Spam Junk email sent to large numbers of email addresses at once

URL Stands for Uniform Resource Locator – the unique web address for a web page

Webmaster The person who runs a website

Website A group of web pages in the same location

First steps

Exploring your family's history is a wonderful adventure. Beginning with your living relatives and any old photographs or documents you can find, you can embark on a journey into the past that will enable you to discover your ancestry and create your family tree. This chapter introduces you to the many resources available to help you.

What is family history?

Your aim may be to draw up a family tree filled with your ancestors. But family history is so much more than that – an enthralling voyage of discovery, back through time, to discover what shaped you.

The growth of the internet and the popularity of television programmes about family history have sparked off huge interest in finding out more about our past. The sense of achievement in tracing our ancestors has added to the appeal of this enthralling hobby, and more and more people are motivated by the desire to create a legacy to pass on to their children and grandchildren.

Family links *Not only does a family share its genes, but it has a vast, shared history, too. Careful questioning will provide vital links.*

Where did it all start?

In early medieval times, fighting knights adopted distinctive symbols, representing their family, to identify themselves. These were displayed on shields and on a surcoat worn over armour: the word 'surcoat' is the origin of 'coat' as in 'coat of arms'. At this time, only the nobility had coats of arms.

Modern times *The arms granted to Dr Norman McIver in 2006 reflect his working life. His service as a Ghurka is represented by the kukri or short sword in the boar's mouth, while the red of the shield indicates a career in finance.*

By the late 13th century, lesser nobility and gentlemen had also started to adopt coats of arms. A specific coat of arms was passed down through the male line of the family, but important marriages were recognised by the inclusion of some of the symbols used by the bride's family, so that new emblems evolved. A daughter was entitled to inherit the family coat of arms intact only if the owner – or 'armiger' – died without a male heir.

In 1530, Henry VIII sent heralds throughout England and Wales to register each coat of arms. Every family using one had to justify its claim through genealogical tables and proofs.

As a result of these investigations – or 'heraldic visitations' – many people had to give up their coats of arms when they couldn't prove their link to nobility. The regularity of

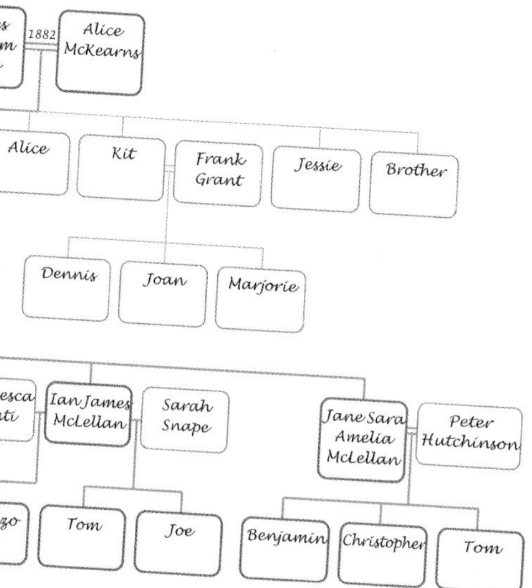

the visitations resulted in a wealth of records, mainly in the form of pedigrees – simple, linear family trees going back three to five generations from the time of compilation. The earliest genealogists were members of wealthy or noble families trying to establish the family's right to coats of arms, by tracing their forebears through heraldic records and thus proving their noble ancestry.

Today, these records are held by the College of Arms in London (see Directory), where royal heralds continue to check claims and issue new coats of arms. There may be a number of coats of arms for any one family, as coats were attached to individuals, not to surnames.

The internet makes it so easy

Until the 1990s, family history research involved visiting local, county and national record offices to trawl through records. Now, with the ease and speed of the internet, it's all so much faster. The internet has chat rooms where you can swap hints and tips, get advice if you are stuck, and where people will share their stories – especially if they discover a link to your family. Message boards are an excellent place to meet people to discuss your findings; you'll find a good selection if you key 'family history message boards' into Google.

Not everything is available online yet – you may still have to visit some record offices – but the advantage is that many of them have exhibitions and displays which may help to bring the past to life for you.

Two routes to choose from

When you decide to start tracing your family's history, there are two main areas you can focus on. One is building a family tree and peopling it with as many ancestors as you can find. The other involves investigating a particular story, or ancestor, in detail.

- To begin with, most people choose the family tree route, because it gives you an overview of your family. The obvious starting point is your paternal line – you probably share the same surname and can track it back into the past. This might be quite straightforward if you have an unusual name.
- If your name is more common – Jones, Smith, MacDonald or Murphy, for example – it might be easier to start several lines of enquiry at once. This way, you'll find as many direct ancestors as possible. Remember that the number of people to think about and trace doubles each time you work back a generation – you have four grandparents, eight great grandparents, 16 great great grandparents, and an impressive 32 great great great grandparents.

Searching through so many generations doesn't have to be daunting, if you start with what you already know – your immediate living family. Start by asking your parents and grandparents, uncles and aunts to tell you what they remember. If they're no longer alive, it's possible you may already have – or can get access to – family documents that will point you in the right direction.

Family history societies

- There are many family history groups you can join. The largest is the Society of Genealogists, which was founded in 1911 and has more than 15,000 members worldwide and a research library in London. Further details of its services can be found on the website **sog.org.uk**.

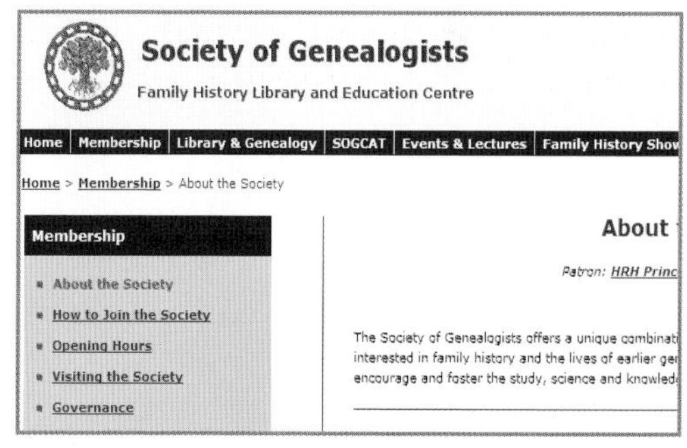

- There's also a vast network of local groups, most of which come under the umbrella of the Federation of Family History Societies (FFHS) at **ffhs.org.uk**. Joining a society gives you access to resources such as surname databases and local indexes. Consider joining several groups, one near you, perhaps, and others in the places your ancestors came from.

Ten sites to get you started

There are hundreds of websites for family historians, but here are ten that are particularly useful as they're easy to use and packed with information – just what you need for your online adventure.

Some of these sites offer good basic information for beginners, others give you useful links to family history material on the web. There are sites to help you to find distant relatives, and sites with the historical information you'll need to build up a picture of your ancestors' lives.

There are, of course, hundreds of other key resources, many of which will be discussed within this book, but these ten represent the wide range of sites you may want to visit. They'll give you an idea of the astonishing amount of material that's available on the web.

A family business
Jewish immigrant Lazar Atlas, with his children Minnie and Maurice, stands in front of his grocery shop in Cheetham, Manchester, in the 1890s. If your ancestors owned a shop in a town or city their names and addresses – perhaps even their ages – would have been recorded regularly in official documents such as tax records and local business directories. These records can be accessed through the sites on the following pages, and may give a good insight into the business successes (or otherwise) of previous generations of your family.

Great websites to begin your search

Most of these sites are free to use and will give you a good idea of the wealth of information available to you online.

familyrecords.gov.uk

FamilyRecords is especially helpful for anyone new to family history as it gives an overview of the collections of records in the UK – census returns, birth, marriage and death certificates and wills – along with descriptions of the records and practical advice about obtaining copies of them (see page 42).

bbc.co.uk/familyhistory

Visit BBC Family History for top tips on getting started. Its content is linked to the television series *Who Do You Think You Are?* and the site provides a list of useful links to other organisations. There are also lively message boards where you can exchange information with other family historians.

genuki.org.uk

Genuki is designed to serve as a 'virtual reference library' of family history that's relevant to the UK and the Republic of Ireland. It's run by volunteers, and there are comprehensive sections devoted to every part of the British Isles, including every county, with details of record offices and links to online material. For many counties, there are even pages for individual towns and parishes (see page 44).

cyndislist.com

Cyndi's List is a comprehensive site that has links to more than 200,000 online resources. Although it's maintained in the USA, Cyndi's List has a strong international section that includes the UK and the Republic of Ireland (see page 46).

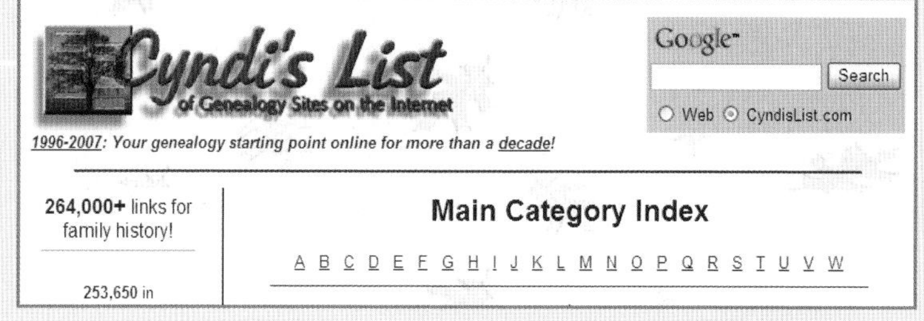

nationalarchives.gov.uk

The National Archives is the home of Britain's historical records. Its extensive website has material for everyone from the novice to the expert. There are basic guides to all the main national records of interest to family historians, and it's an essential site for anyone with ancestors in the army or navy. There's an online catalogue, and directories of both local record offices and the archives that those offices hold.

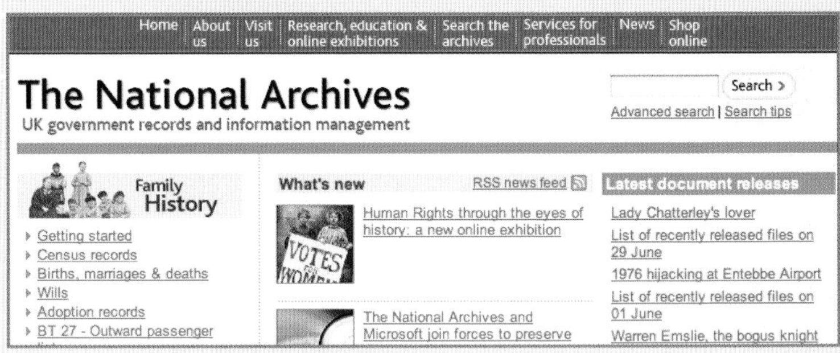

rootsweb.com

RootsWeb is one of the oldest genealogy sites on the web. Its main value is as the home of thousands of family history mailing lists and message boards, devoted to places, surnames, occupations and other useful topics. Its WorldConnect service allows you to put your family tree online free of charge, and it has a good range of guides for beginners.

ancestry.co.uk

For an annual subscription fee, Ancestry provides access to its expanding worldwide collection of records and indexes. Its databases include census returns, birth, marriage and death indexes, Irish and UK probate records, old telephone directories, military service papers, passenger lists and arrival records for the Port of New York (see page 50).

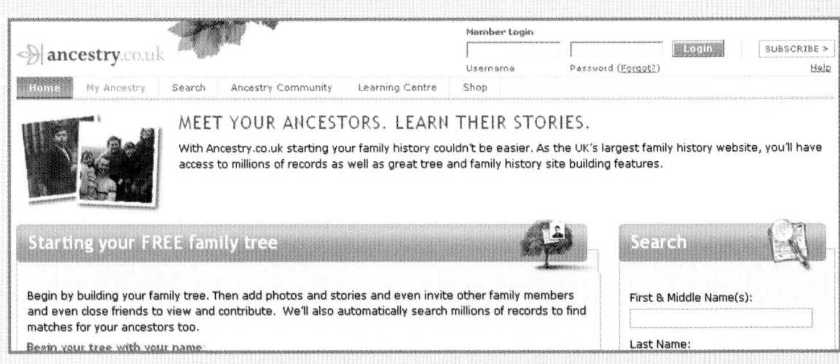

findmypast.com

Findmypast is a rich source of information for family historians looking for English and Welsh records. It holds indexes for civil registration and census returns, military indexes – particularly for the First World War – and migration records, which include passport applications and ships' passenger lists. There's also a wide range of occupational records. For more about the website, see page 52.

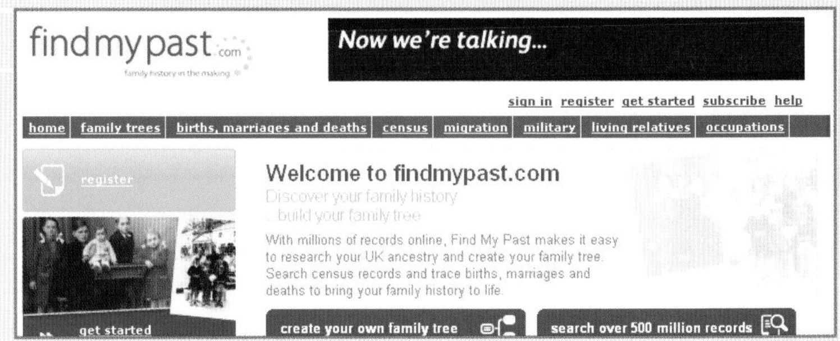

Tracing rural records

A husband and wife labouring in fields might seem impossible to trace, but if they were tenant farmers or workers on the estate of a landowner, the records of their tenancy and the rent they paid may be shown in the estate archives. If the estate has remained in the same family, the archives may still be with them, but often they have been deposited in county record offices. Other useful resources include census records and some school archives, which may hold details of pupils' parents. You'll find links to county record offices and archives on websites such as Genuki and The National Archives.

familysearch.org

Almost all the sites with large data collections are commercial and require payment. But FamilySearch is run by the Church of Jesus Christ of Latter-day Saints (the Mormons) and is free of charge. It has an index to the 1881 census of England and Wales, and millions of baptismal entries from parish registers. The Mormons have ambitious plans to add images to the site and millions more data entries (see page 54).

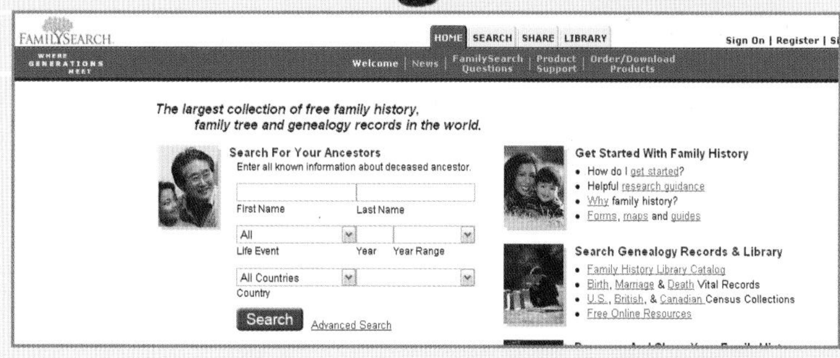

genesreunited.co.uk

GenesReunited is one of the most popular UK sites for family historians. Anyone can upload a family tree for other users to see, and the aim is to help you to find people whose ancestors match yours. You need to register (which is free) to use it, and other people will be able to contact you. But to initiate contact with someone who has put their tree on the site, you'll need to pay the modest subscription (see page 272).

Gathering information

The best place to start researching your family's past is with some careful offline detective work. Then you'll be ready to tap into the amazing resources of the internet.

Start your search offline

You may be surprised by how much you can find out about your relatives even before you venture online. Pulling together this information is vital preparation for the journey further into your family's past.

Picture clues *Notes on photographs can provide important family history clues. Here, they reveal that William Wilcox of Fairford (right) was a handyman. The cottage that he and his father rented can be seen in the background.*

First, write down everything you know about your family – starting with yourself. Then include all you know about your nearest relatives – your parents, siblings, uncles, aunts and grandparents. Include as much detail as you can, making an accurate list of the full names, and dates of birth, marriage and death (where applicable), for all the members of your immediate family.

Add additional data such as where people lived or worked, and how and when they moved around the country. There's a lot of geography involved in tracing your family history, as you'll discover when you begin looking at certificates and census returns, so invest in a good atlas or street map.

Identifying the gaps

This isn't simply a fact-finding mission; you are also highlighting areas that need research. It's unlikely that you'll be given names and biographical detail on all eight ancestors from three generations back, so you'll need to expand on what you're told. This might mean talking to more distant relations, or finding official documents such as birth, marriage and death certificates or census returns.

Family portrait *A tenant farmer, Jacob Pady (left), with his wife and children in a 1900 photograph taken on his farm at Colyton in Devon.*

Set yourself a goal

It's a good idea to set limits, because it's easy to lose your focus as you gather information. Define what you want to achieve, and your research won't get muddled or lose direction. Decide whether you want to concentrate on one strand – a particular ancestor or a specific story – or work back in time and discover relatives you know nothing about.

If you go for the latter, decide whether to work back in a linear fashion, from generation to generation focusing only on direct forebears, or perhaps to branch out sideways and find siblings and cousins.

Whether you choose to concentrate on one side of the family or complete the whole picture, make sure you know exactly what you're looking for and why, every time you start a new search – online or off.

Using record sheets

One way of keeping information is by filling in record sheets, particularly if you're getting details from electronically held data sources. Good examples can be found on the BBC website **bbc.co.uk/familyhistory**. Download and print as many of these sheets as you need.

BBC FAMILY HISTORY

Sheet ....

Contd ....

First information sheet

NAME	Relation to you
Birth date/place	Death date/place
SPOUSE 1	SPOUSE 2
Name	

Keeping records

Organise your findings right from the outset and take clear notes as you do your research. Keep track of the searches you've done, make a note of record offices you've visited and record each website that you search. This will save you wasting a lot of time – and some money – going over old ground.

Organise the paperwork

Once you start building up photocopies, print-outs from websites, notes, photographs and duplicate certificates on different branches of the family or individual ancestors, you'll want to be able to access them quickly. Work out a system of storage folders that suits you. There's no 'correct' method: just be consistent in the way you organise information in each folder. You can then keep your folders in chronological order, or cross-reference them by name.

Collecting family memories

Your parents and grandparents are a living link to the past, so ask them to tell you about the family. They should be able to provide information about more distant relatives – people you may never even have met.

Talking to your relatives is one of the most important ways of finding out about previous generations. Reminiscences will give you the facts – names, dates and places linked to your family. But just as importantly, they add colour. What were these people like? Are there family secrets to be discovered? See what you can find out about the individual characteristics, likes and dislikes, loves and tragedies, occupations and skills, hobbies and pastimes of your ancestors. Capturing this oral history is a vital process that will allow you to preserve and pass on information to the next generation.

You can't rush the early stages of gathering information: it takes time and tact. It also requires careful thought and planning beforehand. Use these guidelines to help you to interview your relatives.

Set clear objectives

Before you talk to someone, think carefully about what you want to find out.

- What do you want to achieve from the interview?
- Do you want to talk about one particular ancestor, or do you want to collect some stories about a range of people?

You may achieve more if you focus on only one line of questioning at a time, otherwise you could confuse your subject.

Write down some questions

A good way to start is to write down some prompting questions in advance. These will help you to maintain your focus and not get sidetracked during the interview.

- Make the questions clear and relevant.
- Focus, where possible, on concrete things to begin with – the person's full name, place and date of birth and where they grew up.

Answering these straightforward questions may 'warm up' a reluctant relative, who'll then decide to elaborate and give you much greater detail or perhaps feel more willing to talk about more sensitive subjects. If you're lucky, a line of questioning will trigger valuable memories.

Record the interview

It's a good idea to record your talk – partly so that you have an accurate record, but also to ensure that you have something to pass on to future generations.

- You can use a simple notebook, but these days there's so much technology available that it would be a shame to miss the opportunity to create a fuller record.
- After obtaining the subject's permission, you could use a camcorder, tape recorder or digital camera. Capturing how the relative looked and sounded will add an enormous amount to the records you create.

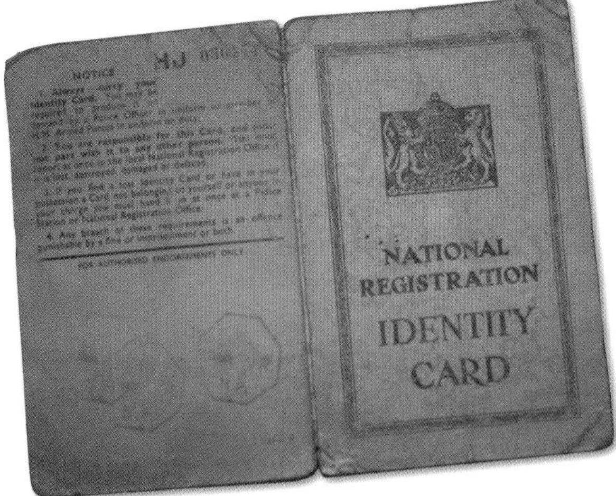

Wartime ID *During the Second World War, everyone, even children, had to carry an identity card like this one, giving the holder's age, occupation, marital status and home address.*

- Later, you might want to incorporate the interview onto your own website (see page 304), but do get permission before putting any personal material online.

Be a good interviewer

Good interviewing techniques are essential. Relatives usually relish the chance to tell stories from their past – but not always, so try to be as sensitive as possible.

- Make sure your subject is relaxed and happy to tell their tale.
- Never push someone on a topic that they are clearly uncomfortable talking about. Respect their wishes if they don't want to talk. You may be able to find the missing information from someone else.
- Be patient, and offer to come back another time, if you sense your relative is tiring.

Verify your facts

Although your relative may be adamant about a date of birth or a family story, don't accept everything you hear as fact. Memories can play tricks on elderly people, and some of what you hear may not be accurate.

- Take the information away and verify everything with official documents, as this will save you problems later.
- Try to compare versions of the same story as told by different relatives. Where accounts overlap, there's likely to be an element of truth. When they vary, do more research.

False relatives and nicknames

Those aunties and uncles being referred to may not necessarily be blood relations. They could be longstanding friends that have earned honorary family status.

- Establish exactly who is a blood relative through official documentation.
- Make sure you find the full, given names, and check official documents, because pet names or nicknames used by the family can confuse your search. The youngest daughter in a family may have been nicknamed 'Dolly' by her sisters, because she was so much smaller than they were – but you won't find her under that name on any birth certificate.

Starting from scratch

Even if you have no living relatives, you can still start creating your own family tree. Begin by looking at your own birth certificate. From this, you might be able to get an approximate date for your parents' marriage, which could lead you to their marriage certificate and details of their parents.

Ten leading questions

Here are some questions you might ask close family members and elderly relatives. Some could release a wealth of memories and vital clues.

1. Will you give me your full name, your date of birth and where you were born, and the date and place of your marriage?
2. What can you tell me about your parents and grandparents? Do you know your grandmothers' maiden names?
3. Did anyone have a nickname?
4. Can you tell me anything about the jobs our ancestors did?
5. How did they look and what were they like? And have you got any photographs I could borrow?
6. Can you remember the house you grew up in? Or even the address?
7. What schools did the family attend? Did anyone go on to university – if so, which one?
8. Did the family go to church – if so, which one?
9. Do you have childhood memories of relatives? Are you sure they were blood relations?
10. Can you remember any family christenings, weddings or funerals?

Often, older people who've experienced traumatic events or difficult childhoods simply refuse to talk about the past. In such a case, you could try, with the utmost tact, to ask them to write down their memories and leave the pages to you in their will.

Discovering the stuff of life

Tracing your family history isn't just about dates and facts – it's also about the real, flesh-and-blood personalities in your family. Rummaging through family memorabilia can tell you a lot about them.

When you look at photographs of your great grandparents or other ancestors, they may seem a little formal and staid. But behind those 'proper' appearances were real characters – brave, weak, adventurous or even totally outrageous. It's only through discovering the things they left behind, or sent to other people, that you start to get a fuller idea of them as human beings.

If you're lucky, your older relations will have a collection of memorabilia that can help you to build up a picture of your family – old football programmes, ration books, letters and so on. These are often kept in drawers or files, a scrapbook or a precious box of 'treasures', and are powerful clues.

OFFICIAL PAPERS Birth, marriage or death certificates are the most obvious starting point. Official documents will usually have clear, verifiable data on them. Find as many as possible, because not only will these help to confirm – or disprove – some of the information you've already been given, but they'll also save you

Hidden treasures *Memorabilia and documents such as letters, wills, medals and certificates are important in rounding out the realities behind the pictures. They tell the story of personalities and circumstances that the official records omit.*

time and money when it comes to buying certificates online. The last thing you want is to duplicate anything that already exists within the family.

WILLS Usually written near the time of death, wills give a snapshot not only of assets and funds, but also of family and friends. A will might tell you more about the person's most treasured possessions. It might mention land, a house or an occupation – or even reveal a long-hidden family secret.

FAMILY BIBLE If you're lucky enough to have a family Bible, it could hold information vital to your search, such as names and dates of former owners and their families. Look in the Bible for its year of publication – any information that precedes that date will have been written down from memory after the Bible was acquired, and needs to be verified.

BITS AND PIECES Printed ephemera, such as cinema tickets and theatre programmes, give an insight into the person's standard of living as well as their pastimes and hobbies. School reports are fascinating, as they show people in their formative years – through the eyes of their witty or acerbic teachers.

Respect people's privacy

Remember that items of family memorabilia, and especially letters and postcards, can be extremely personal. They should never be taken or read without the express permission of the owner. You'll need to be sensitive and diplomatic in this area of your research.

Serving their country

With two World Wars in the 20th century, as well as National Service, your ancestors may well have served in the military. This generates memorabilia such as service papers, medals – often giving details of regiments or ships that your ancestor served with – and uniform insignia. Keep a look out for other items, such as letters and postcards sent home while on active service, ration books and identity cards. It's a good idea to check whether any of your forebears kept diaries: these can give fascinating insights into wartime life, both at home and abroad. To deal with the shortage of manpower for the Army's peace-time commitments, National Service was started in 1949. Young men had to do 12 months' full-time service followed by five years' reserve service. It wasn't long before the 12 month period was extended to 18 months – and in 1950 it went up to two years. The last men were called up in 1960, and National Service finally ended in 1962.

Finding clues in photos

Family photographs are our windows on the past. If you're lucky, you may have one or two portraits dating from the 19th century. Family photo albums can help you to put faces to some of the names in your family tree.

Go through photographs with your elderly relatives and ask them what they can remember about the picture – who's in it, and when and where it was taken. You may find the names of people in a photo or the date it was taken written on the back. This could involve removing a photo from its frame – which may uncover further hidden treasures, such as a newspaper cutting or a revealing letter.

MAKE A COPY If the picture's not yours, borrow it or take a digital shot and download it to your computer; then record any names that appear on the back. Once you've found a name or two, the missing names should fall into place.

Tracing the studio *The photographer's name and address can be useful research tools, particularly if written records survive.*

STUDIO PHOTOS Formal occasions were often captured by a local professional. If you can't recognise people or events in a photo, look for the address of the photographer's studio, as in the pictures shown below. You may be able to find the studio through old local trade directories (see pages 230-3) which could point to when and where the picture was taken. The studio's address might also suggest the area where these ancestors lived, as it was probably within walking distance.

OUTDOOR PHOTOS Cars, buses and buildings in the picture can help you to date or locate the shot. A house or street name may lead you to a family home, as might a photo taken at a local landmark, especially if you can link it to surviving family letters referring to an outing.

FASHION OR 'SUNDAY BEST'? Look at what the subjects are wearing. Your local archive, studies centre or museum, or even the Victoria and Albert Museum (see Directory), may be able to help you to date their clothing. Clothes can also cast light on your ancestors' social standing, but remember that people tended to dress up for a session at the photographer's and their 'Sunday best' could be 20 years out of date.

Harness technology

Faded or damaged pictures can be restored at a photographic or print shop. Digitally scanning your photographs and uploading them onto your computer will allow you to embed them into an online family tree (see page 312), or email them to relatives who may be able to identify people and events.

Military detail *Puttees and the motorbike date this photo to the First World War. Badges, buttons and buckles, if visible, give useful clues. Military websites may be able to help you to identify a regiment* *(see page 192).*

Preserve and protect

Keep precious photographs and documents away from heat, light and damp and, where possible, store them in sturdy boxes. You can buy containers designed for storing fragile memorabilia from **memories-nostalgia.com**.

Digital scrapbooking is another option. You can now create virtual photo albums that can be arranged page by page and printed out. There's a range of software available to help you to do this – from LumaPix FotoFusion at **lumapix.com**.

Other websites, such as Flickr (see page 318) and Nations Memorybank (see page 322), allow you to upload and organise your family photographs online.

Clues in the background

Lots of old family photos are just informal snapshots of the family at home or enjoying a day out. You can often date these photographs – at least to the nearest decade – by looking carefully at background detail as well as what the subjects are wearing and doing.

In this picture, a number of clues tell you that it was probably taken in the 1930s. The chair could have been made in the early 20th century but it has obviously been re-covered and the ends of the arms look a little worn.

The fireplace is a Victorian register grate, a type first used after 1850, but the nursery fireguard is early 20th century. The fire-irons show that it was a working fireplace, typical of most homes until after the Second World War, and the sprigged wallpaper is typical of the period between 1910 and 1920.

Above the fireplace, a selection of photographs pinned to the wall could be of loved ones killed in the First World War. On the mantelpiece, a pocket watch could have belonged to a close family member.

When you look at your own photos, remember that pieces of furniture or grandfather clocks may predate the photo by decades. But other items such as lamps, radios and record players are likely to be contemporary and may be a recognisable and easily dated design. For help with dating items, see page 26.

Period pieces

If you're lucky enough to find items from your family's past tucked away in an attic or drawer, or if you have keepsakes handed down from generation to generation, you may be able to make fascinating discoveries about your ancestors, their lives and their interests.

Uncovering the stories behind inherited objects is as enthralling as investigating the 'official' side of your ancestors' lives, and will open up a whole new area of research. So many items have a story to tell, from everyday articles such as toys, ceramics, pottery and silverware to more cherished possessions like jewellery, retirement clocks, prizes for sports achievement or a family bible.

Sharp dresser *Finding a mini dress like this by Mary Quant from 1967 tells you that a relative kept up with the fashions.*

The way people looked

You may come across clothing that belonged to an ancestor, or military keepsakes such as medals or badges. These are valuable clues that can be dated, enabling you to find a regiment or identify a relative, as well as telling you something about their lifestyle. Even modern items are important: a pair of platform shoes, a mini-skirt or a silk chiffon evening gown will tell you that your relative followed the latest trends.

Old family photos yield clues, too, from clothes, locations or the type of event, such as a wedding or street party. Try your local museum for help on dating items in a photo, or the Victoria and Albert Museum (see box, right), or visit the 'Date an old photograph' pages on **cartes.freeuk.com/**. For military photos, watch for cap badges, ranking insignia and regimental crests.

Getting the picture *If you find old photos but no dates, you might be able to place them by changes in fashion. In the first photo, the woman wears a full, wide dress popular in the 1860s. By the time of the next photo, in the 1880s, dresses were more fitted with tight high-necked bodices, while the final picture shows the wide-brimmed hat popular towards the end of the 19th century.*

Jewellery that has been handed down from generation to generation may have more than just sentimental value. Silver can be identified through its hallmark, and many marks are listed online. The Silvermine website at **freespace. virgin.net/a.data/** will help.

Treasures in the home

Most families have collected some ceramic pieces over time. There's usually information on the base of plates or other items that you can use to either date the piece, or work out the name of the potter or factory. If it's a small, local company, you can start to narrow down where your ancestors might have lived. Websites to help you to date and identify ceramics include the International Ceramic Directory (see box, right).

Toys that have been treasured and handed down over the years also shed light on the childhoods of our ancestors. Those from recent decades are easiest to place, but you may find older toys that could be dated. A hollow-cast lead soldier, for instance, might be marked 'William Britain',

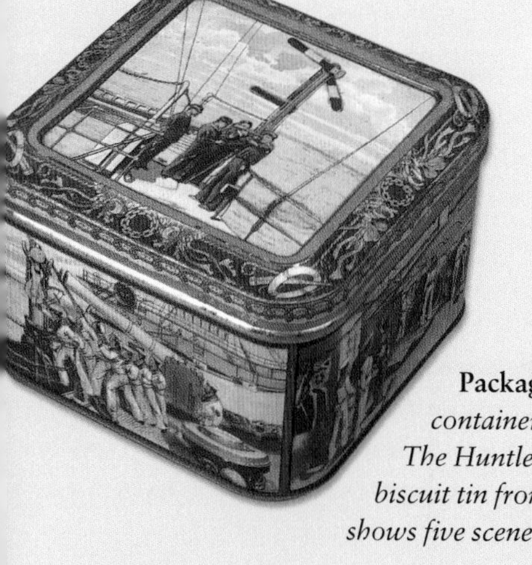

Packaging clues *Even a container can be revealing. The Huntley & Palmer's biscuit tin from 1900, left, shows five scenes of Navy life.*

Boys toys *If you find Dinky toys, they're quite likely to date from the 1950s (right), when they became a huge craze for Britain's boys.*

a British company that started making such figures in 1893. They all stand on a flat base and those made before 1912 are marked simply 'William Britain'. After 1912, 'Ltd.' was included with the name, and after 1917 'England' was added.

You may also find dolls or teddy bears packed away. Many dolls are marked on the back of the neck, below the hairline, with the manufacturer's stamp, which helps to identify both maker and date. The Museum of Childhood (see box, right) has more than 8,000 dolls in its collection, and the website may help you to date any that you find.

Counting the time

Clocks, watches or other memorabilia presented at retirement or on another occasion can provide valuable information about an ancestor. Look for an inscription that might say when your relative received the gift, the company or organisation he worked for, his period of service and the position he held.

If there's no inscription, the style of watch can tell you much: a hunter pocket watch (with a cover) or half-hunter (with a window in the cover) were popular in the mid to late 19th century and could reveal an interest in country pursuits. Wrist watches came to the fore during the First World War, as the most practical kind of timepiece for use in the trenches. Then, as the popularity of motoring spread from the 1920s, curved watches, known as drivers' watches, became fashionable – the driver could still read the face with both hands on the steering wheel.

Show time *Before the wrist watch there was the pocket watch. The example below, from around 1900, has an open glass face, which meant its use was at least partly decorative.*

Websites to use for dating objects

The following organisations and websites can help you to identify and date the memorabilia you find, adding colour and interest to the ancestors on your family tree.

Angels costumiers fancydress.com
A costume-hire company that supplies costumes for films and museums as well as to the general public. A look around their website can help you to date period clothing.

Victoria and Albert Museum vam.ac.uk
The London museum is a great resource for clothing, jewellery and antiques. A visit to the website can get you started dating your fashions and other memorabilia.

Museum of Childhood vam.ac.uk/moc Part of the Victoria and Albert museum, the Museum of Childhood has a wide range of all kinds of toys through the ages, including dolls, teddy bears and games.

International Ceramic Directory ceramic-link.de Pottery and porcelain marks from all over their world can be seen and checked on the website. Use it to help you to identify your finds.

National Maritime Museum nmm.ac.uk
The museum has a large collection of jewellery dating from the 16th to early 20th centuries, including buckles, broaches, rings and watches. It can help you to find out more about the objects in your collection that have an 'official' or 'maritime' look.

Imperial War Museum iwm.org.uk
The website (see also page 195) includes a large collection of medals and other war-related objects. It has pictures and information that help you not only to identify medals, but also to find when and why they were awarded.

Secrets of successful research

When you begin investigating your family history, it's tempting to dive into the first website or record office you come across, to see what you can find. Wait, follow these simple guidelines and you'll be far more successful.

It may not sound thrilling, but you'll find a methodical approach to family history is best. Taking one step at a time helps you to avoid the common pitfalls that often beset newcomers to family research. Starting slowly and gradually going from success to success works best for most people.

Advice from the experts

Experienced family historians use the following research methods to ensure the best possible results.

WORK BACK IN TIME Go back through the generations, starting from as close to the present as possible. To get to your great grandparents, you first need to find out as much as you can about your grandparents. Their life stories will contain clues that will make it much easier for you to find relevant documentation about their parents.

DON'T TAKE A GIANT LEAP BACKWARDS
It's tempting to jump back to the 1901 census and see if you can find anyone who might be a relative. Unless you have researched and identified actual family members in a precise location, you're likely to be disappointed. You may have to pay for some searches to be done, so it would be a waste of money to go after certificates of people who might not be related to you at all.

WORK FROM KNOWN FACT TO KNOWN FACT
If you come across a gap in the trail leading back to an ancestor, don't assume a link. Instead, try to find some supporting evidence from another source. If you can't find any evidence, you'll be unable to prove that particular connection conclusively, which means that any work you do beyond this point will be based on supposition – and will be tainted with an element of doubt. Come back to it later, when you've found evidence.

QUESTION OFFICIAL DATA Family historians rely heavily on official sources such as civil registration certificates for births, marriages and deaths; census records; parish register entries and wills. But this data is only as accurate as the person recording or providing it – and some of your ancestors might have given false information for a variety of personal reasons. An example is the census: these were taken every ten years, but when people's stated ages are compared over the decades, the age gaps often don't add up. Where possible, find at least two different sources that give the same details; that way there's more chance of the 'facts' being true.

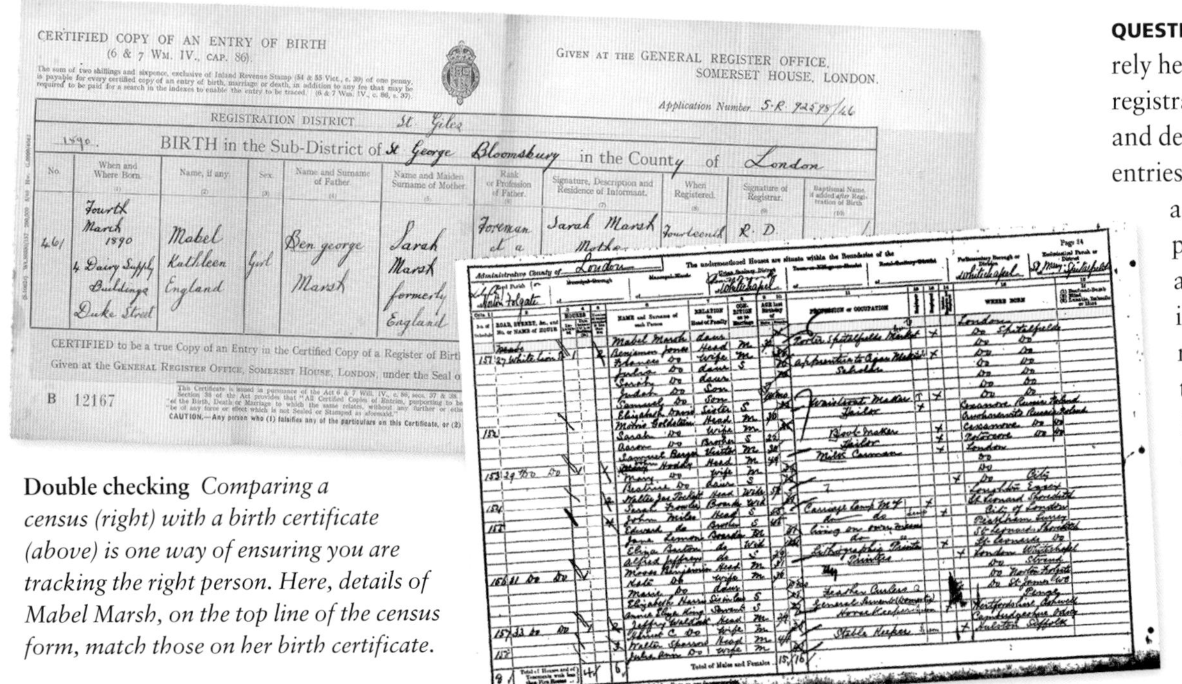

CERTIFIED COPY OF AN ENTRY OF BIRTH (6 & 7 Wm. IV., cap. 86)

GIVEN AT THE GENERAL REGISTER OFFICE, SOMERSET HOUSE, LONDON.

Application Number S.R. 92578/46

REGISTRATION DISTRICT St Giles

1890. BIRTH in the Sub-District of St George Bloomsbury in the County of London

No.	When and Where Born	Name, if any	Sex	Name and Surname of Father	Name and Maiden Surname of Mother	Rank or Profession of Father	Signature, Description and Residence of Informant	When Registered	Signature of Registrar
461	Fourth March 1890 4 Dairy Supply Buildings Duke Street	Mabel Kathleen England	Girl	Ben george Marsh	Sarah Marsh formerly England	Foreman	Sarah Marsh Mother	Fourteenth	R. D.

CERTIFIED to be a true Copy of an Entry in the Certified Copy of a Register of Birt…

Given at the General Register Office, Somerset House, London, under the Seal o…

B 12167

Double checking *Comparing a census (right) with a birth certificate (above) is one way of ensuring you are tracking the right person. Here, details of Mabel Marsh, on the top line of the census form, match those on her birth certificate.*

BE WARY OF ONLINE DATA Information that appears on the internet isn't always true. Errors can creep into any transcribed information, so don't take it as an indisputable fact – verify it by looking on at least one other website.

CHECK THE ORIGINAL SOURCES Individuals who put data online don't always cite the original source of the information they've uploaded onto their website. But if they do, make a habit of verifying it offline, to ensure that it has been transcribed or used in the right way. You certainly don't want to incorporate someone else's mistakes into your own work.

SEE IF THE FACTS REALLY FIT Resist importing data into your own findings unless you're sure there's a link. It's tempting to link into a family tree you've found online when the facts appear to fit. Stick to the rule of working back in time until you've reached the relevant period, and then see if the facts still fit – remembering to double check the sources offline, too.

ASK PERMISSION If you want to incorporate someone else's research work into your own, contact them to ask permission first; many sites are protected by personal copyright. At the very least, you can use this process to check the accuracy of the information by asking questions about their research. If you do use someone else's work, be sure to credit them for their contribution, by showing their internet address properly when you incorporate their data.

Family history in miniature

The practice of having miniature portraits painted was the early equivalent of the studio photograph. Here, a family is able to view the changing generations through painted portraits, bringing it up to date with personal photographs. In the first portrait, Thomas Offspring Blackall is wearing a uniform that could be from Harrow School, so that would be a good place to start searching for his records.

Thomas Offspring Blackall 1832-79

Anne Phoebe Meeres 1867-1954

Kathleen Ruth McColl 1903-66

Anne Christina Snape 1928-

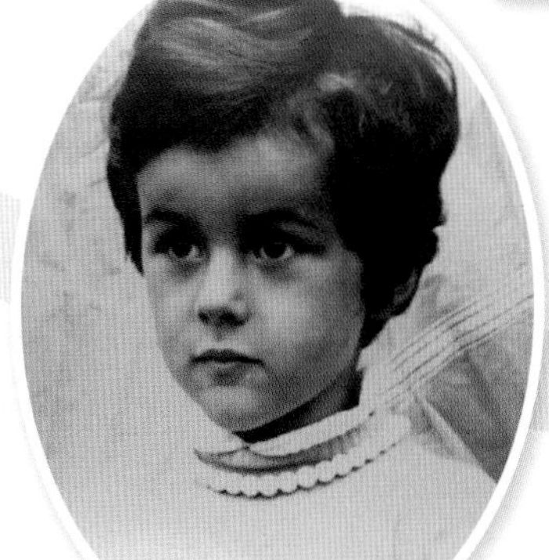

Virginia Mary Snape 1955-

Phoebe Snape 1990-

Keeping a record

It's tempting to plunge in and start pulling together all sorts of random information, but if you're to avoid wasting time and effort by going over old ground, good record keeping is essential.

Take some time to think about how you're going to organise your material right from the start. Whether you're working offline or online, making a note of previous searches avoids time-wasting duplication and helps you to remember exactly where you are with your research. It should prompt you to re-check material after a new discovery or return to areas of work that you deliberately left for another day.

Offline searches

Where records haven't been digitised, you will need to carry out your searches at libraries or archives. Make a note of the document reference for each item you have viewed, the archive in which you found it and the date you examined the document. Write down the page number of any item you quote from or copy. Don't forget that each archive will have its own reference system. If you make any changes to your notes and files, remember to mark down the date and the reason for the amendment.

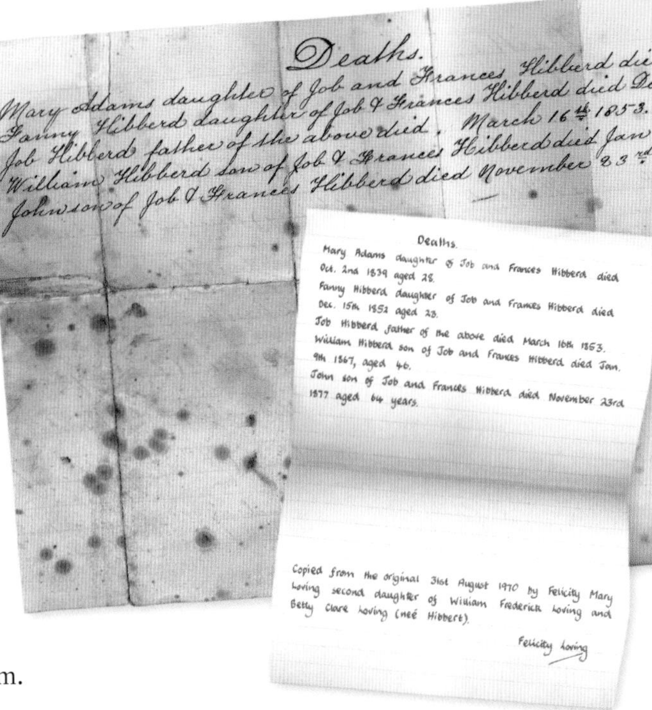

Deaths.
Mary Adams daughter of Job and Frances Hibberd died
Fanny Hibberd daughter of Job & Frances Hibberd died Dec
Job Hibberd father of the above died. March 16th 1853.
William Hibberd son of Job & Frances Hibberd died Jan 9
John son of Job & Frances Hibberd died November 23rd 18

Deaths.
Mary Adams daughter of Job and Frances Hibberd died Oct. 2nd 1839 aged 28.
Fanny Hibberd daughter of Job and Frances Hibberd died Dec. 15th 1852 aged 23.
Job Hibberd father of the above died March 16th 1853.
William Hibberd son of Job and Frances Hibberd died Jan. 9th 1867, aged 46.
John son of Job and Frances Hibberd died November 23rd 1877 aged 64 years.

Copied from the original 31st August 1970 by Felicity Mary Loving second daughter of William Frederick Loving and Betty Clare Loving (neé Hibbert).

Felicity Loving

Treat with care *When you find an old, rather fragile document packed with information, make a transcript of all the details and then work from that, rather than risk damaging the old document with too frequent handling.*

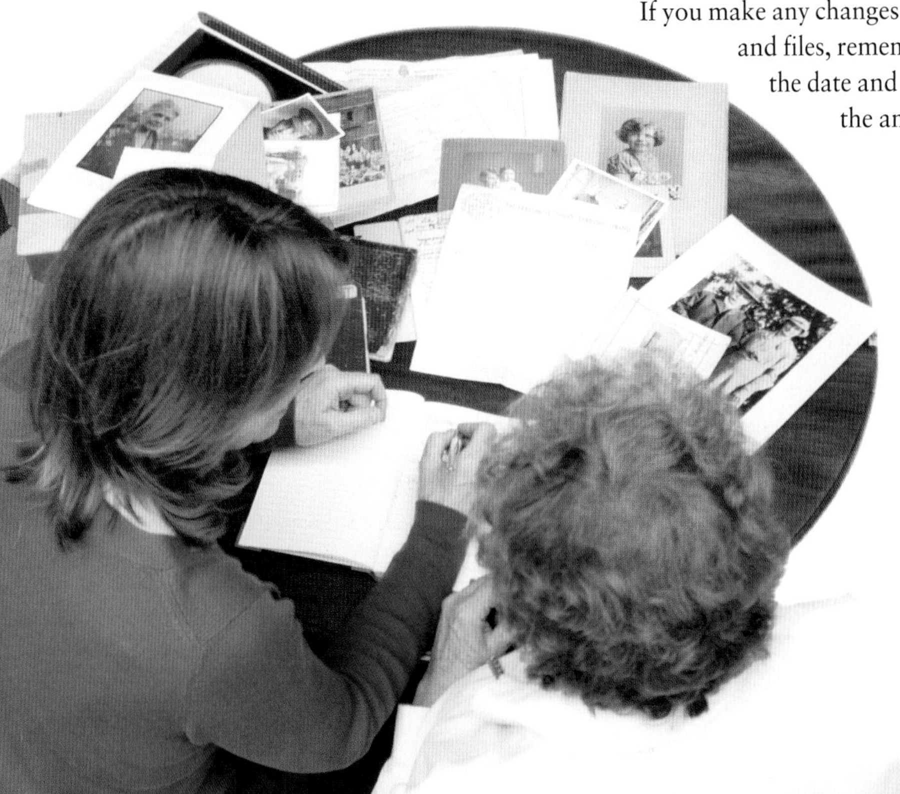

Gather your resources *Ask an older member of the family to go through all the material you have collected so far. Write down any information they can give you and note the areas that will need further research.*

Online searches

Make a list of all the websites that you've visited, and the indexes that you've searched, as you go along. If you don't take this basic step it's all too easy to forget which sites you've seen, and what you've examined when you were there. At the same time, make a list of the pages you've browsed. You can copy and paste these from your browser into a document for filing electronically, or you can print the pages out and store them with any offline records you've collected. Update this record after each set of searches.

Divide up the family

Organise your searches by the name of the ancestor you're researching, and keep separate files or folders for each branch of the family. Under each family member, make a list of websites visited and pages searched. If you're using abbreviations, make sure you keep a key. For a list of family history abbreviations, see page 8.

If you're searching for variations on name spellings, write down each version of the name that you come across and whether you've run a search on it. This will save you time in the long run and avoids duplication of searches.

Try wherever possible to link an event in your files (such as the marriage of a great-grandparent) with the source from which you took this information (marriage certificate, parish register entry or banns, for instance) so that you can revisit the site if necessary.

Practical 'housekeeping'

Make sure you back-up the information held on your PC, and save master copies of your notes in case of loss or corruption of files – there's nothing worse than losing months of work. With this in mind, make sure your anti-virus software and firewalls are regularly updated, too. See page 41 for information about the importance of anti-virus software and firewalls.

Bookmarking the best sites

Here's how to use your computer to bookmark your favourite family history websites.

- Go to the website you want to bookmark.
- On the toolbar at the top of your computer, click on the option for **Bookmark** or **Favorites**. Select the option that lets you save the site.
- The next time you want to access the page, you can find it in the drop-down menu under the **Bookmark** or **Favorites** tab.
- You can then organise these websites into folders or rank them in terms of usefulness.
- If you don't have your own PC, keep a paper trail of your favourite websites so you don't have to go trawling through various search engines every time you want to update your research.

Storing information from the internet

Most software allows you to copy and save useful documents into your own folders for future use. To save text, use the mouse to highlight the text that you want to copy. On the toolbar, go to **Edit**, and then select **Copy**. Find or create the document that you wish to save the information into. Click on this so that the text cursor is blinking. Return to the toolbar, go to **Edit**, and then select **Paste**. Save the document and label it clearly. To find out how to save images, see below.

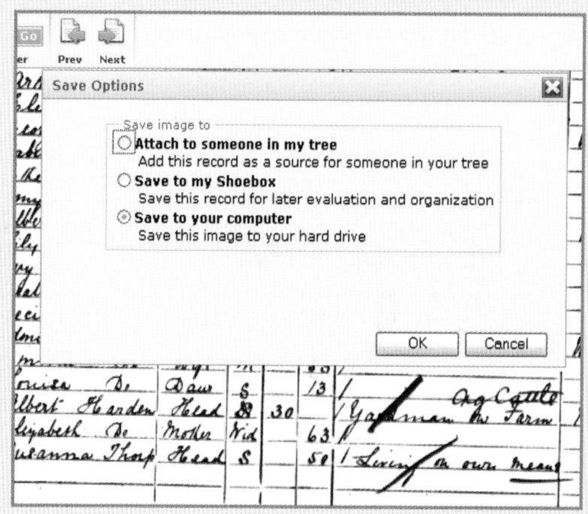

Saving images from the internet

1 Many sites, such as Ancestry, allow you to save images of their original documents to your PC. This means you can view the return as often as you like without having to log back into the website. Select the image that you wish to save – in this case, a page from the 1901 Census. Click on the **Save** icon on the top right-hand side of the image.

Storing saved images on your PC

2 You are then given three options. Select the third option, **Save to your computer**. Click **OK**. You'll then be asked to name the file and select where you'd like it to be stored. It's important to name the file as precisely as possible so that you can recognise it easily for future use. This is how you'd save on the Ancestry site; other webites may offer different methods, but the principle will be the same.

The National Archives – history under one roof

More than 1,000 years of British history is captured within the concrete and glass of The National Archives – if it happened, it's here. Among the collections are documents that have shaped the nation, as well as priceless artefacts, many of which you can see online as well as in person.

Beside the River Thames at Kew in southwest London, a stone's throw from the Royal Botantic Gardens, is the official repository for the records of England, Wales and the UK government. Millions of documents, from wills, census returns and military service records to royal seals and treaties, are kept in 29,000 m^2 of storage, carefully controlled at a temperature of 16°C and humidity of 50°, and protected from sunlight, pests and water or fire damage.

It all began in 1838, when the Public Record Office (PRO) was established in Chancery Lane, London, pulling together many disparate national records. In 1977 a second site was built at Kew, then extended in 1995, with all records transferred from Chancery Lane two years later. The PRO then merged with the Historic Manuscripts Commission in 2003 to create The National Archives (TNA).

To anyone researching family history in England and Wales, TNA is the most important repository. It contains the story of almost all our families spread across a vast array of official records that minute the stages and events of our ancestors' lives from the cradle to the grave.

People who made history

Perhaps the most fascinating treasures at TNA are the records associated with famous or infamous individuals in our history. These documents bring the past vividly to life, and many can be viewed online at **nationalarchives.gov.uk/museum/**.

Ancient and modern *The National Archives (below) holds the records of a millennium of history. The nation's past is stacked in boxes, in 16 repositories on 100 miles of shelving that grows by a mile each year.*

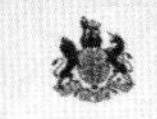

Making history *Edward VIII's 1936 abdication letter can be viewed on The National Archives website.*

Guy Fawkes ranks high in the rogues gallery of British history, and at TNA you can see two versions of his confession to taking part in the Gunpowder Plot of 1605. One he shakily signed 'Guido' straight after torture, the other he marked with a more steady hand eight days later. A miscreant that history has treated more heroically is highwayman Dick Turpin, although the indictment for him held at TNA that led to his final trial and execution was simply for stealing two horses worth four pounds.

Other famed people were the unwitting makers of history. Among the documents at TNA, for instance, is the page from the logbook of HMS *Bounty*, written by Captain William Bligh, that details the dramatic moment of mutiny on Tuesday, April 28, 1789:

'Just before sun rise Mr. Christian, Mate, Charles Churchill, Ships Corporal, John Mills Gunners Mate and Thomas Buskitt, Seaman, came into my cabbin while I was asleep and seizing me tyed my hands, with a cord behind my back and threatened me with instant death if I spoke or made the least noise.'

Nearly 150 years later, on December 10, 1936, another momentous piece of writing secured its place in history. This time it was a typed letter, signed by Edward VIII, declaring his 'irrevocable determination to renounce the Throne for Myself and for My descendants'. This 'Instrument of Abdication', as it's headed, marks the only time an English monarch has voluntarily given up the throne.

The bigger picture

At TNA you'll also find the official documents that have played a key part in the nation's history, many of which you can see online at **nationalarchives.gov.uk/museum/**. Your ancestors are unlikely to appear in these records, but the social or political changes they wrought will have affected them. Understanding these events helps to put your own family history into a wider, national context.

For two of the most ground-breaking documents the story goes back 800 or more years. It begins with the Domesday Book (see page 222) and continues with the Magna Carta or 'great charter', which helped to shape our system of constitutional law. Drawn up in 1215 by the English barons in protest against the arbitrary policies of King John, the Magna Carta's purpose was to restrict the rights of the king and bring them within the law of England. One of the most important clauses – 'no free man shall be seized or imprisoned, or stripped of his rights or possessions ... except by the lawful judgement of his peers' – enshrined the principle of a right to a fair trial by your equals, reflected in today's jury system.

A great wrong righted

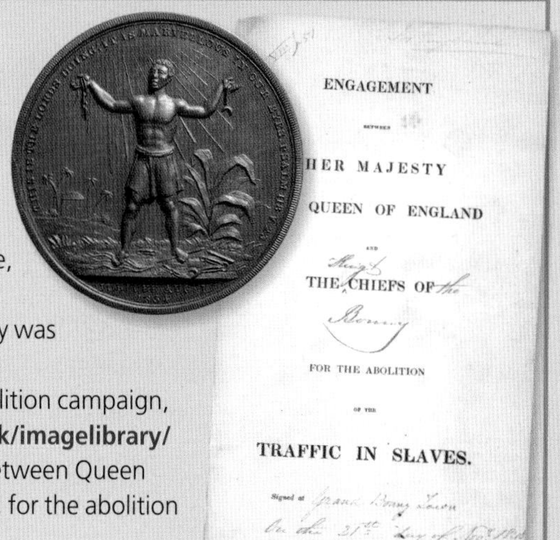

In 1807, an Act of Parliament formally abolished the slave trade. Until then, slaves were bought and sold throughout the British Empire – and the rest of the world – as chattels.

The Act was the culmination of a widespread campaign led by prominent political figures of the time, such as William Wilberforce, Charles Fox and Lord Grenville. A bronze medal (right) was cast when slavery was finally eradicated from the British Empire in 1834.

TNA has hundreds of documents relating to the abolition campaign, some of which you can see at **nationalarchives.gov.uk/imagelibrary/slavery.** This includes a signed 'Engagement' (right) between Queen Victoria and the King and Chiefs of the Bonny, Nigeria, for the abolition of slavery on November 21, 1848.

Getting started online

You're on the brink of a great adventure: rather than remaining faint ghosts of the past, your ancestors are about to join the family you know. Prepare to be enthralled and absorbed by this fascinating journey.

Making the internet work for you

There's a wealth of original material available online, and the scope increases by the day. It's a goldmine of information, just waiting for you to start digging.

Using the internet to research your family tree is the future for family historians. With so much available, and so easily accessible, there should be no stopping you.

You'll find digitised images of an amazing array of documents – civil registration records dating back 170 years, Victorian census returns, elaborately written medieval wills, maps that are hundreds of years old, ships' passenger lists going back to about 1890, First World War service papers and Prisoner of War interviews. And that's just a small part. The range of surviving material that will enable you to piece together the jigsaw of your family heritage is astounding.

Not so long ago, these documents would have been tucked away in inaccessible archives, only to be seen by determined genealogists prepared to spend hours trawling through paper indexes and rolls of microfilm. Now they're accessible to you simply at the click of a mouse.

Get to know the websites

The number of family history-related websites is growing rapidly. If you're new to online research, start by familiarising yourself with some of the most useful sites mentioned in this book. Many of the more popular websites work in a similar way, so once you've mastered a few, you'll be well on your way to finding the records you want quickly and easily.

Most of them explain how to navigate around the website and search each type of record. There's also usually an FAQ (Frequently Asked Questions) page, which can be helpful if you get stuck.

As well as updating their content, many family history sites regularly change the design of their pages, so you may find you'll have to reacquaint yourself with the look and feel of the site every now and then.

Avoiding confusion

There's so much material online that it's easy to get bogged down trying to work out what's relevant to you. You can avoid this if you have a plan before you start, listing exactly what you want to find for each ancestor or family line. There are many different websites that hold similar documents, so once any initial bewilderment has been overcome, you should find it relatively straightforward to find what you're looking for.

The internet has revolutionised the way we access information. Embrace all these newly available resources and you may find that researching your family history becomes your most rewarding hobby.

Across the generations *Using the internet to trace family relatives is fun for all ages. Children will enjoy showing off their computer skills.*

The birth of the internet and the World Wide Web

It all began with the US Government in the 1960s. First they compiled a report outlining a way to link up all the computerised data they used, then followed this, in the 1970s, with a research network that they eventually called Internet.

A decade later, across the world in the Swiss Alps, a young British software consultant named Tim Berners-Lee (left), who was on a six-month contract with CERN (the European Organisation for Nuclear Research), had a moment of illumination. He was trying to find a way to organise his notes by creating a program that would work rather like a brain, monitoring random information. In his own words, he devised a piece of software that would keep 'track of all the random associations one comes across in real life, and brains are supposed to be so good at remembering, but sometimes mine wouldn't'.

He went on to create a system that could link a word in one document to other files on his computer – and from there it was only a matter of time before his files could be linked to others at CERN, and then to other organisations. The concept of the World Wide Web was born – where information could be shared freely, at no cost, around the world. Tim then built the first website while still working at CERN and it went live on August 6, 1991.

Using family history software

Once you've started your research and made some progress with your family tree, you'll want to explore different ways of storing all the details on your computer. No matter how complicated your family's story, there'll be a software package that can hold the information.

Family history software becomes increasingly sophisticated as more and more people are gripped by the fun of discovering their ancestry. There's nothing wrong with keeping records on paper, or typing them up, but there are advantages to using specially designed software to store all that vital information.

Putting it all on the computer

Because these software packages are designed specifically for the needs of family historians, you don't need to keep on repeating the basic relationship and other terms used in family history. A program will have tables already set up to receive the data you want to enter, with all the headings you could ever need for each person. This means it's quick and easy to transfer the information from your handwritten notes into a master database.

For example, a database entry will let you add a person's full name and nickname; their dates and places of birth, baptism, marriage, death and burial; their occupation(s) and various addresses; as well as their children's, siblings' and parents' names. Most packages will usually also allow space to add a photo album with a set number of pictures, a timeline showing the major events in a person's life and a full biography.

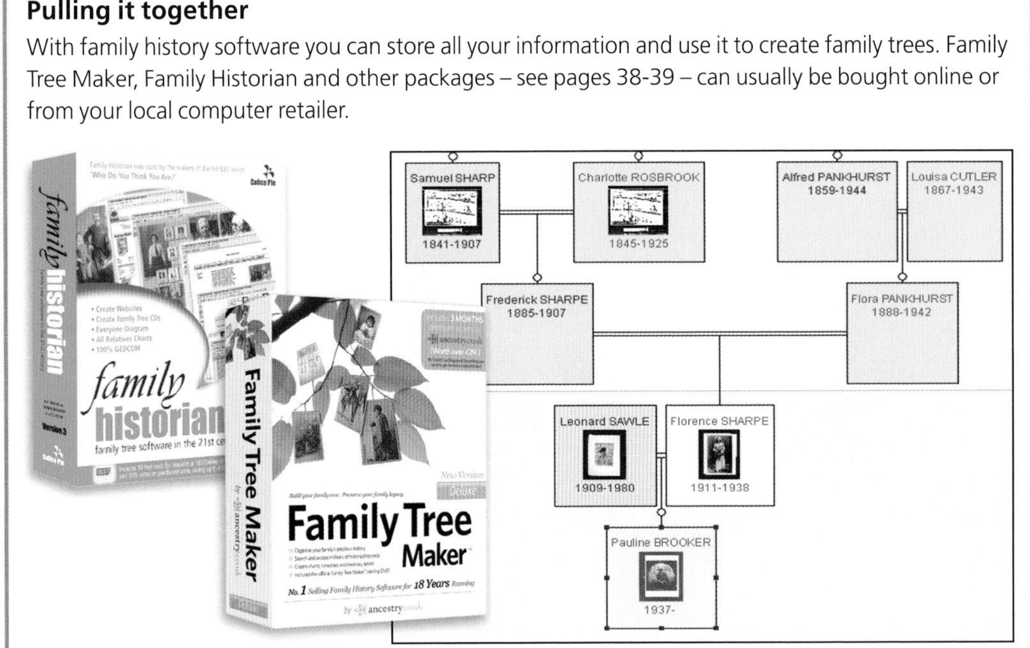

Pulling it together

With family history software you can store all your information and use it to create family trees. Family Tree Maker, Family Historian and other packages – see pages 38-39 – can usually be bought online or from your local computer retailer.

Advantages of digital records

You might wonder why you should bother keeping an electronic record, especially if you've taken thorough, detailed notes and have copies of all the documents that you've found. Although keeping your paper notes is important, especially copies of official documents, there are a number of advantages to having it all recorded digitally as well.

GOOD SOURCES Most family tree-building packages have the facility to add a list of sources to an individual's notes, which is vital when you're researching your family history. It becomes even more relevant if you choose to send your saved tree to another researcher or family member – they can see at a glance that you've used reliable sources and can also double-check them if they want to.

UNLIMITED STORAGE An electronic database offers almost limitless storage of your findings, from statistics and source references to family photographs and images of documents. Most software packages are designed to let you flick from one type of record to another with just a few mouse clicks. Having all the research together helps you to take in the overall picture, so that you can spot any gaps that need filling.

EASY SHARING If you're keen to show snippets of your research to other family members and share the information, you'll probably find that they'll prefer receiving an electronic file to browse and enjoy, rather than wading through a pile of paperwork. With electronic files you can isolate sections and pass them on, without having to copy and post records.

FASTER RESEARCH Sharing your family tree with other researchers is much easier with electronic files. Recent advances in family history software mean that most packages save your data as a Gedcom file (see page 278), which can be shared with other PCs. Most genealogy websites have a family tree-sharing facility where you can upload your Gedcom file and save it on their database (see pages 270-77 for a description of the best sites for this purpose).

Sharing information in this way can help other researchers to learn from your work and may speed up your own research. Perhaps a distant cousin you've never met, who's exploring a branch of your family tree, will find a common ancestor in your two trees and get in touch with you. This may help you to work back even further, or save you wasting time on an ancestral dead-end.

When your family doesn't fit the format

Many software packages are set up for families that fit into a traditional framework. Explaining to a computer package that your grandmother had a child with an unknown American soldier before she married your grandfather, then divorced him two years after your father was born, could be tricky. Nevertheless, software companies are continually refining their products to reflect changing family dynamics so that several, such as 3D Family Tree and GenoPro 2007, now have options to include more than one marriage and explain which children were the product of which marriage. Illegitimacy and adoption are less easy to indicate on computerised family trees, so you may have to resort to making a note on an individual's page about the circumstances of their birth. If you have a high number of unusual relationships in your tree it's worth shopping around to find a package that gives you the flexibility to enter this data.

Much married *Henry VIII married six times and had children by three different wives, which makes his family tree complicated to draw up.*

Choosing the right software

There are many excellent family history software packages on the market, from basic programs for building family trees to more advanced products that also help you to search online records.

Family history software packages make compiling a family tree easier than doing it on paper. They also often offer regular upgrades, which can make them even more effective.

Most packages allow you to upload family photos and scanned images of important documents, as well as video and audio files that will really bring your research and family tree to life. These software packages are specifically designed to simplify the storage of records, with sensible organisation and easy access. The beauty of using a digital package is that you can display as much or as little information as you need to view at any time, and yet have instant access to all the data you've collected.

Gone are the days of rummaging through mountains of paperwork; with modern family history software packages you simply specify what you want and it's presented to you within seconds. Some packages even have direct links to the internet, guiding you to recommended sources and helping you to find vital information.

Check the reviews

There are reviews of several software packages on **familyrecords.gov.uk** (follow the links to **Guides** and then **Genealogy Software**) as well as on **genealogyreviews.co.uk/genealogysoftware.htm**. The website **my-history.co.uk** regularly reviews the latest releases in family history software, and illustrates the main features of each program. Forums hosted by genealogy websites (see pages 280-5) are good for recommendations, too. Browse before buying.

Family tree software packages to consider

The four software products shown here are among the most popular on the market. Remember that this is an ever-changing area – new packages are introduced regularly and older ones are upgraded – so always check reviews and look out for the latest editions.

Family Historian

Family Historian allows you to create different styles of family tree, to which you can add pictures, audio files and videos. If you have a group photo, people within the shot can be linked to one or several individual ancestors. The software also lets you record details of your sources – vital for verifying your research. All the people in your database can be listed in one window, from where you can go into and edit each person's details. You'll find the Family Historian website at **family-historian.co.uk**.

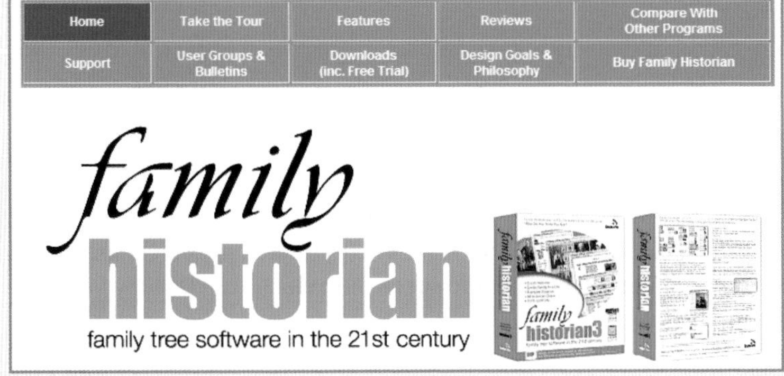

Family Tree Maker

This software allows you to display your data in a diagrammatic form that combines elements of a pedigree chart and a family tree. You'll be able to view your ancestors on a chart that shows up to seven generations at one time. Most versions of Family Tree Maker have an interactive map facility so you can see where your ancestors lived, and you can upload video and audio files as well as digital images. The software can be ordered from **ancestry.co.uk**.

Roots Magic

For a free trial of the Roots Magic Version 3 program, go to **rootsmagic.co.uk**. The software lets you create photo trees, pedigree charts and relationship charts, as well as designing wall charts which you can customise by adding pictures, moving boxes and altering the colour and background. You can publish your family tree in a book format easily with Roots Magic: the software creates an index for you, and lets you choose what information and images you'd like to include.

Legacy Family Tree

You can download a basic edition of Legacy Family Tree free of charge from **legacyfamilytree.com**. It has links to family history sites such as **familysearch.com** and **ancestry.co.uk**. A deluxe version of the software can be bought from the Legacy website and gives you access to useful extra features such as Research Guidance (help with your family research), Publishing Center (where you can publish the results of your research in a book) and Timelines (which provides a chronological review of your ancestors' lives).

Getting the best from the web

When you're searching online, it helps to understand the way your computer interacts with the internet and how to get the most out of your search engine.

There are a number of terms you'll need to know for your searches online.

Browser

A web browser is a software program such as Internet Explorer or Mozilla Firefox that you can use to view web pages and 'browse' websites. All web browsers are the same in principle – they are made up of an address box, into which you type a web address, and an area in which web pages can be viewed. Text and images on a web page often contain links to other web pages on the same or different websites. Web browsers activate these links so you can view the relevant pages.

Cookies

A cookie is a small piece of information that is sent to your computer through your web browser when you've visited particular websites. Cookies store information about you for the next time you go to that site – the pages you visited, any actions you took or links you followed. They're stored on the hard drive of your computer and are dormant until you come back to that site again, at which point they're activated.

When a cookie is placed on your computer, it records the website that will be allowed to open it in the future. For example, if **ancestry.co.uk** places a cookie in its name, only **ancestry.co.uk** will be able to open it. You can set your browser so that it doesn't accept cookies, but the problem with this is that sites that allow payment for instant access, or those with checkout facilities, won't function correctly and you won't be able to get what is called 'user authorisation' unless the settings are reconfigured to accept cookies. As you're likely to need to pay for searches and certificates, this could be really inconvenient.

Plug-ins

A plug-in is a small piece of computer software that a web browser uses to let you view a document, interact with an image, listen to music or watch a video. If your computer doesn't have the correct plug-in, you can't listen to audio footage or see animations and video on-screen. If you need a plug-in that you don't already have on your

How to search effectively

There are many well-known search engines on the internet, including **google.co.uk** and **yahoo.co.uk**. Although you can do simple searches by just typing in words in the search box, this will often bring up far too many results which aren't relevant to what you want.

To get the best from a search engine, there are a few basic techniques that will make finding what you want easier and quicker. If an initial search doesn't turn up what you're looking for, you should try these.

Looking for phrases If you want to search for a particular phrase, you can improve the search results by enclosing the phrase in inverted commas, rather than just typing in the individual words. This isn't so important if the words are often used together anyway (such as 'Bodmin Moor'), but it's useful for finding names. Putting 'Mary Ann Brown' in inverted commas will find only the pages where those three names are next to each other in that order, not just any page which may have Mary, Ann and Brown, in any context, on it.

Looking for alternatives If you have a surname that may have different spellings, it's a good idea to look for all variants. Unfortunately search engines don't know anything about surnames, so you'll have to list all the variants, separated by the word OR (which must be in capital letters) – 'Bishop OR Bishopp OR Bisshopp', for example.

Advanced searching All search engines have a wide range of options beyond the basic ones mentioned here. The easiest way to find out about these is to click on the **Advanced Search** link that most search engines have on their homepage. The Advanced Search page should have a link to a help page which will explain what all the options do and how you should use them.

Incorrect spellings Sometimes you don't find what you want because you've spelled it incorrectly yourself. For example, if you type 'English Sivil War' into a search engine such as Google, it will manage to find hundreds of entries despite a misspelling. Fortunately, Google has a spelling checker and asks you: **Did you mean: 'English Civil War'?**

computer you'll be prompted to install it. Most websites offer step-by-step help to install the program, so don't feel alarmed if you're told you need to load one. There are hundreds of different types of plug-in, but only a handful of family history websites are likely to ask you to install one.

Antivirus software

A computer virus is a piece of code that's capable of copying itself. Viruses spread from computer to computer by attaching themselves to email messages or hiding in the code of some programs. As well as replicating themselves so that you'll inadvertently send them to your friends and contacts, many viruses delete files on your computer, or even disrupt pre-loaded software.

Because of the problems that these viruses can cause, it's absolutely vital that you take steps to protect your computer with antivirus software. It consists of computer programs that identify, thwart and eliminate computer viruses and other potentially harmful software. If the antivirus software spots a virus hidden in an email message or web page, it attempts to disable the virus and prevents it from damaging your computer.

You can download basic antivirus software, free of charge, for personal use from websites such as **free.grisoft.com** from AVG, **avast.com** from Avast or **clamav.net** from ClamAV. If you'd like a higher level of security, you should buy an antivirus software package, such as Norton's antivirus at **symantec.com**, McAfee's VirusScan at **us.mcafee.com** or the commercial version of AVG at **grisoft.com/doc**.

Firewalls

A firewall is a software program that forms a barrier between your computer and the rest of the internet. It protects your computer from hackers, viruses and any other type of harmful element. Quite simply, a firewall has the ability to stop anything you don't know about from passing between the internet and your computer.

Some internet service providers, such as BT and AOL, actually provide a free copy of a firewall program to their broadband customers. You can also buy firewall software just as you'd buy the antivirus software already described, fromMcAfee at **mcafeestore.com** or from ZoneAlarm at **zonealarm.com**. If a firewall isn't provided automatically, you should invest in one.

Using a credit card safely on the internet

If you want to sign up to family history websites and spend money online, there are a few basic security precautions you should take, to avoid becoming the victim of fraud.

First, you'll need to make sure that you're shopping on a site that you can trust. To help you to follow best practice online, take a look at **besafeonline.org** and **consumerdirect.gov.uk**.

Some websites let you see their products and decide what you want before you register. Others will insist that you register first. Where you need to pay is usually known as the 'checkout'. You can pay by either credit or debit card, and to complete the transaction you'll need to enter the card number and expiry date.

Some sites also ask you for the security code (the last three numbers printed on the back of your card) as extra security.

Before you hand over your details, make sure that the site you're using has a safe checkout. Regardless of which web browser you're using, a small padlock should appear in the bar at the bottom of the screen. This symbol indicates that other online users can't see any of the data you're sending to the shop.

Play it safe *Be very careful when you put any of your banking details online. Never give your PIN number or password to anyone. Keep a record of any transaction you make until you've received an email confirmation of your purchase.*

Where to start online

You've decided what you want to research and where you want to end up, but just where do you begin, faced with the treasure trove of information that's available on the internet?

One of the best places to start your search is **familyrecords.gov.uk**, a government website that describes the main types of record and where you can find them online and offline. It also acts as a portal to other family history resources available on the internet. The site covers most of the official sets of information you're likely to need. The **Topics** section deals with civil registration, religious records, census, wills, immigration, emigration, military records and adoption. In the **Partners** section, you can just click on the links to access public sector and government bodies holding original material that could be useful to your research. A third section, **Resources**, provides useful sources for family historians.

Your search usually starts with finding civil registration certificates. FamilyRecords tells you about the information on these certificates, and how it will help you to trace your family tree. There's also advice on how to find relevant certificates in England and Wales, as well as details about Scotland and Ireland, and other registries such as the Isle of Man and the Channel Islands. The site explains why you may not always find what you're looking for in the records, and gives suggestions about where else you can look.

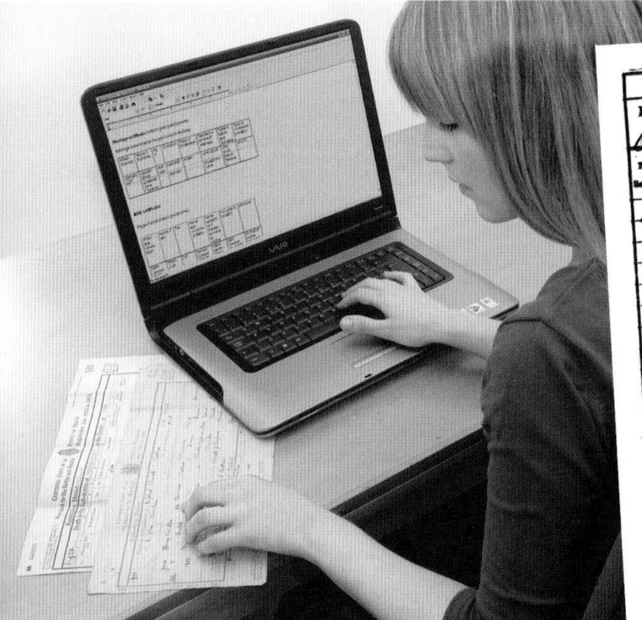

Upload your notes *Transfer information onto your computer as you go along, making sure you record your sources. Details from certificates (above) or a census return (right) will be much easier to access once they are correctly filed on your PC.*

123 [Page 13

The undermentioned Houses are situate within the Boundaries of the

Parish [or Township] of Old Stratford | City or Municipal Borough of | Municipal Ward of | Parliamentary Borough of | Town of Stratford on Avon | Hamlet or Tything, &c., of | Ecclesiastical District of

No. of Schedule | Road, Street, &c., and No. or Name of House | HOUSES: Inhabited, Uninhabited (U.), or Building (B.) | Name and Surname of each Person | Relation to Head of Family | Condition | Age of Males, Females | Rank, Profession, or Occupation | Where Born | Whether Blind, or Deaf-and-Dumb

Total of Houses... 2 | Total of Males and Females... 7 15

Eng.—Sheet D.

The Family Records website is provided by a consortium representing public sector bodies and government departments, including:

- The National Archives (TNA)
- The Public Record Office of Northern Ireland (PRONI)
- The National Archives of Scotland (NAS)
- The National Library of Wales (NLW)
- The General Register Office (GRO)
- The General Register Office for Scotland (GROS)
- The British Library India Office (BLIO).

Top tips for keeping online records

- Keep separate notes for each section of the family, so that they don't become confused.
- Record and keep a reference for all the web searches that you do. This will make it easier to remember details at a later date.
- Record and reference any documents you've viewed online, linked to the original archive from which they were taken.
- Make sure you record the time and date each time you update your research.
- Save your favourite websites into your browser.
- Consider buying scrapbook software to help you keep all your findings together.
- Remember to back up your information regularly in case of computer problems that could wipe out months of work.

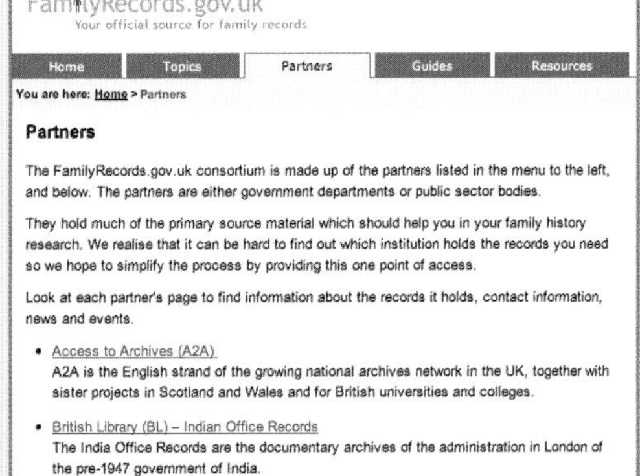

Topics section

1 At the top of the homepage, click on **Topics**. This gives you a list of information subjects including civil registration certificates (for births, marriages and deaths), census returns, wills, religious records, immigration, emigration and adoptions. These are the main types of public record that you'll need to access in order to start building your family tree.

Partners section

2 On the homepage go to **Partners,** where there are links to search engines such as A2A (Access to Archives), an online database that lets you search the catalogues of hundreds of local and county archives by keyword. There are also links to The National Archive's websites, the Commonwealth War Graves Commission and the British Library, among others.

Resources section

3 On the homepage, click on **Resources** at the top. This lets you navigate to additional resources that aren't strictly official sources, but are important further down the line when you may want to connect with other online users or widen the scope of your research.

Finding local knowledge

A number of sites will point you to national information and records, but once you've found out where your ancestors came from, you'll want local information to help you to fill in missing details. This is where Genuki comes in, steering you to the local archives and other resources you may need.

Genuki (at **genuki.org.uk**) is an acronym of Genealogy in the UK and Ireland. It's a free, non-commercial website that provides information and links to online resources for all six regions of the British Isles: England, Scotland, Wales, Ireland (covering both Northern Ireland and the Republic of Ireland), the Isle of Man and the Channel Islands.

The entry for each region holds national information and has links to separate pages for each county. It's these county pages which you'll probably find most useful. They have details of the records offices and libraries where you'll find original records, and many links to online resources for genealogy and history relating to the county.

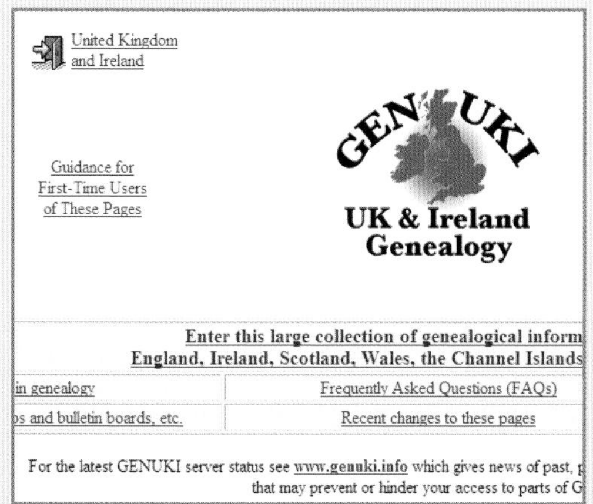

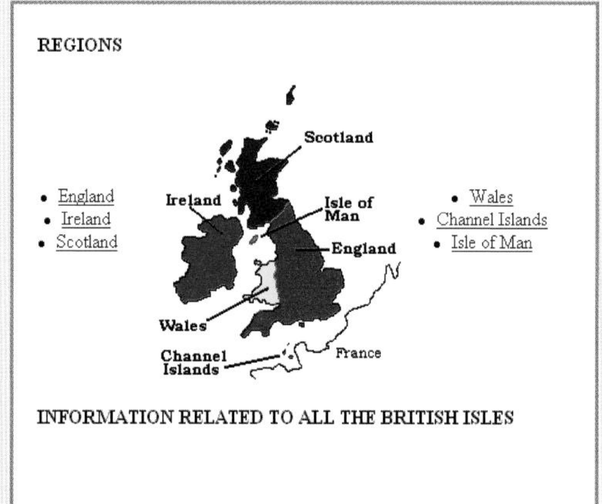

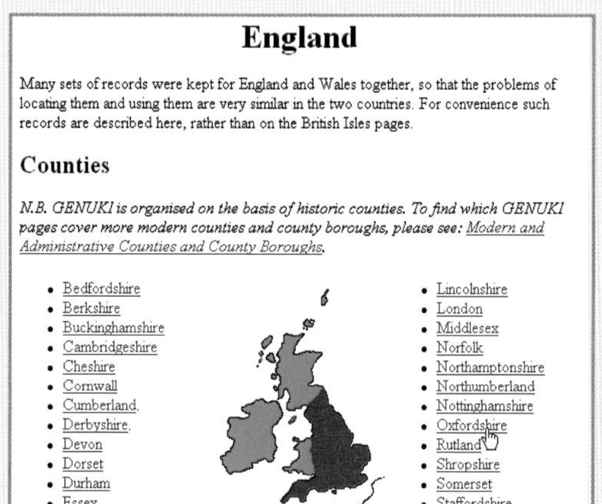

How to search on Genuki

1 Key in **genuki.org.uk** to get to the homepage. To access the site's collections, click **United Kingdom and Ireland** in the top left-hand corner.

Select a region

2 Up comes a map of the British Isles, broken into six regions. There's also a general list offering information on everything from cemeteries to taxation, from which you can choose, without selecting a region. Click on a region to see the specific collections held there.

Find your area

3 In this example, by clicking on **England** you're presented with all the English counties. You'll also be offered links to information relating to all of England.

Every county page has a set of headings such as Church Records, Maps and Occupations, so it's easy to find the topic you're looking for. You'll find links to a list of all the towns and parishes in the county. Many individual parishes have a page devoted to them, with more links to local sites.

Because it's designed for family historians, Genuki is organised around the counties as they were in the early 19th century, so you won't find pages for London Boroughs or post-1974 counties such as West Midlands or Avon. But you can use Genuki's Gazetteer at **genuki.org.uk/big/Gazetteer/** to find out in which county a place used to be – the search results give a grid reference and link to the relevant page on Genuki.

In addition, Genuki has many useful tools and lists that you should visit:

☛ There is a list of all family history societies in the British Isles at **genuki.org.uk/Societies/**

☛ All the mailing lists for British and Irish genealogy are listed at **genuki.org.uk/indexes/MailingLists.html**

☛ The Genuki Church Database (also called the Parish Locator) at **genuki.org.uk/big/churchdb/search.html** lists all the churches within a chosen radius of a particular place – ideal for trying to work out where your ancestor may have been baptised or married.

☛ The Genuki Search at **genuki.org.uk/search/** lets you search all of Genuki, and many other major websites for British and Irish family history research, such as the National Archives, the Society of Genealogists, and most local family history societies.

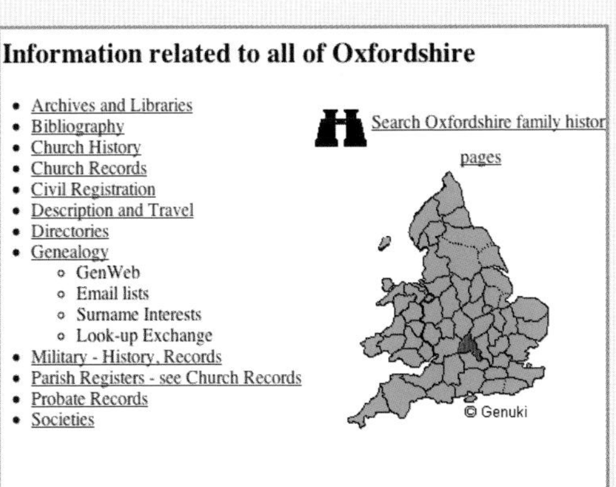

Find your county

4 Click on the county in which your ancestors lived (**Oxfordshire** is shown here). You'll be taken to a brief description of the county, links to the main archives, and any relevant online resources. There's also a list of parishes and often a separate page devoted to each parish.

Tracing your ancestral home

You may come across an old photograph or painting of an ancestor's home – perhaps one that has since been sold and is no longer owned by a family member. With a house name or address, it may be possible to identify the location on an old map. If the house was large enough, it might be named on the map. This can be invaluable in pinpointing the local archives that may contain records of its ownership and when it was sold.

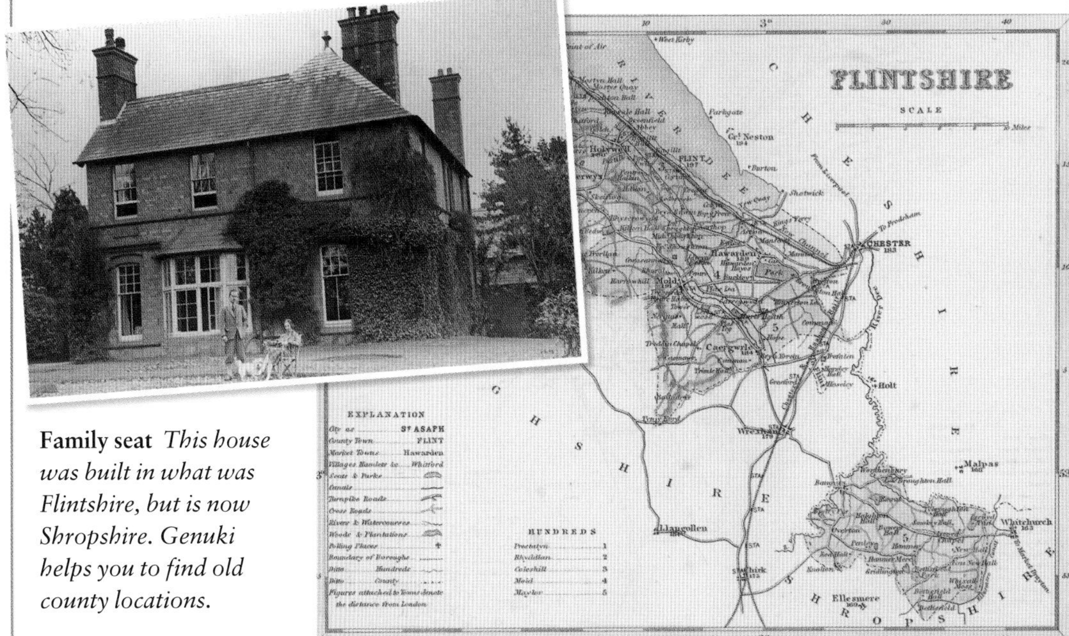

Family seat *This house was built in what was Flintshire, but is now Shropshire. Genuki helps you to find old county locations.*

Cyndi's List – gateway to family history sites

Probably the world's largest family history 'portal' site is run by Cyndi Howells, who has been a genealogist for more than 20 years. Her site provides you with links to a huge range of websites that could help in the search for your ancestors.

There are more than 263,000 web links available through Cyndi's List, all updated and checked regularly. Its value to family historians is enormous and there's nothing else on the internet that quite compares.

One of the most appealing aspects of the website, **cyndislist.com**, is its sense of community – you can contribute to it and edit information that appears, as well as email Cyndi with suggestions and comments. There are links to groups and societies, most of which have message boards or chat rooms putting you in touch with the global family history community. You can also subscribe to Cyndi's newsletter to keep up with news.

The site is an excellent resource if you're stuck for information, or need a little more guidance about where to look. There are links to thousands of websites, so make a note of every site you search; the sheer size of Cyndi's List makes it tricky to find your way back to a site if you haven't recorded your route carefully.

An all-inclusive site

Although it's slightly skewed towards North America, Cyndi's List has plenty of resources that you'll find relevant to your searches. The homepage displays the date when new links were last added, so you can keep up to date with information and not miss anything.

As well as the main index, which categorises entries according to subject matter, geographical location or theme, there are four other main sections to the site that you can access via links on the left-hand side of the homepage.

TOPICAL INDEX Arranged under subject headings, the topical list includes: Computers and the internet; Ethnic groups and people; Help from others; History; Immigration, emigration and migration; Localities; Marketplace; Memorabilia; Military; Miscellaneous; Occupations; Records; Religions; Research tools and reference materials and Wars. Select a heading that interests you, and you'll find numerous links to relevant resources that have been accepted by Cyndi's website.

TEXT ONLY INDEX If you have a relatively slow internet connection, such as dial-up, select from here, as it takes less time to load.

ALPHABETICAL INDEX Topics and links are given in alphabetical order, in a complete index of all of the pages and sub-pages on the site. For example, under F you'll find Family History Centers and Family Newsletters; under G, Genealogy Lending Libraries & Archives.

'NO FRILLS' INDEX As you'd expect, this is a pared-down list of headings, containing no descriptions of what each link contains. This index is useful for a quick browse, or to use when you want to revisit an item.

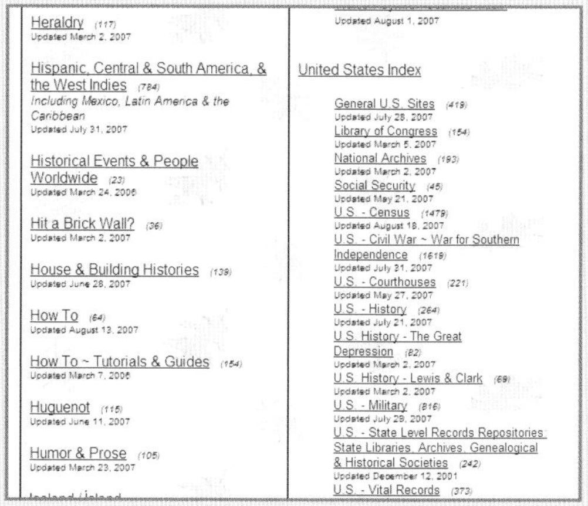

A search for a Huguenot ancestor

1 You can search under a variety of topics using Cyndi's List. For example, if you're looking for an ancestor, Jean du Plessy from Poitiers, who was a Huguenot and who may have escaped persecution by sailing to South Africa, go to the homepage, and click on **H**. This will take you to the link for Huguenot sources.

Using the main index

One of the most useful aspects of Cyndi's List is the ease with which you can research almost anything. For example, if you want to find an ancestor who went to New Zealand in the 19th century, and you believe he became a fireman, click on **New Zealand** on the main index on the homepage (see right). You'll get a long list of topics on the left, and a shorter list of related categories on the right. To find your ancestor, click on **People and families.** The list that's offered has a link for the **Palmerston North firemen in the 1800s.** Click on this, and up comes a list of all the firemen, with their dates of service. When you check the bar at the top of the screen, you'll see you're no longer on the Cyndi's List website, but have been connected directly to **angelfire.com**, the site that offered the information to Cyndi's List. You'll find all the information on the website is contributed by outside sources.

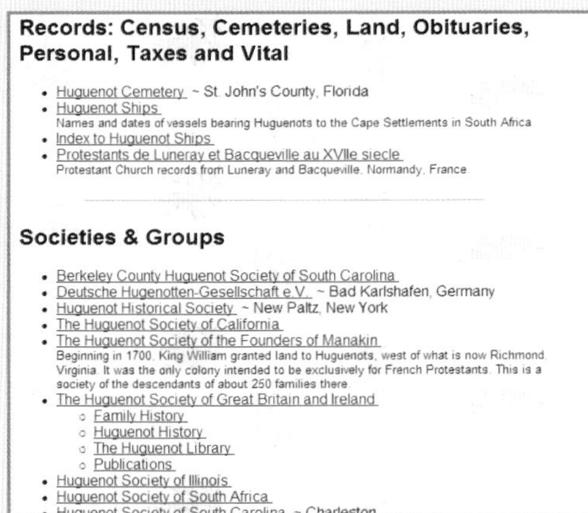

Records: Census, Cemeteries, Land, Obituaries, Personal, Taxes and Vital

- Huguenot Cemetery ~ St. John's County, Florida
- Huguenot Ships
  Names and dates of vessels bearing Huguenots to the Cape Settlements in South Africa
- Index to Huguenot Ships
- Protestants de Luneray et Bacqueville au XVIIe siecle
  Protestant Church records from Luneray and Bacqueville, Normandy, France

Societies & Groups

- Berkeley County Huguenot Society of South Carolina
- Deutsche Hugenotten-Gesellschaft e.V. ~ Bad Karlshafen, Germany
- Huguenot Historical Society ~ New Paltz, New York
- The Huguenot Society of California
- The Huguenot Society of the Founders of Manakin
  Beginning in 1700, King William granted land to Huguenots, west of what is now Richmond Virginia. It was the only colony intended to be exclusively for French Protestants. This is a society of the descendants of about 250 families there.
- The Huguenot Society of Great Britain and Ireland
  - Family History
  - Huguenot History
  - The Huguenot Library
  - Publications
- Huguenot Society of Illinois
- Huguenot Society of South Africa
- Huguenot Society of South Carolina ~ Charleston

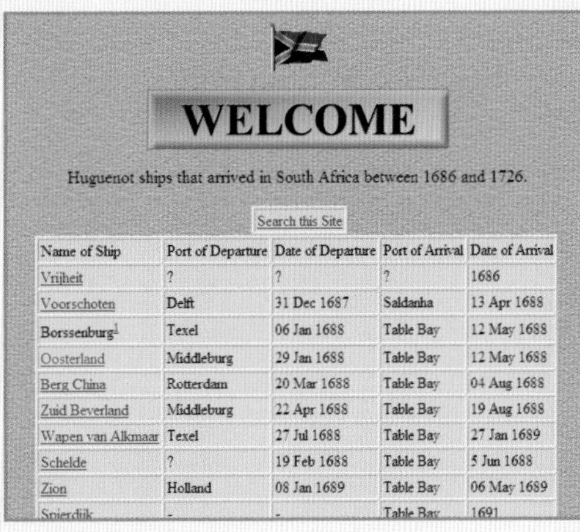

WELCOME

Huguenot ships that arrived in South Africa between 1686 and 1726.

Search this Site

Name of Ship	Port of Departure	Date of Departure	Port of Arrival	Date of Arrival
Vrijheit	?	?	?	1686
Voorschoten	Delft	31 Dec 1687	Saldanha	13 Apr 1688
Borssenburg[1]	Texel	06 Jan 1688	Table Bay	12 May 1688
Oosterland	Middleburg	29 Jan 1688	Table Bay	12 May 1688
Berg China	Rotterdam	20 Mar 1688	Table Bay	04 Aug 1688
Zuid Beverland	Middleburg	22 Apr 1688	Table Bay	19 Aug 1688
Wapen van Alkmaar	Texel	27 Jul 1688	Table Bay	27 Jan 1689
Schelde	?	19 Feb 1688	Table Bay	5 Jun 1688
Zion	Holland	08 Jan 1689	Table Bay	06 May 1689
Spierdijk	-	-	Table Bay	1691

The OOSTERLAND sailed from Middleburg on 29 January 1688 and arrived at Table Bay, South

PASSENGERS

Surname	First Name (s)	Origin	Age	Died	Occupati
Avicé	Sara	Chateaudun	-	-	-
Briet	Suzanne	Chateau Thierry, Champagne	-	-	-
Carnoy	Antoinette[1]	Tournai, Flanders	-	-	-
Clouden	Jean	Condé	-	-	Shoemak
Cochet	Sara[2]	-	-	-	-
de Buiyse (du Buis, Buis,Buys)	Jan[3]	Picardy	-	-	Agricultur
de Savoie or Savoye	Jacques[4]	Ath (Aeth)	52	1717	-
du Plessy (Plessis)	Jean Prieur[5]	Poiters	50	1708	Surgeon
Menanteau (Menanto)	Madeline	Poiters	-	Bef. 1700	-
Nortie (Nortier)	Daniel	Saint-Blaise near Guines, Picardy	-	-	Carpente

Finding Huguenot ships

2 You're now provided with a list of sources that you can search to trace your Huguenot ancestor. Under **Records: census, cemeteries, land, obituaries, personal, taxes and vital**, you'll see a link to Huguenot ships with names and dates of vessels that took Huguenots to the Cape. Click on this link.

Find the ship

3 Up comes a list of ships' names. You'll need to know the name of the ship that your ancestor served on, or you may have to undertake a lengthy search. If you know the name of the ship, in this case the *Oosterland*, and a rough date, click on the ship's name.

Find your ancestor

4 Now you can search through a list of passengers who sailed on the ship that you have chosen. Jean du Plessy is there, and you can see that he was a surgeon. He travelled with his wife, Madeline Menanteau, and their son Charles, who was born on the voyage. The list also tells you the date and port of departure and the date and port of arrival.

What you'll find online

Family history information on the internet is constantly changing. Not all records are there yet, but an amazing number are, and it's growing all the time.

This is an exciting time to be researching your ancestry. You can access ever-increasing amounts of information about your family from the comfort of your own home.

Most key records are available online, to some degree at least, including those listed below. Each of these categories is dealt with in greater detail later in the book. Website addresses for major collections or indexes are given here, but there are other smaller collections on a wide range of sites. You can find these by entering key words such as 'mineworkers' records' or 'methodist ministers' into a search engine such as Yahoo! or Google.

CIVIL REGISTRATION Indexes for birth, marriage and death certificates in England and Wales are available at **findmypast.co.uk** and **ancestry.co.uk**. For Scotland, you'll find indexes for birth, marriage and death certificates, with access to digitised images of the Old Parish Registers and early census books, at **scotlandspeople.gov.uk**.

CENSUS RETURNS For England, Scotland, Wales and the Channel Islands, from 1841 to 1901, go to **ancestry.co.uk**; for Scotland, from 1841 to 1901, visit **scotlandspeople.gov.uk**.

WILLS You can view English wills from 1384 to 1858 at **nationalarchives.gov.uk**. Testaments and wills for Scotland, from 1513 to 1901, are at **scotlandspeople.gov.uk**.

PARISH REGISTERS Transcripts of parish registers prepared by the Church of Jesus Christ of Latter-day Saints (Mormons) are available at **familysearch.org**. Parish registers for England and Wales are searchable by county at **familyhistoryonline.net**.

BURIALS You can access the National Burial Index at the Federation of Family Histories website **familyhistoryonline.co.uk**. Go to **memorialinscriptions.org.uk** to find the location of a grave and its inscription.

PASSENGER LISTS You'll find passenger lists for every ship leaving any British port between 1890 and 1919, including the list of the *Titanic*, at **findmypast.com**.

MILITARY RECORDS First World War service records are at **ancestry.co.uk**. You can search the Medal Card Index for the First World War at **nationalarchives.gov.uk**. For lists of war graves, go to the Commonwealth War Graves Commission at **cwgc.org**.

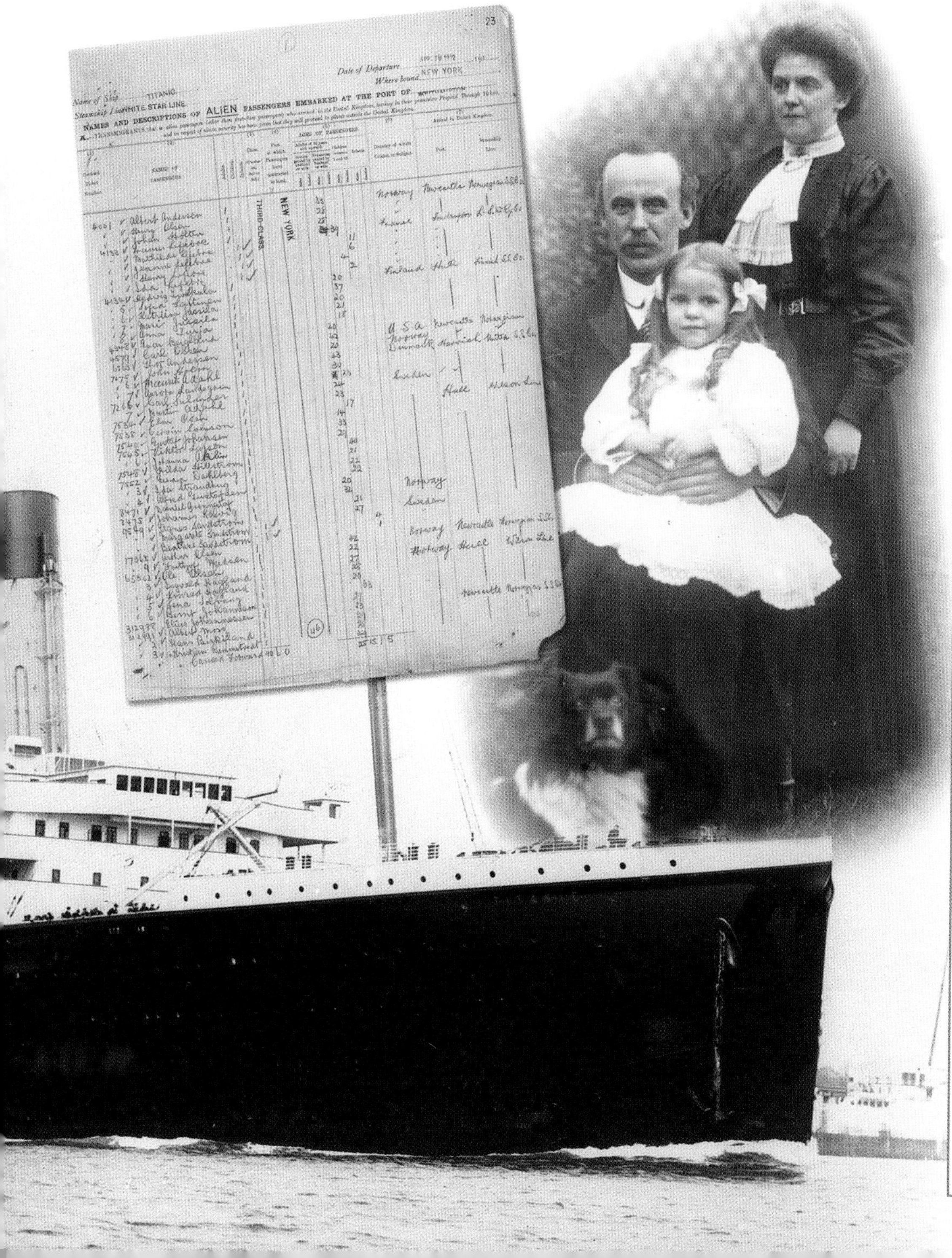

Fateful voyage *The passenger list (far left) for RMS* Titanic *records all those who embarked on her maiden voyage on April 10, 1912. You can see the details at* **findmypast.com.** *Some 1400 passengers and 800 crew were on board when the ship hit an iceberg on her way to New York. More than 1500 people died, including The Reverend John Harper, a widower and a Baptist minister from Glasgow, (left). His daughter, Nina, survived. Here they are seen before the fateful journey, with Miss Jessie Wills Leitch who also survived.*

What's not online yet

Very few local records are online as yet, although they are being digitised. Additions to the online indexes are usually well publicised, but it's best to do a Yahoo! or Google search every now and then to see what's new.

Images of civil registration certificates
Work is in progress on the digitising of images of birth, marriage and death certificates for England and Wales, and the online indexes are growing.

The 1911 census This is due to be made fully available to the public in 2012, after the mandatory 100 years has elapsed. Further information about it can be found at **nationalarchives.gov.uk**.

Most military service records You'll have to view the records themselves offline, though online indexes are available online at **nationalarchives.gov.uk/catalogue**.

Occupation records These are rarely found online, although indexes for some trades, occupations and professions are found on some websites (see pages 180-91).

Using online data services ancestry.co.uk

A number of key websites, including Ancestry, offer vast amounts of information – your ancestors will be in there somewhere. You may have to pay for the information, but it's well worth it.

Some of the information on Ancestry is free – for example, the birth, marriage and death indexes for England and Wales. You can search these indexes by clicking the **Family Trees** link near the top of the homepage. But to access most of the data collections you'll need either to

Ancestry records include:

- UK censuses 1841-1901
- Birth, marriage and death indexes 1837-2005
- UK and Ireland parish and probate records
- Irish immigrants: New York port arrivals
- British phonebooks
- Pallot's Marriage Index for England 1780-1837
- Indian Army records

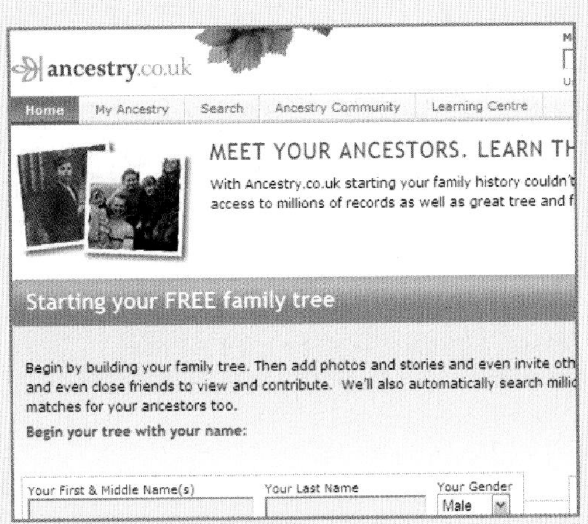

Go to the homepage

1 The design of the **ancestry.co.uk** homepage changes often, but it always gives you details of the records on offer. The tabs at the top provide further information about what you can do on the site. Access is via a registration and subscription service, but you can usually have a free 14 day trial. To register as a member, click on **Subscribe** on the top right-hand side of the page.

Register and subscribe

2 On the registration page you'll be asked to select an annual or monthly membership package, or a pay-per-view system for a set number of images. Pay-per-view is best if you know what you want to search for, but once activated, the subscription allows access for only a set length of time (usually 14 days). If you don't use all your search credits within that time, you will lose them. Select your preferred plan and click on **Sign up now**.

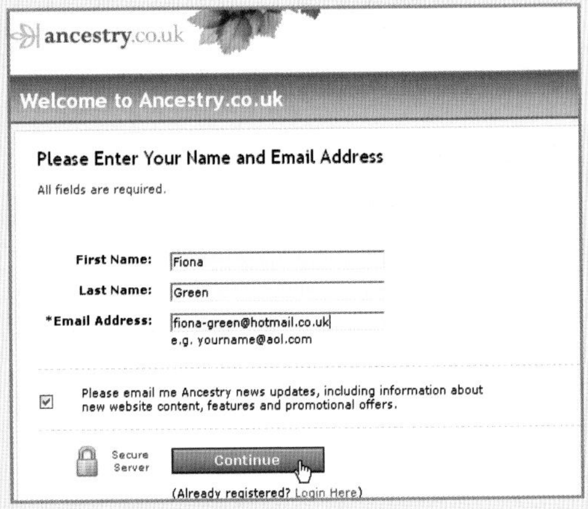

Give your details

3 Enter your name and email address and click on **Continue**. This takes you to another page where you enter your contact details. Then enter your credit card details. Make sure you read and accept the terms and conditions of the site. Once you're registered, you have access to the records via a series of search screens.

take out a subscription (which gives you access to all the records without further payment) or use the pay-per-view system, where you pay for a fixed number of record searches. Whichever you choose, you'll pay by credit card and your subscription will be renewed automatically unless you cancel it.

There are separate UK and World subscriptions, but unless you know that Ancestry has records for a country your ancestors came from or went to, the UK membership should cover all your needs.

What's in the indexes

Take a look at the yellow box opposite, to see what information is held on the Ancestry site. Like most other data services, it has relatively little material for Scotland – most of which is available only on ScotlandsPeople (see page 56).

Ancestry has an enormous number of different datasets, and in many cases they provide not only an index or transcription of the records but also images of the original records. This means you can see all the details for yourself, to check against the information given in the index.

Seeing the images

To display these images, Ancestry has a special image viewer with facilities for saving, printing and zooming. Once you've saved an image on your own computer, you can view or print it as you need.

In addition to the basic image viewer, Ancestry also has an Enhanced Image Viewer, which provides a wider range of options, including a facility for magnifying individual sections of a page. There are also options to download higher-quality images – these take longer to download, but you may be able to read the writing in the image more easily.

The Enhanced Image Viewer is designed to be used with the browser Internet Explorer, version 5.5 or later. It doesn't work with some other browsers, so you may need to switch to Internet Explorer to get the best out of the Ancestry site. To use the Enhanced Image Viewer, you'll need to install a special piece of browser software, or plug-in, on your computer (see page 40). Usually your computer will prompt you to install the plug-ins you need. If your browser settings or anti-virus software try to prevent installation, you'll find Ancestry's help pages have the information to solve the problem.

Lawful union

There's a double chance that you'll be able to trace your ancestors' wedding because most Anglican marriages generate two records: of the banns and of the marriage itself. In the 19th and early 20th centuries, weddings usually took place in the bride's parish church. Then, as now, the banns would be read by the vicar on three Sundays before the wedding. The banns publicly proclaim the couple's intention so help to avoid a bigamous or unlawful marriage. Records of banns and marriages can be found at **ancestry.co.uk**.

DNA testing service

Ancestry offers a range of DNA tests which allow you to find out if others with the same surname are related to you. You can buy a testing kit through the website and send off a simple mouth swab to get the results.

Using online data services
findmypast.com

This website was originally called 1837online, named after the year in which civil registration of births, deaths and marriages began in England and Wales. You may see it referred to by that name on other websites and message boards. Through **findmypast.com** you can access all the indexes held in the General Register Office (GRO), apart from those of the past 18 months, which aren't yet accessible (see pages 78-81). You can also view images of the original indexes. To get all the information you need, you'll have to order the certificates using a GRO reference number, which you can find on the website.

Many hands *Men of the Royal Marine Artillery unload howitzer shells at Ypres in 1917. First World War records on* **findmypast.com** *will tell you about your fighting ancestors.*

Sign in to the site

1 To sign in, go to the **findmypast.com** homepage. Click on the **Register** link, at the top of the page. This will then direct you to the registration screen.

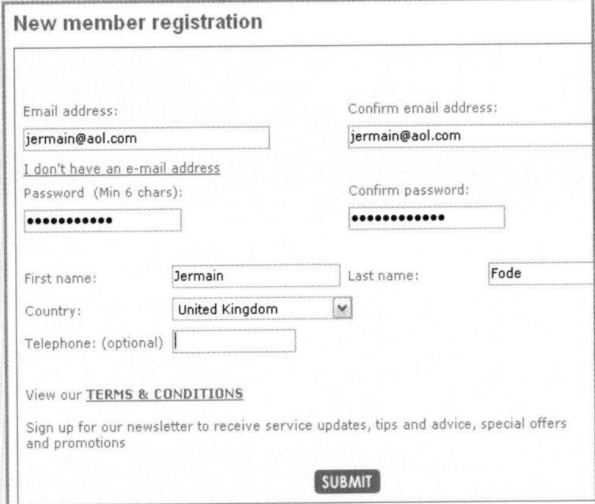

Register your own details

2 You'll be asked to confirm your registration details, which include your email address and a password of your own choosing, as well as your name, country of origin and phone number. As with most sites, you'll also be asked to agree to its terms and conditions.

Download image viewer

If you cannot see the image below you need to download our free and completely safe image viewer.

Download image viewer

If you are a beginner to family history please visit our getting started section to help you with your research.

Good luck with your research!

Download free software

3 After you've registered, you'll be directed to a test screen to discover whether you'll be able to see images on Findmypast. If you can see the image provided, you can move on; if not, you'll be asked to install specialist software that's free and easy to load. This should only take a couple of minutes, and there are step-by-step instructions provided.

The findmypast information includes:

- Civil registration indexes to birth, marriage and death certificates for England and Wales
- Census returns for England and Wales 1841-91
- Occupational resources, including Kelly's Handbook 1901, the Clergy List 1896, Dental Surgeons' Directory 1925, Medical Register 1913 and Medical Directory for Ireland 1858
- Passenger lists of ships leaving the UK 1890-1960
- Indexes of living people, where you can look for a relative, address or business
- Military records, including soldiers who died in the First World War, Army births 1761-1994, marriages 1818-1994 and deaths 1796-1994, National Roll of the Great War, Army Roll of Honour 1939-45 and other Army lists roll calls 1656-1888
- Migration records showing passport applications 1851-1903, as well as several sets of Indian records such as the Bengal Service Graduation list for 1869, the India Office list for 1933, the East India Register and Army list for 1855, the Indian Army and Civil Service list for 1873 and the East India Company's Commercial Marine Service Pensions List 1793-1833

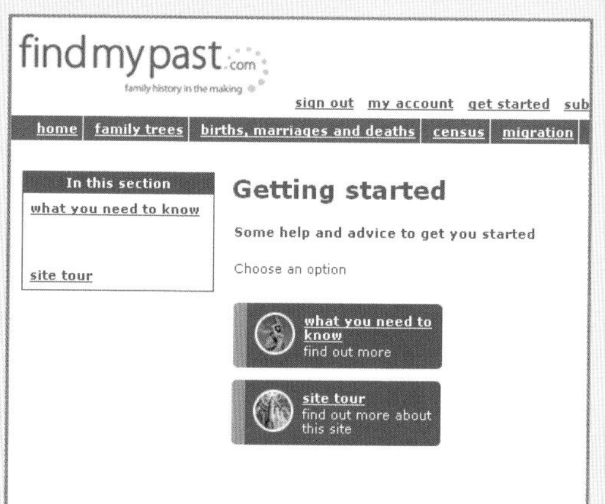

Get to know the site

4 Once this is complete, it's a good idea to familiarise yourself with the site. Click on the **Get started** tab at the top of the page, and you'll be directed to a screen that offers you **What you need to know** or **Site tour** options. Explore both until you feel confident about using the site.

Search all military records 1656-1994

Military records		discov subscrip
Search all military records 1656-1994	search	-
Soldiers Died in the Great War 1914-18	search	-
National Roll of the Great War 1914-18	search	-
Army Roll of Honour 1939-45	search	-
Other army lists roll calls 1656-1888	search	-
Armed forces births 1761-1994	search	-
Armed forces marriages 1818-1994	search	-
Armed forces deaths 1796-1994	search	-

Start your search

5 Once you've familiarised yourself with the site, you can begin your search by clicking on the relevant links at the top of the page. These are arranged by order of topic, so if you wish to search for military records, click on the **Military** link, and you'll be directed to the search page.

Wedding paperwork *A Victorian bride and groom sign the register – the original record of the event, which was forwarded to the GRO. Findmypast lets you view a transcription of the details.*

Using online data services
familysearch.org

The Church of Jesus Christ of Latter-day Saints (LDS), also known as the Mormons, maintains an online resources called **familysearch.org**. You can use its indexes free of charge. Its 'Search for Ancestors' facility is useful if you're looking for ancestors born before civil registration was introduced in the UK in 1837, because LDS has transcribed information, mostly from parish registers, known as 'British Isles Vital Records' from 1530 to 1906. These records appear in their International Genealogical Index (IGI).

FamilySearch records include:

- Census records, including a full transcript of the 1881 English and Welsh census, as well as US and Canadian records
- The International Genealogical Index (IGI) – a list of births, marriages, deaths and burials, transcribed from parish registers around the world
- Family trees, ancestral information and family pedigrees from other users of the website
- Links to Family History Centres world wide

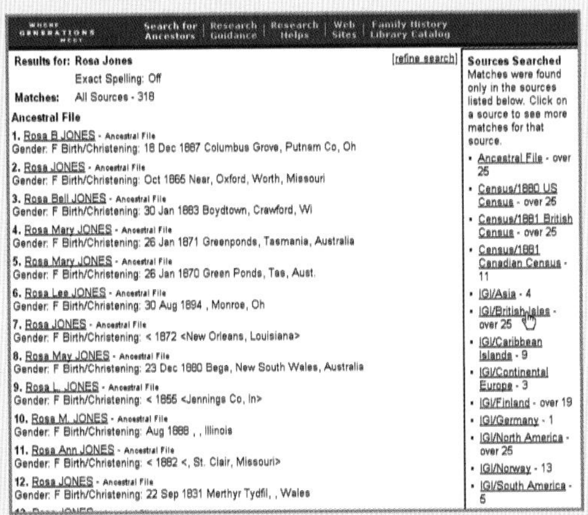

Start your search

1 Suppose you're searching for the birth of Rosa Jones around 1885. On the homepage click the **Search** tab at the top of the page and enter the name. Restrict the date ranges as much as possible. The page is presented in the form of a small family tree diagram; you can fill in as much or as little detail as you like. Select the appropriate country and click on **Search**.

Choose from the matches

2 A list of matches appears, broken into categories. You can view all these resources, or focus on the International Genealogical Index (IGI) by clicking on the relevant link in the **Sources searched** box on the right. Here, the link is **IGI/British Isles**. Click on it to see her name, the date of her birth, names of other relevant parties listed on the original record and details of the person who submitted the information.

Share your information

3 If you want to add to the information on the website, click on the **Share** tab at the top of the page. This takes you to the registration page where you confirm your details. Once you've been accepted, add your ancestral files to the site. As all the information has been voluntarily submitted and is therefore not necessarily accurate, you should verify the findings offline.

Using online data services
origins.net

As well as census records, the **origins.net** site provides access to less commonly found records, such as Irish wills, livery company apprenticeships and court disputes going back at least 400 years. It's able to do this through partnerships with rich archive sources, such as the National Library of Ireland, York University's Borthwick Institute and the Society of Genealogists.

The King's shilling
Recruiting sergeants in Westminster try to encourage young men to sign up. The Origins website holds useful data of the young men who enlisted.

theoriginsnetwork

sign up
login
getting started
what's new
newsletter
origins store
gift subscriptions
help & resources
feedback
libraries

British Origins
Irish Origins
Scots Origins

SPECIALISTS IN BRITISH AND IRISH GENEALOGY RESEARCH
Featuring comprehensive and exclusive British and Irish record collections dating back to the 13th century, as well as rare and unique photos and books to browse
Enter your ancestor's name below to begin your family research!

Getting Started | What's New | SoG Members

Search the most accurate 1841 census for England & Wal

Try a Free Origins Network Search ▸ | Free Search by Nar

Last name (Required) | First name (Optional)
NameX Close variants | NameX Close varia

NEW COLLECTIONS December 2006
○ England and Wales Census 1841 - NOW COMPLETE! About Sea
○ Wonderful London in British Origins Library About Browse

nsnetwork

Origins Network Subscription Packages

The Origins Network offers subscription packages to access British Origins and Irish Origi
Plans are available for a 72 hour access or monthly and annual recurring subscriptions. Pa
unlimited access to the selected databases for the duration of your subscription with no ex

○ Monthly and longer subscriptions to British Origins, Irish Origins or Total Access
a Free E-Booklet on English or Irish genealogy research written by Origins Experts
○ SoG Members Please click here to sign up or log in

Origins Total Access | British Origins | Irish Origins

Change currency: British Pounds | Check currency converter

Origins Total Access *Best value!* Choose pl

Gain access to our exclusive British and Irish databases and Libraries for one low price (note that Scots Origins searches are always free)
Change currency or check converter

▸ 72 hour
▸ Monthly
▸ Annual

Sign up

1 From the homepage you can make a free search by name or place. To access this information, you need to sign up as a subscriber. Click on the **Sign up** link on the top left-hand side of the homepage. Enter your contact information, plus your email address.

Select a subscription package

2 You can choose to subscribe to all of the British, Irish and Scottish collections or you can opt to subscribe to only one area. Prices vary from package to package. You'll subscribe for a set number of days, so have all the information for your searches ready, to save time and money. Click on your chosen package and follow the registration and payment details.

The Origins collections include:

British Origins britishorigins.com
- Marriage Licence Allegations Index 1694-1850
- Militia Attestations Index 1886-1910
- Bank of England Will Extracts Index 1717-1845
- Apprentices of Great Britain 1710-74
- Passenger lists for 1890
- Teachers' Registrations 1870-1948
- Prerogative and Exchequer Courts of York Probate Index 1853-8
- Boyd's Inhabitants of London index

Irish Origins irishorigins.com
- Dublin City Census for 1851
- Irish Wills Index 1484-1858
- Passenger lists: Irish ports to USA for 1890
- Militia Attestations Index 1872-1915
- Griffith's Valuation of Ireland 1847-64

Scots Origins scotsorigins.com
- Access to experts' research of Old Parish Registers, detailing births, baptisms, marriages and death records in Scotland
- The 1861 and 1871 census records
- Free search for Scottish places
- Articles and discussions on Scottish history

Using online data services
scotlandspeople.gov.uk

If you have Scottish ancestors, visit the 'one-stop shop' for Scottish family history, **scotlandspeople.gov.uk**. It's the government-sponsored online resource for Scottish records, and holds most of the birth, marriage and death indexes, known as statutory registers, as well as images of the original documents online.

Original images *Each hand-written two-line entry in the Old Parish Register of births and baptisms records whether the child was 'lawful' or 'natural' – a euphemism for illegitimate.*

The website will give you access to what is known as Old Parish Registers, which are the records kept by individual parishes of the Church of Scotland before the introduction of civil registration in 1855. Some date back as far as 1552. Many parish boundaries were changed over time, often more than once, and on this site you can find information about these changes to ensure you're looking in the right place.

The website also offers research guides, background information about the records, discussion groups and a comprehensive Frequently Asked Questions (FAQ) section. Browsing the contents list is free, but you'll have to pay to access the data (the fee is a contribution to the cost of indexing and digitising the records).

The ScotlandsPeople indexes include:

- Indexes and images of Statutory Registers: births 1855-1906, marriages 1855-1931 and deaths 1855-1956
- Indexes and images of census records for Scotland 1841-1901
- Indexes and images of Old Parish Registers for births, baptisms, banns and marriages 1553-1854
- Indexes to wills and testaments 1513-1901. This area is free to search.

Getting more information

As well as searching for facts about your ancestors, you can read about the significance of the data you're looking at. This is an important aspect of your research as it gives you an overall picture of how your ancestors lived, not just where and when.

The indexes on the site are listed in the box below. To access more recent statutory registers for births, marriages and deaths, as well as burial records from the parish registers, you need to go to the General

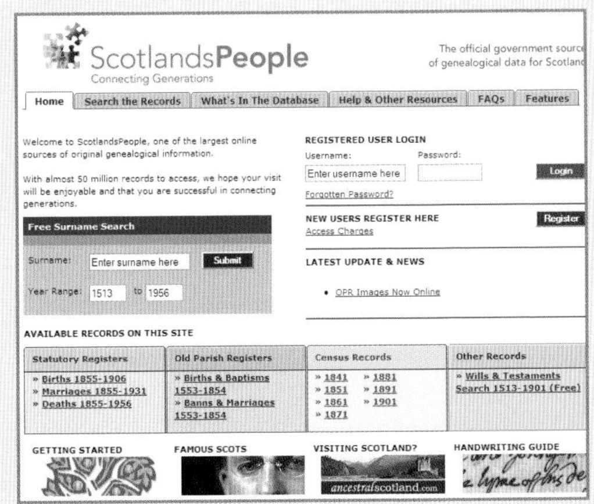

Go to the homepage

1 There's a free surname search offered on the ScotlandsPeople homepage, but you'll need to register if you want to do a more detailed search of the records. Select **Register** from the **New users register here** section on the right-hand side of the homepage.

Register Office for Scotland, in Edinburgh. The website tells you how to do this and the address details are also given in the Directory. Read more about using ScotlandsPeople on pages 96-99, and about searching Scottish parish records on page 144.

For the record *A class of children pose with their teacher at Eddleston School in Peebleshire in 1899. Their names and family details would have been entered in the Scottish records when they were born, and again when they were baptised.*

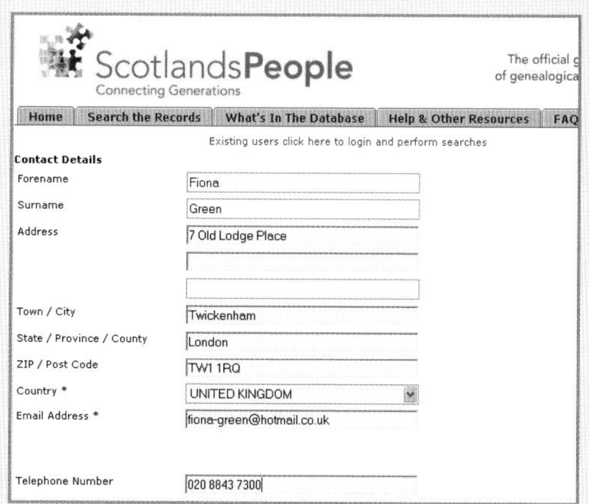

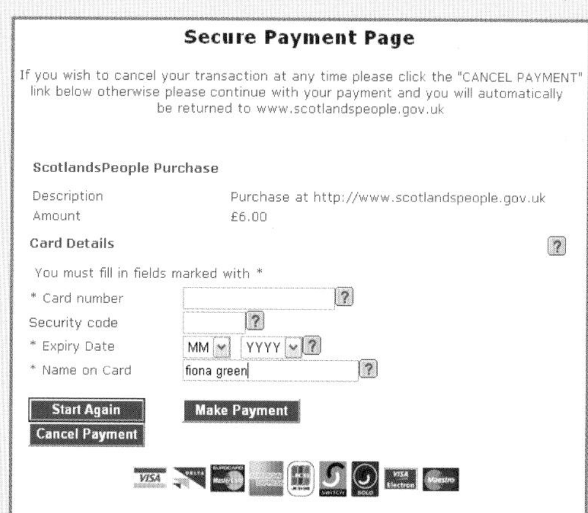

Register and get a password

2 Enter your name, postal and email addresses as well as your username. Your password will be emailed to you, and when you receive it you can start your searches. Once you've filled in the details, click the **Register** button at the bottom of the page. You'll be taken to a page where you can buy credits and choose a payment method.

Buy credits

3 Select the payment method and the number of credits from the drop-down menu and click on **Purchase**. Follow the payment instructions. Once payment is authorised, you'll be taken back to the site and your 90 days of access begin. Return to the search screen and select which one of the sets of data you want to access.

Buy more credits

4 During your 90 days, the icon on the bar at the top of the screen shows how many credits you have, and whether they've expired or not. If you run out, click the **Need more?** link. Select the amount you want to purchase from the drop-down list, and click on the blue **Purchase** button. Follow the instructions to make a further payment.

Using online data services
familyhistoryonline.net

The data at **familyhistoryonline.net** (which is sometimes called FHOL) has been made available by the Federation of Family History Societies (FFHS), which acts as a co-ordinator for a number of family history societies. The information on the website is organised by UK county. It contains more than 67 million records, covering census records, parish registers with births, baptisms and marriages, as well as details of workhouse admissions and deaths. There's also a national list of army deserters and details of wills and probate, and a link to the National Burial Index (see opposite), which has a growing collection of burial details, memorial inscriptions and photographs of gravestones.

Using the site

When you've registered (see right), go to the homepage and click on **Databases**. You'll see an index page that shows you at a glance which counties are covered. Select a county and browse the contents for what you need. At the end of each county list you'll see a link to the National Burial Index for that area (shown as NBI).

The amount of information available for different counties varies a great deal: some counties are comprehensively covered, others may have little or none at all.

Did they go to Australia?

In addition to UK information, FHOL has some Australian records, such as the full lists of 20th-century newspaper funeral notices. There are also details of cemetery burials and memorial inscriptions in Victoria for the period 1835 to 1997. The Victoria lists also contain the names of people mentioned in official Government Gazettes for Victoria between 1858 and 1900. New South Wales lists include details of convicts arriving there between 1788 and 1842.

Mealtime in the workhouse *Seated in unsociable rows, men in a Marylebone workhouse in 1903 eat their dinner. Life was intentionally hard and* **familyhistoryonline.net** *has moving records of men who died in Victorian workhouses, separated from their families.*

The National Burial Index

Burials and monumental inscriptions in England and Wales from 1538 (when parish records started) can be found in the National Burial Index at **familyhistory.online.net**. You'll find the name and age of the deceased, the date of burial and where the burial is recorded. The index covers Nonconformist and cemetery records, too. The inscription shown here is from a monument in Westminster Abbey for a man who died at the improbably old age of 152.

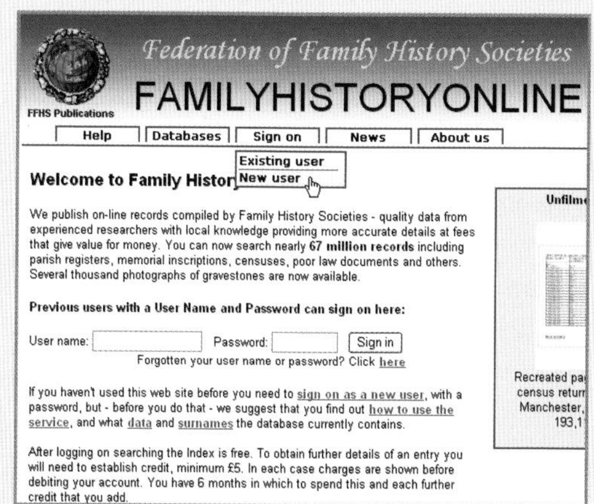

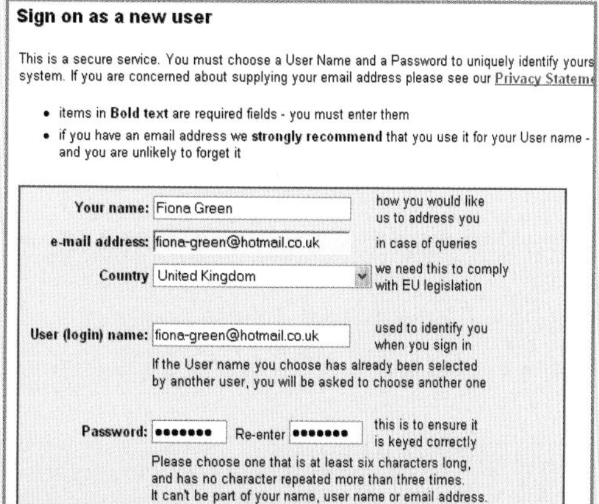

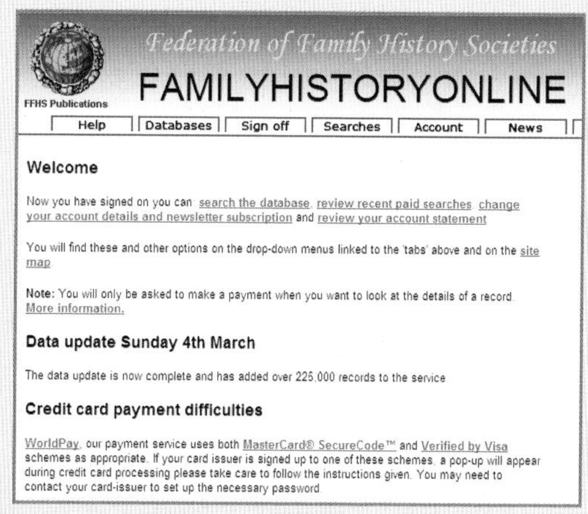

Sign on

1 To gain access to the databases on the site, you need to register as a user. On the homepage, click the **Sign on** link at the top of the page, and select the **New user** option from the drop-down menu. This takes you to the registration page.

Register your details

2 Enter your name, email details, country of residence, username and password. If you want to receive the FFHS newsletter, select the **Newsletter** box. After filling in your details, click the **Sign on** button.

Start browsing

3 You'll be taken to a confirmation screen that tells you what you can browse, free of charge. When you want to see an entry in detail you'll be told what it will cost. Click on the charge shown and follow the prompts to pay by credit or debit card. You have six months to use the credit. When you've paid, fuller information will be displayed, and you can print it out. (For more about costs, see page 140.)

Where did your surname come from?

The starting point for your family research will probably be your surname. Whether it's rare or common, it will tell you something about your family background and help you to trace other ancestors.

The Normans brought surnames to Britain after the Conquest in 1066. Before then, most people simply had Anglo-Saxon or Viking personal names, such as Edgar or Eric. Some Normans took their names from the towns they had left in France, such as the Laceys from Lassy. Others used their fathers' names, adding 'fitz', meaning 'son of', to form new names such as Fitzwilliam. Biblical names, such as John and Peter, were also used. As the population grew, so did the need for surnames, in order to distinguish people.

LOCATION Linking a name to a location started in the 13th century. More than a quarter of English surnames came from the position of a person's home, such as Underwood or Bywater, or from geographical features, such as Banks, Ford, Hill or Wood. Surnames that developed from place names often took the form used in local dialect, so someone from Braithwell in Yorkshire may have been called Brewell. People who moved to a new area were often named after the place they had come from, such as Welshman.

FAMILY NAMES Many surnames came from a father's name – so the son of James may have become known as Jameson. These are called patronymic names. Less frequently, names came from the mother's line – matronymic. This was likely if the woman were a widow or a wealthy landowner. Matronymic last names were also given to children of unwed mothers. Their descendants would adopt a matronym based on her name, such as Marriott from Mary, and Beaton from Beatrice.

FEATURES People were often named after their physical appearance, character or nickname – Sweet, Strong, Short or Ball (a nickname for a bald man), for instance.

OCCUPATION This is the most common derivation of English names. Clerk, Cook, Hunter, Butcher, Baker and Smith are all self-explanatory. Some occupational names are no longer quite so obvious. Cooper, for example, is derived from the maker of casks; Fletcher

The Luttrell Psalter *In the first half of the 14th century, Geoffrey Luttrell, a wealthy Lincolnshire landowner, commissioned a richly illustrated copy of the Psalms. The illustrations give an insight into rural and domestic medieval life and show some of the occupations that later gave rise to surnames used today. This portion shows a butcher, two cooks and two dispensers or butlers.*

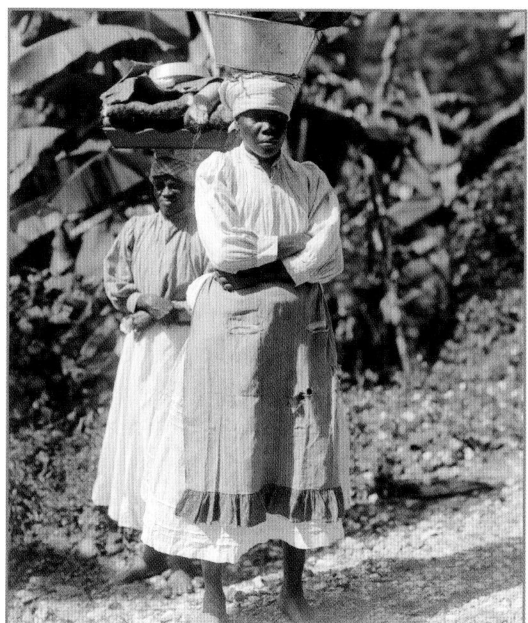

New names imposed

Many people taken as slaves from Africa to the West Indies in the 17th and 18th centuries were deprived of their own family names and given the surnames of the plantation owners or the estate on which they worked.

made arrows; Coward herded cows; Webster was a weaver and Butler, Spence or Spencer were dispensers of food and drink.

NO STANDARD SPELLINGS Until the late 19th century, few people were literate, so names weren't often written down, and when they were, similar-sounding names may have been spelled differently, such as Smith and Smythe. People also changed their names to avoid prejudice. During and after the two World Wars, many German or Jewish names were anglicised – Braun to Brown, for example.

Learning more about your surname

Someone who shares your surname may have already made a start on researching it. The way to find out is to go to the Internet Surname Database at **surnamedb.com**, which is free to use. Enter your name in the search box on the homepage, and if it has been researched, you'll see the results immediately. The information concentrates on the origins of the name, its meaning, its likely geographical source and the changes in its location over time, as well as some of the holders of the name who've appeared in various parish and county records.

Links to other sites

On the **surnamedb.com** homepage there are several links taking you to other sites that will help with family research. One of them is **onegreatfamily.com**. It has a bank of 190 million already researched names, and displays them in the form of a simple family tree.

Origins and meanings

Back on the **surnamedb** homepage, click on **Surname origins** and you'll get a link to **ask.com**. Click on this and a list of family history sites is offered, including **dnaancestryproject.com** and **last-names.net**, both of which are helpful for surname searches.

For an insight into the meaning of surnames, go to **ramsdale.org/surname.htm**. It has a section on modern names and their long-forgotten origins.

The history of English, Irish, Welsh and Scottish surnames, as well as coats of arms, crests and mottos, are offered at **nameseekers.co.uk**.

The spread of a name

The Guild of One-Name Studies researches all appearances of a name (its distribution and frequency of appearance, for example). There are 7000 names on the Guild's site, **one-name.org**, and you can check what's held there by clicking on **Online records** on the homepage. An A to Z index comes up. Choose the first letter of the name you want, and if it's shown, click on it and you'll see who's researching it and how to contact them.

Just for fun

While following up on the surnames in your family history, you may find that a particular first name keeps on cropping up. To satisfy your curiosity, make a short detour to a website that sheds light on the history of first names – **behindthename.com**. Enter the first name you want to check and you're led to a chart that describes the impression it gives to other people, versions of the name as it appears in a number of other languages and comments about the name that have been posted online.

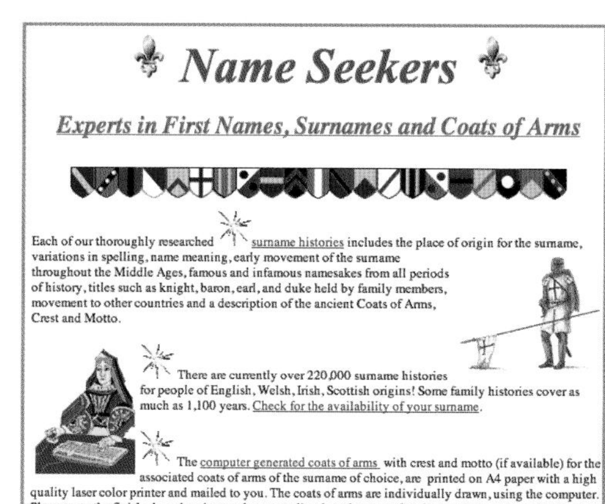

Tracking family names

Your surname provides important clues to your roots, especially if it's derived from a particular geographical region, place or feature.

All but the commonest surnames have a geographical distribution that can help you to trace the origins of your family. Thanks to the large data collections now available, studies in surnames and their worldwide geographical spread can be accessed on a new website, **nationaltrustnames.org.uk**. Just click on **Search for a surname** on this site to get information on 25,000 of the most widespread names.

Family business *Mr Davies stands outside his Cardiff boot shop in 1903. Then, you'd have been hard pressed to find a Davies beyond Wales.*

Find your relatives

Key in your name and you can call up maps of how people with your name were spread across Britain at the time of the 1881 census and in 1998. This will give you clues about how your family has moved over the past century. You'll also be able to pinpoint where most people with your name are concentrated, not only in Britain, Northern Ireland and the Republic of Ireland, but also in the USA and Commonwealth countries, too.

By accessing other census returns in the UK, you can take the research further. And if you want to know more about the history of your surname, try the Internet Surname Database on the website **surnamedb.com**, described on page 61.

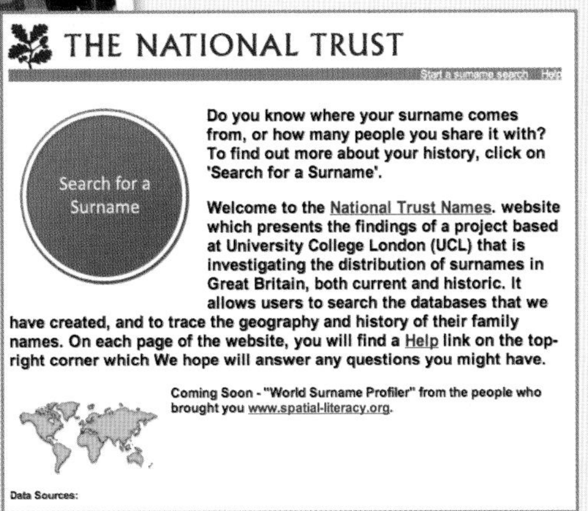

THE NATIONAL TRUST

Start a surname search Help

Search for a Surname

Do you know where your surname comes from, or how many people you share it with? To find out more about your history, click on 'Search for a Surname'.

Welcome to the National Trust Names. website which presents the findings of a project based at University College London (UCL) that is investigating the distribution of surnames in Great Britain, both current and historic. It allows users to search the databases that we have created, and to trace the geography and history of their family names. On each page of the website, you will find a Help link on the top-right corner which We hope will answer any questions you might have.

Coming Soon - "World Surname Profiler" from the people who brought you www.spatial-literacy.org.

Data Sources:

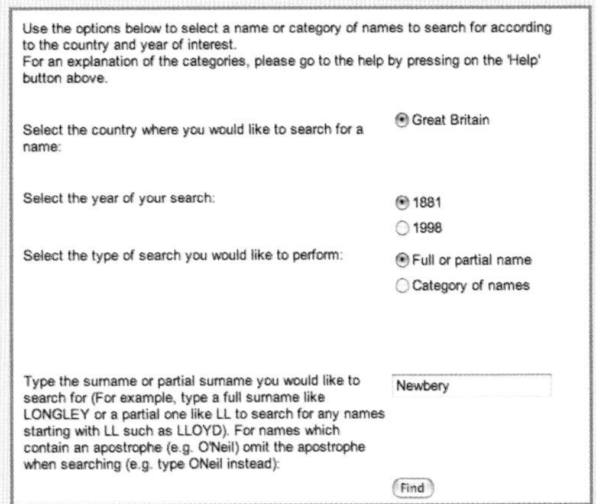

Use the options below to select a name or category of names to search for according to the country and year of interest.
For an explanation of the categories, please go to the help by pressing on the 'Help' button above.

Select the country where you would like to search for a name: ◉ Great Britain

Select the year of your search: ◉ 1881 ○ 1998

Select the type of search you would like to perform: ◉ Full or partial name ○ Category of names

Type the surname or partial surname you would like to search for (For example, type a full surname like LONGLEY or a partial one like LL to search for any names starting with LL such as LLOYD). For names which contain an apostrophe (e.g. O'Neil) omit the apostrophe when searching (e.g. type ONeil instead): Newbery

Find

Start your search

1 To search for the spread in Great Britain of the surname Newbery, for example, go to **nationaltrustnames.org.uk** homepage and click on **Search for a surname** on the left-hand side of the page. The data is taken from the 1881 census and the 1998 electoral roll, so when you start to search, you can choose to see how the distribution of your surname has changed over time.

Fill in your details

2 Great Britain is already selected as the country to check. You then need to select either 1881 or 1998. Once you have your results it's easy to change your selection to see how the distribution of your surname has changed. If you're looking for a specific surname search, select **Full or partial name**. Type the name you're searching for in the box provided – in this case, Newbery. For a wider search, use **Category of names**. Click on **Find** to view the results.

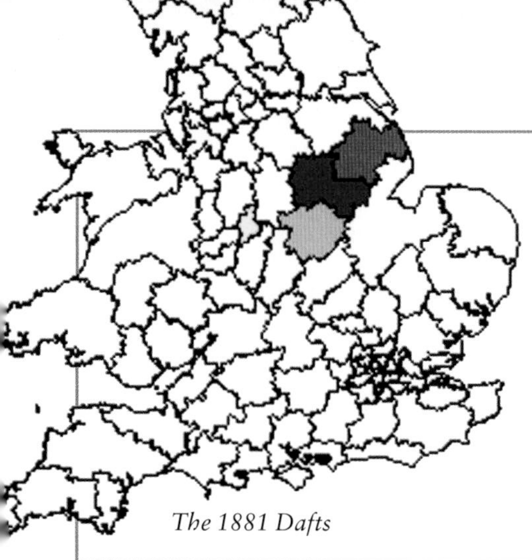
The 1881 Dafts

They weren't daft!

What could the names Cock, Hickinbottom and Smellie have in common? The research behind the creation of **nationaltrustnames.org.uk** reveals that these are among the six least popular surnames in Britain and have disappeared from the records over the past century or so. Another in this category is 'Daft'. Call it up on the distribution map of 1881 (left) and you'll see that the name is concentrated in the east Midlands, in Nottinghamshire, Lincolnshire and Leicestershire. Click on the map of 1998 (right) and the picture has changed little, apart from a small exodus to Dorset. The surname of Daft probably began with a single family – and just to set the record straight, in the Middle Ages it meant 'meek', not 'stupid'.

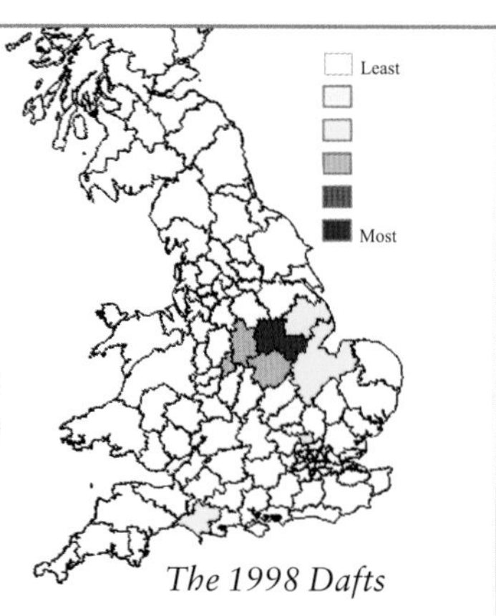

The 1998 Dafts

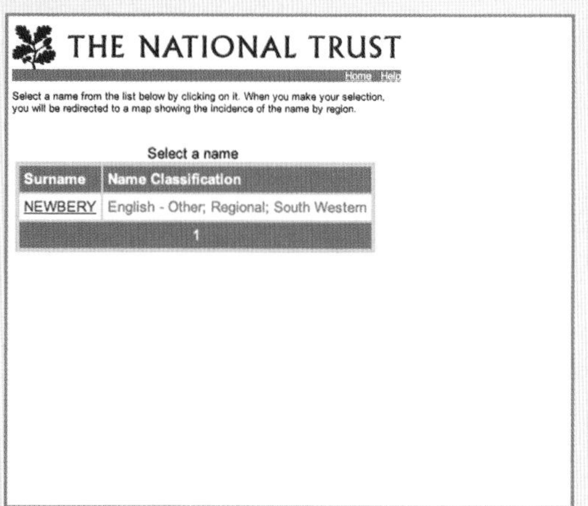

View the spread of a name

3 If you selected **Full or partial name**, you'll be presented with either a single match (as above) or a list of surnames, showing you the basic ethnic and geographical background for each one. If your name doesn't appear in the 1881 search, try again, this time selecting 1998 to see if it appears there. Then select the name and click on the link.

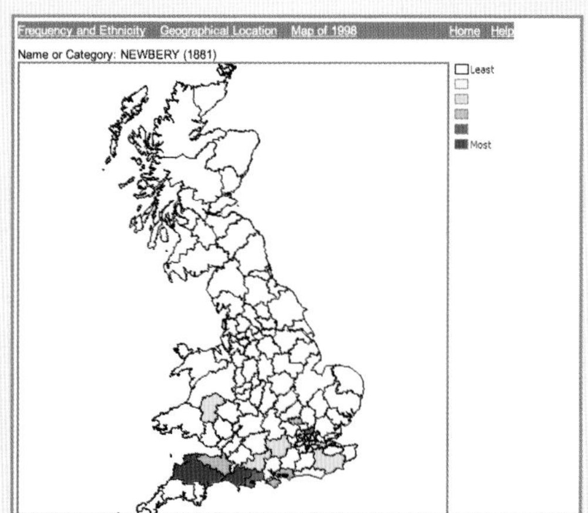

British concentrations

4 This page will show you a map of England, Scotland and Wales, showing the distribution of your surname, colour coded to indicate the areas of the most and least coverage. Now you can begin to build up a picture of where the heartland of your family surname was located in 1881. In this case, you can see Newbery is mostly of southwest origin. At the top of the map, there's an option to view the map of 1998. Click on this link to see the corresponding distribution a century later.

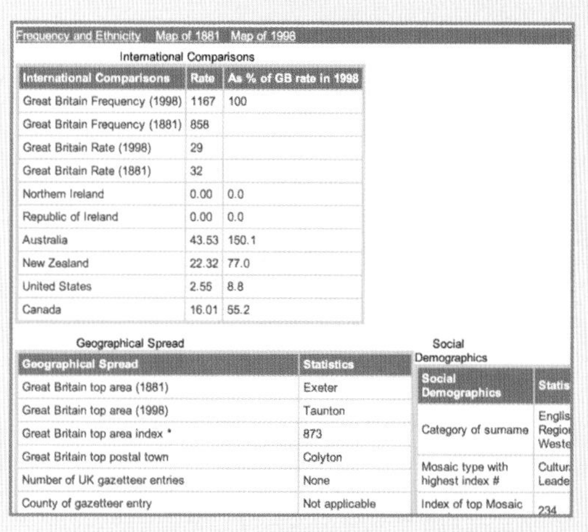
Frequency and Ethnicity Map of 1881 Map of 1998

International Comparisons

International Comparisons	Rate	As % of GB rate in 1998
Great Britain Frequency (1998)	1167	100
Great Britain Frequency (1881)	858	
Great Britain Rate (1998)	29	
Great Britain Rate (1881)	32	
Northern Ireland	0.00	0.0
Republic of Ireland	0.00	0.0
Australia	43.53	150.1
New Zealand	22.32	77.0
United States	2.55	8.8
Canada	16.01	55.2

Geographical Spread

Geographical Spread	Statistics
Great Britain top area (1881)	Exeter
Great Britain top area (1998)	Taunton
Great Britain top area index *	873
Great Britain top postal town	Colyton
Number of UK gazetteer entries	None
County of gazetteer entry	Not applicable

Social Demographics

Social Demographics	Statis
Category of surname	Englis Regio Weste
Mosaic type with highest index #	Cultur Leade
Index of top Mosaic	234

Find out more

5 From the map screen, click on **Geographical location** to see how common your surname is in other parts of the world and for more information on its spread within Britain. This may lead you to broaden your search for family members (see pages 254-61). From this screen you can also click on **Frequency and ethnicity**, to see your surname distribution data in terms of numbers for 1881 and 1998, followed by a listing that shows the ethnic origins of your name.

When a name doesn't match

If you have difficulty finding a match for the surname of an ancestor, it may well be because it has been presented differently in the records or indexes you've been searching. This situation is usually easy to resolve.

One reason your ancestor's surname appears differently in the records could be because the spelling has changed over time. A Shepherd could become a Sheppard, for example, or a Rumball a Rumbold. Or perhaps a census enumerator, encountering someone with an unfamiliar accent, didn't take down the name the way you'd expect. It could also be that a modern data processor has made a mistake reading Victorian handwriting – when you look at the originals yourself, you'll see how hard they are to read. (For more about how to read old handwriting, see page 174.)

Most of the material available online has been created by large groups of people working from digital records or microfilm, rather than the original documents. The reproduction of some of the original images is often less than perfect, making them difficult to read. Add the possibility of simple human error and the 100 per cent accuracy of surname transcription can't be guaranteed.

All of this means you have to be open-minded about surname spellings and be prepared to search for that ellusive person. But looking through huge lists of possible variants is a tedious process, so most data services offer a range of options for finding variants in a single search.

Search tips for finding names

Many websites automatically offer variations on the spelling of a name and you have to select the **Exact match** option if you want to find only the spelling you've entered. The disadvantage in doing a wider search is that you may have too many results to check.

There are ways to widen your search, though, without being overwhelmed by results. If you're having no luck trying to match a name exactly, a Wildcard, Soundex or Namex search can be helpful.

WILDCARD SEARCH One way to improve on an **Exact match** search is to use a Wildcard to stand for any letter or group of letters. Most sites use an asterisk for this purpose. For example, W*lsh will find Walsh, Welsh, Wailsh and so on. Will* finds Will, Wills, Willis, Williams and Willoughby. You can use more than one wildcard: W*l*h will find both Walsh and Welch. Wildcards are particularly useful at coping with transcription errors, as they allow you to ignore letters that have been entered wrongly.

Home | Search the Records | What's In The Database | Help & Other R
Overview | Viewed Images | Previous Searches | Timeline | Shopping Bas
Search Statutory Register Births
Click here for more information.
Search
Surname: *
Use Soundex
Forename:
Return all forenames
Sex: Both
Year Range: 1855 To
County/City/Minor Records: All Records
District: All Districts
ABBEY
ABBEY ST BATHANS
ABBOTSHALL
ABDIE
ABERCORN
ABERCROMBIE
ABERDALGIE
ABERDOUR (ABERDEEN)
SR Births Soundex
If you are unsure of the spelling of the surname, you may wish to check the "Use Soundex" box to activate a soundex search on that surname. Soundex is a system whereby names are grouped phonetically. It works by converting each name into a code or 'key', and retrieving all entries with the same code as the search name. It does, however, have its limitations and can generate a large number of superfluous results. For further information on using soundex and how to calculate the soundex value of a name, see Soundex

SEARCHING WITH SOUNDEX This technique for name-matching was invented in pre-computer days for the US census to try to get round spelling variations. Many records sites, such as ScotlandsPeople (left), make it available as a search option.

Soundex gives each surname a code based on the first letter and the remaining consonants, with similar codes for similar-

Saints' names *Many saints, such as John and Matthew (above), inspired both forenames and surnames. With time, their spelling may have changed, giving variations such as Johns, Johnson and Jonson, or Matthews, Matheson and Mathieson. A wildcard, Soundex or NameX search will help to find a name as it once was.*

sounding names. The code for Walsh, for example, is W420 and a Soundex search for Walsh will look for all names that are coded W420. These will include names like Welsh, Welch, Walch, Walshe as well as many that are less likely to be misspellings or genuine variants of Walsh, such as Wallace, Wells, Wills, Wheelock, Wolsey and Wyles. So a Soundex search will always give you a lot of names to search through. Another limitation of Soundex is that some obvious surname variants have different codes and won't turn up as matches, so Hill has a code H400, while Hills is H420.

SEARCHING WITH NAMEX The surname-matching technique NameX is a more recent option to Soundex. It averages out the results of several name-matching systems to give a score of how closely another name matches what you've searched for. So if you search for Walsh, you'll find Wallsh scores 99 per cent, Welsh 95 per cent, Walshaw 82 per cent and so on. In Soundex, two spellings either match or they don't. But NameX tells you how closely they match. The Origins site, for example, uses NameX to give you a choice between **Close variants** and **All variants.**

Searching for a surname, offline

Don't worry if you can't match a name online. There are surname directories and publications that can help. Here are just three suggestions.

- ☛ Family history magazines (such as *Family History Monthly*) often feature surname studies.
- ☛ If a family history has been researched before, you'll be able to find it in T.R. Thompson's *Catalogue of British Family Histories*, available through your local family history society or library.
- ☛ Many name studies are also available through local and county history studies. *The Genealogist's Internet* gives a list of all the surnames and family studies that have been published since the 18th century, in one handy volume.

The Bard fails the spelling test

William Shakespeare's will is remembered not only for the leaving of his second-best bed to his wife, Anne Hathaway, but also because his name is spelled differently twice in the same document. In one place it's given as 'Shackspeare', but the signature at the end of the will appears as 'Shakspeare'. His name is spelled differently on other documents, too, and illustrates the relaxed attitude towards spelling in many official and private records of the time.

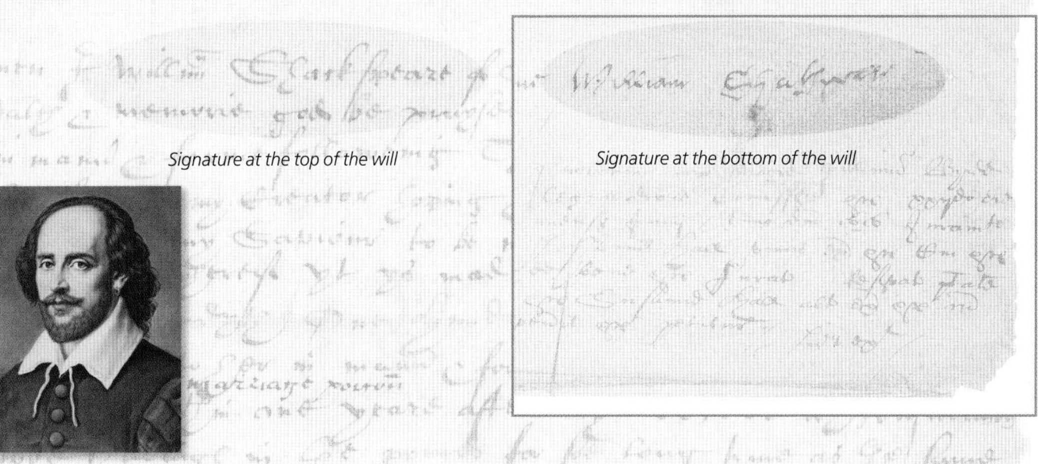

Signature at the top of the will

Signature at the bottom of the will

Building your family tree

Once you've gathered all your preliminary data, you'll want to find and collect the information that links one generation to the next – birth, marriage and death certificates, census forms, church records and other original documents. This is where you turn family history detective, following the clues and making great discoveries.

Setting out your family tree

When you've gathered a certain amount of information about your family going back a few generations, you'll want to start putting it into some sort of order. A family tree is the most obvious and most manageable format for this.

The simplest family tree is known as a pedigree chart or birth brief (see page 70). It starts with one person (usually yourself) and works backwards in time, generation by generation. At its most basic level, a pedigree chart names direct ancestors only – parents and grandparents on both the maternal and paternal line – and to keep things simple, it doesn't include aunts, uncles, cousins or siblings. As your research widens, you may find that you expand your pedigree chart which can encompass these relatives and any new ones that appear as you make progress. You can then work forward in time to record any children or grandchildren you may have.

Putting it down on paper

When you start drawing up your family tree, you'll use the information you've acquired from your family interviews as well as from your initial research. These are your building blocks and should include facts about:

- your children
- your brothers and sisters and their children
- your parents
- your grandparents
- any further generations about whom you have concrete evidence.

Working backwards, write your parents' names above your own, and link them with a double line to indicate their marriage (see the tree-drawing tips, right). Then add the names of your siblings, again linking them to you. As you add each person, list their dates and places of birth under their names for easy reference. Where marriages have taken place, write the date and place of marriage under each entry. And if anyone has died, write the date and place of death, if known.

List your grandparents, using the same principles, and go back as far as you can. Leave spaces for any information you don't know, or insert question marks if you're not certain of the date of an event or the full name of the person. These flagged areas will need follow-up research later on.

Starting your family tree on paper is the obvious way to go, but as you begin to add more and more information, using your computer becomes more practical. You'll find plenty of help in this book to help you to get your family tree into an electronic form, but it's worth waiting until you've amassed quite a bit of detail.

Check and double-check

Make sure that any information you add to your tree is verified and accurate. Remember to double-check everything you've been told against documented sources such as certificates and census records. You'll discover in this chapter how to find all this information and get copies of details. Once you've drawn up your immediate family tree based on interviews, it's a good idea to make it a rule that you add further information only after you've verified it.

Making duplicates

As your family tree expands, it's a good idea to take copies of smaller sections of it with you if you have to go to libraries or record offices in the course of your research. They'll help you to maintain your focus on a specific area of research without becoming bogged down in the larger tree and stop you being tempted to fly off in a dozen different directions on possible wild goose chases.

If you do find new information, add it to the master copy as soon as possible and be sure to date any additions as you write them onto the tree. From time to time, print out or draw up a new tree, so that you always have a clean, up-to-date version to refer to.

Facing hurdles

Be realistic about what you can expect to find. Although the ideal tree traces all lines back as far as possible, you're bound to encounter obstacles – especially as your search widens beyond your immediate family. Sometimes these problems can seem almost insurmountable – and every family historian dreads coming up against a 'brick wall'. But as you gain experience and amass more information, you'll discover that there are ways around apparent dead ends. The key is to be prepared to use the family history community, experiment with new sources and not to give up.

MUM → WEDDING PICS?

MY FAMILY TREE

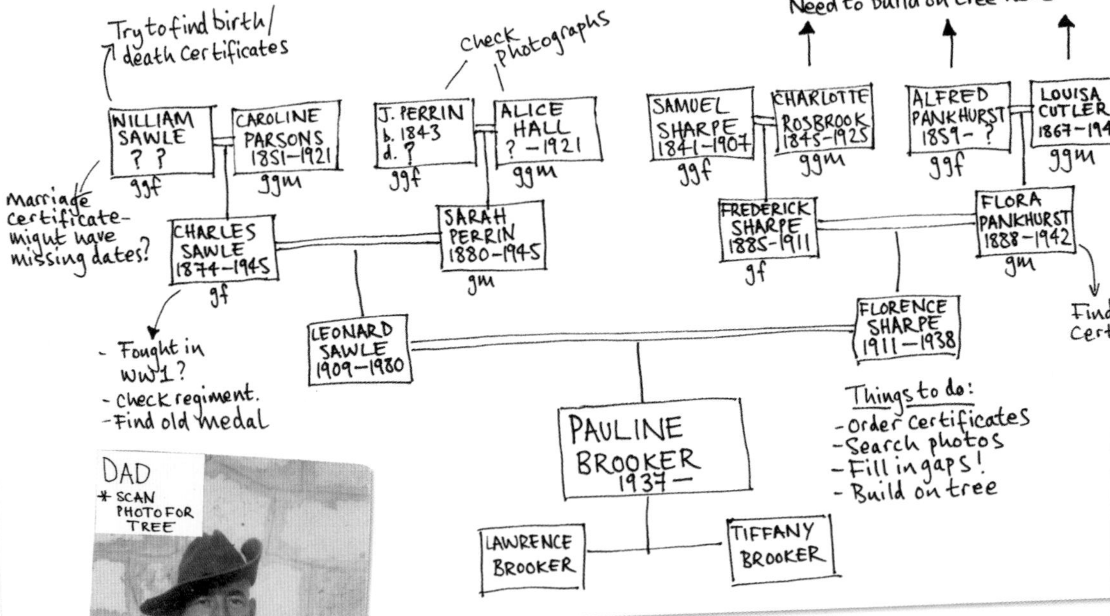

DAD
* SCAN PHOTO FOR TREE

First attempts *Start by putting your family tree together on paper, using all the documents you've collected. At first you may find it easier to write the names of your ancestors on pieces of card, or on sticky notes, so that you can move them around easily on your tree without having to re-draw it.*

Family tree-drawing tips

To make your tree easier to read and understand, it's a good idea to stick to the accepted conventions for showing relationships.

- Women on the tree are given their maiden name, and are linked to their spouse by **=** or **m**.
- A vertical line links children to their parents, beneath the marriage symbol.
- A horizontal line links siblings.
- Children are usually listed in chronological (date) order from left to right.
- Members of the same generation are written on the same horizontal line.

Types of family tree

Family trees come in different shapes and sizes. Once you've compiled enough information to start putting your tree onto your computer (see pages 312-5), you can decide which is best for you.

The most commonly used format is the pedigree chart (see right) that starts with yourself at the bottom of the page and works upwards, and backwards in time. Or, you can display the same information in a horizontal format, called a birth brief (below), which starts with you on the left and has each successive generation moving one step to the right. You can even develop a circular chart, with yourself in the centre. These charts are suitable if you are concentrating on just one branch of the family, excluding any siblings.

If you want to expand your tree to include other branches of your family, a drop line chart – where you start with your earliest-known ancestors at the top and work down through the generations – will be the most suitable. This type of tree can become complicated because there's so much information to include, but it has the benefit of showing a complete family history.

There are a number of accepted symbols and conventions to use when drawing up your tree – see pages 8 and 69.

Birth brief – an alternative view

This horizontal format for a family tree is simple and easy to read. On your computer, you can keep on adding generations as you discover more ancestors.

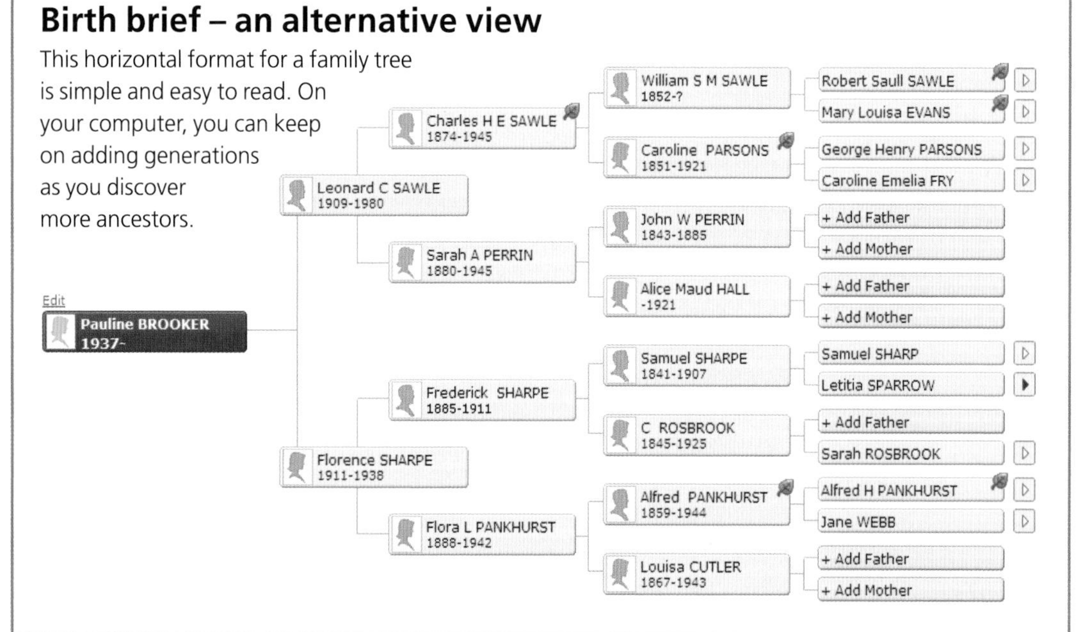

Know your pedigree *The style of tree that concentrates c branch of the family is called a pedigree. Here, the pedigr chart of Pauline Brooker starts at the bottom and works No siblings are shown, just direct ancestors. On Pauline' maternal line, the surname Sharp changed over time to S*

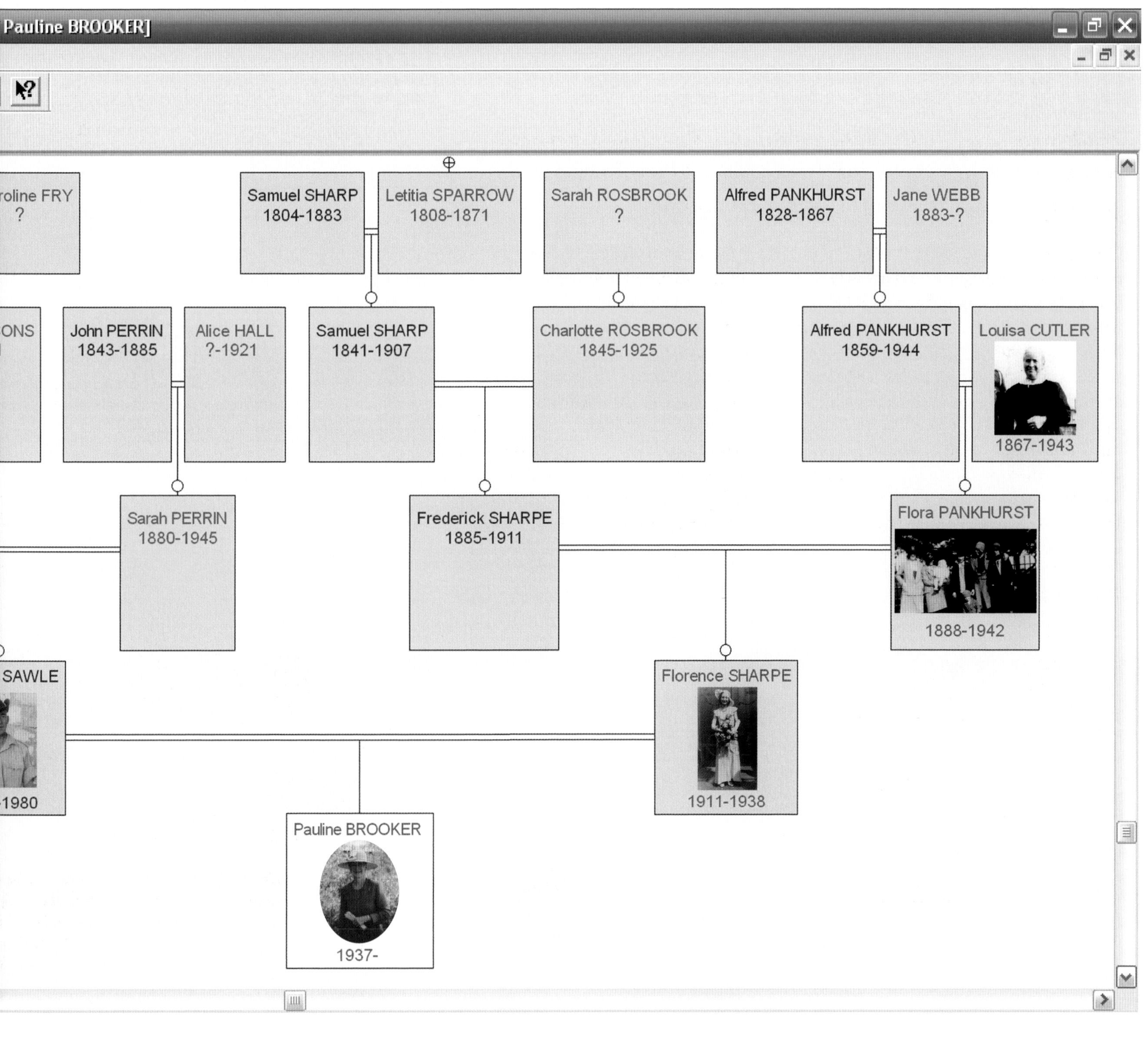
Pauline BROOKER]
roline FRY
?
Samuel SHARP
1804-1883
Letitia SPARROW
1808-1871
Sarah ROSBROOK
?
Alfred PANKHURST
1828-1867
Jane WEBB
1883-?
ONS
John PERRIN
1843-1885
Alice HALL
?-1921
Samuel SHARP
1841-1907
Charlotte ROSBROOK
1845-1925
Alfred PANKHURST
1859-1944
Louisa CUTLER
1867-1943
Sarah PERRIN
1880-1945
Frederick SHARPE
1885-1911
Flora PANKHURST
1888-1942
SAWLE
-1980
Florence SHARPE
1911-1938
Pauline BROOKER
1937-

Births, marriages and deaths

Now that you know how to enter material into your family tree, you can start researching the civil registration documents that hold vital information about your ancestors.

Understanding civil registration

The wealth of information collected by the Victorians sheds light on many aspects of our ancestors' lives, including their professions, their property, the size of their families, their age at death and even what they died of.

The established Church in England and Wales has had to record all of its ceremonies since 1538. Until 1837, baptisms, weddings and burials were registered at the church where the ceremony took place and the recorded information stayed there. But with the spread of nonconformist religious groups there were many births, burials and marriages not recorded in this way.

Registration after 1837

On July 1, 1837, soon after Queen Victoria ascended the throne, a national, centralised system of registering the births, marriages and deaths of everybody in England and Wales was set up for the first time. Scotland and Ireland had later starting dates.

THE FIRST NATIONAL INDEXES The new system introduced the concept of a civil marriage and required all religious establishments to forward records of marriages, and all relatives to register births and deaths at local register offices, where local indexes were created. These were sent each quarter (January-March, April-June, July-September and October-December) to the General Register Office (see page 80) with copies of each certificate issued. National indexes were compiled covering these respective quarters.

MISSING CERTIFICATES If you can't find an early certificate, it may be because your ancestor just didn't register the event. It wasn't until 1875 that the rules were tightened, making it more difficult to avoid registration. A large number of births, marriages and deaths were registered before 1875, nonetheless, and the certificates yield more details than the early parish records.

How civil registration worked

In 1837 a Registrar General was created in London with responsibility for the rest of England and Wales. Registration districts were set up with central register offices manned by superintendent registrars. Each registration district was split into sub-districts with a registrar to record local births, marriages and deaths. The new registration districts reflected the existing boundaries of the Poor Law Unions (see page 210).

REGISTRATION DISTRICT BOUNDARIES This system has not changed greatly since it was first established, but some boundaries have moved. You'll find the English and Welsh registration district boundaries for 1837 to 1851, 1852 to 1946 and 1946 to 1965 on maps published by the Institute of Heraldic and Genealogical Studies (see Directory). If you can't find an ancestor in the registration district that seems logical, look in adjacent districts, in case boundaries have changed.

PAGE 11

RECEIVED: 25 OCT 1901

MARRIAGE solemnized in the Parish Church of S. John, Walworth, in the County of SURREY.

No.	When Married.	Name and Surname.	Age.	Condition.	Rank or Profession.	Residence at the time of Marriage.	Father's Name and Surname.	Rank or Profession of Father.
21	Dec 25 1882	James William Long	full	Bachelor	Driver	2 Brunswick Place	James Long	Boot Maker
		Alice McKearns	full	Spinster		2 Brunswick Place	Bernard McKearns	deceased

Married in S. John's Church, according to the Rites and Ceremonies of the Established Church, after Banns by me, G. F. Cotham Vicar

This Marriage was solemnized between us: James William Long, Alice McKearns — in the presence of us: Eliz Lee, Amelia McKearns

The above is a true Copy of the Marriage Register of the Parish aforesaid.—Witness my Hand, this 25 day of December 1882

Wedding days *English artist, Sir Samuel Luke Fildes, painted this picture (left) of a village wedding taking place in high summer in 1883. By contrast, a marriage certificate from 1882 (right) shows that two domestic servants from Walworth in London were married on Christmas Day – their only free day.*

What registration certificates will tell you

First prize in the treasure hunt for your family's records must be the discovery of birth, marriage and death certificates. Not only do they confirm names, dates and places, they may often yield a wealth of other information, too.

Sometimes a certificate may uncover a long-hidden family secret. If, for example, you come across a birth certificate where the father's name has been left blank, this suggests that the child was illegitimate and the father was not present at the registration (the mother couldn't give his name in his absence). When this happened the child usually took the mother's surname.

You can double-check this information by searching for that child's marriage certificate and seeing if the father's name is blank on that, too. Thanks to the Victorians' scrupulous record-keeping, you can find details of the births, marriages and deaths of many of your ancestors in the records of the General Register Office (GRO).

The National Archives in Kew have microfiche copies of the indexes from 1837 until 1992, and many local record offices and public libraries also have copies. If you'd rather do your research from home, several websites provide online access to the indexes (see pages 82-93). You'll need to use data from the indexes when you order copies of certificates from the GRO (see page 94).

DoVE: improved access to indexes

The General Register Office (GRO) is undertaking a major project, known as DoVE – Digitisation of Vital Events. It'll create a searchable database of all birth, marriage and death records from 1837 to 2006, as well as records of stillbirths from 1927 to 2006. Once DoVE is complete, it'll be easier to track down the details of your family's past, and the process of buying registration certificates will be streamlined. To find out more about its progress, go to **gro.gov.uk** and click on the DoVE link in the **Shortcuts** box.

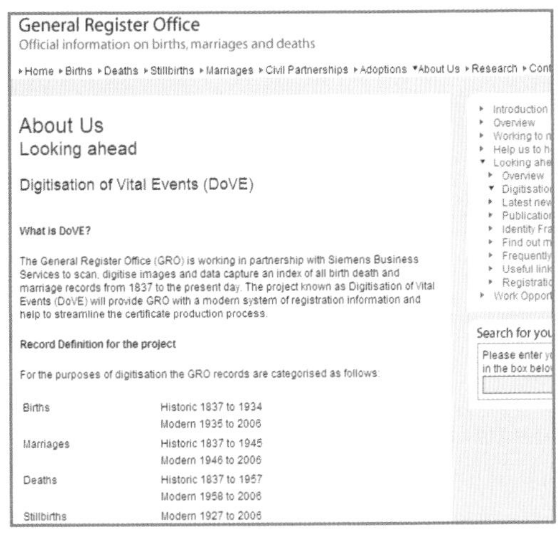

The importance of baptismal records

Before civil registration was introduced in 1837, births would not have been recorded officially. But as most babies were baptised within weeks in their local church (left), baptism records act as a guide to the birth date. If your ancestor was born after 1837, you can expect to find a record of both birth and baptism. After 1874, by law, births had to be registered within six weeks of the event.

CERTIFIED COPY OF AN ENTRY OF BIRTH

GIVEN AT THE GENERAL REGISTER OFFICE

Application Number G209162

REGISTRATION DISTRICT Amesbury

1858 BIRTH in the Sub-district of Orcheston in the County of Wilts

Columns:-	1	2	3	4	5	6	7	8	9	10
No.	When and where born	Name, if any	Sex	Name and surname of father	Name, surname and maiden surname of mother	Occupation of father	Signature, description and residence of informant	When registered	Signature of registrar	Name entered after registration
418	Fourth March 1858 Tilshead	Edward	Boy	Thomas Mead	Ellen Mead formerly Payne	Shoemaker	Ellen Mead Mother Tilshead	Tenth March 1858	Edw. Wilson Turner Registrar	
①	②	③	④	⑤	⑥	⑦	⑧	⑨	⑩	

CERTIFIED to be a true copy of an entry in the certified copy of a Register of Births in the District above mentioned.

Given at the GENERAL REGISTER OFFICE, under the Seal of the said Office, the 13th day of March 2007

BXCC352896

CAUTION: THERE ARE OFFENCES RELATING TO FALSIFYING OR ALTERING A CERTIFICATE AND USING OR POSSESSING A FALSE CERTIFICATE ©CROWN COPYRIGHT

WARNING: A CERTIFICATE IS NOT EVIDENCE OF IDENTITY.

PDP

039887 10107 08/05 SPSL 012033

What you'll find on a birth certificate

First, you'll see where the birth was registered – the registration district, the sub-district and the county. Then ① the GRO reference number ② where and when the child was born (this can be revealing, as most children were born at home until the National Health Service was set up in 1948, when hospital births became more common) ③ the child's first names ④ the child's sex ⑤ the father's full name ⑥ the mother's full name and maiden name ⑦ the father's occupation ⑧ who registered the birth, their relationship to the child and their address ⑨ when the birth was registered and ⑩ the registrar's signature. The last column is for any later notes. It may show that a child was adopted or that they changed their surname.

CERTIFIED COPY OF AN ENTRY OF MARRIAGE

GIVEN AT THE GENERAL REGISTER OFFICE

Application Number Y006395

1910. Marriage solemnized at the Ea. Ham Baptist Church, Plashet Grove East Ham in the District of West Ham in the County of Essex West Ham C.B

No. (1)	When Married. (2)	Name and Surname. (3)	Age. (4)	Condition. (5)	Rank or Profession. (6)	Residence at the time of Marriage. (7)	Father's Name and Surname. (8)	Rank or Profession of Father. (9)
84	Ninth September 1910	Archie Edgar Hibbert	28 years	Bachelor	Secretary Public Company	130 Clements Road East Ham	John Rison Hibbert	of no Occupation
		Louie Alice Beatrice Mead	26 years	Spinster	/	76 Bristol Road East Ham	Edward Mead	Commercial Clerk

Married in the (10) Baptist Church according to the Rites and Ceremonies of the Baptists by certificate by me,

This Marriage was solemnized between us, (11) A. E. Hibbert, L. A. B Mead; in the Presence of us, Jno R. Hibbert, E. Mead, G. Mead; Frank Williams, S. Mawer Registrar

CERTIFIED to be a true copy of an entry in the certified copy of a register of Marriages in the Registration District of West Ham

Given at the GENERAL REGISTER OFFICE, under the Seal of the said Office, the 6th day of September 2001

MXA 895057

This certificate is issued in pursuance of section 65 of the Marriage Act 1949. Sub-section 3 of that section provides that any certified copy of an entry purporting to be sealed or stamped with the seal of the General Register Office shall be received as evidence of the marriage to which it relates without any further or other proof of the entry, and no certified copy purporting to have been given in the said Office shall be of any force or effect unless it is sealed or stamped as aforesaid.

CAUTION: THERE ARE OFFENCES RELATING TO FALSIFYING OR ALTERING A CERTIFICATE AND USING OR POSSESSING A FALSE CERTIFICATE. ©CROWN COPYRIGHT

WARNING: A CERTIFICATE IS NOT EVIDENCE OF IDENTITY.

Form MXA Series Dd 0730 90M 04/01 SPSL(000153)

What you'll find on a marriage certificate

First, the name of the town and county where the marriage took place. Then (1) the GRO reference number (2) the date of the marriage (3) the full names of the groom and bride (4) the ages of the groom and bride ('full age' means they were over 21, 'minor' means they were under 21) (5) the marital status of the groom and bride (6) the groom's occupation or social status (7) where the groom and bride were living before they married (8) the groom's and bride's fathers' names (if the father has died, the word 'deceased' will normally be written underneath the name) (9) the groom's and bride's fathers' occupations or social status (10) where the marriage took place, whether it was in a church, synagogue or registry office, and under which religious denomination the ceremony was performed and (11) the signatures of the groom, bride and two witnesses.

CERTIFIED COPY OF AN ENTRY OF DEATH

GIVEN AT THE GENERAL REGISTER OFFICE

Application Number Y 006395

REGISTRATION DISTRICT Ilford

1946 DEATH in the Sub-district of Ilford North in the County of Essex

Columns:–	1	2	3	4	5	6	7	8	9
No.	When and where died	Name and surname	Sex	Age	Occupation	Cause of death	Signature, description and residence of informant	When registered	Signature of registrar
459	Seventeenth April 1946 King George Hospital	William Loving	Male	73 years	of 26 St. Margarets Road Barking a Council Lavatory Attendant	Broncho pneumonia due to fractured Right femur. Knocked down by motor cycle on highway when crossing on foot. PM Accidental Cause	Certificate received from P. Bernard Skeels Coroner for Metropolitan District of Essex Inquest held 20th April 1946 25th April 1946	Twenty seventh April 1946	G A Norkett Registrar
①	②	③	④	⑤	⑥	⑦	⑧	⑨	⑩

CERTIFIED to be a true copy of an entry in the certified copy of a Register of Deaths in the District above mentioned.

Given at the GENERAL REGISTER OFFICE, under the Seal of the said Office, the 6th day of September 2001

DXZ 894350

See note overleaf

What you'll find on a death certificate

It will start with the registration district, the sub-district and the county. Then ① the GRO reference number ② when and where the person died ③ the deceased person's full name ④ the deceased person's sex ⑤ the deceased person's age (death certificates issued after1984 show the person's date and place of birth instead) ⑥ the deceased person's occupation (women's death certificates prior to 1984 usually state the husband's name and occupation instead of the woman's occupation) ⑦ the cause of death ⑧ who registered the death, their relationship to the deceased person and their own address ⑨ the date the death was registered and, finally, ⑩ the registrar's signature. If the cause of death is a condition or illness that's unfamiliar to you, see how to get help with understanding the terminology on page 74.

How to use General Register Office indexes

Your search for family records is about to get really exciting. The records of the vast majority of births, marriages and deaths in England and Wales since 1837 are listed in the indexes of the General Register Office (GRO), and the information gets easier to access every day.

You can already view many of the indexes online through the pay-per-view websites that appear on the following pages. The ultimate aim is for everyone to be able to search online for images of real certificates.

What the indexes are

The GRO indexes are lists rather like the index in a book. Entries for all certificates are arranged in chronological order, and then alphabetically, by surname. In the past, they were held in book form at the Family Records Centre in Islington, London, but now you can see them on microfiche at The National Archives (TNA) at Kew or through the websites that are making them available online.

Before you begin looking for your family's certificates, you'll need to understand exactly how the indexes are arranged and what information they contain. The page opposite tells you how to find birth certificates; see page 80 for marriage and death certificates.

Don't be misled by the date

Even if you know the exact date of an event such as a birth, the index entry will not necessarily appear in the quarter in which it happened: it will be in the quarter in which it was registered. Births may be registered several weeks after the event.

BETWEEN 1837 AND 1983 In this period, the indexes are arranged in year order, with each year divided into quarters: January-February-March; April-May-June; July-August-September; and October-November-December. Each quarter is known by the name of its last month – so the first quarter is referred to as 'March quarter'. Within each quarter you'll find an alphabetical index of surnames. So if, for example, you know that your ancestor, Grace Abbots, was born on August 4, 1920, find the section of books

How to order a certificate by phone

Having found an entry in the indexes, you may want to order a certificate. You can do this online by visiting the GRO website, **gro.gov.uk** (see page 94) or, if you're unsure about the information you have and would feel happier speaking to someone about it, you can order by phone (0845 603 7788). If you have the index entry number, which will be a volume and page number, that will be very helpful, but if you haven't found a reference in the indexes, staff at the GRO will look it up for you. There's a cost of £3 for this service.

You can pay by credit or debit card over the phone. Certificates are posted to you after five working days at a cost of £8.50 a certificate. This is £1.50 more than it costs if you order it over the internet. Or you can use a priority service, which despatches the next working day at a cost of £24.50 for each certificate if you order by phone, or £23 if you order on the internet.

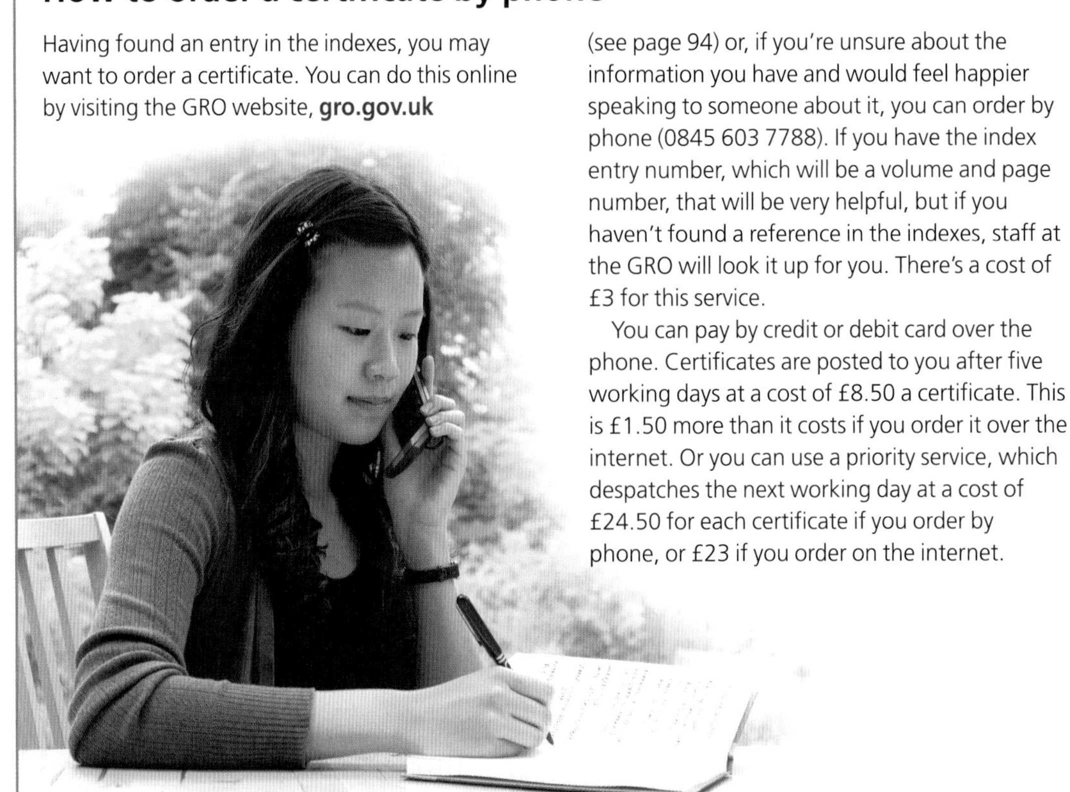

covering 1920 and then the quarter covering July, August and September (but see 'Don't be misled by the date', opposite). Now look under 'A' for Abbots and then find 'Grace' in the sub-heading under 'Abbots'.

AFTER 1984 In this period, the books are arranged chronologically by year, then alphabetically by surname and forename, with no quarterly breakdown. To find Mary Abbots born August 4, 1991, find the books covering 1991 and then look under 'A' for Abbots; there's no need to know the quarter in which she was born.

Searching the birth indexes

The birth indexes from September quarter 1837 until June quarter 1911 give only the child's first names, surname, father's name and the registration district of the birth, along with the GRO reference code that you'll need if you intend to order a copy of the certificate.

From September quarter 1911, the indexes will also show the mother's maiden name, making it easier to identify the correct entry. It will also make it possible for you to trace relatives from her side of the family.

WHAT TO WRITE DOWN If you think you've found the entry you want in the birth indexes, and want to order a certificate, make a careful note of:

- the first name and surname of the child
- the year (and quarter, if before 1984) in which the birth was registered
- the registration district in which the birth was registered
- the page number of the entry and the volume in which it appears – all of which will be shown on-screen. These details are essential if you're going to order a copy of the birth certificate from the GRO and you want to be sure that they'll send you the right one. (For information on ordering, see box, left.)

Given a name *Birth certificates and baptismal records are the earliest official appearance of a person's name. You should be able to find details of your ancestors in the GRO indexes at* **gro.gov.uk** *(see page 94).*

Searching for marriage and death details

These two key life events will form an important part of your family history research. The General Register Office's indexes for marriages and deaths are a rich source of the information you need.

Using the GRO's marriage indexes for England and Wales since 1837 will enable you to find the date of a family marriage. It will also allow you to verify other dates, places and names that you may have found from less reliable sources, such as a letter.

Searching the marriage indexes

These are organised in year order, under the 'quarter' system described on page 78. Marriage indexes covering ceremonies that took place before the end of December quarter 1911 will show the name of the person you are searching for (but not the surname of their spouse), the registration district in which the marriage took place and the GRO reference number. The spouse's surname was included from the beginning of the March quarter 1912, making these indexes much more helpful.

BOTH NAMES KNOWN If you're hunting for a marriage that took place before the end of December 1911, and you know the full names of both the bride and groom, you can do two separate marriage searches using each of the names. Then cross-reference the list of possibilities that comes up until you find a pair with matching registration districts and reference numbers for the same year and quarter. This saves you wasting time as well as money.

Love at the double *Although it's traditional for brides to take the surname of their husband, some couples combine their surnames and create a new, shared name that will go into the records. If you're looking for a double-barrelled name, try searching the GRO indexes for both names, separately.*

ONLY ONE NAME KNOWN If you know only one of the surnames, you'll need to order certificates for all possible marriages for the person whose name you do know, and then use the certificates to find a match for the correct forename – a more expensive route. Before buying certificates, it's a good idea to cross-check your information on a free-to-use website, such as **freebmd.org.uk** (see page 82), with a database of transcribed index entries.

Once you've found the details

When you're sure that you've found the right marriage record, but before you attempt to order a copy of the certificate from the GRO, make a careful note of the information that you get from the index – or you could end up paying for a certificate that isn't what you really wanted.

WHAT TO WRITE DOWN These are the details you'll need to note:

- the full name of at least one of the people on the marriage certificate – the bride's first name and surname or the groom's full name are sufficient. Having both is even better
- the year and quarter in which the marriage was registered
- the registration district in which it was registered
- the volume and page number of the entry.

Searching the death indexes

If it's a death certificate you're after, the GRO's indexes from 1837 until the end of December quarter 1865 give the name of the person who died, the registration district in which the death was registered and the GRO reference number you'll need when ordering.

From March quarter 1866 until the end of March quarter 1969, the indexes also give the age of the person who died, making it much easier to identify the correct entry, especially if you have either of the relevant birth or marriage certificates. From June quarter 1969 the death indexes are even more detailed, giving the date of birth of the deceased person rather than just their age. So if a relative died after April 1969 and you know the date of death, you can quite quickly and easily discover their date of birth.

End of the thriller *Agatha Christie's death in 1976 would, like all deaths, have been recorded where she died, and not necessarily where she lived or was buried (below). Her death certificate is held at the GRO and can be accessed online.*

WHAT TO WRITE DOWN To order a copy of a death certificate from the GRO, you need the following information from the index:

- the first name (or names) and surname
- the age at death or date of birth if given, although this isn't essential
- the year and quarter in which the death was registered
- the registration district
- the volume and page number of the entry.

Suspicious deaths

Sometimes a death certificate may indicate that the death wasn't due to natural causes and therefore a coroner's order was made. It's definitely worth following up on this lead by looking for details of an inquest or inquiry in the local newspaper of the time (see page 216). Some coroners' records are held in the county record offices, but aren't accessible for at least 75 years after the death.

Using the national indexes freebmd.org.uk

If you're after the birth, marriage or death certificate of an ancestor, the best place to start searching is this free-to-use website. It holds transcriptions of the GRO indexes.

FreeBMD has transcribed the indexes of all registered births, marriages and deaths in England and Wales from 1837 up to 1983, with more being added daily. Transcriptions are held in a database that's searchable by name, which saves you having to trawl through scanned pages of original indexes, searching for the name you want.

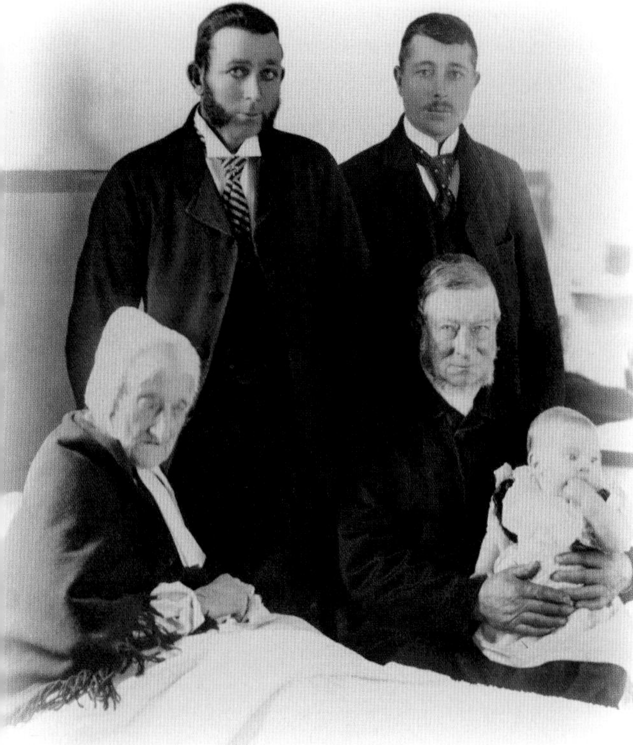

To search the registers, click on the **Search** button on the homepage. The website also offers links to FreeCEN (census data) and FreeREG (parish registers).

Using the searchable database

The transcriptions on FreeBMD are held in a database that you can search by first name and surname, or surname only if you're not sure of the person's first name. Narrow down the list of search results by including the county and registration district, if you can, and restricting the range of years.

For searches in the birth index after September quarter 1911 – when the mother's maiden name began to be included – restrict your results by asking the database to find only those entries that include the mother's correct maiden name. Similarly, if you are looking for a marriage from March quarter 1912 – when the spouse's surname was first included in the index – narrow down the results by searching only for entries that include the spouse's correct surname.

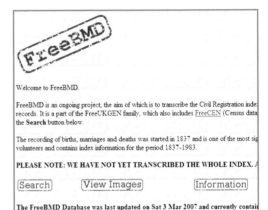

Five generations *An elderly woman with her son, grandson, great grandson and great great grandchild. A photograph that captures several generations is a wonderful find, matching faces to the names you'll see on sites such as FreeBMD.*

Welcome to FreeBMD.
FreeBMD is an ongoing project, the aim of which is to transcribe the Civil Registration inde
records. It is a part of the FreeUKGEN family, which also includes FreeCEN (Census data
the Search button below.
The recording of births, marriages and deaths was started in 1837 and is one of the most sig
volunteers and contains index information for the period 1837-1983.
PLEASE NOTE: WE HAVE NOT YET TRANSCRIBED THE WHOLE INDEX.

View Images
Information
The FreeBMD Database was last updated on Sat 3 Mar 2007 and currently contai

All entries should have a link to a scanned image of the original index. Click on the spectacles symbol next to the entry if you'd like to see the scanned page. Download the image to your computer (see page 31), free of charge, and then you can enlarge it to read the entry more easily.

Facts to bear in mind

This website is a great short cut for getting started with a 19th-century birth, marriage or death search, but you won't get all the details until you can see the certificate itself. If you find a promising lead, make sure you note the district, volume and page numbers, as you'll need these to order original certificates (see pages 78-81 and 94).

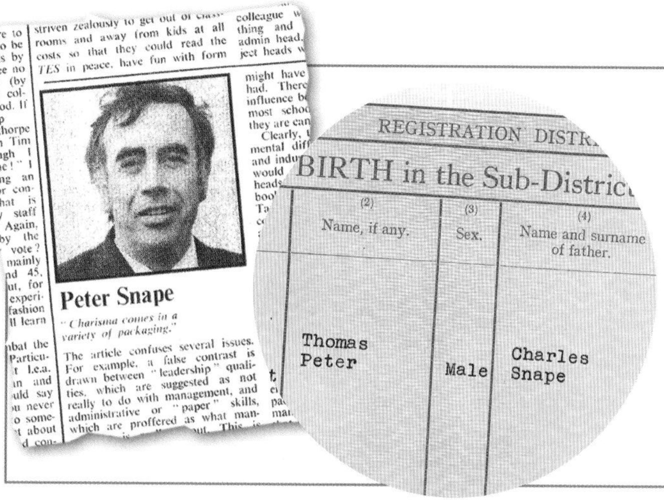

Thomas or Peter?

Confusion over the name by which a person is known can make your search trickier. Headmaster Thomas Peter Snape was always known to both his family and his colleagues as Peter, but looking for a 'Peter Snape' in various records and indexes would have drawn a blank. Always try to search using both forenames.

Search guidelines to help you

- Enter what you know into the search engine.
- If you're looking for the birth of someone with a common name, restrict the search by entering a county or registration district of birth.
- If you're doing a general search for the deaths of everyone with an unusual family name, just enter that surname and a date range.
- If you can't find an ancestor, it may be that the transcriptions are incomplete or contain mistakes. Instead, return to **gro.gov.uk** (see page 94).

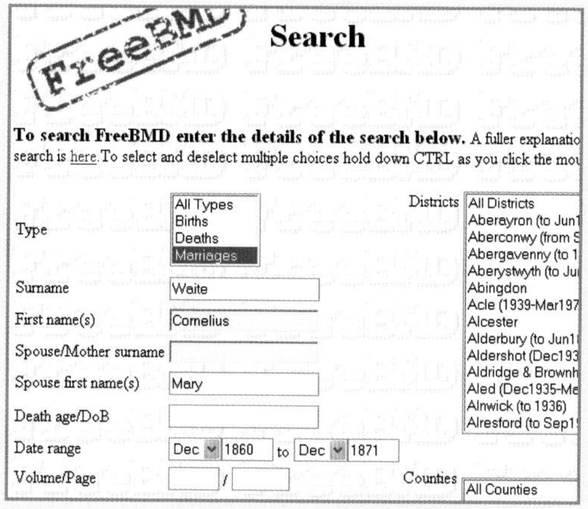

Search for the name of a spouse

1 In this case history, you know that Cornelius Waite married a woman called Mary Ann some time between the 1861 and 1871 censuses, but you don't know her maiden name. To find their marriage in the indexes, go to the **freebmd.org.uk** homepage and click **Search**. This takes you to a page where you enter all the details you already know. Choose **Marriages** from the **Type** list. Select the registration district and county if you know them. Click on **Find**.

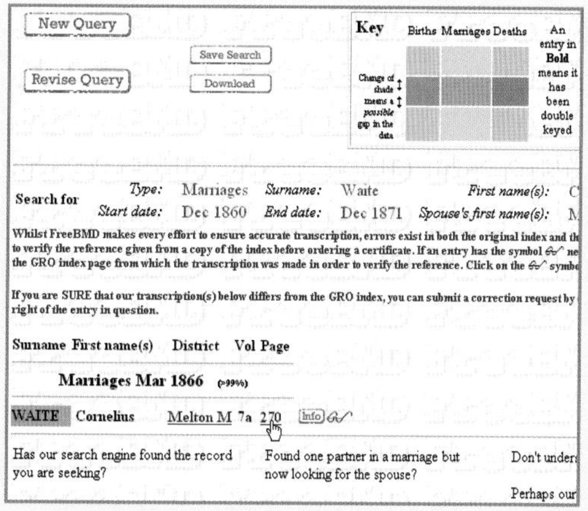

Possible matches

2 You entered 'Waite' in the **Surname** box and 'Cornelius' in the **First name(s)** box, narrowed down the search by entering the years 1860 and 1871 in the **Date range** boxes and put 'Mary' in the **Spouse first name(s)** box. The search engine produces a list of possible results under the name 'Waite'. Click on the highlighted page number. Here, it's page 270.

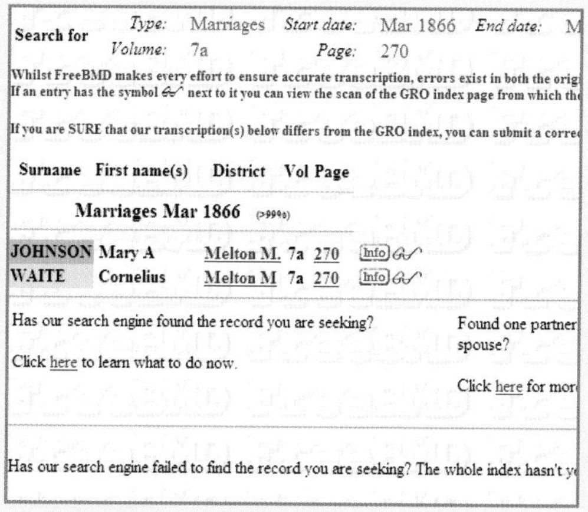

Spouse's name found

3 You'll see any other names whose reference matches Cornelius Waite's, and find that Mary Ann's maiden name was Johnson. Click on the spectacles icon for a scanned image of the entry. If you were researching a more common name, you could get several results. In that case, you'd need to order all the marriage certificates to discover which was the right one.

Using the national indexes

findmypast.com

On **findmypast.com** you'll find all the digital images of the General Register Office (GRO) indexes from 1837 until 1983, as well as the indexes from 1984 to 2005 in a searchable database. But what makes it particularly useful is that it also has details of births, marriages and deaths of British subjects that occurred overseas between 1761 and 1994. It wasn't compulsory for a British subject living abroad to register these events, so the indexes aren't necessarily complete. The website also has indexes of births, marriages and deaths that happened at sea in the second half of the 19th century, as well as divorce proceedings that took place between 1858 and 1903. There's a section that deals with military records – you can search all records from 1656 to 1994, for example, as well as armed forces records for births, marriages and deaths going back as far as the late 18th century. All these indexes are free to search, but there's a small charge to view the image or database transcription. You need to do this, to make sure you've found the correct entry, and to get the references you require for ordering certificates from the GRO.

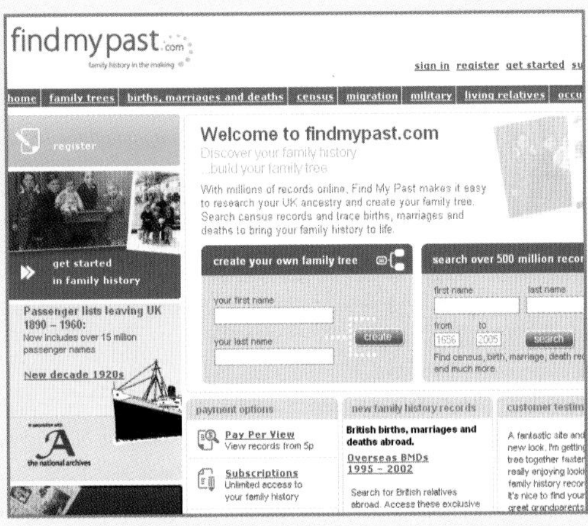

Go to the homepage

1 Here's how to do a search for details of the departure from the UK of a relative, John Jones, some time between 1890 and 1919. Go to **findmypast.com** and register, as shown on page 52.

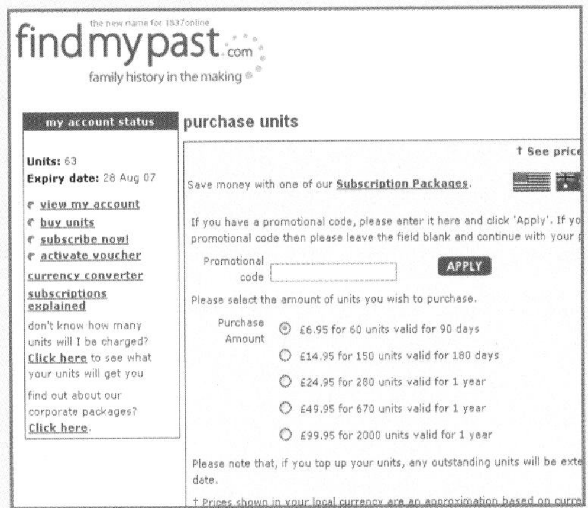

Buy units

2 Having registered you can search all the indexes on the site for free, but to see relevant entries in more detail you'll have to buy credits. Click on **Buy units** in the left-hand box. Give your credit card details. The units are valid for a limited time. (See opposite for how to set up an account.)

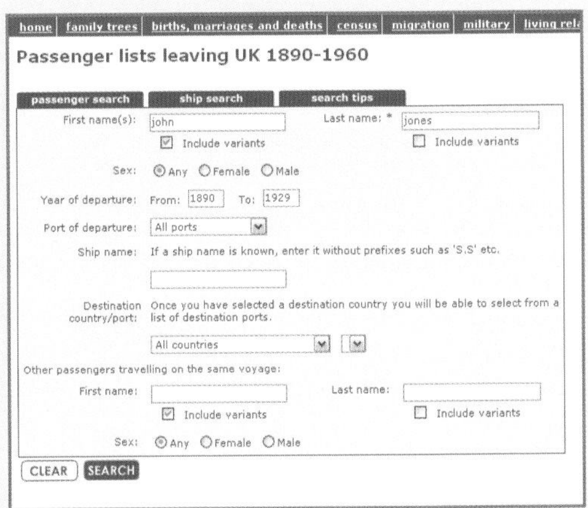

Enter search details

3 Enter the first and last names of your ancestor. Tick the **Include variants** box, to widen the search in case his name was entered wrongly. Click on **Male**. Set the date range between 1890 and 1919. Click on **Search**.

THE 1837-1983 DATABASE The births, marriages and deaths search engine for 1837 to 1983 looks only for the index pages that cover the surname you're looking for, and doesn't locate an individual entry. Type in the name and the date range you wish to search. The Search Results page shows you a list of all the quarters and years that cover the period for the name. Click on **View** to have a closer look at the scanned image of each quarter to see if you can find your ancestor's name and details.

THE 1984-2005 DATABASE If you're looking for a birth, marriage or death between 1984 and 2005, narrow the search by including the person's middle name, the district in which the event was registered, the mother's maiden name for a birth, the spouse's surname for a marriage and the date of birth for a death search. The Search Results page will give you a list of possible entries but will provide only name, registration district and year of registration. Click **View** to see the full entry, for 1 unit.

Setting up an account

To view images on the Findmypast website you have to register, open an account and buy £5 worth of units – which gives you 50 units at 10p each. There's step-by-step advice for this below, left, and on page 52. You can pay online, using your credit or debit card, or by using BT's Click & Buy service that adds the charge to your phone bill. You can also buy monthly or annual price plans from the site. One unit is deducted from your account each time you view an image.

Passenger list search results

Search criteria used:

Last name: **Jones**
First name(s): **John (including variants)**
Year of departure: **1890 to 1929**

Results:

- 2710 records shown include exact matches.
- **6800 records** include initial J and exact matches.
- **12702 records** include unstated first name, initial J and exact matches.

Cost:

You will be charged 5 units to view a transcript and 30 units for an image unless y subscription for this set of records.

Viewing Page 1 of 55 [1

Last name	First name	Age	Sex	Year of departure	Departure port	Destination country	Destination port
JONES	A L St John			1918	Liverpool	Canada	Saint John Nb
JONES	Albert John	25	M	1922	Liverpool	Canada	Halifax
JONES	Albert John	36	M	1925	London	Australia	Adelaide
JONES	Albert John	36	M	1929	Liverpool	Canada	Halifax
JONES	Alfred John	12	M	1920	Liverpool	Canada	Quebec
JONES	Alfred John	30	M	1922	Southampton	USA	New York
JONES	Arthur John	27	M	1922	Liverpool	USA	New York
JONES	Arthur John	18	M	1927	London	Australia	Sydney
JONES	Cyril John	39	M	1925	London	Australia	Melbourne
JONES	David John	40	M	1895	London	Australia	Sydney
JONES	David John	31	M	1919	Liverpool	India	Calcutta
JONES	David John	37	M	1923	Southampton	Canada	Halifax
JONES	David John	35	M	1924	London	India	Calcutta
JONES	David John	4	M	1926	London	Australia	Fremantle
JONES	David John	28	M	1926	Liverpool	Canada	Quebec
JONES	David John	29	M	1926	Liverpool	Canada	Quebec
JONES	David John	50	M	1927	Southampton	USA	New York
JONES	David John	39	M	1928	Liverpool	USA	New York
JONES	David John	26	M	1928	Southampton	USA	New York

Choose from the results

4 Your results will be presented as a list that shows you the name, age, sex, year of departure, port, destination country and destination port. Select the entry that seems most likely. Decide whether you want to see a transcript or the image of the entry and click on **View** in the appropriate column on the right. You'll need to use your credits, or register for a voucher. It costs 5 units to see a transcript and 30 to see the image.

World travellers *Your ancestors may have roamed about the world or been migrants. Ships' passenger lists are useful in tracking down the details, providing information on ports of embarkation as well as destinations. Extensive lists of travellers to and from the UK are held on* findmypast.com.

Using the national indexes bmdindex.co.uk

The BMD site specialises in births, marriages and deaths, holding scanned images of the General Register Office (GRO) indexes from 1837 to 1983 and a database of transcriptions from the GRO indexes for 1984 until 2005. You'll have to pay to use **bmdindex.co.uk**, but it's not expensive.

Searching the records

There are four ways to search the records. You can choose from the basic search engine, an advanced search engine or two 'SmartSearch' options – one for births and one for deaths. There's also a facility that displays your results as a printable map.

BASIC SEARCH ENGINE This searches the indexes for all records between 1837 and 1983 by surname, forename and year range. You'll get a list of results with links to scanned images of the pages on which your entry might be found. The search engine looks for initials only, even if you've supplied full details of the first names, so there may be two or more pages to check for one quarter, particularly if the surname is a reasonably common one. It's best to use this type of search when the surname is uncommon.

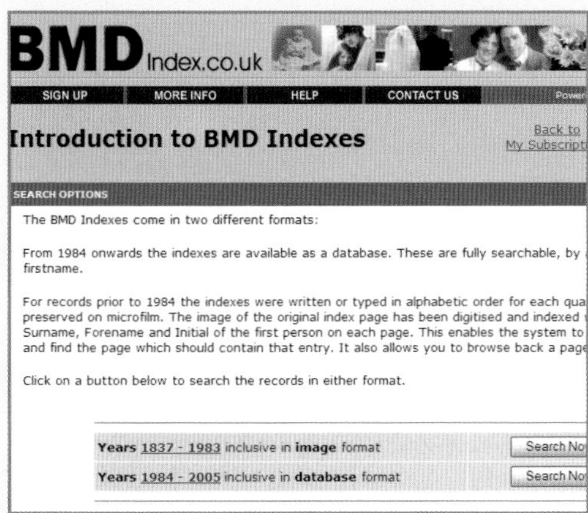

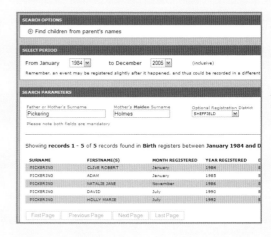

Log in and set date parameters

1 In this case history, the search is for the children of a John Pickering and a Janet Holmes, whom you know were born after 1984, probably in Sheffield. On the homepage click on **Log in**. You'll be taken to The Genealogist website. Enter your email and password or **Register** if you're a first-time user. Press the **Search** link that takes you back to BMD Indexes 1837-2005. Under **Search options** click on the **Search now** button for records between 1984 and 2005.

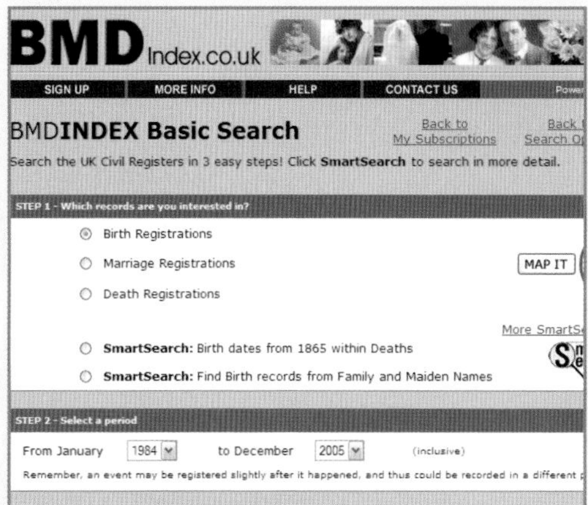

Choose your search method

2 The BMDindex Basic Search page shows how you can search the records. Choose from birth, marriage and death registrations, SmartSearch for birth dates from 1865 within the deaths list, or SmartSearch to find birth records from family and maiden names. Click on the second **SmartSearch** option, and the search engine will be displayed. Set the dates to cover 1984-2005 in the **Select period** panel.

SEARCH OPTIONS
Find children from parent's names
SELECT PERIOD
From January 1984 to December 2005 (inclusive)
Remember, an event may be registered slightly after it happened, and thus could be recorded in a different
SEARCH PARAMETERS
Father or Mother's Surname: Pickering
Mother's Maiden Surname: Holmes
Optional Registration District: SHEFFIELD
Please note both fields are mandatory
Showing records 1 - 5 of 5 records found in Birth registers between January 1984 and D

SURNAME	FIRSTNAME(S)	MONTH REGISTERED	YEAR REGISTERED
PICKERING	CLIVE ROBERT	January	1984
PICKERING	ADAM	January	1985
PICKERING	NATALIE JANE	November	1986
PICKERING	DAVID	July	1990
PICKERING	HOLLY MARIE	July	1992

First Page | Previous Page | Next Page | Last Page

Find the children

3 Under **Search parameters** enter 'Pickering' in the **Father or mother's surname** box. Type 'Holmes' in the **Mother's maiden surname** box and scroll down the **Optional registration district** list to find Sheffield. Click on **Find children from parent's names** under **Search options**. Five children come up with the surname Pickering and mother's maiden surname Holmes born in Sheffield between 1984 and 1992.

ADVANCED SEARCH ENGINE Records from 1984 to 2005 can be accessed by an advanced search engine. To narrow down the list of results – useful if you are searching for a common name – enter a middle name and mother's maiden name for birth searches, or partner's surname for marriage searches, or a date of birth for death searches. If you click the link to the spouse's surname in a marriage search, for example, you'll see the page showing the groom's or bride's entry – and discover his or her first name.

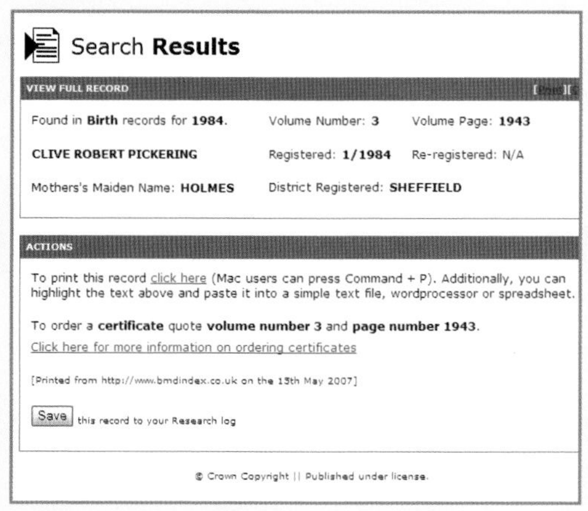

Search Results
VIEW FULL RECORD
Found in Birth records for 1984.
Volume Number: 3
Volume Page: 1943
CLIVE ROBERT PICKERING
Registered: 1/1984
Re-registered: N/A
Mothers's Maiden Name: HOLMES
District Registered: SHEFFIELD
ACTIONS
To print this record click here (Mac users can press Command + P). Additionally, you can highlight the text above and paste it into a simple text file, wordprocessor or spreadsheet.
To order a certificate quote volume number 3 and page number 1943.
Click here for more information on ordering certificates
[Printed from http://www.bmdindex.co.uk on the 15th May 2007]
Save this record to your Research log
© Crown Copyright || Published under license.

View the records

4 Click the **View** icon to find the GRO references needed to order each birth certificate, which is the only way you can be sure that all the children have the same parents. You can print the onscreen record, or cut and paste it into a document on your computer (see page 31).

USING SMARTSEARCH FOR DEATHS To find death records between 1984 and 2005, use the first SmartSearch option. Its death records contain the dates of birth, so a search for one will yield the other. You'll be given a list of surnames, first names and the month, year and district of registration for anyone matching your criteria who died between 1984 and 2005. Click **View** to see the fully transcribed record, which confirms the date of birth and the GRO reference. On the **Full record** page, you'll find an option to view the page in the birth indexes where your ancestor's birth entry should be found. For the death registration for a married woman, you need to enter her maiden name in the **Surname at birth** box to find her birth date.

USING SMARTSEARCH FOR SIBLING BIRTHS Trace the births of siblings born between 1984 and 2005 by using a second SmartSearch option. This finds children whose surnames and mother's maiden names match. You can narrow down the results by restricting the year range.

Bear in mind that people shown as sharing surnames and mother's maiden name are not necessarily siblings. To cut out confusion, restrict the district search to the area in which the parents married if you think they might have stayed in the same region.

How to pay

It's free to search the site's indexes and view results pages, but you'll have to register and buy a subscription before you can access the search engines. Credits are deducted from your account every time you view a new image of the indexes or a full transcription.

There's a range of price plans for viewing the information held by **bmdindex.org.uk**. A low-cost, pay-as-you-go subscription lets you view the birth, marriage and death indexes. You get 20 credits, valid for 90 days – it costs one credit to view an image. If you want to view the same image more than once in a 30 day period, you won't be charged a second time. There's also an option to have a year's subscription, which works out cheaper if you have a lot of searching to do.

Bear in mind that your account can be activated only on one computer – so you can't access the search engines unless you're using the computer on which you signed up to the account. But you can change your registered computer as many as three times, if you find you have to.

A final farewell *Parish burial records are important in tracing the dates of deaths occurring before the start of civil registration in 1837.*

Using the national indexes familyrelatives.com

The wide range of information available at **familyrelatives.com** includes some of the more unusual records, such as overseas births, marriages and deaths, and Army, Navy and RAF deaths from the two world wars. In addition, records from hundreds of parishes have been transcribed.

The civil registration indexes for England and Wales from 1837 to 2005 are being transcribed, and the site has divided the period into four sections: 1837 to 1865, 1866 to 1920, 1921 to 1983 and 1984 to 2005. You can access the site's 400 million records by subscription or by a pay-per-view system.

BEFORE YOU BEGIN Before you can search the site's databases you'll need to register – which won't cost you anything. Just as with most other sites, the registration form will ask for your email address, a password, your name and contact details. Once you've filled in the form, click on **Continue** to be taken to the **Search** page, where you can choose which database you're interested in.

It makes sense to buy units or set up a subscription before you begin searching. You'll need credits to be able to view any

Life in the colonies *In the late 19th century, the three Hewitt sisters went out as nurses to what was then Rhodesia. Annie Hewitt (centre) married Joseph Nesbitt on October 10, 1900. Many colonial marriages can be found in the overseas records.*

The Holy Catholic Church.
Province of South Africa.
Diocese of Mashonaland.

This is to Certify that
Joseph Alexander Nesbitt
and
Annie Hewitt
were Married in accordance with the Rites of the Church at
St. John's Umtali
on
Wednesday Oct: 10th 1900.
Witnesses.
J. H. Birchell
J. A. Palmer. M. Birch
By me, W. J. Roxburgh

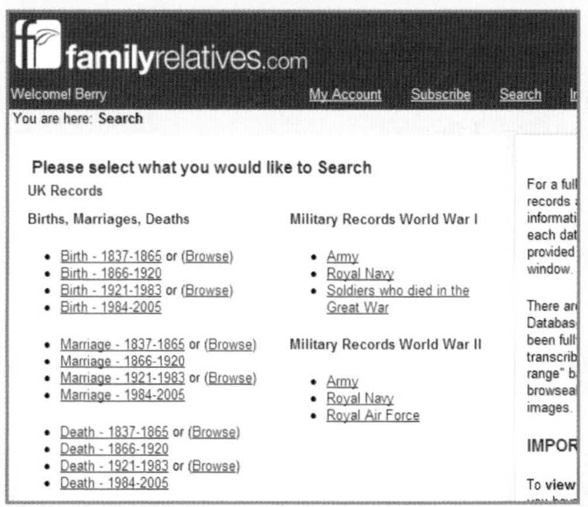

Search for a birth

1 Once you've registered (see above), go to the search page and choose the type of event and year range you wish to search. For example, if you want to search the website's transcriptions for the birth of a Mary King born between 1911 and 1915, click on the **Birth – 1866-1920** link.

of the results you find that could help your research, and it's frustrating to have to stop and set up your credits when you've actually found what you want to see. Click the **Subscribe** link along the top panel and you'll be offered a choice of an annual unlimited subscription for £37.50, or units in blocks of 50 for £5, or 150 for £12.

INCOMPLETE TRANSCRIPTIONS The periods 1837 to 1865 and 1921 to 1983 aren't yet fully transcribed, but you can browse the scanned index pages. You can use the search engine for these years free of charge, but you'll have to pay one unit (about 10p) to download each scanned page. You can search the two databases by surname, first name, year and quarter. You'll get a list of all the pages you need to download and browse for the entry you're looking for. It costs two units to view a page of up to 20 transcribed results showing the name, year, quarter, district and reference number, plus one additional unit to view an image of the index page.

FULLY TRANSCRIBED INDEXES The indexes for 1866 to 1920 and 1984 to 2005 have been fully transcribed and can be searched by name, district, year and quarter range (see page 73). You can also opt to match a person's name with the spouse's surname in the indexes that cover information after 1912, and a child's name with the mother's maiden name if you're searching after 1911. As the number of fully transcribed indexes increases, so do your chances of finding your relatives.

England & Wales - Births 1866-1920

Forename(s): Mary
Last Name: King

District: All Districts / Aberayron / Abergavenny / Aberystwith / Aberystwyth / Abingdon / Alderbury / Alnwick

From Year: 1911
To Year: 1915

From Quarter: All Quarters
To Quarter: All Quarters

☐ Select Unique Quarter

Mother's Maiden Name (from 1911): Payling

Enter the details you know

2 Enter 'Mary' in the **Forename(s)** box, 'King' in the **Last name** box, restrict the **From year** to 1911 and set the **To year** to 1915. You know her mother's maiden name was Payling, so enter that, too. You can further restrict the search by **District** and **Quarter** if you know these details. Click on **Search records**.

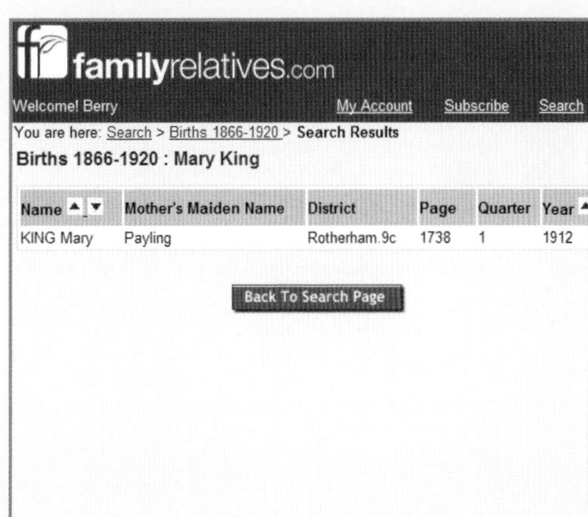

familyrelatives.com

Welcome! Berry | My Account | Subscribe | Search

You are here: Search > Births 1866-1920 > Search Results

Births 1866-1920 : Mary King

Name	Mother's Maiden Name	District	Page	Quarter	Year
KING Mary	Payling	Rotherham 9c	1738	1	1912

Back To Search Page

Read the results

3 The next page shows the results that match your search criteria in a table format. Only one match was found for the birth of Mary King, with the mother's maiden name Payling. If your search gives more results, you can choose to arrange them chronologically or alphabetically by clicking on the up and down arrows next to the **Name** or **Year** fields.

FEBRUARY AND MARCH 1912.

	Mother's Maiden Surname.	District.
King, Margaret T.	Blake	Wallingford
— Marguerite E.	Easton	Edmonton
— Marian E.	Watkin	Peterbro
— Marie Y.	Rose	Dewsbury
— Marjorie F.	Street	S.Stoneham
— Marjorie M.	Leach	Guildford
— Mary	Tyrrell	Norwich
— Mary	Payling	Rotherham
— Mary	Bisatt	Thorne
— Mary	Fowler	Fulham
— Mary A.	Beal	Wigan
— Mary A.D.	Barlow	Kingston
— Mary A.M.	Downes	Tynemouth
— Mary E.C.	Fermor	Burton
— Mary E.	Buckle	Islington
— Mary E.	King	Shipston
— Mary H.	Porritt	Tynemouth
— Maud	Robinson	St.Olave
— Maud A.	Dewson	Holborn
— Maud A.	Mills	W.Ham
— Maud E.E.	Lewin	Eastry
— Maude M.	Burns	W.Ham

View the transcription

4 The transcribed result gives you all the information you need to order Mary King's birth certificate from the General Register Office (see page 83). But if you want to make sure the transcription is accurate, click on **View image** and, for the price of 1 unit, you'll see a scanned image of the original index page showing Mary's birth. To see the image, you'll be prompted to download the free DjVu viewer, available from the 'Information' page.

Using the national indexes

ancestry.co.uk

Access to online birth, marriage and death (BMD) indexes is completely free on **ancestry.co.uk**. Scan the indexes to see if the information you want is there, then just register your name and email address on the site, when you're prompted, if you want to view the actual images of the documents you've found.

The website has three types of search engine for the indexes of the General Register Office (GRO).

- A complete set of scanned images of the GRO indexes from 1837 to 1983.
- Access to the partially transcribed FreeBMD indexes (see page 82) for 1837 to 1983 with links to scanned images.
- A database of indexes from 1984 to 2005.

Complete BMDs for 1837-1983

This set of scanned index images is searched in the same way as the original GRO indexes (see page 94). Choose whether you want to research births, marriages or deaths. The search engine will ask you for the name you are looking for, as well as the appropriate years and the quarters to search.

You'll then see a list of pages that you can search. Click on **View** to see the scanned image of each page from the indexes and search the page to see if your ancestor is there. Many family history websites charge you to look at these pages; here it's free, so this is a good site to start with.

A MISSING QUARTER Check that the search engine has found all four quarters for each year. Sometimes one or two quarters may be left out, because the search engine has been confused by something such as an entry being added to the page by hand, so the names are no longer in alphabetical order. If this happens, you can find the missing quarter by going back to the search engine and keying in a surname that's close in spelling to the one you're looking for in the missing year and quarter. If you're looking for the surname Berry, for example, a useful trick is to ask the search engine to find Barry instead, which is

Search for a death

1 To trace the death of a Sinah Price between 1928 and 1930, go to the homepage and from the 'Search' panel on the right, click on **Search birth, marriage and death records**. On the next page, under the heading 'Deaths', click on **1911 to 1983**. Then enter 'Sinah' in the **First Name** box and 'Price' in the **Last Name** box. Select **All** from the **Quarter** drop-down list, enter '1929' in the **Year** box and select **1** from the **+/-** drop-down list. Click on **Search**.

— Samuel	56	Liverpool	8	b	54
— Sarah	72	Birmingham S.	6	d	118
— Sarah A.	66	Wirral	8	a	794
— Sarah A.	85	Ashton	8	d	1402
— Sarah E.	76	W.Bromwich	6	b	1322
— Sarah E.	36	Worksop	7	b	76
— Sarah J.	87	St.Geo.H.Sq.	1	a	1000
— Sarah J.	78	Stourbridge	6	c	54
— Sarah J.	67	Hereford	6	a	882
— Sarah L.	62	Oxford	3	a	2082
— Sarah R.	30	Chester	8	a	722
— Sinah	86	Manchester S.	8	d	515
— Sophia	86	Holywell	11	b	293
— Stanley	1	Prescot	8	b	1204
— Stanley	1	Dudley	6	b	1729
— Stanley W.	0	Stourbridge	6	c	9
— Susan	86	Brentford	3	a	337
— Susan A.	64	Bristol	6	a	160
— Susannah	75	Brentford	3	a	197
— Susannah	27	Swansea	11	a	1449
— Sylvia M.	4	Cardiff	11	a	576
— Teddie	0	Newport M.	11	a	392
— Terrence	0	Bridgend	11	a	1152
— Thomas	74	Pontypool	11	a	208
— Thomas	81	W.Bromwich	6	b	1547
— Thomas	80	Brecknock	11	b	134
— Thomas	55	Bridgend	11	a	1167
— Thomas	66	Hampstead	1	a	1273
— Thomas	67	W.Derby	8	b	884

Scan the results

2 The results list has links to 12 pages of Prices in chronological order. Click the **View Image** icon for each quarter, and check the index entries. Sinah Price's death appears on the fifth image,and gives the information needed for ordering her death certificate. Note down the date of death (March quarter 1929), the district (Manchester S), the volume (8d) and the page (515). See pages 78-81 and 94 if you want to order a copy of the certificate from the GRO.

earlier in the list than Berry. On the page that comes up, keep clicking on the **Next** button until you find the page with Berry on it.

Partial BMDs for 1837-1983

When you use this search engine, there's no trawling through pages of surnames until you find the right first name. Here, your search takes you directly to the name and gives you a list of transcribed names and references from the indexes and links to scanned images of the pages. The drawback is that it's not as comprehensive as the Complete BMD as it uses transcriptions from FreeBMD that aren't yet complete.

The search engine will also find transcriptions of names that look or sound similar to the one you're looking for, unless you restrict your search instructions to include exact matches only.

Complete indexes for 1984-2005

Unlike the other two, this database contains no scanned images, because all the data was entered electronically to start with. The death indexes, for example, show the person's name, the year and quarter of registration of the death, the registration district and the deceased person's date of birth. These pieces of information will help you to widen your search for further details.

Common ground *The population of Britain grew significantly in the 19th and early 20th centuries, and an increase in leisure time, affordable public transport and a delight in new and exciting events drew people of all classes together. Your ancestors could have been among the crowd flocking to see the spectacle of a hot-air balloon ascent at Crystal Palace Park in Sydenham, in London.*

Discovering local indexes ukbmd.org.uk

For fewer transcription errors, try this website, linked to local authority and family history society sites, which goes direct to local register copies.

The acronym UK BMD stands for United Kingdom births, marriages and deaths. The site is valuable if you're tracing your family, because it transcribes from original sources of information, significantly reducing the chances of errors that arise when material is re-transcribed by the General Register Office (GRO). Use of the UK BMD website is free.

What's on the website

The site provides links to 465 other websites that have transcriptions from local civil registration birth, marriage and death indexes. The website suggests that, whenever possible, you search these local indexes first, before consulting the GRO indexes, to cut down the chances of coming across transcription errors.

The best links on the website for tracing your ancestors fall into three general categories: Local, GRO and County.

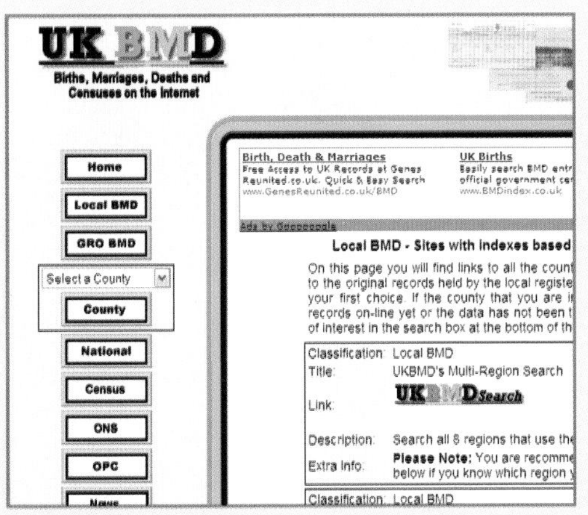

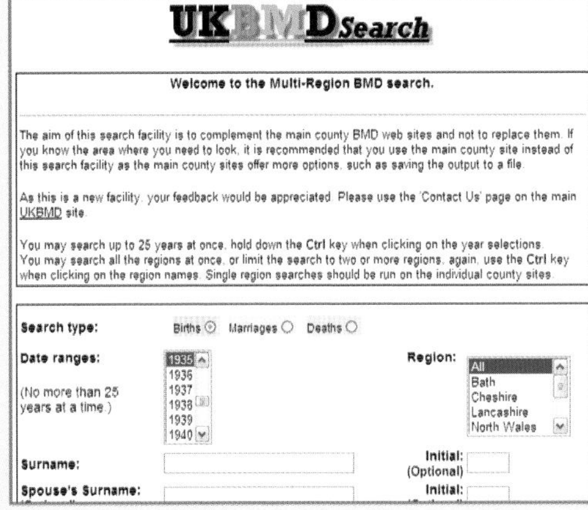

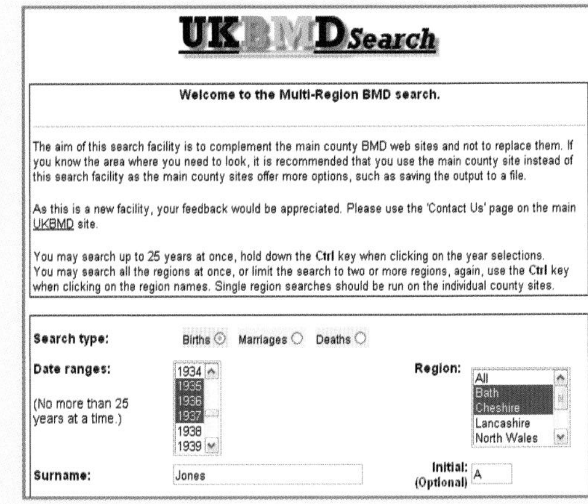

Start your search

1 To search for the birth of an Alan Victor Jones in Bath or Cheshire between 1935 and 1937, click **Local BMD** in the left-hand margin of the homepage. The next page has links to each county's database. Click on **Select a county** and choose one from the list. Alternatively, to search more than one county's records at once, click on the **UKBMDSearch** link in the **UK BMD's Multi-region search** panel on the right.

Give the event and date

2 Click **Births** in the **Search type** section. Scroll down, using the arrows to the right of the **Date ranges** box, to find the years you want. Then hold down the left mouse button to highlight the years in the box. If you hold the left button of the mouse down over the year **1935**, you'll make it active and ready to select.

Add name and place

3 If you decide to spread the search, in terms of years, select all three years, **1935**, **1936** and **1937**. In **Regions** highlight **Bath** and **Cheshire** in the same way. Type 'Jones' in the **Surname** box, 'A' in the **Initial** box and click on **Search** at the bottom of the screen.

Local BMD

Here you can access websites that provide free indexes for whole counties. Search these individually by county or as a whole via the UK BMD multi-region search engine (see the case history, below). Local BMD also provides links to records transcribed by smaller areas, but you'll have to consult these individually – they aren't associated with a centralised search engine.

Various local authorities and family history societies are creating new indexes based on the local register offices, rather than taking information from the GRO's national indexes. There are millions of entries, with more added each day. Each local area website shows how complete its online records are.

GRO

This service provides links to sites whose records are based on the GRO national indexes. Most are commercial 'pay-per-view' sites, though some – such as FreeBMD – are run by volunteers and are free of charge.

County BMD

Find out which websites from both the Local and GRO categories have online records for your county by selecting the name of the county from the drop-down list on the left-hand side of the homepage and clicking **County**. This displays links to all the websites that hold records relevant to the county you've chosen, with brief descriptions.

UKBMDSearch

In the results below, the reference number will be a link to a printable application which can be used to order the certificate for the index entry. Full details of the charges and the Register Office address can be found on the form.
Please note that due to the manner in which some of the Cheshire indexes were compiled into groups of years, you may see results from years outside of the range that you requested in the results from Cheshire.

Surname	First Name(s)	Mother's Maiden Name	Year	District	Region	Registers At	Reference
JONES	Alan Edward		1936	Mottram	Cheshire	Tameside	MOT/40/11
JONES	Alan Frank		1936	Stockport Third	Cheshire	Stockport	ST3/37/100
JONES	Alan Stanley	ROBERTS	1935	Keynsham	Bath	Bath	KEY/30/295
JONES	Alan Trevor		1935	Stockport First	Cheshire	Stockport	ST1/61/54
JONES	Alan Victor	BLACKER	1936	Norton Radstock - First Series	Bath	Bath	NR1/1/163
JONES	Alan		1933	Denton	Cheshire	Tameside	DEN/63/78
JONES	Alan		1933	Mossley	Cheshire	Tameside	MOS/36/70
JONES	Alan		1936-1938	Crewe	Cheshire	Cheshire Central	CR/1B/472
JONES	Alan		1936-1938	Northwich	Cheshire	Cheshire Central	NO/2A/194
JONES	Alan		1937	Ashton	Cheshire	Tameside	ASH/1/6
JONES	Alan		1937	Dukinfield	Cheshire	Tameside	DUK/1B/7
JONES	Alan		1938	Cheadle	Cheshire	Stockport	CHD/2/4
JONES	Albert Joseph		1937	Chester City	Cheshire	Cheshire West	CHC/31/43
JONES	Albert		1934	Chester City	Cheshire	Cheshire West	CHC/26/11
JONES	Albert		1936-1938	Crewe	Cheshire	Cheshire Central	CR/25A/224
JONES	Alexander Hamilton		1937	Chester City	Cheshire	Cheshire West	CHE/1/67
JONES	Alfred		1934	Stockport First	Cheshire	Stockport	ST1/59/40
JONES	Alfred		1935	Audenshaw	Cheshire	Tameside	AUD/101/41
JONES	Alice Emma		1936	Chester City	Cheshire	Cheshire West	CHC/29/92
JONES	Alison Elizabeth		1938	Chester Castle	Cheshire	Cheshire West	CAS/2/34
JONES	Alison Mary Bradley	TAGGART	1936	Twerton - Second Series	Bath	Bath	TW2/14A/267

Scan the first results

4 You'll see the births of all Joneses with first names starting with 'A', in alphabetical order. Alan Victor Jones' transcription shows that his mother's maiden name was Blacker, and his birth was registered in 1936 in Norton Radstock district, which is in the Bath region. Not all counties' transcriptions include the mother's maiden name. Bath does; Cheshire doesn't. Click on the underlined **Reference** next to the entry.

APPLICATION FOR A BIRTH CERTIFICATE
PLEASE READ THESE NOTES before completing this form

1 TO BE COMPLETED BY THE APPLICANT
Name of applicant Mr Mrs Miss/Ms (STATE NAME IN FULL)
Full postal address
Post Code: Telephone no: e-mail address:

2 Are you applying for your own birth certificate? Yes/No
If not please state your relationship to the person:

3 DETAILS OF BIRTH CERTIFICATE REQUIRED

FULL NAME AT BIRTH	FATHER'S FULL NAME	MOTHER'S FULL N
FORENAME(S) Alan Victor	FORENAME(S)	FORENAME(S)
SURNAME JONES	SURNAME	SURNAME
		MAIDEN SURNAME BLAC
DATE OF BIRTH	PLACE OF BIRTH (Full address or name of hospital)	
DAY MONTH YEAR 1936	Norton Radstock - First Series	

4 REQUIREMENTS — Send this Applicatio
BIRTH CERTIFICATE £ 7.00
I require NUMBER birth certificate(s)
The Superintendent Registrar, Bath and N
Register Office, The Guildhall, High Stree

5 REMITTANCE ENCLOSED *(POSTAL APPLICATIONS ONLY)*
UK: applications should enclose an SAE. Postal order or cheque made payable to :
Overseas: applications should enclose a self addressed envelope and two IRCs, with payment by Bankers Sterling Draft payable to :
Please note: Bath & N.E. Somerset RO charge a £1 supplement for Credit & Debit Card Orders.
The Superintendent Regi
for £

Order your certificate

5 Up comes a printable form containing all the details of the birth. Print it off and send it, with the £7 fee, to the register office whose address appears on the form, and they'll send you a copy of the birth certificate.

Bonny baby *Christina McColl with her son Hugh in 1893. At this time, baby boys wore dresses, so it's hard to tell from a photo whether you should be searching online for the birth of a boy or a girl.*

Ordering certificates from the GRO

If you're researching family history at home, it's quick and easy to go online and order birth, marriage and death certificates from the General Register Office (GRO) website.

The General Register Office (GRO) website, **gro.gov.uk**, provides information on all aspects of civil registration and is a great help to the family historian. When you're ready to order a certificate for a birth, marriage or death, it's the GRO you turn to.

How to use the service

You can order certificates online, by post or by phone or fax. Before you can use the online service you need to register; your email address and chosen password will be your log in details for all future transactions.

Buying certificates isn't free of charge. The standard service charge for a certificate is £7 and the certificate is posted to you four working days after receipt of your order; the priority service costs £23 and the certificate is dispatched the next working day.

Certificate choice

Please select a certificate type and provide any additional information requested. We then choose the appropriate application form.

Certificate Types

For events registered in England and Wales

1. Birth Certificate (England & Wales)
2. Marriage Certificate (England & Wales)
3. Death Certificate (England & Wales) — Age at death in years
4. Adoption Certificate (England & Wales) — Current age of adoptee

For overseas events which were registered with the British authorities

5. Birth Certificate (Overseas events)
6. Marriage Certificate (Overseas events)
7. Death Certificate (Overseas events) — Age at death in years

For all events

Delivery address details

Please enter the delivery address details below.

Unless a DX Address is given, Address Line 1, Town and Country MUST be completed. All other required fields are followed by the * character.

This will be the delivery address for this individual application only.

After completing, please press the 'Submit' button to continue.

Delivery address details

Title

Forenames* Fiona

Surname* Green

DX address (not sure what this is? see our faqs. if you have one, you will not need to complete postal details below)

Address line 1* 7 Old Lodge Place

Ordering a certificate online

1 Suppose you wish to order a death certificate for Sinah Price, the ancestor you discovered in Ancestry online's index (see page 90). You know that she died March quarter 1929, district Manchester S, volume 8d, page 515. You need this information to place your order. Go to **gro.gov.uk**. On the homepage, click **Ordering certificates online**. This takes you to the 'Certificate ordering service' page.

Putting in the detail

2 Click **Order a certificate online now**. Give your login details, and when the 'Certificate choice' page opens click on **Death certificate (England & Wales)**. Click **Yes** next to the question 'Is the General Register Office index known?' and put '1929' in the **Year in which the event was registered** box. Now click **Submit**.

Giving delivery instructions

3 You'll then be asked to fill in the address you'd like the certificate sent to. You'll also be asked for your phone number in case there are any problems processing your order. When you've completed this page, click **Submit**.

Add extra detail where possible

To make sure you get the right certificate, add as much detail as you can. Click the **Reference checking** option at the end of the order form and add at least one of the following details – more, if possible:

- date of death
- place of death
- date of birth of deceased
- occupation of deceased
- marital status (if female)
- other checking point of your choice (for example, the father's name on a birth certificate).

If the office can't find matching detail, you won't be sent the certificate but you'll get a partial refund of the certificate fee. After you've completed the form, click **Resume Application**.

Preparing to order
Certificates are quite expensive, so make sure that you have all the details ready to hand, as well as your credit card, before you go online. Keep a record of what you've ordered – it's easy to lose track when making multiple orders.

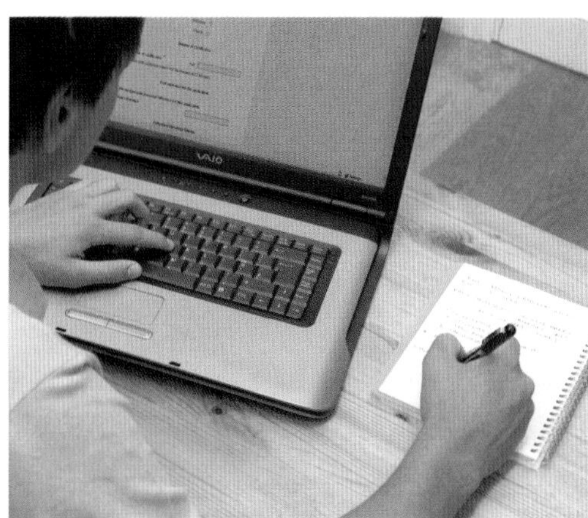

Surname of deceased * — Price
Forenames of deceased * — Sinah
Relationship to the deceased
Date of death (dd/mm/yyyy)
Age at death in years (for infants less than 1 year please state 0) — 86
Place of death or last known address
Father's surname
Father's forenames
Mother's surname
Mother's forenames

Reference information from GRO Index

Year — 1929
Quarter* — Jan, Feb, Mar
District name* — Manchester

Basket summary

The table below contains summary details of all applications currently in your basket.

Each row in the table represents an individual application.

Please use the buttons at the bottom of the table to 'checkout' or to continue with your order. The butto the right of each application row can be used to delete or edit an individual application.

If you wish to assign a reference number to the order then please enter this at the top of the form and the button marked ' Set Ref ' to do so.

Order Reference [Set Ref]

Name on Certificate	Certificate Type	Number of Certificates	No. Ref Checks	Despatch Date (Est)	Customer Ref	Price	Actions
Sinah Price	E/W Death	1	0	06 Jun 2007	FG_1_TR	£7.00	Edit Del

Year	Qtr	District	Vol	Page	Reg	Ent No	DOR
1929	Mar	Manchester	8d	515			

£7.00

[Checkout] [Add to order]

Proceed with payment

[Return to basket]

Do not use the back button to return.
If you wish to return to your basket now then please click the 'Return to basket' button.

Please confirm the contents of your basket and then click 'Proceed with payment'. You will be allowed 15 minutes to complete the process.

Please Note - Once you press 'proceed with payment' to complete and pay for your order, we regret that there is no facility to cancel or amend an order. Orders feed directly into our production process, leaving us unable to stop the system. Please therefore take extra care to check the details you have supplied before you click on the 'proceed with payment' button.

Name on Certificate	Certificate Type	Number of Certificates	No. Ref Checks	Despatch Date (Est)	Customer Ref	Price
Sinah Price	E/W Death	1	0	06 Jun 2007	FG_1_TR	£7.00

Year	Qtr	District	Vol	Page	Reg	Ent No	DOR
1929	Mar	Manchester	8d	515			

£7.00

[Proceed with payment] [Return to basket]

Filling in the application

4 This takes you to the 'Application' page, where you have to complete the boxes marked with a red asterisk * – and any further information you have. Put 'Price' in the **Surname** box and 'Sinah' in the **Forenames** box. Choose **Jan, Feb, Mar** from the **Quarter** drop-down list; key 'Manchester ' in **District name**; put '8d' in **Volume number**; and '515' in **Page number**. At the bottom of the form, choose whether you want **Standard** or **Priority** delivery service.

Finalising your order

5 The 'Basket summary' page shows your order. Check that the details are correct. Click **Edit** if you need to go back and change anything. To order further certificates, click **Add to order**. You'll be taken back to the 'Certificate choice' page, where you can fill in another set of forms. When you've finished, click **Checkout**.

Making a payment

6 If you're happy with your order, click **Proceed with payment**. If you need to adjust your order, click **Return to basket**. On the 'Secure payment' page choose the appropriate credit or debit card to reach the next page, where you can enter your card details. Finally, select **Make payment**. Your payment will be processed and you'll receive an email to confirm this.

Civil registration in Scotland

The civil registering of births, marriages and deaths began in Scotland in 1855. If you've Scottish ancestors, you're in luck, as the records offer you more family history information than those for anywhere else in the UK.

On January 1, 1855, the recording of baptisms, marriages and burials by Church of Scotland parishes was replaced by civil registration for all denominations. In the first year people had to provide extensive detail – a real boon to family historians. This proved impossible to sustain, so from 1856 the level of information reduced, although the post-1856 records are still more detailed than English and Welsh certificates.

The extra information means that when you find someone in the Scottish registers you can be confident it's the right person. This then saves time when you start looking for the birth, marriage and death certificates for the rest of that branch of your family.

The paper records, known as Statutory Registers, are held in the General Register Office for Scotland (GROS) at New Register House, Edinburgh (see Directory). But thanks to ScotlandsPeople, **scotlandspeople.gov.uk**, the official government website, you can now search online. The website contains indexes and images of the Statutory Registers for births 1855-1906, marriages 1855-1931 and deaths 1855-1956. Its other records include census returns, wills and parish records – and some digital images of paper records from New Register House. ScotlandsPeople is the only website which holds this material.

STATUTORY BIRTH REGISTERS The registers include all the information you'd normally find on English and Welsh birth certificates, plus the family's home address.

If your relative was born in 1855, you may discover much more – any other siblings, the parents' ages and birthplaces, and where and when they married. Although much of this information was dropped from 1856 for practical reasons, the date and place of the parents' marriage was re-introduced on the registers from 1861.

All Scotland's people *Your Scottish ancestors may have lived in dilapidated buildings like these, which were to be found in the West Bow area of Edinburgh in the 1900s. Wherever they lived, you should be able to find records relating to the significant events in their lives at the GROS.*

1855. MARRIAGES in the Parish of Stornoway Page in the County of Ross Registered by [illegible] Registrar.

When, where, and how married.	Signatures of the Parties.	Residence. Present.	Usual.	Age.	Rank or Profession, and Relationship of Parties (if related).	Condition. If a Widower or Widow, whether Second or Third Marriage.	Children by each former Marriage. Living. Dead.	Birthplace, and when and where registered.	Parents' Names.	Rank, Profession, or Occupation.	If a regular Marriage, Signatures of Officiating Minister and Witnesses.	If irregular, date of Extract Sentence of Conviction, or Decree of Declarator, and in what Court pronounced.	When and where registered, and Signature of Registrar.
On January ... At Garrabost. Marriage after Banns was solemnized between us according to the Forms and Ceremonies of the Free Church of Scotland	signed George Montgomery His × Mark; signed Ann Murray Her × Mark	Garrabost	Garrabost	25; 24	Tenant; Tenant's Servant			Born but not Registered on 1830 at Garrabost; Born but not Registered on 1831 at Stornoway	John Montgomery and Isabella Montgomery Maiden name MacDonald; John Murray, Ann MacLeod	Tenant; Tenant	signed Donald Murray Minister; signed John Graham Witness; signed Angus Mackenzie Witness		1855 January 18 At Stornoway [illegible] Registrar
On January ... At Manse of Knock. Marriage after Banns was solemnized between us according to the Forms and Ceremonies of the Free Church of Scotland	signed Donald MacDonald His × Mark; signed Isabella MacPhail Her × Mark	Bernera; Goat Hill	Bernera; Goat Hill	33; 33	Fisherman; [illegible]			Born but not Registered on November 1821 at [illegible]; Born Registered at February 1832 at Shawbost	Angus MacDonald and Ann MacDonald Maiden name MacArthur; Norman MacPhail and Ann MacPhail Maiden name MacLeod	Tenant; Domestic Servant; Tenant	signed Donald Murray Minister; signed Angus Mackenzie Witness; signed Rachel Graham Witness		1855 February 2 At Stornoway [illegible] Registrar

[illegible] Registrar

STATUTORY MARRIAGE REGISTERS On the registers you'll find details of the bride's and groom's names, ages, marital status, occupations, addresses, date and place of marriage, both their fathers' names and occupations, the witnesses' names and the name of the officiating clergyman.

If your relatives were married in 1855, you'll again discover a great deal more. You may find out if the bride and groom were related to each other (cousins, for example), what their mothers' names and maiden names were, where they were born, and whether either was married before and had any children by that marriage. All of which information is a huge boost to your research.

After 1855, the GROS stopped including the couple's birthplaces and previous marriages. Then from 1972 the number of former marriages was shown in the registers again, adding further valuable details to help you in your search.

STATUTORY DEATH REGISTERS In all these registers, you'll find the date, time and place of death, the person's name, sex, marital status, age, occupation, cause of death, duration of last illness, doctor's name and informant's details. Again, if your relative's death was registered in 1855 itself, you'll find a wealth of extra detail: their address, place of birth, spouse's name, the names and occupations of their parents and whether they, too, had died, the names and ages of any children (including the age and year of death of any children that had died before the parent), when the doctor last saw the person alive, the burial place and undertaker's name.

From 1856, the deceased's birthplace, names of children and spouse's name were no longer recorded. Then, from 1860 the burial place, name of the undertaker and when the doctor last saw the deceased alive was also omitted. But after 1861, the registers once again showed the spouse's name.

The detail of marriage *Two entries in the 1864 marriage register for the parish of Stornoway provide far more information than would be found in registers in either England or Wales – although by then it was no longer necessary to show the couple's bithplaces and any previous marriages.*

When a record is unavailable online

To research births after 1906, marriages after 1931 and deaths after 1956, you'll need to visit the General Register Office for Scotland (GROS) in Edinburgh in person. You can find out how to do this at **gro-scotland.gov.uk**.

If you want to order extracts of entries from modern birth, marriage and death registers, you have a choice of methods. You can fill in an application form at New Register House in Edinburgh; apply in writing to the GROS (see Directory); apply at the local Registration Office where the event was originally registered; or phone the Certificate Ordering Service at New Register House on (0131) 314 4411.

Scottish registers scotlandspeople.gov.uk

If you have Scottish ancestors, you'll find the ScotlandsPeople website a big help in your researches. It's a vast online source of original genealogical information, well organised and remarkably user friendly. Before you start searching, you'll need to register (see page 56) and choose a password. Then you can search for a name in the birth, marriage or death records, free of charge. You're told whether any matches have been found. But if you want to look at the results, you'll need to buy credits. You'll see more about how you do this on page 56.

Viewing the register

Before charging you to view a page, the site will always tell you how many credits it will cost and asks if you're sure you want to go ahead. If you want to proceed, click **Yes**, and the 'Search Returns' page will list the transcriptions for every match.

- Births – you're told the year of the entry, the child's full name, the sex of the child and the district name, county and General Register Office for Scotland (GROS) data.
- Marriages – you get the year of the entry, the man's and woman's full name, as well as the district name, county and GROS data.
- Deaths – you're given year of the entry, the deceased's full name, the mother's maiden name, other surnames the deceased may have had (in the case of a woman who has married more than once), the sex of the deceased, the age at death, as well as the district, county and GROS data.

From here you can choose to view an image of the Statutory Register for each match (see page 96). It costs 5 credits but what you see is marvellous – a scan of the original register page containing the handwritten entry you're interested in, along with any other entries on that page (see opposite). It's exciting when you realise that you've found the right record, and that there's much more information about that person than you had before. You can save the image to your desktop or just print it out.

Search Statutory Register Deaths
Click here for more information.
Search
Surname: * Fyfe
Use Soundex
Forename: Alexander
Return all forenames that begin with these characters
Other Surnames:
Mothers Maiden Surnames:
Sex: Both
Year Range: 1921 To
Age Range: 58 To 62
Include Unrecorded Ages in Age Range
Birth Year: ± 0 Years
County/City/Minor Records: All Records
District: ST ANDREW (DUNDEE) ST ANDREW (EDINBURGH)

Find the death registration first

1 Say you want to trace the birth, marriage and death of an ancestor, Alexander Fyfe, who died in 1921, when he was about 60. You also know that the Fyfes had strong links with St Andrews, in Fife, and that Alexander's oldest son, Arnet, was born in 1893. Start by finding Alexander's death certificate. Go to **scotlandspeople.gov.uk** and click **Deaths 1855-1956** in the pink box. Then type 'Fyfe' in the **Surname** box, 'Alexander' in the **Forename** box and '1921' in both of the **Year range** boxes. Under **Age range**, put '58' to '62'. Then click **Search**. There's just one match, which you can view for the price of 1 credit. It's in St Andrews, Fife, which seems appropriate. Now for 5 credits you can look at the page. You can discover Alexander's profession, his wife's name (Jessie Mason), when and where he died, his parents' names, his father's profession and his mother's maiden name. You're also told how he died, how long he'd been ill and that his death was reported by his son, Arnet. You now have enough information to search for Alexander's marriage and his birth records.

Your SR Marriages Search Returns
Click here for more information

You searched for: Male Surname: **"Fyfe"**; Use Male Soundex: **Off**; Male Forename: **"alexander*"**; Female Surname: **"mason"**; Use Female Soundex: **Off**; Female Forename: **"jessie*"**; Year From: **1883**; Year To: **1893**;

Page 1 (Free) of 1 (1 records)

No	Year	Surname (M)	Forename (M)	Surname (F)	Forename (F)	District	City/County/MR	GROS Data	Image
1	1892	FYFE	ALEXANDER	MASON	JESSIE	DENNISTOUN	GLASGOW CITY/LANARK	644/03 0362	VIEW (PAID)

Click here for printer-friendly version

Page 1 (Free) of 1 (1 records)

Statutory Registers	Old Parish Registers	Census Records	Other Records
» Births 1855-1906 » Marriages 1855-1931 » Deaths 1855-1956	» Births & Baptisms 1553-1854 » Banns & Marriages 1553-1854	» 1841 » 1881 » 1851 » 1891 » 1861 » 1901 » 1871	» Wills & Testaments Search 1513-1901 (Free)

Find the marriage record

2 Click **Marriages 1855-1931** in the pink box and then key the known facts into the relevant boxes – Fyfe/Alexander/Mason/Jessie. Alexander and Jessie's firstborn, Arnet, arrived in 1893, so key in a year range of ten years preceding this date – '1883-1893' – to cover the probable years of marriage. Click on **Search**. Interestingly, this registration isn't in St Andrews but in Dennistoun, Glasgow. Following Scottish tradition, it's likely that Alexander's father was also called Arnet. As it's the only match, it's probably worth investing 5 credits to look at the page. All the information correlates to the information you found earlier on the death registration, confirming it to be the entry you want. What it adds is Alexander's home address in Glasgow, the date and place of the marriage, Jessie's home address, her profession and her parents' details.

Your SR Births Search Returns
Click here for more information

You searched for: Surname: **"fyfe"**; Use Soundex: **Off**; Forename: **"alexander*"**; Sex: **"Male"**; Year From: **1861**; Year To: **1863**; District: **ST ANDREWS (FIFE)**;

Page 1 (Free) of 1 (1 records)

No	Year	Surname	Forename	Sex	District	City/County/MR	GROS Data	Image
1	1862	FYFE	ALEXANDER	M	ST ANDREWS AND ST LEONARDS	/FIFE	453/00 0100	VIEW (PAID)

Click here for printer-friendly version

Page 1 (Free) of 1 (1 records)

Statutory Registers	Old Parish Registers	Census Records	Other Records
» Births 1855-1906 » Marriages 1855-1931 » Deaths 1855-1956	» Births & Baptisms 1553-1854 » Banns & Marriages 1553-1854	» 1841 » 1881 » 1851 » 1891 » 1861 » 1901 » 1871	» Wills & Testaments Search 1513-1901 (Free)

Search for the birth record

3 Click **Births 1855-1906** in the pink box and then key your known facts into the relevant boxes. You know from the death registration that Alexander was 59 when he died in 1921, so he must have been born around 1862. Put '1861' and '1863' into the **Year range** boxes and St Andrews, Fife in **District**. There's one match.Click **View** to see the handwritten entry in the register, for 5 credits. This shows Alexander's name, address and date of birth, both his parents' names, including mother's maiden name, and the date of his parents' marriage – four months before his birth. His father's name is, as suspected, Arnet – the final confirmation, if any were needed, that you've found the correct entry.

Civil registration in Ireland

When researching your Irish ancestors it's important to be sure of your dates, so that you can go straight to the correct source of the records. Ireland was divided in 1922, and so were its records.

This doesn't mean that tracking down births, marriages and deaths before 1922 is trouble-free, as not all of these events were registered. Until April 1, 1845, only Catholic baptisms, marriages and deaths were registered, by the church itself. Then, in 1845, registration was extended to include non-Catholic marriages. It was not until January 1, 1864, that the registration of all events – births, marriages and deaths – whatever the denomination, was made compulsory.

Until the partition of Ireland in 1922 into the Irish Free State (later the Republic of Ireland) and Northern Ireland, records were held in Dublin. After 1922, they were split between Dublin and Belfast.

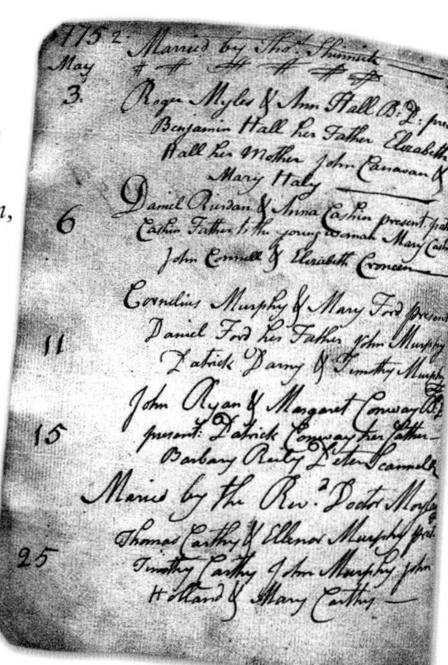

1752 Married by [illegible]
May
3 Roger Myles & Ann Hall [illegible]
Benjamin Hall her Father Elizabeth
Hall her Mother John Canavan &
Mary Haly
9 Daniel [illegible] & Anna [illegible] present [illegible]
6 [illegible]
John [illegible] & Elizabeth [illegible]
Cornelius Murphy & Mary Ford present
Daniel Ford her Father John Murphy
11 Patrick [illegible] & Timothy Murphy
John Ryan & Margaret Conway [illegible]
present Patrick Conway her father
15 Barbary [illegible]
Married by the Revd. Doctr. [illegible]
Thomas Carthy & Ellenor Murphy [illegible]
25 Timothy Carthy John Murphy John
[illegible] & Mary Carthy

Deciphering the past *Many Catholic parish registers, written in Latin, have been copied into the indexes.*

How to find the records

Records for 1864 to 1921 for the whole of Ireland, and from 1922 onwards for the Republic of Ireland, are held at the General Register Office (GRO) in Dublin; the website is **groireland.ie**. Northern Irish records, since 1922, are held at the GRO in Belfast; the website is at **groni.gov.uk**. Both sites give you contact details – or see the Directory.

Few Irish records have been digitised, so if you're researching your Irish roots you'll need to visit the archives. Alternatively, you can hire a researcher to trace your family history from the Irish archives.

What the records contain

The records from 1864 to 1877 are indexed chronologically by year; those from 1878 onwards are indexed quarterly. The registers contain all the information you'd expect: names, ages, dates, addresses, witnesses or informants and details about fathers' professions. In birth records you sometimes get a baptismal name if one was added after registration of the birth.

Understanding the registration

To research your Irish ancestry, it helps to understand how the registration districts worked. Under the Irish Poor Law Act of 1838, the country was divided into 159 areas called Poor Law Unions. Each area centered on a market town and covered a radius of about 10 miles – often crossing county boundaries. Every union was responsible for providing relief to the poor and destitute within its boundaries. In the 1850s, the Poor Law Unions were subdivided into smaller 'Dispensary Districts' as part of a nationwide public health system and, in 1864, each Dispensary District also became a local registration district. A registrar sent the records to a superintendent registrar who was in charge of assembling all the records within his Poor Law Union boundary. These were then sent on to Dublin, copied into a central index at the Office of the Registrar General and then returned to the local offices. It's this central index that you'll use to find birth, marriage and death records.

As well as the master indexes for the entire country, the Dublin GRO also holds microfilm copies of all the local registers.

Searching the indexes

In Dublin, you can search for a particular name over a five-year period for a fee of €2, or you can have access to all the indexes for up to 7 hours for €20, but it'll be only the indexes that you can view. To see a full entry, you'll have to pay €6 per entry for a microfilm print. Or you can buy the certificate of any entry for €10, but this tells you no more than the microfilm copies.

The GRO in Belfast has computers with indexes to all births, marriages and deaths from 1864 and non-Catholic marriages from 1845. To view them, it's wise to book a place in the search rooms (tel: 02890 252 128). It costs £10 to search the computerised indexes for a 6 hour period. This includes four verifications of entries by staff – further verifications cost £2.50 each.

To make it easier, the GRO staff will give you an hour's help in searching as many records as you like, for £24, or the staff will conduct searches on your behalf. They charge £5.50 for each five-year search. You can order birth, marriage and death certificates online from the Belfast GRO website at £11 each. If you apply in person, a certificate can be produced within an hour, for £27, for you to take away.

LOCAL OFFICES Every county in the Irish republic has a Superintendent Registrar's Office (SRO) where staff will search the original registers rather than the indexes for you. Because they have fewer requests to deal with, they often respond more quickly than the GRO in Dublin. You'll find addresses for SROs at **groireland.ie**; click on the **Local Registration** tab on the left-hand side of the homepage.

HERITAGE CENTRES Each county also has a local Heritage Centre that will provide search services for a fee. You'll find them by going to **groireland.ie**.

FAMILY HISTORY CENTRES The Church of Jesus Christ of Latter-day Saints (the Mormons) has made copies of most of the Irish indexes and registers, which can be viewed at its local Family History Centres. Details of how to find a Family History Centre are found on the Mormon website **familysearch.org** (see page 137). You'll probably have more success with these records than searching the indexes at the GRO in Dublin, because you can search the indexes and the registers simultaneously.

The Mormons have also transcribed birth and marriage registrations, from as early as 1530, into their family history database.

Heritage in flames
Thousands of records were destroyed when Dublin's Four Courts building went up in flames in 1922. The loss was catastrophic, but you can still acccess much of the information through Family History Centres.

What to do when data is missing

Sometimes, an ancestor may prove elusive. You know the person lived – you have several pieces of information to confirm it – but they're lost in the records. Don't worry – help is at hand.

There's an art to searching indexes for birth, marriage and death records, especially when looking for early 19th-century events. English and Welsh civil registration may have begun in 1837, but it wasn't until 1875 that the system began to be really efficient. In the early days, it was possible simply to avoid registration, which explains why some names are missing from the indexes of that period.

Why you might not find a name

There are also some other obstacles to finding information. These guidelines will help you to track down your ancestor.

EXTEND THE NAME SEARCH Variations in spellings, of both forenames and surnames, may explain why you can't find your ancestor in the indexes, or that person may have been known by their middle name. Try looking in the indexes under a variety of spellings. If you can't find Mary Ann Price, try looking for her under Mary Ann Pryce. Search for shortened versions of forenames – for example, Sarah Ann was sometimes shortened to Saran, Elizabeth might be recorded as Betsy, and many a Margaret was known as Peggy. Also, try looking for a person under a middle name.

Gypsy wedding *Romany or gypsy weddings like this one in Holsworthy, Devon, in about 1910, were traditionally held in the open air. Despite the elaborate ritual, it was unlikely that anyone would offer the details for registration.*

Britons abroad

If your ancestor doesn't appear in any UK records, he may have spent time overseas, perhaps with the British Army, such as these soldiers (right). They were stationed in Egypt during the First World War, to protect the Suez Canal and keep it open for the transport of troops from the Colonies to the Western Front.

Many sites, including The National Archives have indexes of regimental births, marriages and deaths online (see also FindMyPast on page 86).

CHECK REGISTRATION DETAILS When looking for a specific date, remember that the record will be found in the quarter in which the event was registered – which isn't necessarily the quarter in which it occurred. Search the quarter that includes the month in which the event took place and also the following quarter: it's perfectly legal to register a birth or a death up to six weeks after the event. When checking dates given to you by elderly relatives, remember that it's possible they've got their 'facts' wrong.

WIDEN THE DATE RANGE Even if you're fairly sure of the date, widen the year range you're searching by a decade or more. Some people in the 19th century simply did not know when they were born, so ages on census returns may not be accurate. Others lied about their age on marriage certificates, claiming to be older. And for a death, the person reporting it may not have known the deceased's true age and just guessed at it.

WIDEN THE AREA Try using local indexes (see page 92) rather than national ones, as the national indexes are more likely to contain errors, having been retranscribed. Alternatively, if you've been looking in a specific region because a census return told you the person was born there, it could be that they grew up in that place but were actually born elsewhere. For example, Manchester and other large cities have many registration districts very close together, so search a range of districts in the general area in which your family lived.

LOOK EVEN FURTHER AFIELD Migration around the country was fairly common during the Victorian period, as people moved from villages and farms to industrialised towns looking for work. When searching for records of someone's marriage and death, bear in mind that these events may have occurred some distance from the village or town where they were born.

CONSULT ORIGINAL SOURCES Sometimes the transcriptions are wrong, often simply due to human error. If you're having no luck in finding a person, you may have to consult the original paper indexes at the relevant archive. With more and more people transcribing information onto the internet, the margin of error becomes greater, so always double check your findings.

Living rough *It's hard to trace relatives who fell on hard times. This homeless woman, sitting outside a workhouse in the late 19th century, may not have appeared in the census and could have had an unrecorded death.*

The census

Details about Britain's inhabitants have been recorded in a census every ten years since the early 19th century. After 100 years, each census is released to the public and provides vital information about our ancestors and fascinating insights into the way they lived.

Understanding the census

When the first census was taken in 1801 its main aim was military. Napoleon was regarded as such a serious threat that the British Government needed to know how many men could be mobilised if French forces invaded.

Since that first head-count, a census has been taken every decade (apart from 1941, when the Second World War prevented it). Census records include personal and, sometimes, sensitive information – such as names of couples who weren't married – which is why the data remains confidential for a century. The 1901 census is the most recent that we can access, so you have to trace your family back to the beginning of the 20th century, using civil registration certificates, before the census comes into play.

What the census contains

Before 1841, the census was simply a head-count that – with a few regional exceptions in 1821 and 1831 – contained nothing about individuals. After 1841, the census included details about individuals, such as name, age, sex, occupation, place of birth and any relationship to others in the house, which you can now use to trace family history.

On rare occasions the census takers, known as enumerators, compiled their own lists of the heads of each household; these usually survive only in local record offices.

Mass information *19th-century censuses give a wonderful insight into the social and economic changes experienced by the growing British population.*

When you start to delve into census records, you'll find they're like a snapshot taken on a given night of the year. They capture information about the people residing at a specific address, along with any visitors, servants and lodgers present on the night in question. It also records information about people who were away from home, in institutions such as prisons, schools and workhouses, or on naval vessels.

Inconsistencies in the returns

Levels of detail in census returns can vary according to the whim of each enumerator. Also, it was usually the responsibility of the householder to provide accurate information – and this wasn't verified in any way. Householders were simply asked to fill in forms that were then collected and transcribed by the enumerators. This accounts for some of the oddities in the returns – such as people's names spelled wrongly and discrepancies in the way people's ages progressed, from one census to another.

Britain was divided into census enumeration districts, which were further broken up into sub-districts. From 1841, these were the same as civil registration districts, which makes it easier to move between the two sources in your search.

Census dates

The census returns were recorded on a particular night of each year:

1841 – June 6	1851 – March 30
1861 – April 7	1871 – April 2
1881 – April 3	1891 – April 5
1901 – March 31	1911 – April 2

It may be useful to keep these dates to hand for working out and checking the ages of your ancestors.The figures for the 1911 census will become available in January 2012.

A right puzzler *The early census forms often came as an unwelcome piece of officialdom. In this* Illustrated London News *cartoon, from the 1840s, a bemused householder is visited by the enumerator.*

"WHAT'S THIS?"

Census records online – a priceless resource

All the major censuses are now available on the internet, so you can search this vast store of records from home on your computer. Here are some of the best websites on which to start your investigations.

You can get to original census images online through databases that are searchable by the name of a person. Access to the census collections is rarely free – companies such as Ancestry and FindMyPast (see below), which have digitised the censuses, will charge you a subscription to view their images. If you don't want to pay, you'll have to visit local archives to view microfilm versions, or look at the digitised records at The National Archives (TNA) in Kew, in London.

What's in the census records?

All census returns tell you who was staying in a specific property on the night of the census – wherever they normally lived. In addition to the basic information listed by all censuses, the census returns from 1851 to 1901 include marital status, relationship to the head of household and place of birth (county and parish). They declare whether an individual is 'deaf-and-dumb' or 'blind', and by 1891, whether they're 'lunatic, imbecile or idiot'.

By 1901, the records also show a person's employer or employee status. The 1841 census is different; the ages of children under 15 were recorded accurately, but ages over 15 were rounded down to the nearest five-year band – so someone aged 34 in 1841 would be recorded as being 30. Place of birth isn't given, other than whether or not they were born in the county of residence. If someone was born elsewhere, this was indicated with **I** for Ireland, **S** for Scotland or **F** for Foreign.

The National Archives
Sample Forms
Download blank Census forms.
You can fill out the form with information on your ancestor, or just use it to

Lists of census returns and links to relevant websites are provided at the TNA website, **nationalarchives.gov.uk/census**. The links take you to census data at either **ancestry.co.uk** (see below) or **1901censusonline.com**. If you're accessing the records from home, you'll need to pay to view the images; if you're researching at TNA at Kew, you can access all the census records free.

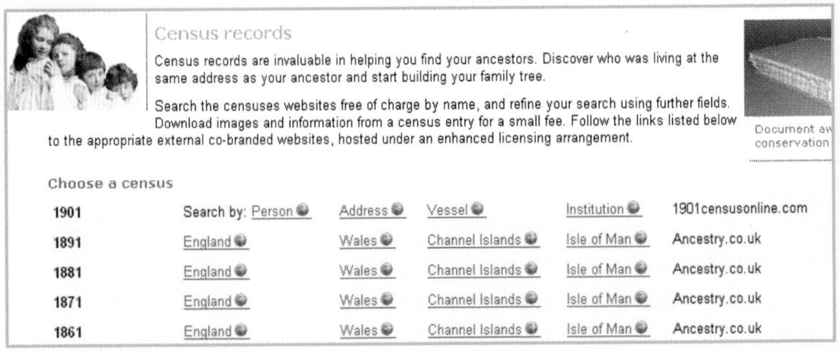

Census records
Census records are invaluable in helping you find your ancestors. Discover who was living at the same address as your ancestor and start building your family tree.
Search the censuses websites free of charge by name, and refine your search using further fields. Download images and information from a census entry for a small fee. Follow the links listed below to the appropriate external co-branded websites, hosted under an enhanced licensing arrangement.
Choose a census
1901 Search by: Person Address Vessel Institution 1901censusonline.com
1891 England Wales Channel Islands Isle of Man Ancestry.co.uk
1881 England Wales Channel Islands Isle of Man Ancestry.co.uk
1871 England Wales Channel Islands Isle of Man Ancestry.co.uk
1861 England Wales Channel Islands Isle of Man Ancestry.co.uk

Ancestry

The Ancestry website, **ancestry.co.uk** (see page 112), holds all the census returns for Britain as well as records for Canada and much of the USA. Each census has been individually transcribed. The 1881 England and Wales census index can be searched free of charge; otherwise you'll need to buy a monthly or annual subscription, or pay-per-view if you only want to use the facilities for a limited period.

Civil Parish or Township

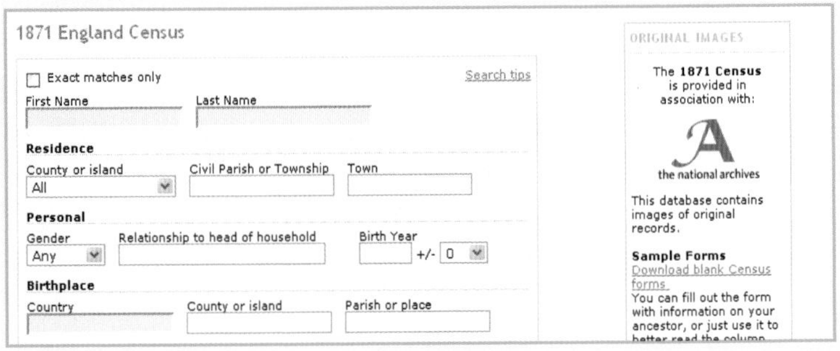

Origins

At **origins.net** (see page 114) you can look at census collections for different parts of the British Isles. British Origins holds the 1841, 1861 and most of 1871 census for England and Wales. Scots Origins holds censuses transcriptions for 1861 and 1871, but not online. Irish Origins has partial censuses and 'census substitutes' (see page 126). You can subscribe to the entire website, or to one geographical area only, on a 72 hour, monthly or annual basis.

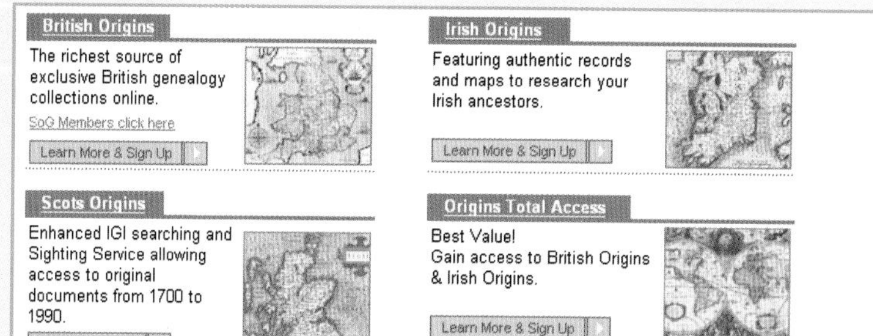

FindMyPast

The website **findmypast.com** (see page 120) allows you to search the 1841, 1861, 1871 and 1891 censuses for England and Wales, and offers the useful function of searching by address as well as by name. You can search the indexes without registering or paying, but if you want to view a transcript or an original image, you'll need to subscribe – which you can do on a monthly or yearly basis.

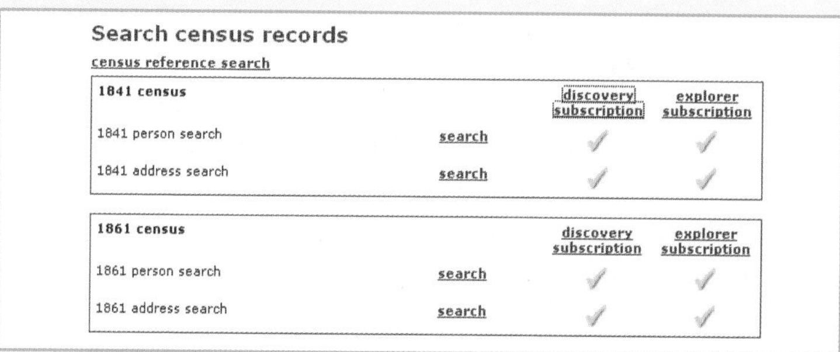

ScotlandsPeople

Scottish censuses from 1841 to 1901 are at **scotlandspeople.gov.uk**. You can search the collection indexes free of charge once you've registered your details, but you'll need to buy credits to view your search results and the original images (see page 124).

Search the Records

Please read the latest news before continuing.
LATEST UPDATE & NEWS

- RCE Images now online / Voucher Payments
- OPR Images Now Online

Choose from one of the index searches below. If you'd like to read more about the searches before you start, please visit our "Help and Other Resources" section, or to read more about tracing your family history, read our Getting Started guide.

Statutory Registers	Old Parish Registers	Census Records	Other Records
» Births 1855-1906 » Marriages 1855-1931 » Deaths 1855-1956	» Births & Baptisms 1553-1854 » Banns & Marriages 1553-1854	» 1841 » 1881 » 1851 » 1891 » 1861 » 1901 » 1871	» Wills & Testaments Search 1513-1901 (Free)

About ScotlandsPeople | Terms & Conditions | Copyright | Accessibility | Contact Us | Site Map | Search Site

1901censusonline

The usefulness of this website lies in its excellent index, which you can search not only by name, but also by address, institution and navy or merchant vessel (see page 116). You can search **1901census.online.com** free of charge and without registering. You'll need to buy credits only if you want to view an original image. The website is run by GenesReunited and can be accessed via their site, too (see page 270).

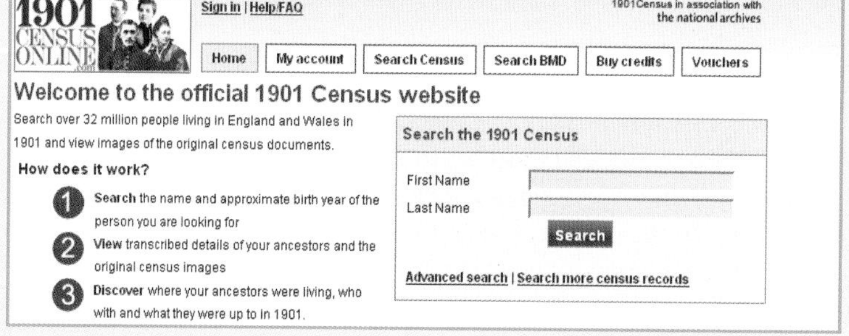

The men behind the census

It was Napoleon who pushed Parliament into the first census. The concept had been around since Roman times but it took the fear of French invasion during the Napoleonic Wars to make it happen. But the unsung heroes of the censuses were the army of men who gathered the mountain of information.

In 1800 Parliament decided it needed to know how many men could be called on to defend the country against the French camped just across the Channel – and also how many aliens were living here. So the first official census was taken on March 10, 1801.

As we scour the records now for information about our ancestors, though, we give little thought to the people who gathered all this detail. The census takers, known as enumerators, had the onerous task of visiting every home in their district on a particular night and recording the occupants' details – and they did it every ten years.

How the enumerators' task grew

At first, from 1801 to 1831, all the enumerator did was record the size of the population of his local parish, based on the number of people living in each house, the numerical breakdown of their occupations, how many houses were occupied and the total number of baptisms, marriages and burials in the parish.

He was usually chosen because he had some standing in the community, perhaps having served on the parish council or undertaken the role of an assessor of local rates. Because the enumerator was part of the community, he'd have known much about the neighbours he was counting and they, in turn, would have trusted him to come into their homes – and perhaps share a little light refreshment with them.

Some enumerators took their jobs so seriously that they made personal notes as they went around. Richard Stopher, for example, the enumerator for Saxmundham, Suffolk, in 1831, and a keen local historian, added biographical notes to the names of householders as he travelled throughout the parish. It was such men, gathering personal data as well as the basic statistical information, who

No one left out *Even Queen Victoria was included in the 1851 census (left), with Prince Albert and her large family at Buckingham Palace. On the other end of the social scale, a gypsy family are counted by an enumerator in 1901 (right).*

helped to change the way the census was perceived and brought about new categories of information, such as the names, ages, occupations and birth places of each occupant, introduced in the 1841 census. This census was also the first to use forms that were filled in by the head of the household, with the help of the enumerator, if necessary. On the night of June 6 that year, 35,000 enumerators recorded the names and biographical data of almost 16 million people.

More trouble than it's worth

Unlike Richard Stopher, not all census takers knew their community. Some enumerators in the large towns and cities encountered suspicion from householders who resented the intrusion, or they were simply not taken seriously. One householder listed 'Dick the Canary' as a member of his household. Sometimes enumerators described the difficulties and

Famous names at home

Despite the difficulties of the job, enumerators could always claim to have met renowned people, even if they were little-known at the time. In 1901, for instance, Charlie Chaplin (right) was recorded as a 12-year-old 'music hall artiste' in south London, at 94 Ferndale Road, Lambeth.

As they carried out their jobs, enumerators also encountered every walk of life – one day, quite possibly, a slum, recording prostitutes and beggars, the next royalty in their palaces. Despite being the ruler of the British Empire, Queen Victoria is recorded on the 1851 census (far left) simply as 'The Queen', with her husband Prince Albert listed as 'Head of Household'. Other enumerators would have had the pleasure of meeting such notables as Florence Nightingale (left, 1861), H.G. Wells (1891), and W.G. Grace and Claude Monet (1901).

frustrations they'd encountered at the end of their written returns. In one such record for Isleworth, Middlesex, the enumerator, Mr Abott, wrote 'This is the first and last of W. Abott's taking the census of England and Wales, unless the price goes up'. It seems the job wasn't worth the 2s 6d for every 100 persons counted, and it was this discouragingly low rate of pay that led to the recruitment of women enumerators from 1891.

There's no accounting for people

Census gathering may have been streamlined over the years, but the task of the enumerator becomes no less problematic. During the foot-and-mouth crisis in 2001, enumerators in Scotland weren't allowed past security cordons for fear of spreading the disease through their door-to-door visits. And despite improvements in technology, and changing ways in which the data is collected, the census still causes controversy. Also in 2001, an online campaign ensured that 390,000 people stated their religion as 'Jedi Knight'. As a result, official reports into the state of the UK were forced to include Jedi on the list of practising religions.

Using the census

All you need to search the census are your ancestor's name and a few basic details. Then get off to a flying start with a choice of websites.

Once you've established information about your family going as far back as the early 20th century, you can access the 1901 census to find out more. To make the most of census returns, you'll need to use the information you've gathered from civil registration certificates (see pages 74-77). For example, by establishing someone's date and place of birth from a birth certificate, you can then work out how old he or she would have been in a particular set of census records and narrow down the likely area in which they might have been living. Bear in mind that people did move around from town to town. The reverse is also true: you can use what you find out from the census to track down further civil registration certificates. For example, by looking at the ages of children born to a couple, you can usually predict a marriage date. A combination of census and certificate information allows you to work backwards through the returns to widen your family tree. You can also use the information to fill out the branches by including siblings listed on the returns.

Online census indexes

In addition to the websites described on pages 106-7, you could try visiting Family Search at **familysearch.org** (see page 54). It has an excellent index to the 1881 census.

Many family history societies have created census indexes for their local area – go to the FFHS website **familyhistoryonline.net** or visit their online shop at **genfair.com** for more information.

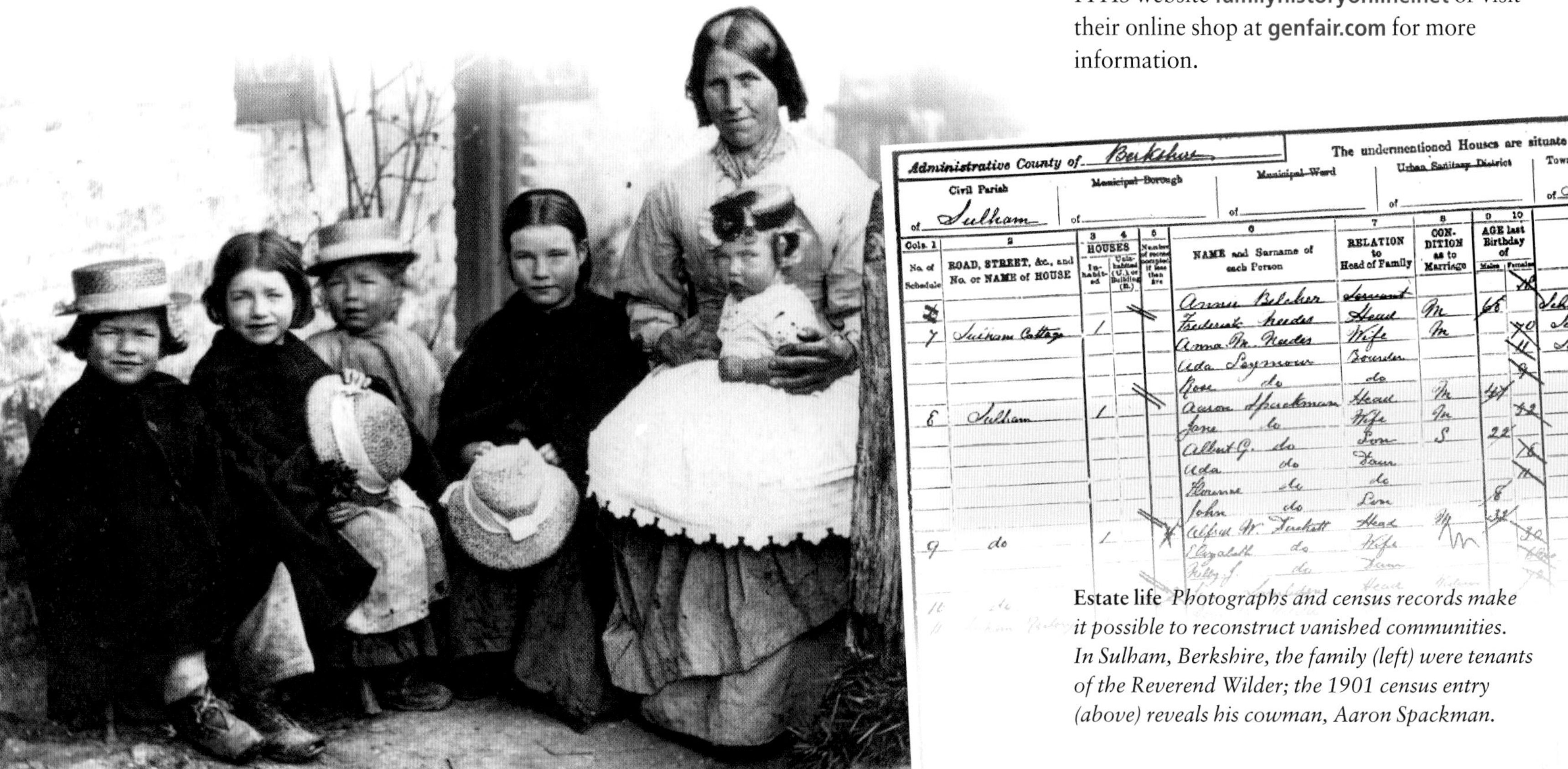

Estate life *Photographs and census records make it possible to reconstruct vanished communities. In Sulham, Berkshire, the family (left) were tenants of the Reverend Wilder; the 1901 census entry (above) reveals his cowman, Aaron Spackman.*

Online search facilities are extremely useful tools, but some of them may have a few transcription errors, which can make it hard to find what you're looking for. If this happens, try another website.

Online census images

You can view the images and transcripts in various ways. Some sites allow you to download the images direct to your PC so that you can view them electronically as often as you like. You can also print most of the images straight from the website. You'll find detailed instructions about the main sites on pages 112-29.

Some of these sites allow you to store your family tree information on their software, and sites such as **ancestry.co.uk** also allow you to upload census images to your family tree to back-up your findings.

A picture of life in the past

The information you discover from census returns can be a great help if you want to put your research into a wider social context. Look at the occupations of your relatives. For example, were trades or professions handed down from generation to generation within your family? Whether they were miners or solicitors – or anything in between – you often find several generations following in the previous one's footsteps.

You'll also notice unfolding social trends brought about by economic change. The rapid industrial growth of the 19th century may have drawn ancestors to towns and cities. Some may appear as railway workers – benefactors of the Victorian 'railway mania'.

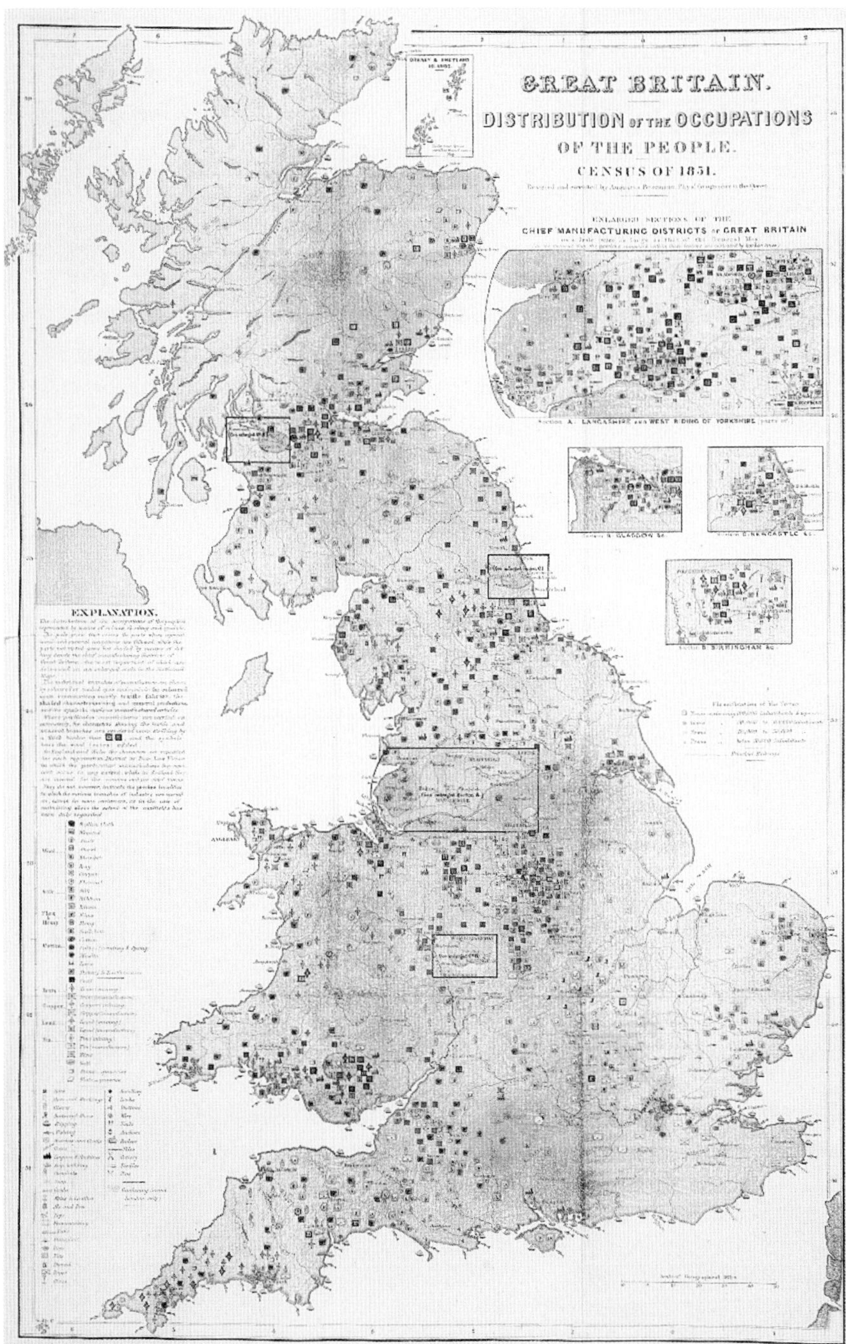

The bigger picture
Census data can reveal information of all kinds. The map, left, created from 1851 census detail, shows how occupations were distributed across Britain in the year of the Great Exhibition. Britain was undergoing an industrial transformation and the censuses show vividly how the lives of even the most ordinary families were affected by the big changes of the day.

Using the census
ancestry.co.uk

Ancestry's census indexes cover England, Wales, the Channel Islands, Isle of Man and Scotland. You can search the whole census collection or choose a specific year and region. All the indexes are free to view, once you've registered your details (see page 50). If you're lucky enough to be searching for an unusual name, you can conduct a simple name search on Ancestry's census search page. But if the name is fairly common, you could end up with a lot of matching results, so it's better to fill in any other details you have – the more you enter, the narrower and more accurate your results will be.

As well as your ancestor's name, add anything else you know – such as his mother's name, where and when he was born and his relationship to the head of the household. If you tick the 'exact match' box, then that's what you'll get – which could be a blank, if the entry was mistranscribed.

When you draw a blank

If you don't get any matching results, don't worry – just delete some of the information in the boxes and try again. It's also a good idea

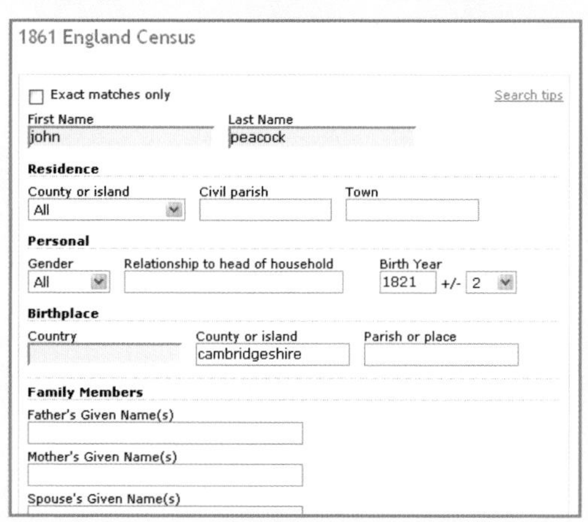
1861 England Census

Exact matches only | Search tips

First Name: john | Last Name: peacock

Residence
County or island: All | Civil parish | Town

Personal
Gender: All | Relationship to head of household | Birth Year: 1821 +/- 2

Birthplace
Country | County or island: cambridgeshire | Parish or place

Family Members
Father's Given Name(s)
Mother's Given Name(s)
Spouse's Given Name(s)

Fill in the known facts

1 To find a John Peacock, born around 1821 in Cambridgeshire, in the 1861 census, go to the homepage and click on **1861 England** under UK census records. Enter 'John' in the **First name** box and 'Peacock' in the **Last name** box. Enter **Cambridgeshire** in the **County or island** list. For his birth year, allow a bit of leeway, so enter '1821' and select **+/– 2** because the ages given on census forms aren't always accurate. Click **Search**.

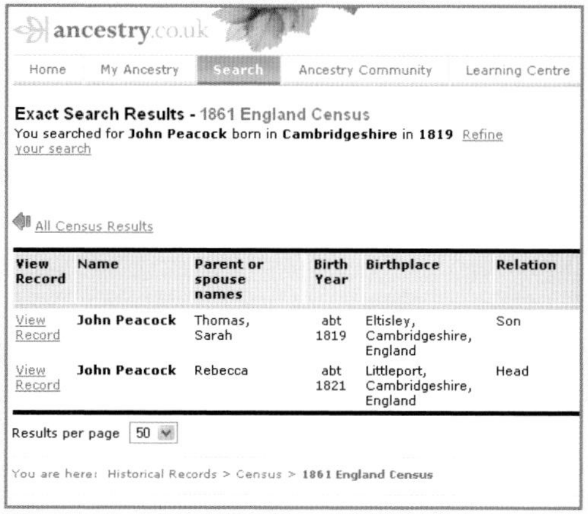

ancestry.co.uk

Home | My Ancestry | Search | Ancestry Community | Learning Centre

Exact Search Results - 1861 England Census
You searched for **John Peacock** born in **Cambridgeshire** in **1819** Refine your search

All Census Results

View Record	Name	Parent or spouse names	Birth Year	Birthplace	Relation
View Record	John Peacock	Thomas, Sarah	abt 1819	Eltisley, Cambridgeshire, England	Son
View Record	John Peacock	Rebecca	abt 1821	Littleport, Cambridgeshire, England	Head

Results per page 50

You are here: Historical Records > Census > 1861 England Census

Refine your search

2 The search finds far too many matches because you didn't specify **Exact matches only**. Click on **Refine your search** and resubmit the original form, but this time tick the **Exact matches only** box. Then click on **Search**. The matches are narrowed down to just two John Peacocks, as shown above.

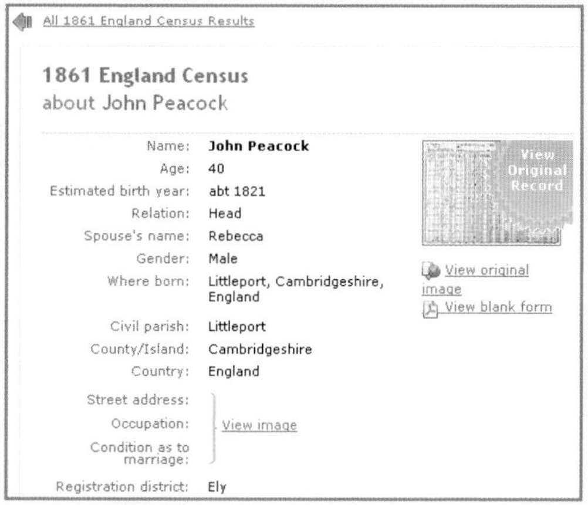

All 1861 England Census Results

1861 England Census
about John Peacock

Name: John Peacock
Age: 40
Estimated birth year: abt 1821
Relation: Head
Spouse's name: Rebecca
Gender: Male
Where born: Littleport, Cambridgeshire, England
Civil parish: Littleport
County/Island: Cambridgeshire
Country: England
Street address:
Occupation: View image
Condition as to marriage:
Registration district: Ely

View Original Record
View original image
View blank form

Look at the details

3 You know that the John Peacock you're looking for was married, so the second option (shown as the head of the household) is more likely to be the right one. Click **View record** to learn more. From here you can also opt to view the original image.

to remove the tick from 'exact matches', so the search engine will look for close variations of names and other data you've keyed in – which may find you hundreds of possibilities. You'll need to experiment with your search, but that's what makes it so thrilling when you get a positive result.

Counting heads *Every person in every household would be counted on the night of the census, including servants who 'lived in', such as the driver of this wealthy family's 1910 Humber.*

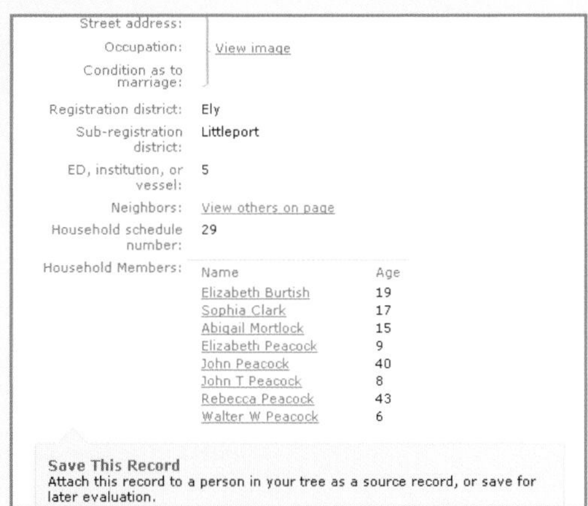

Street address:
Occupation: View image
Condition as to marriage:
Registration district: Ely
Sub-registration district: Littleport
ED, institution, or vessel: 5
Neighbors: View others on page
Household schedule number: 29

Household Members:

Name	Age
Elizabeth Burtish	19
Sophia Clark	17
Abigail Mortlock	15
Elizabeth Peacock	9
John Peacock	40
John T Peacock	8
Rebecca Peacock	43
Walter W Peacock	6

Save This Record
Attach this record to a person in your tree as a source record, or save for later evaluation.

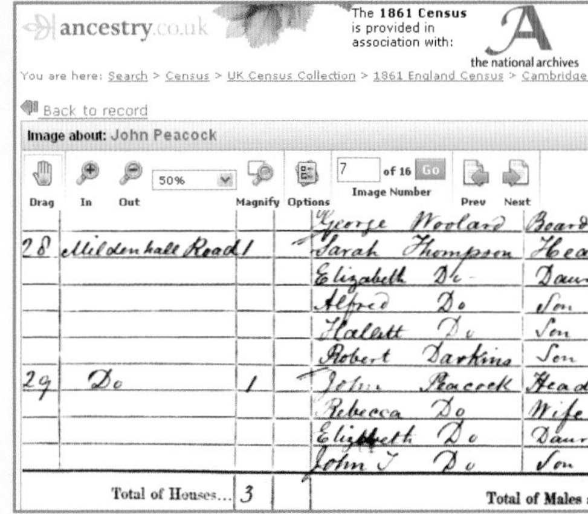

ancestry.co.uk
The 1861 Census is provided in association with: the national archives
You are here: Search > Census > UK Census Collection > 1861 England Census > Cambridgesh
Back to record
Image about: John Peacock
Drag In Out 50% Magnify Options 7 of 16 Go Image Number Prev Next

Who else lived there?

4 Scroll to the bottom of the page about John Peacock to see who was staying at that address on census night 1861. There was 40-year-old John, his wife Rebecca, two sons, a daughter and three servant girls. You can also see who your ancestor's neighbours were, by clicking **View others on page**.

View the original

5 If you select **View original image** shown near the top of the page – on the right in Step 3 – you'll see the handwritten census page, including other houses in the same street. You may need to scroll up or down to find your ancestor. The magnifying glass tool at the top left of the page will allow you to zoom in so you can read the entry.

Locate your ancestor

6 Scroll down until you find John Peacock near the bottom of the page. The double diagonal lines drawn at the top left of John Peacock's name indicates the start of a new household. When a household begins near the bottom of the page, it often continues on the next page. If you wish to check, click on the green arrow with **Next** beneath it. You can also print the image or save it to your computer.

Using the census origins.net

The Origins Network has a wide range of UK and Ireland data collections (see page 55 for more details). They're arranged geographically, with links to British Origins (meaning English and Welsh), Irish Origins and Scots Origins at the top of the homepage. The Irish Origins section is particularly valuable as an online resource if you're researching your Irish ancestry.

IRELAND Because of the destruction of virtually all Ireland's 19th-century census returns in a fire at the Public Record Office in Dublin in 1922, a whole range of different sources (known as 'census substitutes') have become vital to the family historian with Irish roots. The Irish Origins holdings include many of these records – which are searchable online – and they include:

- **Elphin 1749 census** Records for nearly 20,000 people living in the Diocese of Elphin in 1749 tell you the occupation and religion of the head of household, size of the family, who had servants and how many they had.
- **Irish 'strays' in England and Wales** Lists of people identified as Irish in both the 1841 and 1871 England and Wales censuses.
- **Griffith's Valuation 1847-64** An all-Ireland property survey, county by county, published between 1848 and 1864, that holds detailed information about land and buildings – who owned, let or occupied them.
- **William Smith O'Brien Petition 1848-9** A petition listing more than 80,000 names and places from the time of the Great Famine.
- **Dublin City 1851 census** An index of the heads of households in Dublin, which was compiled by a local doctor in order to help old age pension applicants prove their age and make claims.
- **Dublin City Rotunda Ward 1901 census** Details of 13,556 individuals living in more than 1,334 properties in the Rotunda Ward.
- **Irish Wills Index (1484-1858)** Online access to wills and related documents.
- **Transatlantic migration (1858-70)** Lists of passengers returning to Ireland from the USA.
- **Irish Origins library** Collection of rare vintage photos, books, maps and other publications of interest to family researchers.

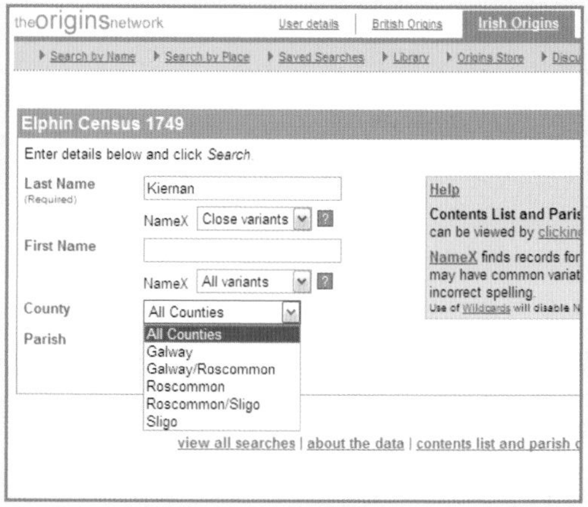

Heavy work *Many Irish migrants came to the UK to work on large construction projects such as the Manchester Ship Canal. Here, 'navvies', or labourers, are shown at the start of the excavations in 1887.*

Search the Elphin census

1 To search the census for a Sarah Kiernan, go to **origins.net**, log in or register (see above, opposite), and then choose the Irish Origins site. Click on **Click here for all Irish origins collections**. Then select **Search** next to **Elphin census 1749**. Enter 'Kiernan' in the **Last name** box. You can search by county, but the Elphin census covers only Galway, Roscommon and Sligo. You can also search by parish. Once you've entered any details that you know, click on **Search**.

ENGLAND AND WALES Origins holds transcriptions and scanned images of the English and Welsh censuses for 1841 and 1861, and part of the 1871 census.

SCOTLAND Access to the Scottish records is free of charge but what you can find there is limited. The site gives free access to an index of place names in the 1881 census, but not to any other census transcriptions. You can request a search of the 1861 and 1871 Scottish censuses and order transcriptions by sending in an order form with details of your search criteria, which must include at least your ancestor's name and where you think they lived.

Researching with Origins

To search the network's indexes for British or Irish ancestors you need to register your email address and a chosen password on the site. The minimum subscription is £7.50, which gives unlimited access to the records for 72 hours. You can look at all the census records for one country at the same time. Whether you're searching the censuses or a census substitute, the principle is the same. Enter your ancestor's name and select a specific year range. If you get too many results to sort through, you can narrow down the results by clicking on **Refine search** next to the dataset (census return) you wish to search. You can then expand your search criteria by entering parish and county of residence, birthplace and age range. The website will lead you through other options.

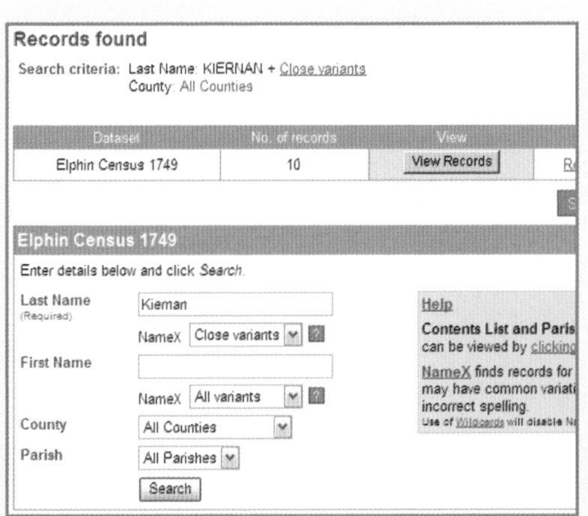
Records found

Search criteria: Last Name: KIERNAN + Close variants
County: All Counties

Dataset	No. of records	View
Elphin Census 1749	10	View Records

Elphin Census 1749

Enter details below and click *Search*.

Last Name (Required): Kiernan — NameX: Close variants

First Name: — NameX: All variants

County: All Counties

Parish: All Parishes

Search

Help

Contents List and Paris... can be viewed by clicking...

NameX finds records for... may have common variati... incorrect spelling

First findings

2 At the top of the page you'll see that ten results have been found for your search. You can then choose to refine your search, or view all the results. If you want to view all of them, click on the **View records** button at the top of the page.

View records - Elphin Census 1749

Search criteria: Last Name: KIERNAN + Close variants
County: All Counties

Click column heading links to change order of results

Last Name	First Name	County	Parish	Page number	Row number	Image
Kiernan	Edmond	Roscommon	Kilmore	66	114	Image
Kiernan	Laurence	Galway	Kilbegnet	302	293	Image
Kiernan	Margar	Roscommon	Kilmore	66	116	Image
Kiernan	Margret	Galway	Kilbegnet	302	300	Image
Kiernan	Mark	Galway	Kilbegnet	302	283	Image
Kiernan	Patrick	Galway	Kilbegnet	302	289	Image
Kiernan	Patrick	Galway	Kilbegnet	302	299	Image
Kiernan	Sarah	Galway	Kilbegnet	302	290	Image
Kiernan	Sarah	Galway	Kilbegnet	302	294	Image

Find your ancestor

3 You'll see a screen, displaying the names, counties, and parishes of the people with the surname you've asked for, as well as the page number for the census return. Scan the list to find the person with details that most closely match your ancestor's. If there's more than one likely name, you may need to check all of them. In this case, the match is the first Sarah Kiernan, the eighth name on the list. Click on the **Image** button next to her name.

THE CENSUS OF ELPHIN 1749

See the scanned image

4 If you haven't used the site before, you'll be asked to view a test census image. This is so the site can check that you have the appropriate software. Once you've viewed the test image successfully, the census image will be displayed. It will show you the county, place of abode, name and religion, profession, number of children over and under 14, and number of male and female servants in the house on the night of the census.

Using the census
1901censusonline.com

Some websites only let you search by name, but with this pay-per-view site you have the bonus of getting at information in the 1901 census for England and Wales through an address, institution or ship's name – and even by place, so you can see the census return for a whole area.

The 1901 census was the first census to be digitised and made available to the public online. It was launched on January 2, 2002, by The National Archives (then known as the Public Record Office) and its project partner QinetiQ. They underestimated the popularity of the subject matter, and the site crashed within seconds – it was unable to cope with the millions of family historians who logged on, not only from the UK but from right around the world. Since it was restored, it has proved to be extremely popular and totally reliable.

Types of search

The 1901 census search engine offers several different types of search, each of which has links to scanned images of the census return. If you start with the site's **Search census** link at the top of the homepage it will take you straight to **Person search** – but using the tabs along the top of this page you can change the basis of your search, and choose other criteria, such as a vessel or institution.

The **Address** search allows you to look for a house name, house number, street name and place. So if you're having trouble finding your ancestors when you search for them by name – and this will often be because the name has been mistranscribed – you may be able to find them by searching an address found on a marriage or birth certificate dated 1900 or earlier. You can also use the address search to discover the names and other details of people who were living in your own home at the time of the 1901 census. Both types of search are shown overleaf, on page 118.

Using advanced searches

If you're not sure of the spelling of an ancestor's name, the **Advanced search** option allows you to tick an **Include synonyms?** box next to the person's name. The results will include variants on the name you have entered, which will greatly widen your search.

You may find you get too many results. If this happens, you can narrow the results list by specifying the occupation of the person you're looking for, their relationship to the head of the household, and their marital status.

Street life *A crowded London tenement would house hundreds of people, many of them extended families. Pinning down who lived there would have been a full-time job for an enumerator and mistakes were often made.*

If you're looking for an address, the **Advanced search** lets you narrow the search right down to the ecclesiastical parish and parliamentary borough the address should come under. But it's important to remember that restricting your results may in fact make

it harder to find the correct entry. If, having entered all the known criteria into an advanced search, you still have no luck, try reducing the number of details you fill in. This will widen the search.

The cost of searching

It costs nothing to make a simple search of the indexes. This will let you see, for free, lists with transcriptions of names, ages, places of birth, county and town of the census return and occupations. But if you find a possible ancestor or place you'd like to investigate more fully, you'll be prompted to register and buy credits to see more detail or to view the digital image of the actual census page. You can buy credits using your credit card, or there's the option of buying vouchers, which is explained onscreen. For most people, using a credit card is the quickest and easiest option.

The minimum amount you can spend is £5.50, which buys you 550 credits that are valid for seven days. It costs 50 credits to view the transcription of a page and 75 credits to view the scanned image of the page. Once you've paid, your search continues.

Other censuses on the site

The website also has online indexes and scanned images of the 1841 to 1891 England and Wales censuses. The search engines for these census returns are less sophisticated than those of the 1901 census and allow you to search only by first name, last name and year of birth.

1901 CENSUS ONLINE .com

Sign in | Help/FAQ

Home | My account | Search Census | Search BMD

Search 1901 census for an institution

Reveal who was living in hospitals, barracks, orphanages, workhouses and prisons in 1901.

Person search | Address | Place | Institution | Vessel

Easy institution search

You may use wildcard characters (*) in the search conditions but you must supply at least 2 characters before the wildcard.

Institution name: guys — e.g. Blenheim Barracks

Place Keywords:

Results per page: 10

Search

Advanced search

Clear form

Start your 1901 census search

1 To search for an Adelaide Archdale in Guy's Hospital, London, in the 1901 census, first sign in and check that you have enough credits to order original material (see above). On the homepage, click on **Search census** button. Next, click on the **Institution search** button and enter 'Guys'. Add any other details you have. Click on **Search**. If you have a lot of detail for your search, use the **Advanced search** option by clicking the link at the bottom of the page.

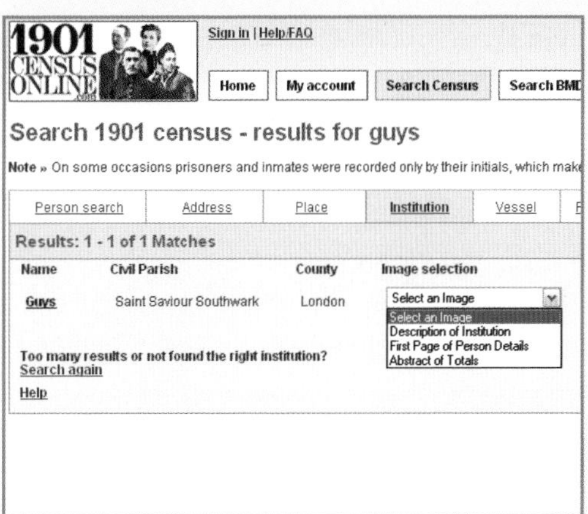

See the first results

2 It takes a few minutes for the results to download, so be patient. The results will come up and you'll be offered a number of viewing options: you can view a description of the institution, the total number of people in the institution or the first page of person details. But if you're searching for a person, it's best to click on the name of the institution – in this case, **Guy's**.

Full transcription details for Adelaide Archdale

National Archives Reference

RG Number, Series	Piece	Folio
RG13	362	112

Adelaide Archdale

Language	
Relation to Head of Family/ Position in the Institution	Nurse
Condition as to Marriage	Single
Age Last Birthday	26
Sex	F
Profession or Occupation	Hospital Nurse
Employment Status	
Where Born	Norfolk Colhshaw
Infirmity	
Institution Name	Guys

Find your relative

3 A list of names of all those present in the hospital on that night will come up. Click on the name you're looking for – in this case, Adelaide Archdale. You'll see that she was a single nurse, aged 26 and born in Colhshaw, Norfolk. To see an image of the original census page, go back to the previous screen and click on the census icon next to her name.

Using the census
1901censusonline.com

The address search feature of **1901censusonline.com**, mentioned on the previous page, can help you if you're battling to find an ancestor using a name search. When you do an address search you're asked for the house or street name and the place. It's a good idea to omit the words Road, Avenue, Hill, Street or Lane because the spellings of these can vary. 'Avenue', for example, may have been transcribed as 'Ave', 'Av' or 'Avn'. So if you're looking for East Street, for example, just key in East.

Once you've found the name of the people who were at the address on census night in 1901, why not try entering that name into the indexes for the 1891 census, to see if they were living there then. If the house had been passed down through the generations, you could be lucky enough to find a string of census entries in the name of the same family, as you work backwards through the censuses for previous years. You can then build up a vivid picture of the family who lived there.

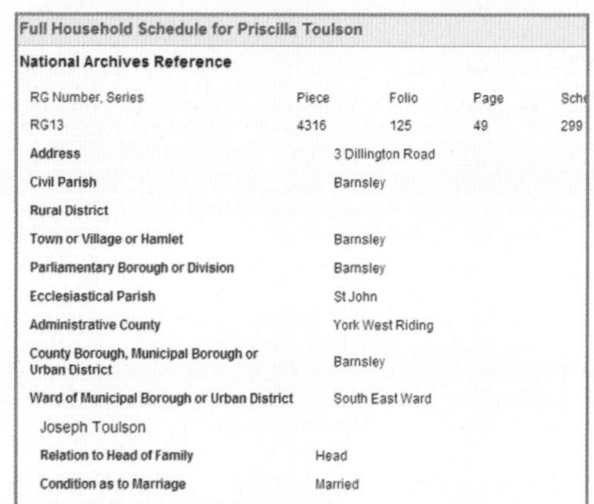

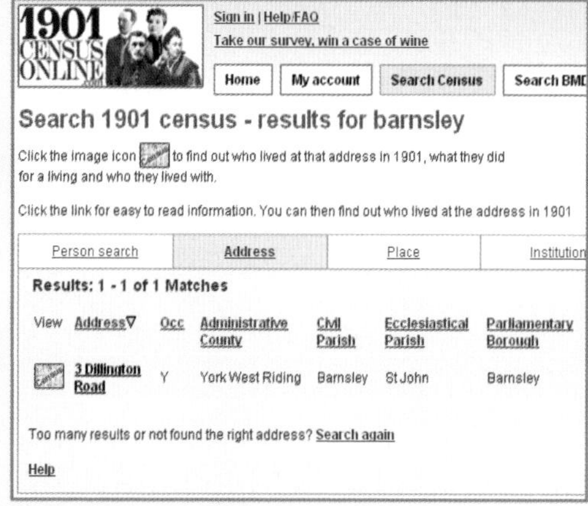

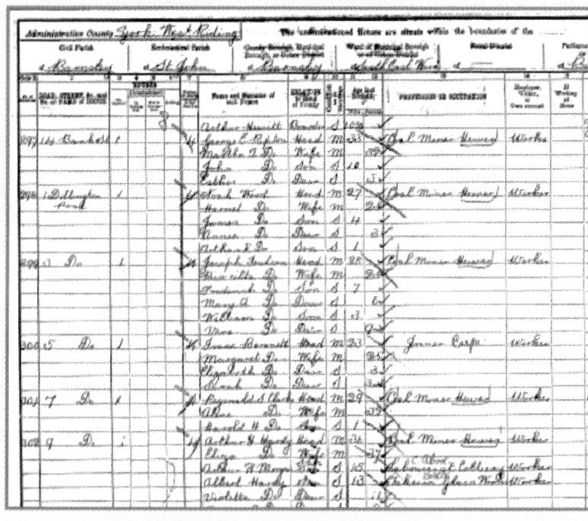

Finding people using an address

1 Say you're having difficulty locating a Priscilla and Joseph Toulson in the 1901 census, but you know their daughter Vera was born in 1900 at 3 Dillington Road, Barnsley. On the homepage, click the **Address search** link at the top. This takes you to the address search engine. Enter '3 Dillington' in the **House and/or street** box and 'Barnsley' in the **Place keywords** box and click **Search**.

View the results as a list

2 The results page shows that there's only one match for '3 Dillington' in Barnsley, and it's 3 Dillington Road. Click the address to see a full transcription of all the occupants there on the night of the 1901 census. This will cost 50 credits.

View the results as an image

3 Alternatively, click on the census icon to see a digital image of the whole census page. You'll find Priscilla and Joseph Toulson living at 3 Dillington Road with their daughter Vera and the rest of their children. This will cost 75 credits. To read the entry easily, use the toolbar along the top of the image to zoom in. You'll have access to this page for seven days, so it's worth making a copy of it to save to your computer (see page 31).

Who was living in The Hermitage in 1901?

On census night, 1901, The Hermitage in Tonbridge was a full house. The occupants were George and Kate Dain, their five school-age children, George Dain's younger brother, Harry – employed by his brother and presumably a permanent resident – and two servants. The house had four bedrooms, used by the family members, as well as two attic rooms for the servants. Until the 1980s, there were still bell-pushes in the main rooms that rang bells on a labelled board in the kitchen. The 1901 census is the only one that lets you find occupants when you know only the address and not their names.

1901 CENSUS ONLINE

Sign in | Help/FAQ

Take our survey, win a case of wine

Home | My account | Search Census | Search BMD

Search 1901 census for an address

Look for an address in the 1901 Census and see who was living in your house at that time.

Person search | Address | Place | Institution

You may use wildcard characters (*) in the search conditions but you must supply at least 2 characters before the wildcard. You can use a maximum of 2 wildcards per search.

House and/or Street: 22 The Hermitage

Place Keywords: Kent

Results per page: 10

Search

Advanced search

Clear form

Click the link for easy to read information. You can then find out who lived at the address in 1901

Person search | Address | Place | Institution

Results: 1 - 5 of 5 Matches

View	Address	Occ	Administrative County	Civil Parish	Ecclesiastical Parish	Parliamenta Borough
	22 The Hermitage	Y	Kent	Tonbridge Urban	St Peters & St Pauls Tonbridge	Sth Western Tonbridge D Of Kent
	By The Gas House	Y		Hadlow	Hadlow St Mary	South Weste Tonbridge D Of Kent
	By The Gas House	Y		Hadlow	Hadlow St Mary	South Weste Tonbridge D Of Kent
	The Hermitage	Y		Hadlow	Hadlow St Mary	South Weste Tonbridge D Of Kent
	The Hermitage Near Woodside Rd	Y	Kent	Tonbridge	Tonbridge St Stephens	South Weste Tonbridge O

Searching for previous occupants

1 If you're researching the history of the house where you grew up – for example, The Hermitage, 22 East Street, Tonbridge. Assuming that it was built and occupied by the time of the census in 1901, you can use the address search. From the homepage click the **Search census** tab, then click on **Address** at the top of search page. Enter '22 The Hermitage' in the **House and/or street** box and 'Kent' in the **Place keywords** box. Click **Search**.

Select from the possible matches

2 There are three matches from this search. The transcribed index gives the addresses, whether the buildings are occupied (Y or N), and administrative details of the county and town of the census return.

View the entry

3 Select **22 The Hermitage**, the entry that most closely matches your criteria. You can then read full transcription details of the ten occupants on census night 1901. If you want to see the original census image, click the census icon at the top of the page.

Using the census
findmypast.com

Searching the indexes of **findmypast.com** is free, but you have to pay a small amount to see detailed information (see page 84). You can search for evidence of your family's past, either by person or by address, in the indexes and images of the 1841, 1861, 1871 and 1891 census records for England and Wales. If you know the TNA document reference number for the image you want, click **Census reference search** to go straight to it.

Searching for a person

A **Basic person search** (see step 1, right) lets you restrict the census search by first name and surname, age range, occupation (in 1861 and 1891), place of birth, residence and county. Results can be arranged by age or alphabetically. You can narrow them down by choosing **Advanced person search** (see step 3, below). This lets you include middle name, sex, marital status, exact residence and relationship to head of household. Also, you can add the name of another person who should be in the same household, which is helpful if you're looking for people with fairly common surnames – knowing the names of other family members will help to filter the search results. Opting to include variants in name spellings may help to cover enumerator errors or mistranscriptions.

The results list is free and displays the address type (household, institution or vessel), the person's name, age (but this would be rounded up or down to the nearest five years in the 1841 census), sex and the

Search tips

It's better to fill in fewer fields and read all the results rather than ask the search engine to restrict the results. Only fill in more fields if a list of results is really long or you're searching for common names.

Some names have been transcribed with the surname first, particularly census returns for institutions. If you can't find someone, try entering their surname in the first name field and their first name in the surname field.

In cases where the **findmypast** transcribers have been unable to decipher certain words, they've typed **'999'** or **'...'** instead – which explains why you may sometimes not be able to find an ancestor in the census return.

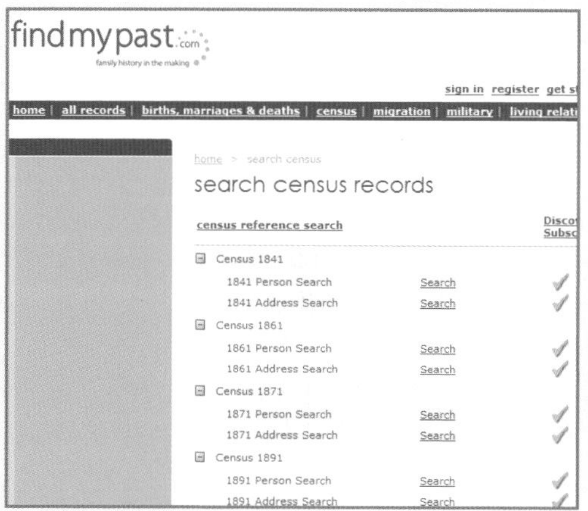

Start your basic search

1 You want to find a Joseph Lilly on the 1841 census, but the only information you know is that he was 28 years old in 1841 and that his wife's name was Elizabeth. He travelled around a lot so you're unsure where he may have been living in 1841. To start with a basic search for his name, go to the **Census** link along the top panel of the homepage and click the **Search** link next to the **1841 person search** option.

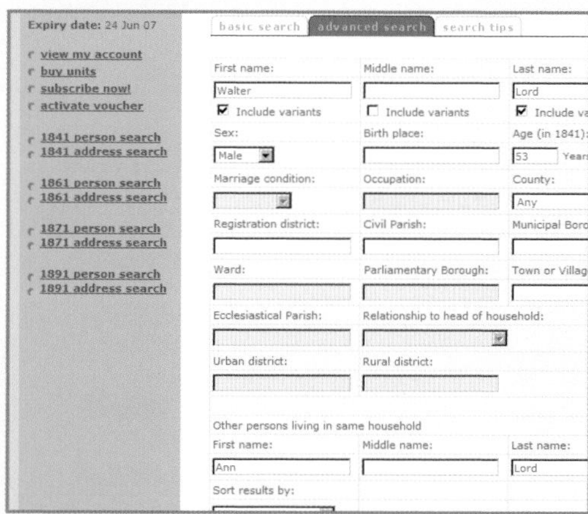

Assess the first results

2 The **Basic search** window will appear. Enter 'Joseph' in the **First name** field, 'Lilly' in the **Last name** field, tick the **Include variants** box for both the first name and surname, enter '28' in the **Age** box and set the +/- age range to '5' (because the 1841 census enumerators rounded adult's ages up and down). Now press **Search**.

registration district. To see a household transcription or view an image of the page, buy units (the minimum purchase is 60 units, costing about £7) or subscribe to the website. A download costs 3 units; a subscription gives you unlimited access for a specific period – £25 for 30 days, for example.

Searching for an address

A **Basic address search** asks for the street name, the place of residence and a county. An **Advanced address search** narrows the results by asking you for more information; use this option when a basic search yields too many results. If you simply can't find an address, it could have been mistranscribed. Try doing a 'wildcard' search (in which you type * to replace one or more letters) in either the basic or the advanced address search engine.

The results page provides the census schedule number, house number, street name, civil parish, town, registration district and ecclesiastical parish. It'll show you who was staying at the address on census night.

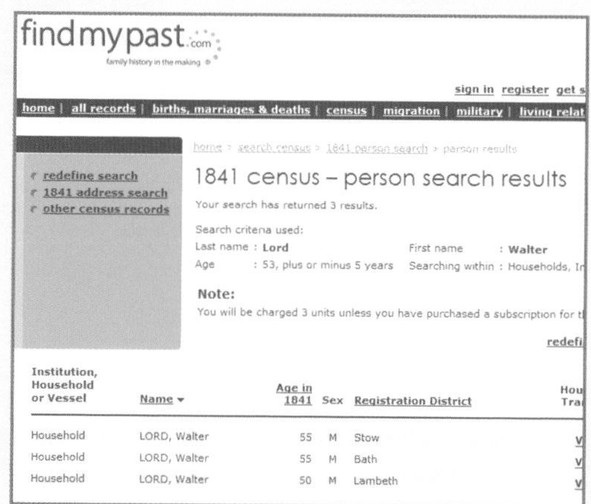

findmypast.com
family history in the making
sign out my account get started subscribe
home | all records | births, marriages and deaths | census | migration | military | living relat

1841 census person search results

Your search has returned 1 result.
Search criteria used:
Last name : Lilly First name : Joseph
Age : 28, plus or minus 5 years Searching within : Households, Institutions, Vessels

Note:
You will be charged 3 units unless you have purchased a subscription for this set of records.
redefine current search

Institution, Household or Vessel	Name	Age in 1841	Sex	Registration District	Household Transcript
Household	LILLY, Joseph	30	M	Newark Union	VIEW

1841 address search new 1841 person search

© 2006 Intelligent Image Management Inc. and The Origins Network

Do an advanced search

3 Four Joseph Lillys are found with the correct name and roughly the right age, although none are exactly 28 years old. Click on the **Redefine current search** link, then on the **Advanced search** tab. Add Joseph's wife's name: under **Other persons living in same household** put 'Elizabeth' in the **First name** box and 'Lilly' in the **Last name** box. Press **Search** to be taken to the results page.

Your ancestor is found

4 Only one of the Joseph Lillys listed previously are now displayed, which means he was the only one living with an Elizabeth Lilly. To view the original census page press the **View** link in the **Original census** image column.

(Form A.)

LIST of the CREW and OTHERS on BOARD of the SHIP or VESSEL called the

	NAME and SURNAME	CONDITION	AGE OF		RANK or OCCUPATION
	Write, after the Name of the Master, the Names of the other Officers and Crew; and then the Names of Passengers and Visitors (if any).	Write "Married" or "Unmarried," "Widower" or "Widow," against the Names of all Persons except Young Children.	Males	Females	State here the rank of the Officers, and the rating of the Men and Boys of the Crew. The rank or occupation of Passengers and Visitors should be stated as fully and clearly as possible.
1	George Smith	Un	above 20		Master
2	Thomas Smith	Do	16		Mate

Life on the river *If your ancestors worked the rivers on a barge, you'd expect them to be hard to find on a census. But as the census entry above shows, some bargemen were recorded.*

Using the census familyhistoryonline.net

Known as FHOL, **familyhistoryonline.net** is the data service for the Federation of Family History Societies (FFHS). Through it you can access records transcribed from local record offices and county archives, and search its geographically arranged databases by surname. You'll have to register (see page 58) before you can search the site. Searching the indexes is free, but you have to pay a few pence to see full details of some entries. To do this, you'll need to buy a minimum of £5 credit.

Work is still ongoing on this project, so FHOL's census indexes are not complete for every year or for every county. But for those entries that you can find, the transcriptions may be more accurate than those found on some other internet sites, because they have been transcribed by people with local knowledge.

Searching for a year and county

To check whether the site has a census index for a particular year and county, click **Available databases** from the **Databases** tab in the top panel of the homepage. Click the relevant county name to see a list of all the databases the site holds for that county. Then click on the link to the relevant census for more information about the coverage, the names of places that have been indexed and a list of abbreviations used in transcriptions and what they mean.

Searching for a relative

To find an ancestor in the census index, go to **Searches** along the top panel of the page and select **New search**. The form will ask for a surname and first name, and you can also use 'wildcards' (see page 64) or select variants if the name is a more common one.

Specify a county of residence and a range of years. Ticking the boxes that let you choose **est. births** and **others of this family** widens the search to include entries which may give the person's estimated birth.

Every search you do may take a slightly different path, but the site will help you by offering choices and prompting you to the next step. Each transcription that you end up with includes forename and surname; relationship to head of household; condition (**M** for married or **U** for unmarried); gender;

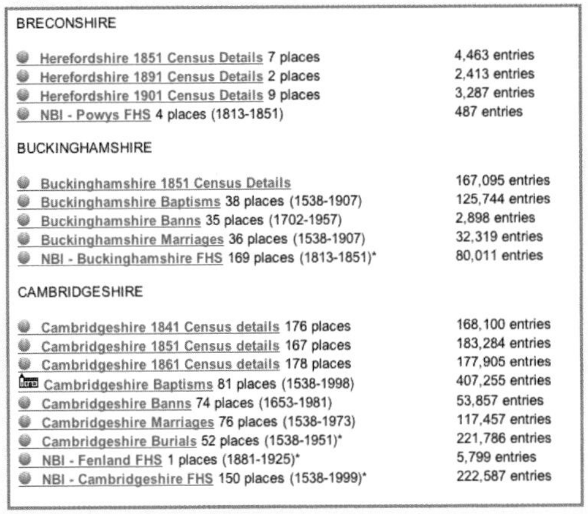

BRECONSHIRE

Herefordshire 1851 Census Details 7 places	4,463 entries
Herefordshire 1891 Census Details 2 places	2,413 entries
Herefordshire 1901 Census Details 9 places	3,287 entries
NBI - Powys FHS 4 places (1813-1851)	487 entries

BUCKINGHAMSHIRE

Buckinghamshire 1851 Census Details	167,095 entries
Buckinghamshire Baptisms 38 places (1538-1907)	125,744 entries
Buckinghamshire Banns 35 places (1702-1957)	2,898 entries
Buckinghamshire Marriages 36 places (1538-1907)	32,319 entries
NBI - Buckinghamshire FHS 169 places (1813-1851)*	80,011 entries

CAMBRIDGESHIRE

Cambridgeshire 1841 Census details 176 places	168,100 entries
Cambridgeshire 1851 Census details 167 places	183,284 entries
Cambridgeshire 1861 Census details 178 places	177,905 entries
Cambridgeshire Baptisms 81 places (1538-1998)	407,255 entries
Cambridgeshire Banns 74 places (1653-1981)	53,857 entries
Cambridgeshire Marriages 76 places (1538-1973)	117,457 entries
Cambridgeshire Burials 52 places (1538-1951)*	221,786 entries
NBI - Fenland FHS 1 places (1881-1925)*	5,799 entries
NBI - Cambridgeshire FHS 150 places (1538-1999)*	222,587 entries

Start your search

1 You want to find a Charles Stafford on the 1851 census. You know he lived in Dinton, Buckinghamshire, in 1841. Go to the homepage and click on **Databases**. Select **Available databases** and click the **Buckinghamshire 1851 census details** link. The 1851 census is the only one available for this county. Click on **Searches** on the top panel of the page and choose **New search** from the drop-down list.

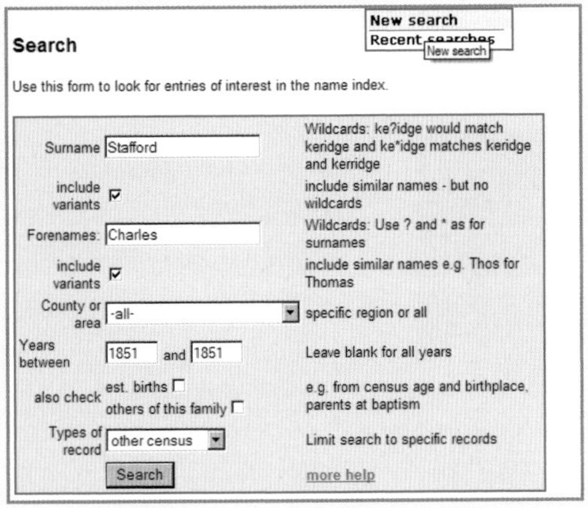

New search
Recent searches
New search

Search

Use this form to look for entries of interest in the name index.

Surname	Stafford	Wildcards: ke?idge would match keridge and ke*idge matches keridge and kerridge
include variants	☑	include similar names - but no wildcards
Forenames:	Charles	Wildcards: Use ? and * as for surnames
include variants	☑	include similar names e.g. Thos for Thomas
County or area	-all-	specific region or all
Years between	1851 and 1851	Leave blank for all years
also check	est. births ☐ others of this family ☐	e.g. from census age and birthplace, parents at baptism
Types of record	other census	Limit search to specific records
	Search	more help

Fill in details

2 On the form enter 'Stafford' in the **Surname** box, tick the **include variants** box, type 'Charles' in the **Forenames** box and tick the second **include variants** box. You can restrict the search to Buckinghamshire in the **County or area** drop-down list, or you can let it scour all areas in case he moved. Restrict the **Years between** to '1851' and '1851'. Choose **other census** from the **Types of record** drop-down list and click **Search**.

age; occupation; place of birth; address; and any disability. Most of this information is abbreviated, except for the names of people and places. These details are followed by the census reference numbers. Images of original enumeration books aren't available yet.

A rainbow nation *Since 1991, census forms have included a section that covers ethnicity. With the increase in families from various ethnic backgrounds, this information will be invaluable to researchers in a century's time.*

Person 1

1 What is your name? (Person 1 in Table 1)

2 What is your sex?
Male
Female

3 What is your date of birth?

4 What is your marital status (on 29 April 2001)?
Single (never married)
Married (first marriage)
Re-married
Separated (but still legally married)
Divorced
Widowed

5 Are you a schoolchild or student in full-time education?
Yes ► Go to 6
No ► Go to 7

6 Do you live at the address shown on the front of this form during the school, college or university term?

7 What is your country of birth?
England
Wales
Scotland
Northern Ireland
Republic of Ireland
Elsewhere, please write in the present name of the country

8 What is your ethnic group?
A White
British
Irish
Any other White background, please write in
B Mixed
White and Black Caribbean
White and Black African
White and Asian
Any other Mixed background, please write in
C Asian or Asian British
Indian
Pakistani
Bangladeshi
Any other Asian background, please write in
D Black or Black British
Caribbean
African
Any other Black background, please write in
E Chinese or other ethnic group
Chinese
Any other, please write in

9 This question is not applicable in England.
► Go to 10

10 What is your religion?
This question is voluntary.
None
Christian (including Church of England, Catholic, Protestant and all other Christian denominations)
Buddhist
Hindu
Jewish
Muslim
Sikh
Any other religion, please write in

11 Over the last twelve months would you say your health has on the whole been:
Good?
Fairly good?
Not good?

12 Do you look after, or give any help or support to family members, friends, neighbours or others because of:
• long-term physical or mental ill-health or disability, or
• problems related to old age?
No
Yes, 1 - 19 hours a week
Yes, 20 - 49 hours a week
Yes, 50+ hours a week

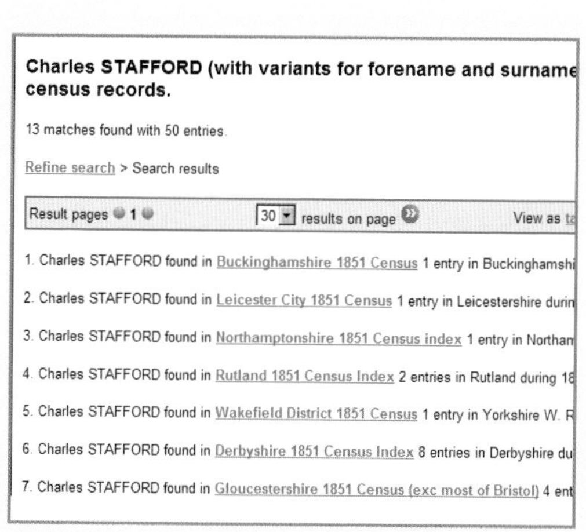

Charles STAFFORD (with variants for forename and surname census records.

13 matches found with 50 entries.

Refine search > Search results

Result pages 1 | 30 results on page | View as t

1. Charles STAFFORD found in Buckinghamshire 1851 Census 1 entry in Buckinghamshi
2. Charles STAFFORD found in Leicester City 1851 Census 1 entry in Leicestershire durin
3. Charles STAFFORD found in Northamptonshire 1851 Census index 1 entry in Northam
4. Charles STAFFORD found in Rutland 1851 Census Index 2 entries in Rutland during 18
5. Charles STAFFORD found in Wakefield District 1851 Census 1 entry in Yorkshire W. R
6. Charles STAFFORD found in Derbyshire 1851 Census Index 8 entries in Derbyshire du
7. Charles STAFFORD found in Gloucestershire 1851 Census (exc most of Bristol) 4 ent

Browse the first results

3 In the list of results, you'll see that for some counties, such as Derbyshire, more than one entry has been found and you're asked to pay to view all of them at once rather than one at a time. But, one entry reads 'Charles STAFFORD found in Buckinghamshire 1851 Census', so it makes sense to look at this first. It will cost 10p to view the details. Click the **Details £0.10** link to see a full transcription.

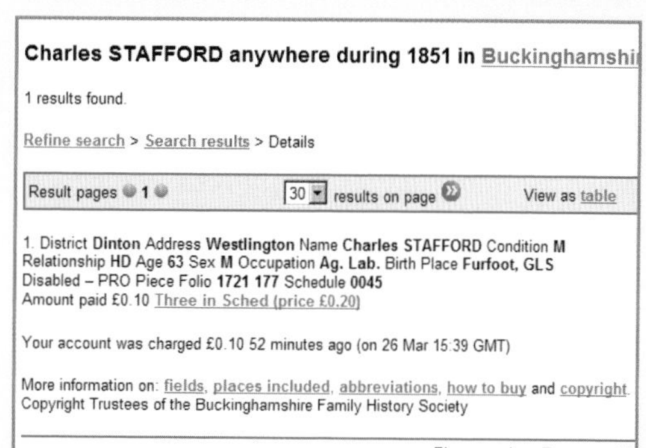

Charles STAFFORD anywhere during 1851 in Buckinghamshi

1 results found.

Refine search > Search results > Details

Result pages 1 | 30 results on page | View as table

1. District **Dinton** Address **Westlington** Name **Charles STAFFORD** Condition **M** Relationship **HD** Age **63** Sex **M** Occupation **Ag. Lab.** Birth Place **Furfoot, GLS** Disabled – PRO Piece Folio **1721 177** Schedule **0045**
Amount paid £0.10 Three in Sched (price £0.20)

Your account was charged £0.10 52 minutes ago (on 26 Mar 15:39 GMT)

More information on: fields, places included, abbreviations, how to buy and copyright.
Copyright Trustees of the Buckinghamshire Family History Society

Visit our e-commerce shop at: GENfair™ www.genfair.com

Please read our Terms and C
and Privacy and Copyright s
© 2002-2007 FFHS Publications Ltd
Page updated 26 Mar 2

View a transcription

4 Charles Stafford was living at Westlington, Dinton. He was married ('M' under 'Condition') and head of the household ('HD' under 'Relationship'). He was 63 and an agricultural labourer ('Ag. Lab.'). He was born in Furfoot, Gloucestershire ('GLS'). Click on **Three in sched (price £0.20)** to see who else was in the house that night. To make the transcription easier to read, click **View as table** on the right, in the blue band above the entry.

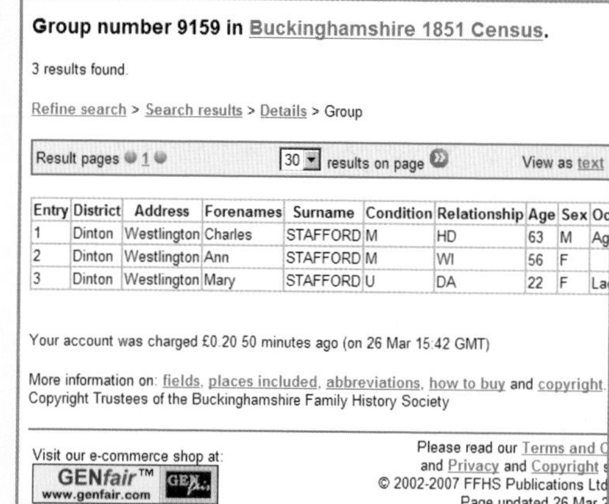

Group number 9159 in Buckinghamshire 1851 Census.

3 results found.

Refine search > Search results > Details > Group

Result pages 1 | 30 results on page | View as text

Entry	District	Address	Forenames	Surname	Condition	Relationship	Age	Sex	Oc
1	Dinton	Westlington	Charles	STAFFORD	M	HD	63	M	Ag
2	Dinton	Westlington	Ann	STAFFORD	M	WI	56	F	
3	Dinton	Westlington	Mary	STAFFORD	U	DA	22	F	La

Your account was charged £0.20 50 minutes ago (on 26 Mar 15:42 GMT)

More information on: fields, places included, abbreviations, how to buy and copyright.
Copyright Trustees of the Buckinghamshire Family History Society

Visit our e-commerce shop at: GENfair™ www.genfair.com

Please read our Terms and C
and Privacy and Copyright s
© 2002-2007 FFHS Publications Ltd
Page updated 26 Mar 2

See the detailed results

5 Charles is shown to have been at home on the night of the 1851 census, with his wife Ann, aged 56, and his 22-year-old unmarried daughter, Mary – who was a lacemaker.

Using the census scotlandspeople.gov.uk

The entire collection of Scottish census returns – from 1841 to 1901 – has been indexed and made available online. They can be accessed, along with other Scottish data, at **scotlandspeople.gov.uk**.

Before you can view the census index, you need to register as a new user, choose a password and log in (see page 56). Making a search is free, but you have to pay to view the results pages and each page of the census return, which involves buying credits.

So far, the 1881 census is the only one that has been transcribed on this website. The others have to be viewed as original records, which means there's no option to search for and view a whole household. If the household is spread over two pages, you may not realise that it's incomplete – and to view the following page, just to be sure, will cost you a further 5 credits.

Reading the handwriting

Just about everything you see, apart from the 1881 census, will be in the handwriting of the time. For more information about reading handwriting click the link to **Help and other resources** from the homepage. This takes you to a page of useful links, including one to **Handwriting** where there is a further link to **ScottishHandwriting.com**. This website offers 'online tuition in the palaeography of Scottish Documents'. It covers the 16th, 17th and 18th centuries, but the information contained in the site, especially the 'letter finder' section, is invaluable for deciphering the handwriting in some of the 19th-century census returns. See also pages 174-5 for help with reading old handwriting.

Spelling the name correctly

When you begin searching for an ancestor, the search facility page gives you the option to search by name, sex, age range, year, county and district. You'll also see a **Use Soundex** box beneath the surname. If you don't tick the Soundex box, which widens the search to names that are similar, the search engine will locate only exact matches.

Suppose you believe your ancestor was called James Fyffe. By ticking the Soundex box on the surname and entering his forename, the database will return all entries containing that forename at any position in the forename record. So the results will include James Fife, Alexander James Fyffe, James Robert Fyfe and so forth. This can help you to locate family members whose names were wrongly recorded in the census – but the only disadvantage is that it can give you an excessively long list. In that case it's worth limiting the search by district, if you can.

Note that looking for 'Mac' surnames with the Soundex box ticked will not return any 'Mc' versions of the name, but a search for 'Mc' surnames with Soundex enabled will find both 'Mc' and 'Mac' versions.

Why you may not find a match

Sometimes a search may yield no records, despite the fact that you know that the person you're looking for definitely existed. This may be because the name wasn't recorded in the way you might have expected – either due to a different spelling or because of illegitimacy. The person may not have been staying where you expected to find them – or even living in Scotland. Sometimes it can help to broaden your search by being less specific and ticking the **Soundex** box.

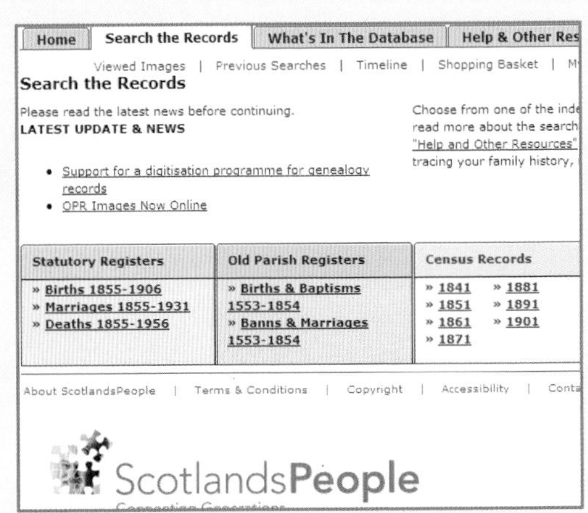

Searching in the 1861 census

1 If you want to search for a Donald John MacDonald in the 1861 census, go to **scotlandspeople.gov.uk** and log in or register. Click **Search the records** at the top of the homepage. This will take you to the records that are available to view online. Click on the census year that you wish to search, 1861.

A jumping-off point

It's a good idea to use the information you find in the 1881 census to do some detective work that will take your family research considerably further.

- The birthplaces and ages recorded in the census can be used to look for the registered births or baptisms of these people.
- Because you know the age of the householder you can work out roughly when he married, and find the names of his parents in the marriage indexes.
- The disappearance of an elderly relative or a young child between census years might indicate a death to be pursued.
- A woman might have returned to her family home for her first confinement, therefore the given birthplace of the eldest child might be an indication of where her parents lived.

Son of Perth *John Buchan, author of novels such as* Greenmantle *and* Mr Standfast, *was born in 1875. You can find his name and details in the Perth 1881 census returns.*

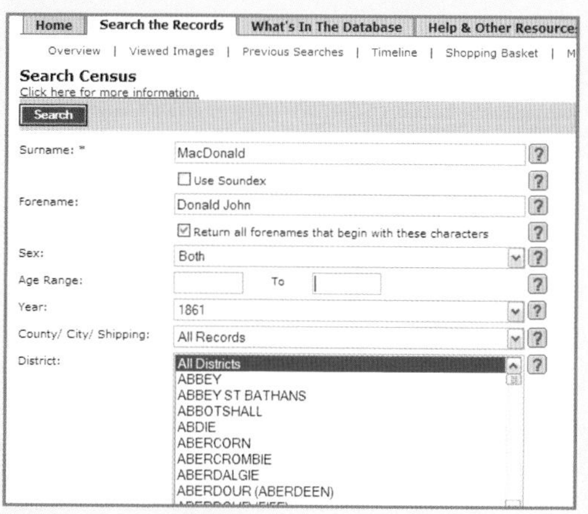

Fill in the details

2 On the search page enter 'MacDonald' in **Surname**, 'Donald John' in **Forename** and '1861' in **Year**. Then click the **Search** button at the top left of the search page.

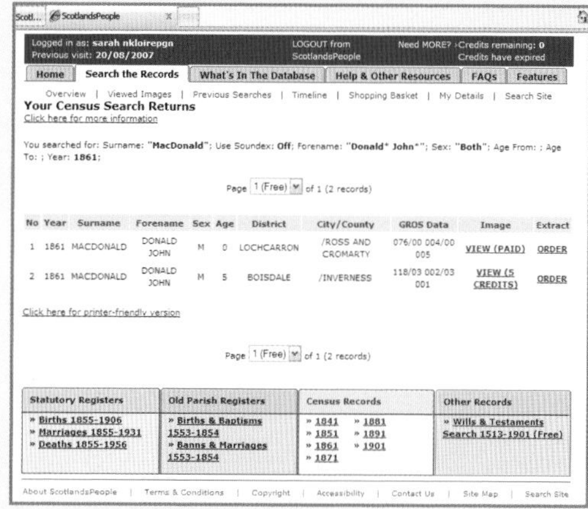

First results are shown

3 The index has returned two results for this search. It will cost you 1 credit to view them. Click on **View (1 credit)**. If you haven't already done so, you'll then need to buy credits (see page 56). Having clicked the **View** link, the next page will ask if you want to go ahead. Click **Yes**.

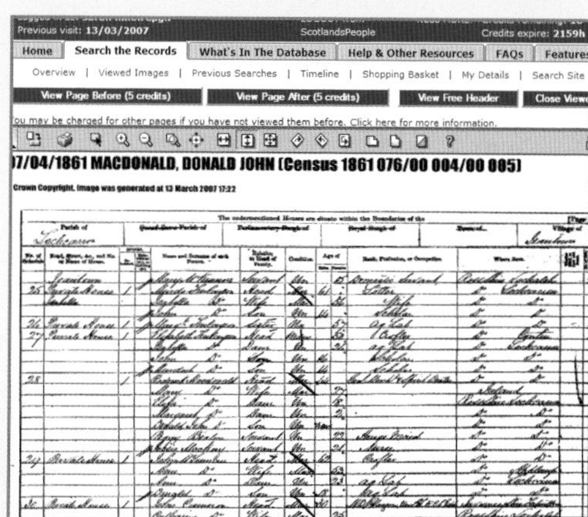

Viewing the results

4 If you see a match, you can view the original for 5 credits. If you click the **View (5 credits)** link, you'll be asked again if you want to proceed. Click **Yes**. You'll find the infant Donald John at home with his parents, two sisters and two servants. Clicking on the appropriate icons at the top of the screen will allow you to save the image to your computer for future reference or to print out the page.

Using the census
irishorigins.com

Census records for Ireland are sparse, but this site gives you access to the best alternative there is – Griffith's Valuation.

Although censuses were taken in Ireland from 1821 to 1911, many returns haven't survived. Those for 1861 to 1891 were deliberately destroyed and pulped for paper during the First World War, and most of the census returns for the preceding years – 1821 to 1851 – were lost in the catastrophic fire in Dublin's Public Record Office in 1922.

Fortunately, the returns for 1901 and 1911 are in the public domain, and although they may not be available yet online on this site, you can view them if you visit the National Archives in Dublin or go to the Public Record Office of Northern Ireland (PRONI) in Belfast.

Irish property records

Luckily, the gap left by the destruction of the census returns has been partly filled by another important source of information – 19th-century Irish property records, which can be accessed through **irishorigins.com**. They're known as Griffith's Valuation, and are the most comprehensive survey of

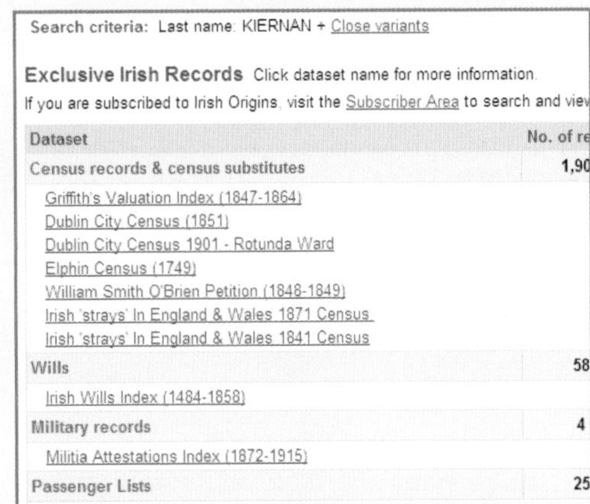

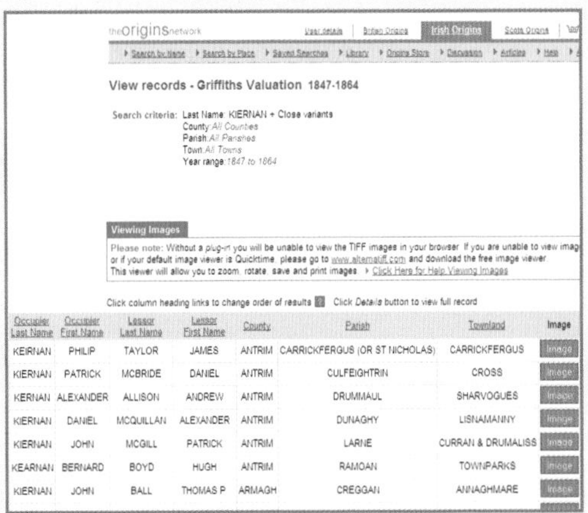

VALUATION OF TENEMENTS.

PARISH OF CULFEIGHTRIN.

Search Griffith's Valuation Index

1 Once you've subscribed to **irishorigins.com** (see **origins.net**, page 55), you can search Griffith's Valuation. To search for a Patrick Kiernan, go to the homepage and enter the surname in the **Last name** box. You can choose to search by exact match or, if you're not sure of the spelling, by close variants. Once you've entered the name, click on **Search**. You'll be offered the screen shown above. From the datasets offered, select **Griffith's valuation index**.

Choose an image to view

2 The results for your search appear. The list shows name ranges, so you need to select the correct range for your ancestor's name. Patrick Kiernan falls within the ranges of the second line down. To view an image of the valuation survey page for the entry that best fits your search criteria, click on the **Image** button, to the right of the name.

Find the address you want

3 You'll then be given an image of the valuation return. The image may look a little fuzzy, but Patrick Kiernan is about a third of the way down the page, and it includes a description of his dwelling. You can print this out for your records. Return to the search page to find out if a map is available. If it is, click on the button to help you to locate the property

Dispossessed

Many tenant farmers and their families were evicted from their homes when agricultural depression hit Ireland in the late 19th century. Sometimes force was used and the house was destroyed. The cottage (right) of Mathias Magrath in County Clare was demolished by battering ram (a great log slung from a wooden frame) in the late 1880s. Facing homelessness and destitution in Ireland, thousands of people emigrated and made new lives elsewhere. You'll be able to track down stories such as this in the Griffith's Valuation Index.

households for the period covering the years between the Great Famine and the start of civil registration (1848-64). The records cover the entire country: every property in Ireland was included in the valuation, along with the occupier's name and, if the property was rented, the house owner's name.

What's more, the valuation covers not only houses, but every building, as well as land – it lists everyone who paid rates. This linking of land, landowners, property and family members is what makes it such a valuable 'census substitute' for family historians. But before you can make the best use of these property records, you need some idea of where your ancestor lived. Unless he had a very unusual surname, you'll need at least a county of origin.

Accessing the records

To access the Griffith's Valuation records, go to **irishorigins.com** and click on **Irish origins**. You'll also be able to access other Irish census substitutes such as the Dublin City censuses for 1851 and 1901. You can search the index for free, but to view any detailed information, you'll need to register your name and email address, and pay a subscription (see page 100). The site operates on a pay-per-view voucher system.

Finding out more about Irish records

These websites have a lot of useful information about using Irish family history records:

☛ The Public Record Office of Northern Ireland (PRONI) at **proni.gov.uk** has information about freeholders' records.

☛ Genuki's site for Ireland at **genuki.org.uk** gives county-by-county detail.

☛ The family history website, **movinghere.org.uk**, provides a free online catalogue of material related to migration from local, regional and national archives, libraries and museums. Click on **Tracing your roots**, then on the **Irish** button.

Can't find an ancestor?

Don't despair if you have trouble finding a relative on census returns. There are many ways of getting round this brick wall.

When you're hunting for a particular census return, be prepared for two common stumbling blocks: errors made when the original returns were transcribed into a database, and mistakes in the original census returns. Both are most often simply a result of human error. A good way to lessen the effect of any of these mistakes, and get the best results, is to use the census returns along with the civil registration certificates that you'll probably have acquired already.

Tackling transcription errors

Always remember that the online census index you search may not be accurate. The original information has gone through many steps before you see it – from householder to enumerator, then stages of transcription and digitising. Look out for these three areas.

- Bad handwriting – in some cases the original returns may have been illegible, in others careless mistakes were made.
- Abbreviations – in some cases names were abbreviated, with William recorded as Wm and Thomas as Thos, for example.
- Dittos – the form 'do', rather than today's ditto marks, was used by the enumerator when the information in consecutive entries on the same page was the same.

The 'less is more' approach often yields the best results. If you use the **Advanced Search** facility on the Ancestry website, for example, rather than entering the full range of information, including dates of birth, counties and other people that you expect to be in the household, you can widen your search by omitting some of your 'facts'.

DIFFERENT CENSUS, DIFFERENT INFORMATION
Some census indexes can be searched in ways other than by name. For example, the 1881 census on the Ancestry site lets you search by occupation, and the 1901 census on The National Archives site allows you to search by address and street. This will help you to learn more about the local area and your ancestors' neighbours.

NAME SPELLINGS: VARIANTS AND SOUNDEX
If you aren't sure of a spelling, some sites offer Soundex (see page 64), and others list all the variations of a name if you click the appropriate option from a drop-down list. For example, the Origins search engines use NameX, where you can choose **exact matches only**, **close variants** or **all variants** when you're searching.

NAME SPELLINGS: WILDCARDS When using wildcards (see page 64) you usually have to enter a specific number of characters to make the search work. For example, The National Archive search for the 1901 census specifies a minimum of two characters before a wildcard entry. So if you're hunting for Louisa, say – which is often mistranscribed Lousia – try entering **Lou*** for a better result.

Errors in the original returns

If you've tried all these search tips and still can't find who you are looking for, it could be a problem that dates back to the night on which the original census was taken.

STAYING AWAY The most common reason that people don't appear where they should is that they weren't at home on that particular night. Your ancestor could have been staying with friends or relations so won't be listed in his own home. Another reason for a non-appearance in the census is that many people travelled about to look for work.

IN AN INSTITUTION An ancestor may have been in an institution. Remember to search the returns for barracks, if you know someone was in the military. A child might have been at boarding school, some distance away from home. Or perhaps your ancestor was in a workhouse or in prison.

DIFFERENT NAMES Although the enumerator may have abbreviated names, it was more common for householders to provide the information themselves, and they may well have used pet names or shortenings. So James is often recorded as Jim, and Elizabeth as Lizzy or Betsy. People were often known by their middle names, too, so the 'John William' you are searching for could well be listed in the census return as 'Bill'. Use lateral thinking in your search.

RELATIONSHIP DISCREPANCIES A householder may have listed someone as a 'brother' or 'cousin', but this doesn't tally with your research. Bear in mind that these terms were sometimes used to describe relations acquired though marriage, or even distant relatives.

ENUMERATOR PROBLEMS Enumerators might have recorded names phonetically; a variant name search or a wildcard can help to overcome this. Examples of phonetic names recorded in the census include Sarah as Sahra or Sara, and Kathrine as Catherine.

MISSING RETURNS Occasionally the page has been lost – between 5 and 10 per cent of the 1861 census is missing. It's most likely that the final page dropped off the enumerator's book – and as there was only one set of returns recorded, your best bet is to search the censuses before or after the one you're in.

There are also a variety of reasons, ranging from being deliberately omitted by the householder, to being homeless and on the streets at the time, that mean at least 5 per cent of the population doesn't appear in census returns.

Top 5 causes for a 'missing' ancestor

1. The person was away from home that night
2. Your relative travelled a lot, so is hard to trace
3. The person was listed under a different name
4. The householder lied on the census return, perhaps to hide evidence of an illicit relationship or a fugitive
5. The person was away from home on a vessel or in an institution (a boarding school, perhaps, or even a prison).

Multiple identities

Tracking an ancestor can be hard if details have been wrongly recorded or transcribed. Edward Mead, wearing his hat on the beach (right), was a particular challenge. His birth in 1858 in the small village of Tilshead in Wiltshire was registered (below, left) by his mother, Ellen. As a three year old he was recorded as Edwin (instead of Edward) Mead in the 1861 census. At the age of 13, he appears in the 1871 census as E. Mead, scholar, born in Tilshead, living in the household of a baptist minister in Worcestershire (below, middle). But the digital version of the census document (far right) describes him not as a male scholar, but as the granddaughter of the minister. Having his place and date of birth firmly fixed helped his great-granddaughter to solve the puzzle.

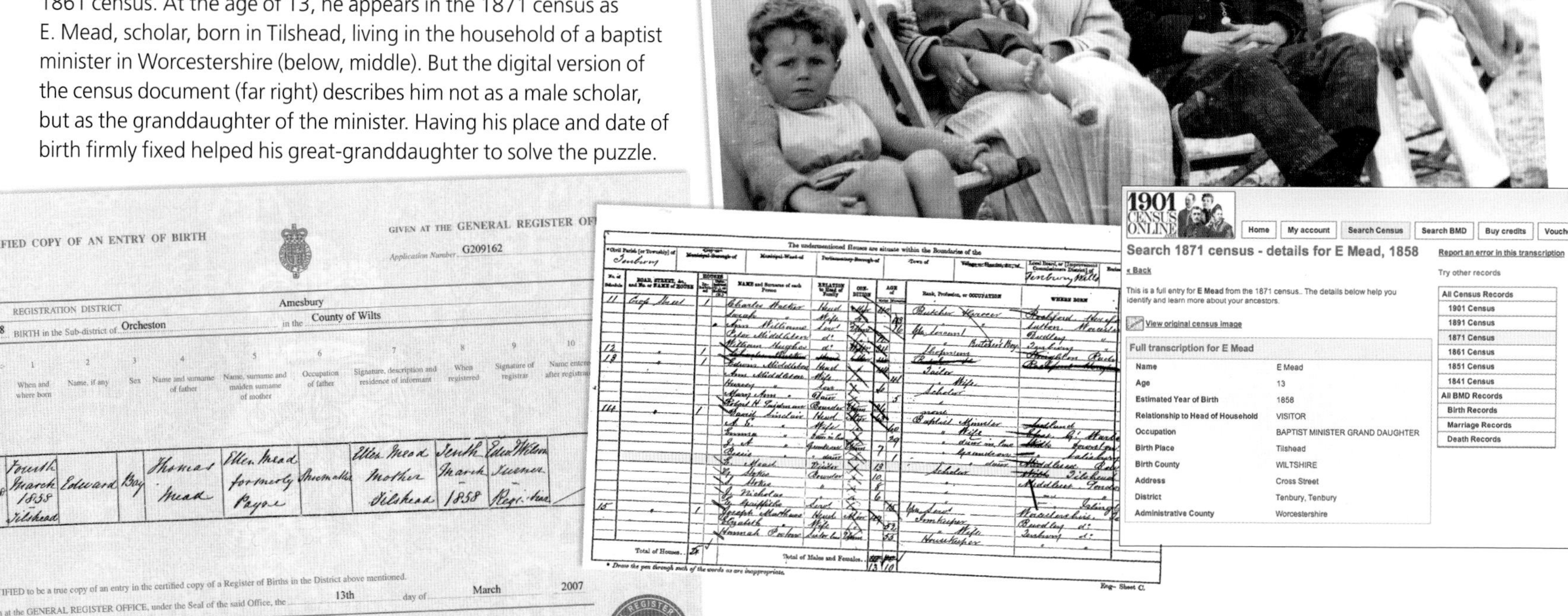

The Red Cross – in peace and war

For almost 150 years, the Red Cross has helped people suffering through military conflict, many of whom appear in its archives. Just as important is its peacetime role, bringing relief to those caught up in flood, famine, earthquakes and other disasters around the world.

In 1859, a Swiss businessman, Henry Dunant, witnessed horrific scenes on the battlefield of Solferino in northern Italy. He was so appalled by the misery of the thousands left to die that he founded the Red Cross in 1863 to protect the victims of armed conflicts, including the wounded, prisoners of war, refugees and civilians. The British Red Cross was established in 1870, following the start of the Franco-Prussian War.

Wartime roles

When war broke out in 1914, the British Red Cross joined forces with the Order of St John (founder of the St John Ambulance first-aid service) as the Joint War Committee, to work in hospitals, medical supply depots and convalescent homes. They also replaced the old, slow horse-drawn ambulances with motorised ambulances in battlefields. One volunteer driver was the writer Ernest Hemingway who drew on his experiences to write *A Farewell to Arms* after the war. The volunteers helped to keep prisoners of war in touch with their families and, at the end of the war, organised the safe return home of more than 420,000.

The Red Cross fulfilled the same role during the Second World War but was prevented at first from applying pressure on the Nazis about their treatment of Jews in the concentration camps for fear that reprisals would affect its freedom to help other prisoners of war. Some 20 million of the famous Red Cross food parcels were dispatched to prisoners from the UK alone and, in November 1943, it received permission to send parcels to inmates of some concentration camps. As the parcels were often signed for by other internees, the Red Cross managed to compile a list of more than 100,000 camp prisoners.

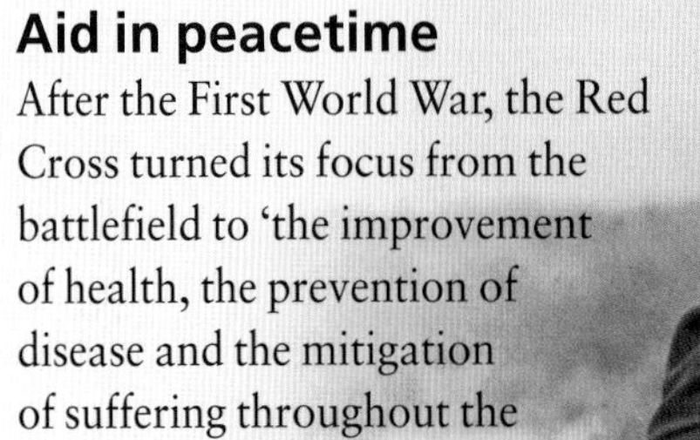

For exceptional service *The Florence Nightingale Medal is awarded to nurses who've shown remarkable bravery. It was instituted in 1912 by the International Committee of the Red Cross in Geneva to commemorate the work of Florence Nightingale.*

Aid in peacetime

After the First World War, the Red Cross turned its focus from the battlefield to 'the improvement of health, the prevention of disease and the mitigation of suffering throughout the

Helping hand *A Red Cross nurse (right) lends her support to an injured soldier, a sailor and a pilot wounded during the Battle of Britain in 1940.*

world'. It began fulfilling this ambitious role at home by setting up Britain's first blood transfusion service in 1921. Overseas, the Red Cross provided help and relief to millions of people displaced during the Second World War, and continued to support refugees from conflicts such as the Hungarian Revolution in 1956 and the Vietnam War.

Natural disasters have also spurred the Red Cross into action. Many thousands affected by cataclysms such as the Indian Ocean tsunami of 2004 and Hurricane Katrina in 2005 are grateful for the relief provided by the volunteers wearing the red cross.

Records held by the Red Cross

If someone in your family trained or served in the Red Cross, or was caught up in warfare somewhere around the world, you may find you can discover more from the Red Cross Museum and Archives, which holds records dating from its foundation in 1870. Among these are personnel records for the Voluntary Aid Detachments (VADs) – including those who trained in military hospitals and as nurses. Records since the Second World War are scant and there are none for the inter-war years. The archive also has medals and emblems, posters, postcards and photographs – many of which can be viewed on the website at **redcross.org.uk**.

Researching with the Red Cross

From the homepage at **redcross.org.uk** (below), go to **About us** in the top bar and choose **History & origin** from the drop-down menu. Then click on **Historical factsheets**, where you'll find a link to **Collections**. You'll be able to see what archives are held. There's no online catalogue, but you can make an appointment to visit the museum and archives in London (see Directory). Research hours are from 10am to 1pm and from 2pm to 4pm, Monday to Friday.

Tracing a volunteer or a POW

To find out about an ancestor who worked for the Red Cross, email **enquiry@redcross.org.uk**, giving as much information about the person as possible, or write to the address in the Directory. The records of prisoners of war and civilian internees are held by the International Committee of the Red Cross (ICRC) in Geneva (see Directory). You can write to them and ask for a search, but this can take a long time. You'll need to give the person's name and nationality as well as date and place of birth, father's name, date of capture, regiment and army number, if you have them. Searches are carried out free of charge, but the Red Cross suggests that you make a voluntary donation, if you can, to contribute to the cost of the service.

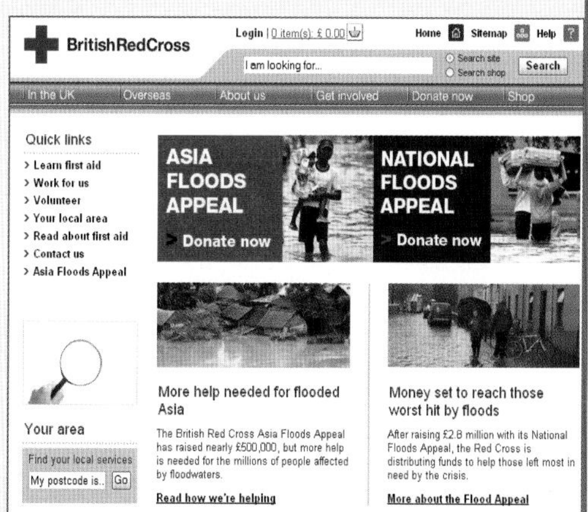

Church records

To go beyond the early 19th-century limits of civil registration and census records, you'll need to look at parish registers of baptisms, marriages and burials. These could carry you back to the mid 16th century.

Understanding parish registers

A parish is a specific area with its own church where all local baptisms, marriages and burials were once recorded. Its size could range from just a few city streets to a large part of the countryside.

In England and Wales, the process of registering births, marriages and deaths within a parish began in 1538, as decreed by Thomas Cromwell, Henry VIII's chief minister. Few parishes still have information dating back to that time as records were often kept on loose sheets that haven't survived.

In 1597, Queen Elizabeth I ordered that a special register should be kept, and that all existing records be transcribed into 'fair parchment books, at least from the beginning of this reign'. In most cases, parish registers begin in the mid 16th century. The registers that have survived are usually held in city or county record offices. If a register has been lost, you may find the missing details in copies of the registers, called 'bishops' transcripts'. The 1597 Act also stipulated that the events registered should be copied annually and sent to the bishop of the appropriate diocese. These bishops' transcripts provide a valuable back-up.

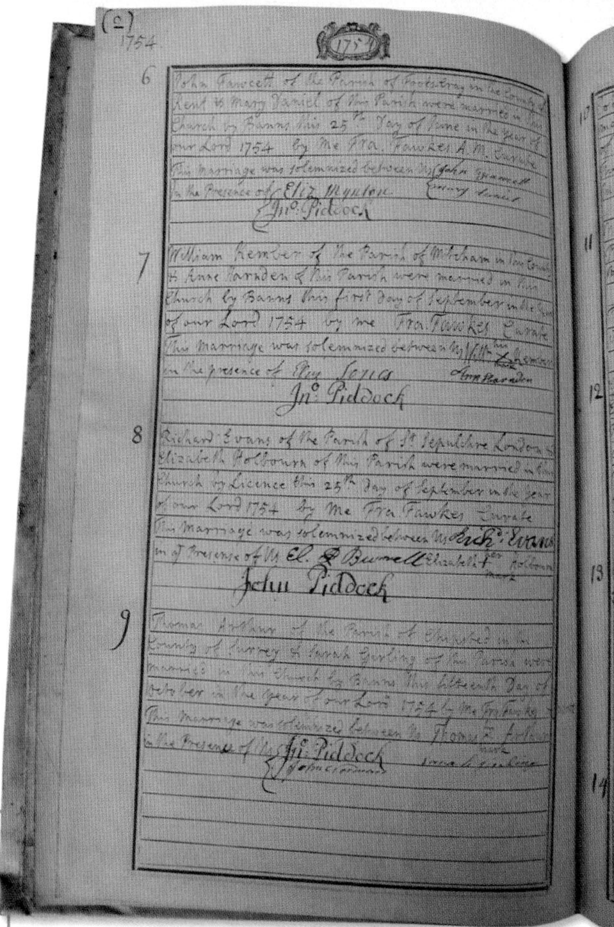

1754

6 John Fawcett of the Parish of [illegible] in the County of Kent & Mary Daniel of this Parish were married in this Church by Banns this 25th Day of June in the Year of our Lord 1754 by Me Fra. Fawkes A.M. Curate
This Marriage was solemnized between Us John [illegible]
In the Presence of Eliz. Mynton
Jno. Piddock

7 William Kember of the Parish of Mitcham in the County & Anne Haraden of this Parish were married in this Church by Banns this first Day of September in the Year of our Lord 1754 by me Fra. Fawkes Curate
This Marriage was solemnized between Us Willm [illegible]
In the presence of [illegible] Jones Ann Haraden
Jno. Piddock

8 Richard Evans of the Parish of St Sepulchre London & Elizabeth Holbourn of this Parish were married in this Church by Licence this 25th Day of September in the Year of our Lord 1754 by Me Fra. Fawkes Curate
This Marriage was solemnized between Us Richd. Evans
In the Presence of Us El. [illegible] Burnell Elizabeth Holbourn
John Piddock

9 Thomas Arthur of the Parish of [illegible] in the County of Surrey & Sarah [illegible] of this Parish were married in this Church by Banns this [illegible] Day of October in the Year of our Lord 1754 by Me Fra. Fawkes
This Marriage was solemnized between Us Thomas Arthur
In the Presence of Us Jno. Piddock

Parish records on the internet

As parish records for England and Wales were created and are retained locally, there's no central internet site containing all their details. Online parish data is limited to a number of key sitesthat may prove useful in your search:

ancestry.co.uk Here you'll find databases for parish records, including Pallot's Marriage Index (more than 1.5 million marriage entries 1780-1837, mainly for the London area) and a dedicated section for parish and probate records (containing more than 15 million names).

familysearch.org The major online resource for parish information is run by the Church of Jesus Christ of Latter-day Saints (also known as the Mormon Church). The transcription of these parish records, mainly baptisms, is known as the International Genealogical Index (IGI) and is free to use. Always double-check any information found against the original parish register, as there are some errors in transcription. The IGI is not a comprehensive database of all parish registers.

origins.net A subscriber-only website, this has transcriptions of both Boyd's London Burial Index and Boyd's Marriage Index (see page 143).

familyhistoryonline.net Contains more than 66 million family history records on its pay-per-view website. It also holds a large amount of parish information.

parishregister.com Data from the parishes surrounding the London docklands area is available on this free-to-search website.

Record keeping *Thomas Cromwell (right, in a drawing by Hans Holbein) prescribed how parish registers should be kept from 1538 onwards. The parish had to provide and pay for its own register, so many of the earliest records were written on scraps of paper which were easily lost or damaged. After 1597, events were written down in more durable registers, like the one above for the parish of Croydon in Surrey.*

The parish and its records

Parish records relate to the established Church of England, so if your ancestors were, like most of the population, Anglican, you'll find their names there – after a bit of detective work. The first step is to find the parishes where your ancestors lived.

What you'll find in parish registers varies considerably. The earliest entries contain little information; baptisms may only give the name of the child and the father, with no mention of the mother. The quality of the data also depends on the work habits of the clerks – some entered the information as it occurred, others did it at the end of the year.

It wasn't until 1813 that uniformity was brought into the process, when every parish had to buy specific books from the 'King's printer', into which they entered each birth, marriage and burial in much greater detail than had previously been recorded.

How to use the records

Parish records are usually a rich source of material, but you need to understand how to use them to get the best out of them:

DATING Until January 1, 1752, parish registers followed the established practice of starting the New Year on March 25 (Lady Day) rather than January 1. All the dates you find before 1752, from January 1 to March 24, need to have an extra year added to become modern dates. So an event occurring on February 18, 1705, should be noted as February 18, 1705/6. Dates after January 1, 1752, are as we would recognise.

Safe keeping *After 1538, records of all baptisms, marriages and burials in each parish were kept in a chest, like this Welsh one, shown left. Each chest had to have two or more separate locks, with keys held by the vicar or curate and churchwardens, so that at least two people were present when it was opened.*

Finding the right parish online

Before you can search the parish registers for your ancestor's details, you'll need to establish which parish he belonged to. Parish boundaries often changed through the centuries, but you can get help in establishing the right parish by consulting online gazetteers.

A good place to find details of parishes is at **visionofbritain.org.uk**. The website contains information from maps, statistical trends and historical descriptions covering 1801 to 2001.

The website **genuki.org.uk** has lists of parishes for each county and its church database at **genuki.org.uk/big/churchdb/search.html** is useful for locating the nearest church to a place.

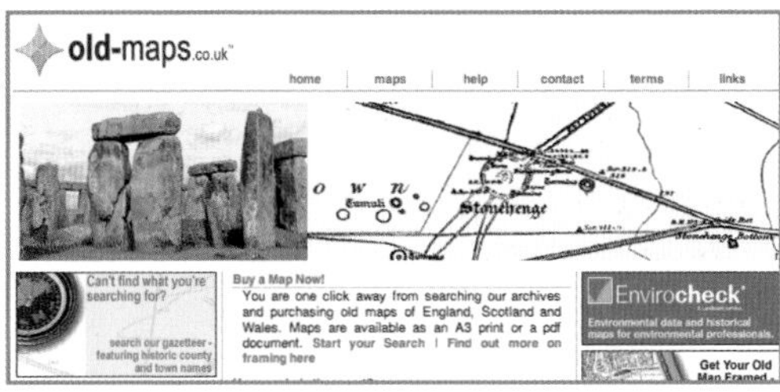

At **old-maps.co.uk** you can enter a specific address or a place name to view a map for that area, or you can browse by county for a church you're interested in. Some private individuals have also placed historical maps on the internet. Look at **freepages.genealogy.rootsweb.com** to see some examples of these – they're fascinating.

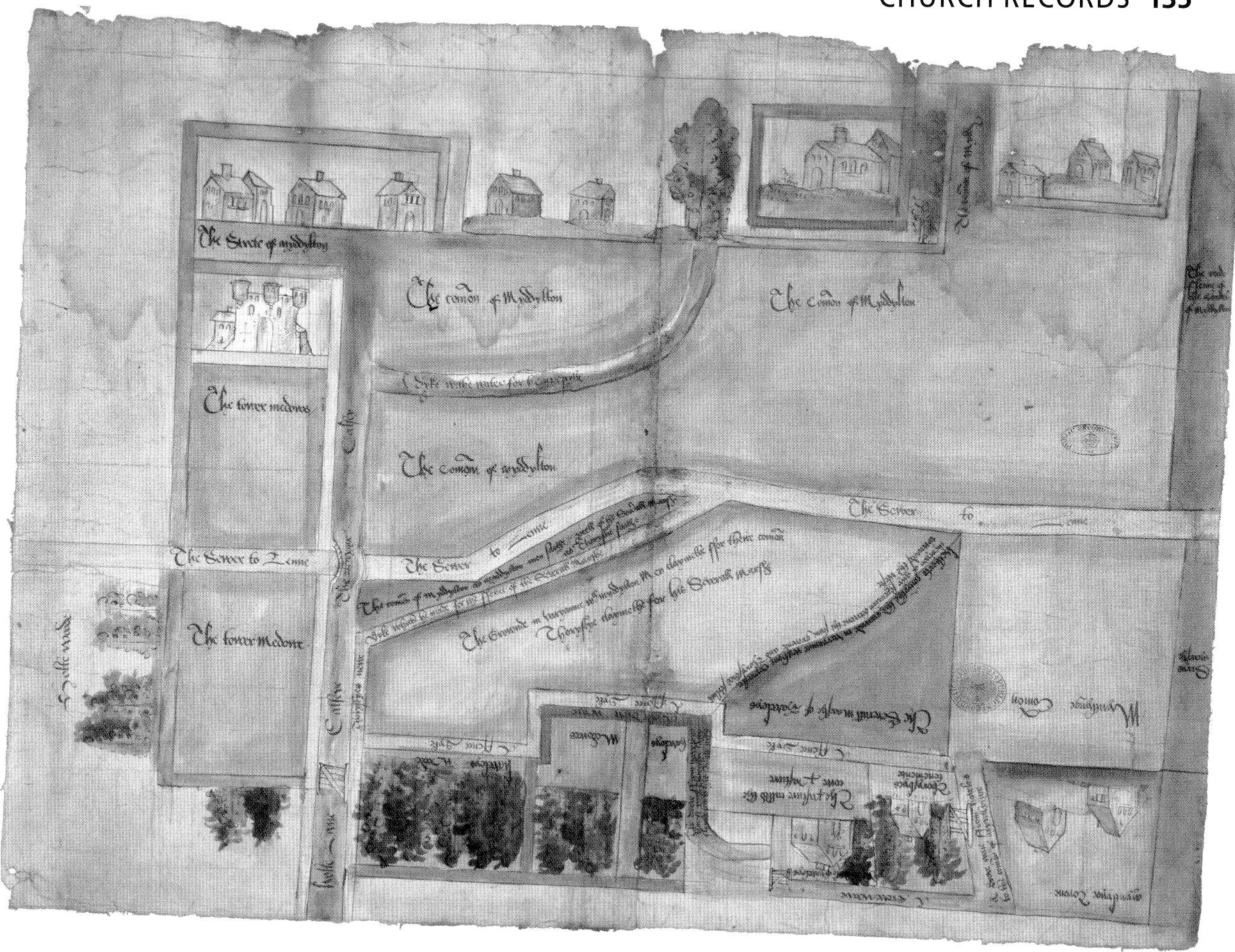

Changing fortunes *This 16th-century map shows the parishes of Mintlyn and Middleton in Norfolk. Mintlyn's church is now a ruin and its parish part of that of nearby Gaywood, while Middleton has remained independent with its own church.*

LEGIBILITY You may find reading the earlier 16th and 17th-century registers difficult. For help with reading old documents, see page 174. The earlier registers are very often in Latin, so it's useful to understand the key phrases (see page 146).

WHERE AND HOW FAR TO LOOK
Until the early 19th century, people didn't move about very much. They tended to stay in the same parish for most of their lives and would have moved to nearby parishes, if at all. If you don't find your ancestor immediately, extend your investigations to nearby parishes. Remember that parish boundaries may have changed over the years, and many new parishes were created in Victorian towns and cities.

Significant movement began during the 19th-century industrial surge, when the labour market moved to the expanding urban areas, speeded up by introduction of the railways. You'll need to link your search to the census returns (see right) if you think your ancestors left home to look for work.

Getting help from other sources

- The CD *Historic Parishes of England & Wales: An Electronic Map of Boundaries before 1850 with a Gazetteer and Metadata*, by Roger J.P. Kain and Richard R. Oliver, is a thorough collection of parish maps and boundaries. The CD is accompanied by a book, which you can order through your local library or family history society.
- Census returns, which are now available online from 1841 to 1901, are also important sources for identifying the parish of your ancestor's birth. They often give the name of the parish where the individual was born, so you can go directly to the appropriate parish register. They also give specific details about the location of each address, along with information relating to neighbouring districts, thereby helping to pinpoint exactly where your ancestor lived.
- *The Phillimore Atlas and Index of Parish Registers* contains countywide parish maps along with information as to where the parish registers are now deposited. There may be a copy in your local library.

Tracking down parish records

From grand city cathedrals to tiny rural parish churches, they all have registers that can be traced and searched for your ancestors' records. Websites and search engines make it easier to pin down where they are.

Once you have the name of the parish you want to research, you need to know where the registers are. A good place to look is at **genuki.org.uk**.

Searching with Genuki

Say you want to discover where the parish register is deposited for St Mary's Parish, Harrow-on-the-Hill, Middlesex. First, navigate to the contents page and choose the country page – **England**. Click on the appropriate county page, **Middlesex**. Next, click on the link for **Middlesex parishes** at the top of the page. Up comes an alphabetical list of the parishes held in the county of Middlesex. You want Harrow, so click on **H**, and find Harrow-on-the-Hill. On the page for the parish is a list of links. Click on **Church records**. This takes you to information for all the churches in the parish, and tells you that the records are deposited at the LMA (London Metropolitan Archives). It also gives a link to the London Generations database, a good site for family historians who are researching the capital.

Searching with Google

If you know which repository or archive holds your registers, you can find the location using an online search engine. For example, you can search for Nottinghamshire archives using **google.co.uk**. Call up the Google search page if it isn't already on your screen. In the search bar enter the words 'Nottinghamshire archives'. Beneath the search bar, click on **Pages from the UK**. Click on the **Search** button to bring up a list of links to Nottinghamshire archives; click on the top link and navigate through the site. You can also search for archives through the database **a2a.org.uk**.

Getting help from the Mormons

The Church of Jesus Christ of Latter-day Saints (the Mormons) holds information that can help you to search for parish records – see page 138 for more about their website **familysearch.org**. The church also has Family History Centres throughout the UK that contain most of the information available in its main library. To find your nearest centre and what it contains, follow the instructions for searching opposite.

Full house *An 1809 illustration of the church of St Martin-in-the-Fields in London, which was designed and rebuilt by James Gibbs in 1726. It shows the church crowded with the people flocking to hear a popular preacher.*

Keeping a record *Church registers became more detailed as record-keeping was standardised. The 18th-century burial register (right) gives the bare minimum – and sometimes not even a name – whereas the 1863 marriage certificate (far right) provides a wealth of infomation.*

Using the NRA

The National Register of Archives' database at **a2a.org.uk** gives details of more than 400 repositories, as well as the scope of their contents and the contact details of each archive. For example, here's how to find the address details of the Nottinghamshire archives:

Enter **a2a.org.uk** in the address bar of your web browser. Towards the top of the website's homepage there are eight options. Click on the option **About a2a**. On the following page there are further options listed on the left-hand side of the page, ranging from 'What are Archives?' at the top, to 'Legal Disclaimer' at the bottom. Select the fourth option **a2a contributors**. This page lists all the contributors alphabetically.

Scroll down to find **Nottinghamshire archives** and click on it. This will bring you to a page with all the details for this archive and how to go about contacting it.

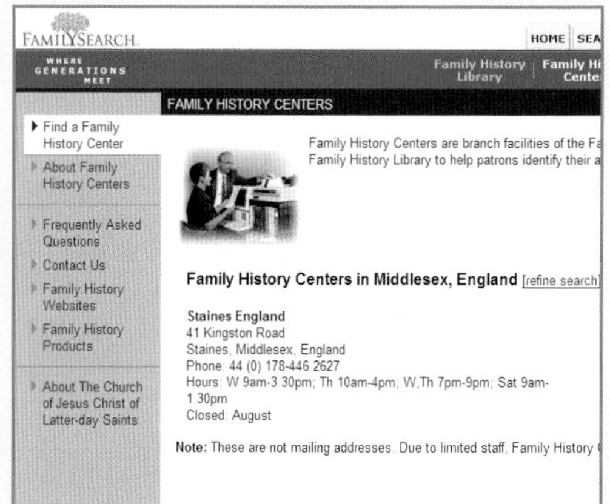

Finding a Family History Centre

1 Go to the **familysearch.org** homepage. At the top of the page you'll see four tabs. Click on the **Library** tab. On the library page you'll see four further options below the library tab you've just clicked. From left to right they read Family History Library, Family History Centers, Family History Library Catalog and Education. Click on **Family history centers**.

Search for the nearest

2 You'll find the nearest Family History Centre by filling in the information in the boxes provided. For example, to search for centres in Middlesex, England, select the **Country** by scrolling down to find 'England'. In the **County** box enter 'Middlesex' and click the **Search** button. The website will list all the Family History Centres in the county with their contact details.

Using parish register indexes familysearch.org

Several websites help you to search parish register indexes online, and most of them have similar information. The trick is to find one that suits you and seems to hold the type of information you want. The free website **familysearch.org**, run by the Church of Jesus Christ of Latter-day Saints (LDS – the Mormons), is a good place to start. For more details about what the site contains, see page 54. To use this site to find an LDS Family History Centre near you, see page 137.

The information in this website comes from three main sources. Two, the Ancestral file and Pedigree Resource file, consist of information submitted by users on a voluntary basis, which means that you'll need to verify it. The third, the International Genealogical Index (IGI) is the most useful: a vast collection of parish record transcriptions for the UK and other countries throughout the world. Some other websites will automatically link you to it.

Below are two examples of the types of parish register search you can do on **familysearch.org.** One is a simple search to trace a baptism, and the other is an advanced

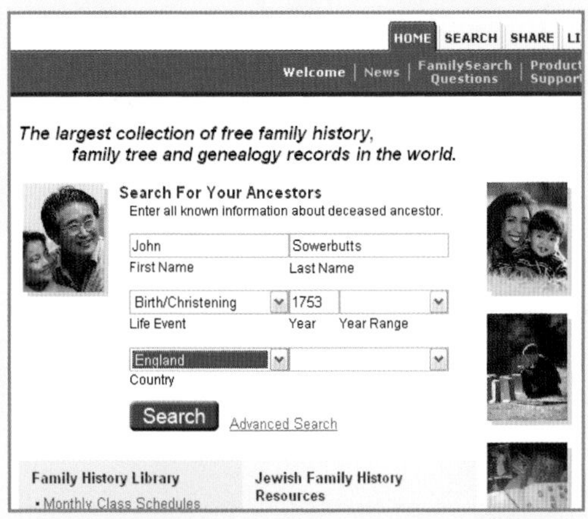

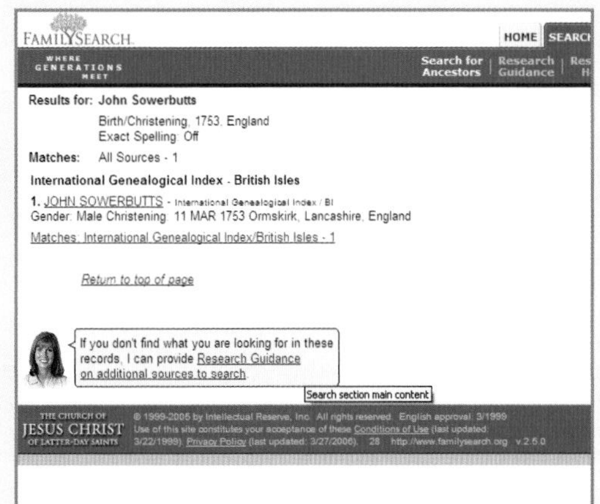

FAMILYSEARCH
HOME SEARCH
WHERE GENERATIONS MEET
Search for Ancestors | Research Guidance
IGI Individual Record
Search Results | Download | Pedigree
JOHN SOWERBUTTS
Male
Event(s):
Birth:
Christening: 11 MAR 1753 Ormskirk, Lancashire, England
Death:
Burial:
Parents:
Father: THOMAS SOWERBUTTS
Mother: ELIZABETH
Messages:
Form submitted by a member of the LDS Church. The form lists the submitter's name and address and m
know the batch and sheet number.

Start a simple search

1 To find the baptism of a John Sowerbutts in Lancashire in 1753, go to the homepage and start a simple search. Enter 'John' for the **First name** and 'Sowerbutts' for the **Last name**. Choose **Birth/christening** for **Life event**. Enter '1753' in the **Year** box. From the **Country** list choose **England**. Click on the blue **Search** button.

Success with the first result

2 One possible entry comes up in the International Genealogical Index (IGI). This John Sowerbutts was christened on March 11, 1753, at Ormskirk parish in Lancashire. Click on his name for more details.

Father and mother revealed

3 This screen gives us the names of John Sowerbutts' parents: Thomas Sowerbutts and Elizabeth. You can find out if any more information on them is held in the records by clicking on their names.

search to find a marriage. To go straight to the more detailed search, select the **Advanced Search** option on the homepage next to the large blue search button, or just click on the tab at the top of the page.

Parish duties *Keeping accurate records of all baptisms, marriages and burials was required of all Anglican clergymen. The legibility of hand-written parish registers is sometimes poor, but fortunately many of the records have been transcribed and are available online.*

Using the IGI – what to bear in mind

- Although the IGI contains many millions of entries, it's not complete for the UK. Entries are mostly for baptisms, with a few marriages and almost no burials. Some parishes are only partially indexed whereas others aren't indexed at all. If your ancestor isn't listed, you may still be able to find them in the original parish registers.
- The IGI has some transcription errors, so don't enter any information into your files until you've checked it against the original parish record.

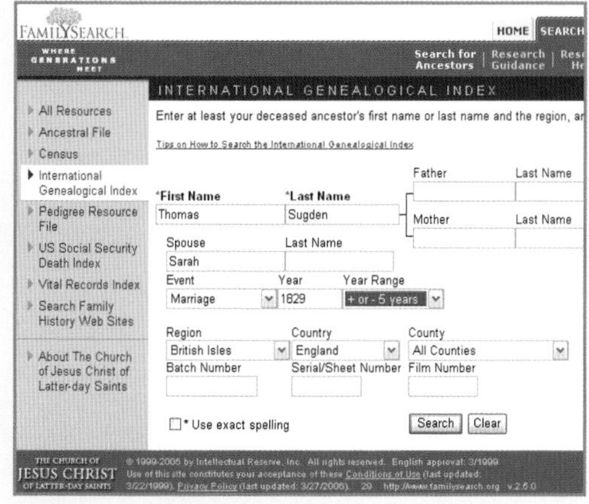

Start an advanced search

1 To search for the marriage of a Thomas and Sarah Sugden, whose daughter Nancy was born in 1829 in Bradford, go to the homepage and click on the **Advanced search** button. Then click on the **International genealogical index** on the left of the screen. Enter the parents' full names in the appropriate boxes. Choose **Marriage** for the event. Enter a marriage date five years prior to the baptism with a range of **+ /–5 years**. Under **Country**, choose **England**.

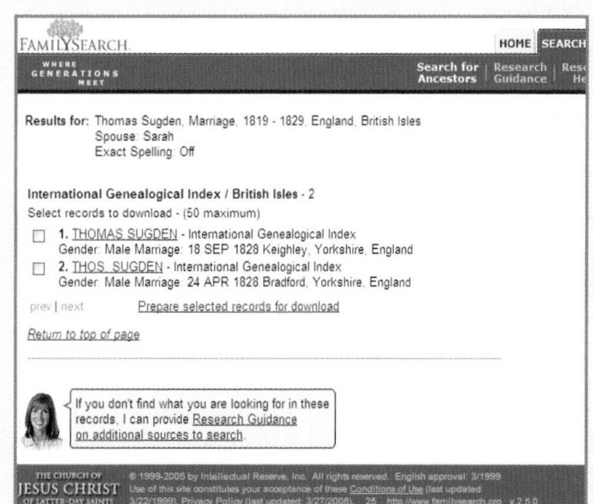

View the first results

2 The search comes up with two results. The second one is in the same parish as the baptism of Nancy Sugden, in Bradford. Click on the second link, **Thos Sugden**, for more details of the marriage.

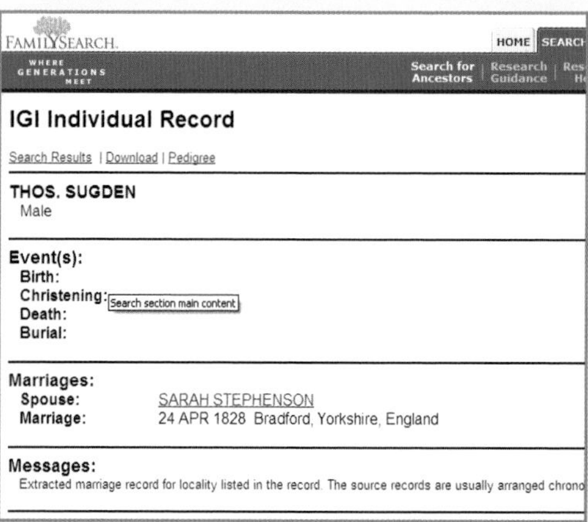

The marriage date revealed

3 The 'IGI Individual Record' page reveals that Sarah Sugden's maiden name was Stephenson and that she and Thomas were married in Bradford on April 24, 1828.

Using parish register indexes
familyhistoryonline.net

The data website of the Federation of Family History Societies, **familyhistoryonline.net**, is a good place to search for parish registers, because it has access to numerous databases for many of the counties of England and Wales, including records up to the 20th century. It even has a number of Australian databases, which are useful if your ancestors emigrated. The many different databases provided on the website include information received from parishes for births and baptisms, marriage indexes, indexes for marriage licences, burial indexes, memorial inscription indexes and census indexes.

Using the site

First, you need to register (see page 59). Then, when you've found a record through the search index, you can pay to view the complete record. The cost of an individual search varies, but it's usually between 5p and 7p. You can open an account online (£5, £10, £20 or £50 using a credit or debit card) or buy prepaid vouchers from some family history societies, from the postal service run by the Federation or from GENfair (the online shop also run by the Federation).

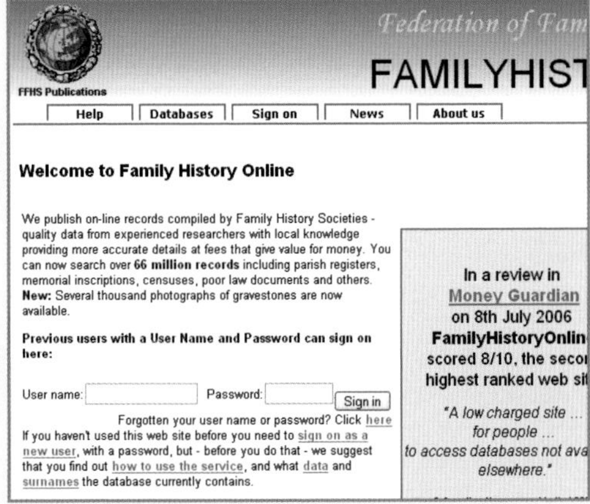

Sign in on the homepage

1 Here's an example of a search for the baptism of a Jane Wiggins, around 1775, in Sussex. Go to **familyhistoryonline.net** and register (see page 59). Enter your **User name** and **Password** and click on the **Sign in** button.

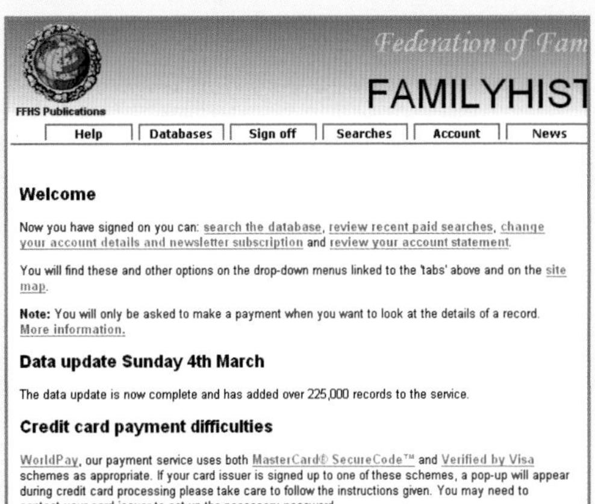

Begin your search

2 Start the search for Jane Wiggins by clicking on the **Search the database** link near the top of the page. You can search the information by date, location and type of record.

FFHS Publications
FAMILYHIST
Help | Databases | Sign off | Searches | Account | News

Search
Use this form to look for entries of interest in the name index.

Surname	wiggins	Wildcards: ke?idge would match keridge and ke*idge matches keridge and kerridge
include variants	☐	include similar names - but no wildcards
Forenames:	jane	Wildcards: Use ? and * as for surnames
include variants	☐	include similar names e.g. Thos for Thomas
County or area	Sussex	specific region or all
Years between	1770 and 1780	Leave blank for all years
also check	est. births ☐ others of this family ☐	e.g. from census age and birthplace, parents at baptism
Types of record	baptisms	Limit search to specific records
	Search	more help

Enter the details you know

3 Key in the name details for Jane Wiggins, and choose 1770 to 1780 from the **Years between** section. From the **County or area** list, choose **Sussex.** From **Type of record,** choose **Baptisms**. Now click **Search.** If you're not sure of the spelling of the names, tick the two **Include variants** boxes, too.

Always double-check the information

As with any transcribed index it's absolutely essential to cross-reference the information you find against what's in the original registers. This is explained quite thoroughly on the website, on the **Terms and conditions** page, found under the **About us** tab on the homepage. Here you're told that there may be inaccurate transcriptions as a result of human error or the illegibility of the original record.

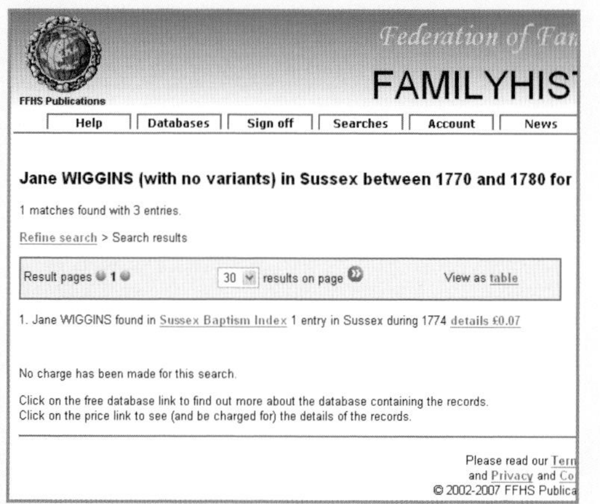

Read the results

4 The results of the search are displayed. Click on **Sussex baptism index** to view the record in the free database. You can see details of the full record by clicking on **Details £0.07**. Your account will be charged 7p.

Christening Sunday *Families leave church with their newly baptised infants in this painting by Charles James (1851-1906). Until the introduction of civil registration in 1837, baptism was the first appearance of an individual in the records.*

Using parish register indexes
origins.net

Another website with access to a large amount of parish data is **origins.net**. It holds a wealth of genealogical records for England, Wales, Scotland and Ireland subdivided into subsections: British Origins, Irish Origins and Scots Origins. The general databases are compiled from numerous sources, dating from 1209 to 1948, and are constantly being added to. The section covering British Origins alone contains more than 53 million names. Despite this, the site doesn't offer a huge amount of information on baptisms, although its marriage and burial records are excellent. As with other indexes, it's always advisable to check the information against original records.

Marriage records

MARRIAGE LICENCE ALLEGATIONS – VICAR GENERAL INDEX 1694-1850 An allegation was an oath, sworn by the groom, usually, in which he stated there was no impediment to the marriage. It would also state the location of the forthcoming marriage. Not every allegation resulted in marriage. The records of the earliest allegations are more detailed, and many give the ages of the two parties and details of next of kin. These records are indexed by name only and relate to licences issued by the Archbishop of Canterbury.

Modesty or caution?

Not every wooing ended in a wedding and wealthy women, in particular, had to be wary of false suitors. After 1837, a marriage was only considered legally valid if banns indicating the intention of the couple to marry had been announced in church beforehand, or if a licence to marry had been issued. In order to buy a licence, a marriage allegation or bond had to be sworn stating there was no reason why the marriage could not take place. The wording was solemn to emphasise the gravity of the oath, as a false declaration leading to a bigamous marriage, for example, was considered to be a serious offence.

In 'The proposal' (left) by Sir James Dromgole Linton (1840-1916), a bashful woman receives her kneeling suitor's proposal. The fact that it's happening in a secluded place, with a friend or chaperone posted at a discreet distance, suggests that an illicit courtship is in progress. The chaperone may be keeping a watchful eye open for the approach of a disapproving parent – or ensuring nothing improper takes place.

MARRIAGE LICENCE ALLEGATIONS – FACULTY OFFICE, 1701-1850 These records are similar in their content to those of the Vicar General Index, but with the advantage that both forename and surname are shown.

BOYD'S MARRIAGE INDEX In the early 20th century, Percival Boyd compiled an index to parish register marriages of all English counties (none complete), from 1538 to 1840. The level of coverage of each county varies considerably, as does the accuracy.

Burial records

BOYD'S LONDON BURIAL INDEX This is another index compiled by Percival Boyd, in 1934. Various parishes are included for the London area covering the years 1538 to 1840. It's not a complete resource and there may also be transcription errors in the index.

CITY OF LONDON BURIALS About 36,000 burials in 76 parishes in the City of London for the period 1813-54 are indexed, with a few earlier ones and some for 1855-1904.

Subscribing to the website

You have to pay to use the Origins site. For details of how to sign up, see pages 55 and 115. It's possible to carry out a simple name search on the homepage, but you need to subscribe in order to view the results from this free-of-charge search. There are three levels of subscription that you can choose from:

- a 72 hour subscription costing £7.50
- a monthly subscription costing £10.50
- an annual subscription costing £47.

Start a search for a marriage

1 Once you've subscribed to the website (see above, right), you can start to search. If, for example, you wanted to search for the marriage of your ancestor, a William Inge, to an Elizabeth Adams in the 1760s, click on **British origins**, then on the **Search** button to the right of 'Marriage records'.

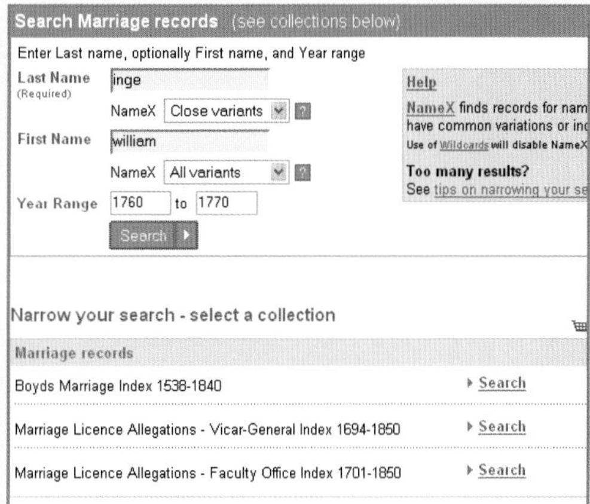

Fill in the search details

2 Next, enter the information about your ancestor. It's possible to search for an exact spelling or for variations on the name, too. It's also possible to filter the date. Once you've entered all known information, you can search the marriage records. Searches will be made in all three sets of records (see above).

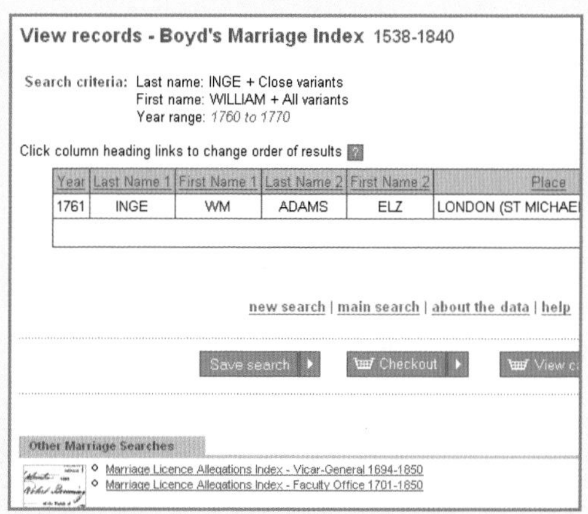

Results from a marriage index

3 In this example, Boyd's marriage index has produced the information required. If there are a number of results, navigate to each individual record to view the information. To order a copy of the original, click on the **Add to cart** button and following the checkout procedures.

Using parish registers
scotlandspeople.gov.uk

Scottish wedding
A piper walks ahead of a bride and groom at a traditional Scottish wedding in July 1960.

Searching parish registers for your Scottish ancestors is relatively straightforward, because the General Register Office for Scotland (GROS) has been collecting parish records, as well as the records for civil registration (the Statutory Registers), since 1855. The GROS has placed the majority of records on one website, **scotlandspeople.gov.uk**, a government-run resource that contains births, baptisms, banns and marriages from 1553 to 1854, known as the Old Parish Registers. For more information about what else the website holds, see page 56.

In Scotland, the parish records are sometimes called parochial records. The oldest records date back to 1553, but they are few and far between – only 20 survive from before 1600. Some records begin in 1690, when Presbyterianism finally achieved dominance over the Episcopalian church and became the established church in Scotland. Unlike England and Wales, where hardly any details of banns survive, Scotland has a few pre-1754 banns surviving, often in banns books.

Since 1855, the Old Parish Registers have been housed in the General Register Office for Scotland, in Edinburgh (see Directory). Some 4000 volumes from 1000 parishes survive, but the quality of information varies: for example, some entries are brief, stating only the bare necessities.

Subscription charges

You have to pay to use ScotlandsPeople. It costs £6 to buy 30 'page credits' to search the parochial registers. You can pay online using a variety of credit or debit cards. The cost of viewing one record is 6 credits. For details of how to sign up, see page 56.

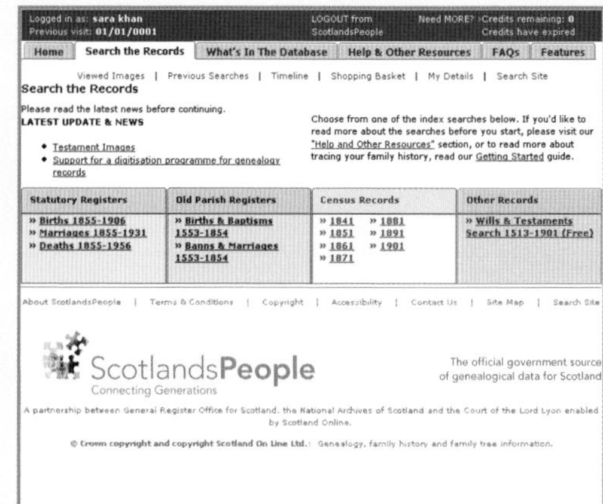

Searching for a baptism

1 If, for example, you want to search for the baptism of a William Jardine in the parish of Stoneykirk, around 1785, first register on the site (see pages 56-57). Then click on the **Births & baptisms 1553-1854** link under the blue **Old parish registers** heading.

Home baptism

In 1783, a duty of threepence was charged on every baptism that was registered. Some families were simply unable to pay the fee, so the minister would take pity on them and baptise the child at home, without entering the event in the parochial register. Registered paupers also evaded the charge, and thus the records. So you may not always be successful in your search for an ancestor's baptism.

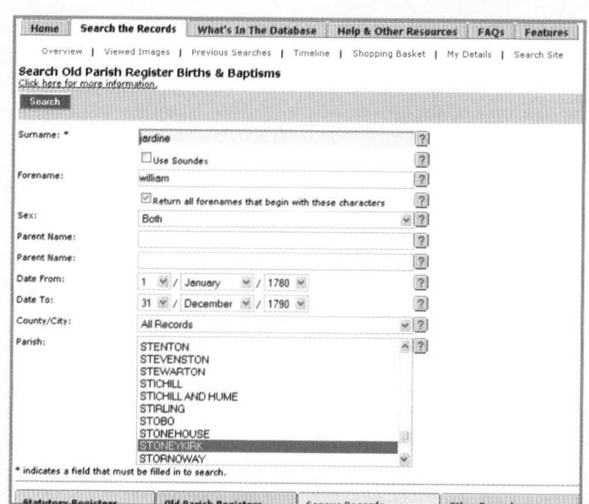

Give the details

2 Enter all the information you have in the relevant boxes. Set a date range (here, '1780' to '1790' to allow for variations) and also choose a parish, if you know it (in this case, Stoneykirk). Click the green **Search** button at the top left of the page.

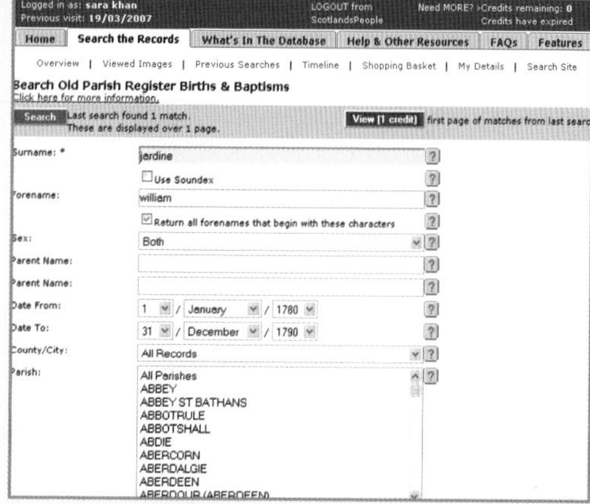

What the search finds

3 The results of the search are displayed in the blue strip at the top of the page. Click on the blue **View (1 credit)** button towards the top right of the page to see the results. It will cost 1 credit to see the transcription of the search result.

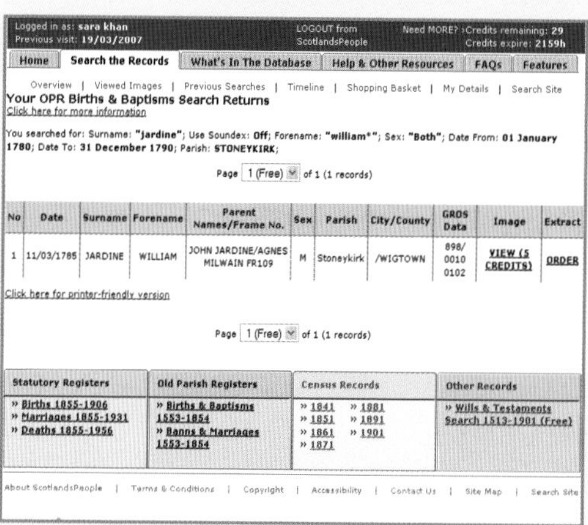

View all the information

4 William Jardine has been found. He was born in 1785 in Stoneykirk, Wigtown. His parents were John Jardine and Agnes Milwain. It will cost 5 credits to view an image of the register. Click on the **View (5 credits)** link under the heading **Image**, to the right of the page. This shows you the actual page from the register. Zoom in to find the record you want to see.

Finding Catholic records

Most early parish records relate to the Church of England, but you should still be able to find Catholic ancestors before civil registration began in 1837. Here's how to start the search into their often difficult lives.

In the early 16th century, Henry VIII broke with the Roman Catholic Church and made himself head of a newly formed Church of England, so that he could divorce Catherine of Aragon and marry Anne Boleyn. Since then, the Anglican church has been the official and established form of worship in England and Wales.

But not everyone approved of his changes, and many Catholics continued to worship in what they called 'the true faith', despite running the risk of being punished for heresy. They practised their faith in secret, and held private and secret masses, often hiding and protecting the few remaining Catholic priests. For a brief spell, after Henry died and while his Catholic daughter, Mary, was on the throne, Catholics weren't persecuted.

King's hiding place *Charles II hid from Parliamentarian forces for two days after the Battle of Worcester, in 1651, in this priest hole in Old Moseley Hall in Wolverhampton. It was concealed beneath the floor of the closet and had been built to protect the family's Catholic priest.*

Early Roman Catholic records

But in 1559, Queen Elizabeth I made it illegal to celebrate a Catholic mass in England and Wales. Her wishes were carried out with such vigour that many Catholics feared for their lives and kept their religion a closely guarded secret. Despite this, the secret practice of Catholicism survived in England for several hundred years. The only Catholic chapels were those that were kept by the Catholic gentry who could afford to keep a priest, often as a tutor for the sons of the family. The priests took on the care or 'curacy' of Catholics scattered over a wide area, and continued to be protected and hidden, when necessary, by the families they served.

This constraints on Catholics remained in force until the Catholic Relief Act of 1778. Few registers were kept for English Catholics during this period because of the fear of prosecution, so it may help to search court records (see page 202) to see if your Catholic ancestors were caught and prosecuted. As often happens when you try to trace your

Understanding Latin terms in Catholic documents

Some Roman Catholic documents were written in Latin, so it's worth knowing some of the terms that were used. Here's a list of the most commonly used names and terms, with their meanings.

aetatis	age
Alianora	Eleanor
anno	in the year
baptizatus/ baptizata or *bapt.*	baptised
Brigida	Bridget
conjugo, conjugum, conjunxi or conji. and *in matrimonio*	joined (in matrimony) or married
de	of
defunctus/defuncta	dead
die (20)	on the (20th) day
et	and
filia/filiam	daughter
filius/filium	son
Hannoria	Hannah
Jacobus	James
Joannis	John
Josephus	Joseph
matrina	godmother
mensis	in the month
olim	née or previously (to show maiden name in married women)
Patricius	Patrick
patrinus	godfather
sepultum est	buried
sponsori or sp.	sponsors (godparents)
vidua	widow
Xtopherus	Christopher

ancestors, it's when they came up against the law that their names and details would have entered the records. Also, as Catholics were subject to extra taxes and fines, consider searching the tax records held in The National Archives (TNA) and at local record offices. Because Catholicism was stronger in northern England, the local archives there will be of particular value in your search.

Catholics cradle to grave

From the beginning of the 19th century, Catholic churches began to keep registers of baptisms, marriages and burials. When civil registration began in 1837 only a small number of them were deposited in central archives, along with other non-parochial records. You'll find those that were deposited are mainly from northern England and are in TNA, among the other sets of registers found in a record series called RG4 (see page 148).

The rest of the registers are either still with the individual churches or in local record offices. It's also worth remembering that, in the middle of the 19th century, about three-quarters of Catholics were of Irish origin, so your Catholic ancestors from that era are likely to have come from Ireland.

Tracing your Catholic ancestors

Apart from TNA indexes, a number of websites offer help in tracing Catholic records.

Two specialist sites are the Catholic Record Society at **catholic-history.org.uk/crs** and the Catholic Family History Society at **catholic-history.org.uk/cfhs**.

There are also some established sites such as **ancestry.co.uk** and **movinghere.org.uk** that will help. The Society of Genealogists at **sog.org.uk** and *The Irish Times* at **ireland.com** have good indexes of information about Catholic records.

You may well find, though, that most of your searching will have to be done offline. For books about Catholic records, try the Institute of Heraldic and Genealogical Studies (IHGS) online Family History Bookshop at **ihgs.ac.uk**. It holds a number of books that you'll find helpful in tracing Catholic ancestors. Also, you might try the Westminster Library at **westminster.gov.uk**, which offers more family search suggestions, under their Libraries and Archives section on the homepage.

Risky mass *For many years Roman Catholics were forced to worship in secret, knowing that not only their priest, but they, as well, would be severely punished for participating in unlawful rituals. Often the priest lived with a sympathetic Catholic family and his presence was kept hidden. Restrictions introduced in the 16th century were only lifted in the 18th and 19th centuries.*

Tracing your Nonconformist ancestors

If your ancestors belonged to one of the Nonconformist religions, it's unlikely you'll find them in the records of the established Church. But there's plenty of information available elsewhere to help you to track them down, whatever their beliefs.

The term 'Nonconformist' was used from the 16th century onwards to describe people who refused to conform to the rites and disciplines of the Anglican church. They included many religious groups – Presbyterians, Unitarians, Congregationalists, Baptists, Methodists, Puritans and other smaller groups – who were fined and penalised for not attending Anglican services. Although Charles II had promised an amnesty to all dissenters when he was restored to the throne in 1660, he increased persecution and discrimination by introducing the Act of Uniformity two years later. At this point many Nonconformists sailed to North America for refuge; the Quakers, for example, founded Pennsylvania as a haven of religious freedom.

Indexes of Nonconformists and Dissenters (as they were also called) may be found on the website of the Church of Jesus Christ of Latter-day Saints, **familysearch.org**, which has transcribed the registers of a number of independent churches among the records held in its International Genealogical Index or IGI (see page 138). Another informative website is **spartacus.schoolnet.co.uk/religion.htm**. It has information about various religions.

The Toleration Act of 1689 made life a little easier for Nonconformists, but until 1828 they were debarred from holding political office. And in 1837, when civil registration began, most Nonconformist registers were collected and deposited with the General Register Office (GRO).

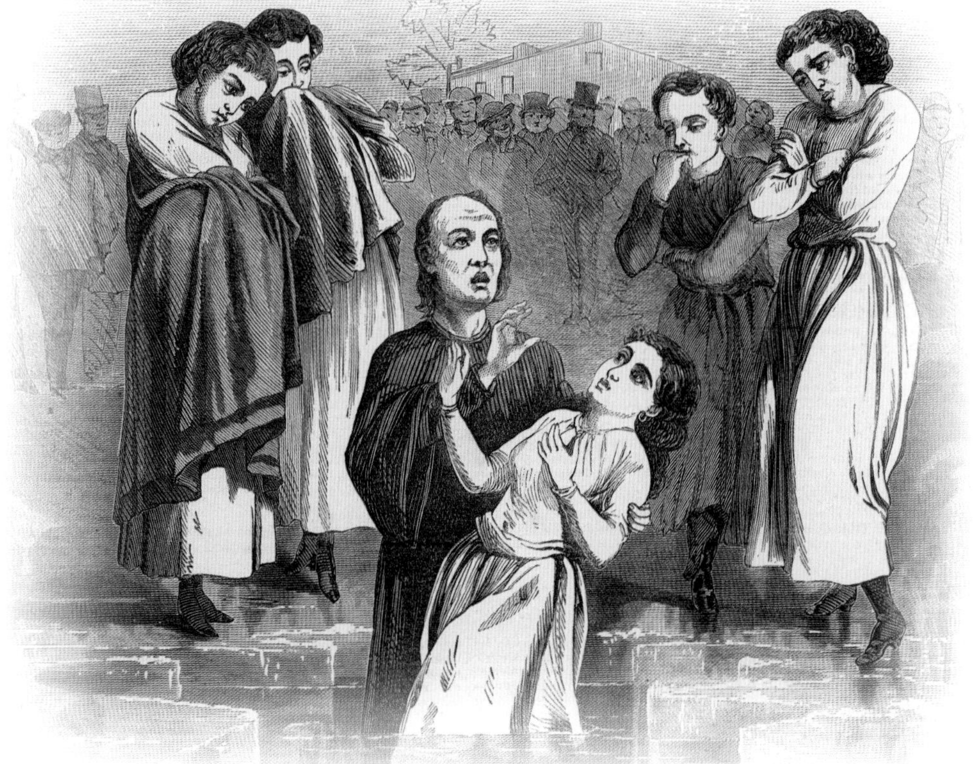

Finding a relative in TNA indexes

Most of the Nonconformist birth, marriage and death records are held in The National Archives (TNA) under the department code RG (see right). Even if you don't know the name of the church or chapel that your ancestor attended, it's still possible to find relevant records. The records are listed by county, so try doing a search by county or town. This is how the records are grouped:

A different way of baptising *The Baptist movement began in 1612 and was based on the concept of adult baptism and universal access to salvation. One of its greatest supporters was John Bunyan, whose 1678 allegory* Pilgrim's Progress *enhanced the credibility of the movement. Baptist records can be found in series RG4 and RG5 at The National Archives.*

- RG4 holds registers of births, marriages and deaths surrendered to the Non-parochial Registers Commissions of 1837 and 1857, 1568-1857. Also the Protestant Dissenters' Registry or 'Dr William's Library' of Baptists, Congregationalists and Presbyterians in the London area from 1742
- RG5 has birth certificates from the Presbyterian, Independent and Baptist Registry and from the Wesleyan Methodist Metropolitan Registry, 1742-1840
- RG6 contains Society of Friends' Registers, Notes and Certificates of Births, Marriages and Burials, 1578-1841
- RG7 has the registers of Clandestine Marriages and of Baptisms in the Fleet Prison, King's Bench Prison, the Mint and the May Fair Chapel, 1667-c.1777
- RG8 holds registers of births, marriages and deaths surrendered to the Non-parochial Registers Commission of 1857, and other registers and church records, 1646-1970.

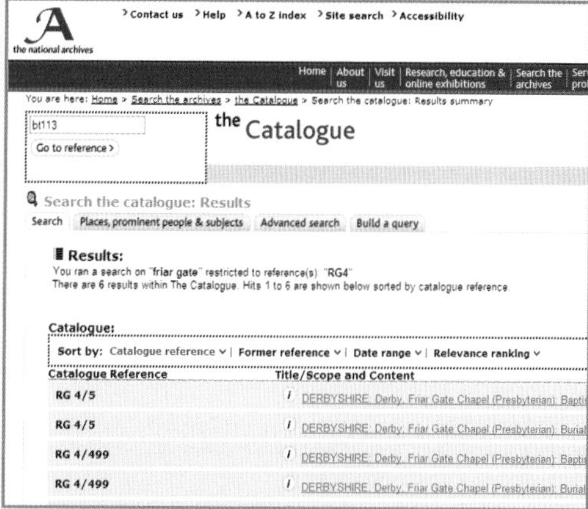

Searching for a chapel

1 To find the location and details of the Friar Gate Chapel in Derbyshire, for example, go to **nationalarchives.gov.uk**, select **the Catalogue**, and then **Search the catalogue**. In the **Word or phrase** box enter 'Friar Gate'. To narrow the search, enter 'RG4' into the **Department or series code** box. Click on **Search**.

Accessing the chapel's records

2 You will then be given a list of all the records in this series that relate to Friar Gate Chapel. They're arranged in chronological order, by record number. Make a note of the number on the left of the entry you're interested in. These records are available only on microfilm at TNA, and you'll need this unique reference number in order to locate and view the records you've chosen.

A quiet new faith

The Society of Friends, or the Quakers, was established by the dissenter George Fox in the 17th century. Early Quakers worshipped without preachers or any liturgy, as they believed God would speak to them through members of the congregation. As well as rejecting the established Church, Quakers refused to bear arms or take oaths, and believed in the equality of the sexes.

Violent persecution forced many Quakers to emigrate to North America. Many others stayed, with some, such as the chocolate magnates and industrial reformers, Joseph Fry and George Cadbury, making their mark on British life. The Society of Friends was the first Nonconformist organisation to start using registers and began recording births, marriages and deaths from the mid 17th century. In addition to series RG6 at TNA, Quaker records can also be found at **rootsweb.com/~engqfhs**. Not every register has survived, and you may find gaps in the records when you search for your Quaker ancestors.

Quaker wedding *Surrounded by 'Friends' in a meeting house, two Quakers make a commitment to a lifelong, equal partnership, without any need for clergy.*

Memorial inscriptions

Finding the words from a tomb or gravestone for an ancestor is poignant, as well as informative. Inscriptions can be traced online, as many local family history societies have transcribed them from graveyards and cemeteries.

Inscriptions on your ancestors' gravestones often contain far more detail than you'll find in official records or parish documents. For example, you may find out their date of birth and age at death, as well as where they lived and what job they did. Many of them give information about the parents and children of the person, helping you to extend your family tree.

A memorial inscription may tell about the travels of the person, because not all burials take place where the person died. Sometimes a body is brought back to a parish from many miles away, to be interred with other family members. This can help where you have a 'missing' relative, or answer the question 'Where did he get to for all those years?'

Inscriptions online

The online indexes of transcribed memorial inscriptions should tell you the graveyard where the inscription was found. This in turn helps you to find further information in the parish burial register of the church associated with the graveyard.

A good place to search for memorial inscriptions is on **familyhistoryonline.net**, a website run by the Federation of Family History Societies (FFHS – see page 58). The Federation has been transcribing inscriptions throughout England, Scotland and Wales since 1978 and many are now available online. You have to pay a modest fee to use the website, but once you've registered it's possible to use just the index free of charge.

Inscriptions offline

Although there's plenty of help available for online searches, not all inscriptions have been transcribed yet, so sometimes you simply have to visit a graveyard, church or crematorium to track them down. It could prove a fruitful journey, because graves and monuments offer up hidden treasure to the persistent explorer. Many churches have detailed memorial inscriptions about past parishioners and dignitories on their walls and set into their floors. You may also be

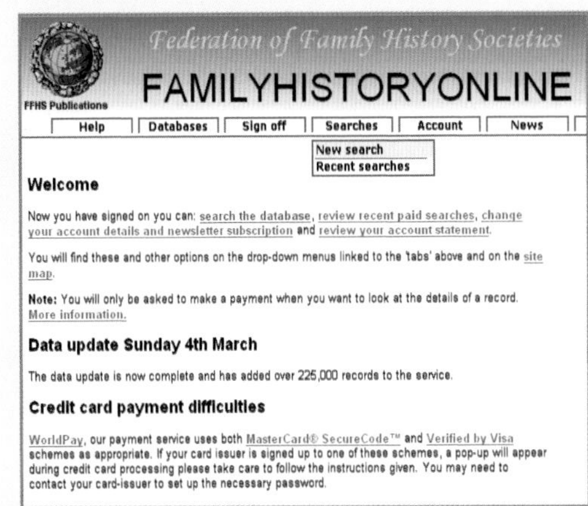

Searching for an inscription

1 Say you want to search for the memorial inscription of a Richard Wilkinson, in the Cheshire area, who may have died between 1800 and 1850. Go to **familyhistoryonline.net**, sign on (see page 59) and click on **Searches** and then on the **New search** button.

Give the details

2 Click on the **Search the database** option and you can start searching the index. Enter all the known details, such as the surname and forename. Choose the county from the drop-down box and set the approximate dates. Choose **Inscriptions** in the drop-down box for **Types of record**. Click the **Search** button.

able to find out about an ancestor at a crematorium, where ashes are interred in urns in a garden of rest.

Closed or redundant graveyards

You may find that the graveyard in which you expected to find your ancestor's gravestone and inscription has been built on or paved over. Before any old or redundant graveyards can be re-used in this way, the information on the gravestones has to be recorded in great detail and deposited with the local council or records office. Sometimes the stones will have been preserved and may still be accessible.

Some closed graveyards are maintained by the council in the area or by a group of local volunteers, and through them you may be able to find a list of the inscriptions of gravestones and monuments that are still there. Many local libraries have lists of memorial inscriptions of gravestones that have long since vanished or have become illegible with the erosion of time.

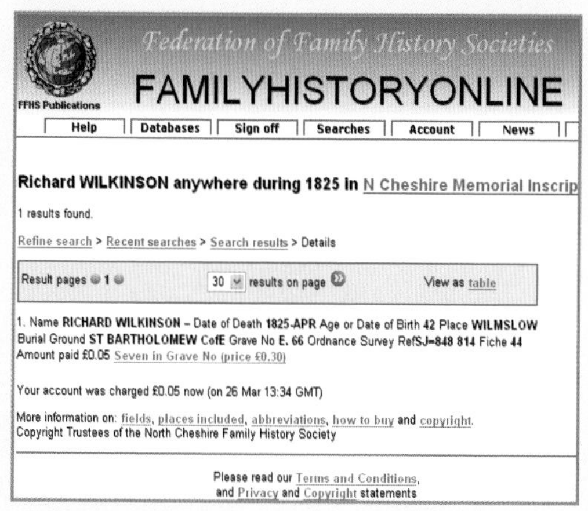

See the results

3 One entry has been found. Click on the link **Details £0.05** to view the information and you'll find out that Richard Wilkinson died in 1825 aged 42, and is buried at Wilmslow. This gives you an approximate year of birth (c.1793). The location of the burial ground and details of the grave are also provided. For 30p, you can view other family members buried with him. Click on the link **Seven in grave no**.

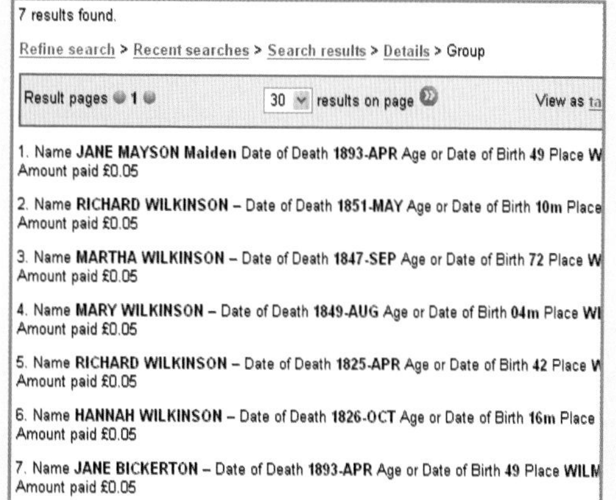

Other family members

4 The results of this search give details of six more family members, including three children who died before they turned two. These are valuable extra details that can be used to extend the family tree.

How to prepare for a graveyard visit

- Take a camera, notebook and pencil with you, so that you can record the information accurately. Note the position of the grave you are interested in within the graveyard, too.
- Some old inscriptions are difficult to read, especially if the stone has weathered. Go either early or late in the day, when the sun's slanting rays will light the inscription to best advantage.
- You may be tempted to brush off moss and lichen if they're obscuring the inscription, but be aware that old headstones are fragile, and you must take care not to damage them at all.
- Some graveyards are overgrown, so wear sturdy shoes and have a pair of secateurs in your pocket in case you need to cut back weeds or brambles to expose your ancestor's memorial inscription.

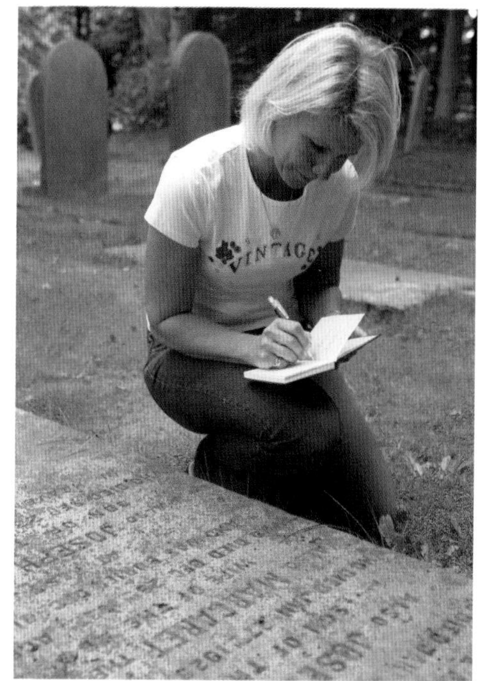

Searching for inscriptions

As more and more local record offices digitise information, the search for memorial inscriptions gets easier and more exciting. The material available online could include the words on your ancestor's gravestone.

Compiling databases of the inscriptions on memorials is a slow business, often carried out by volunteers and students. Tapping into a database that covers memorials in the area you're searching is the family historian's equivalent of finding a seam of pure gold. The discovery of a detailed memorial inscription can open up new directions for you to explore, and can help you to fill in details of other relatives.

Using NAOMI

The Heritage Lottery Fund supports the National Archive of Memorial Inscriptions (NAOMI).This is an organisation based at De Montfort University in Bedford, which is compiling a database of monumental inscriptions mainly from Church of England parish churchyards for family historians to search by name and place. At first, only monumental inscriptions from Norfolk were available, with more than 102,000 inscriptions and 142,000 names, and work

Searching for a memorial

1 In the 1901 census, a John Robert Chettleburgh, aged 55, appeared as a farmer living in Hardwick, Norfolk, with his second wife Patience. To find his memorial inscription, go to the homepage of **memorialinscriptions.org.uk** and choose **Search criteria**. Enter 'John' in the **First name** box, 'Chettleburgh' in the **Last name** box, set the **County** to Norfolk and type 'Hardwick' in the **Place** box. Click on **Search**.

Getting a result

2 John Chettleburgh died in 1925 aged 79, and is buried in St Margaret's burial ground in Hardwick, Norfolk. To see a transcription of the inscription, click on **View**. You'll be offered a list of options and prices. Seeing a transcription of the inscription and the grave reference costs £4. A plan of the burial ground may be available for £1, and a photo of the church costs an extra £1. Make your selection, click on **Continue**, and follow the instructions to pay by debit or credit card.

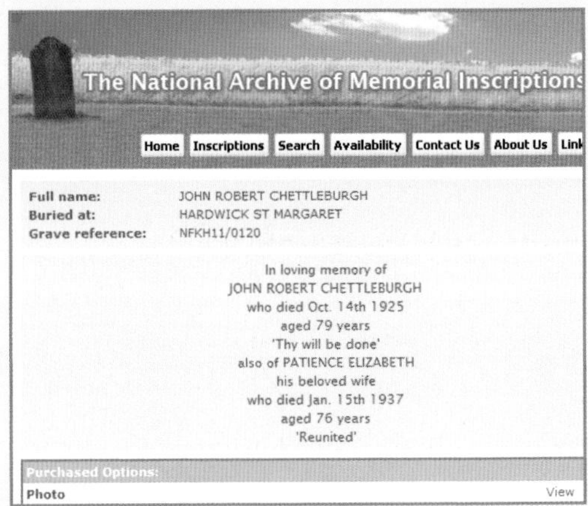

To see the inscription

3 The transcription of the memorial inscription at St Margaret's appears. It's useful because it also tells when his wife died. Their grave reference is given, which can be used to find their grave. If the church doesn't have a map on website, the church office should have a map they can post to you, or the local authorities can put you in touch with whoever holds the cemetery records.

has started on inscriptions from Bedfordshire. But as it's a work in progress, it's a good idea to check regularly for names and places relevant to your research. It's free to search the database by name, date range, county and place, but a fee is charged to view the full entry. Groups of people collect this data from Anglican and Nonconformist churches, cemeteries and war memorials. Visit the website at **memorialinscriptions.org.uk**. It gives you the option to receive a newsletter and promises not to disclose your details.

Searching local sites

Most areas in Britain have a local record office and many have websites that provide the family historian with detail of memorial inscriptions. If you can't find what you are looking for, don't despair – you may be able to get help direct from your local records office. Below are three examples of good local sites.

Bath Record Office

If your ancestors lived in or near the city of Bath it's worth visiting the website for the local record office, **batharchives.co.uk**. Clicking on **Family History** at the top of the page will take you to a section of the website where there's a separate page covering memorial inscriptions. Click on **Monumental inscriptions** on the right-hand side of the page and you'll find details of which memorial inscriptions have been transcribed for which parishes around the area. As most of these records are still being compiled, it's worth checking regularly.

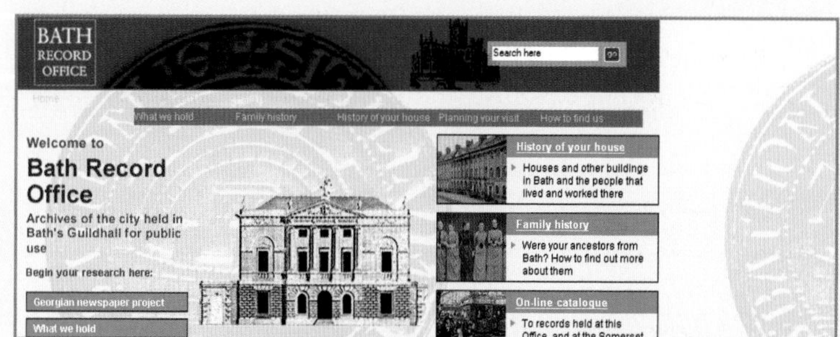

Kent Archaeological Society

For gravestones and monuments in and around Kent, try the Kent Archaeological Society archive of transcriptions at **kentarchaeology.org.uk**. Go to **Research** from the homepage then click on the **M.I.** (Memorial Inscriptions) link. There are parish maps of West and East Kent and an alphabetical list of locations. Clicking on a link to a place in Kent – Bexley, for example – will take you to a list of all the graveyard inscriptions at St Mary's church, Bexley. Some links also show sketch maps of graveyards, so you can identify the exact plot.

Hertfordshire Family History Society

Memorials from many of the parish churches within its county borders have been transcribed by the Hertfordshire Family History Society, at **hertsfhs.org.uk**. It lists the parish churches it has covered, and the cost of transcriptions, under the **Publications** section of the website. Click on the link at the top of the page. Now click on **Monumental inscriptions** for a list of parish churches.The list is updated regularly, so check from time to time to keep updated on what information has become available recently.

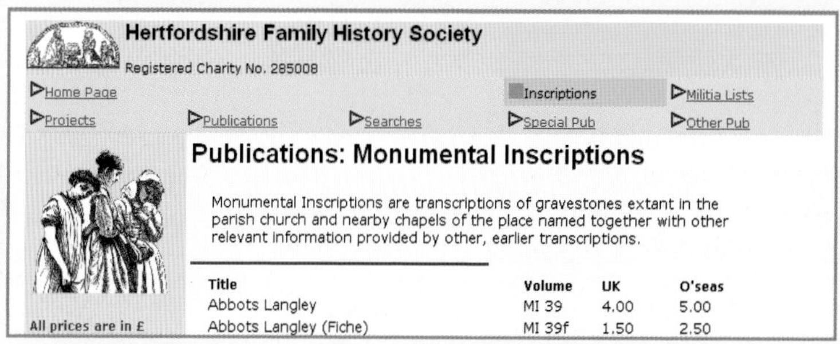

Wills

A will is a uniquely personal document, and can reveal a wealth of information about your ancestor and the family. Finding one could be a huge boost to your research.

Understanding wills

Reading ancestors' wills reveals not only their financial state, but an enormous amount about what was important to them in their lifetime.

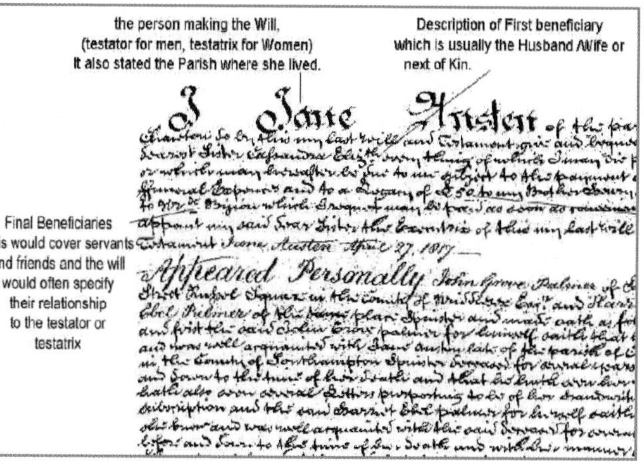

A will is often used to thank people, or to show appreciation of a spouse or children. Sometimes a nominal gift suggests that the deceased was angry with the recipient, so that they were almost cut out of the will. In some wills, the eldest son inherits just a token shilling because he has already taken over a family business or lives in the family home.

A husband's prerogative

Until 1883 a married woman could not make a will without her husband's permission. Once she married, all her property became part of her husband's estate, which meant that, by law, she had no property to leave. So before 1883, you're unlikely to find a will for a married woman – though you might find one for a widow or a spinster.

Wills made before 1858

You'll need to be quite tenacious to find a will made before 1858, because until that date, there was no central system of 'proving' a will – a term that came into use when a Church court validated the will, allowing the executor or administrator to carry out its instructions. Where this process (which is called 'probate') took place, depended on the value of the assets left by the deceased person and where the person had lived. You're not likely to find wills from among the poorer sections of the community – if you had no valuables, you'd have had little or no reason to draw up a will. But anyone with £5 or more to their name would have made a will.

Almost 300 Church courts were responsible for disposing of the possessions of people who had drawn up wills, and most of these wills are still held in local record offices.

There were several kinds of court, ranging from local archdeacon's courts to the Prerogative Courts of Canterbury and York, which dealt only with the wills of the very wealthy. The official records that survive are usually registered copies of 'proved' wills – not the orginals, which may no longer exist.

You can't take it with you *Wine is tasted and valued (left) to assess the amount of tax due on an estate in a 1947 painting entitled* Inventory and valuation for probate *by Frederick W. Elwell.*

A writer's bequests *Jane Austen's will of 1817, with explanations of the terms used, can be viewed on The National Archive's website.*

Wills made after 1858

It's not too difficult to track down wills made since January 1858, as this was when today's centralised system for dealing with legacies began. Unlike census records that stay closed for 100 years, the contents of a will are in the public domain. Copies of all English and Welsh wills from 1858 to the present day are held at the Principal Registry in London (see Directory). In Scotland, most records are held by the individual courts that granted probate; in Ireland, the records are at the National Archives in Dublin or the Public Record Office in Belfast (see Directory).

When there's no will

Any ancestor who failed to make a will is said to have 'died intestate'. What should be done about the assets – or liabilities – was usually settled by a legal process known as administration. An administrator, often the deceased's brother, eldest son or widow, was appointed to pay the debts and distribute the assets, according to the law.

Despite the fact that there may be no will for you to track down, there'll be legal records of what happened to the estate after death – probably held in the local record office.

What wills can tell you

An ancestor's will is a really exciting find. The document is likely to contain a wealth of detail that you wouldn't get from census returns or registration certificates – and you can reveal the real person behind the name.

Wills or legacies left by your ancestors add layers of colour and texture to simple names and dates, and often tell you so much about their lives and families. You'll find out how well off they were, or discover relationships and even children you never knew existed. In addition, you'll find out where they lived, what they owned, whom they loved, what they cared about. Beneficiaries in the will may include institutions such as schools and hospitals or charities, and even a mistress or previously unacknowledged illegitimate child. Then there are the wills that reveal a vindictiveness which can be breathtaking – a husband, for example, leaving his money to his wife on the condition that she does not marry again or co-habit with another man.

Whatever it reveals of the writer's nature, finding a will is a great windfall when you're tracking down long-lost ancestors.

In the solicitor's office *The secrets of a will are revealed in this Victorian illustration. Wills can yield a surprising amount of information about your ancestors.*

Where probate took place

Probate is the official process of validating a will (see page 155), which takes place in the area in which they lived or died.

If your ancestors lived in southern England or Wales and died between 1384 and 1858 (when the centralised probate system was established) and owned assets that were worth more than £5, or stretched over more than one diocese, any will they made would have been proved at the Prerogative Court of Canterbury, in Kent.

Start your search for a will

1 Here's how you'd search for the will of a Richard White, an ancestor from Farnham in Surrey, who died between 1700 and 1720. Enter **nationalarchives.gov.uk** into your web browser. On the homepage click on **Documentsonline** from the **Learning & research** panel on the left. Then choose **Wills** from the drop-down menu under **Family history** on the left-hand side.

The wills of people who lived in northern England were proved at York. Bequests below £5 were handled in other courts by bishops, and you should be able to find those wills in a local archive.

Most wills were proved within a year or two of the person's death, but it could take several years for probate to be granted, particularly if the terms of the will were disputed. If you don't find the probate records you're looking for, try looking in the records for a year or so later.

The earliest wills are likely to be in Latin; English became more widely used by the 17th century. The records that survive are usually registered copies of 'proved' wills – not the orginals. The copied wills vary in length: most are one or two pages long, but if your ancestor was a wealthy aristocrat with vast estates and investments, his will might have run to as much as 15 or 20 pages.

The National Archives has a fascinating collection of more than a million wills online. You can search them using various criteria: name, place, occupation and date of probate. Search these fields together or individually. The index is free to search, but if you find the will you're looking for, it will cost £3.50 to download. Remember that there may be transcription errors. Also, names may not be spelled as you'd expect them, so it's wise to search all variants of a name.

To have a look at some old wills, go to **nationalarchives.gov.uk**, and enter 'sample wills' in the **Search** box. You'll be offered a huge amount of information about them.

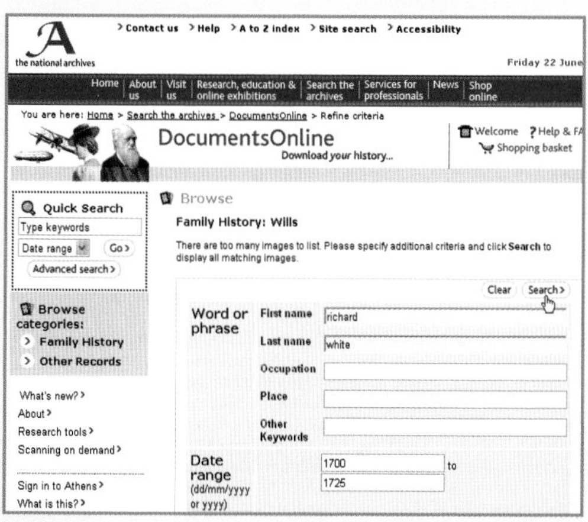

Fill in the details

2 Enter the ancestor's first name and last name. As White is a fairly common name, you should include a **Date range**. Put in the earliest and latest possible dates – in this case '1700' and '1725' – bearing in mind that probate may have not been granted for a few years. If you enter a location it may make the search too limited, so leave it blank and click on **Search**.

Assess the first results

3 From what you know about your ancestor, you can dismiss most of the Richard Whites on the results page. The most promising entry is the will for one from Farnham, Surrey, proved on October 3, 1715. But you can't eliminate the will proved on December 23, 1706, for which no parish name is given. Look at the most likely record first, by clicking **See details**.

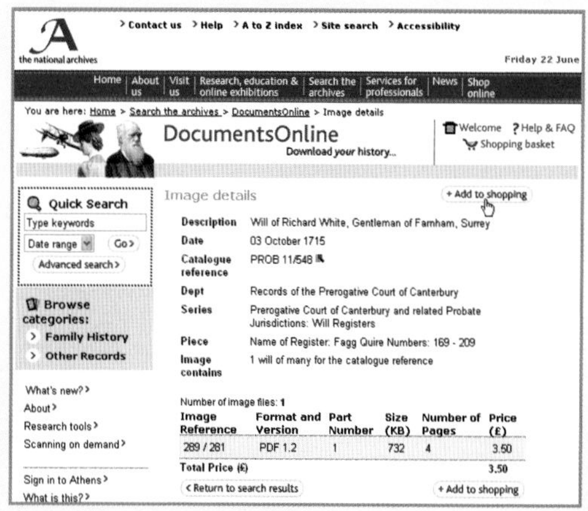

Buying the record

4 The result looks right, so buy the record by clicking **Add to shopping**. You'll be taken through a series of screens that guide you to making an online payment of £3.50. Once your payment is accepted, you can download the will.

Looking for wills

You may think your family was too poor to have left any property, but it's always worth searching for a will. Even if your more recent forebears were humble, you could discover more distant ancestors who were wealthy.

The earliest wills were generally left by the rich, but farmers and craftsmen often left wills, too. A blacksmith or a master carpenter might have wanted the tools of his trade to go to a particular son, for example. By the 18th and 19th centuries, you'll find wills made by soldiers and sailors, and in the 20th century, people from all walks of life, whatever their income or assets, were making wills.

The law makes searching easier

On January 12, 1858, responsibility for the granting of probate was shifted from the Church Courts to the State (see page 155). Since then, probate has been granted in district offices across the UK. Wherever probate is granted, a copy goes to the Principal Registry in London. Calendars giving details of all grants of probates and letters of administration have been published every year since 1858, and these can be searched at the Principal Registry (see Directory) or at major city libraries nationwide.

Looking for older wills

Before the law changed, wills were proved in numerous Church Courts, so pre-1858 you should begin your search at a local or county record office. But before you do, check the online index of The National Archives (TNA) at **nationalarchives.gov.uk** for wills for the Prerogative Court of Canterbury, where many English and Welsh wills were proved between 1384 and 1858. This quick search could save you time and effort.

Using local record offices

Record offices throughout the British Isles hold collections of wills proved in local courts. Few wills are available online, but county record offices are gradually transcribing and uploading indexes of the will collections in their possession. As the work is ongoing in many counties, you'll need help

A possible shortcut

Until 1906, taxes known as death duties were payable on estates over a certain value. Death Duty Registers containing details of these taxes have been kept since 1796. Before 1805, death duties were charged on about 25 per cent of all estates; by 1815 almost 75 per cent of beneficiaries had to pay some death duties on their inheritance. The Death Duty Registers are now held at TNA, and there's an online index covering 1796 to 1811 at **nationalarchives.gov.uk/documentsonline**. You can search the index free of charge and if you find your ancestor, you can download the details – including which court granted probate – for £3.50.

Reading the will *An 18th-century family wait expectantly to hear who has benefited from the will of a relative. Details of wills from this period are often held at local record offices.*

to find the records you need, so try the ARCHON directory (see below). It's accessed through TNA's website. If you find what you're looking for in an online index, the record office will send you a photocopy of the document for a small fee. The following counties have made this information available online through their record offices.

CHESHIRE AND CHESTER The archives and local studies offices for these two counties, at **cheshire.gov.uk/recordoffice/wills** hold on their database more than 130,000 wills that were proved at Chester from 1492 to 1940. Only the index is available to see online, so if you find your ancestor's will listed and want to see a copy, you'll need to order it. You'll receive onscreen prompts to help you.

WILTSHIRE AND SWINDON The record office at **history.wiltshire.gov.uk/heritage** contains 105,000 wills proved in Salisbury between 1540 and 1858. At that time, the diocese covered the whole of Wiltshire and parts of Dorset, as well as the parish of Uffculme in Devon. You can search the index online and order photocopies of the wills you want.

HAMPSHIRE To find wills on this site, go to **calm.hants.gov.uk/record.office/catalog/**. The database includes the records for all probate granted at Winchester (excluding the Archdeaconry of Surrey). As with the other sites mentioned, you can search the index but you can't view the wills themselves online; these can be ordered and posted to you.

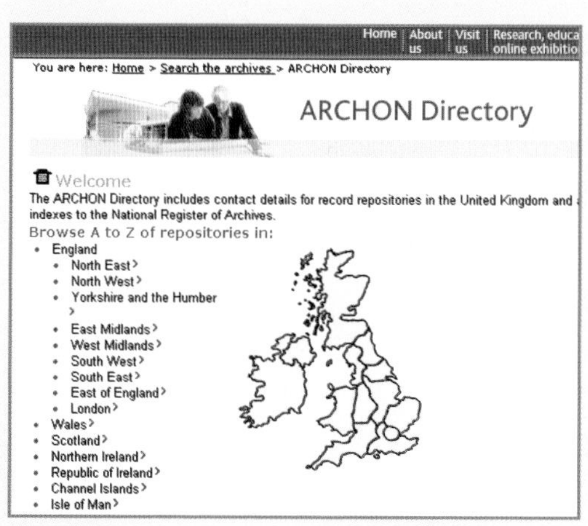

Which record office do you need?

1 If you're not sure where the local record office that holds your ancestor's documents might be, then use the ARCHON directory within TNA's website, **nationalarchives.gov.uk/archon/**. On the homepage, choose **Search the archives** and then click on the **Search ARCHON directory** button.

Search the ARCHON directory

2 If you're searching for archives in the Lichfield area, for example, key in 'Lichfield' in the **Repository name** field and click on **Search**. Four results appear, but only one looks suitable. Click on it to get its contact details.

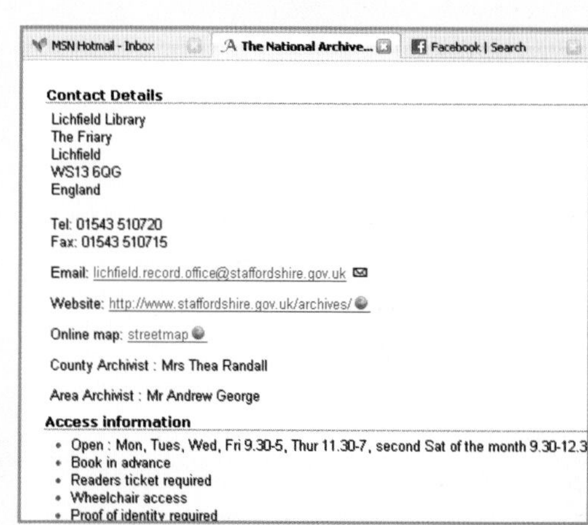

Choose a repository

3 If you selected the 'Lichfield Record Office' (part of the Staffordshire and Stoke-on-Trent Archive Service), you'll see full contact details and access information. There's also a website link through which you can discover more about the library's holdings.

Other sites to search for wills

If you've had no luck searching for ancestors' wills on The National Archives website, there are other sites to try. Wills were proved in a number of different places, and the trick is to track down the one you want.

You'll find the search for a will enthralling and the results, when you get hold of them, worth all the effort. Knowing where to look is half the battle, and so it helps if you can understand the types of will that were made in the past, and can define what type of will you're after.

Looking for English wills

A good variety of wills is held on **origins.net**. Along with an index for the Prerogative Court of Canterbury (see pages 155-7), there's also an index for wills proved in London and at the Prerogative Court of York. About 325,000 names are mentioned in Origins' section for wills, and there are a number of sections you can search, listed below.

Knowing some details about your ancestor will help you to assess which of the indexes is most likely to hold the details of his will and make it easier and quicker to choose from the options that are offered to you.

BANK OF ENGLAND WILLS EXTRACT INDEX
The years 1717 to 1845 are covered in this index. Entries include individual stockholders who were declared bankrupt, as well as people who'd invested money in public funds – this includes people from all over England, not just London. It will cost you a little more to order copies of these wills.

PREROGATIVE COURT OF CANTERBURY INDEX
You'll find this index covers the years 1750 to 1800. Wills were proved in the Canterbury court – that is, probate was granted (see page 155) – until the responsibility was taken over by the State in 1858. It's possible for you to buy hard copies of these original wills.

ARCHDEACONRY COURT OF LONDON WILLS INDEX This court in London was responsible for proving wills in the city. Wills were usually proved in an archdeacon's court if the property involved lay solely within that archdeaconry. The index covers the first half of the 18th century and contains the wills of many sailors.

YORK MEDIEVAL PROBATE INDEX Wills proved in the province of York from 1267 to 1500 are held here. Most of the index's coverage is of individuals with estates in Yorkshire, but there are also entries for people who lived in other parts of England. The hard copies for the index are held at the Borthwick Institute in York (see Directory).

YORK PECULIARS PROBATE INDEX 'Peculiar' is a term used to describe a church or parish that was under the control of a diocese other than the one in which it lies. This index is rare and not widely available. Wills proved in the peculiar courts within the province of York are included in this index. It covers the years 1383 to 1883. Hard copies of these original wills can be bought.

PREROGATIVE AND EXCHEQUER COURTS OF YORK PROBATE INDEX The Prerogative Court of York was the northern counterpart of the one in Canterbury. If property was in one or more diocese but all these dioceses were in York, the will would be proved in York. The Exchequer Court of York dealt with probate

Search for a will

1 To search for the will of a John Stevenson who died sometime in the first half of the 18th century in Bolton, Lancashire, go to **origins.net** and log in. Select **British origins** and, from the list of options you're offered, click the **Search** button next to **Wills records**.

matters for certain laymen and members of the clergy with property in the province only. Indexes are available only for 1853 to 1858, but as this is an ongoing project, the entire index will be available eventually.

How to find a Scottish will

If you're researching a Scottish ancestor it's possible to find the will through an index on **scotlandspeople.gov.uk**. As a large number of Scottish family history records have been placed on this website, searching for Scottish wills is quite easy. The site holds an index for more than 600,000 wills, proved between the years 1513 to 1901.

The index itself is free to search, but you have to log on first (see page 56 for details). Then click on **Wills and testaments search 1513-1901 (free)** to begin the search. Enter everything you know about your ancestor in the appropriate boxes and begin the search to see if any records are held. If you find the will you're looking for, you'll have to pay to get a copy of it.

Finding an Irish will

The loss of so many Irish records in 1922 makes this tricky. But go to **ancestry.co.uk** and click on **Search** at the top of the page, then choose **Browse by location**, and you'll get an interactive map. Click on **Ireland** and you'll be offered a long list of links. Under **Ireland court, land, probate records**, you'll find a couple of links to Irish wills indexes – one is for wills from 1536 to 1857. Click on one of these and you'll be offered a search page on which to fill in your search details.

Enter the details

2 Enter your ancestor's details in the box at the top and click on **Search**. Alternatively, you can search the entire collection of wills by going straight to a specific database, if you know which one you want, and clicking on it.

First results look promising

3 Results have been found in three databases: Bank of England Wills Index, Prerogative Court of Canterbury and the York Peculiars Probate Index. It's most likely that the correct result will be among the York Peculiars Probate Index, but you may want to check the other findings by clicking **View record** in order to rule them out. Otherwise just click on **York peculiars probate index (1383-1883)**.

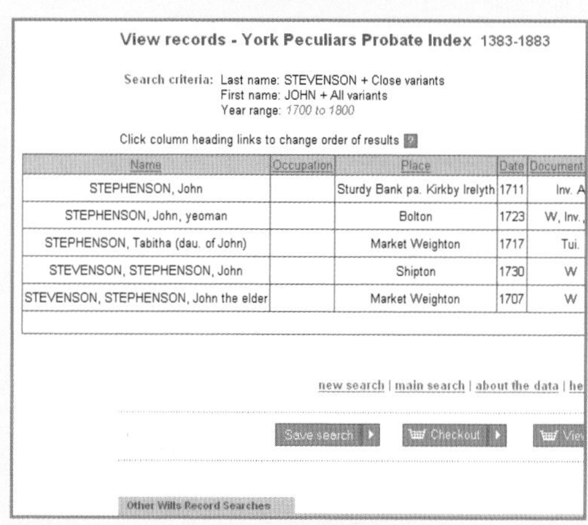

View records - York Peculiars Probate Index 1383-1883

Search criteria: Last name: STEVENSON + Close variants
First name: JOHN + All variants
Year range: 1700 to 1800

Click column heading links to change order of results

Name	Occupation	Place	Date	Document
STEPHENSON, John		Sturdy Bank pa. Kirkby Irelyth	1711	Inv. A
STEPHENSON, John, yeoman		Bolton	1723	W, Inv.
STEPHENSON, Tabitha (dau. of John)		Market Weighton	1717	Tui.
STEVENSON, STEPHENSON, John		Shipton	1730	W
STEVENSON, STEPHENSON, John the elder		Market Weighton	1707	W

new search | main search | about the data | he

Save search | Checkout | View

Other Wills Record Searches

Your ancestor's will is found

4 As your ancestor was from Bolton, it's likely that the correct will is the one dated 1723 for John Stephenson, yeoman. To buy a copy of the original will, click on the **Add to cart** icon. Follow the prompts you're given to pay for the will and a copy will be sent to you.

Consulting original records

Once you've made initial discoveries about your ancestors, you may want to see, and even touch, original documents that relate to them. It can be exciting and inspiring to view the proof of their existence.

Record offices and repositories

National archives and libraries hold an extraordinary amount of detail about your family in official government records. Once you've explored your local archives, the next step is to visit national institutions.

It's always worth phoning before you visit to confirm opening hours and to make sure the archive holds the records you require. You will usually need to give proof of identity before being allowed access to files. Charges will be made for photocopying.

The National Archives

Based at Kew in southwest London, The National Archives (TNA) – formerly known as the Public Record Office – is the central archive for England, Wales and the UK Government (see page 32).

Its records exist in different formats. There are original paper and parchment documents, microfilm and microfiche copies, and digital scanned images. Viewing any of these can give you detailed insights into your family's past.

If, for example, your ancestor was a railway worker, or applied for naturalisation as a British subject, or was transported to Australia as a convict, or spent time in one of London's debtors' prisons, you should be able to find out more from the archives. There's also a wealth of material on the Metropolitan Police, Army, Royal Air Force, Royal Navy and Merchant Navy, Coastguard and railway company records – most of whose records include service histories.

Information is power *The National Archives at Kew holds the more than 900-year-old story of the nation and its people, from the Domesday Book to the present day.*

Catalogue reference codes

Each document held at TNA has a unique reference code which you'll need if you want to order it. The first part of the reference always refers to the government department responsible for the record. So 'HO' stands for Home Office and 'WO' for War Office.

Finding a document

The National Archives Catalogue provides online descriptions of more than 10 million documents that you can search for by keyword, such as a surname or place name. You can narrow the search by year range and by departmental code – such as HO for Home Office records. The results list will give you a brief description of the document's content, the covering dates for each record and the catalogue reference code.

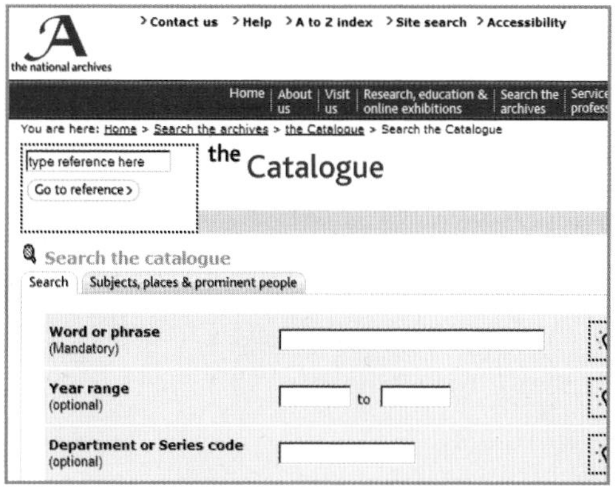

Making a visit to TNA

If you can't find a document online, you'll need to go through the paper catalogues at TNA. But if you've found a document that you'd like to view, you can place an order for it, in advance of your visit, by going to **Visit us** on the top panel of the homepage and selecting **Order documents in advance of your visit** from the list. Once you're at TNA, you register for a Reader's Ticket, which allows you to use the Reading Rooms and order more documents.

You can order up to six documents – for which you'll need to have found reference numbers – by email or over the phone.

What's available online?

Among the records now available online are First World War British Prisoner of War interviews, Victorian Prisoners' photographs, Death Duty registers, First World War Campaign Medals, Second World War Seamen's Medals and Alien Registration Cards – and the scope is increasing.

To see what else has been digitised, go to the homepage at **nationalarchives.gov.uk**. Select **Search the archives** on the top panel of the homepage and choose **Documentsonline** from the drop-down list. If you find what you're looking for, you can download it for £3.50, or view it free of charge if you choose to visit The National Archives.

Searching for records in Scotland

Scotland has its own National Archives, which holds government records stretching back 800 years, quite separate from birth, marriage and death registers of the General Register Office for Scotland.

Strange though it may seem, it's always much easier to find ancestors who fell foul of the law. So if you know that one of your Scottish ancestors was a thief or a bigamist, you're likely to find him recorded in the National Archives of Scotland (NAS). You'll also find lighthouse keepers, coal miners, Catholics and canal workers among the esoteric collections on its website at **nas.gov.uk**.

Like England, Ireland and Wales, Scotland has a local record office for each county or shire, with the main repository – the National Archives of Scotland – based in Edinburgh (see Directory). It holds Scottish government records going back as far as the 12th century, along with a variety of records deposited by businesses, landed estates, families, courts, churches and other institutions. The NAS doesn't duplicate any of the information held at the General Register Office for Scotland (GROS) – so you won't find any civil registers of births, marriages and deaths, Old Parish Registers of the Church of Scotland or census returns (see right) among its archives.

Most of the NAS records have been indexed and can be searched using the Online Public Access Catalogue (OPAC) – see right. The OPAC database searches by keyword, surname, place name, date and reference number (if you happen to know it); you can fill in one or more fields in the general search engine. So if you suspect that one of your Scottish forebears may have come into contact with the Scottish government at some time, you may find them with a search on OPAC. Getting to the point where you can begin to find relevant information is quite a long-winded process, but it's worth persevering.

There's a technique to searching OPAC, because the records aren't catalogued under the most obvious headings. For example, if you entered 'Highland Clearances' into the search engine, you'd get very few results. But if you put in names, dates or places that were relevant to the event, you'll get what you're looking for.

Pride of Scotland *The declaration of Scotland's independent status was drawn up at Arbroath Abbey (left) in 1320 – a copy is held in the NAS.*

Other archives that hold Scottish records

- The most important resource for anyone researching their Scottish ancestry is the General Register Office for Scotland, **gro-scotland.gov.uk**, which holds birth, death and marriage registers, and census returns (see pages 96-99).
- Many of Scotland's local authorities, universities, health boards and other corporate bodies have historical records and maintain archive services. The Scottish Archive Network (SCAN), at **scan.org.uk**, is compiling a unified online catalogue to many of these records – including those held by the National Archives of Scotland.
- The National Library of Scotland (NLS), **nls.uk**, in Edinburgh, holds UK legal deposits (a copy of every British and Irish publication), as well as collections of manuscripts, maps and Scottish newspapers.
- Some historical documents for Scotland are held at The National Archives (TNA) in Kew (see page 163), at **nationalarchives.gov.uk**. They include military service records after the union of Scotland and England in 1707, ships' passenger lists from 1890 and records of immigration to the UK. Using the keyword **Scotland** will reveal hundreds of documents that may be relevant; knowing a date will narrow down your search.

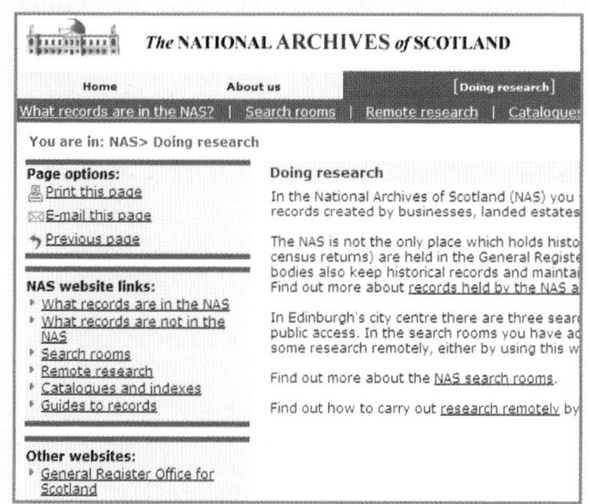

How to access OPAC

1 Go to the NAS homepage **nas.gov.uk**. Click on the **Doing research** tab at the top of the screen. It takes you to a page with tips for starting out. On the left-hand side of the screen, click **Catalogues and indexes**. From the next screen choose the **Online public access catalogue (OPAC)** link that's in the text on the page. Next, click the **Search** link from the bar at the top of the NAS catalogue page.

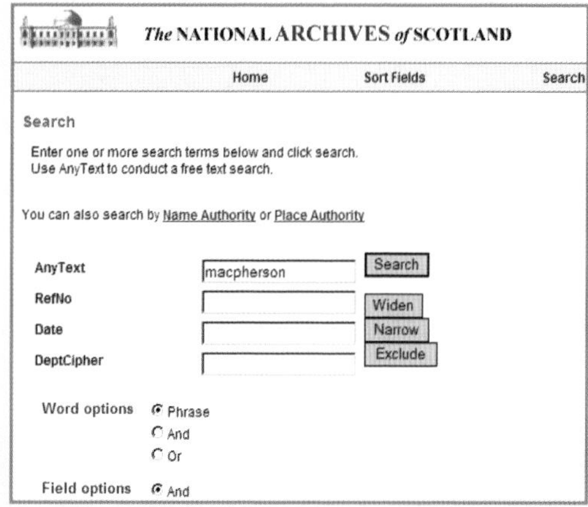

Enter your details

2 To do a search for a MacPherson ancestor who was a petty criminal in the 19th century, enter the name in the **AnyText** box. If you want to search a specific date range, key the relevant years into the **Date** box – '1840-1854', for example. Then click on **Search**.

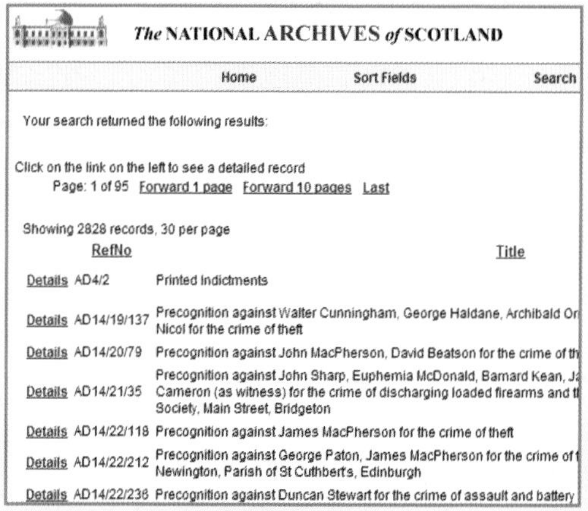

Narrow down the results

3 A general search for your relative has yielded 95 pages of results. To narrow these down, either restart the search using additional words in **AnyText** or click on the **Search** button. This will keep your original search but allows you to narrow the search. Add a first name, click on **Narrow**, and your hit rate will be significantly reduced.

Record offices and repositories
Ireland, Northern Ireland and Wales

If your ancestors were transported from Ireland to Australia, or signed the Ulster Covenant opposing home rule for Ireland in September 1912, or were buried in a Welsh churchyard, you're likely to find the event recorded in the relevant country's national archive. They'll probably be there even if their lives were quietly unremarkable.

Searching the record offices in these three areas can be very rewarding once you know how to go about it. Here's an overview of what you can expect to find.

Republic of Ireland archives

The National Archives of the Republic of Ireland, in Dublin, holds official records for the whole of Ireland as well as records relevant to Irish genealogy and local history. The archive is in the process of digitising the 1901 and 1911 Irish censuses, and has an informative website, **nationalarchives.ie**.

Online indexes to the archive's collections are held in 19 searchable databases, so you can visit the archive armed with a list of references you'd like to look up. The Ireland-Australia Transportation database – which lists Irish convicts transported to Australia between 1780 and 1868 – is an especially valuable resource. You'll find more about emigration to Australia on page 254.

Northern Ireland explored

Documents relating to Northern Ireland's history are held at the Public Record Office of Northern Ireland (PRONI) in Belfast. The names of people and organisations that have deposited papers in the archives are listed alphabetically on the website, **proni.gov.uk**, and a subject index describes the records available to researchers – such as 18th and 19th-century census substitutes, which are valuable because of the destruction of so many census records for Ireland.

There are several ways you can search. If you're trying to work out the exact location of a parish, Poor Law Union or county, use the Geographical Index – which gives you Ordnance Survey reference numbers. Or, if you're looking for someone of historical interest, the Prominent Persons index has around 5000 entries, some of which have digitised images that are free to download. You can also check the alphabetical index of Church of Ireland parishes or Presbyterian churches whose records are on microfilm.

Keeping the records *A country's national library is the guardian of its history – accessible and invaluable to the lay person and specialist alike.*

A record of Wales

The National Library of Wales (NLW), also known as Llyfrgell Genedlaethol Cymru, based in Aberystwyth, is the main Welsh archive. You can browse its website, **llgc.org.uk**, in Welsh or English – choose a language when you start using the site. Its electronic records are free to view online.

From the website you can search the NLW collections by clicking on the **Catalogues** link on the top panel of the homepage. Links will appear to the **Library catalogues, Electronic resources** and **Other resources** (A-Z).

The Library Catalogue has a main database known as **The full catalogue** that can be used to search for books, periodicals, newspapers, electronic publications, maps, graphics and digitised records. Eventually, all of the library's collections will be searched from this catalogue, but until then there are four other catalogues that you can look at for additional material.

- Archives and Manuscripts catalogued before 1999 are searchable by key word.
- Archives and Manuscripts catalogued after 1999 are searchable by name, subject, place name and key word.
- The Theses Catalogue has records of more than 15,000 theses presented for Higher Degrees to the University of Wales since 1984 and the University of Glamorgan since 1999.
- The National Screen and Sound Archive of Wales holds information about the television and radio programmes recorded by the Archive over the past 20 years, as well as a cross-section of the Archive's film collection.

The full catalogue is searchable by keyword, author, title and subject. Try using wildcards (see page 64) to broaden your search, or use the **My search limits** link to the left of the search engine to narrow down your results if you get too many.

The **Electronic resources** section is extremely useful. If you click on the link you'll be taken to a list of databases containing images that are free to download.

For family research, you'll find the most useful of these are the **Digital mirror** database, where selected manuscripts, archives, videos, pictures, maps and photos have been digitised, and the **Marriage bonds** search engine, where you may find an ancestor's marriage, if he applied for a marriage licence between 1616 and 1837.

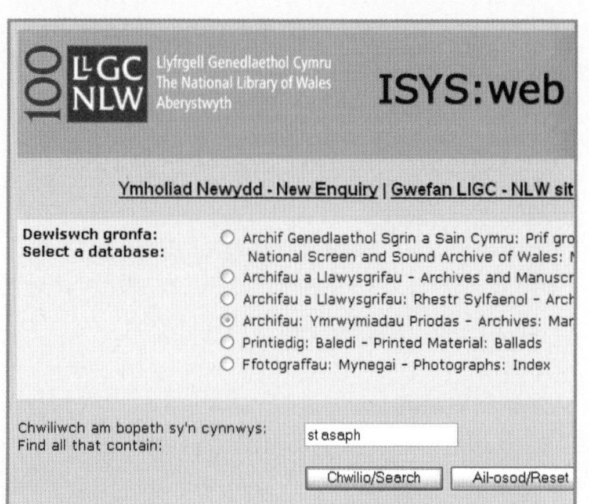

Starting a search in Wales

1 To find the marriage of a Sarah Capper at St Asaph in North Wales before 1750, go to **llgc.org.uk**. Under the **Family history** tab, select **Search archival database**. On the next screen click on **Marriage bonds**. Enter 'Sarah Capper' into the **Find all that contain** box. Click on the '**&**' symbol next to **And which also contain...** and enter 'St Asaph' in the text box that appears. Another box will appear, entitled **The current query is:** confirming the details. Click on **Search**.

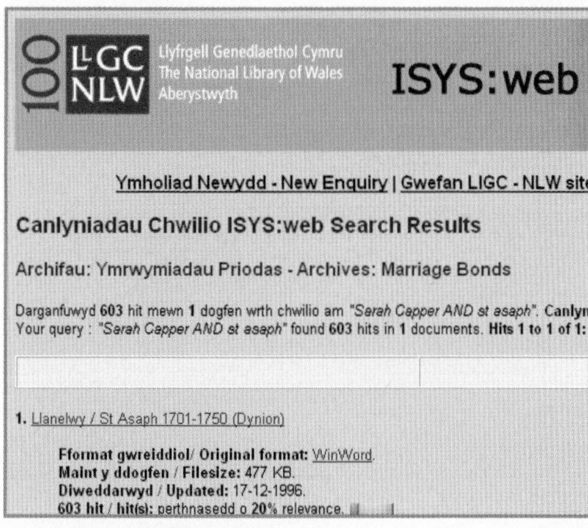

Read the results

2 The results page shows only one page of marriage bond transcriptions with a match in the database for Sarah Capper at St Asaph. The result is displayed as **Llanelwy / St Asaph 1701 – 1750 (Dynion)**. Click on this link to see a list of transcriptions of all the marriages on that page for the St Asaph region between 1701 and 1750.

ALLBONE, George, bach., Llanrwst, DEN. 1750, Aug 30. At Wrexham. Mary Edwards. B. 26/94.
ALLIN, Anthony, miner, Ysgeifiog, FLN. 1744, Jun 4. At Y. Mary Hughs. B. 20/45.
ALLEN, Francis, Northop, FLN. 1740, Apr 26. At N. Elizabeth Pierce. B. 15/35.
ALLEN, John, miner, Ysgeifiog, FLN. 1748, Jul 18. At Mold or Nannerch. Jane Clag. B. 24/67.
ALLIN, Thomas, miner, Ysgeifiog, FLN. 1739, Jan 1. At Y. Elizabeth Hughes. B. 15/1.
AMES, David, miner, Ysgeifiog, FLN. 1742, May 7. At Meliden or Bodfari. Jane Parry. B. 18/21.
ANDERTON, William, yeoman, Eccleston, CHS. 1721, Aug 7. At Gresford, DEN. ←**Sarah Capper**→. B. 8/43.
ANDREW, David, Tregynon, MGY. 1746, Sep 14. At Tregynon or Manafon. Jane Woosnam. B. 22/85.
ANDREW, Richard, husbandman, Penmachno, CAE. 1726, Sep 23. At Ysbyty Ifan, DEN. Margarett Ellis. B. 9/74.
ANDREW, Thomas, Selatyn, SAL. 1747, Jan 21. At S. Mary Jones. B. 23/141.
ANSON, John, 1743, Apr 4. At Llanymynech, MGY. Mary Parry. B. 19/2.
ANWYL, Hugh, husbandman, Abergele, DEN. 1723, Dec 31. At A. Margaret Jones. B. 8/197.
APLETON, Francis, joiner, Wrexham, DEN. 1701, Jun 7. At Wrexham or Rhiwabon or Gresford. Jane Valentine. B.
ARTHUR, John, Selatyn, SAL. 1742, Jan 17. At Selatyn or St. Martins. Mary Philips. B. 18/183.
ARTHUR, Robert, tanner, Wrexham, DEN. 1716, May 19. At [Wrexham]. Mary Jones. B. 6/74.
ARTHUR, Robert, Llansanffraid Glyn Ceiriog, DEN. 1748, May 25. At Llangollen. Margaret Edward. B. 24/35.

Find the marriage

3 Every time a word you included in your search is found it will be highlighted. Scroll down the screen until you come across the highlighted name Sarah Capper. The entry shows that on August 7, 1721, at Gresford in Denbighshire, (indicated by the county abbreviation DEN), Sarah Capper married William Anderton, a yeoman of Eccleston in Cheshire.

Using online catalogues to explore the archives

Being able to search an archive's catalogue online not only helps you to decide whether a visit to that archive will be worthwhile, but speeds up your search when you get there. This type of preparation pays dividends.

There's a vast array of archives in the UK, many of which may contain useful information about your family and the areas of research that interest you. In the past, as cataloguing techniques varied from one archive to another, you'd have needed an experienced archivist to decipher the index and find material on your behalf. Now, many archives have begun to upload their catalogues into online databases, with searchable indexes, making the catalogues easy for the first-time family researcher to use. The development of integrated online catalogues, where archives across the UK have compiled their indexes onto one database, means that you can locate documents in archives that you may not have considered visiting. Links from one catalogue to other search engines broadens your scope.

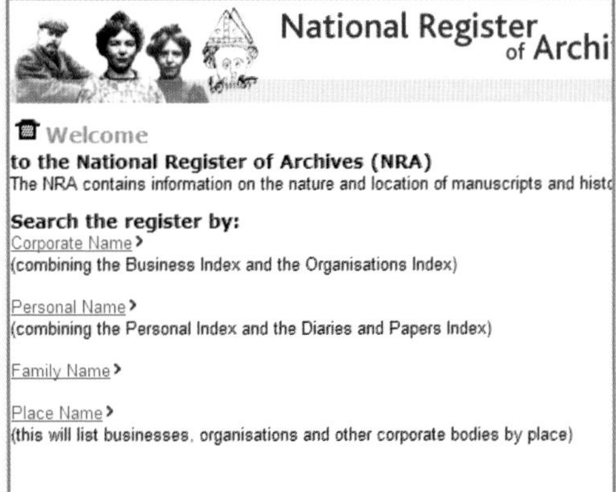

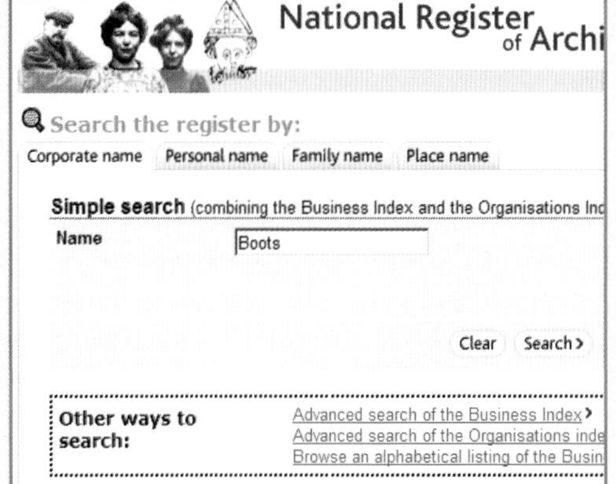

Search by corporate name

1 If you had a relative who worked for Boots Pharmaceuticals in the past, you can try to track down their work record. You need to start by finding out if Boots has a company archive and what kind of records it might hold. Go to **nationalarchives.gov.uk/nra**. From the homepage, select **Corporate name** from the list of possible search options.

Find the company

2 Because Boots is a well known name, start off with a **Simple search** by entering 'Boots' in the **Name** field and clicking on **Search**.

Read the results

3 There are two results, one in Nottingham for 'Boots Co. Ltd. pharmaceuticals, manufacturers and retailers', and one in Newmarket, Suffolk for 'Boots The Chemist, chemists'. The number in brackets next to the company name indicates how many records have been found for each business, but neither tells you where the archives are held. Click on each company name to see a description of the records and their location.

Archives across the nation

In 1869 the Royal Commission on Historical Manuscripts was formed to produce surveys of British historical records held in private collections, known as the Reports and Calendars. So much material was collected that it was necessary to create the National Register of Archives (NRA) as a means of maintaining catalogues and indexes. Since 1995, the NRA has been available online, at **nationalarchives.gov.uk/nra**, and it updates its collections and provides links to electronic catalogues. The NRA now holds indexes to more than 44,000 unpublished lists and catalogues for archives, both in the UK and overseas, and contains information about the historical records kept by around 46,000 individuals, 9,000 families, 29,000 businesses and 75,000 organisations. There is a printed copy of the NRA catalogue available for consultation in the reading rooms at The National Archives (TNA) in Kew, which has been indexed under five headings: Business, Organisations, Personal, Diaries and Papers, and Families and Estates. The online database has put them into four types of search engine:

Life at work *A big company such as Boots will often have archives where an ancestor might appear. Jesse Boot, who founded the business in 1849, was a generous donor to his home town of Nottingham, giving a large area of land (above) to its University College.*

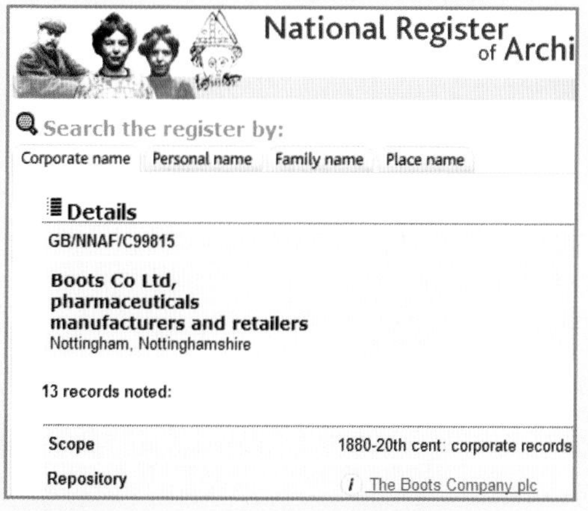

Company archives are found

4 The first of the 13 records in Nottingham reveals that this repository holds corporate records, staff records and photographs. Click on the link to that repository, and you'll be supplied with an address, phone number and map showing the location of the company archive. You can now contact the archive and arrange a visit to see if you can find out more about your ancestor.

CORPORATE NAME You can search the Business and Organisations indexes (see left) using a **Simple search**, which only requires a name or keyword from the organisation's title. Alternatively, you can conduct an **Advanced search** of either index. The advanced search for businesses allows you to specify a sector, town, county and date. The advanced search for organisations can restrict the results by category, town, county and date. You can also browse an A to Z of both the Business and Organisations indexes.

PERSONAL NAME Here, the search engine combines the Personal index and the Diaries and Papers index. Only a name or description of the papers you're looking for is needed for a **Simple search**. You can also search the Personal index using an **Advanced search**, which restricts the search by name and description, gender and date. There's also a link to an alphabetical list of the combined Personal index and Diaries and Papers index.

FAMILY NAME To search the Family and Estates index, you can do a **Simple search** with just a surname. An **Advanced search** lets you enter a name, the family's seat, a county, country and date. There's also an alphabetical list of the Family and Estates index that you can browse.

PLACE NAME All five indexes are combined in this search engine, which you can search by town and county to see what archives are held for a business, organisation, individual or family from a specific area, and what diaries or papers are relevant to that place.

Finding the archives a2a.org.uk

For a good guide to where records are held, use Access to Archives (a2a), which provides online catalogues of many local archives in England and Wales, some dating right back to the 8th century. Not every archive is catalogued, but new ones are added all the time.

Like the National Register of Archives (see page 168), a2a is a database only. That means it provides catalogued descriptions of documents held in local record offices, archives, museums, universities and libraries around England and Wales – and tells you how to access them. It doesn't contain full transcriptions of documents or digital copies of manuscripts or historical records, but at least you'll know where to start looking.

The database includes descriptions of about 10 million records from more than 400 repositories. You'll be able to search them by keyword, repository, area and date range.

Working underground *A 'putter' puts his weight behind a steel tub. He's watched by an overseer at Fourstones Colliery near Hersham in the 1920s. A putter's job was to push the coal to where it could be hauled to the surface by machine or horse.*

Using the search engine

The **Keyword** search on the main search page (see below) is usually the best way to find documents relevant to your research. But if you'd rather search for a specific archive's catalogues, you can select that archive from the **Location of archives** list on the same page and leave all other fields blank. To ensure the widest range of results, set the **Dates of archives** to look for records added since June 2001. As with most search engines, the more detail you enter, the more specific the results.

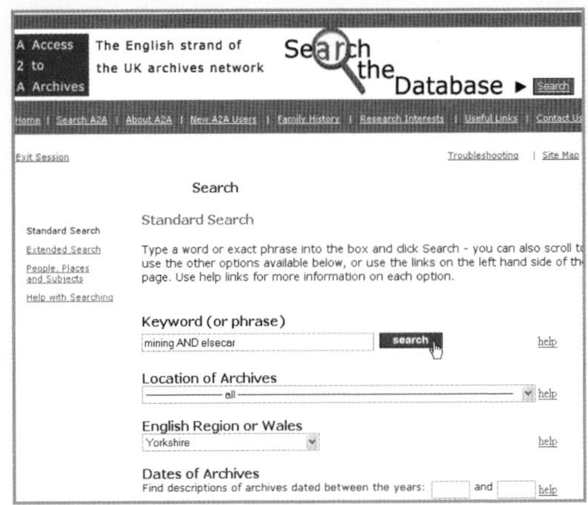

Enter your keywords

1 To find the mining records of Elsecar in Yorkshire, click on **Search a2a** near the top of the homepage. Enter 'mining AND elsecar' in the **Keyword** box. Choose **Yorkshire** from the **English region or Wales** drop-down list. Leave the date range blank and the **Dates of catalogues** to its default (June 2001). Then click on **Search.**

Plans for the future

To forge closer links between archives and local communities, a2a is developing a huge variety of detailed catalogues under the umbrella heading Archives 4 All – click on the **a4a** link from the homepage for more information. Among the records that will become available, you'll be able to research business, estate and trade union papers from the West Midlands; records of the International Harvester, Massey and Wallis and Stevens agricultural machinery companies; veterans' memories from the Queen's Royal Surrey Regiment; and records of the London Borough of Lambeth's local schools, churches and housing associations, as well as the borough's West Norwood Cemetery.

And for anyone researching their Jewish ancestry, 20 of the main catalogues of the Weiner Library – the oldest Holocaust memorial institution – will be put online, including records of the Kitchener refugee camp at Richborough, in Kent.

ARCHON – the local archives directory

You'll find links on some websites to archon, at **nationalarchives.gov.uk/archon/**, part of The National Archives website. It holds contact details of vast numbers of local archives in the UK, the Republic of Ireland, the Channel Islands and the Isle of Man. It also offers an index of foreign record repositories. You can search archon in a number of ways, including by county, by A to Z index and by keyword through the **Search archon** facility.

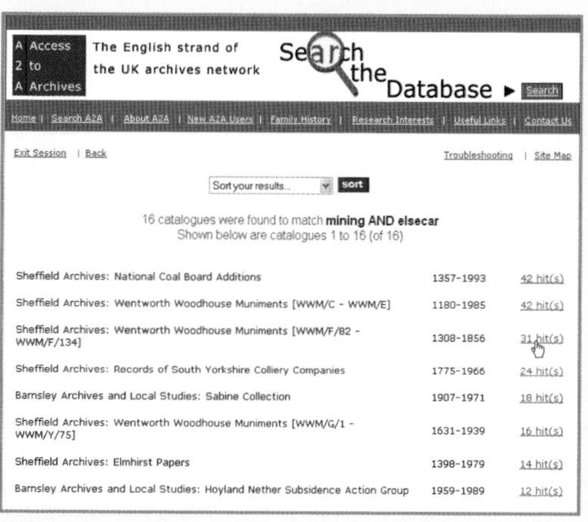

Examine the matches

2 Restricting the search to Yorkshire gives you 16 matches that tell you where the archive is stored, its name, the date range covered by that catalogue, and a link to the 'hits' found. Click on the blue link, on the right, for the third catalogue result to view a detailed description of that collection and the conditions of access.

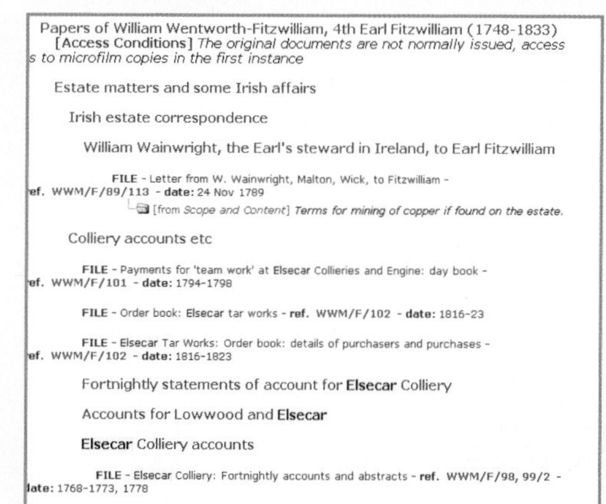

What's held in the archives

3 Scroll down this page to a list of files, along with the reference codes needed for ordering them from the archives. If you want to contact the archive ahead of a visit, in this case the Sheffield Archives, then click on the red link near the top of the page.

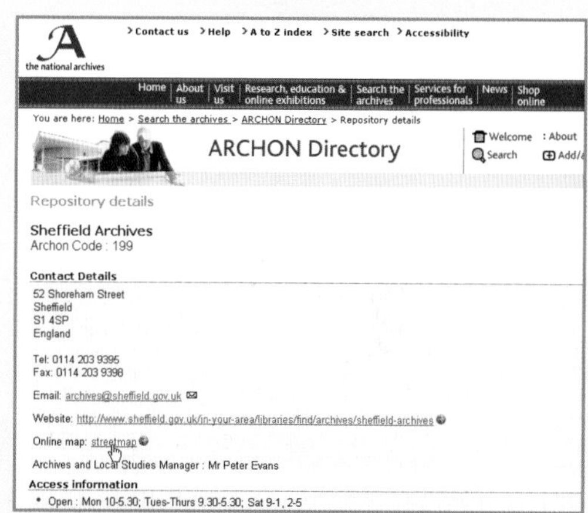

Getting the archive details

4 This takes you to the Archon Directory page for that archive, where you'll find its postal address and phone number, website, access information and a link to an online streetmap.

Finding and using libraries

When you're trying to flesh out the picture you have of your ancestors, a local library's records can prove invaluable. You'll be able to read about their trades or professions, as well as discover what local issues affected their lives.

Many libraries hold local archive material, including newspapers, deposited research notes and electoral lists. If your library has a local study centre, it may also hold rare books, trade directories or maps. Library services are usually free of charge.

Most libraries with source material on microfilm or microfiche will supply you with copies, for a fee. Remember that most family history material can't be borrowed – it's for reference use on library premises only. But there's likely to be a photocopier, so you should be able to buy copies of anything that you find useful for your research.

Making the most of Familia

This is an impressive directory of the family history resources that are held in public libraries in the UK and the Republic of Ireland. Its website, **familia.org.uk**, has links to and details about most local libraries and is free and simple to use. You don't need to register any details or pay a subscription to see information. The website offers an alphabetical index of libraries, so you can see if there's a library in your chosen location, whether it has any relevant family history information, what that information is and which years the records cover.

Familia also tells you whether you need to book an appointment, or require a library ticket to view the information you're searching for. It will also give you the address for the library you want to visit.

Once you click on the link to your chosen library, the site will list all the information sources available to you. There's also a guide for those using a library for family history research, including the following advice:

- When visiting a library for the first time, contact it in advance to confirm what it holds and when it's open.
- Check whether you'll need proof of identity.
- If a library offers a booking service, book a microfilm or microfiche reader, or a computer terminal, before your visit.
- Plan your research beforehand by reading the guide you'll find under **Visit us** at **nationalarchives.gov.uk**.

Using the Mormon researches

You may live within reach of one of the more than 100 or so Family History Centres of the Church of Jesus Christ of Latter-day Saints (LDS – the Mormons) spread across the UK and Ireland. If so, it would be worthwhile visiting the centre to see what research resources it has. There's information about the organisation and its holdings on page 54, and on page 138 you'll see how to use its website. To search for the Family History Centre nearest to you, see page 137.

Getting help with your research from major libraries

The contact addresses for these libraries are given in the Directory and on their websites.

☛ **The British Library** Known as 'the world's library', this extraordinary facility holds more than 13 million books, manuscripts, journals and newspapers. It's based in London and its website is **bl.uk**.

☛ **The National Library of Scotland** Preserving the history and culture of Scotland is the main aim of the library, which holds a large collection of rare books and manuscripts.The library is in Edinburgh and its web address is **nls.uk**.

☛ **The National Library of Wales** Material specific to Welsh history is held here, including photographs, manuscripts and films. Based in Aberystwyth, its website is **llgc.org.uk**.

☛ **National Library of Ireland** Based in Dublin, the library holds microfilm collections of Roman Catholic parish registers up to 1880, as well as Gaelic manuscripts and estate records. There's a good online catalogue at **nli.ie**.

☛ **Manx National Heritage Library** The library archives contain manorial records, maps and plans. The library is in Douglas and its web address is **gov.im/mnh**.

☛ **Catholic National Library** Mission registers with details of baptisms, confirmations, marriages and deaths dating back to 1694 are held in London. The website is **catholic-library.org.uk**.

A haven for family historians

The Society of Genealogists (SOG) is a charitable organisation that encourages the study of genealogy. Its library holds family trees, pedigrees and research notes deposited by other researchers, and a wealth of records from county sources, including indexes and transcripts of parish registers. It also has poll books, directories, local histories, the International Genealogical Index (IGI) on CD, Scottish civil registration indexes, Boyd's Marriage Index for 2,600 parish registers, and some overseas records – particularly for the British empire.

The Society's library in London (see Directory) charges visitors £4 for an hour's use of its facilities, or £18 for a full day. Alternatively, annual membership costs £43 plus an initial £10 joining fee.

You can search the collections through the SOG's online catalogue. Click on **Sogcat** in the bar at the top of the homepage, **sog.org.uk**, and follow the instructions under 'How to use the catalogue'. It's wise to consult Sogcat to make sure the library has what you're looking for, before making the trip to London. The library's collections are arranged by title in alphabetical order, so just enter the beginning of a phrase when you search. It will then take you to the point in the list nearest to the first few letters of the phrase you've entered.

Click on **Library & genealogy** at the top of the homepage, and then **Library index** in the left-hand panel, to see an index of the collections held, including wills, overseas records or surname studies.

Montagu links with Scotland

Edward Douglas Scott Montagu – whose home is Palace House at Beaulieu – inherited the title of Lord Montagu from his father, John. His coat of arms (right) includes the three parts of his surname (below), each representing the family's history. The Scott connection links the family to a distant kinsman, Sir Walter Scott. You can trace your own family's history through reference books available in local or national libraries.

Douglas

Scott

Montagu

Family affair *The present Lord Montagu inherited his father's passion for motoring, founding the National Motor Museum at Beaulieu in 1952. He is seen below with his family.*

How to read old handwriting

Don't be put off by old-fashioned writing on original records and old letters. You can decode it, and doing so will be immensely satisfying.

At first glance, the handwriting you'll find in early documents – from parish records to personal letters – can look illegible. But the websites shown below can help you to decipher them. If you're looking at documents dating from before the mid 18th century, they may be written in Latin. Photocopy difficult documents so that you can take them home to work on them, bearing these points in mind:

- Start building up an alphabet of letters from words you can read and use these to decipher more difficult words.
- Some letters were written differently, such as 's', which was written as 'f' or 'ss' which appeared as 'fs'. The letters 'I' and 'J' were regarded as different forms of the same letter. 'U' and 'V' were treated similarly.
- Capitals and punctuation were arbitrary, and apostrophes were used to show where a letter had been missed out.
- Numbers were often written in Roman numerals, in capitals or lower case – I, i or j = 1; V or v = 5; X or x =10; L or l = 50; C or c = 100; D or d = 500; and M or m = 1000.

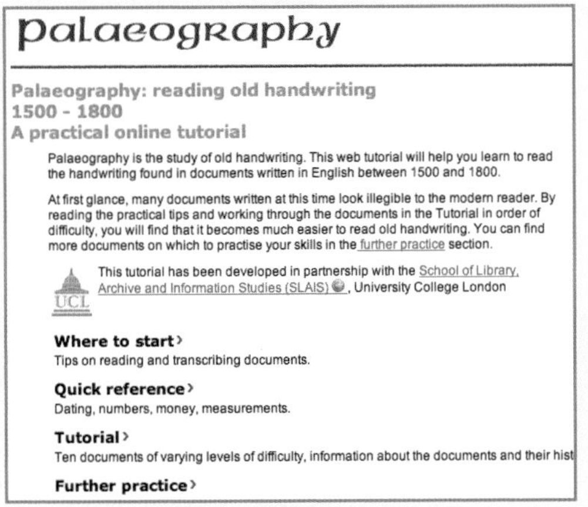

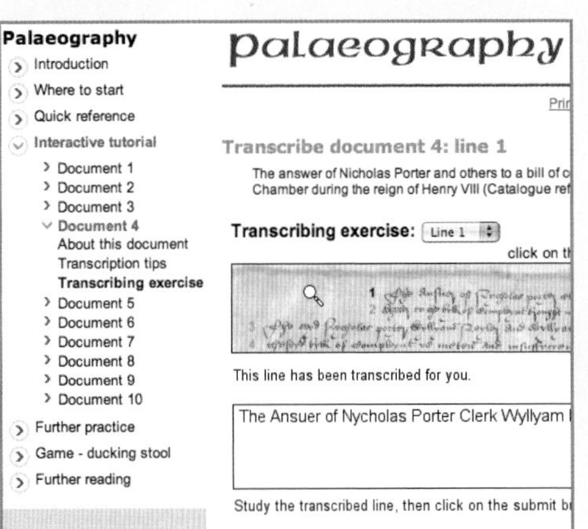

Sample I

Transcription with silent extensions

Received of Mr John Savadge for a pencion
going out of the South parte of the Church
there due to the Kinges ma[jes]tie for the yeare ~
ended at the feast of St Michaell the Arch
Angell last past the somme of Twoe shillinges

Take an online handwriting tutorial

1 Go to **nationalarchives.gov.uk/palaeography/**. There is a choice of links. **Where to start** tells how letters were once used and common words abbreviated. **Quick reference** explains the Julian and Gregorian calendars (see opposite), tells you how to read Roman numerals, explains the old monetary system and gives a list of historic counties with abbreviations. Once you've read these sections, click **Interactive tutorial**.

Learn and practise

2 The interactive tutorial provides ten exercises to work through. To access the text illustrated, click **Document 4**, which takes you to information about the document and some vital transcription tips. When you're ready to have a go, click **Interactive transcribing exercise**. This manuscript has 13 lines. A magnifying glass tool allows you to zoom in and move left or right, and you can fill in your transcription in the box beneath.

Learn more about early documents

The University of Leicester has developed a handwriting website at **paleo.anglo-norman.org**. From the homepage click on the Edward I silver penny for medieval palaeography, the Henry VIII half groat for early modern palaeography. In both time-frames, you'll find sample documents and tutorials. To view the text shown here, click **Sample text 1** from the left-hand column.

Dating documents using the Julian calendar

We now use the Gregorian calendar, but when you're reading dates in early documents, remember that until 1752 Britain used what was known as the Julian calendar. With this calendar, each new year began on March 25 – Lady Day.

So instead of being the tenth month of the year, October was regarded as the eighth month – and was often written in a combination of Roman numerals and letters to give 'VIIIber'; likewise, December was written 'Xber'.

Adjusting the dates you find

If you're looking at a document from 1728, for example, you'll need to bear in mind that with the Julian calendar, December 31, 1728 was followed by January 1, 1728. The last day of the year fell on March 24, and the new year, 1729, began on March 25. To make things even more complicated, the Scots changed to the Gregorian calendar as early as 1600. And in some indexes, transcribers have already adjusted the dates.

Double dating

If you're studying transcripts of documents and events drawn up before 1752, you may find that dates between January 1 and March 24 have been written covering two years – 'February 15, 1728-9', for example. This means that the date was originally February 15, 1728, according to the old Julian calendar, but would be February 15, 1729, by the Gregorian calendar, which was adopted in 1752.

English Handwriting 1500-1700

an online course

Course Lessons

The slate of course lessons offered below has been carefully structured around a selection of resources. Each lesson includes a central manuscript, for which the student is invited to supply a semi-diplomatic transcription in a workspace provided within the course. Alphabets of minuscule and majuscule letter-forms and of brevigraphs and other abbreviations are available, as are a zooming function. Students may also consult supplementary information on dating and describing the hand(s) of the manuscript. Each lesson concludes with a short test, usually of about ten questions, that examines students' abilities to transcribe short selections from the manuscript, afterwards supplying the 'correct' answer along with commentary and suggestions for further consideration. Students may at any time consult an exemplary transcription of each course manuscript, and are especially urged to do so once the lesson is otherwise complete; a PDF version of this file may be downloaded (and printed) to take away as a model. A student who has experienced particular trouble with a given lesson, or who would like further practice of a similar kind, may like to pursue the 'follow-up' suggestions available in the toolbar in the bottom frame.

The efficacy of these course lessons depends on the application and resourcefulness of the student. Suggestions for good use of the materials, and help (both palaeographical and technical) is available at all times; simply click on the question-mark icon at the bottom right of the lesson.

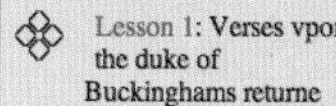

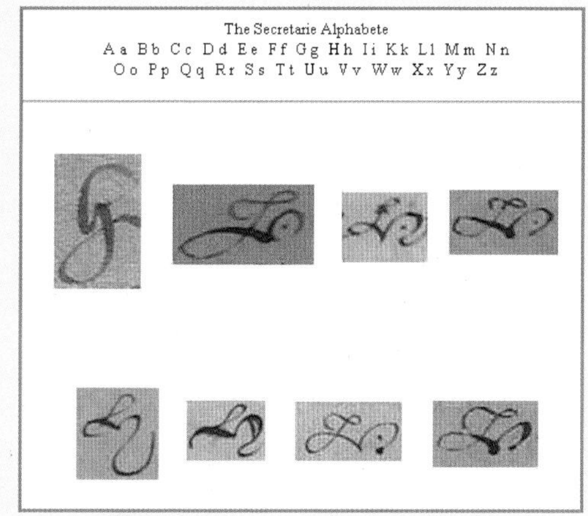

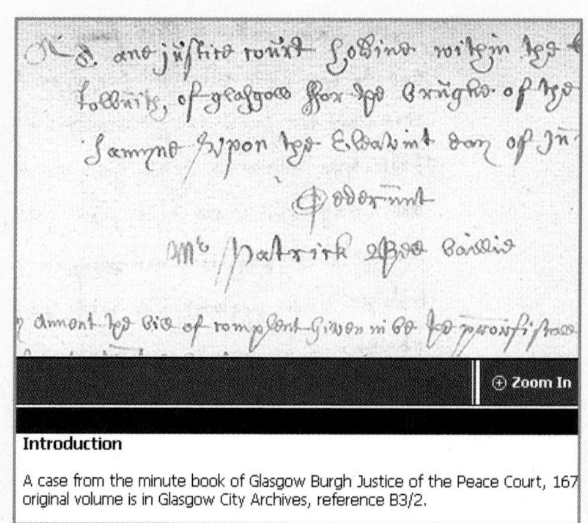

Focus on 1500 to 1700

1 If you fancy an academic challenge, try the online tutorial of 28 lessons that Cambridge University has put together. It concentrates on handwriting from 1500 to 1700. Go to the homepage at **english.cam.ac.uk/ceres/ehoc**. From there, click **Historical introduction** to learn about inks, pens and dating manuscripts, or **Course lessons** to begin the tutorial. The interactive lessons have difficulty ratings of 1 to 5 and can be 'marked' at the end.

Recognise historic alphabets

2 From the Cambridge University site's homepage click **Alphabets**. The modern alphabet is displayed here, and by clicking on any letter, a window will appear showing how the letters used to be written centuries ago. Click the capital **H** to see the images shown here.

Deciphering Scottish handwriting

Scottish documents dating from 1500 to1750 are interpreted in an online tutorial at **scottishhandwriting.com**, a website created by the Scottish Archives Network (SCAN). From the homepage click **Tutorials** and then work your way through the excellent **1 hour basic tutorial**. When you feel more confident, you can test your knowledge on some 17th-century Scottish court records by clicking on **Glasgow Burgh Court**. Click on **Case 4** to see the manuscript shown here.

27

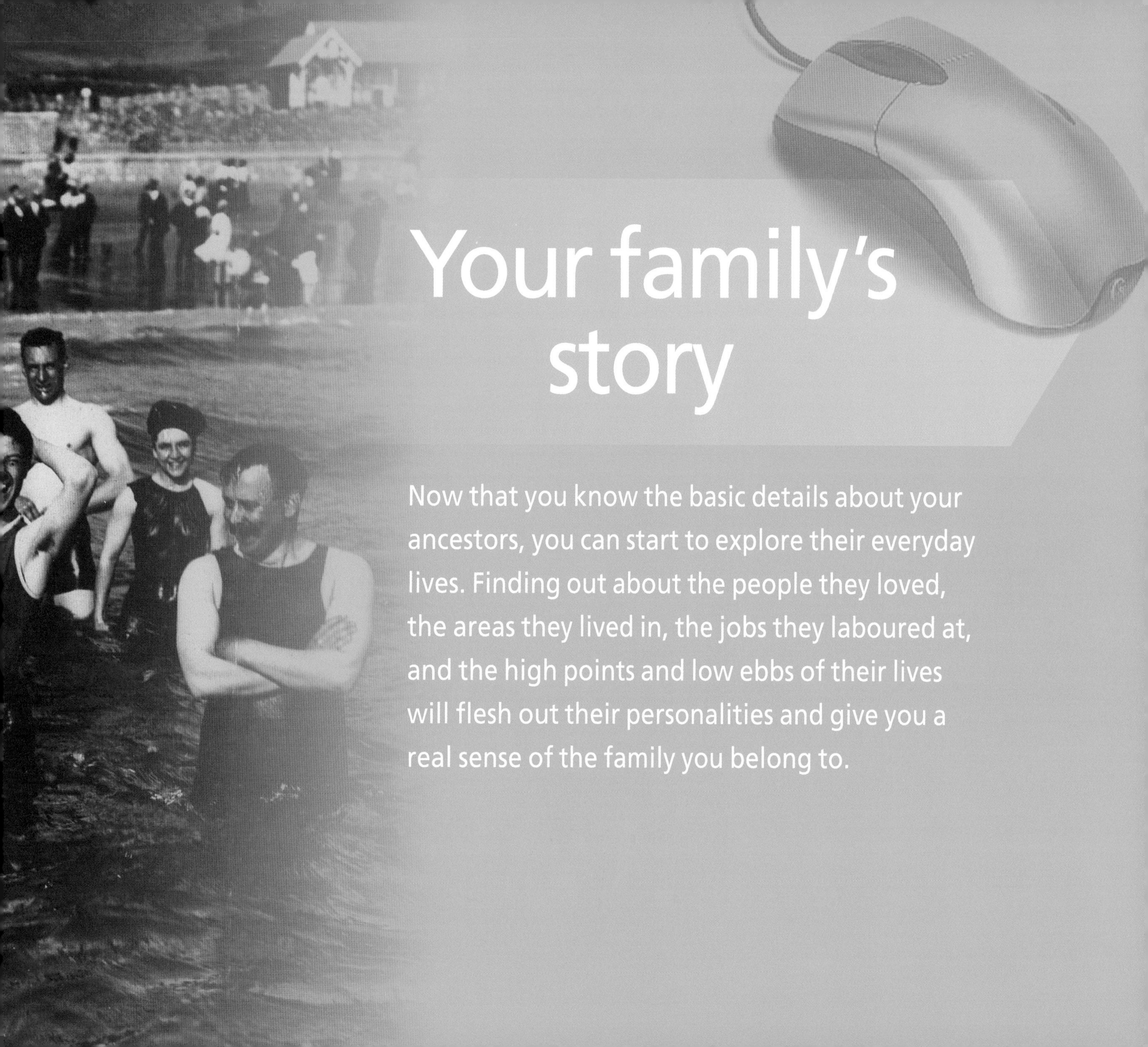

Your family's story

Now that you know the basic details about your ancestors, you can start to explore their everyday lives. Finding out about the people they loved, the areas they lived in, the jobs they laboured at, and the high points and low ebbs of their lives will flesh out their personalities and give you a real sense of the family you belong to.

Real people, not just names

Once you begin to discover more about the lives of your ancestors, they become real people who worked, played and loved, lost and grieved. Only then do the names in your family tree become flesh-and-blood characters.

Finding out more of the daily lives of your ancestors isn't difficult, and you'll find a great deal of help online and in local libraries and archives. You can discover what sort of homes those ancestors lived in, what jobs they did and what was going on in their wider communities. Who was on the throne in their lifetime, and which party was in government? Were they affected by national issues, such as strikes, depressions and even wars?

Where they lived

There are different ways to find out where your ancestors lived, depending on when they were alive. Online censuses from 1841 to 1901 can help, and for 20th-century relatives, you can use civil registration documents (see pages 72-77) and electoral rolls (see page 294).

Until the 20th century, few people owned their homes, most renting in some way or another. In rural areas, people rented houses from wealthy landowners or lords of the manor. Estate and manorial court records were often deposited in a local library or archive. They can tell you about the transfer of property, the names of occupiers and how much rent they paid. You might also find title deeds, estate maps and surveys.

People also rented from landlords in towns and cities – many wealthy families would leave their country homes to rent in London 'for the season'. You may be able to track down tenancy agreements in local archives. Street and trade directories (see page 230) were widely published from the 19th century onwards. Similar to modern phone books, the early directories listed people by trade, and later ones covered neighbourhoods on a street-by-street basis. Some of these are available online; others can be viewed at national and local libraries and archives.

The National Archives (TNA) holds a collection of nationwide street and trade directories in its library at Kew. You could also visit libraries and archives in the areas where your ancestors lived. Or go online to **historicaldirectories.org** for details of English and Welsh directories from 1750 to 1919.

What they did for a living

Where you begin your search for an ancestor's work history depends on what he did. Was he in the Navy or the Army,

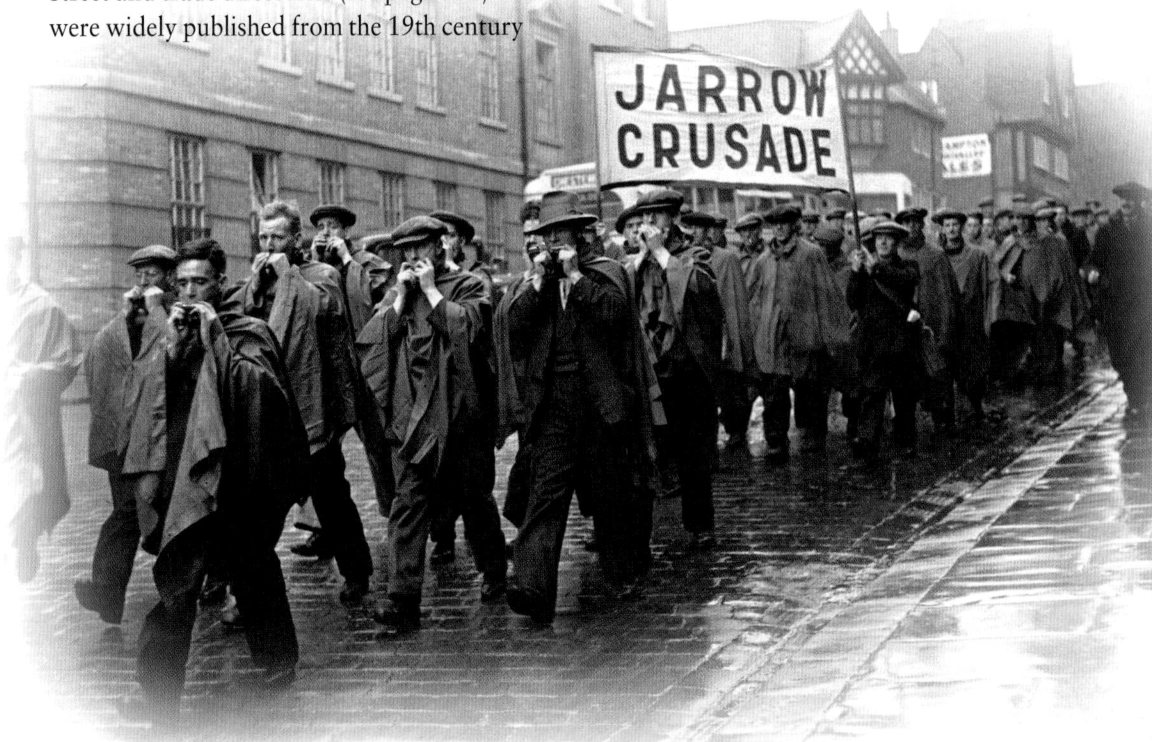

On the march *Playing their harmonicas, 200 unemployed shipbuilders marched from Jarrow, near Newcastle-upon-Tyne, to London, in 1936. Their protest was sparked off by the closing of Palmer's shipyard, after years of worsening industrial conditions. You can find out more about the whole story when you enter 'Jarrow March' in* **bbc.co.uk***'s search engine.*

Ancestors in uniform *Men of the Merchant Navy pose formally for a group photo. You can search records at The National Archives for details of your ancestor's service career, the ships he sailed in, as well as when and under what circumstances he left the service.*

Rich discoveries in local libraries

Most local libraries have local studies collections, where you'll find written histories of towns and many villages, with maps of the area, past and present. These give useful clues about the homes of your ancestors, and you may be able to look at historic local postcards and photographs, and copies of old local newspapers.

For example, the Local Studies collection at Leicester library includes:

- information about Leicestershire and Rutland towns and villages
- individual village and town histories arranged in alphabetical order by place name
- a selection of street directories, giving the names of householders and tradesmen in Leicester and Leicestershire in the 19th and 20th centuries.

a tradesman or a master craftsman with apprentices, an agricultural labourer or a doctor? Most military service records are stored at TNA (see page 196). If your ancestor served in the forces, try to find out what his rank was. Army and naval officers were, by and large, educated and wealthy. 'Other ranks' generally came from poorer backgrounds. If they're not in the digitised records at **nationalarchives.gov.uk**, you can view them at TNA, in person.

If your ancestor was in the Metropolitan Police or the Merchant Navy, an employee of HM Customs and Excise or worked for one of the railway companies, his records are probably stored at TNA.

From the 14th century, apprenticeship schemes (see page 186) were common. The Origins site has the largest online collection of apprentice records, and TNA has 18th-century records, though not as yet online.

Other professions are recorded in more specialised places. For example, the Wellcome Library (see page 182) holds records for doctors and surgeons; and records for the Anglican clergy are held at the Lambeth Palace Library at **lambethpalacelibrary.org**.

Did they emigrate?

You may find a branch of your family moved abroad – sometimes, but not always, through choice. The reasons for their departure tell you something about their circumstances. People tended to emigrate voluntarily because they were poor and felt they stood a better chance of success in North America, South Africa, Australia or New Zealand. Or they might have followed their adventurous spirit and indulged a desire to see the world.

Transportation, the other extreme, was the 'humane' alternative to the death penalty for many convicted criminals (see page 254).

Wherever your ancestors ended up, you'll find records to help your research. There are online indexes to a range of Australian archives covering both voluntary immigrants and people who arrived on prison ships.

If you want to find out what 'crime' your ancestor committed, local record offices and TNA hold criminal records and details of transportation. It's believed that 3 per cent of Britons have ancestors who were transported, many for such misdemeanours as fishing in a private river, or setting fire to undergrowth.

Anyone leaving the UK was recorded on ships' passenger lists (see page 255) – now stored in archives in the UK, Canada and Australia. Some are available online and searchable by name at **findmypast.com**; others can be viewed at TNA.

How they lived

Through talent and hard work, our ancestors turned Britain into a world power. Fortunately, many of them left copious records of their lives and achievements.

What did your ancestors do for a living?

Over the centuries people have earned their livings in many ways, some of which might seem strange today. By discovering your ancestors' occupations, you'll get a clear idea of their social class and probable standard of living.

Before the Industrial Revolution, beginning in the late 18th century, most people worked on the land, whether as land-owning farmers, tenant farmers or agricultural labourers. Their occupations might be recorded in tenancy agreements, census returns and sometimes on their gravestones. If you come across a job you've never heard of, you may find it explained online – try **genuki.org.uk** or go to **rmhh.co.uk/occup/a.html**.

Palisters, todmen and telynors

Some job titles are more obvious than others. Most people know what a smith or a collier did for a living, but fewer will recognise a palister as a park keeper, or a wainwright as a wagon-maker. Your Scottish ancestors might have even odder sounding occupations – a chowder sold fish, a fethelar was a fiddle player, a hetheleder gathered and sold heather for fuel, and the todman was responsible for keeping down the tod (Scottish for fox) population on the laird's estate. In Wales, your ancestor might have been described as a bugail (shepherd), crydd (shoemaker), telynor (harpist) or ysgolfeistr (schoolmaster).

Factory life *Vast numbers of people worked in factories such as the Singer sewing machine works in Glasgow (left), where their employment history would have been scrupulously recorded.*

Companies and industry

From the mid 19th century, factories sprang up all over Britain. The irresistible lure of employment triggered a mass migration from the countryside to the towns. Factories offered work for both the skilled and unskilled.

The Singer Manufacturing Company, for example, began making sewing machines in Glasgow in 1867. It soon grew out of its premises and, by 1883, had built the biggest sewing machine factory in the world – with a distinctive clock tower – at Kilbowie on Clydebank, which provided work for 12,000 men and women by the early 1900s. Then, during both the First and Second World Wars the factory produced munitions for the armed forces alongside the sewing machines.

Industries such as this generated a wealth of employment records and many of the documents survive. The National Register of Archives (see page 168) lists the location of records for around 25,000 companies. Access the index at **nationalarchives.gov.uk**.

Working for the government

If your ancestors were government employees – whether in the civil service or the armed forces – it's likely that their employment records are held at The National Archives (TNA), the UK government's official archive. They may even be available online, among TNA's centuries of records from parchment scrolls to digital files and websites. If your ancestors worked in one of the British colonies or for one of the many railway companies that sprang up across Britain in the 19th and 20th centuries, TNA could hold their employment records, too.

Work in town, live in the country

From the mid 19th century the burgeoning railway network enabled people to commute to work in the cities, while continuing to live in the country. In particular, from 1863 the construction of the London Underground network saw the city's suburbs spread rapidly outwards from the commercial centres. So people's work and home life became more separated, making it harder to work out your ancestors' social standing from their homes and the type and place of their employment.

Early commuter chaos *Workers bound for the City crowd Baker Street station, which opened in 1863 on London's first underground line.*

Occupational directories

Over the centuries, many jobs, trades and professions have kept records of the people who worked in them. If you know the occupations of your ancestors, these records can give you an intriguing insight into their lives.

In this section, you'll find out more about where to search for the records of working people, including the clergy, the medical profession, apprentices, industrial workers and rural labour. They'll give you valuable information about what your ancestors did.

Many professional and occupational bodies have excellent records. You can search websites such as **findmypast.com** for some of them (see opposite), but most are available only in local libraries or archives (see below).

Clerical records

Members of the clergy are ordained and allocated to a parish by a bishop, and these appointments are recorded in the bishops' registers. If the ancestor you're looking for was a member of the Anglican clergy, it's likely he was listed in *Crockford's Clerical Directory*. Crockford's was first published in 1858, and is an annual publication that gives biographical details of all members of the clergy, as well as a list of the Anglican parishes throughout the British Isles. For a fee, you can search the website, **crockford.org.uk**, although online records go back only to 1968. To find someone registered before 1968, you'll have to view the original directories, which are available in most local libraries.

Another useful clerical website is **theclergydatabase.org.uk**. Although it's not yet complete, this site intends to list all members of the Anglican clergy from 1540

JOHN McCOLL (Small: II, 528), born 30th Sept. 1863 at Glasgow, son of Hugh M. and Janet Roberton; educ. at Glasgow Pollokshields P.S., High School, Univ. of Glasgow, M.A. (1882), U.P. College, Edinburgh; student missionary, Edinburgh John Ker Memorial 1884-5; licen. by U.P. Presb. of Glasgow South 1885; ord. and ind. Paisley Lylesland U.P. 20th Dec. 1886; trans. to Queenstown Presb. Church, South Africa,
1920

Man of the cloth *Scotland has its own directories, or 'fastis', of clergy and congregations. John McColl (top) appears in* The Fasti of the United Free Church of Scotland: 1900-29. *His entry (above) charts his progress from a childhood in Glasgow to a posting to South Africa in 1910.*

Offline directories

Many occupational directories aren't available online but are accessible in institutions throughout the UK. The addresses for many of them are in the Directory.

Local record offices and archives Local trade directories listing individuals by profession are held, probably in paper form.

Ham's Yearbooks If your ancestor was in either HM Customs or Excise in the late 19th and early 20th centuries, try consulting the yearbooks for these professions. It's possible to trace the career of your ancestor using these sources at The National Archives (TNA).

The Business Archives Council This organisation aims 'to promote the preservation of business records of historical importance', including records for shipbuilding and brewing. Its library can be used by the public, but an appointment is necessary.

Medical profession Records and directories for medical practitioners may be held at local libraries. Alternatively, the Wellcome Library holds an extensive collection of sources. The library is open to the public and has compiled a detailed guide to its sources that you can download from its website **library.wellcome.ac.uk** to study before you decide to make a visit.

The Law List There are various directories for people who were members of the legal profession. The Law List has been published annually since 1798, and gives details of lawyers in England and Wales. It's usually available in larger reference libraries.

to 1835. Its free-to-use website allows you to search for individuals, locations and bishops, using well-designed drop-down menus, in addition to an A to Z list.

Medical records

The medical profession was divided into three specialist areas until the 19th century: apothecaries, physicians and surgeons. Right up to the late 18th century, they were all regulated by the Church and licensed by its bishops. The issue of each licence was recorded in bishops' registers and held in county record offices. From 1550 to 1875, the details were also held by the Archbishop of Canterbury. Strangely, apothecaries belonged to the Grocers' Company in the Middle Ages, but formed their own society in 1617. Their records are held in the Guildhall Library in London (see Directory).

Midwives also had to be licensed by their bishops and, from 1825 to 1965, their names were published annually by the Royal College of Surgeons.

The *Medical Register*, which lists qualified medical practitioners, was first published in 1859 by the General Medical Council, and *The Roll of the Royal College of Physicians of London, 1518-1825*, was compiled in 1878. The *Medical Directory for Ireland* was first published in 1852. Registration of dentists didn't begin until 1878 – from which time they're listed in the *Dentists' Register*. The British Medical Association Library and the Wellcome Library hold many of the archived records (see Directory).

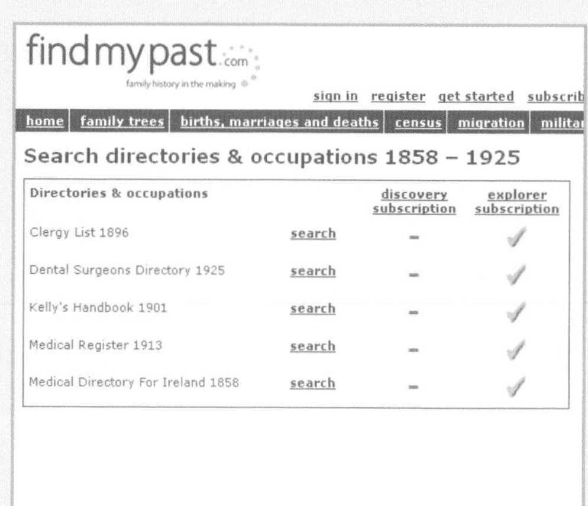

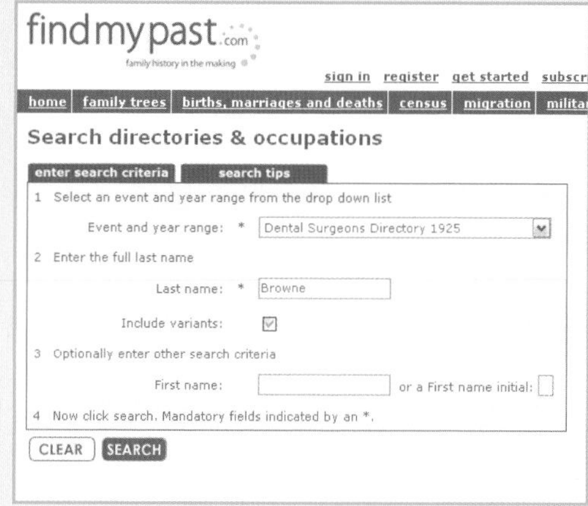

(*Birm.*); Hon. Dent. Surg. St. Edward's Home, Huntingdon & Hunts. Co. Hosp.; Dent. Surg. Hunts. Bd. of Guard.
BROWN, William, Box 30, Mafeking, Cape Province, S. Africa—L.D.S. R.C.S. Ed. 1908; (*Ed.*).
BROWNE, Arthur Leslie, "Heswall," Wentworth Rd., Harborne, Birmingham—L.D.S. Birm. 1922.
BROWNE, David, 107, Avenue Louis Lepoutre, Brussels—L.D.S. Ed. 1885.
BROWNE, David John, Shannon House, Athlone, co. Westmeath—L.D.S. R.C.S.I. 1918; (*Ed. & Dub.*).
BROWNE, Ellis Gardner, 99, Mutual Bldgs., Port Elizabeth, S. Africa—L.D.S. R.C.S. Eng. 1919.
BROWNE, Hy. Montague, Crescent Chambers, Darlaston, Staffs. (*Tel.* Darlaston 62)—L.D.S. R.C.S. Eng. 1914; (*Univ. & Dent. Hosp. Birm.*); late Ho. Surg. Birm. Dent. Hosp.; Dentist W. Riding Co. Counc.
BROWNE, Herbert, 61, Masons Hill,

Select a directory

1 The **findmypast.com** website has a number of searchable occupational directories. To search the site you need to buy credits (see page 52), although use of the index is free. Here's how to search for an ancestor, David Browne, who was a dentist somewhere in the British Isles in the 1920s. Click on **Occupations** at the top right of the homepage, then choose a directory, here **Dental surgeons directory 1925**, and click on **Search**.

Enter the details you know

2 The **Event and year range** will be entered for you, from the previous step. Now enter 'Browne' in the **Last name** box. As Browne can be spelled in more than one way, click on **Include variants**. Now click on the blue **Search** button.

See the entry in the directory

3 In this case, there are two David Brownes. Click on **View** and you'll be offered the chance to see the actual entry in the directory. You'll find that by 1925 your David Browne was living and working in Athlone, county Meath, having qualified in 1918. His address is given as Shannon House, which will help you to find him in a local directory.

The Guildhall – a home to masters of their trades

In the 1420s, London's most famous Lord Mayor, Dick Whittington, set out in his will the foundations of the city's Guildhall. Rooted in the Anglo-Saxon word 'geld', meaning payment, the Guildhall was the place where citizens would come to register their trades when they formed trade associations or 'guilds'. Look in its library for your London ancestors.

The members of merchant guilds, together with the Lord Mayor, effectively ran the City of London and controlled commerce. Each guild had its own hall and coat of arms, but in overall control was the Guildhall, in the heart of the City, where representatives of the guilds met.

The present Guildhall, dating from 1411, now plays a more ceremonial role, used for state and civic banquets, as well as for meetings of the City of London's elected assembly. Its library has many archives that are a great source of information for the family historian. So if you have a craftsman, merchant or trader in your family tree, the Guildhall may have relevant records, and at the least should be able to offer an insight into how they lived and worked.

The importance of guild membership

The earliest guilds were established in the 12th century, in London and other cities such as Bristol and York. Young men entering the trades were given apprenticeships, regulated by local town guilds of merchants and artisans. Once an apprentice became a master of his trade and so a guildsman, he gained certain privileges, such as the right to vote. He could also leave his master and was free to work wherever he wanted, all over the country. Much like the trade unions of today, the guilds looked after the welfare of their members and families. But the great power of the guilds meant that if a tradesman was expelled from his guild, it was almost impossible for him to earn a living elsewhere.

All trades *The earliest reference to a guildhall in London dates from 1128. The hall has long been the centre of trade life for many London livery companies such as the Gardeners (see inset).*

London's ancient guilds

The earliest London guilds, such as the Weavers and the Drapers, are, unsurprisingly, related to ancient crafts or trades. The number of guilds grew as trades such as butchers and goldsmiths became more organised. The Ancient Guild of Apothecaries, for instance, was founded in 1617 but dates back to 1180, when it was linked with the Guild of Pepperers and, from 1316, with the Guild of Spicers, who joined in 1316. The word 'apothecary' comes from the Latin *apotheca* – meaning a storehouse, often for wines, spices and herbs. By the 16th century, the guild was more concerned with medical supplies, rather like the pharmacy of today, and also offered general medical advice and services such as minor surgery.

The Guildhall Library has extensive records relating to the Apothecaries and many other London guilds. It holds, for example, the library and all historic records of the Clockmakers' Company, founded in 1631, including details of 18th and 19th-century apprenticeships.

The special identity of the companies

Each London guild adopted a distinctive style of dress – or livery – to set one apart from the other, and so became known as livery companies. By the early 19th century there were more than 70 companies, each with its own patron saint. St Dunstan, for instance, was adopted by jewellers, locksmiths and armourers, St Boniface protected brewers and tailors, and St Matthew took care of tax-collectors and bankers.

Many of the old livery halls were either destroyed or badly damaged in the Blitz, although some survive, such as the Apothecaries Hall and the Coopers Hall, both dating from the 17th century. Street names in the City echo the early guilds – Milk Street, Bread Street, Ironmonger Lane, Cloth Fair and Mason's Avenue among them.

Today the City of London has more than 100 livery companies, which include more modern professions such as Environmental Cleaners and Management Consultants; their titles are usually prefaced by the phrase 'The Worshipful Company of...'. Changes in the scale of industry and commercial activity mean that they no longer wield the same political or financial power as they once did, but the companies still work to support and champion their trades, as well as raising money for worthy causes.

Finest livery *Each year, at the Lord Mayor's Show, guild members parade through the City of London streets dressed in their livery costumes.*

Using the Guildhall Library

You'll find many original documents relating to London in the Guildhall Library, ranging from parish registers to records of breweries and football clubs. But its collections aren't just restricted to the capital: it holds many journals from local history societies, as well as county, town and village histories, making it valuable for any family historian. You need to register as a reader to see the library's collections, but they're free to use (see Directory for address). The details of opening times and how to register, as well as information on guided tours, are all on the website at **cityoflondon.gov.uk**. Although you can't view documents on the site, you can discover what they hold, and the reference numbers you'll need to locate documents when you visit. Go to the homepage, click on **a-z** in the top bar, select **G** and then scroll down to click on **Guildhall Library.**

Records of apprenticeships

From the 14th century onwards, apprenticeship was an essential stage in a number of trades and crafts, and copious records were kept. So if your ancestor was apprenticed in his youth, you'll be able to find out what he did.

Apprenticeship was a valuable experience for any young man – and some girls – and so had to be paid for, usually by the parents. The young people would be legally bound, for a period of about seven years, to a master from whom they would learn a trade. In 1563, this system was made official by the Statute of Artificers and Apprentices, which stipulated that no one could practise a trade without having first served as an apprentice.

Where to find apprentice records

The National Archives (TNA) has a central register of apprentices, going back as far as 1710. Many apprenticeship records are held in local and county record offices and aren't online yet, so it's a good idea to check what's held in your local archive. The British Origins section of **origins.net** holds a large number of apprentice records, and has two databases.

LONDON APPRENTICESHIP ABSTRACTS This covers 1442 to 1850 and includes the records of the Livery Companies of London. They give the name of the apprentice's father and state the parish of his residence.

APPRENTICES OF GREAT BRITAIN This database covers the years 1710 to 1774. It has been compiled from the Inland Revenue tax records now held at TNA. It provides similar information to what you'll find in the London Apprenticeship Abstracts database, but covers the whole of Great Britain. You'll also be able to see digitised images of the originals.

Unusual professions

Many old professions and occupations have disappeared or changed almost beyond recognition. Coopers (makers of barrels), frobishers (restorers of armour) and mercers (cloth merchants) are just some of the less familiar. If you come across an obscure occupation, a book you'll find helpful is *A Dictionary of Old Trades, Titles and Occupations* by C. Waters, Countryside Books, 1999. Or visit **olivetreegenealogy.com/misc/occupations.shtml** and search their list of **Obsolete occupations**.

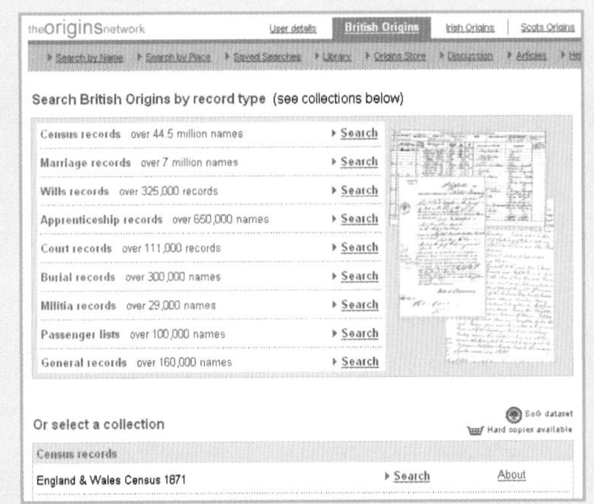

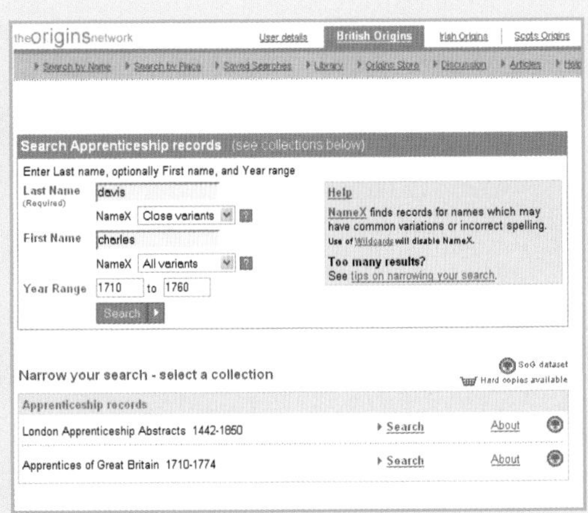

Search the apprenticeship records

1 Here's how you'd search for Charles Davis, who was apprenticed between 1700 and 1760. Go to **origins.net** and click on **British origins**. Then click on the **Search** link alongside **Apprenticeship records**. You'll be asked to sign in (see page 55) or log in.

Enter the details you know

2 On the main search page, enter 'Davis' in the **Last name** box and 'Charles' in the **First name** box. As it's a fairly common name, it's best to add the date range, 1710 to 1760. Click on the blue **Search** button.

Irish and Scottish apprenticeships

The completion of an apprenticeship in Ireland qualified you as a freeman. Many such craftsmen and tradesmen are named in the list of free citizens of Dublin from 1225 to 1918, which is held in the Dublin City Archives (see Directory).

Serving out an apprenticeship in Scotland qualified a man to become a burgess in certain chartered cities, giving him voting rights. Records are kept in the National Archives of Scotland (in Burgh records, ref B).

Trainee cobbler *An apprenticeship was a chance to learn a trade with a master. The records show that young people would travel quite a distance to take up an apprenticeship.*

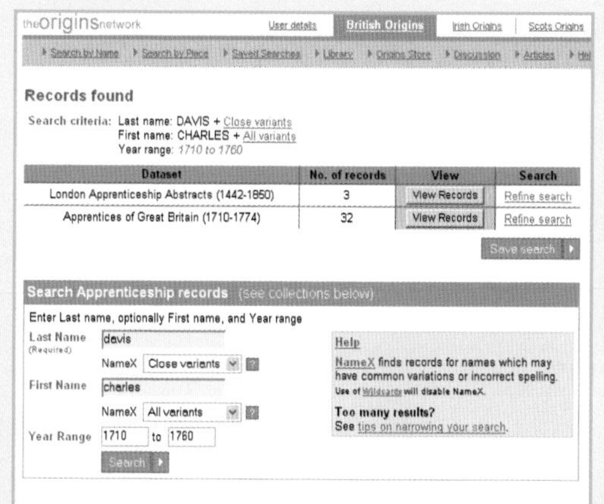

Choose the database

3 The search results are shown by database type. If you think Charles may have been in London, click on the first grey **View records** button to see what has been found.

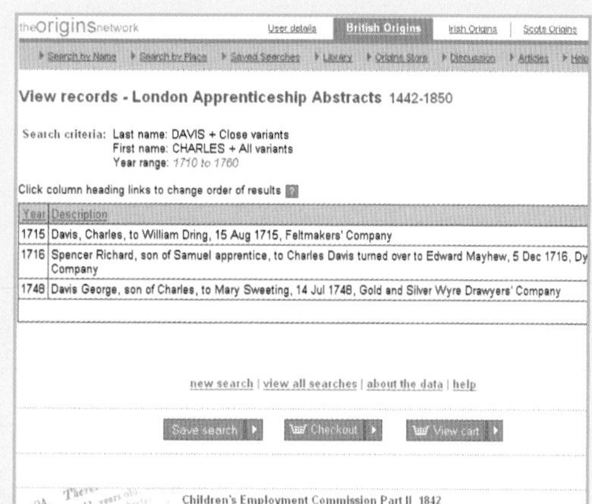

View the records

4 The records for the London Apprenticeship Abstracts are shown and the top one on the list looks most likely. Charles Davis was apprenticed to a feltmaker on August 15, 1715. To see an image of the entry, click on **Checkout**.

anes	Top Last Name	Top First Name	Bottom Last Name	Bottom First Name	Image
1	DAKING	ANN	DAYKINS	THOS	Image
1	DALLIMAN	PET	DULMARE	JACOB	Image
1	DARRAC	JOHN	DERBIE	JAS	Image
1	DAVIES	BEN	DAVIS	DAN	Image
1	DAVIES	DAVID	DAVIS	EDW	Image
1	DAVIS	EDW	DAVIS	EDW	Image
1	DAVIES	EVAN	DAVIS	GEO	Image
1	DAVIS	GEO	DAVY	HEN	Image
1	DAVID	ISA	DAVYS	JAS	Image
1	DAVIS	JAMES	DAVIS	JN	Image
1	DAVIS	JOHN	DAVIS	JN	Image
1	DAVIS	JOHN	DAVIS	JN	Image
1	DAVIS	JOHN	DAVIS	JN	Image
1	DAVEY	JOHN	DAVY	JN	Image
1	DAVID	JOHN	DAVIS	JN	Image
1	DAVIS	JOHN	DAVY	JOS	Image
1	DAVIS	MARY	DAVIS	REBECCA	Image

View Apprentices of Great Britain

5 If you view the records for Apprentices of Great Britain (above), you'll see a page with a list of name ranges that may or may not include the name you want. The range you want for Davis is on the third row down. Click on the **Image** button to the right of the name range to view the actual page, which is a photograph of the record.

Industrial trades and skills

The Industrial Revolution at the beginning of the 19th century completely changed British people's lives and aspirations. Your ancestors may have left their rural homes to work in the new trades that sprang up in towns and cities.

The rise of factory labour meant that more people than ever entered the work force. Records of their employment give rise to information that will prove invaluable to you now. There are some excellent websites with mailing lists that you can visit for information about specific occupations. If you know what your ancestor's job was, one of these occupational websites can give you an insight into how they lived.

The textile industry

If you think your ancestor was a textile worker, **spinningtheweb.org.uk** is a good place to look. Dedicated to the large textile industry of northern England, Spinning the Web gives a thorough history of the cotton manufacture in Lancashire and is divided into different sections, each with a tab at the top of the homepage.

- **Overview** outlines the rise and decline of the industry, divided into chronological periods, from 1760 to the present day.
- **People** analyses the living and working conditions of the many thousands of people employed by the industry, including the use of child labour.
- **Places** describes the environmental and cultural impact of the textile industry.
- **Industry** explains the technical innovation that powered the industry.
- **Clothing & products** shows the industry's products, including clothes and furnishings.
- **Interactives** tells stories related to the cotton industry.

Coalmining

The website of the National Coalmining Museum for England, **ncm.org.uk**, is dedicated to an industry that was one of the country's largest employers in the 19th and 20th centuries. It offers a virtual tour of its museum and provides access to its library catalogue. This fascinating collection includes documents that relate to the history of coalmining, but not the employment records for the miners. Where these survive, they've been deposited with local archives.

Other trades

When researching the kind of work your ancestor may have done, it's useful to visit the following collections. See the Directory for their addresses, or visit their websites.

The People's History Museum

The origins of this museum lie in the Trade Union, Labour and Co-operative Society. It focuses on preserving the history of ordinary working people of Britain and is located in Manchester on two sites. To see its website go to **phm.org.uk**.

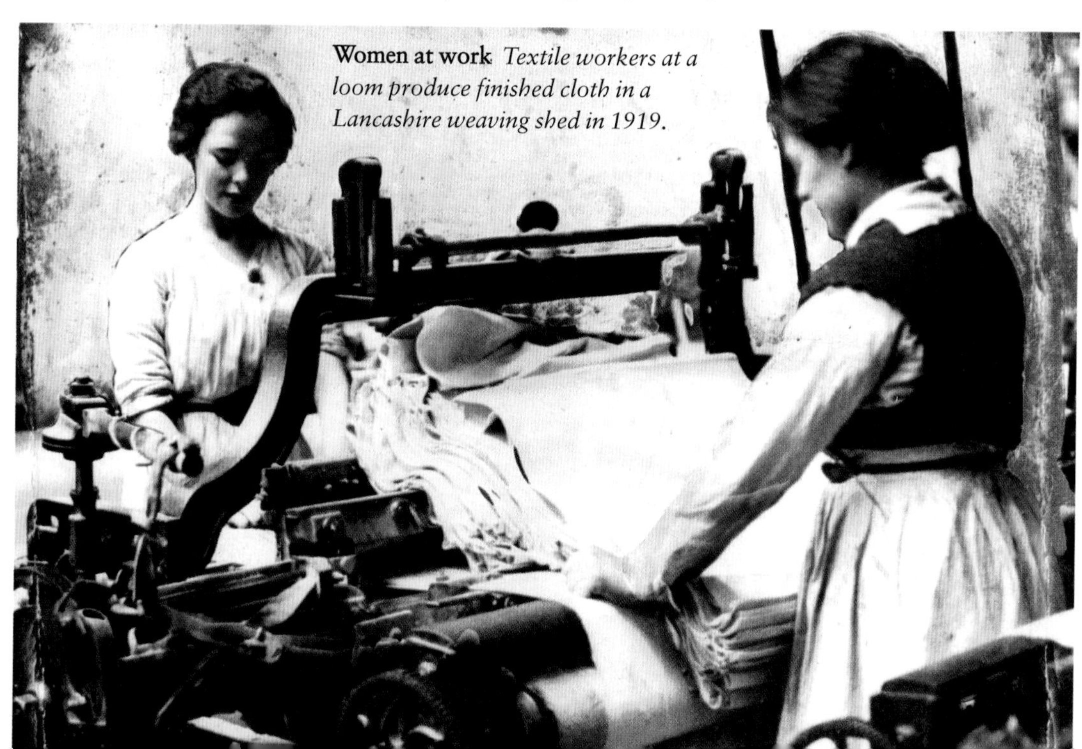

Women at work *Textile workers at a loom produce finished cloth in a Lancashire weaving shed in 1919.*

The modern records centre

The University Library of Warwick hosts **modernrecords.warwick.ac.uk**, a free-to-use collection of social, economic and political history archives, mainly from the mid 19th century onwards. For the family historian who's keen to get into the detail of their ancestor's working lives, these records should prove a rich hunting ground. They include:

- Records of trade unions, which include the archives for the Trade Union Congress (TUC) and similar institutions.
- Records of trade associations, which include archives of the Confederation of British Industry (CBI), employer organisations and related bodies.

THE JOHN RYLAND'S LIBRARY Located in the University of Manchester, the collection holds more than 4 million printed books and manuscripts. The library has a comprehensive selection of material covering economic and industrial history. This includes archives of the coal industry, the pharmaceutical industry, large mill producers and trade unions, as well as a wide range of other industries.

The website is at **library.manchester.ac.uk**. Go to the homepage and click on **Subject** and then **Subject information** on the left. This takes you to an A to Z list of subjects, from which you can choose the trade or profession that you wish to research. In addition, you can choose to search by category and select from engineering, the humanities, life sciences, and medical and human sciences.

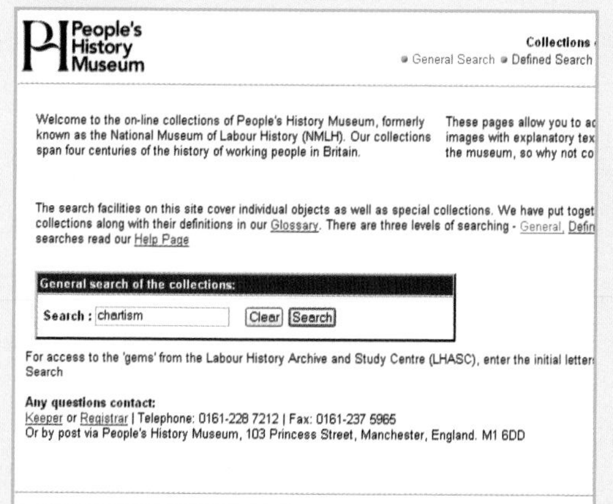

New Search | Contact sheet

Image	Catalogue Number	Object Name
	LHASC : Vin/1/1/1 Minikin/Vincent	letter
	Collection Record: photographs NMLH.2000.10; plus other items: not catalogued	Sample of some of the items in the Communist Part Great Britain Picture Collection: photograph; print, political; certificate; souvenir serviette; poster; pampl
	LHASC: VIN/6, Vincent/Pickles Collection	The People's Charter, 1838
	NMLH.1992.469	jug, ceramic
	NMLH.1993.770	notice, poster
	NMLH.1993.371.120	medal, Feargus O'Connor

New Search | Contact sheet

"The People's Charter, 1838" [LHASC: VIN/6, Vincent/Pickles Collection]

LHASC: VIN/6, V

Object Name	The People's Charter, 1838
Title	Being The Outline Of An Act To Provide For The Just Representation of the Pe Qualification ....
Collection Title	Labour History Archive And Study Centre (LHASC)
Key Word	Chartism Chartists Images Of Labour Condition of England
Place	London
People	Lovett, William; Heatherington, Henry; Cleave, John; Watson, James
Date Created	1838
Associated Date	1838
Text	Many British working people were disappointed when the 1832 Reform Act faile when the reformed House of Commons passed the Poor Law of 1834. In June 1

Search the People's History Museum

1 Here's how to do a free online search of the collections. Go to the homepage and click on **Search our collections**, on the left-hand panel. Say you had an ancestor involved with the radical 19th-century Chartism movement, and you want to know more about it. Enter 'Chartism' into the **General search of the collections** box, and then click on **Search**.

Choose a subject record

2 The results are displayed as a table of 'thumbnail' images, catalogue numbers and object names. The third entry is a digitised copy of The People's Charter of 1838. Click on the image in the left column to display details of the charter.

See the image and description

3 Information about The People's Charter and its purpose are displayed, as well as a thumbnail image of the charter. Click on the image to view a copy of the original charter.

Life on the land

Not everyone left the country to flock to the new factory jobs on offer in towns. Your farming ancestors may have stayed where their families had always lived and worked the soil. In times of war, this proved invaluable to the nation.

The rich history of Britain's rural life is well documented in museums, art and literature, as well as through cherished collections of old farming tools and well-preserved barns. Ancient building, farming and animal husbandry skills are valued and preserved. These were the stuff of life and survival to your ancestors; the tools and skills they used shaped their lives and attitudes. By visiting the museums, websites and resources listed below, online or in person, you'll gain valuable insights into their daily existence.

The levels of farm worker

Not all rural workers were the same, so it helps to be able to distinguish between them. There was a difference in status between farm servants and farm labourers. A farm servant was employed by the year from about the age of 14, and lived and worked on the farm. A farm labourer was usually a married man, employed on either a regular or casual basis, who lived off the farm, sometimes in a tied cottage that belonged to the landowner.

There were also regional differences in earnings. People working on the land in the north of England had the highest pay because of the competition from industries. The worst-paid farm labourers were found in the southwest counties, such as Somerset.

Rural England captured

The Museum of English Rural Life, at the University of Reading (see Directory), charts the history and importance of England's agricultural life. Entrance is free to the public.

The collections are built from various archives, books, artefacts, photographs and sound and film recordings that have been collected over the years. It's a wonderful resource if you want to research the history of food and farming, and understand how your rural ancestors may have lived.

The museum's library contains more than 40,000 different books, pamphlets and journals relating to country life and work. To help you to find what you want, the collection has specific sections on agricultural surveys, the history of British farming, the technology and engineering involved in farming, and conservation.

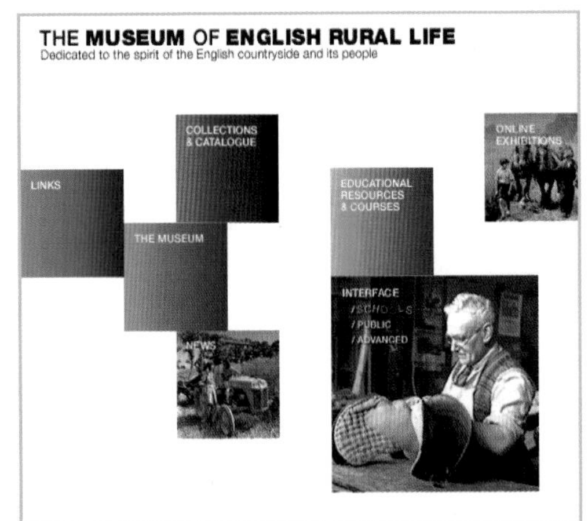

Explore the museum *Changing exhibitions mean that there's always something new to discover on the Museum of English Rural Life website, as well as details of the permanent collections.*

SEARCHING THE DATABASE You can search the online database of the museum at **merl.org.uk**. On the homepage click on **Online Exhibitions** and choose from a selection displaying different aspects of agricultural life and history, on subjects such as gypsy life or farm animals in art. Exhibitions change regularly.

A moment in farming history

Early in the Second World War, Winston Churchill commissioned a survey to find out whether the farms of England and Wales were providing enough food to feed a war-torn nation. The resulting National Farm Survey, completed in 1943, is both an important snapshot of the state of farming during the war and a source of revealing information about your farming ancestors.

The survey tells you about the type and scale of food production on each individual farm (nearly 300,000 or them in total), and includes forms filled out by the farmer and detailed field maps. The records are held in The National Archives (TNA). If you know the name of a farm owned by members of your family at the time, you can learn much about how those ancestors lived and worked the land while the world was at war.

The 'land girls' take over

The Women's Land Army was founded in the First World War to make up the shortfall of male agricultural labour. When war was declared again in 1939, the Land Army was re-established. The women – commonly known as 'land girls' – were recruited from all spheres of life including shops, offices and factories. Many of them had lived all their lives in a city, but by 1943 more than 80,000 women were working on the land. They did a vital job in keeping the country fed during and after the war, often facing prejudice and hostility from farmers and male farm workers.

Although the conditions were often dismal and the pay low, the women had a cheeky 'grin and bear it' attitude that kept their spirits high and earned respect. So many women enjoyed their work on the land that some of them stayed on after the war.

The Land Army was finally disbanded in 1950, and although the service registers don't survive, index cards for the service records do, and are retained by the Imperial War Museum (see Directory, and page 194). You can also view microfiche copies of the cards in person at TNA, although only for the years 1939-45.

Salt of the earth *If you come across a photo of a female relative wearing headscarf, jersey and overalls – and looking muddy and cheerful – she was probably a Land Girl. You might find her records at the Imperial War Museum.*

Did your ancestors fight for their country?

It's likely you'll have ancestors who served in the British Army at some point in history. Searching for their records is much easier when you understand the structure of the army and its regiments.

Before the English Civil Wars (1642-51), an army was raised only when the country faced a specific danger, and it was usually made up of local militia units. Oliver Cromwell created his professional New Model Army in 1644, but the first full-time Army dates from the restoration of Charles II in 1660.

The naming of regiments

Initially, each regiment was named after the colonel that commanded it. Numbering and ranking was introduced in 1694, when the named regiment also acquired a number – for example, the 'Fifth Regiment of Foot'.

By 1751, regiments were no longer known by the name of their colonel, but instead were given a descriptive name. By 1782, this often related to a place or county, but could just as likely reflect a ceremonial link to the sovereign or Royal Family. These descriptions gradually replaced the old regimental numbers so that by 1881 numbering was abolished. Many regiments were merged, and often took the names of the county where they were raised. This means that one regiment might have been known by a number of names over time, so you'll need to investigate fully when looking for a service history of an ancestor.

In addition, there were different types of regiment within the British Army, such as Cavalry, Infantry, Foot Guards and Artillery. Special corps included the Royal Engineers, as well as nursing personnel.

Showcase for the British Army

The National Army Museum in London is dedicated to the army, its regiments and history, and has an online collection of

Joining the regimental ranks *The Royal Fusiliers, painted in 1876 (below), was formed from two companies of the Tower of London Guard.*

records and images that can be accessed via its website at **national-army-museum.ac.uk**. These will help you to identify the correct regiment and understand in more detail the Army's organisation.

The museum itself has a large collection of private, regimental and business papers that tell the story of more than 500 years of regimental history of the British and Commonwealth armies. It also holds information relating to uniforms and medals. The curators of the museum are happy to answer individual questions, which you'll find helpful if you've come across an old medal or a picture of an ancestor in the course of your research.

Finding regimental museums

Many regimental museums have their own websites. To check if the regiment you're interested in has one, take a look at the Army Museums Ogilby Trust website at **armymuseums.org.uk**. It's a great resource for regimental history, approved by the Ministry of Defence, which describes itself as the 'definitive guide to the regimental and corps museums of the British Army'. The website's search engine lets you find museums across the UK, either by regiment or location, so you can see if there's a dedicated museum for your ancestor's regiment. It will spell out the location and contact details of any existing regimental museum and provide a brief description of what it holds, along with links to other useful websites that may be pertinent.

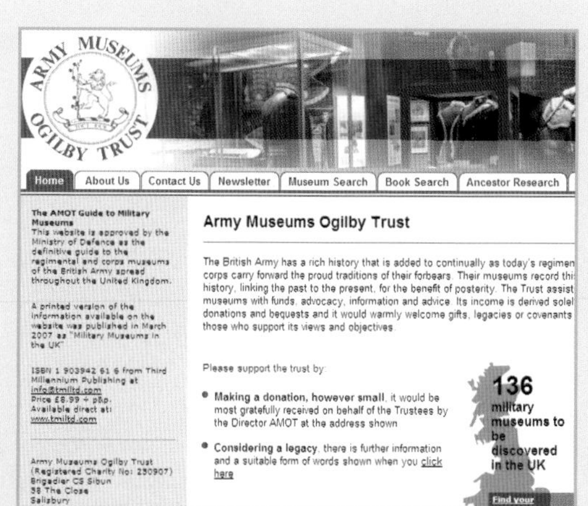

Search for a regiment

1 To search for the details of the Duke of Cornwall's Light Infantry, for example, go to **armymuseums.org.uk**. On the homepage, click on the link for **Museum search** from the tabs along the top.

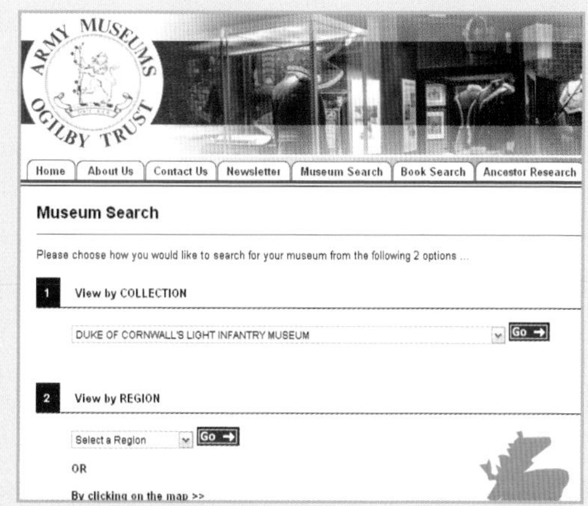

Choose a regiment

2 You'll be offered a search page that gives you the options of searching the collection or the region, both from drop-down menus. To search for a regiment by name, select one from the list. In this case, select **Duke of Cornwall's Light Infantry museum**. Then click on **Go**.

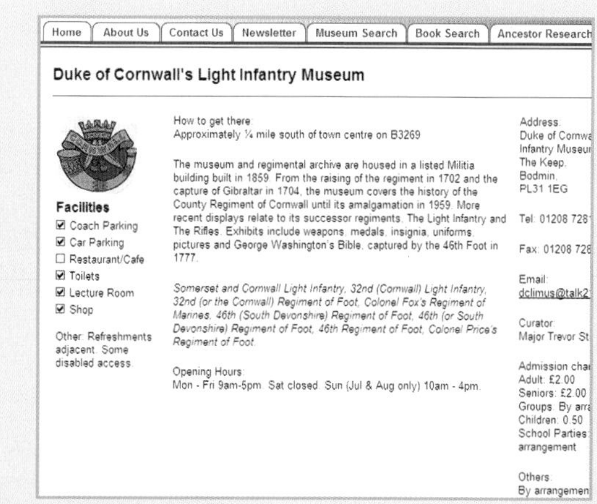

See the details

3 You're taken to a page which gives you a brief description of the Duke of Cornwall's Light Infantry Museum, what it holds (including, among other treasures, George Washington's Bible, captured in 1777), its opening hours, location and contact details. The page will also point you to the museum's website or email address, if it has them.

Imperial War Museum – serving and surviving

The exhibits and archives at the Imperial War Museum give remarkably vivid insights into what life was like for those who fought for Britain – and the people they left back home. The museum can also help you to identify military memorabilia, such as medals and badges.

War has affected most families in some way over the past 100 years, so a visit to the Imperial War Museum (IWM) in London is enthralling for people interested in their ancestors. As well as the collections of military hardware and memorabilia, there's an ever-changing programme of exhibitions that can cover subjects as diverse as propaganda, the Falklands War and the work of war artists.

The imposing building, fronted by two huge 15 inch naval guns from the First World War, was once the central portion of the old Bethlam Royal Hospital – better known as Bedlam. IWM was founded in 1917 as a tribute to those who fought in the First World War, and today the size and importance of the collections are such that they're spread over several other sites: HMS *Belfast*, moored on the River Thames near Tower Bridge; the Churchill Museum and Cabinet War Rooms, in Whitehall; Duxford in Cambridgeshire, which has a superb aviation collection; and the Daniel Libeskind-designed Imperial War Museum North, in Salford, which opened in 2002.

People caught up in war

The museum's permanent displays cover both World Wars and conflicts since 1945, and include permanent exhibitions on key areas such as the Holocaust and the role of espionage. The many testimonies from people who experienced war at first hand on the battlefield or on the home front make it an important resource if you want to understand more fully what your family went through in wartime.

One example describes a soldier's unforgettable Christmas dinner. Peter Roylance Noakes, who served in 1st Battalion Northamptonshire Regiment in India, Ceylon and Burma, remembers December 25, 1943. He was in the Indian jungle at Dimapur when he received a surprising gift from the Gurkhas. They'd shot a deer and cooked it over an open fire. The soldier had 'never tasted anything like it. Smoked venison if you'd like to call it … a change from bully beef and biscuits'.

To find this and more than 13,000 other records on IWM's documents database, you can use the website (see box, right). The document archive (in the section under IWM Collections) holds letters and diaries, as well as photo albums – with pictures of people or the camps where they were stationed – and identity cards.

It also holds prisoner of war listings, including the Singapore Changi Civilian Internment Camp register, kept until the end of 1942. Here you'll find an internee's full name, age, marital status, occupation, date of internment, and name and address of next of kin.

Identifying medals

If you've unearthed medals that you can't identify, the IWM's display of awards and decorations will help you to identify yours. Shown here is the Victoria Cross awarded posthumously to Boy (1st Class) Jack Cornwell (right) for staying at his post on the cruiser HMS *Chester* during the Battle of Jutland on May 31, 1916. The ship was shelled by four German cruisers and all Cornwell's crewmates were killed.

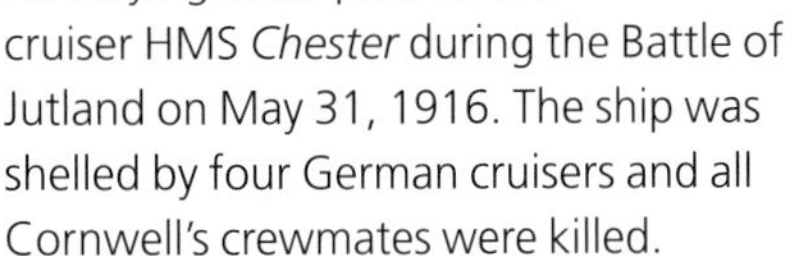

Of men and machines *Visit the Imperial War Museum in London to see planes, tanks, armaments and vast amounts of wartime memorabilia. A Spitfire and a Messerschmidt (above) dominate the entrance hall.*

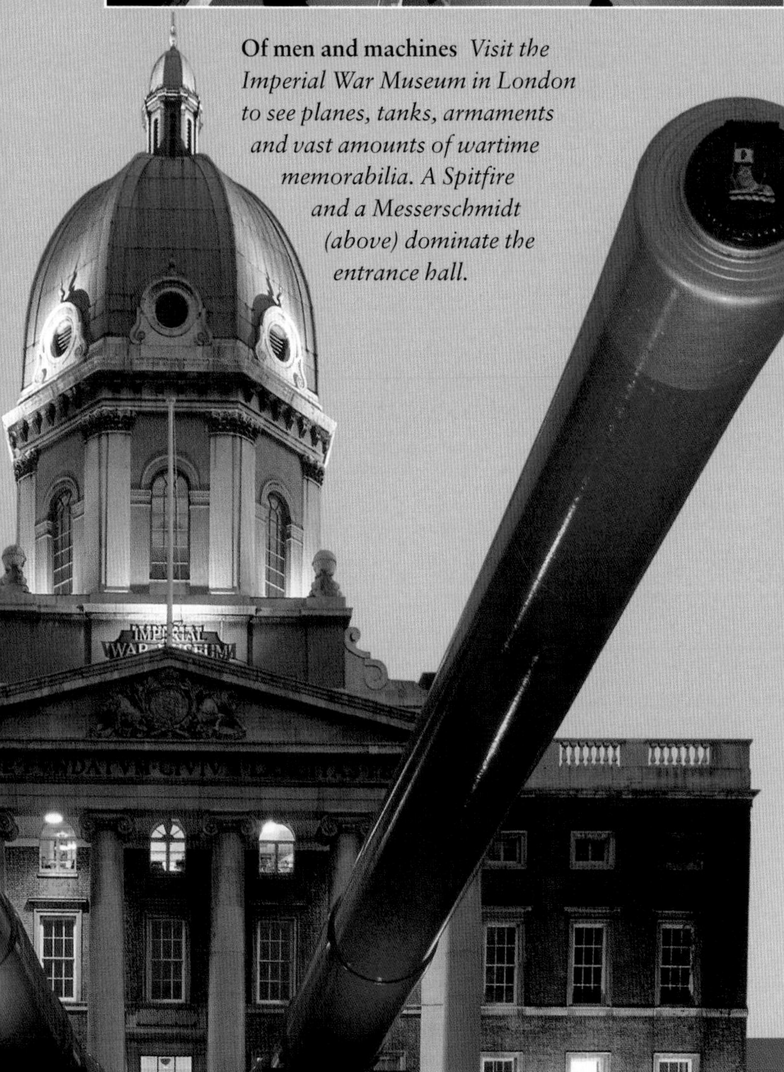

Keeping the home fires burning

The shortage of men back home, in both World Wars, meant that women took on many jobs that had traditionally been done by men – from running the public transport network to farming and even mining. They also operated machines in factories, including the often dangerous manufacture of munitions. The Women's Work Collection at IWM focuses on the involvement of women in the First World War and includes photographs and letters. It can also be seen online (see below).

Women also had to carry on the role of looking after children unwittingly caught up in the dangers and privations of living on the home front. At IWM a long-term exhibition called The Children's War looks at how war affected children – the excitement and disorientation of evacuation, the terror of blackouts and the joyless experience of rationing. This period is made vividly realistic in the 1940s house – a life-size recreation of a surburban house at the time of the Blitz.

Wartime online

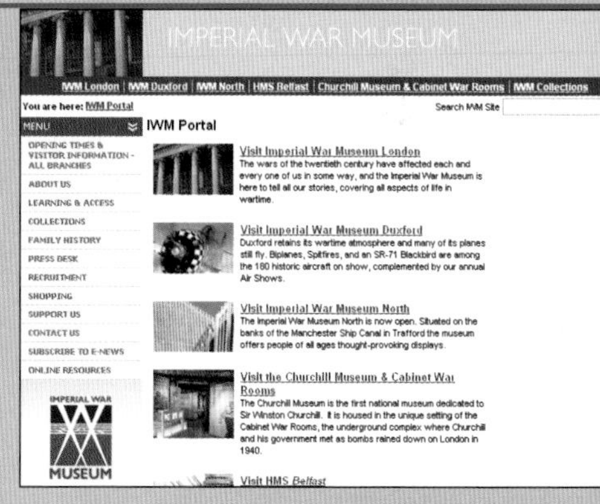

The IWM's website, at **iwm.org.uk**, has a **Family history** page with links to numerous collections, including war graves, rolls of honour, gallantry awards, journals, photos and a section called Women's Work. You can also find advice on how to research your ancestors who may have served in the air force, army, navy or merchant navy, or who were held as prisoners of war. There's a link on the website that takes you to the UK National Inventory of War Memorials, which has the details of the 55,000 war memorials that have been recorded so far. You can also access the site direct at **ukniwm.org.uk**.

Access to all the other IWM sites, in Whitehall, Duxford and Salford, is through the IWM homepage. The website is both easy to use and free to search and could add immensely to your research into your family history in wartime.

Tracing military records

If you have ancestors who took an active part in either of the World Wars, there should be records that provide details about their service.

The First World War saw the largest ever mobilisation of soldiers in Britain: more than 7 million people served in the conflict. Almost everyone who saw service abroad was awarded a campaign medal at the end of the conflict. The National Archives (TNA) has a large set of service records for the Army, some of which are available online. Most online material is from the First World War or earlier. The TNA research guides on army records are worth looking at.

Medal index cards

The index cards for First World War medals have been digitised. You can view and download them at **nationalarchives.gov.uk** under the **Documentsonline** section. The cards give the rank, unit and area of operation of each soldier, as well as details about which medal he was entitled to. Because a large number of other service records were destroyed by enemy bombing in 1940, these cards serve as an effective back-up roll call of all those serving in the First World War. Overall, they consist of more than 5.5 million records.

Searching the index

You can search the medal index free of charge. If you find a document you want to download, it will cost you £3.50.

To search for a medal index card, go to **nationalarchives.gov.uk** and click on **WW1 campaign medals**. Click the **search** link, then enter the name of the soldier. As there are so many cards, it helps to enter the regimental details and army number, if you have them. Most soldiers joined their local regiment, but this was not always the case, so you may have to widen your search to other regiments.

First World War officers' records

Army personnel records are organised under commissioned officers and non-commissioned officers/other ranks, so TNA has divided its records on this basis, too. The main officer service files were among those destroyed in 1940, but supplementary 'correspondence

First World War pension records online

The National Archives, working in partnership with **ancestry.co.uk**, has begun to put online all the First World War pension records that are found in TNA series WO364.

Ancestry is a subscription-based website but once you've registered, the index for the records can be searched free of charge. If you want to view the actual record, you'll have to subscribe first (see page 50).

On parade *Lord Kitchener reviews troops lined up for inspection at the beginning of the First World War. By January 1915, more than a million men had enlisted in the British Army.*

files' were also created and they survived. These files are catalogued by surname and the first initial of each officer, and you can search them by name. They're held in TNA series WO339 (the majority of files for the regular Army and emergency reserve) and WO374 (most of the files for the Territorial Force).

To search for an officer's file, go to **the Catalogue** on the **nationalarchives.gov.uk** homepage, click on **Search the Catalogue** and enter the surname of the officer. Also enter the series you wish to search, in this case WO339 or WO374. Click on the **Search** button. Each result will have a catalogue number, starting with WO (for War Office).

Other ranks before 1914

TNA also retains the surviving service records for other ranks that joined the army, prior to the First World War. They're found in the series WO97, and cover the years from 1760 to 1913. Records kept before 1883 have survived, but only for soldiers who were discharged to pension (commonly known as 'Chelsea pensioners').

It was only after 1883 that service records for almost every serving soldier were kept in a systematic fashion. The surviving records contain attestation and discharge papers and often give the soldier's place of birth, age and next of kin – which is very useful extra information if you're not sure of his connection to your family.

The earliest sets of records in WO97, covering the years 1760 to 1854, have been individually catalogued. It's possible to carry out a name search for a soldier discharged to pension between those years, on TNA's Catalogue. Just navigate to **the Catalogue**, click on **Search the Catalogue** and enter the name of the soldier you're researching. Then put WO97 in the box for **Department or series code**. Enter a **Year range** of 1760 to 1854 to limit the search. Each result gives the parish of birth and the regiment of the soldier which, along with his full name and age, should be enough information to confirm that you have found the correct record. If you'd not already found your ancestor's parish of birth, this is doubly useful.

Army personnel after 1922

Service records for army personnel who remained with the army after 1922, or who joined after that date, are still held by the Ministry of Defence in Glasgow and aren't available online.

For a fee, the Ministry of Defence will search for the service record of your ancestor, and provide you with the information you want. You'll need to contact the Army Personnel Centre; the address is shown in the Directory.

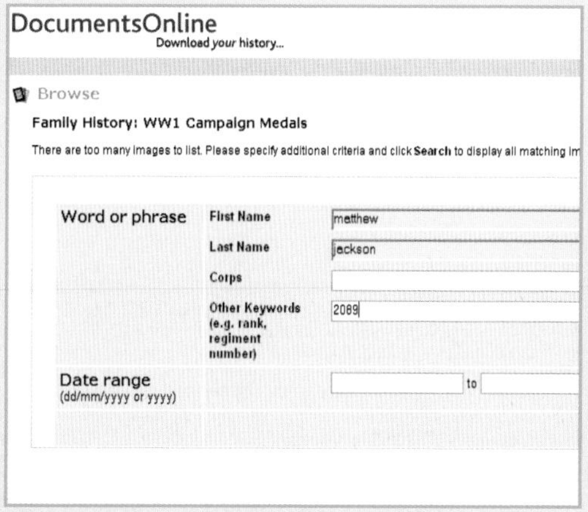

DocumentsOnline
Download your history...
Browse
Family History: WW1 Campaign Medals
Word or phrase — First Name: matthew; Last Name: jackson; Corps; Other Keywords (e.g. rank, regiment number): 2089
Date range (dd/mm/yyyy or yyyy) to

DocumentsOnline
Download your history...
Image details
+ Add to shopping
Description: Medal card of Jackson, Matthew

Corps	Regiment No	Rank
Liverpool Regiment	2089	Private
Machine Gun Corps	24456	Serjeant

Date: 1914-1920
Catalogue reference: WO 372/10
Dept: Records created or inherited by the War Office, Armed Forces, Judge Advocat[e] bodies
Series: War Office: Service Medal and Award Rolls Index, First World War
Piece: Holland D - Jobling H V
Image contains: 1 medal card of many for this collection
Number of image files: 1

Image Reference	Format and Version	Part Number	Size (KB)	Number
182199 / 26589	PDF 1.2	1	158	1

Total Price (£)
Refine search >

Search for a campaign medal

1 To search for the medals awarded to an ancestor, Matthew Jackson, go to the **nationalarchives.gov.uk** homepage, choose **Documentsonline** and click on **WW1 campaign medals**, then on **Search**. Fill in his first and last names. If you know his service number, enter it in **Other keywords**. Enter any other details in the appropriate boxes and click **Search**. The more detail you enter, the more successful your search will be.

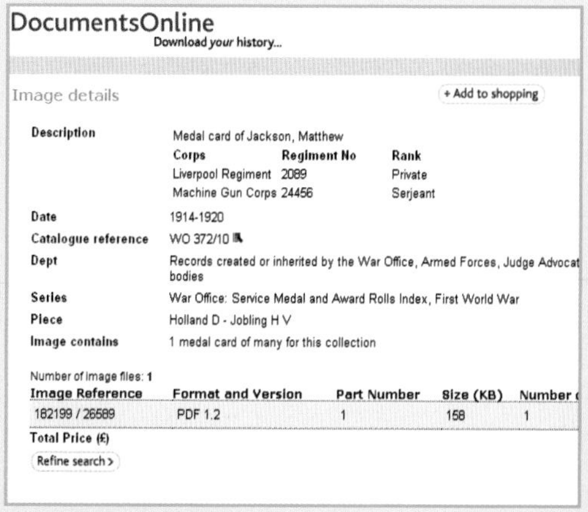

View the details

2 Without the service number, 37 results would have appeared. But with the service number entered, the correct card appears. Click on the **+Add to shopping** button and follow the appropriate steps to download and view an image of the card.

Finding sailors and airmen

Britain has a long seafaring history, and many of your ancestors may have served their country in the Royal Navy. The Royal Air Force is much younger, but it has its records, too, and serving ancestors are traceable.

Few centralised records of seamen were kept before 1853, and if you're trying to track down an ancestor from this period you'll need to know the name of at least one ship on which he served and some details of his life. For example, did he go to sea as a cabin boy or did he join as an adult? Did he have officer training or was he an unskilled, unwilling conscript? The National Archives (TNA) is the place to start. Most naval records have the prefix ADM (for Admiralty) followed by a particular code (see opposite). When using the indexes, note whether the service number ends with the letter A or B, or has no letter at all. This will tell you which register you need to order. It's sometimes given at the top of the index page as Series A or Series B.

Naval service before 1853

Until the introduction of continuous service in 1853, men often moved between naval and merchant ships, which makes tracing them

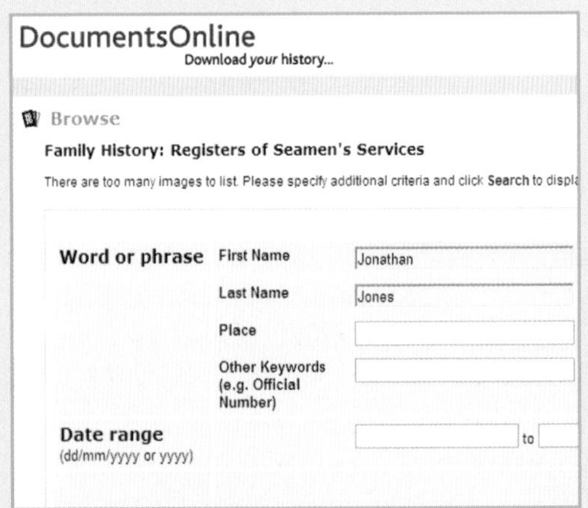

DocumentsOnline
Download *your* history...

Browse

Family History: Registers of Seamen's Services

There are too many images to list. Please specify additional criteria and click **Search** to displ

Word or phrase First Name: Jonathan
Last Name: Jones
Place:
Other Keywords (e.g. Official Number):

Date range (dd/mm/yyyy or yyyy) to

Start your search

1 To search for the naval records of an ancestor, a Jonathan Jones of Lancashire, go to nationalarchives.gov.uk and choose **Documents Online** from the homepage. Click on **Royal Naval Seamen** and then on **Search now**. Then enter the name of your ancestor, Jonathan Jones, into the appropriate boxes and click on **Search**.

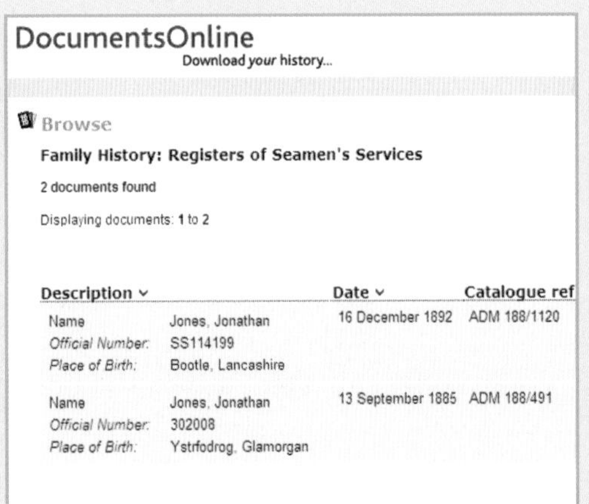

DocumentsOnline
Download *your* history...

Browse

Family History: Registers of Seamen's Services

2 documents found

Displaying documents: 1 to 2

Description		Date	Catalogue ref
Name	Jones, Jonathan	16 December 1892	ADM 188/1120
Official Number:	SS114199		
Place of Birth:	Bootle, Lancashire		
Name	Jones, Jonathan	13 September 1885	ADM 188/491
Official Number:	302008		
Place of Birth:	Ystrfodrog, Glamorgan		

First results

2 Jonathan Jones was born in Lancashire, so the correct record is the first one, with the catalogue reference ADM188/1120. You can view the document by either visiting The National Archives in person, or getting a copy of the record. To obtain a copy of the file click on **See details**.

DocumentsOnline
Download *your* history...

Image details

Description	Name: Jones, Jonathan; *Official Number:* SS114199; *Place of Birth:* Bootle, Lancashire
Date	16 December 1892
Catalogue reference	ADM 188/1120
Dept	Records of the Admiralty, Naval Forces, Royal Marines, Coastgu
Series	Admiralty: Royal Navy Registers of Seamen's Services
Piece	114001-115000
Image contains	1 document of many for this catalogue reference

Number of image files: 1

Image Reference	Format and Version	Part Number	Size (KB)
199 / 100	PDF 1.2	1	199

Total Price (£)

< Return to search results

Buy a copy

3 Jonathan Jones's full record will be displayed and you'll see that a copy will cost you £3.50. Click on the **Add to shopping** button on the page and then click on **Checkout**. You'll be asked to give your email address and a credit card number, and then you'll be able to access a page from where you can download the document.

Ancestors in the RAF

The Royal Air Force was formed in 1918 as an amalgamation of the Army's Royal Flying Corps (RFC) and the Navy's Royal Naval Air Service (RNAS). If your ancestor served in the Royal Air Force before the mid 1920s, you'll be able to search the records on TNA's website by following the links to **Military history** and selecting **Royal Air Force**. You can then choose from **Officers**, **Other ranks** and the **Women's Royal Air Force**. Each of these sections is divided by date and whether people were in the RFC or RNAS. Some information is available online, but full details can only be accessed by visiting TNA.

TNA has a number of excellent leaflets relating to the RAF, which can be accessed and ordered online. On TNA's homepage, select **Research, education and online exhibitions**, then choose **Research guides** and look under **R**.

The RAF records of airmen who served after the mid 1920s are held by the Ministry of Defence (MOD). A contact address is given in the Directory. The MOD will release information to the next of kin for a fee.

The records held by the MOD include details of everyone who served in the RAF, such as these men (right), seen re-arming a Spitfire in 1940.

difficult. Most ships had muster rolls, listing the men on board. To find an ancestor, start with the muster roll and pay books of individual ships (you need to know the name of at least one ship he served on, and a rough date). The muster roll shows where he was before and after his service on that ship.

From 1764 onwards, a muster often provides a man's age and place of birth. From about 1800, description books (which give age, height, complexion, scars and tattoos) may be included with musters. Where a muster is missing, you can use the ships' pay books to confirm that a man served on a particular ship. To trace a muster roll, go to **nationalarchives.gov.uk**, select **Military history** and click on **Royal Navy**. From there, navigate to **Before 1853** and you'll find the series numbers you need.

If you think your ancestor may have fought in the Battle of Trafalgar on October 21, 1805, choose the **Trafalgar Ancestors** link offered on TNA's website. This fascinating database can be searched by surname, and also by first name, age on October 21, 1805, birthplace, ship's name, rating and rank.

Naval service 1853-72

From 1853 onwards, seamen joining the navy were given a Continuous Service Engagement, or CS, number. The Continuous Service Engagement Books are held in ADM139; the books list the CS numbers and their holders' date and place of birth, physical features on entry and a service summary.

Naval service 1873-1923

TNA holds records for those who joined the Royal Navy as regular servicemen between 1873 and 1923 in the Registers of Seamen's Services (ADM188). Service details are recorded up to 1928. Here, you should be able to find your ancestor's year and place of birth, period of service, and on which ship or ships he served. Records of those serving from 1892 onwards also contain details on occupation, physical appearance, wounds received, and notes on character and abilities. Records for those who joined after 1923 are not yet open to the public. If your ancestor was in the navy between 1928 and 1938, see the Directory (under Ministry of Defence) for a contact address for further information.

Other sources of information

Sailors who applied for a navy pension gave details of which ships they served on and for how long. Certificates of Service were then compiled and sent to the Admiralty. They are now held in ADM29. To find an ancestor, go to **the Catalogue** on the TNA homepage. Type in the name and put ADM29 in the last box.

Certificates recording the admission of seamen's children into the school known as the Royal Naval Asylum at Greenwich are in ADM73 and are another valuable resource.

Looking for world war heroes

Most families had to make sacrifices in the two World Wars, and many paid the ultimate price of losing a loved one. The 1.7 million British and Commonwealth men and women who served and died are recorded on the Debt of Honour Register – search it online to reveal the fate of lost relatives.

In your family there may be an uncle, cousin or brother who was alive at the time of the First or Second World Wars but whose fate is a mystery. Or maybe you find a medal or other reminder of conflict bearing a name long forgotten. The poignant and sobering Debt of Honour Register, administered by the Commonwealth War Graves Commission (CWGC) **cwgc.org**, allows you to search for those who died in the two wars and also leads you to the names of the fallen who are buried in more than 23,000 war cemeteries around the world. As well as the military casualties, there are listings for more than 67,000 Commonwealth civilians who died as a result of enemy action during the Second World War. If you're armed with some basic information about a relative, the free CWGC website makes it easy to search for that person, investigate the circumstances of the death, and even find a specific location for a grave.

Using medals to trace relatives

Many servicemen and servicewomen were awarded medals, either for a specific campaign, or to acknowledge their acts of gallantry. Mrs Redmond (right) wears her late husband's impressive array of medals with pride.

- Finding a medal can narrow down your search for an ancestor. Along the edge of the medal is usually inscribed a regimental or service number, which can be used as a cross-reference to the CWGC entries.
- A medal can identify the conflicts in which a relative may have served. For example, the 1914 Star, 1914-15 Star, Victory and British War medals belong to the First World War. The medal card index can be searched online at The National Archives **nationalarchives.gov.uk** via the **DocumentsOnline** link under **Search the archives**. Or visit **gazettes-online.co.uk**, the archive of the *London Gazette*, which has the official announcements of all gallantry medals.

Take your search further

Once you've found a relative, you can extend your research. You might want to check at The National Archives for a First World War service record, or investigate the circumstances surrounding the death of a relative by examining the final unit war diary entry. The relevant regimental or service museum may be able to supply additional details. You could also pay your respects in person by using the Debt of Honour Register to find the grave or memorial reference for your relative, and the name of the war cemetery where he lies. The Royal British Legion organises trips to war cemeteries – see **remembrancetravel.com**.

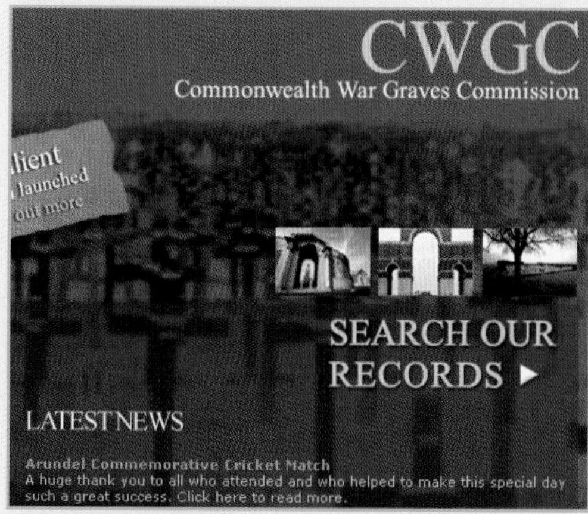

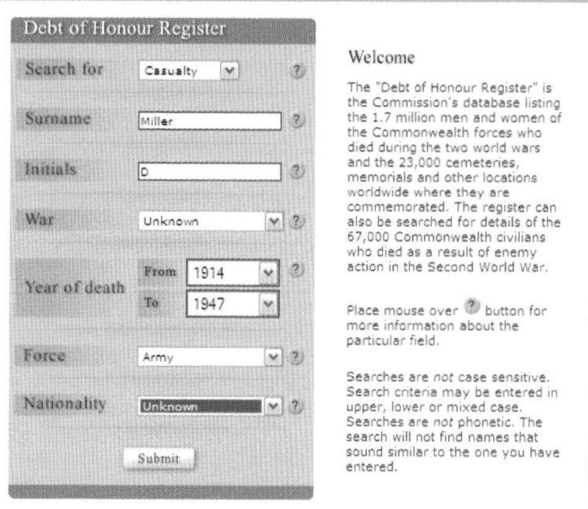

Debt of Honour Register

Search for: Casualty
Surname: Miller
Initials: D
War: Unknown
Year of death: From 1914 To 1947
Force: Army
Nationality: Unknown
Submit

Welcome

The "Debt of Honour Register" is the Commission's database listing the 1.7 million men and women of the Commonwealth forces who died during the two world wars and the 23,000 cemeteries, memorials and other locations worldwide where they are commemorated. The register can also be searched for details of the 67,000 Commonwealth civilians who died as a result of enemy action in the Second World War.

Place mouse over ? button for more information about the particular field.

Searches are *not* case sensitive. Search criteria may be entered in upper, lower or mixed case. Searches are *not* phonetic. The search will not find names that sound similar to the one you have entered.

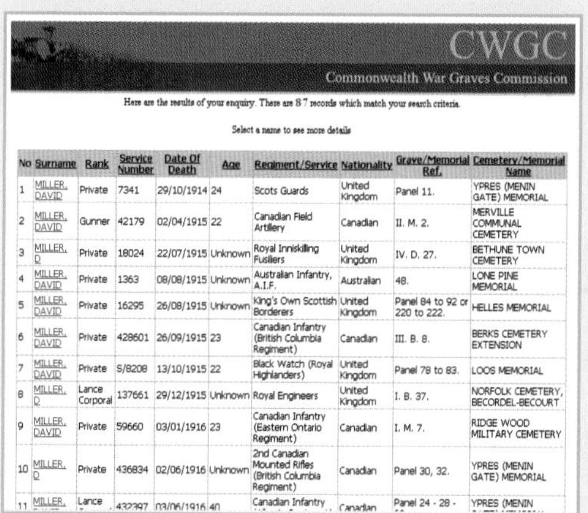

CWGC
Commonwealth War Graves Commission

Here are the results of your enquiry. There are 87 records which match your search criteria.

Select a name to see more details

No	Surname	Rank	Service Number	Date Of Death	Age	Regiment/Service	Nationality	Grave/Memorial Ref.	Cemetery/Memorial Name
1	MILLER, DAVID	Private	7341	29/10/1914	24	Scots Guards	United Kingdom	Panel 11.	YPRES (MENIN GATE) MEMORIAL
2	MILLER, DAVID	Gunner	42179	02/04/1915	22	Canadian Field Artillery	Canadian	II. M. 2.	MERVILLE COMMUNAL CEMETERY
3	MILLER, D	Private	18024	22/07/1915	Unknown	Royal Inniskilling Fusiliers	United Kingdom	IV. D. 27.	BETHUNE TOWN CEMETERY
4	MILLER, DAVID	Private	1363	08/08/1915	Unknown	Australian Infantry, A.I.F.	Australian	48.	LONE PINE MEMORIAL
5	MILLER, DAVID	Private	16295	26/08/1915	Unknown	King's Own Scottish Borderers	United Kingdom	Panel 84 to 92 or 220 to 222.	HELLES MEMORIAL
6	MILLER, DAVID	Private	428601	26/09/1915	23	Canadian Infantry (British Columbia Regiment)	Canadian	III. B. 8.	BERKS CEMETERY EXTENSION
7	MILLER, DAVID	Private	S/8208	13/10/1915	22	Black Watch (Royal Highlanders)	United Kingdom	Panel 78 to 83.	LOOS MEMORIAL
8	MILLER, D	Lance Corporal	137661	29/12/1915	Unknown	Royal Engineers	United Kingdom	I. B. 37.	NORFOLK CEMETERY, BECORDEL-BECOURT
9	MILLER, DAVID	Private	59660	03/01/1916	23	Canadian Infantry (Eastern Ontario Regiment)	Canadian	I. M. 7.	RIDGE WOOD MILITARY CEMETERY
10	MILLER, D	Private	436834	02/06/1916	Unknown	2nd Canadian Mounted Rifles (British Columbia Regiment)	Canadian	Panel 30, 32.	YPRES (MENIN GATE) MEMORIAL
11	MILLER,	Lance	432397	03/06/1916	40	Canadian Infantry	Canadian	Panel 24 - 28 -	YPRES (MENIN

Enter a name

1 To search for the details of a Denis Basil Miller in the CWGC site, go to **cwgc.org** and on the homepage click on **Search our records**. In the **Search for** box select **Casualty** from the drop-down menu. If you're unsure of the spelling of the surname, type '*' after the name in the **Surname** box. Enter the first initial in the next box to maximise the chances of finding the right person. For example, Denis Basil Miller may be listed only as D. Miller on the database.

Refine the detail

2 In the **War** field, select **First World War** or **Second World War** from the list. If you're unsure, choose **Unknown**. Select dates from the drop-down lists under **Year of death**, if you can, to narrow down the search. Otherwise, select **Unknown**. If you know the branch of the Armed Forces in which your relative served, choose it under **Force**. Select the nationality of the force in which the person served. Click **Submit**.

Read the results

3 Your results appear as a grid, with all the names that match the criteria you entered on the search page. The information is displayed according to the name of the deceased; his rank and service number; his date of death and recorded age, if known; the regiment or service in which he served; his nationality; and the grave or memorial reference followed by the cemetery in which he's buried.

Crime and punishment

If one of your distant ancestors was a criminal you're in luck – there are far more detailed records for convicted felons than for most other people. Though tracking them down can be challenging, it's well worth the effort.

The National Archives (TNA) has a range of research guides that deal with crime and punishment. If your ancestor appeared in court, was charged with a crime, went to prison or was transported to the colonies, you should be able to find out more. On the other hand, you'll also be able to find out more about any ancestors involved in the criminal justice system, as the documents also refer to judges and jurors, witnesses and policemen – along with the innocent victims.

Maker of the law *The First Earl of Rosslyn is shown here in his role as Lord Chancellor, head of the legal system. He is portrayed in all his finery by Sir Joshua Reynolds in 1785.*

Different types of court

Understanding the varying courts your ancestor may have attended will make your research much easier.

QUARTER SESSIONS From the middle of the 16th century until 1972, quarter sessions were held every three months (quarter year) in every county in England and Wales. They tried the less serious crimes such as arson, assault, burglary and petty theft. They didn't have the power to hear the most serious crimes – treason, murder or manslaughter, for example – though offenders might be brought there for preliminary hearings. Quarter session records are held in local county archives, which can be searched by going to the Access to Archives (A2A) website at **a2a.org.uk** (see page 170).

ASSIZES The assizes were periodic criminal courts held by judges travelling in 'circuits' around England and Wales. Assizes were generally held twice a year, from the 16th century until 1972. A judge and 12 jurors would try serious crimes, including murder, infanticide, theft, highway robbery, rape, assault, coining, forgery and witchcraft. A serious offence brought to a quarter session would be referred to the assizes and the accused would then be held in custody until a circuit judge arrived.

CROWN COURTS These replaced the assizes and quarter sessions in 1972. Crown Court records are held at TNA, but generally speaking, case files remain closed for at least 30 years. In certain circumstances, permission to access a closed file is granted under the Freedom of Information Act.

Shortfalls in the system

Unfortunately, the system isn't always helpful when you're trying to trace an ancestor. One of the problems is that not many assizes records survive, and before 1732 most of them were written in Latin, which makes deciphering them difficult for most people. In addition, very few counties have surviving witness statements from before the 19th century, and few Midlands circuit records survive before 1818.

As a rule, neither the age of the accused nor details of their family were included in the court reports. Not surprisingly, aliases were widely used, and you can't always rely on the accused's stated occupation or home town either.

Tracking down a case

Assize records aren't indexed by surname, but are arranged by county, grouped into a number of circuits within the county. In this instance, a circuit refers to a group of places within a county. Kent, for example, would fall in the South Eastern circuit. To find a case, you need to know the name of the accused, the county or circuit where they were tried, and the rough date of the trial.

If you're unsure of this, and are searching for a 19th-century case, check the Criminal Registers for England and Wales. These are at TNA in record series HO27 and cover dates 1805 to 1892. After 1868 you can check the calendars of prisoners tried at assizes and quarter sessions in HO104.

Once you know where and when the trial took place, you can begin your search. Bear in mind that many of the Welsh assize records aren't held at TNA but have been relocated to The National Library of Wales (see page 166).

Youth justice *A young boy stands in the dock as his case is heard in 1891. By then, more enlightened attitudes meant children were no longer treated as severely as adult criminals.*

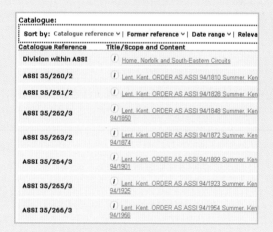

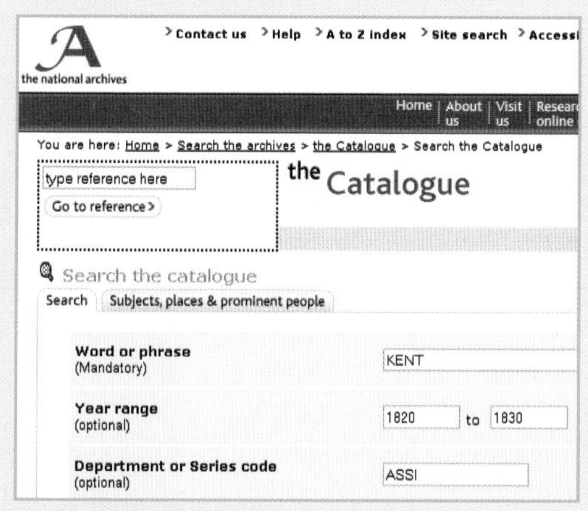

Catalogue:

Sort by: Catalogue reference | Former reference | Date range | Releva

Catalogue Reference	Title/Scope and Content
Division within ASSI	Home, Norfolk and South-Eastern Circuits
ASSI 35/260/2	Lent. Kent. ORDER AS ASSI 94/1810 Summer. Ken
ASSI 35/261/2	Lent. Kent. ORDER AS ASSI 94/1828 Summer. Ken
ASSI 35/262/3	Lent. Kent. ORDER AS ASSI 94/1848 Summer. Ken 94/1850
ASSI 35/263/2	Lent. Kent. ORDER AS ASSI 94/1872 Summer. Ken 94/1874
ASSI 35/264/3	Lent. Kent. ORDER AS ASSI 94/1899 Summer. Ken 94/1901
ASSI 35/265/3	Lent. Kent. ORDER AS ASSI 94/1923 Summer. Ken 94/1925
ASSI 35/266/3	Lent. Kent. ORDER AS ASSI 94/1954 Summer. Ken 94/1956

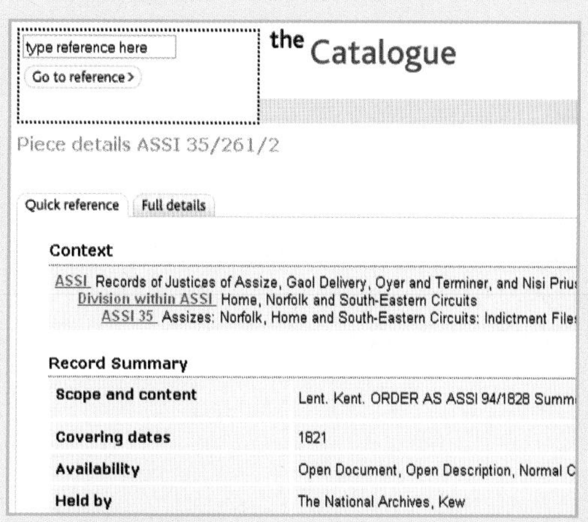

Searching for assize records

1 To search for assize records for a particular county, such as Kent, go to TNA's online catalogue at **nationalarchives.gov.uk/catalogue**. Enter 'Kent' as a keyword. You can also add a date range to narrow down the search. Then enter 'ASSI' in the **Department or series code** box (ASSI refers to the department code that's unique to these records at TNA). Click on **Search**.

View the results

2 You'll be taken to a screen that lists the results for the county you're searching, arranged in chronological order. Once you've found the relevant document, make a note of the number on the left-hand side of the screen – ASSI35/261/2, for example. This is a unique TNA document reference. You can't see these original documents online, but if you go to TNA in person, or order copies online, you'll need to quote this reference number.

Check the details

3 Clicking on the link to your particular record will give you a brief catalogue description of what it contains, usually the date and county. You can now confirm that you've found the right document before you decide to take a trip to TNA or order it.

The Old Bailey – a world-famous criminal court

Our ancestors lived in brutal times. Punishments for crimes included burning at the stake and deportation; even children were hanged. The corpses weren't wasted, though – from 1752 to 1809, the bodies of those executed for murder were taken to Surgeon's Hall in the Old Bailey where they were publicly dissected. Relatives could later buy them back for burial.

The first Old Bailey courthouse was built in 1539 but its history goes back to medieval times, when the site was occupied by the notorious Newgate gaol. 'Hanging breakfasts' took place at the alehouse opposite the gates of the gaol, where diners watched the hangings while they ate.

The court takes its name from the street, Old Bailey, which followed the line of the original fortified wall, or 'bailey', of the City of London. The courthouse has been rebuilt several times – the first time was after its destruction in the Great Fire of 1666.

The present-day court was built in 1907, incorporating stone blocks reclaimed after Newgate prison was demolished to make way for the Old Bailey in 1902. It's still used for major criminal trials – including those of serial killers Harold Shipman and Fred West.

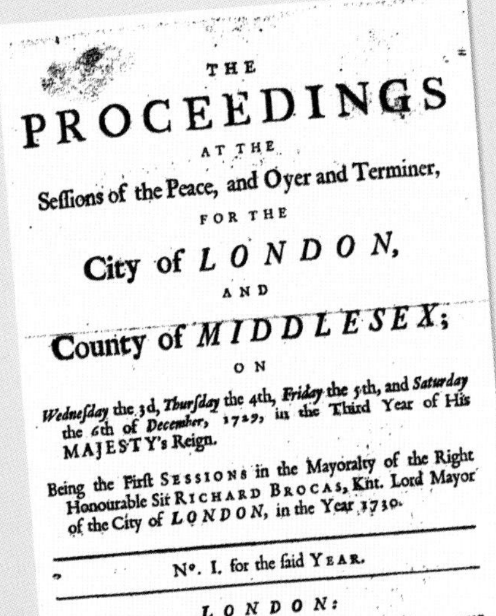

THE
PROCEEDINGS
AT THE
Seffions of the Peace, and Oyer and Terminer,
FOR THE
City of *LONDON*,
AND
County of *MIDDLESEX*;
ON
Wednefday the 3d, *Thurfday* the 4th, *Friday* the 5th, and *Saturday* the 6th of *December*, 1729, in the Third Year of His MAJESTY's Reign.

Being the Firft SESSIONS in the Mayoralty of the Right Honourable Sir RICHARD BROCAS, Knt. Lord Mayor of the City of *LONDON*, in the Year 1730.

N°. I. for the faid YEAR.

LONDON:
Printed for T. PAYNE, at the *Crown* in *Ivy-Lane*, near *Pater-nofter-Row*, MDCC.XXX.
(Price Six Pence.)

Reading the Proceedings

From 1674, transcriptions of Old Bailey trials were published as *The Proceedings*, (right) eight times a year, after each session at the court. During the 1670s, the paper was printed for a popular audience and ran to just a few pages. It was a cheap and popular periodical, publishing descriptions of only the most lurid trials, such as this, from 1679: '*...brought to Tryal, was an unhappy Wench, whom the Devil had seduced to endeavour, to cover the filthy sin of Fornication, with the Scarlet Mantle of Murder, having made away her own new-born Bastard-Child, and in a very barbarous manner cut the Throat of it...*'. The unfortunate girl was sentenced to death.

No hiding place

A century later, *The Proceedings* ran to hundreds of pages, recording most of the evidence presented – apart from the more salacious details of sex crimes. At this time the courtroom layout emphasised the conflict between the defendant and the court. The accused stood at the bar facing the witness box. He was spotlit by a mirrored reflector, which hung above the bar and reflected light from the windows on to his face – so that the court could better examine his facial expressions as he gave his testimony. His voice was amplified, too, by a sounding board positioned over his head.

Symbol of the court *Poised on the dome of the Old Bailey in London, the gilded statue* Justice *represents the rule of law and impartial justice. Major cases from all over England are tried here, including more than a third of all murders.*

Blood-chilling crimes *Among the notorious criminals tried at the Old Bailey were Dr Crippen in 1910 (below), William Joyce ('Lord Haw-Haw') in 1945, the Kray twins in 1969 and Peter Sutcliffe ('the Yorkshire Ripper') in 1981.*

Death by hanging

The unluckiest of the accused were sentenced to execution. More than 200 crimes were punishable by death in 1800 – including impersonating a Chelsea pensioner and damaging London Bridge – although, in practice, people were only executed for 17 of them, with murder, attempted murder, arson, rape, sodomy and sheep stealing among the crimes on the list.

When the grim moment came, the blindfolded convicts stood in a horse-drawn cart, had the noose placed around their necks and the cart pulled away. Death was slow and painful, and convicts' friends often put them out of their misery by pulling on their legs to hasten the moment. The introduction of a 'sharp drop' system in 1783 made death a quicker business.

Until 1783 most of the condemned were hanged at Tyburn – today's Marble Arch. Then, because of the rowdiness that accompanied these grisly events, the site moved to Newgate or nearby, where, by 1902, a total of 1169 people (1120 men and 49 women) had been hanged. Public hangings were only stopped in 1868.

Morbid curiosity *A Hogarth engraving of 1747 captures perfectly the raucous spectacle of a public execution at Tyburn. Its triangular gallows could hang up to 21 people at a time.*

The Old Bailey online

If you're lucky – or unlucky – enough to have a criminal ancestor in your family, take a look at **oldbaileyonline.org** (right). Details of more than 100,000 Old Bailey criminal trials from 1674 to 1834 have been transcribed and can be searched online, free of charge. You can use names (of victims and witnesses as well as defendants), dates, places and subject keywords, and you can also view digital images of the 60,000 original pages of *The Proceedings*. The intimacy of the reports can be astounding, including verbatim transcripts of dialogue in the courtroom. A further 100,000 trials – from December 1834 to April 1913 – are being digitised, a process that should be complete by the end of 2008.

Homepage
Search the Proceedings
About the Proceedings
Historical Background
For Schools
About this Project
Contact Details
Sitemap
Copyright Information and Citation Guide

SEARCH THE PROCEEDINGS
The Proceedings of the Old Bailey

Homepage » Search

The **Old Bailey Proceedings** contain accounts of over 100,000 criminal trials, as well as the text from the front and back cover and advertisements. They can be searched in several different ways.

Advertisement: *Tales From The Hanging Court* Now Available: A new book based on accounts contained in the Old Bailey Proceedings. Click Here to Order from Publisher

If you are just getting started you may wish to browse the history of the Proceedings, or see our notable trials page - specially selected trials of particular historical interest.

- Keyword Search
- Name Search
- Place and Map Search
- Crime, Verdict and Punishment Search
- Browse by Date
- Advanced Search
- Statistical Search
- Reference Number
- Search the Associated Records
- Manuscripts and Ordinary's Accounts Keyword

Further advice on searching for members of specific London communities can be found in the **communities** section of this website:

- Black Communities of London
- Homosexuality
- Gypsies and Travellers
- Irish in London
- Jewish Communities

Transportation

During the 17th century, overcrowding in prisons began to be dealt with by transportation. At first, miscreants were sent to the North American colonies, but after American independence in 1776 that was no longer an option.

With the wide open spaces of America no longer available to them, prison authorities turned to newly acquired lands in Australia. On May 13, 1787, what became known as the 'First Fleet' set sail for Australia with six transport ships, two warships and three store-ships, carrying more than 700 convicts, of whom 48 died en route. They arrived at Port Jackson in January, 1788. Many of them would have been convicted and transported on the flimsiest of evidence – but others had cheated death and welcomed the chance of a new life. For more information look at **convictcentral.com**.

All at sea *Jails became so crowded that prison hulks were moored in The Thames estuary and off the south coast. TNA series HO8 and HO9 cover prisoners held in hulks from 1802 to 1876.*

THE "DEFENCE" HULK AND THE "UNITĒ" CONVICT HOSPITAL SHIP, OFF WOOLWICH.

The 'First Fleeters'

There is no single, authoritative list of convicts, but if you think that one of your distant ancestors may have been on that First Fleet, there are some Australian-based sites that may be useful in your search. The First Fleeters Society has a searchable database at **firstfleet.uow.edu.au/search.html**. Another site you might find useful is **members.pcug.org.au/~pdownes/dps/1stflt.htm**. The First Fleet Fellowship offers more information at **home.vicnet.net.au/~firstff/info.htm**.

Transportation was formally abolished in 1868, but it had effectively stopped by 1857. During those 80 years 158,702 convicts arrived in Australia from England and Ireland, and 1321 from other parts of the Empire, making a total of 160,023 men and women transported. Sometimes even teenagers were sent, often for crimes that would be considered petty today. The theft of a loaf of bread could be enough to send a starving Briton to the colonies.

Read more about it

The National Archives has copies of books that you may find useful. The names of the convicts transported are listed in *The First Fleeters*, edited by P.G. Fidlon and R.J. Ryan (Sydney, 1981).

A list of convicts transported on the second fleet of ships, which left in 1789, during which 278 died, is contained in *The Second Fleet Convicts*, edited by R.J. Ryan (Sydney, 1982).

Searching for a transportee

The National Archives (TNA) holds various sources relating to transportation, but there's no single index of the names of those who were transported. Very few of these records are searchable online and you'll need to visit TNA if you want to consult them – so it helps to know where to start.

ESTABLISHING A DATE AND SHIP To discover more about a convicted ancestor, you need to know when they were tried and/or the date and ship in which they sailed to Australia. To find this, use one of the published Australian censuses or musters (official rolls) of the penal colonies, which often indicate the place of conviction and the date and ship of arrival in Australia. Censuses were taken periodically between 1788 and 1859, and are in the record series HO10. The census of 1828 (HO10/21 to HO10/27) is the most thorough and contains the names of more than 35,000 people with details of their age, religion, family, place of residence, occupation and any stock or land held. In addition, the census shows whether each settler came free or as a convict (or was born in the colony), and the name of the ship and the year of arrival are also given.

ARRIVALS IN NEW SOUTH WALES The microfiche index to the New South Wales Convict Indents and Ships records the names and aliases of the convicts who arrived in New South Wales and Van Dieman's Land (now Tasmania) between 1788 and 1842. It also indexes ships recorded on the same documents. A copy of this is available at the National Archives library, on a CD.

Taking a risk *If they were caught, even young pickpockets such as these would have been transported overseas to Australia.*

Convict registers held at The National Archives

These registers have information about convicts, their trials and where they were sent.

- **HO11** contains transportation registers listed by ship and date of departure 1787-1871. They tell you where and when the convict was tried, and may lead you to records of the trial.
- **HO26** contains registers of Middlesex prisoners 1791-1849.
- **HO27** contains registers of those Middlesex prisoners who were not tried at the Old Bailey 1809-11, all Middlesex prisoners 1850-92, as well as provincial prisoners 1805-92.
- **HO17** 1819-39 and **HO18** 1839-54 contain petitions for clemency. You'll need to use the registers in **HO19** to find the right one.
- **HO48, HO49, HO54** and **HO56** contain petitions that haven't been indexed.
- **HO47** contains judges' reports 1784-1829 and **HO6** contains circuit letters 1816-40.

Finding the date and place of trial

Prison registers indicate where the prisoner was held before trial, and any movements from prison to prison. Many include an index of prisoners. You'll need to consult the following series:

- **HO23** for registers of county prisons 1847-66.
- **HO24** for prison registers and returns 1838-75.
- **HO9** for miscellaneous registers relating to convict prison hulks 1802-49.
- **HO8** for quarterly returns of convicts in prisons and hulks 1824-76.
- **T38** for material on convict hulks 1802-31, with lists of crews and convicts.
- **HO77** for lists of prisoners tried at Newgate 1782-1853.

Further information

Some wives applied to be transported with their convicted husbands. If their petitions were made between 1819 and 1844, they'll be in **PC1/67** to **PC1/92**. Those from 1849 are in **HO12**, and can also be found in the registers in **HO14** under 'miscellaneous'.

- **CO360** and **CO369** contain other names that are held in New South Wales Registers, from 1849.
- **CO202** contains names from the Australian Entry Books from 1786.
- **HO11** contains convict transportation registers 1787-1867. The registers provide the name of the ship on which the convict sailed as well as the date and place of conviction and the term of the sentence. Contracts with agents to transport prisoners, with full lists of ships and convicts, are in **TS18/460** to **TS18/515** and **TS18/1308** to **TS18/1361** with a few stray lists 1840-3, in **PC1/2715** to **PC1/2719**.
- **CO201** has further lists of convicts, together with emigrant settlers 1801-21, in New South Wales Original Correspondence.
- **CO207** has Entry Books relating to convicts 1788-1825. Both of these are available only in microfilm.

Some of the lists from these records have been printed in L.L. Robson's, *The Convict Settlers of Australia* (Melbourne, 1981).

Sources in Australia

The Australian National Archives doesn't hold records on convicts or colonial migration, but suggests you should contact the 'First Fleeters' at the web address given opposite, if you want to trace individual convicts.

Hard labour and houses of correction

From the early 18th century, any ancestors convicted of serious crimes would have been sentenced to swift and brutal punishment. After 1853 you're more likely to find them serving a long-term prison sentence instead.

Until 1853, people convicted of a serious offence were dealt with quite simply – by execution, or by transportation to North America or Australia. Lesser criminals, such as vagrants or debtors, were kept off the streets and put to work in houses of correction, while people awaiting trial or sentence, or anyone convicted of a minor offence, were kept in county gaols, sometimes with short, sharp spells of hard labour. Then in 1823, houses of correction and county gaols were amalgamated and renamed 'prisons'.

Prisoner or convict?

People held in prison were known as prisoners, but those sentenced to transportation or hard labour were convicts. John Little (above), aged 17, was sentenced to six weeks hard labour in Lambeth prison in 1873 for stealing two sixpences.

Prisons take the strain

The Penal Servitude Act (1853) substituted the transportation of convicts to the colonies with a term of imprisonment in Britain – though in practice, convicts were still being transported until as late as 1867. Prison sentences ranged from three years to life and usually included hard labour. This was meant to show offenders the errors of their ways and teach them to be industrious; it was also extremely unpleasant, with a view to deterring others from a criminal path.

Forms of hard labour

The most soul-destroying aspect of most forms of hard labour was their uselessness. Prisoners were sometimes put to working a water pump for hours on end; others were set far more unpleasant tasks.

THE CRANK MACHINE A prisoner had to turn a handle that forced paddles through sand inside a drum several thousand times a day, while a counter registered the number of turns. The guard could make the work harder by tightening a screw – which explains the slang term 'screw' for a prison warder.

THE TREADMILL A vast elongated drum, resembling the wheel of a paddle steamer, had steps instead of paddles. The prisoners had to stand in individual booths over these steps hanging onto a bar or strap. As the wheel turned under their weight, the prisoners had to keep climbing or fall off.

SHOT DRILL In this exercise a row of prisoners had to pick up heavy cannon balls in time with each other, without bending their knees,

Harsh lessons *Prisoners, overseen by a warder, are forced to pump cold water inside Coldbath Fields Prison, London, in the early 1800s.*

and bring them up slowly to chest level. They then took three steps to the right, put the ball down on the ground, took three paces to the left and started again.

Tracing a prisoner

To find an ancestor whom you believe was imprisoned, it helps to know the name of the prison and the date of their imprisonment or release. Don't assume that an individual would have been incarcerated near their home, because prisoners were often moved between prisons, depending on where there was room for them.

Surviving prison records are held at individual county and city record offices and at The National Archives (TNA).

Records at The National Archives

The criminal registers held at TNA list just about everyone accused of a criminal offence – regardless of the verdict – in the 19th and 20th centuries. They're arranged by county and include the following information:

- the result of the trial
- the sentence, in the case of conviction
- the date of the execution of a prisoner who was sentenced to death
- personal details about the prisoner, though these are only occasionally given.

You can see these records at TNA, where the microfiche indexes are arranged alphabetically and by county. Those with the reference code HO27 cover England and Wales from 1805 to 1892. Records in HO26 cover Middlesex from 1791 to 1849 (records from 1850 onwards for Middlesex are in HO27).

Information about finding records for the convicts who were transported to Australia is given on page 206.

PRISONER REGISTERS There are specific reference codes at TNA for prisoner records:

- PCOM2 covers 1770 to 1951
- HO23 records inmates held in rented cells in county prisons from 1846 to 1866
- HO24 records prisoners held in Millbank, Parkhurst and Pentonville prisons in London from 1838 to 1874.
- PRIS1 to PRIS11 include records for King's Bench, Marshalsea and Fleet (London debtors' prisons) during much of the 18th and 19th centuries.

JUDGES' REPORTS These are in HO47 and cover 1784-1829. To search these records, go to **the Catalogue** on the TNA website. In the box on the top left of the screen, type 'HO47' and click **Go to reference.** Then click on the **Browse from here** button. HO47 is the second entry on this page.

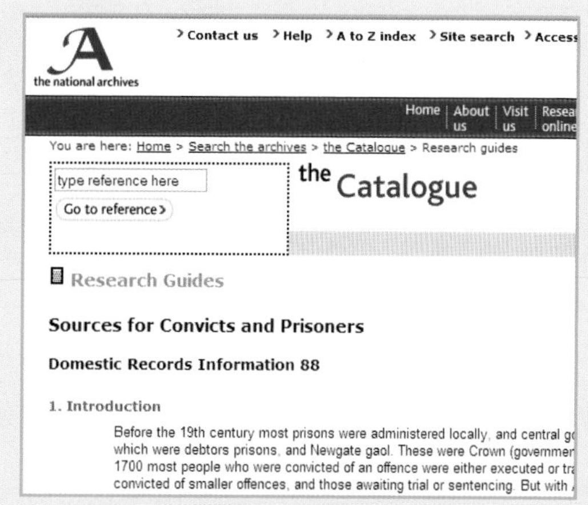

Finding a catalogue reference

1 Go to **nationalarchives.gov.uk**, the TNA homepage, and click on **Search the archives** on the top bar, then select **the Catalogue**. Click the **Research guides** link at the top right of the screen and from the alphabetical list that appears, choose **Convicts and prisoners,1100-1986**. Up comes an online guide (above) that includes a list of reference codes detailing exactly what records each series contains.

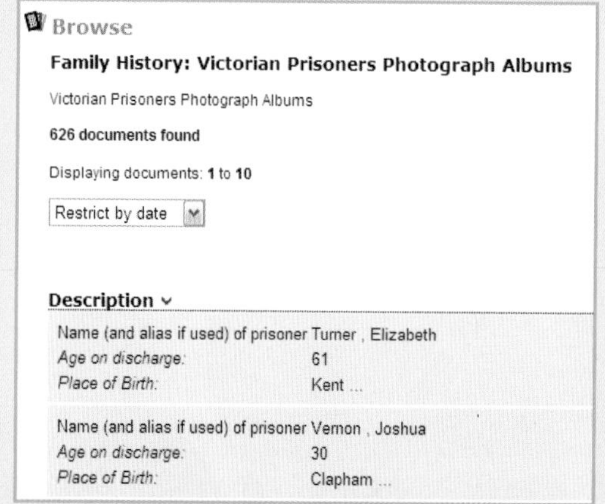

Did your relative have a photo album?

2 The National Archives also has more than 600 Victorian prisoners' photograph albums online. From the TNA homepage, go to the drop-down menu at **Search the archives** and select **Documents online**. From the next screen click **Search documents online** and then choose the link to **Victorian prisoners photograph albums** from the **Family history** section.

The poor and the destitute

You may find you have ancestors who fell upon hard times and had to ask for what was called 'poor relief'. Sometimes local parishes helped, but often the shame and hardship of life in the workhouse was all that lay ahead.

Until Henry VIII dissolved all the monasteries in the 1530s, the poor were usually cared for by the monks and nuns of religious houses.

With these havens burnt or ransacked, the poor were meant to be cared for by individual parishes, but the system was haphazard and ineffective. Parishes were expected to raise money from their parishioners to provide for the poor and for orphaned children.

Dealing with the poor

The rules for the care of the poor in England and Wales were formalised by the Poor Law Act of 1601, and lasted for more than 200 years. Records cover the system of outdoor relief for the so-called 'deserving poor' (where money or food and clothing were given, but people remained at home) and the houses of correction (see page 208) for those who were considered the 'undeserving poor'.

For records of the Elizabethan Poor Law, outdoor relief or houses of correction you'll need to go to county record offices. A useful reference book is *An Introduction to Poor Law Documents before 1834*, by A. Cole.

The dreaded workhouse

Between 1832 and 1834 the Poor Law was reformed and rationalised, with parishes organised into Poor Law Unions, each with its own workhouse. The official view now was that the poor were largely responsible for their own plight, so the workhouse was designed to be a harsh place, discouraging the poor from seeking relief there. Controversy over workhouse conditions led to a New Poor Law in 1847, which imposed a rigorously implemented, centrally enforced, standard system for all, which centred on the workhouse. The records generated all relate to admission to these dreaded institutions.

Hard times *The extremes of poverty that affected many people are captured in illustrations from Henry Mayhew's 1862 book* London Labour and the London Poor.

The officers of poverty

The website **nationalarchives.gov.uk** holds information about the records of the governing bodies – the Poor Law Board and the Poor Law Commission – under the code MH (Ministry of Health). If you have an ancestor who was a workhouse official, you'll find records of the staff between 1837 and 1921, with details of dates of appointment and salary, in MH9. In MH12 you'll find the names of thousands of individuals listed by poor law union, with notes of the dates of correspondence, but with no indication as to the subject.

The 'lucky' poor in Scotland

Scotland was way ahead of England and Wales when it came to caring for their poor. The Poor Law (Scotland) Act came into force in 1579. Although records are sparse, it seems that the poor were cared for by wealthy landlords of the parish, who were known as 'heritors'. Payments were noted in the minutes, accounts and heritors' records of the parish Kirk Sessions. Names of the

Searching the quarter sessions

Poor Law records can also be found from searching the records of the quarter sessions. These were the courts in England and Wales that supervised and implemented the Poor Law. The Access to Archives site, **a2a.org.uk**, contains information relating to the quarter sessions.

Go to the search page and enter **Quarter Sessions** into the search tool bar. Then key in the location that you wish to search and you'll be taken to local studies and records for the area.

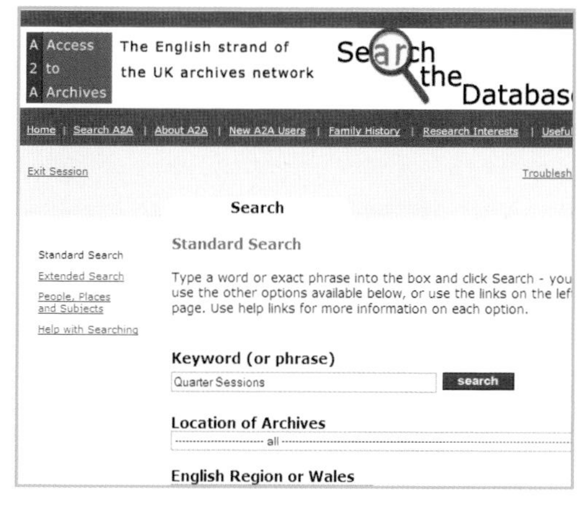

poor receiving relief appear on the Poor Rolls, which are held by the National Archives of Scotland (see Directory). The Poor Rolls show the amounts paid and the recipients' disabilities – which can add poignancy to your research.

Ireland and its poor

Before 1838, when Poor Law Unions were formed in Ireland, private and religious charities took care of the poor. Some towns had almshouses where records may have been kept, but generally, few records were kept of recipients. When the Poor Law Unions were introduced in Ireland, there was only 'indoor relief', which meant that paupers were taken into grim workhouses.

Each Poor Law Union kept records of the people it helped. In many cases, inmates were encouraged to emigrate to North America, Canada, Australia and South Africa, to get them off the list. Details of who went, their ages, names and where they came from, as well as who went with them and where they were going, can be found among individual Poor Law Union records. Many are held at the Public Record Office of Ireland. You can find out more about the Irish Poor Law Unions at **ancestry.co.uk**, **rootsweb.co.uk** and in the civil registration lists at **genuki.org.uk**.

Map of distress *Poor Law Union boundaries are shown on this faded 1890 Ordnance Survey map of Ireland. It was once hand-coloured to show the degrees of anticipated distress – acute, severe or light – even 40 years after the Irish Famine.*

Life in a workhouse

If your ancestors were unfortunate enough to suffer from incapacitating ill health, or were unemployed for long periods of time, they may have ended up within the grim walls of a Victorian workhouse.

Based on the unforgiving sentiment that the poor were feckless and had brought their fate upon themselves, workhouses were forbidding and uncomfortable places. They were nationally established by the Poor Law Amendment Act of 1834 (see page 210), although many individual workhouses existed before this. Under the Act, local parishes were grouped into Poor Law Unions and each union had to provide a workhouse.

The workhouse system was eventually abolished on April 1, 1930, but the records hold fascinating information and can add heartbreaking details to a search for an ancestor whose life took a turn for the worse.

Inmates were free to come and go as they liked, but life within the workhouse was deliberately made as austere and mortifying as possible so that layabouts and vagabonds would not be tempted to use them as a free hotel. Only those who were truly desperate would apply to live there.

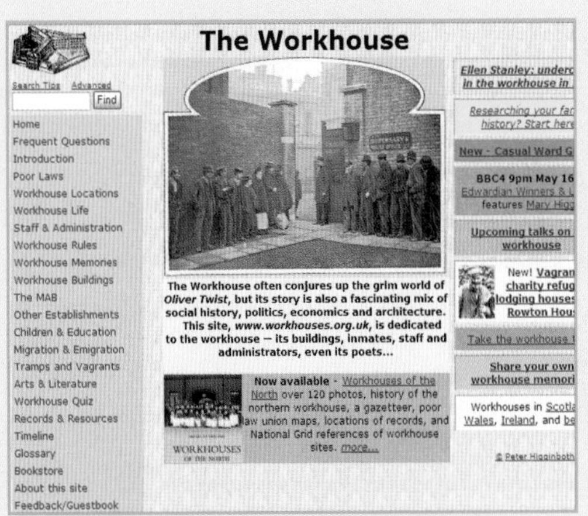

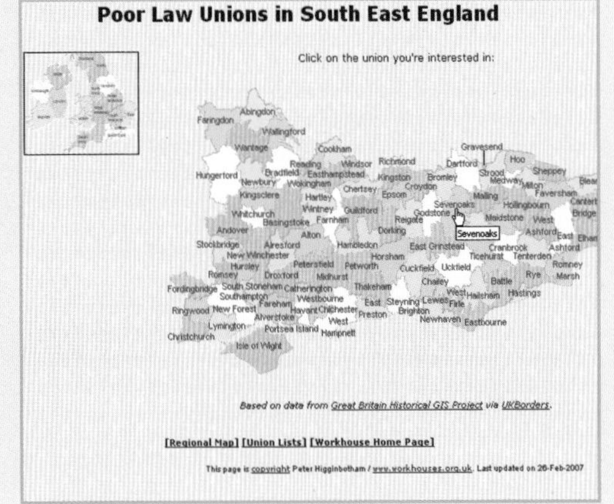

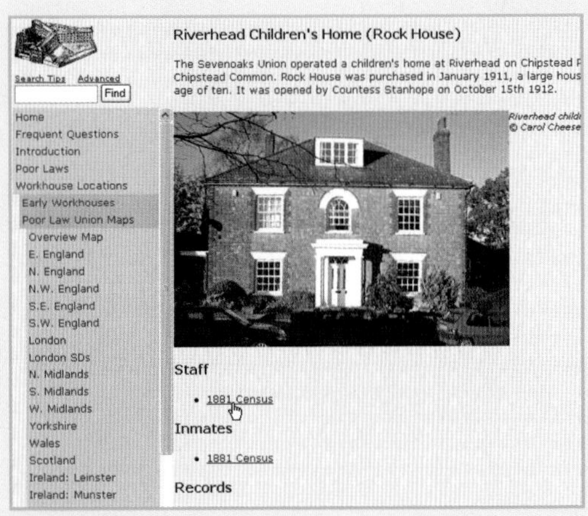

Searching for a workhouse

1 To find an ancestor, for example a James Brown who worked in a workhouse in Kent, go to the homepage **workhouses.org.uk**. Enter his name into the search menu, top left. You'll see a list of all those with this name who were recorded within a workhouse. If it's a very common name, you'll need to refine the search by adding a location. If you're not sure whether there was a workhouse in your town, click on **Workhouse locations**, then on **Poor law union maps**.

Choose a location

2 This will open another menu, which has organised the nation into regions. You know James Brown was in Kent, and think it was Sevenoaks. Choose **S.E. England**. Click on the region for **Sevenoaks**, shown on the map.

Find the workhouse

3 The page reveals a brief history of the workhouse in Sevenoaks, with maps and photographs of the building, both past and present. There's also a link near the bottom of the page under 'Records' to relevant county records – here the Centre for Kentish Studies. From the links at the top of the page, click on **Staff** to be taken to the section of the site that deals with workhouse staff and inmates.

When people went into a workhouse, they were given a thorough medical examination, and if they weren't found to be infirm or chronically ill, they were put to work breaking stones or picking hemp, crushing bones, digging ditches or cutting firewood. Women were given lighter tasks, such as mending and laundry. Elderly men were put to work in kitchen gardens.

Families were split up and the sexes were segregated, making the experience particularly traumatic for children. The only good thing that can be said for the institution was that vulnerable people were given basic shelter and food, and rudimentary medical care – which was better than being out on the streets.

Researching online

To find out more about workhouses, go to **workhouses.org.uk**. It has lots of detail about the Poor Laws, the English, Welsh and Irish Poor Law Unions, as well as maps, locations and photographs of all known workhouses. There are examples of workhouse rules and links to relevant archives. It's an extremely easy-to-use website with a wealth of interesting information, even if you're not searching for a particular person.

Young, poor and infirm *The grim comforts of the workhouse are evident in this 1897 photo of inmates of the Ormskirk Workhouse in Lancashire. Workhouse registers, such as that from Whitechapel (right), provide invaluable detail on the circumstances leading to admission.*

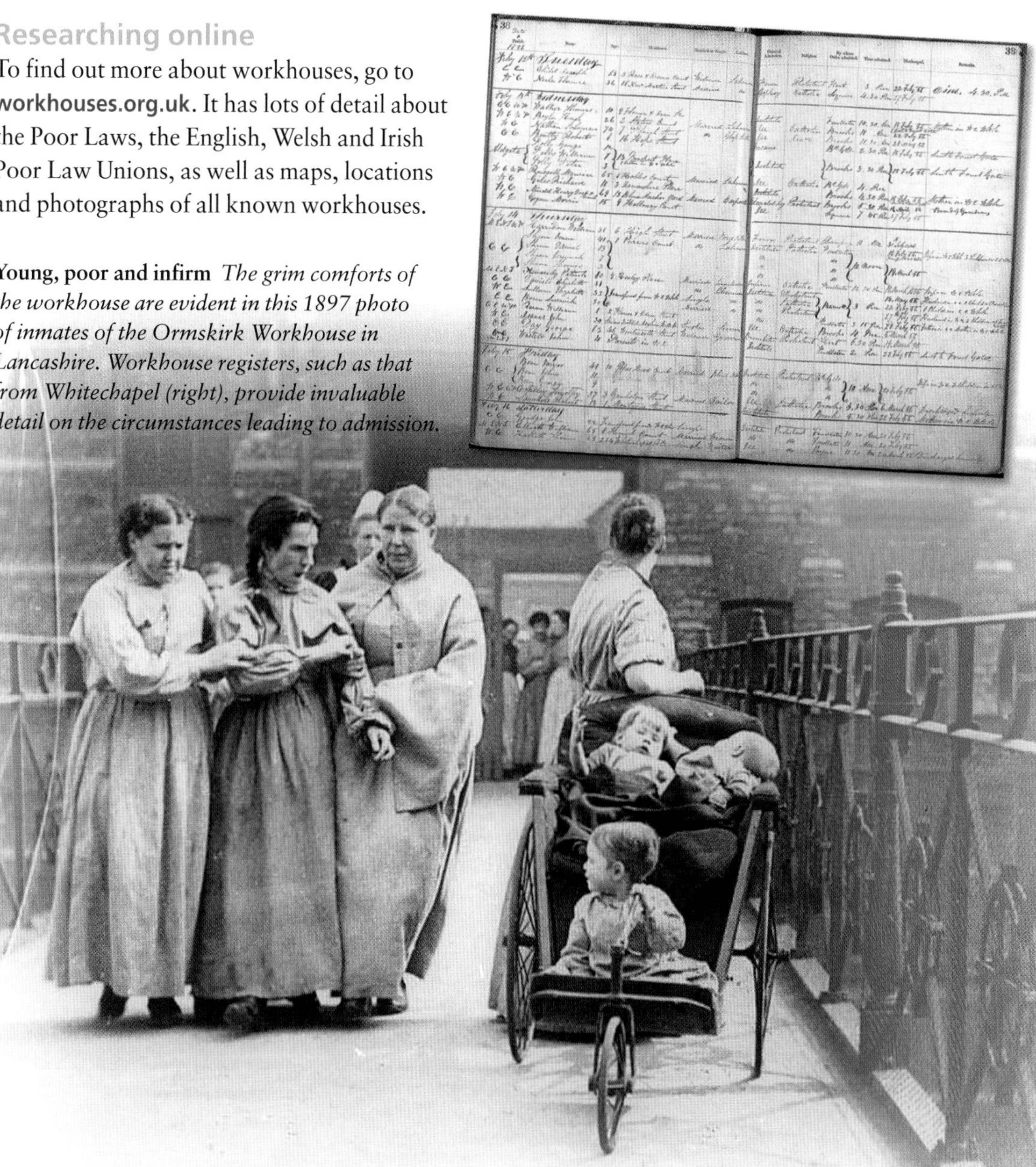

Search Tips Advanced
Find

Home
Frequent Questions
Introduction
Poor Laws
Workhouse Locations
Early Workhouses
Poor Law Union Maps
Overview Map
E. England
N. England
N.W. England
S.E. England
S.W. England
London
London SDs
N. Midlands
S. Midlands
W. Midlands
Yorkshire
Wales
Scotland
Ireland: Leinster
Ireland: Munster

1881 Census: Residents of Sevenoaks Union W Kent

Name	Mar	Age	Sex	Relation	Occupation
Staff					
James BROWN	W	59	M	Master	Master Of The Workhouse
Phillis ROBERTSON	U	38	F	Matron	Matron Of The Workhouse
William Arthur BRAILEY		6	M	Visitor	
Frederick HICKS	M	33	M	Porter	Porter Of Workhouse
Rosalie HICKS	M	32	F	Nurse (Wife)	Hospital Nurse
Selina CONWAY	W	35	F	House Nurse	House Nurse
CARD	U	23	M	Schoolmaster	Schoolmaster
Inmates					
Ann ALLEN	W	71	F	Inmate	No Occupation
John ANNETT	W	66	M	Inmate	Agricultural Labourer
Charles BAKER		8	M	Inmate	
Charles BAKER		11	M	Inmate	
Elizabeth BAKER		4	F	Inmate	
Ann BALL	W	83	F	Inmate	No Occupation
Joseph BARTHOLOMEW	U	61	M	Inmate	Housekeeper
William BARTHOLOMEW	U	61	M	Inmate	Pot Boy
William BELL	W	54	M	Tramp	Rope Maker
Hannah BERRY	W	63	F	Inmate	Hawker
Frederick BOAKS		13	M	Inmate	
Jane BOAKS	W	40	F	Inmate	Domestic Servant
Louisa BOAKS	O	13	F	Inmate	
Alice BOND	O	12	F	Inmate	

See the staff and inmates

4 This gives you the option to view the staff or inmates, as shown in the 1881 census. Clicking on **1881 census**, under **Staff**, will reveal a list of staff in order of position. Here we find James Brown, Master of the Workhouse, and further details about him, his marital status, age, relation to others in the workhouse and occupation or position. Directly below this are records of the inmates in alphabetical order.

Taxpayers and their records

Nothing can be certain except death and taxes, so the saying goes. What's also certain is that both yield excellent information for the family historian.

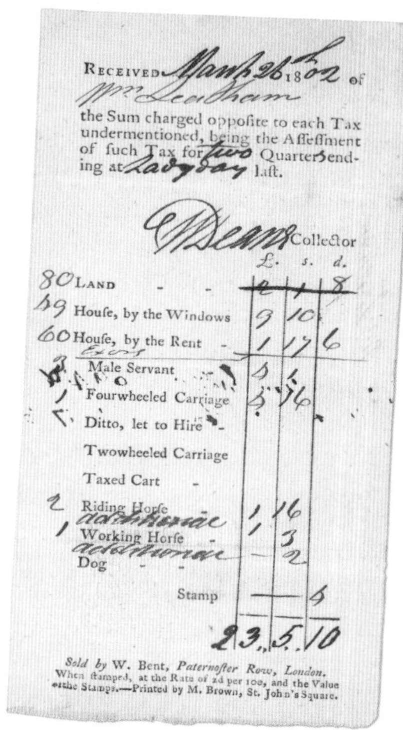

RECEIVED March 26th 1802 of
Wm Leatham
the Sum charged oppoſite to each Tax undermentioned, being the Aſſeſſment of ſuch Tax for two Quarters ending at Ladyday laſt.

W Dean Collector

		£.	s.	d.
80	LAND	2	1	8
59	Houſe, by the Windows	9	10	
60	Houſe, by the Rent	1	17	6
	Male Servant	5	1	
1	Fourwheeled Carriage	4	16	
	Ditto, let to Hire			
	Twowheeled Carriage			
	Taxed Cart			
2	Riding Horſe	1	16	
1	Working Horſe	1	3	
	Dog	—	2	
	Stamp	—	—	4
		23	5	10

Sold by W. Bent, *Paternoſter Row, London.* When ſtamped, at the Rate of 2d per 100, and the Value of the Stamps.—Printed by M. Brown, St. John's Square.

Proof of payment *Dated March 25, 1802, a tax receipt for the two quarters ending on Lady Day includes £9 10s for the number of windows in the house and £4 16s for a four-wheeled carriage.*

Taxation goes back a long way and so do its records, offering a wealth of detail about people and their social status. The records of particular interest to family historians include the intriguingly named Fifteenths and Tenths, as well as returns from Poll Tax, Hearth Tax and Tithes. Many tax records can be searched online at The National Archives (see opposite).

Taxes of the Middle Ages

Records of medieval taxes are plentiful, but most are written in Latin and relate almost entirely to England. Wales was only included in the taxation system by the Act of Union in 1536. At this time, the king could tax people only to subsidise unusual expenditure, such as a war. He could also impose taxes directly, in the form of feudal levies or forced loans.

The Fifteenths and Tenths

In 1332, Edward III imposed a tax known as the Fifteenths and Tenths. It was levied at the rate of a fifteenth of income in the country and a tenth in the city. Two years later, he levied it again, at the same rate, and the amounts that he collected in 1334 became the basis of all taxes for the next three centuries. A system of fixed quotas on individual townships was introduced, and the same amount was due every time Parliament granted the king's request for a tax to be imposed.

The much-hated poll tax

Poll taxes were levied on individuals, rather than property. Everyone over a certain age had to pay a given amount, so documents including them may have information about your ancestors. The widely loathed poll taxes, introduced in 1377, 1379 and 1380, led to the Peasants' Revolt in 1381. These records aren't online, but *The Poll Taxes of 1377, 1379 and 1381* by Caroline Fenwick (British Academy Records of Social and Economic History, new series, 1998-2004), contains surviving receipts from these taxes.

The Tudors tax movable goods

The early Tudors changed taxation, assessing the value of a person's movable goods or income from land (whichever was the greater) and taxing it at a given rate. Under Henry VIII, these taxes became the norm. From 1523, the names and contributions of individual taxpayers were recorded.

After 1563, the threshold was fixed at a higher rate and so only wealthier people were required to contribute – which means records beyond this period are less extensive.

Counting the hearths

Between 1662 and 1689, a levy on hearths was levied. Each householder had to pay a shilling for each hearth in their property, every year. Many of the records also include lists of those who were exempt – so you'll find records of hearth taxes a good source of names. You can search the records in series E179 at TNA (see opposite, far right) – just select **Hearth tax** from the drop-down menu.

Tithes – a tenth of income

Tithes were payments to the church of one-tenth of a person's crops or livestock; they reveal how wealthy people were. In 1836, payment in kind was dropped in favour of money payments – a process known as 'commutation'. The resulting Tithe Files include letters to the Tithe Commissioners and records of the commutation in some areas. The records are usually only available on microfilm at TNA, in series IR29. Tithe maps are held in IR30 and you can look at the original maps, in person; some more fragile maps can be seen as microfilm copies only. Some County Record Offices will have tithe projects, so check your local office.

A tax on the land

If your ancestors were landowners, they should appear in the Land Tax records, but remember that owners weren't necessarily resident on their land. The Land Tax was introduced in 1692 and abolished in 1963; its records list the landowners (and occupiers) in each parish and give some indication of their social status. Survival of land tax records varies from county to county and the most complete records cover 1780 to 1832.

Land Tax records are kept in the relevant County Record Office, but can be searched at **a2aorg.uk**. Go to the **Search** page and enter **Land tax** as a keyword. Then, using the drop-down menu, find the relevant archive.

How to search tax records at TNA

The most informative tax-related documents at TNA are in series E (for Exchequer) 179, which contains the majority of records relating to tax assessment and collection in England and Wales from the 13th to the 17th centuries. These records show how taxes were administered and also reveal much about the people who paid them.

You can search E179 by place, date, tax and document type, or a combination of these. Although names of individual taxpayers aren't included in the database E179, it can be used to identify documents containing the names and you can then consult this document in person at TNA. The database is also linked to both the online TNA catalogue and, for visitors to Kew, to the document ordering service (see page 163).

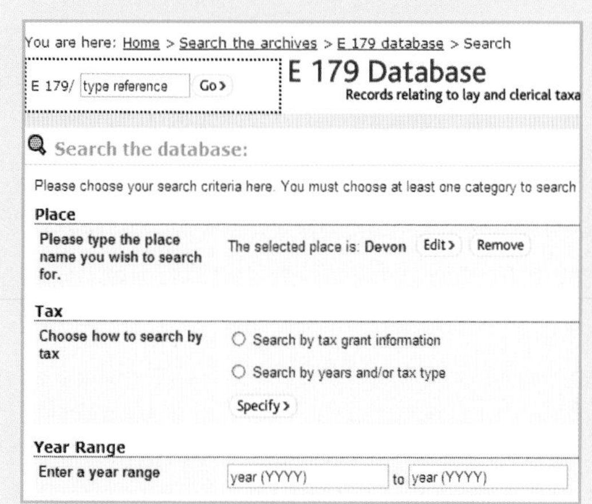

Search for a Fifteenth tax record

1 To search for Fifteenths relating to Devon, from 1550 to 1559, go to **nationalarchives.gov.uk/e179**. Then click on **Search E179**. Enter 'Devon' in the **Place** box and confirm it as a selection. Under **Tax**, click on **Search by years and/or tax type**. Click on the **Specify** button, then use the drop-down box under **Tax** to select **Fifteenth** and enter '1550' and '1559' into the **Year range** boxes. Click on **Search the database**.

You are here: Home > Search the archives > E 179 database > Search > Results

E 179/ type reference Go >

E 179 Database

Records relating to lay and clerical taxation

Search the database:

There are 7 results within E 179 Database, grouped below by Piece reference.
Page: 1 of 1

Piece reference	Document date
E179/100/345	[1555 Nov 30 or later]
E179/100/346	[1553 June 29 or later]
E179/100/347	[1555 Nov 30 or later]
E179/100/348	[1555 Nov 30 or later]
E179/100/349	[1555 Nov 30]
E179/100/352	[1558 Nov 10 or later]
E179/298/1	[1559 - 1569]

Choose a document

2 You'll see a list of documents. To find out more about the document you're interested in, click on the link on the left-hand side. You'll be shown a document that you can see by visiting The National Archives (TNA). Make a note of the details.

Insurance records

Fire was a great hazard when most houses were thatched. With open fires and candles in every house, the chances of a fire breaking out were high. Enterprising characters established fire insurance offices in London in the late 17th century and in the wider country a few years later. The registers contain details of thousands of businesses and homes. Local record offices hold the records for local companies, and the Guildhall Library (see Directory) holds those for more than 80 London-based insurance companies. You'll need to know the policy number to find the right entry in the register.

The A2A site, **a2a.org.uk**, can help you to find insurance records. Click on **Search a2a** and enter **Insurance records** and a county as keywords. Follow the links that are offered.

Read all about them

Newspapers are a rich source of information for the family historian, not only for notices of births, marriages and deaths, but also for news items about events that might have affected our ancestors.

It's likely that your ancestors will have made the odd appearance in the newspapers of their day, and it's fascinating to try to trace them through national and local papers.

The earliest papers were no more than news sheets and, in the 17th century, were largely political, taking sides in the Civil War. But in the 18th century, they became of more interest to the upper classes, professional people and merchants who looked to them for political and business news. By 1785, there were eight morning papers in London alone; one of them, *The Daily Universal Register*, was renamed *The Times* in 1788.

Spreading the words

Most 18th and early 19th-century papers published outside London were called 'provincials'. One of them, the *Norwich Post,* first published in 1701, ran both national and local news. By 1750, most counties had their own papers. They played an important role, keeping people up to date with new laws and taxes that might affect them, as well as with the latest news, both local and from London.

The rapid expansion of the railway network in the mid 19th century made it easier to get newspapers, hot from the press, to all parts of Britain, and meant that local papers could incorporate national and international news. And when the stamp duty on papers was repealed in 1855, the lower production costs meant newspapers became affordable for the masses. This got *The Daily Telegraph* off to a flying start in 1855.

Reduced costs had a marked effect on local papers: the number of titles proliferated and most areas had at least two, taking opposing political stances and vying with each other to carry the most interesting stories. Local news now included news of sudden deaths, inquest reports, funeral notices and obituaries of both well-known and even more ordinary people.

News of the ancestors

Towards the end of the 19th century, local papers carried news of flower shows, sporting events, the arrival and departure of doctors and clergy, and reports on societies – all rich hunting grounds for news of your ancestors.

The obvious place to search is in the births, marriages and deaths section of the paper, but remember that most local people wouldn't have appeared, as they had to pay to have a notice published. So your ancestors may be found if they were wealthy and important, or had reached a grand old age, worked for the gentry for many years, had died suddenly or in suspicious circumstances – or had left a number of orphans for the parish to care for. By the 1880s, far more middle-class families were prepared to pay for announcements.

DAILY SKETCH.

ONE HALFPENNY.

HISTORY'S MOST WONDERFUL DERBY: FIRST HORSE DISQUALIFIED: A 100 TO 1 CHANCE WINS: SUFFRAGETTE NEARLY KILLED BY THE KING'S COLT.

Dramatic moment *Suffragette Emily Davison flings herself in front of the king's horse at the Epsom Derby on June 4, 1913. Although not online, some original papers can be viewed at local archives and libraries.*

Limitations of online searches

Most local papers aren't online, so to access this rich source of information, you may have to visit newspapers' archives, or your local library, and leaf through collections of old papers. They're usually stored in date order, so you'll need a rough idea of the date of the event you're researching.

If you're not sure which newspaper archive you want, or where it is, go to the Access to Archives website, **a2a.org.uk**, which allows you to search local newspaper archives by location, keyword and date. Another impressively comprehensive source of information is the the British Library's Newspaper Library at Colindale, in London.

The British Library catalogue

The British Library lists its huge collection of newspapers in its catalogue, which has entries for more than 52,000 newspaper and periodical titles. The collection includes all UK national, daily and Sunday newspapers from 1801 to the present; most UK and Irish provincial newspapers, some dating from the early 18th century; selected newspapers from around the world in European languages, some dating from the 17th century; and a range of periodicals from the UK and Ireland covering fashion, music, hobbies and trades.

Go to **bl.uk/catalogues/newspapers** to see what papers are held, but to view the actual journals you'll have to travel to the British Library's reading room in Colindale, north London (see Directory).

Searching the catalogue online

Each entry in the British Library's newspaper catalogue shows the title, place of publication and the dates held. The catalogue may be searched by entering a keyword – such as a title or place name – or by a combination of keywords. The search results you receive may be sorted and displayed alphabetically, by title or place of publication, or by year of publication. You can limit your search to a specific period of time by combining a keyword search with a date search. Simply select the **Date search** facility and enter the appropriate keyword(s) and year(s). The results will list the relevant newspapers in the collection, and tell you whether they're kept on microfilm, microfiche or hard copy.

Visiting the British Library

On your first trip to Colindale, you'll have to apply for membership of the library for a minimum period of three months. You'll need ID and a plan of what you intend to research. Some newspapers are kept on open shelves, and you'll be given a shelf-mark to help you to find them. Most will need to be ordered from the stacks. The items you select can only be read in certain reading rooms.

If you are unable to visit, the British Library offers a newspaper search service. For £50, a researcher will search up to four newspapers and report on articles found. You can then order copies if you want to.

The word on the street *A group of newsboys in 1910 wait for fresh supplies of the latest papers to sell to a public hungry for news and sensation.*

Newspapers in Scotland and Wales

For national and local newspapers of Scotland and Wales, check the collections held by the National Library of Wales at **llgc.org.uk** and the National Library of Scotland **nls.uk**.

National newspapers online

Some national newspapers have digitised their early editions and scanned their images. This has created a wonderful resource for you to search for news of your ancestors or find about the lives they led.

The newspapers described on these pages have the best online collection of early newspapers. Most national papers have their own website with online archives available to search by keyword, but they rarely go further back than the date that they first began publishing current issues on the website, usually from the late 1990s. The National Archives, at **nationalarchives.gov.uk** doesn't hold collections of newspapers, although it does have a few papers that might have been sent to government departments because they were considered politically sensitive.

The Times online

Of all the online collections of digital records, *The Times* has the most comprehensive. It has been split into three periods, each with its own search engine.

☛ Recent editions of *The Times* are free to search online at **timesonline.co.uk**, but only as far back as 2000.

☛ *The Times* and *The Sunday Times* have an online archive that can be searched back to 1985, at **newsint-archive.co.uk.** It's free to search by keyword, date range, headline, writer and section, but if you find pages you'd like to view, you'll need to subscribe. This costs a minimum of £10 for 10 downloads, but each download is cheaper if you invest in a more expensive subscription.

☛ The Times Digital Archive is a digital edition of *The Times* from 1785 to 1985 that you can search by keyword to find facsimile images of either a specific article or complete page. It contains a wealth of birth, marriage, death and funeral announcements, obituaries, court summaries and criminal reports, as well as details about change of name and address, and advertisements that may have been posted by one of your ancestors' businesses.

This archive can only be accessed via the InfoTrac database, which is a subscription-only facility designed for institutions. To use it, you can visit the British Library or The National Archives (see Directory) and use their subscriptions, free of charge, on computers in the reading rooms.

In addition, many local libraries hold subscriptions, which you may be able to access online from home, using your library card number and a pin number the library will supply you with. Contact your local library to find out how to access their InfoTrac system from home.

The Scotsman digital archive

If you have Scottish forbears, you'll find **archive.scotsman.com**, *The Scotsman*'s digital archive, really helpful. The paper was first published in Edinburgh on January 25, 1817, as a liberal weekly, pledged to 'impartiality, firmness and independence'.

The past, online *These three news websites are treasure troves of valuable and fascinating family history – not just for details of births, deaths and marriages, but also for the exciting times that framed the major events in your ancestors' lives.*

It's now a well-established daily national newspaper, and every edition of *The Scotsman* from 1817 until 1950 can be searched online.

You can search the **Calendar** to find issues from specific dates, or use the **Search** facility to look for a keyword, within a date range, from advertisements, articles and pictures. It also contains birth, marriage and death announcements.

The newspaper is free to search, but to view full articles you'll need to take out a subscription. An Archive Pass can be bought online for about £8, which gives 24 hours' unlimited access, or longer periods can be purchased at discounted rates. Students who've been provided with an ATHENS Login password by their educational institution can access the digital archive free of charge.

Penny Illustrated Paper

The British Library's Collect Britain website, **collectbritain.co.uk**, a lively virtual archive of some of its exhibits, includes a complete digitised and indexed run of the *Penny Illustrated Paper*. This paper, published in London between 1863 and 1913, reported news from across Britain and the Empire to many eager readers and is an enthralling source of information.

To access the 52,000 pages and 500,000 images, go to the **Collect Britain** homepage and either search the site by keyword and date, or use the **Quick link** to the *Penny Illustrated Paper*. That takes you to a page offering a range of editions, as well as the option to search the collection. You can download the results free of charge.

Official news in the Gazettes

From the late 17th century onwards, all legal notices in the UK were published in *The London Gazette*, *The Belfast Gazette* and *The Edinburgh Gazette*. These publications may sound rather dry, but they're essential if you're searching for important events in your ancestors' lives. Not only do the Gazettes contain information relating to State, Parliament and ecclesiastical issues, including official appointments, but you'll also find insolvency and bankruptcy notices, deed polls, name changes, and military medal and honours awards – any of which could apply to one of your ancestors.

The historic archive covering the 20th century – and even earlier for *The London Gazette* – has been uploaded by The Stationery Office (TSO) to provide free access for everyone. Go to **gazettes-online.co.uk**, where you can choose to visit the homepage of *The London Gazette*, *The Belfast Gazette* or *The Edinburgh Gazette*.

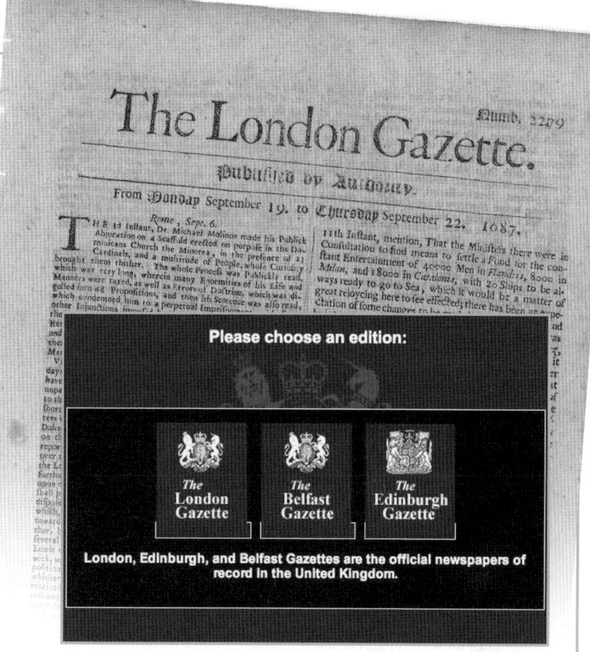

Searching the Gazettes

On the homepage of the Gazette you've chosen, go to the **Archive** tab at the top. Select **Full search** from the drop-down list and click on the **Search archive** link.

To make a simple search of all the notices, enter a keyword, such as a name you're looking for, in the **Find** box. Narrow the date range and then click on the **Search** button.

Alternatively, if you'd like to find a record of a relative who received a civilian or military medal, enter their name in the **Find** box and narrow the date range to cover the war years you're interested in, such as 1939 to 1945. For *The London Gazette*, simply select **World War II records**, and choose the type of medal you believe your relative was awarded, from either the **Civilian medals** or **Military medals** drop-down list.

The **Archive search results** page will show a list of the issue numbers and dates that your search criteria match, with a link to view the page from the Gazette. Download each page by clicking on **View edition in PDF format** and search for your keyword on the page.

The keyword won't be highlighted on the page, so if you have difficulty finding the word, click on the binoculars symbol and type your keyword into the **Find what** box, which will highlight that word on the page.

The London Gazette can be searched up to 1997, *The Belfast Gazette* up to 1999 and *The Edinburgh Gazette* up to 2001 using this search engine. To search issues later than these dates click on the relevant link, such as **Search London Gazette notices post 1997**, and you'll be taken to a separate search engine for that period.

The news from Ireland

The Dublin Gazette, known as *Iris Oifigiuil* since 1922, has a website at **irisoifigiuil.ie**, but its online archive goes back only to 2002.

Where they lived

Finding out where in the British Isles your ancestors lived is crucial to your search. It can be a puzzle working through the administrative and geographical changes over the years, but there are plenty of websites to help you.

How the British Isles divides

Over the centuries the boundaries of counties, boroughs and other administrative areas have varied. When researching, you need to understand the changing divisions – this can affect where old documents are kept, how they are arranged and what survives.

The British Isles are divided into the major administrative regions of England, Wales, Scotland, Northern Ireland, the Republic of Ireland, the Channel Islands and the Isle of Man, but the administrative geography of individual regions has changed several times. Once you understand the changes, you'll be able to target your search better. It will also help to explain why there's so much material available on the internet for some parts of the country and not for others.

The Republic of Ireland

In 1922, when Ireland was divided, 26 of the 32 counties became the Republic of Ireland, and the remaining six counties stayed under UK administration. This means that records for Ireland are split according to time and place: material for all Ireland until 1922 and the Republic since then is located in The National Archives of Ireland in Dublin; material for Northern Ireland after 1922 is in the Public Record Office of Northern Ireland, in Belfast (see page 100).

Pancake day *Local customs and traditions exist throughout the British Isles, and your ancestors will certainly have watched or taken part in some. Here, women in Olney, Buckinghamshire, celebrate Shrove Tuesday in 1951 with their annual pancake race. The tradition began in 1445 to celebrate the final day before Lent.*

Isle of Man and Channel Islands

All these islands are self-governing. Of the Channel Islands – Jersey, Guernsey, Alderney and Sark – only Sark doesn't have its own administrative centre (see Directory).

Mainland counties

In England and Wales, the administrative districts are the counties (also referred to as shires), and most documents relating to local areas will be found in the relevant County Record Office. Counties are made up of smaller administrative districts whose boundaries have often changed. Knowing about changes in the past will help you to find records at the relevant County Record Office.

THE 'HUNDREDS' Ancient counties in England and Wales had sub-divisions known as 'hundreds' that were used in census-taking until 1834 when many gave way to Poor Law Unions (see page 210). In 1889 Municipal Boroughs and Urban and Rural Districts, governed by County Councils, were introduced. This new system brought the number of counties to 62.

COUNTIES AND GREATER LONDON By 1965, the total number of counties had decreased to 58, and the boundaries of Greater London were established. Some towns that are now in Greater London, such as Harrow and Barking, were officially in Essex, Kent, Hertfordshire, Surrey or Middlesex before 1965. The administrative county boundaries were abolished in 1974 and replaced by six Metropolitan counties and 39 counties that were non-Metropolitan.

Scotland

In the 17th century, Scotland was divided into counties and burghs, which were ancient urban settlements given trading privileges by the Crown. Burghs of Barony were granted to some landowners, Royal Burghs were mainly sea ports, and Police Burghs had a town council to take care of policing, paving, lighting and cleaning. The numbers of burghs increased with time and boundaries moved. County Landwards and Parish Landwards were areas of land within a county or parish that did not fall within a burgh.

Knowing what type of burgh or county your ancestor lived in is helpful, because separate valuation and electoral rolls were compiled for Royal Burghs and Police Burghs until 1975. After that, burghs were replaced by district councils, and then by local authorities in 1996. Burghs also produced court books, guild records, registers of deeds, financial accounts and records of Burgh institutions such as schools and libraries.

A land captured in the Domesday Book

More than 900 years ago the new Norman masters of England created one of Britain's oldest public records, full of names and details of places, many of which still exist. The priceless original is housed in Kew at The National Archives – but you can read the entries online.

When William the Conqueror urgently needed to raise funds to prepare to combat a threatened Scandinavian invasion in 1085, he commissioned the Domesday Book. Commissioners were sent all over England, and asked such detailed questions that landowners likened the process to the Last Judgment – or 'Doomsday' – described in the Bible. The data recorded was deemed 'final proof' of legal entitlement to land – and in some cases still is. As recently as the 1960s, information in the Domesday Book was used to settle a dispute over land and property rights.

The first draft, completed in August 1086, held records for 13,418 settlements in the English counties south of the rivers Ribble and Tees; many northern counties were exempt from royal taxation, or were not yet fully under Norman administration. The Domesday Book is, in fact, two volumes (see right): Little Domesday – a detailed survey of Norfolk, Suffolk and Essex – and Great Domesday, comprising the rest of England. London and Winchester (the capital of England in 1086) were surveyed, and spaces left for them in Great Domesday, but for reasons that are unknown today were never entered. Bristol and Tamworth were also omitted.

Domesday online

The National Archives (TNA) has transcribed each entry from the Domesday Book into a database that's searchable by place or person, at **nationalarchives.gov.uk/domesday**. This means that local and family historians can learn about the medieval history of a settlement and its population, as well as something about what life was like in the 11th century. If, for example, you enter Halnaker in West Sussex, you get a transcription of the original entry listing the names of people mentioned, such as 'Guntrum' and 'Thorkil, free man', and the village's Domesday name – Helnache; you can also download an image of the original for a small fee.

Answer the following questions…

Domesday was not a population census. Instead it itemised land and landowners at various points in time – at the death of Edward the Confessor (1066); when the new owner received the land; and at the time of the survey (1085-6). Each landowner,

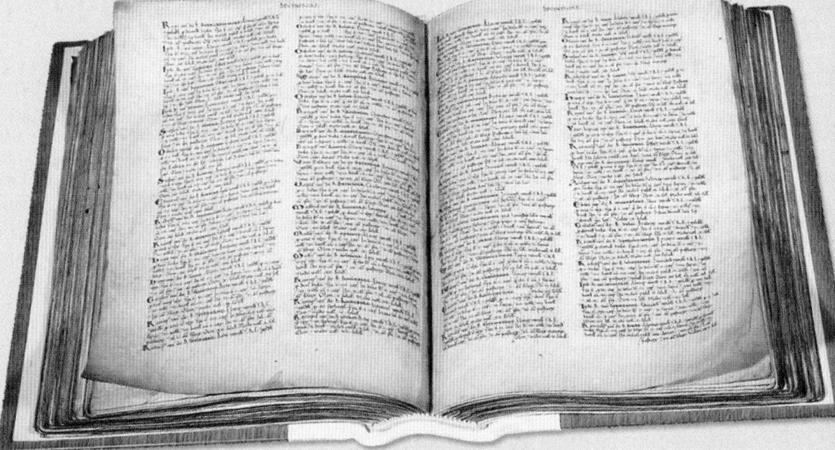

Not so small
Little Domesday (right) may not be as big as Great Domesday (above) but its entries contain more information.

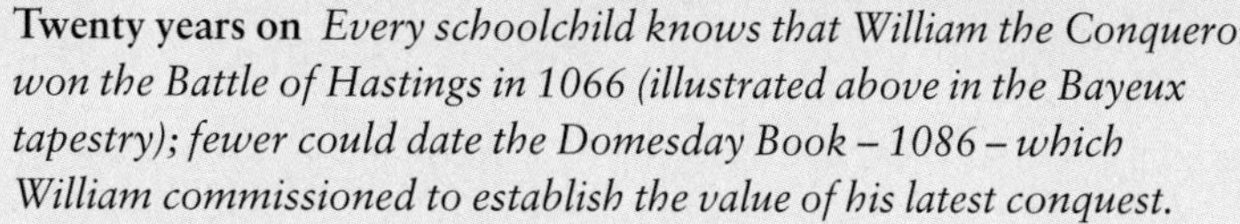

Twenty years on *Every schoolchild knows that William the Conqueror won the Battle of Hastings in 1066 (illustrated above in the Bayeux tapestry); fewer could date the Domesday Book – 1086 – which William commissioned to establish the value of his latest conquest.*

In your best hand *Little Domesday took around six scribes up to 12 weeks to write using quill pens. Great Domesday was mostly the work of one scribe, with help from five others, who would often have to go back and make corrections.*

or a designated representative, had to visit the local court and, after being sworn in, would be asked a series of questions by commissioners-under-oath in front of a jury of barons and villagers. The questions included:

> What was the name of the manor?
> Who held it in the time of King Edward?
> Who holds it now?
> How many hides [land measurement]?
> How many ploughs?
> How many men, either free, tenant or slave?
> How much wood, meadow and pasture?
> How many mills and fishponds?

The information was recorded in Latin in black and red ink on sheepskin parchment by one or more scribes, and then double-checked by another. According to the contemporary *Anglo-Saxon Chronicle*, 'there was no single hide nor a yard of land, nor indeed one ox nor one cow nor one pig which was left out'.

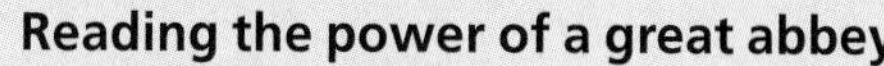

Reading the power of a great abbey

A number of local history societies have used the Domesday Book to reconstruct a picture of local life in the 11th century. Details of the entry for Peterborough Abbey can be seen at **cottinghamhistory.co.uk/domesdaybook.htm**. The transcript reads: 'Land of Peterborough Abbey. The Church itself holds in STOKE Hundred COTTINGHAM. 7 hides. Land for 14 ploughs, in lordship 2; 4 slaves; 29 villagers and 10 smallholders with 10 ploughs. A mill at 40d; meadow, 12 acres; woodland 1 league long and ½ league wide. The value was 10s; now 60s'. The website explains what each entry means and gives a map of the area.

Old money *From Domesday until the Dissolution of the Monasteries in the mid 16th century, Peterborough Abbey was rich and powerful, and owned large areas of fertile – and taxable – farmland.*

Local history – and how to find it

Once you know where your ancestors lived, it's really rewarding to explore websites about their locality. These sites provide useful information and fascinating details about the lives they led.

When you start trying to find out about a particular area in the British Isles, you'll need to consult some of the websites that can help you to identify local administrative boundaries, research local history and locate records. Here are a few of the more comprehensive.

genuki.org.uk

Genuki has an excellent breakdown of information about the whole of the British Isles on its county, town and parish pages, with links to family history websites, history societies and archives. For more about the site, see page 44. From the United Kingdom and Ireland homepage you can choose to search the administrative regions of England, Wales, Scotland, Northern Ireland, the Republic of Ireland, the Channel Islands and the Isle of Man.

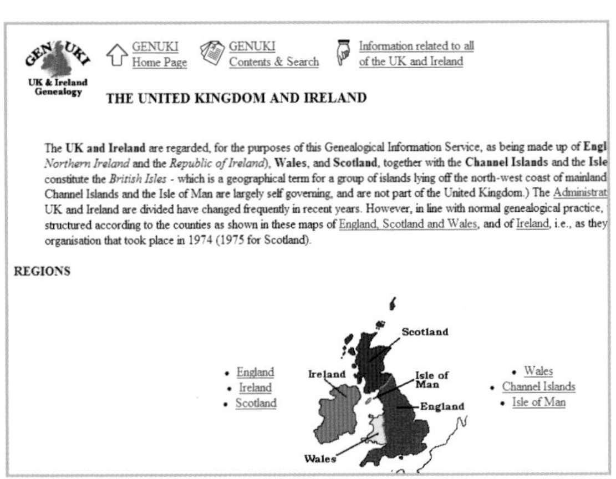

curiousfox.com

Curious Fox is a website aimed at helping family and local history researchers with interests in the same villages or towns to connect with each other and share their knowledge. You're free to search the database of posted entries, which you do by location, but to make the most of the site, it's best to become a paid-up member for £5 a year. This allows you to send messages to other members who may have information useful to your research, and it allows you to search the posted entries by surname. The website covers England, Wales, Scotland and Ireland.

victoriacountyhistory.ac.uk

Known as VCH, Victoria County History was founded in 1899 in honour of Queen Victoria, and is an encyclopedic record of England, arranged by county, from the earliest times to the present day. Information on the VCH website is based on original documents and work done by historians across England and tells what life was like in each area of England, give detailed accounts of cities, towns and villages, and explain the social and economic history of each county.

The VCH index is arranged by county. It lists the publications that are available for each county, with a description of the topics discussed. It has links, via British History Online (a digital history library), which enable you to read many of the publications free of charge. If the volume you're interested in is still in print, you can order it online, but you'll find most libraries have copies of the volumes that cover their local area. Although the VCH website concentrates on England, you'll find Scottish records and documents are also accessible through the site's link to British History Online.

Local gems *Information about every section of the British Isles is there on the Genuki website (left). It will be a great help to your quest for ancestors and information about how they lived.*

Curiosity satisfied *Searches on Curious Fox (right), by county, town, village or surname, should yield details of that elusive ancestor and his home, lifestyle and times.*

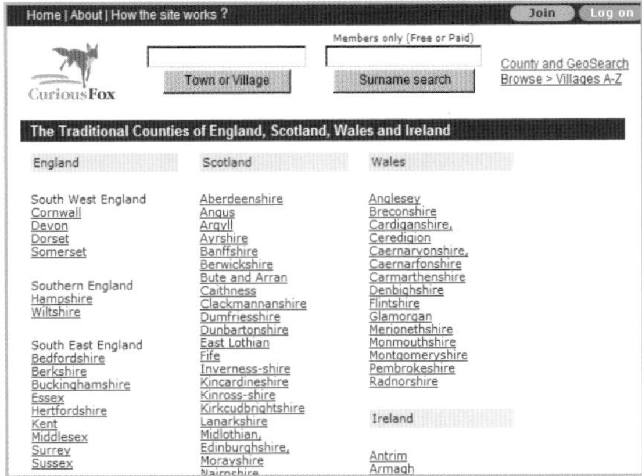

Blair Castle *The archives held in this Scottish castle include letters from Charles Stuart, the Young Pretender, and Queen Victoria's childhood notebooks. Many other documents are there, too – such as the letters Sir Harold Goodeve Ruggles-Brice wrote to his wife while fighting in the Boer War. You can access these documents through ARCHON on The National Archives website (see below).*

nationalarchives.gov.uk/archon

The ARCHON directory, which is accessed via The National Archives (TNA), holds contact information for archives around the British Isles, as well as details of institutions from all over the world that hold manuscripts and documents that are useful for local history research.

Use the interactive map to get an alphabetical list of repositories for each county, or use the search engine to find archives in a specific town or county. For example, select Scotland from the map, and scroll through the alphabetical list of record offices and archives to Blair Castle. Click on the name for full details of what is held in the repository and you'll be swept up into another world (above). It includes address and contact details, a street map and a list of what National Register of Archives indexes are held in the castle. The wealth of information is encouraging if you want a picture of what your Scottish ancestors' lives were like, and the events that affected them.

visionofbritain.org.uk

The Vision of Britain Through Time website was created by the Great Britain Historical Geographical Information System Project, and is a wonderfully detailed site designed for people interested in local history. Its resources describe Britain and its localities, showing how they've changed over the centuries.

The site has used statistics from census returns between 1801 and 1961, information from 19th-century gazetteers and travellers' tales dating back to the 12th century to create a wealth of local histories that can be searched by a village or town name.

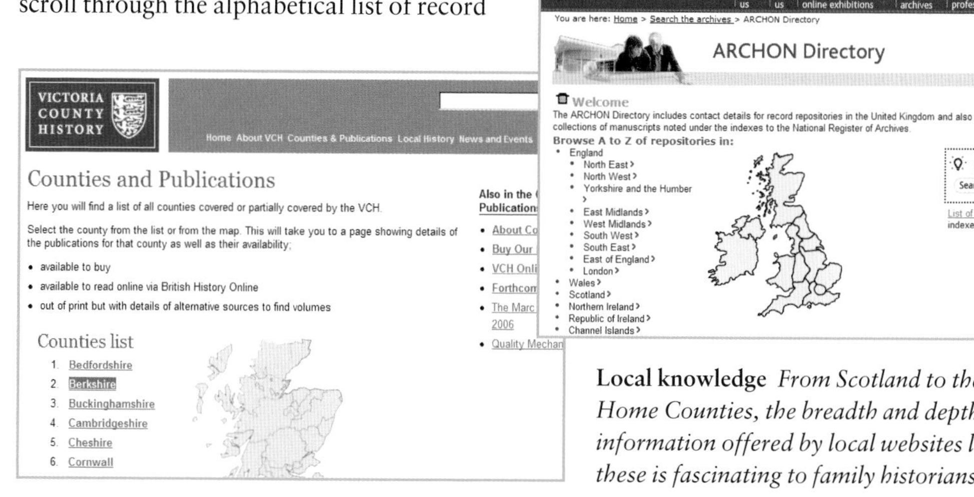

Local knowledge *From Scotland to the Home Counties, the breadth and depth of information offered by local websites like these is fascinating to family historians.*

Getting down to the grass roots

When you start to reveal those missing ancestors, it's enthralling to find out how they lived day-to-day in their communities. Local history websites can bring those worlds to life.

How did the village where your relatives lived look all those years ago? What were their workplaces like, or their houses, and can you still visit them? What kind of clothes did they wear? Seeing pictures of other people who lived in the same area in the same period, or reading contemporary personal accounts, can give you a vivid impression of the daily life your ancestors might have led.

More and more local authorities and history societies are building websites with photographs, moving images, personal documents and oral history that provide deep insights into a local area. Check the local history society, record office, library or county council websites in the area of interest to you, to see if they have projects as packed with information as these examples.

Handsworth – village to suburb

The Digital Handsworth Project at **digitalhandsworth.org.uk** holds an online collection of historical material about the ancient parish of Handsworth near Birmingham. The project charts the area's change from a rural village with medieval roots to its urbanisation from the 1850s to the 1940s, and its later development into a multicultural suburb. There are valuable contributions from local libraries, archives, museums and community groups who've uploaded photographs, prints, personal documents, newspaper extracts, old maps, and video and audio clips.

You can search these resources by keyword or theme – **People, Place, Subject** and **Time**. There's also a quick-search facility which is useful for finding out about a particular event, such as the Blitz. A map explorer helps to find information about a specific location in or around Handsworth.

Handsworth's history *Browsing the Digital Handsworth site for historical events on Handsworth's past yields a wealth of information, backed by first-person accounts, pictures of people and places and enthralling journeys into bygone days. If your ancestors lived here, this will be a gold mine for you.*

The website has an interactive timeline with key events that have occurred in the local area from the Roman period to the present day.

Digital Handsworth is one of seven projects forming the Digital Midlands initiative. The other projects are: Exploring the Potteries, Literary Heritage West Midlands, Revolutionary Players, Secret Shropshire, Staffordshire Past Track and Windows on Warwickshire. See the website **digitalmidlands.org.uk** for details.

Spotlight on south London

The history of six London boroughs and their people are the focus of the Ideal Homes website, **ideal-homes.org.uk**. On the site, Bexley, Bromley, Greenwich, Lambeth, Lewisham and Southwark are explored through old maps, photos and historic documents. Ideal Homes explains the history behind suburbia and what it would have been like to live in these residential developments, using places such as Streatham and Norwood to show how suburbs were created and why. There are also personal memories, such as tales of Coronation street parties in 1953.

It's through these personal documents that life in south London suburbs springs vividly to life – and even if your ancestors aren't mentioned by name, you'll understand more about how they lived and the sorts of things they cared about. A link to each of the six

Life in the suburbs *London's borough of Lambeth was once a country village and may have taken its name from 'lamb' and 'hythe', suggesting a landing place for sheep on the river bank. Pearly kings and queens (below) add to the colourful traditions of the area. The website,* **ideal-homes.org.uk**, *brims with colourful facts.*

boroughs at the top of the page takes you to a summary of the history of each area, with further links to other places within the borough where you can find more specific historical accounts and photos.

You can contribute your own photos, documents and memories of south London to the website and search other people's contributions. The website also plans to offer a keyword search facility.

Great ports of England

A breath of sea air seems to sweep through **portcities.org.uk** as it takes you on a journey through the history of five of our great maritime centres – Bristol, London, Hartlepool, Liverpool and Southampton.

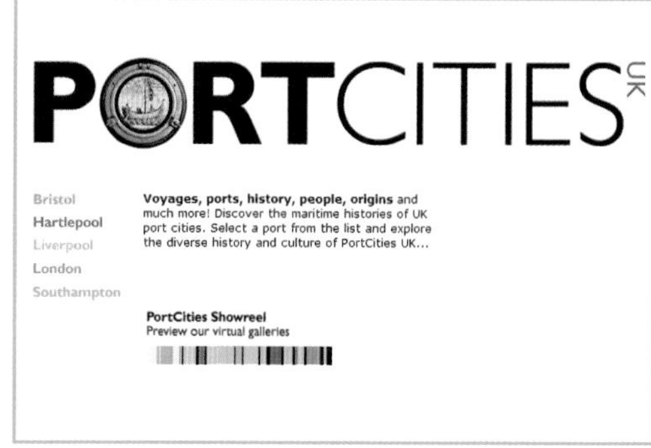

Sailing into the past *From the Romans to the 20th century, PortCities explores Britain's maritime past and its impact on people's lives.*

As an island nation with ancient seafaring traditions, Britain has been hugely influenced by its ports. PortCities explains the impact of the maritime world on British culture by telling the stories of people who lived and worked in port communities, looking at the key events that affected their lives and the industries and leisure activities that grew up around these commercial hubs.

The PortCities website is supported by museums, libraries and archives from across the UK. You can search all five ports at once, or just explore one in detail.

The site's contents can be browsed by time and by topic, and its collections can be searched by keyword. PortCities holds photos, images, stories, videos and expert information about all aspects of maritime life. If your ancestor was a mariner, you can look for images of the ships he may have worked on. Even if your family didn't live in one of these centres, the website is a wonderful place to get a feel for what life would have been like living in big ports around Britain.

Going local in Scotland, Ireland and Wales

Local authorities and history societies in these countries are doing a great job of digitising material about their areas. Online photographs, documents and personal experiences give a real flavour of how your ancestors lived.

Local history sites are easy to use and are often interactive, with links to forums, offline and online, where you can contribute your own memories. The following websites are good examples of the wealth of online material about places and people.

Life in the Highlands

The Gaelic Village, or Am Baile, website, **ambaile.org.uk**, created by the Highland Council, is a digital archive of the history and culture of the Scottish Highlands and Islands. Its material is gathered from archives, libraries, museums and private collections.

An alphabetical subject index allows you to browse tales of Scotland's history, such as the story of the Scottish clans, complete with a Highland clan map. If you have even a scrap of information about the clan your ancestors belonged to, you'll be able to use a keyword search to find images, maps, audio, film footage or narratives about people, objects, themes or places. There's also a page where you can read other people's memories.

Highland highlights *The Gaelic Village site is a must for those with Scottish ancestors. It's an entertaining way to find out all about the heritage and culture of the Highlands and Islands of Scotland.*

Gateway to Ireland

The Island Ireland site, **islandireland.com**, is full of valuable information for researching your Irish local history, with links to many aspects of Irish life, including architecture, archaeology, folk culture, language and music. It's broken down into Irish counties, and the links take you to websites that are rich in detail. For example, the link to the Limerick's Life website provides information about Limerick's colourful history, as well as old and new images of the city, extracts from historic quarter sessions records and some old newspaper excerpts.

Island Ireland also has links to genealogy sites, in and beyond Ireland, along with details of Irish local history societies that you can join.

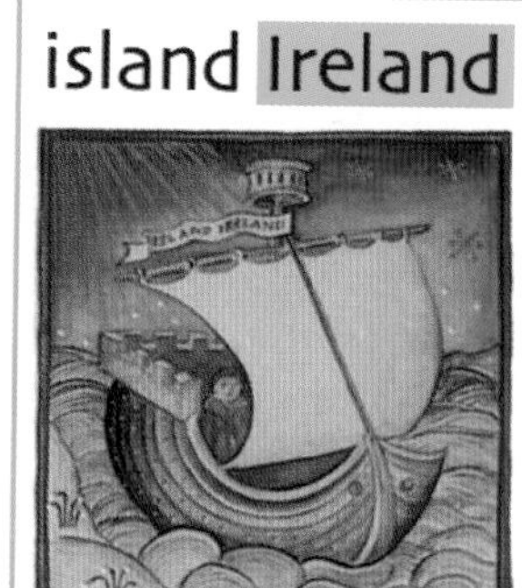

Emerald enlightenment *An enthralling cross-section of all things Irish is stored on this site. You can browse the index list for directories.*

Wales revealed in all its glory

Welsh Wales offers an enthralling history of Wales and its people on its colourful website, **welshwales.co.uk**. It contains links to specific parts of Wales, with particular emphasis on Swansea. As much of the information is written by local people with a passion for their roots, this is a valuable resource for your family research.

Click on the link to **History**, for example, and you'll find a comprehensive history of Swansea describing its many industries from ship-building to mineral exploitation. The site contains fascinating images of the town as it was, and compares old buildings with their present-day appearance. The **Golden yesterdays** section is an illustrated history

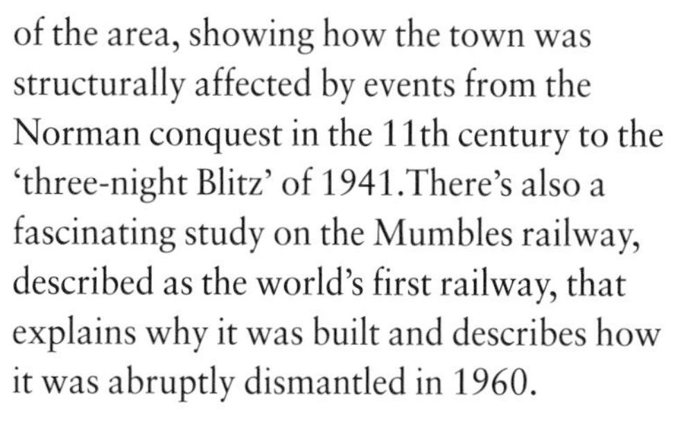

of the area, showing how the town was structurally affected by events from the Norman conquest in the 11th century to the 'three-night Blitz' of 1941. There's also a fascinating study on the Mumbles railway, described as the world's first railway, that explains why it was built and describes how it was abruptly dismantled in 1960.

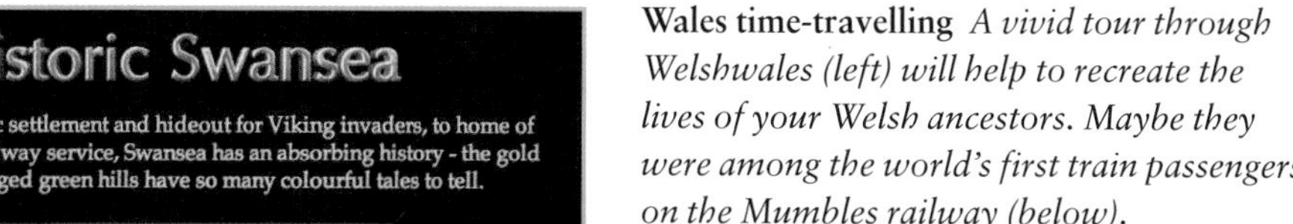

Historic Swansea
From a pre-historic settlement and hideout for Viking invaders, to home of the world's first railway service, Swansea has an absorbing history - the gold sand and rugged green hills have so many colourful tales to tell.
In Swansea's own lifestory, a history of ship building in the 14th Centu
turned to considerably more delicate porcelain manufacture and follow
by exhaustive oyster harvesting; mineral exploitation and copper expor

Wales time-travelling *A vivid tour through Welshwales (left) will help to recreate the lives of your Welsh ancestors. Maybe they were among the world's first train passengers on the Mumbles railway (below).*

The Mumbles Train
- World's first railway service
On 25 March 1807, a railroad carriage converted to carry people was conveyed by horse along the perimeter of Swansea Bay, travelling between "the dunes" at Swansea, and destined for Mumbles, an oyster harvesting and fishing village on the west of the bay. The people who undertook this journey were unknowing pioneers - they were the first railway passengers in world history.
The story of the "Mumbles Train", as it came to be known, is as heart breaking as it is fascinating. Considering its myriad achievements and world records, it's incongruous that the railway isn't more famous. It is disgraceful also that the railway was abruptly dismantled in 1960 (at that time electric tram powered) - 153 years after those historic first steps in 1807. To the commuter age and the world of

Forgotten faces *You may be able to recognise an ancestor in a group photograph. This procession in Wales in 1911 is to celebrate the coronation of George V.*

Trade, postal and street directories

Family historians love finding the right local directories, because these old records can often provide an exact location of a business or home address of a relative. Most are in local libraries and record offices, but some are online.

A few trade directories exist from the late 18th century, but most were produced from the early 19th century up to the 1970s. They began as an aid for commercial travellers, and as the 19th century wore on, the information in them became more comprehensive. From the 1860s directories included private residences as well as tradesmen.

Early trade directories

The first trade directories tended to focus only on a specific town or region. But greater co-operation between directories and the Post Office made compiling the directories more efficient, which led to the emergence of large-scale directories covering substantial areas of the UK. The best known of these were Pigot & Co.'s Directories that date from 1820 and Kelly's Post Office Directories, organised by county and published from 1845 until the mid 20th century.

Annual directories are the most useful. They're a wonderful resource for tracing people's movements, and for filling in missing information for the ten years between each of the censuses. They also play an important role in tracing relatives after 1901, because census records since then are closed – 1911 records won't be fully available until 2012.

Useful for Scotland and Ireland

You'll find directories especially helpful for tracing your ancestors in Scotland and Ireland, particularly in those areas where fewer genealogical sources are available. There's good coverage for both countries from the 1890s, with one directory for Dublin and one for Glasgow dated 1846. There are also the odd directories available for earlier dates, such as Pigot & Co.'s 1824 Directory of Ireland.

Detective work with directories

Local directories can contribute to your research in two ways. First, they can be used to find the address of a person when you only know a name. But more importantly, they can help you to find the person's name when you only have an address or company name to go on. Once you have that name, you'll be able to locate your ancestor in other sources, such as electoral registers and in the census.

Types of directory

Directories were organised in a variety of ways – usually in alphabetical order, by town, by street name and house number, by occupation or by surname. Some directories included more than one type of index, which makes your hunt easier.

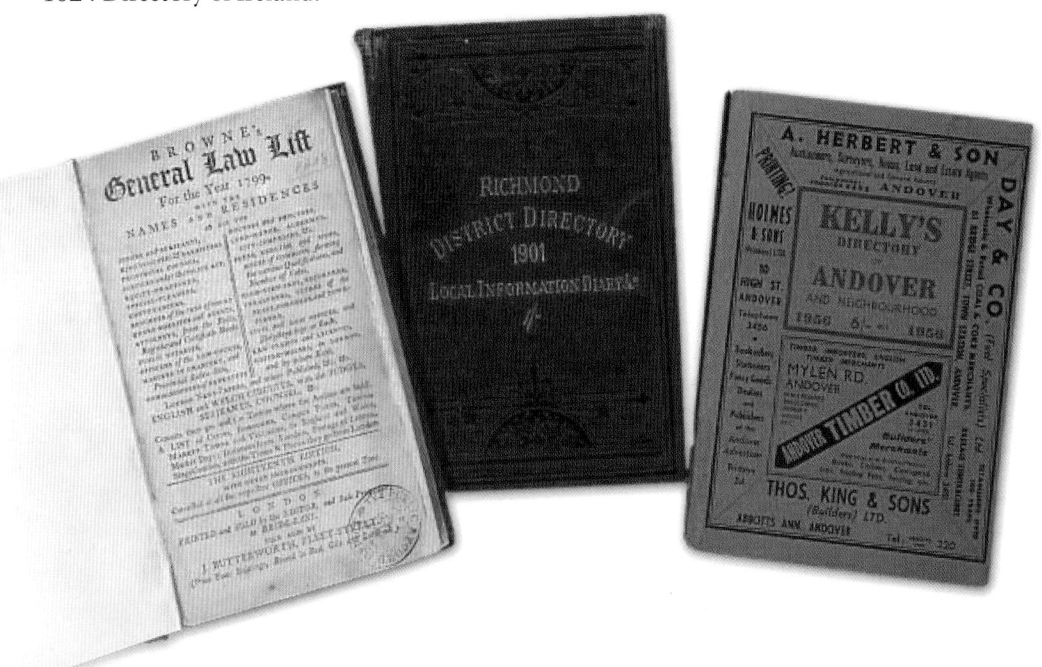

Invaluable resources *Ranging from the late 18th century to the mid 20th century, trade and street directories such as these can be searched for fascinating details about your ancestors.*

The Post Office and its workers

Ever since Charles I established the 'royal mail' in 1635, there's been a need to have a record of people's names and addresses.

With the growth in literacy, followed by the dispersal of people during the Industrial Revolution, the Post Office was kept busier and busier delivering letters. By the late 19th century, it employed around 170,000 people. Their records, showing appointments, pensions and dates of retirement, may also reveal birth date, wages received and reason for retirement. You can find out more about them at **postalheritage.org.uk**.

Mass communication *Postmen in 1930 sort through millions of parcels during the annual Christmas rush. Accurate use of addresses was never more important.*

TRADE DIRECTORIES These were most often arranged by town and then alphabetically by trade, sometimes with a second index of surnames. They give the name of the business, its address and the owner's name. They sometimes have a residential section as well, supplying the names of people not listed in the commercial section. This combination is particularly helpful to family historians.

POSTAL DIRECTORIES Arranged by county and then alphabetically by town, these directories usually give a short description and introduction to each place, with the names of local gentry and prominent people and institutions, a list of local traders grouped by occupation and, sometimes, even a residential list.

STREET DIRECTORIES All types of premises were covered, arranged by town, and then alphabetically by street name and numerically by house number. This kind of directory can be particularly useful if you're looking into the history of your own home (see page 234), because you can go straight to the address in the directory, without needing to know the name of the person who lived there.

Points to bear in mind

When using directories to help you to find an ancestor, there are some limitations to the information they can provide. For example, trade directories give only the head of the household or owner of the business, not the names of everyone living or working at the address. Consider these facts, too:

- House numbers and street names have changed over time, which can make it difficult to pinpoint a modern address. For example, most streets named after Nelson Mandela will have had an earlier name. Using directories in conjunction with old maps (see page 242), electoral lists (see page 294) and rate assessments helps to identify how and when the name changed.
- People renting rather than owning a property weren't usually listed.
- Private residents could choose not to be listed, which can confuse your search.
- It's easier to trace men than women through directories, as women were less likely to be listed as the head of a household or the owner of a business, or to own property of any kind.

Finding old directories

Your search will be speeded up if you know just where to look for trade, postal and street directories. Help is available, online or offline.

Most local archives and libraries hold the directories relevant to their area. You may be able to find them on the shelves, or ask to see copies that have been kept on microfilm. They are usually arranged chronologically.

If you can't track down the directory with information you want, there are some useful specialist reference books on the subject. Try looking in *British Directories – England & Wales, 1850-1950* by Gareth Shaw and Allison Tipper (2nd edition, 1997) or in *Guide to the National and Provincial Directories of England and Wales, excluding London, published before 1856* by J. Norton (Royal Historical Society, 1950). Your local reference libary should have copies of them for you to check.

Sweet treats *Customers line up to buy in a Victorian grocer's. This and all other shops would have appeared in a local trade directory.*

Websites that help in the search for a directory

These sites will help you to find the old postal, trade and street directories that may be able to take you further in your search for relatives. You could also try the Society of Genealogists' Library at **sog.org.uk** (see page 173).

The Digital Library of Historical Directories

The University of Leicester is compiling an online database of English and Welsh trade, postal and street directories from 1750 to 1919, available at **historicaldirectories.org**. There's no charge for searching the scanned directories by location, date or keyword.

The keyword search is particularly useful if you're not sure of where your ancestor lived, because it lets you search for a surname even if the directory is indexed by occupation or address. You can find out which directories are available for each county by selecting the **Find by location** search option.

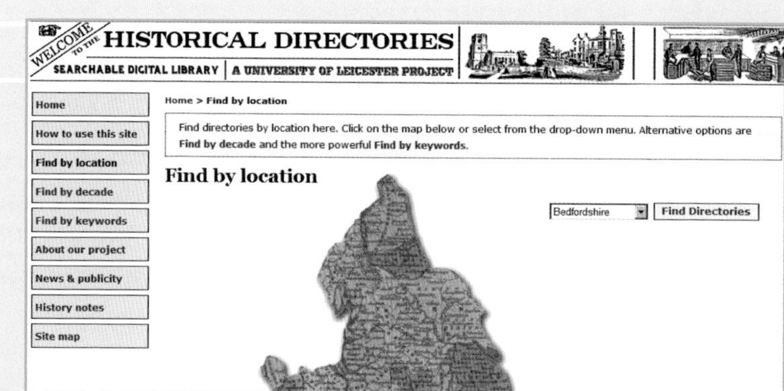

Genuki

Genuki has transcriptions and surname indexes to some trade directories at **genuki.org.uk**. Navigate to the relevant county page and then look under the **Directories** section to see if there are any indexes or transcriptions for that county. For example, the Kent County page has transcriptions of part of Pigot's 1840 and Kelly's 1936 directories, as well as surname and place name indexes for Pigot's 1823 and 1839 Kent directories. Choosing Kent, for instance, will bring up a screen with 19 options.

Directories

Pigot and Co.'s Royal National and Commercial Directory

The flysheet of the 1839 edition continues ...

"... comprising classified lists of all persons in trade, and of the nobility, gentry and clergy, resident in the towns and principal villages in the above counties. An account of every mode of convenance by railway, road and water; Post-Office regulations, &c."

Alec Whitfield has compiled indexes to surnames and place names for the Kent volume of the 1823 and 1839 editions which have been republished are fairly readily available to researchers.

1823 (available on CD from S&N Genealogy Supplies)
Pigot 1823 (Kent) surname index
Pigot 1823 (Kent) place name index

1839 (available on CD from Archive CD Books)
(facsimile edition published 1993 by Michael Winton - ISBN 0-9504069-5-3, now hard to find)
Pigot 1839 (Kent) surname index
Pigot 1839 (Kent) place name index

1840 Janet and Richard Mason have transcribed parts of the Pigot 1840 Directory.

Fáilte Romhat

This privately run site, at **failteromhat.com/pigot.htm**, has scanned copies of Pigot & Co.'s *Provincial Directory of Ireland, 1824*. You can search the site by province and town, and can choose from Connaught, Leinster, Munster and Ulster. Click on the one you want and an alphabetical list of towns and counties will appear, with links to scans of the pages for that town or county.

Pigot & Co's Provincial Directory of Ireland 1824

Connaught

Scanned images of Pigot & Co's Provincial directory of Ireland 1824. These are in PDF format so that they can be more easily viewed. Please note these files are large. The average size is 250k. Pigot & Co's directory goes through the towns of Ireland alphabetically. It lists a detailed description of the town or city, post office information and shows the names of nobility and gentry living in or close to the town. The traders of each town are arranged according to their trade. Pigot & Co's Directory was first published in 1820.

Province of Connaught	Castlerea	Gort	Sligo
Ballina	Castlerea	Jamestown	Strokestown
Ballinamore	Colooney	Killala	Swineford
Ballinasloe	Drumsna	Loughrea	Swineford
Ballisodare	Elphin	Manor-Hamilton	Tuam
Ballymote	Eyrecourt	Manor-Hamilton	Ballinrobe
Boyle	Galway	Roscommon	Ballinrobe
Carrick-on-Shannon	Galway	Sligo	Westport
Castlebar	Galway	Sligo	

Who's been living in your house?

Tracking down your ancestors' homes and learning more about them helps you to build up a more personal picture of your relatives. It can also reveal what their social status was and what sort of lifestyle they enjoyed.

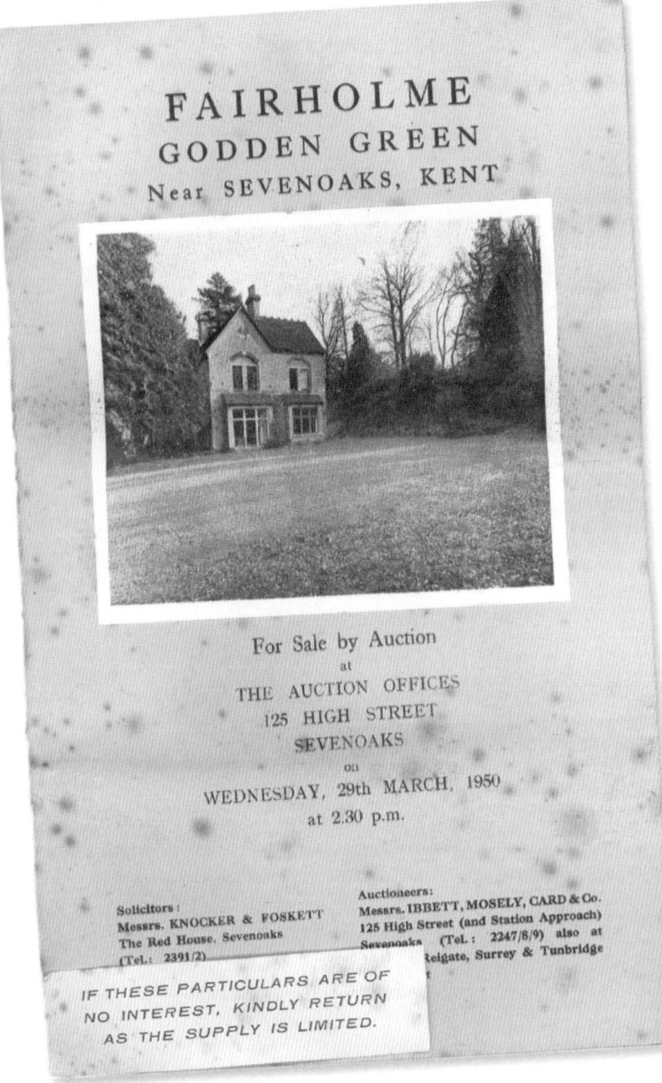

FAIRHOLME
GODDEN GREEN
Near SEVENOAKS, KENT

For Sale by Auction
at
THE AUCTION OFFICES
125 HIGH STREET
SEVENOAKS
on
WEDNESDAY, 29th MARCH, 1950
at 2.30 p.m.

Solicitors:
Messrs. KNOCKER & FOSKETT
The Red House, Sevenoaks
(Tel.: 2391/2)

Auctioneers:
Messrs. IBBETT, MOSELY, CARD & Co.
125 High Street (and Station Approach)
Sevenoaks (Tel.: 2247/8/9) also at
Reigate, Surrey & Tunbridge

IF THESE PARTICULARS ARE OF NO INTEREST, KINDLY RETURN AS THE SUPPLY IS LIMITED.

Did they live in a grand detached house with acres of garden, or was it life above a shop? Was their home situated in suburbia or did it jostle its neighbours in a former slum? There's a variety of resources available online to help you to make a start with researching the history of the homes your ancestors lived in – or, perhaps, finding out more about who lived in the house that you're living in now.

Where do you start?

The census and civil registration certificates you'll have already found are the best starting point. You can trace the addresses given on these documents on old maps (page 242), in electoral registers (page 294), in rate books, in street directories (230-3) and land tax documents (page 214) to learn more about the building, how long your family lived there and what it would have looked like. If you're really lucky, you may even find the deeds, original plans and old photos of the property. Then, using modern maps, you can establish whether the house you're looking for is still standing and if the street has the same name. The highlight of the search will be visiting that street and seeing the house for yourself. If the present owners are friendly, you might even get a chance to look inside.

Desirable property *It's wonderful when you come across the sale particulars of your ancestors' home. Often they'll give you details of the interior, as well as the size of the grounds and the benefits of living in the area. This house was built by the Blackall family in 1864, and it wasn't put on the open market until 1950.*

Searching online

By using the aids available online, you can start to build a good foundation for your research. The websites shown on the right help to map a home today and yesterday, and fill in colourful social detail of many areas.

Need help?

If you get stuck with your house history research and need some expert help, go to the Hidden House History site at **hiddenhousehistory.co.uk** where there's an **Expert's archive** link. It takes you to a page where you can post your queries and receive an expert's answer. Alternatively, you could visit the **Online house detectives** at **house-detectives.co.uk** to find out about the seminars and workshops they run or to commission them to further your findings.

Mapping the history of a home – online

Map websites are a great start. Once you've found the place you're looking for, you can zoom in or out to find your house, and you can cross-refer old and modern maps, to see how areas change over time. Note any outstanding landmarks, like railway lines or large institutional buildings. Not only will this help you to find the house, but these are the features that alter with time. Always make a note of the date of a map, especially if you're printing it.

Multimap

Begin with a modern map site. Multimap, at **multimap.co.uk**, allows you to search by postcode, and will provide you with the location of your property, as well as a larger view of the surrounding area. This will be useful when matching up a house with older maps.

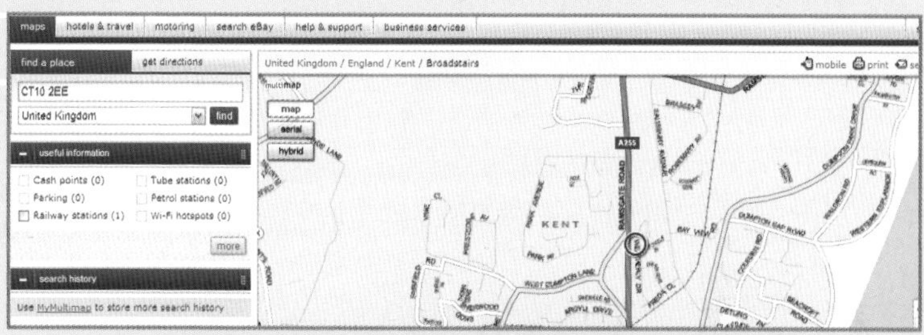

Old Maps

Once you've found your property on a modern map, try to match it up with an earlier map. Old Maps, at **old-maps.co.uk**, has a vast number of historical maps. It's searchable by county, or map co-ordinates. Click on the appropriate county, then on a place within the county, and this should give you a picture of a historic map. For example, when searching for Broadstairs, you need to look under **Kent**, then **B** to bring up an image of the map.

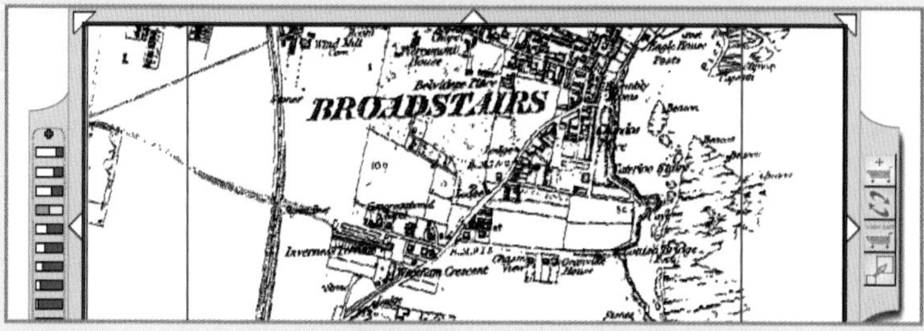

The Francis Frith Collection

It's a good idea to look at the Francis Frith collection at **francisfrith.com**. It has historic photographs of more than 7000 towns as well as maps and shared memories of specific places. This site is easy to search: just type in the place you're looking for, such as **Broadstairs**, and it will direct you to the relevant page. If you're lucky, there'll be old photographs, maps that you can buy online and information about the town and how it has changed.

Vision of Britain

Information about the parish where the house stood is invaluable. Vision of Britain, at **visionofbritain.org.uk**, lets you search parishes by place name or postcode. Here, a search under the Broadstairs postcode 'CT10 2EE' takes you to a history of the Isle of Thanet and describes the changes through time. There's a topic index that covers population changes, land use and mortality rates. You'll be able to see if your ancestors were typical of their time.

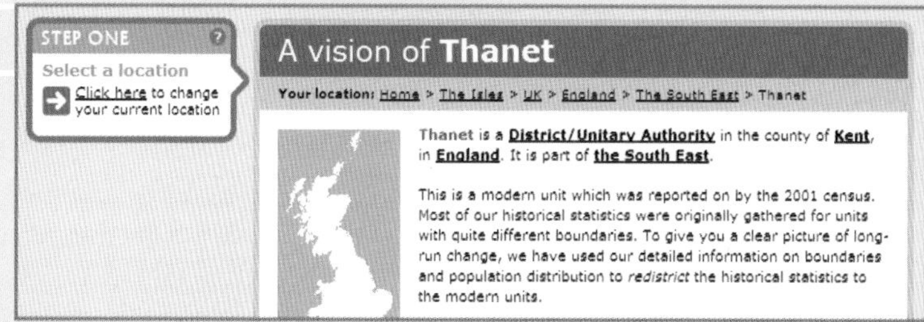

Maps – portraits of a landscape

You can discover much about the lives of your ancestors through maps of the local world they inhabited. These documents give you a sense of the landscape, the size of villages and towns and the rivers, roads and railways that gave access to the area – snapshots in time of how places looked.

Whether researching a local area, or the history of an ancestor's home, you can use past and present maps to find out where people lived, how an area has changed, whether the streets still have the same names – even whether or not the streets still exist and the houses still stand. Great swathes of residential housing were demolished in the late 19th century to make way for railways, stations and goods yards. Other areas were obliterated by bombing during the Second World War. Then, in the 1960s, row after row of Victorian 'slum' terraces were bulldozed and their inhabitants rehoused in shiny new tower blocks.

Maps to augment documents

When a census return or trade directory doesn't give a house number, but you want to find out exactly which building your ancestor lived or worked in, you can use a contemporary map to provide that vital clue. Look on the map for a labelled building, such as a pub or post office, that's near your ancestors' home. Then find that building in the census return or trade directory. You can work your way along the street on the map, following the households listed in the census return or trade directory, and find out exactly which building your ancestor lived in. For more information about using census returns and trade directories, see pages 104-129 and 230-233, respectively.

Surveying the scene *This dapper surveyor and his fine theodolite, of around 1900, were essential to the detailed and extensive work carried out by the Ordnance Survey map-makers.*

Using old maps with new maps

If you compare a modern map with old maps of the same area, you'll soon notice that historical landscape features are echoed by modern ones. Former field boundaries and ancient footpaths dictate the routes of modern roads and the boundaries of housing estates, keeping the old shapes but in new guises. You can use these repeating patterns to help you to pinpoint a specific landmark from map to map, regardless of how extensively an area has been built up. Look out also for permanent landmarks such as rivers and lakes – they're unlikely to change, however much the areas around them do.

Maps online

The internet has made finding and using modern maps easy – all you need to do is key in a postcode, street or place name into a map-finding search engine (see page 242) to see an instant image of the area. A number of websites offer this free service.

Using Ordnance Survey maps

A marvellous aid to tracking your ancestor's whereabouts are the detailed, accurate and to-scale surveys of Great Britain's countryside and towns, dating from the early 19th century, especially the Ordnance Survey (OS) maps that now cover every inch of Britain.

Taking the high road *An Ordnance Survey map of 1929 shows an evocative Cairngorms view. The OS one-inch-to-the-mile map series was trusted by motorists and walkers alike.*

Back in 1791, in response to fears of invasion by France during the French Revolution, the Board of Ordnance (the government body responsible for military stores and weapons) was ordered to create an accurate map of the south coast of England. The first OS map, covering Kent, was published in 1801. Between 1867 and 1870, the OS undertook mapping for the whole of Great Britain in what became known as the 'First Edition Ordnance Survey Map'. Since then, regular surveys have recorded changes to Britain's countryside and towns. On a large scale map, you can even work out the dimensions of individual buildings and houses. By comparing maps of the same area from different years, you can track alterations or extensions to any house or other building.

You'll find historical OS maps in most major archives, local libraries and record offices. Free online access to its modern digital maps is available on the OS website at **ordnancesurvey.co.uk**. These can be searched by place name, postcode or grid reference.

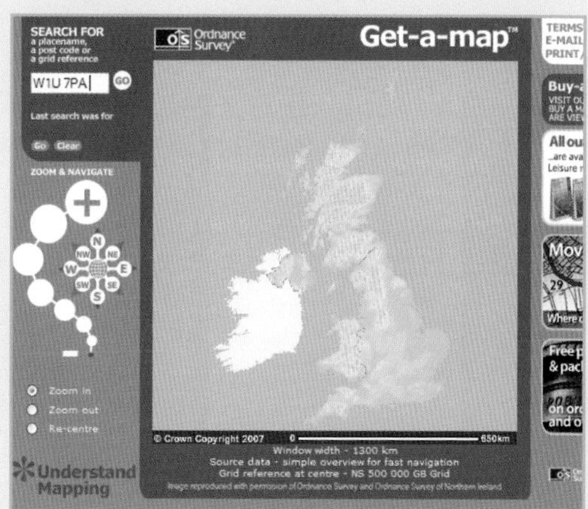

Finding an OS map

1 Enter your search criteria in the box on the homepage at **ordnancesurvey.co.uk** under **View maps online**. Alternatively, click the **Get-a-map** link; then, from the information screen that appears, click the big pink button. Enter the place name or postcode you want in the box on the left at the top – in this case 'W1U 7PA'. Click **Go**.

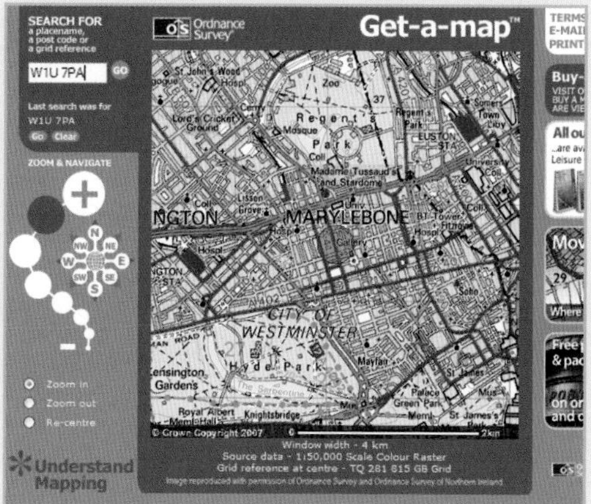

View your chosen map

2 A pop-up of the area map in question appears in the middle of the screen and you can use the tools on the left to move around the map and zoom in or out, save or print, free of charge. If you want information about buying a more detailed map of the area, click the **Buy-a-map** link to the right of the screen to go to the online mapping shop.

The digital miracle of modern maps

Thanks to the internet you can have unprecedented access to modern maps of all kinds, from simple street maps to stunning satellite images which allow you to see the very buildings in which your ancestors lived, worked or worshipped.

A number of websites allow you to view modern maps online, free of charge. Most can be searched by postcode or place name and let you zoom in and see an area close up in great detail, or zoom out to see a building or street in its wider context and in relation to other places. This makes searching for your ancestors' homes far easier than if you were limited to printed maps and atlases. Before you start searching one of the digital map websites for an address that you're not too sure of, it's a good idea to have a 'dry run', and look for your own home, your old school or your workplace. Once you're confident, you can start your search in earnest.

Using Streetmap to search for a map

On **streetmap.co.uk** you can search UK maps by a range of categories including place name, street name, postcode and phone code. Enter a postcode, for example, and click **Search**. This will take you to a map of the area, from which you zoom in and out, using the control functions below the map. If you want to enlarge the map area, click the **Large map** link. To see further in any direction, press the relevant arrow at the edge of the image.

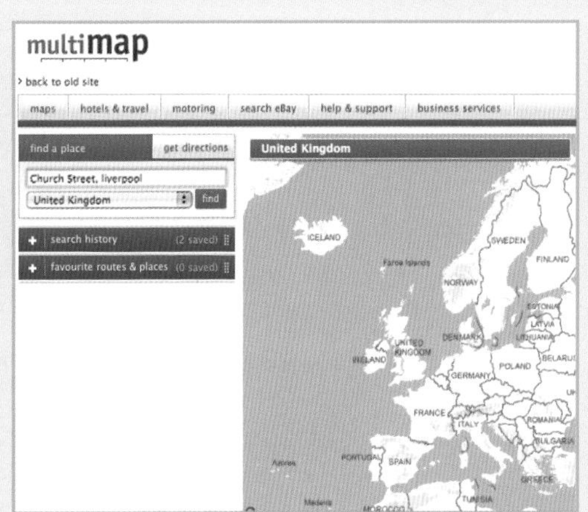

Search Multimap for your street

1 You can use **multimap.com** to search the UK by postcode or place name, and also carry out international searches by selecting an alternative country from the drop-down menu. Key in your search address and click **Find**. A straightforward street map appears.

Get an even better view

2 Multimap also lets you see your chosen area as an aerial photograph; click the aerial button to the left of the screen. If you click the **Hybrid** link, you'll see the aerial photo overlaid with a small section of map, which you can move around with your mouse to display road names. By ticking the boxes to the left of the map, you can discover useful information such as the locaton of schools.

How to download Google Earth

If your PC is less than four years old and has Windows 2000 or XP as standard, you should be able to download Google Earth to see wonderful aerial shots of places anywhere in the world, such as Hampton Court, Surrey (left).

This broadband 3D application is free of charge. Go to **earth.google.com**, click on the green **Download google earth (free)** button and follow the instructions to install the software.

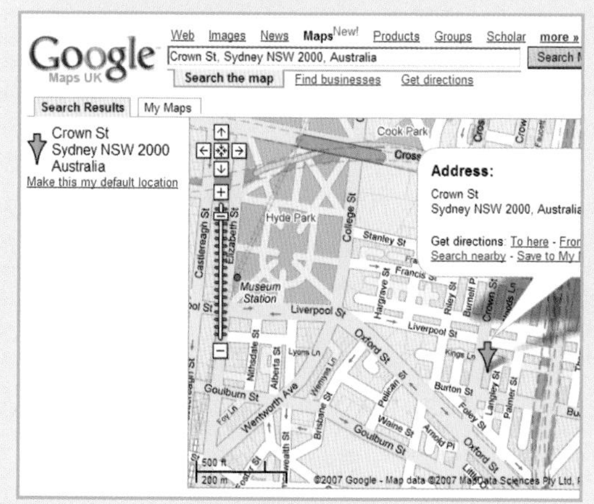

Using Google maps

With **maps.google.co.uk** you can search by street name, place name or postcode, worldwide. Enter the address into the **Search the map** box and click **Search maps**. A green arrow points to your location and a bubble gives the full address, with links to enable you to get directions. You can zoom in and out and move around. If you click on the **Satellite** button an aerial photo of the area will replace the street map; click on the **Hybrid** button and the street map is overlaid on the aerial map.

Google Earth for the big picture

1 On **earth.google.com** there's a breathtaking map of the world, created using satellite images and aerial photographs. It lets you zoom from a country overview to a photographic image of a well-known landmark – or even your own home – close up. Having installed the application on your PC (see box above), double-click the **Launch google earth** icon on the desktop. A satellite photo of the Earth appears with a **Fly to** box, into which you key the address you want.

Explore with Google Earth

2 When you click on the magnifying glass, the screen zooms in to your chosen location, which may take a couple of seconds to appear. You can zoom in more closely and look at individual buildings using the control features at the top right-hand corner of the image, and the map can be 'grabbed' and moved around using your mouse.

Watching Britain evolve

By comparing maps through the ages, you can see just how and when the green and pleasant acres that your ancestors knew were smothered by buildings and restructured by industry, transport and all the facilities of modern life.

The earliest-known English county maps were drawn by Christopher Saxton in the late 1500s. They're fascinating and beautiful but not very useful to the family historian, as few are to scale and none show any roads.

In the early 17th century, a cartographer called John Speed changed all that. He was born in Cheshire in 1552 and worked as a tailor in the family business. After a while he moved to London and began mixing in academic circles, which stimulated a passion for history and map making. Speed joined the Society of Antiquaries, where he found fellow enthusiasts more than willing to advise him, and soon he was able to give up tailoring and become a full-time cartographer. His maps of 1605 to 1610 are more comprehensive and detailed than Saxton's, and include the first town plans of England and Scotland.

Enclosure maps, 1750 to 1830

The earliest detailed surveys of most parishes are enclosure maps – large-scale maps of rural Britain drawn up between 1750 and 1830. The enclosure scheme was introduced by the government to make farming more efficient, in order to cope with the population explosion in the 18th and 19th centuries.

Before enclosure, most English peasants owned a few strips of land on which they grew their food. These strips were redistributed every year – so if you got poor land one year, you'd get a fertile strip or two the next. And every villager had commoners' rights, which meant that even the poorest could graze their animals and cut turf and wood for fuel. Enclosure took away these rights, consolidated all the strips of land and redistributed them as permanent plots. If you got an infertile plot, you were stuck with it. It also obliged the new landowners to fence their plots, which many couldn't afford to do, so they sold their land. Many people lost what little independence they'd had and ended up labouring for the new landowners, or migrating to the growing cities to staff the burgeoning factories. Enclosure maps were drawn up to show how the land had

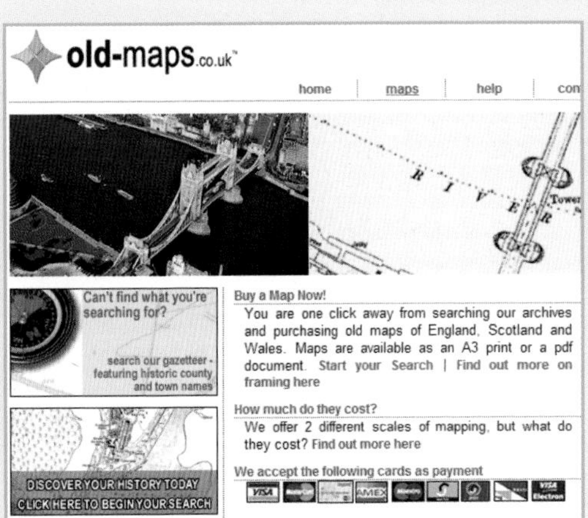

Search for old maps

1 The best place for viewing national historic maps online is at **old-maps.co.uk**. The site holds the digital Historical Map Archive for Great Britain and has collections of historical maps from the OS County Series at scales of 1:2500 and 1:10 560, dating from 1840 to 1948. Click on the link at the bottom left on the screen, where you see **Click here to begin your search**.

Four ways to search the site

2 You can enter an address – town name, modern postcode or street name and number; or use British National Grid co-ordinates, remembering to enter first Easting and then Northing; or use the gazetteer to search by county and then town name (click on the **Gaz** button); or choose from the **Places of interest** drop-down menu.

been divided into 'awards' – 5341 in England and 229 in Wales. They outline fields, farms and settlements, land ownership and parish and township boundaries.

The National Archives (TNA) holds some enclosure maps and tithe maps (see box, right), but the best information as to their location is on **hds.essex.ac.uk/em/**, a free online database, complementing the book *The Enclosure Maps of England and Wales, 1595-1918* by R.J.P. Kain, J Chapman and R.R. Oliver (Cambridge University Press, 2004).

Official taxation maps

After the Finance Act of 1910, the Valuation Office used Ordnance Survey maps (see page 237) to devise a new tax based on property values. It surveyed houses, farms and workshops. Each property was identified and numbered. Details about the property, including its owner, occupier, how many rooms it had and its value were entered into a 'Field Book'. Valuation Office maps for England and Wales are at TNA (series IR121 to IR135); Field Books are in series IR58.

Using tithe maps to track the land

Tithes were originally payments in kind (see page 214). The Tithe Act of 1836 brought in cash payments, and maps were drawn to show the areas on which a tithe was payable. Every map shows the boundaries of woods and fields, roads and waterways and the location of buildings. With the maps were tithe apportionment books, whose numbers correspond to plots on the maps. From these you can find out addresses, names of occupiers, landowners and types of property.

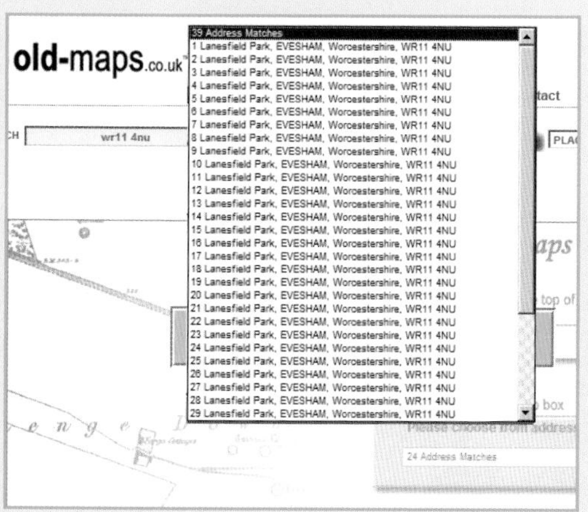

Using a modern postcode

3 To match a postcode of today with an old map, go to **Maps** along the top panel of the homepage and enter, for example, the postcode 'WR11 4NU' into the **Search** bar. Press the **Go** button. This brings up a results page – in this case with 39 matches – from which you can choose an address match, say 21 Lanesfield Park; click the **Down** arrow next to your address result.

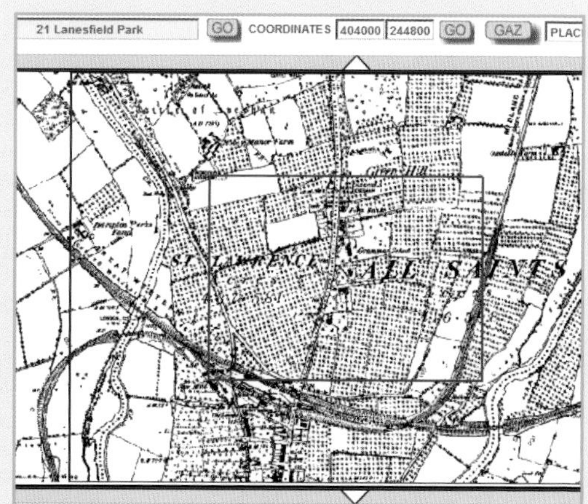

Pinpoint the house

4 To see the location of 21 Lanesfield Park on an old map, choose the map from the drop-down list. The image of the map will then be downloaded. You can zoom in or out and move in different directions around the map.

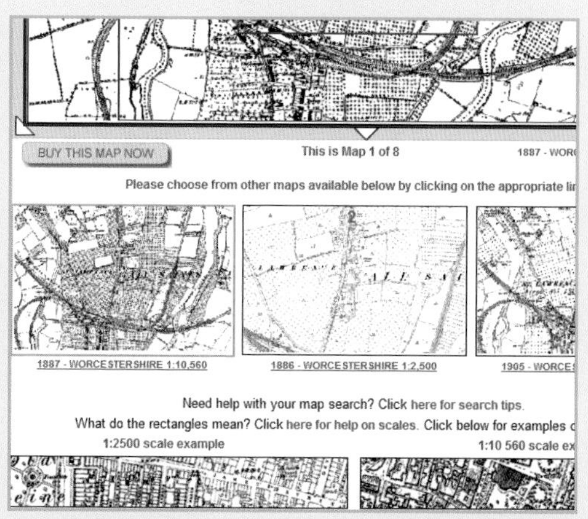

Choose alternative maps

5 Scroll down the page. You can look at other historic maps whose dates are shown along the bottom of the map image, compare the old map with a modern map or buy a printed map. The collections are free if you're using only the earliest 1:10 560 scale map. If you want more detailed or later maps you'll have to pay for them. Images can be sent to your PC via email within an hour, or prints can be posted to your home within 48 hours. Follow the prompts for payment.

Finding old maps online

You can use old maps to help you to work out exactly where your ancestors lived. From a location on a census return you can use current or historic Ordnance Survey maps, and tithe or enclosure maps to take you back in time.

Some family history societies are putting local historical maps online and the process is a continuing one. So if you don't find what you're looking for at first, it's worth checking regularly for new material. The following websites provide access to local historical maps or information about where to find them. For more information on tithe and enclosure maps, look back at pages 214 and 240.

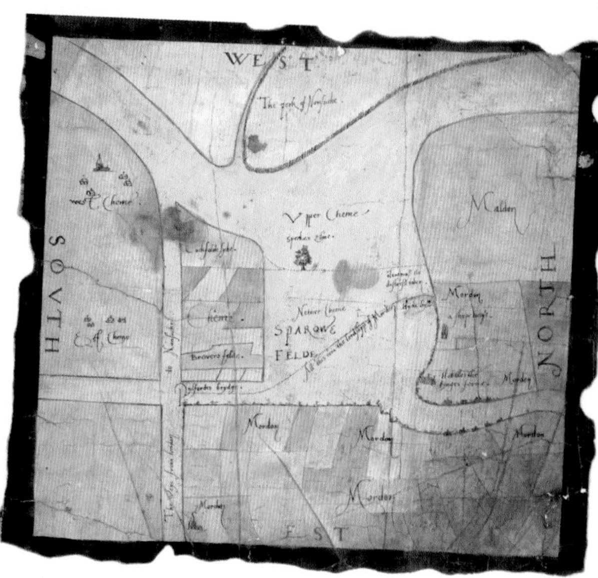

Nonsuch Park *In 1538, Henry VIII built a great palace and park here. This map was drawn up after his death to settle a property dispute.*

Tracking down your ancestors' homes

The following websites will make it easier for you to find the elusive map that will give depth to the detail you've already collected.

Genuki

You can check what's available online in a specific locality at **genuki.org.uk**. For example, if you want to find a map of an area of Cumberland, go to the United Kingdom and Ireland homepage; select **England**, then **Cumberland**, and choose **Maps** from the alphabetical topics list. This takes you to a page of map links – from Saxton's 1607 map of Cumbria to state-of-the art 2007 satellite images from Flash Earth.

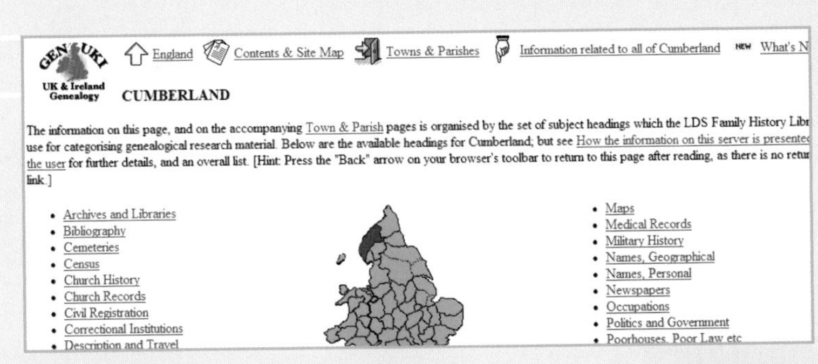

Your Old Books & Maps Online

There's a great range of old maps and etchings, as well as digital facsimiles of old historical and military books, available both on CD and online at **yourmapsonline.org.uk**. You have to pay to use the site: a year's access, suitable for broadband users, is around £13. For dial-up connections, there's a cheaper subscription of about £4.

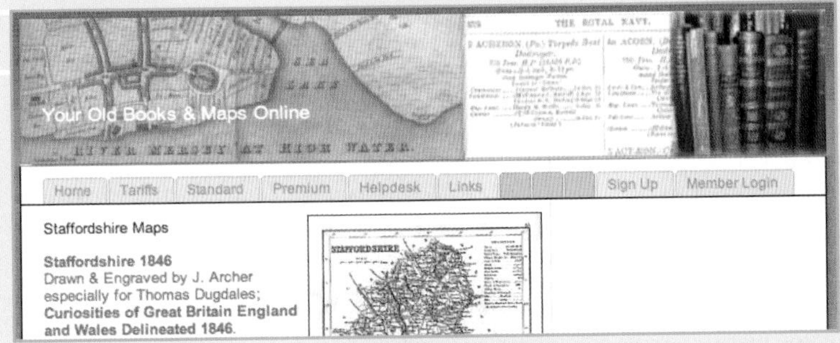

MAPCO

The MAPCO website, **archivemaps.com/mapco**, holds images of 18th and 19th-century maps of London, the British Isles and Australia that you can view for free; shown here is Bett's map of Scotland, 1847. Either key a place of interest into the Google search bar at the top right-hand corner of the page, or click the links on the page to access your area of interest. Once you've chosen a map, you can see close-ups of different areas by clicking on the relevant square in the interactive grid.

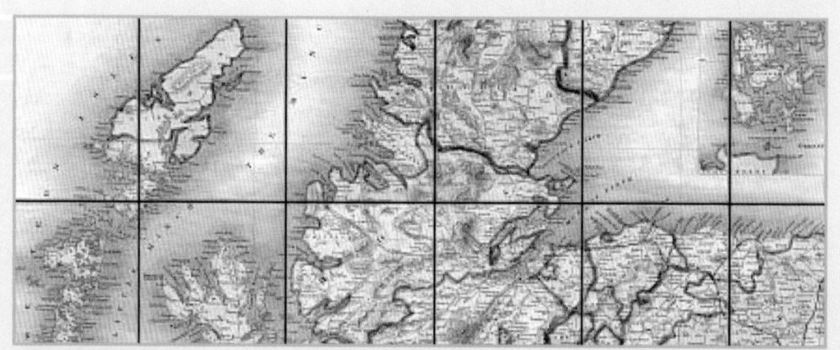

MOTCO

If you're interested in London, go to MOTCO, at **motco.com**, where several maps can be viewed online for free – four of them are linked with contemporary surveys of the city. Click on the link from the homepage to **Maps – reference database**, where you can scroll through the descriptions and choose the map you'd like to see; shown here is part of a map of Westminster and Southwark in 1746. Use the link to the left of the page to access the index of places on your map.

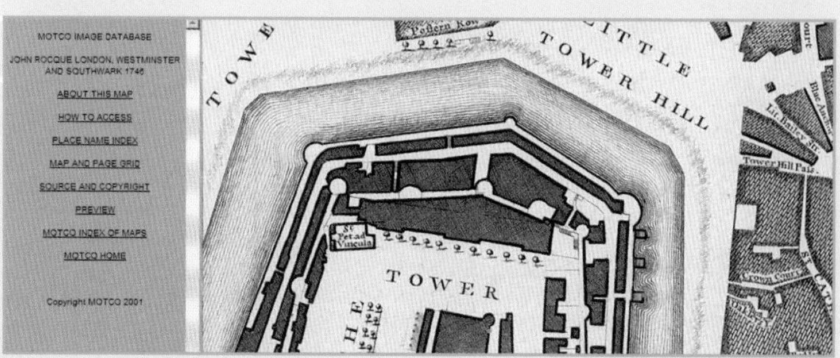

British Library

To access the British Library's map collection, go to the homepage at **bl.uk** and click **Collections**. Scroll down the list and click **Maps**. Some maps are available online, others are held at the British Library in London (see Directory). To see which maps can be viewed online, go to **collectbritain.co.uk**, and click **UK map search**. Then go to **Advanced search** and click the **Object search** tab, where you can choose the type of search you wish to make, such as postcode or date. A links page, at **bl.uk/collections/map_links.html**, provides access to other useful sites.

The National Archives

Although The National Archives (TNA) holds maps from the 16th to the 20th centuries, you can't view them online, but you can find out what's in the collection via the catalogue at **nationalarchives.gov.uk**. From the homepage, choose **Search the archives** from the drop-down menu and click on **the Catalogue**. Click on the **Search** link, top right. In the **Word or phrase** box type 'map AND [place name]' or 'plan AND [place name]'. You'll then see a page of results and codes. Click on the code to see a description of the document(s). If you want to see any items at TNA, write down their reference numbers.

Photographic collections online

Historic photos are a great way of adding colour to your family story. You might not find photos of your relatives in an online collection, but you can supplement your own pictures with images of places that they knew, to give depth to your discoveries.

Two views of Bournemouth *The photo below was taken in 1904, and the smaller inset in 1925. Although taken from a similar viewpoint you can see how the area has changed in the intervening years.*

Picture libraries often hold photographs of workplaces, railway stations, football grounds, streets and buildings with which your ancestors may have been associated. Try looking for something specific to your family, such as a place of worship, a sports club or a factory.

Public photo albums

Pictures of ordinary people from a particular era can give you a good idea of how your ancestors lived and dressed. The Francis Frith or Mary Evans (see right) libraries have pictures dating from the beginnings of photography, 150 years ago.

You'll find the Francis Frith Collection at **francisfrith.com**. It's the result of one man's ambition to photograph every town and village in the UK. Frances Frith was a Quaker born in Chesterfield, Derbyshire, in 1822. Originally a grocer, then a printer, in 1855 he sold all his businesses to devote himself to his photographic ambitions. At first he took the photos himself but, as the business grew, he hired assistants. He liked to include people in his views, both to give a sense of scale and to say something about contemporary fashions, transport and pastimes. Today, the library is an invaluable record of the changes in Britain's towns, villages and countryside from 1860 to 1970. You can search the website by place name, postcode or through the online gazetteer.

On the website **nationsmemorybank.com** you can see a wide variery of collections of family photos and memories. Search for photographs by name, geographical location or type (see pages 322-25).

Local photographic collections

Right across the UK there are valuable local picture collections that will enhance your view of the past. Some are accessible online; others you need to visit.

☛ **Glasgow Museums Photo Library, glasgowmuseums.com/photolibrary**, holds more than 15,000 art and photography images. Use a keyword to search its online images, then sort the results using the subject titles Art & Design, Transport & Technology, Natural History and Human History.

☛ **PhotoLondon, photolondon.org.uk**, lists addresses and searching information on how to locate images from archives such as the Guildhall Library, Museum of London, London Metropolitan Archives and Westminster Archives. There's also a section to help you to trace individual photographers working in London between 1841 and 1908.

☛ **Manchester Local Image Collection**, at **images.manchester.gov.uk**, contains more than 80,000 historical photos from the past 100 years that you can search online.

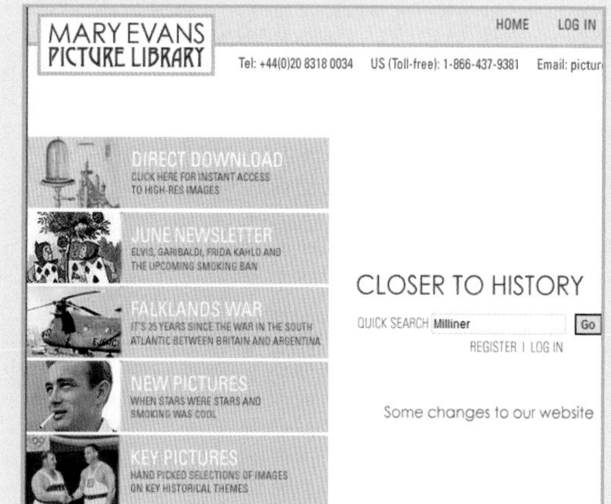

Visit the Mary Evans Picture Library

1 There are more than 200,000 images available online at **maryevans.com**, with around 500 new ones added every week. There's a broad spectrum of topics and subject areas, which often extend far beyond the traditional notion of a historical picture.

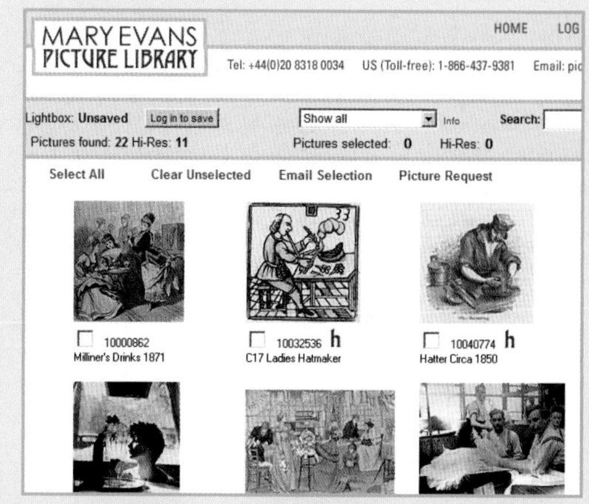

Search the online collection

2 To make a free search of the online collection, key a word, such as 'milliner', into the **Quick search** box and press **Go**. A selection of thumbnail pictures appears, each of which can be clicked on to enlarge the image and display the date of the image and a detailed description.

In search of a better life

For hundreds of years people have been coming to the British Isles, often to escape religious or political persecution – and many Britons left to find work and greater opportunities elsewhere. So there's a good chance of finding a migrant somewhere in your family tree.

A story of new peoples

From Saxons, Vikings, Normans and 16th-century Huguenots to Jews escaping persecution in the 19th and 20th centuries, and post-war West Indians and Asians, Britain's story is closely linked to immigration. The documents generated include many potential ancestors.

The records made when people first arrive in Britain are key sources of information – they include passenger lists, certificates of arrival and naturalisation records. There was no official registration of foreigners, or 'aliens', until the 19th century, but some documents do exist as far back as 600 years ago.

Where to start looking

A good place to begin your search for immigrant ancestors is The National Archives (TNA). It has some of the oldest records for immigrants, which are filed under a wide range of series codes (see below).

NATURALISATION CERTIFICATES An important TNA resource is the series of naturalisation certificates issued by the Home Office from 1844 to 1948. They were issued to people once they had satisfied certain criteria, such as length of stay, other family members living in the UK or having performed some sort of service to the nation. The records are a great help if you're trying to trace the records of an ancestor who arrived in Britain in the late 19th or early 20th century. But records after 1922 are officially closed for 100 years – although in some instances the Home Office will review an individual file's status if there's a sufficiently good reason.

New lives *Thousands of Jews left Eastern Europe in the late 19th century. Many settled in cities such as London, Leeds and Manchester, establishing new communities and businesses.*

Multi-cultural London *People from all over the world flocked to London, bringing with them their cultural and religious identities. The London Muslim Centre (left), opened in 2004, was the realisation of an idea born in 1910. Russian steam baths (below) in London's Brick Lane, maintained the propriety of 'Ladies only' days.*

Most of these files would have been the concern of the Home Office, so they have the prefix HO preceding the file number. The certificates fall into four groups, depending on the date on which they were granted.

- HO1 – from 1844 to 1871
- HO45 – from 1872 to 1878
- HO144 – from 1879 to 1934
- HO405 – from 1935 to 1948 (Some of this series is still retained by the Home Office; you should contact them if you require access. The address is in the Directory.)

SEARCHING ONLINE FOR A CERTIFICATE You can search the appropriate series to find your ancestor's records using TNA's online catalogue at **nationalarchives.gov.uk**. It's possible to do a search by surname, but unless you're looking for a rare name, it's a good idea to narrow the field before starting your search by adding details such as a person's forenames, date of birth and place of birth. This will save time by making your search much more effective.

Immigrant communities

Arrival records of individuals date from the Napoleonic wars, when legislation was introduced to monitor people entering the country. The mass of paperwork that immigration generates is a rich hunting ground.

There has always been a steady flow of people into the British Isles, but in modern times it has increased. For example, from 1948 to 1962 any citizen of the British Commonwealth was automatically entitled to British nationality upon arrival. After 1962, there was a tightening of the immigration rules, though large numbers of people continued to arrive throughout the 1960s and 1970s. Several websites can help you to trace the 'new Britons' who arrived at this time.

A website that tells it as it was

Funded by the Heritage Lottery and supported by The National Archives, the Moving Here website, **movinghere.org.uk**, looks at the history of 19th and 20th-century migration to England. To help minority ethnic groups to document their own history of migration it provides free access to an online catalogue of material related to migration history. The material is divided into four broad themes – stories, a gallery, migration histories and help with tracing your roots.

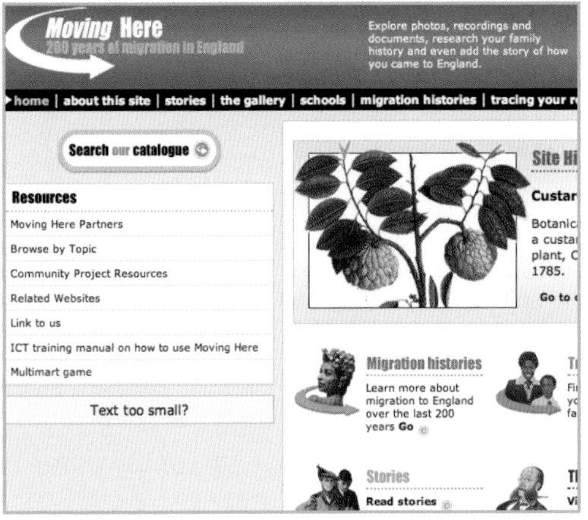

STORIES In this collection of immigrants' oral histories, you can listen to people telling their own tales or simply read transcripts of the recordings. There are hundreds of stories, ranging from a Pakistani's memories of moving to Huddersfield to a Caribbean migrant's experiences after arriving on the SS *Empire Windrush* in 1948.

If you have a story to tell, you can do it – the website tells you how. In the **Stories** section you'll also find themed collections of memories on a wide range of subjects. These have been compiled by museums and family history organisations working with the Moving Here project.

THE GALLERY You'll find this wonderful collection contains the most diverse images, arranged by theme and reflecting different aspects of migration. Subjects include food and drink, faith, faces, war, politics and identity. You can download the images free of charge, and even send them as e-postcards.

'No blacks. No Irish. No children.'

England was not as welcoming to the new Britons as some might have hoped. One Jamaican man, Owen, recalls his brother's hunt for lodgings: '...he went to this house and he knocked and the lady said, "No, there is no vacancy". Soon as he walked out on the pavement, she came over with a bucket of water and throw (*sic*) water on stairs outside and start scrubbing it. He was really shocked'. His experience wasn't unique.

MIGRATION HISTORIES The experiences of four immigrant communities – Caribbean, Irish, Jewish and South Asian – are looked at in fascinating detail. Each immigrant history talks about why people migrated from their home country, finds out what their journeys were like, asks about people's experiences of arriving and settling in England, and asks how people make contact with their family's original home country. A timeline for each community gives the story a historical perspective, so that you'll get the whole picture. You can download some of the sources – such as newspapers and photos – that were used to compile the histories.

TRACING YOUR ROOTS Perhaps the most important section, if you're tracing your family, is the section on tracing your roots. After an excellent introduction, there are sections devoted to Caribbean, Irish, Jewish and South Asian groups. Each of these gives a thorough guide to researching your roots within that community. For example, if you click on **Tracing Caribbean roots**, you're offered links to life events, occupations, land and property information, a section on slavery and another on migration. Within each of these there are more options and the depth of information is remarkable. For example, the land and property page gives you information that includes deeds and patent registers, maps and plans, probate records and plantation records. Pictures, subject overviews and first-person accounts add to the comprehensive amount of detail.

Brightening up Britain *The austerity of 1950s Britain was enlivened by newcomers from the Caribbean with their different cultural traditions.*

The Channel 4 history website

In 2000, Channel 4 launched a campaign to consolidate a range of local black history projects that were already under way across the UK, and to encourage new initiatives. They invited secondary schools and other groups and individuals to get involved. This thriving resource can be found at the **Untold** area of the website **channel4.com/history**.

There are links to other websites about Black and Asian history, as well as one to Channel 4's helpful guide to genealogy. Like the Moving Here website, the Channel 4 site has sections covering different communities – in this case Jewish, African-American, West Indian, African and Asian immigrants. Click on the community you're interested in for specific information on how to trace your family's history.

In addition, there's a feature called the Black and Asian History Map of the British Isles (below) that links to a number of other websites. You can search them by time, place and subject for more about the experiences of Black and Asian immigrants. It's interactive, so you can add your own stories, too.

Not all 'criminals' committed crimes

If you're researching your West Indian ancestors, don't overlook criminal records: Many islanders were labelled criminals for violating the smallest law – such as a black woman wearing a silk slip (only white women were allowed to wear silk). Slaves or servants could also be arrested just for whistling in public. Your ancestor just might be listed as a 'criminal' for doing something very minor. The only positive legacy of this harsh system is that it makes people easier to trace.

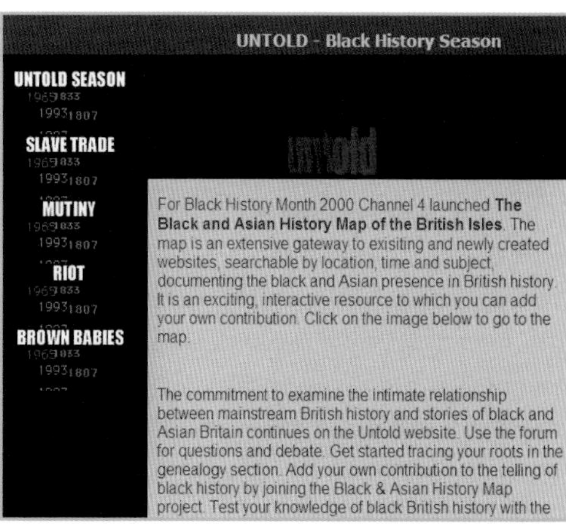

UNTOLD - Black History Season
UNTOLD SEASON
SLAVE TRADE
MUTINY
RIOT
BROWN BABIES
For Black History Month 2000 Channel 4 launched The Black and Asian History Map of the British Isles. The map is an extensive gateway to exisiting and newly created websites, searchable by location, time and subject, documenting the black and Asian presence in British history. It is an exciting, interactive resource to which you can add your own contribution. Click on the image below to go to the map.
The commitment to examine the intimate relationship between mainstream British history and stories of black and Asian Britain continues on the Untold website. Use the forum for questions and debate. Get started tracing your roots in the genealogy section. Add your own contribution to the telling of black history by joining the Black & Asian History Map project. Test your knowledge of black British history with the

Jewish resources online

Over the centuries, many Jewish people have settled in Britain and there's a wealth of information about them available on the internet. Much of it has been collected by charitable organisations and is free to access.

The first Jewish communities in England can be traced back to the 11th century. At that time the Jewish population was largely made up of Norman-French Jews who were followers of William the Conqueror and had travelled to England in 1066, acting as the king's financiers. But in 1290 Edward I's Edict of Expulsion meant Jews were expelled, forcibly converted or killed. It wasn't until the mid 17th century that Jewish immigrants were permitted to settle here again.

Large numbers of Jewish refugees came to Britain during the last two decades of the 19th century, fleeing from the persecution inflicted on them in parts of Eastern Europe under the Russian Tsars, Alexander III and Nicholas II. Then in the 1930s, the Nazi persecution of Jews brought a further wave of refugee immigrants.

Seeking the Jews of Britain

This migration of Jewish people into Britain over the centuries has generated a great deal of information, and there are a number of websites that can help those researching their Jewish ancestors. You can start your search in conventional civil registration and census documents. But it's important to remember that many Jews changed their names, especially during the two world wars, to anglicise them. The unusual sounding names were often misspelled on official documents, so you may need to do a little lateral thinking. Also bear in mind that some Jewish marriages would have gone unrecorded as Jews were not subject to the Marriage Act of 1753, which stated that weddings must take place in an Anglican place of worship.

Jewish records at TNA

The National Archives (TNA) has various sources relating to Anglo-Jewish history in its collection, found within many different records. The earliest records occur in the Home Office (HO) collections, while the Colonial Office (CO) and the Foreign Office (FO) records contain information for Jewish communities abroad, both in British colonies and foreign lands. TNA's records for immigration and naturalisation could also be relevant, particularly for the large influx of Jewish refugees in the late 19th century.

To search TNA's indexes, go to **nationalarchives.gov.uk** and select **the Catalogue**. Click on **Research guides** and then use the alphabetical list to find the section on **Jewish history**. The list that comes up describes the different sources available and where to access them.

Child refugee *Tired and alone, 8-year-old Josepha Salmon, the first of 5,000 Jewish and non-Aryan refugees, arrives at Harwich on December 2, 1938 in an exercise known as the* Kindertransport. *She'd come from Germany, and was destined for Dovercourt Bay camp.*

Websites that help you to trace your Jewish ancestors

In addition to Cyndi's List (at **cyndislist.com/jewish.htm**), which will give you many links to Jewish resources all over the world, you may like to try these websites.

Genealogy Resources on the Internet

American genealogist John Fuller has developed an extensive database of genealogy resources on the internet. His site provides you with mailing lists for Jewish genealogy from many parts of the world, including Britain, America, Israel, Germany and Russia. Enter **rootsweb.com/~jfuller/gen_mail_jewish.html** into your web browser, then click on any links that interest you.

Genealogy Resources on the Internet

JEWISH MAILING LISTS

URL: http://www.rootsweb.com/~jfuller/gen_mail_jewish.html

Last update: June 29, 2007 by John Fuller, johnf14246@aol.com

Register Resource | Update Resource | Report a Broken Link

- AUSTRIACZECH (Jewish genealogy in Bohemia and Moravia plus parts of Austria)
- AUSTRIA-HOLOCAUST (Austrians interned in German Holocaust camps)
- AUSTRO-HUNGARIAN-JEWISH (Austro-Hungarian Jews)
- BDS&V: (Jewish residents of Borislav, Drogobych and Sambor, Ukraine)
- BELARUS (Jewish family roots in Belarus; more specifically former Russian Gubernii of Grodno, Minsk, Mogilev, and Vitebsk)

JewishGen

The website **jewishgen.org** is dedicated to Jewish genealogy throughout the world. JewishGen is a non-profit-making organisation that aims to share as much information as possible. The site has a number of online databases, such as a Worldwide Burial Registry, Holocaust Database and Communities Database, as well as discussion forums and various ongoing projects. The website is free to search, but you'll need to register.

Home

JewishGen: The Home of Jewish Genealogy

An affiliate of the Museum of Jewish Heritage - A Living Memorial to the Holocaust

Learn

- JewishGen FAQ – *Frequently Asked Questions about Jewish Genealogy – How to do Jewish genealogical research. An extensive discussion of methods and resources.*
- JewishGen InfoFiles – *A comprehensive directory of information resources, organized by both topic and country.*
- JewishGen Tools – *Calculation aids (soundex, calendar, distance).*

London Metropolitan Archives

London has long been an important home for the Jewish community and the website **lma.gov.uk** has links to various resources. For a time, from the 1650s to the 1730s, most Jews in England were based in London, so the archives also have sources important to Jewish genealogy covering this period, including some synagogue records. From the LMA homepage, select the link to **Information leaflets** and choose **Jewish genealogy sources.**

Information Leaflet No.32

Jewish Genealogy: A summary of Sources for Jewish Genealogy at London Metropolitan Archives and Elsewhere

This leaflet explains some of the major ... *World Jewish Relief*

The Jewish Genealogical Society of Great Britain

This volunteer-run, non-profit-making organisation has its own website at **jgsgb.org.uk**. The website is free to use, although there's also a members-only area which has databases that can be viewed online. The website has details of a number of family trees that it holds in its library, but they can't be viewed online.

Jewish Genealogical Society of Great Britain

WELCOME TO THE JEWISH GENEALOGICAL SOCIETY OF GREAT BRITAIN - JGSGB

To ensure your place book early as seats were sold out last year - click here for information and booking form

JGSGB LIBRARY

ABOUT JGSGB

The Society encourages genealogical research and promotes the preservation of Jewish genealogical records and resources.

JGSGB QUARTERLY PUBLICATIONS which are sent by post or electronically to members

Finding new homes

If your family came from the Caribbean, West Africa or Asia, or ancestors emigrated to Commonwealth countries or worked in colonial India, these websites may help you to understand more about them and their new lives.

The family historian who's interested in the records of Britain's colonial past and the slave trade can get hold of a vast amount of material online. But this is only the tip of the iceberg. There's so much more – hundreds of thousands of pages – stored on microfilm and microfiche, or in the form of letters and other papers, books and photographs. Much of this material can be viewed only where it is stored – at libraries such as the Commonwealth Institute in London, at family history societies all over the UK and at a variety of other museums and archives. The good news is that what is available online is increasing, as dedicated volunteers locate, transcribe and upload the data.

New citizens *People from the Caribbean began to arrive in Britain as early as the 17th century. Many Jamaicans, like those seen here arriving at Plymouth in 1955, were eager to enjoy a new way of life in England. If your family came from the West Indies, you'll find their records through one or more of the websites here.*

The Commonwealth Institute website (see below) and the four websites shown opposite are primarily concerned with immigrant and emigrant communities. While they may not help you to draw your family tree, they will provide valuable and often moving insights into the background of your community, and help you to establish lines of inquiry.

The Commonwealth of countries

The Institute of Commonwealth Studies in London (see Directory) has a website at **commonwealth.sas.ac.uk**. It has no simple 'find your roots' links, or lists of names for you to search, but the library (catalogued online) holds more than 160,000 items of Caribbean, Southern African and Australian information. For those with West Indian ancestors there's an online exhibition at **commonwealth.sas.ac.uk/carib_web/default.htm**, called Routes to Roots, which covers Caribbean history, explaining what archives are available and providing links to other relevant websites.

Searching farther afield

World Gen Web

One of the most important resources for all family historians is WorldGenWeb, at **worldgenweb.org**. It's a project run by volunteers, and is designed to provide genealogical and historical records and resources to the public, via the internet. Eventually it hopes to have every country in the world represented online, hosted by researchers who are familiar with the records in their own country. It's divided up into countries, then each area within that country, and is free and simple to use.

The National Archives

An online exhibition, **nationalarchives.gov.uk/pathways/blackhistory**, focusing on black history in Britain from 1500 to 1850, has been created by The National Archives (TNA) in partnership with the Black and Asian Studies Association. You'll find six separate 'galleries' to visit and superb interactive 'learning journeys', such as a virtual tour of the Black and Asian influence on three English cities – London, Bristol and Liverpool. Follow the links to maps of each of the cities, with further links to the Black and Asian presence in particular areas.

The British Library India Office Records

The British Library is the home of the records and archives of British families in South Asia from the early 17th to the mid 20th centuries. Start your search at **bl.uk/collections/orientaloffice.html**. Then click on **Asia, Pacific and Africa Collections** (shown, right), for links to numerous family history sources such as records for British families who settled in India during the colonial period. And there's an informative section on the Asians in Britain before the large-scale immigration that began in the 1950s and 1960s.

London Metropolitan Archives

The London Metropolitan Archives has researched groups of immigrants, including French, Irish, Black and Asian, living in London over the past 500 years. An online exhibition at **cityoflondon.gov.uk/corporation/lma_learning/schoolmate/bal/sm_bal.asp** opens on Black and Asian Londoners, with links to Irish and French communities, too, and insights into the lives and times of all groups. The **Images** link takes you to a set of illustrations dating back to the 18th century. Click **Maps** to see historic maps of London, India, Ceylon, Liberia, France and Ireland.

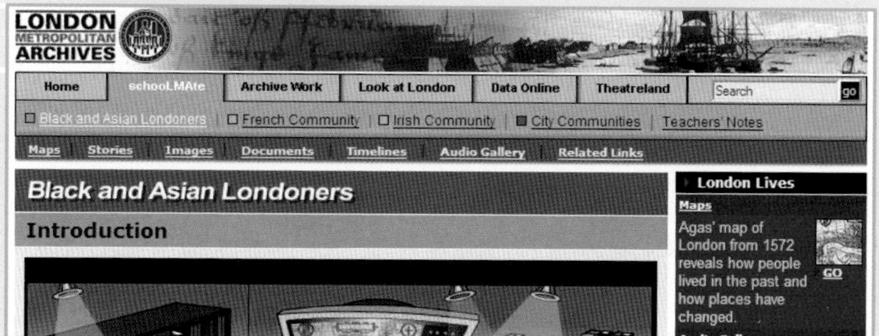

Emigration and the colonies

As Britain expanded its empire, so the opportunities for Britons to live or work overseas increased. Some people chose to go, others were forced – but whatever the reason for their departure, a wealth of documentation exists to help you to track down emigrating ancestors.

Large-scale voluntary emigration from Britain began with the establishment of the colonies from the 17th century onwards. Before then, only small numbers of people had left to settle in Europe, including those from England and Scotland who were encouraged to colonise Ireland in the 1600s. Records about the settlement of Ireland during this period can be found at The National Archives (TNA). They include Irish state papers, muster rolls and poll tax records – all of which give snapshots of how many immigrants there were in different Irish counties at any one time.

People on the move

Both voluntary and forced emigration increased in the 17th and 18th centuries. Penal colonies were set up in the New World and many convicts were transported there. After the American War of Independence in the 1770s, new destinations were needed and Canada, the West Indies and newly colonised Australia became home for large numbers of transported convicts (see page 206). Transportation was discontinued in 1868, but by then about 160,000 convicts had been sent to Australia and Van Diemen's Land (Tasmania) alone.

If you have ancestors who went to the New World voluntarily in the early years, their records may exist in the archives of the countries where they settled. But these are

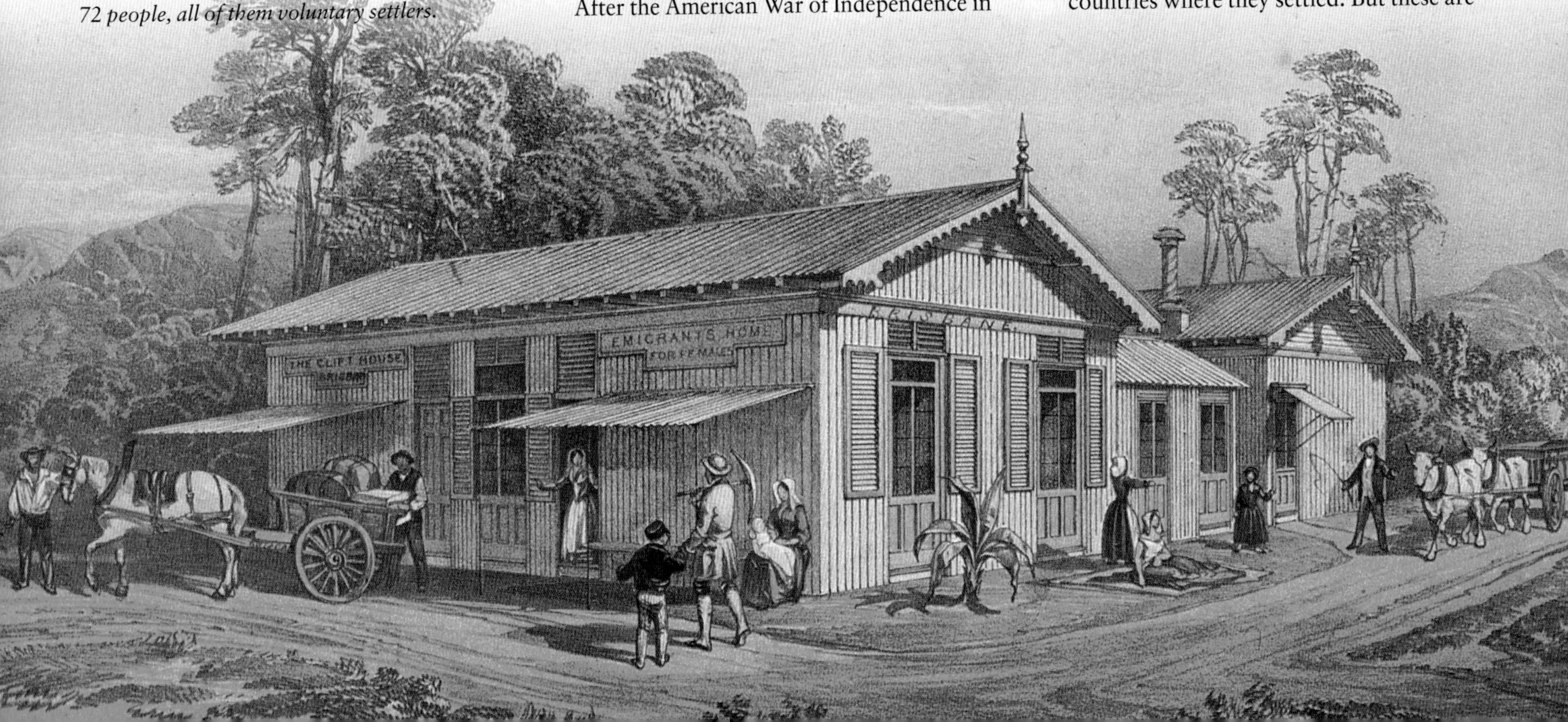

Pioneer homes *This 19th-century immigrants' house in Sydney, Australia, accommodated 72 people, all of them voluntary settlers.*

largely incomplete as there was no systematic record keeping. Detailed passenger lists for voyages out of Britain weren't kept until very late in the 19th century, so their departure may have gone unrecorded.

You'll find Cyndi's List and WorldGenWeb are helpful for this type of search. See page 260 for examples of how to use these sites.

A new life in the sun

The numbers who chose to leave the British Isles peaked in the 19th century, with as many as 10 million people leaving for the USA, Canada and Australia during this period to seek their fortunes in farming and gold-mining. Others spread across the British empire, mostly employed in running the colonies, or to join civil engineering projects, such as the building of bridges and railways in India. Soldiers and sailors were granted land at the end of their period of service, if they agreed to settle in the new colonies.

The government's introduction, after 1832, of specially reduced passages from the UK to the colonies enticed still more people to emigrate.

More controversially, from the late 1800s, orphanages sent children abroad to help to populate Australia, Canada and New Zealand (see page 300) with 'good British stock'.

Convict records

Because of the nature of officialdom, you've a much better chance of tracking down your emigrant ancestors if they were deported as convicts than if they left of their own volition. In contrast to the records for voluntary emigration, far more detail was amassed for those forcibly removed from Britain. Many of their records are held by Australia's state archives. (See also page 206.)

Websites to help you to trace ancestors in Australia

Both New South Wales and Queensland have websites to help you to find ancestors. So if they settled there, you should be able to find them.

New South Wales Try **bdm.nsw.gov.au**. It's the registry for births, marriages and deaths. Then there's **records.nsw.gov.au** for census returns.

Queensland For births, marriages and deaths, go to **justice.qld.gov.au**. For information about assisted passages to Australia between 1814 and 1912, visit **archives.qld.gov.au**.

If you don't know the state in which your relatives lived, one of the following family history sites may help. They are gateway sites that will link you to archives in various states and territories. Start with **coraweb.com.au**, which has a section dedicated to immigration. Or try the Australian Family History Compendium at **cohsoft.com.au/afhc**. It will link you to other sites that are geared towards family history research.

In addition, the National Archives of Australia (NAA) holds a quantity of information on its website, **naa.gov.au**. The site has a free online catalogue with descriptions of about 6 million documents, posters, photos, maps, films and sound recordings that you can search by keyword, name and date. Go to the homepage, choose the **Record research** link on the left and then **Search now as a guest**.

Emigration records at TNA

The National Archives holds a variety of emigration records dating from the 1600s. Records from the 19th century are the most comprehensive, including not only passenger lists for voluntary emigrants but also detailed criminal records of the convicts and their transportation papers.

It's a good idea to read TNA's guide at **nationalarchives.gov.uk/catalogue/leaflets/vi2272.htm** before you begin looking for emigrant records. Scroll down to E and choose **Emigrants**. You'll discover a wealth of information and you can choose to look more closely at the most appropriate section for your search. For example, passenger lists can be very helpful. Everyone boarding a specific ship was registered on its passenger list. The lists often give extra family history information, such as age and usual place of residence. If you think you have ancestors who set sail for a new life abroad between 1890 and 1919, you should be able to find their records in the online passenger lists, but not every record has survived and they're not all kept and catalogued together.

Series BT27 holds passenger lists compiled by the Board of Trade (hence BT) for outward passengers from 1890 to 1960, and series BT26 lists all the incoming passengers. The whole list – more than 30 million names – is being digitised by TNA in partnership with the family history website, **findmypast.com**. When the project is complete, it will provide a body of information of enormous value to you if you're tracing an emigrant ancestor.

Tracing family members in India

Britons went out to India in droves, as traders, planters, soldiers or government officials. Although there was no mass emigration at any one time, your ancestors could have been among the 4 million who were born, married or died there.

Britain's influence in India and neighbouring regions goes back a long way. If some of your ancestors lived there for a time, you should be able to trace them.

Birth, marriage and death records, similar to those found in UK parish registers, were kept by both the East India Company and the British Government's India Office. Chaplains of the Company began compiling records from the late 17th century as Christian churches became established in India. You'll need to know where your ancestors lived, as the records are split according to region – the three main areas being Bengal, Madras and Bombay – and cover mainly European and Anglo-Indian Christians. The British Library (see right) holds sets of the registers, but they're not yet available to search online.

East India Company records

Up to 1858 British interests in India were controlled by the East India Company, which recorded a vast amount of information about its activities and its staff – merchants, traders, mariners and soldiers. Annual army lists were compiled, detailing both native regiments and those commanded and staffed by Europeans.

If your ancestor was a soldier, it helps to know his rank, as one set of records covers commissioned officers and another encompasses 'other ranks' – including non-commissioned officers. The entry papers for officer cadets – the rank held by military cadets during their training to become commissioned officers – provide valuable genealogical information, such as the names of cadets' parents and details of their births or baptisms.

Starting to piece together the service records for 'other ranks' is rather less straightforward. But you can gather together information by using embarkation lists, depot registers, muster rolls and registers of the East India Company's soldiers.

British life abroad *So determined were Britons in India to 'maintain standards' that they even took their foxhounds along on board. You can search for details of their military and business careers in India on* bl.uk *and* fibis.org.

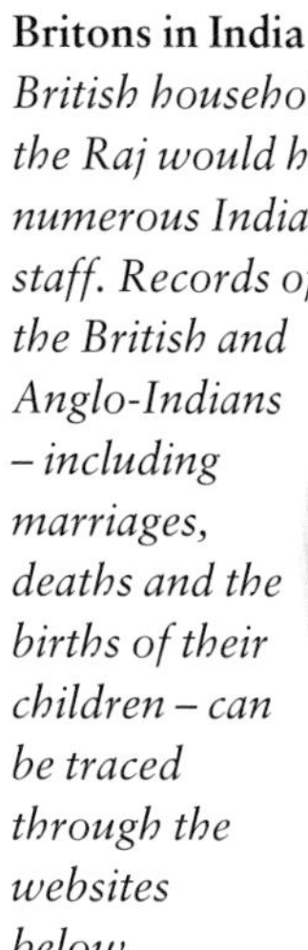

Britons in India *A typical British household at the time of the Raj would have included numerous Indian staff. Records of the British and Anglo-Indians – including marriages, deaths and the births of their children – can be traced through the websites below.*

Two phases of British rule in India

British involvement in India can be divided into two distinct periods. Records for both periods are now held at the British Library (see below).

- 1600-1858 Britain conquered and controlled India through the East India Company.
- 1858-1947 India was governed directly by British government through the India Office. This period was known as 'The Raj' – from a Hindi term for 'rule'. In its prime, the Raj included not just present-day India, but Pakistan, Bangladesh, Sri Lanka, Nepal, Bhutan and Burma. Britons lived and worked in all these countries, so your ancestors may show up in the records.

Searching online for your ancestors in India

The National Archives, at **nationalarchives.gov.uk**, is a natural starting point. Its research guides will help you to understand why people emigrated, and it will give you links to related websites. In addition to the TNA site, you may find that the three websites described here can be helpful in your search for family relatives in India and the surrounding regions. They can be searched online and should help you to track down or piece together the lives of your ancestors.

British Library

A wealth of British Government records exists, from the private papers of the Viceroys of India to key documents about the partition of India. The records have been given alphabetical classifications. Class N, for example, covers baptisms, marriages and burials 'relating mainly to European and Eurasian Christians in India, Burma and other areas administrated by the East India Company and the Government of India' from1698 to 1969.

You can make a limited search of the information held in the British Library's online collections at **bl.uk/collections/oiocfamilyhistory/family.html**. Then click on **Asia, Pacific and Africa Collections** and select a link that looks suitable, to carry on your search. For a much wider search, go to the homepage, **bl.uk**, and key in 'India Office' in the search box. You'll be offered a huge amount of information that you can browse through for the information you're looking for.

Families in British India Society

The website of Families in British India Society (FIBIS), at **fibis.org**, gives free online access to the records you'll need if you decide to research ancestors who lived or served in the Indian sub-continent from 1600 to 1947. Its database of transcriptions is still somewhat limited, but this is an on-going project so the scope will broaden.

On the homepage, click on **Fibis search**, then select the section in which you'd expect to find the records you want. The website has transcriptions of military and maritime records, wills, photos, personal papers and directories. Most have been taken from the British Library's India Office Records Section (IOR). You can use a simple search, a person search, an image search or an advanced search.

If you're a beginner, the website offers links to research guides that help you to find resources that may not yet be available on the FIBIS website. To find detailed research guides on civil, military and other occupational records that are being updated all the time, click on the **Fibiwiki** link along the top panel of the homepage.

Moving Here

You'll find great tips for tracing your Indian ancestors on the website **movinghere.org.uk**. It gives online access to case studies and records that you can search for free. There's a specific section on Indian ancestors that you can visit by keying in **movinghere.org.uk/galleries/roots/asian/asian.htm**.

Ellis Island – a new start in America

For thousands of immigrants nearing New York by sea, the Statue of Liberty, torch lifted high in her hand, was guiding them to a better life in America. At her feet lay Ellis Island, their first port of call.

From January 1, 1892, to November 12, 1954, this small patch of land, just off the southern end of Manhattan Island, opened its arms to more than 12 million people fleeing poverty, oppression and disease. The island is named after Samuel Ellis, a local farmer and merchant, who owned it in the 1770s. In its early years it was used for many purposes, including a hanging site for pirates and a coastal fort to stop fleets sailing directly into New York harbour as the British had done in 1776 during the War of Independence.

The US government bought the island from New York State in 1808 and used it as a military base until 1890, when $75,000 was allocated to build the first immigration centre. Landfill was used to double the size of the island, and while it was under construction, the Barge Office at the Battery, on the southern tip of Manhattan, processed nearly 406,000 immigrants.

Symbol of freedom *Dominating Ellis Island, the Statue of Liberty was a gift from the people of France in recognition of American support during the French Revolution. Inscribed on it is a verse by Emma Lazarus that begins 'Give me your tired, your poor, your huddled masses yearning to breathe free...'. True to that promise, a poor Italian family arrive at Ellis Island (right).*

The rough and the smooth of immigration

Not everyone who came to America was a refugee in dire straits. Turmoil in parts of late 19th-century Europe could also affect well-off families, who took advantage of increasingly sophisticated and comfortable ships to travel together to America in search of a safer life. For them, the immigration process was relatively easy. An upper-class family paying first or second-class fares wouldn't have had to visit Ellis Island at all. Instead, the wealthy underwent brief questioning and medical examination on board their ship, and then disembarked at the Hudson or East River Piers on Manhattan Island. The US government calculated that if you had the means to purchase an expensive ticket, then you would not be a financial problem.

Life was different, though, for those in third class or steerage. Once the first and second-class passengers had disembarked, they'd be transferred to a ferry, taken to Ellis Island and put through a medical and legal inspection. Even if you were in good health, with all your paperwork in order, the whole process could take up to 5 hours. And yet, even in the peak year of 1897 with 1.25 million immigrants pouring in, a positive effort was made to treat all who arrived with courtesy, and hospital wards built for those who were ill.

For some, though, the arduous journey across the Atlantic was a wasted

Welcome to America *Some descendants of immigrants to the USA trace their families' names on Ellis Island's Wall of Honor.*

experience. About 2 per cent of people never made it through the immigration process and were returned to their country of origin, usually because they were judged to be of bad character and a potential burden to the state. Others with chronic contagious diseases were also rejected as a danger to public health. To these people and their families, Ellis Island became known as 'The Island of Tears'.

First and famous arrivals

When the Ellis Island immigration centre opened in January 1892, the first person to be processed was Annie Moore, from Cork, in Ireland. She was just 15 years old and described by officials as 'A rosy cheeked Irish girl'. She was just one of 700 people who arrived in New York on that day.

Among the millions, some notable names passed through Ellis Island over the years, and they can all be found online (see right). Walt Disney was one of them. He arrived on September 23, 1919, aged 19, from France, where he'd served as a Red Cross ambulance driver during the First World War. He then headed for Kansas City to concentrate on his career as a cartoonist. Another was Sigmund Freud, who sailed from Bremen, Germany, in 1909, to deliver a series of lectures. This was his first and only time in America, declaring later that 'America is a mistake, a giant mistake'. More appreciative of this new land were Harry Houdini, Albert Einstein and English entertainers Charlie Chaplin, Leslie Hape (Bob Hope) and Arthur Jefferson (Stan Laurel), who were all to find fame in Hollywood.

Perhaps luckiest of all the arrivals at Ellis Island was the less-famous Barbara West. She arrived, aged just 10 months, on the RMS *Carpathia*, which had rescued her from a freezing sea on the night of April 14-15, 1912. The ship that she'd been aboard was the *Titanic*.

Star immigrant *A 16-year-old stilt-walker called Archibald Leach arrived at Ellis Island from England on July 28, 1920. By 1931 he had arrived in Hollywood and changed his name to Cary Grant.*

Ellis Island ancestors online

The website **ellisisland.org** is a great resource if you have immigrant ancestors who arrived at Ellis Island. It has a free searchable database, and all you have to do is register your email address to search the records. By using a simple name search, you can trawl the passenger lists or ships' manifests – the shipping companies' records of all passengers. You can also download and print a certificate for your family history records.

The website (right) also links you to the site of the American Immigrant Wall of Honor at Ellis Island (above), a permanent memorial of individual or family names. There are 700,000 names on the wall and more are being added all the time. Your ancestor or family may be eligible for addition to the wall if they arrived at Ellis Island in the past.

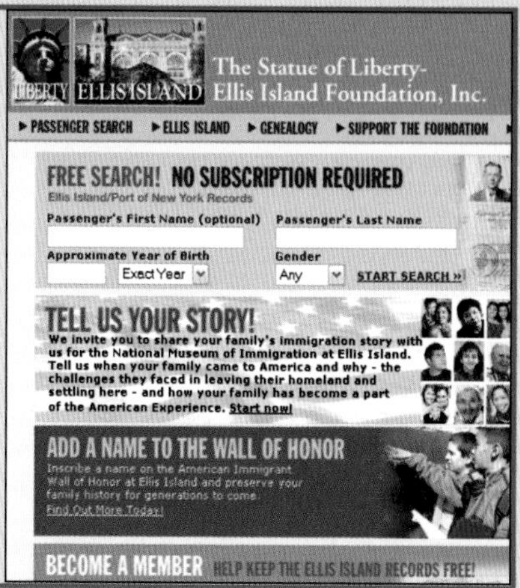

Did your ancestors go adventuring?

The thrill of striking out into the unknown was irresistible to many men during the 19th century. They dreamed of bringing the benefits of 'civilisation' to great swathes of the world that made up the British Empire. Sometimes their families went along for the ride, too.

Although most British emigrants settled in the colonies of North America and Australia, some people went to places with far smaller British communities. Those who went as missionaries often ventured into previously uncharted regions.

As the Empire expanded during the 18th and 19th centuries, many people were bound to explore new territories abroad through their service in the armed forces, as civil servants or as traders in places as far flung as Kenya and Malaya. Others were motivated to go overseas to heal the sick or teach.

Searching for ancestors abroad

When you start on the trail of these daring relatives, remember that only a few records were kept, so searching can be quite difficult. As always, the more information you have – such as a date of departure, arrival, a ship name or a destination – the more chance of success you'll have.

Many primary resources that would be useful to you are located overseas. If you can't find what you're searching for online, you may want to consider hiring a researcher abroad, or even visiting the land of your forefathers yourself. If the adventurous blood that coursed through your ancestor's veins still runs in yours, you'll find the challenge exciting and, with luck, rewarding.

The websites shown here may be helpful if you're trying to track down ancestors in other parts of the world. In most cases, they will have travelled to far-off countries by ship, so it makes sense to start by looking at passenger lists of people leaving the UK. If you know which ship your ancestors sailed on, you may be able to track their passage at **ancestorsonboard.com** (which is part of FindMyPast) or **ancestry.co.uk**.

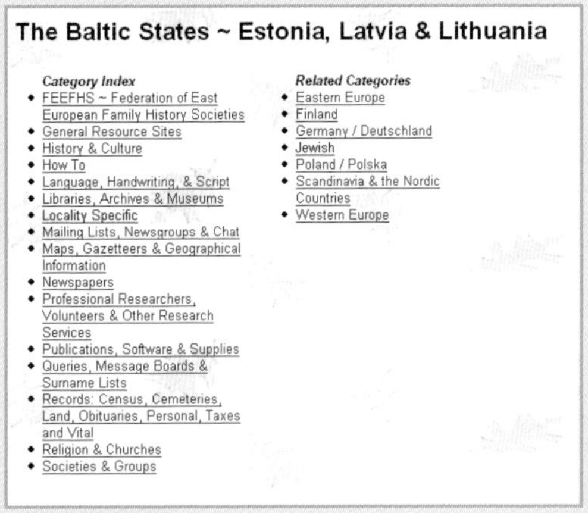

The Baltic States ~ Estonia, Latvia & Lithuania

Category Index
- FEEFHS ~ Federation of East European Family History Societies
- General Resource Sites
- History & Culture
- How To
- Language, Handwriting, & Script
- Libraries, Archives & Museums
- Locality Specific
- Mailing Lists, Newsgroups & Chat
- Maps, Gazetteers & Geographical Information
- Newspapers
- Professional Researchers, Volunteers & Other Research Services
- Publications, Software & Supplies
- Queries, Message Boards & Surname Lists
- Records: Census, Cemeteries, Land, Obituaries, Personal, Taxes and Vital
- Religion & Churches
- Societies & Groups

Related Categories
- Eastern Europe
- Finland
- Germany / Deutschland
- Jewish
- Poland / Polska
- Scandinavia & the Nordic Countries
- Western Europe

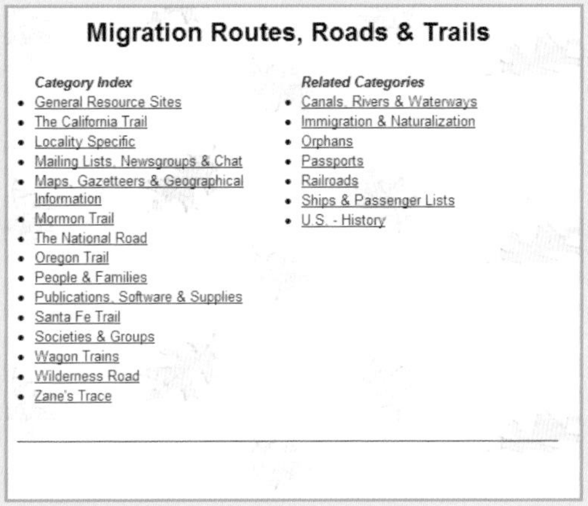

Migration Routes, Roads & Trails

Category Index
- General Resource Sites
- The California Trail
- Locality Specific
- Mailing Lists, Newsgroups & Chat
- Maps, Gazetteers & Geographical Information
- Mormon Trail
- The National Road
- Oregon Trail
- People & Families
- Publications, Software & Supplies
- Santa Fe Trail
- Societies & Groups
- Wagon Trains
- Wilderness Road
- Zane's Trace

Related Categories
- Canals, Rivers & Waterways
- Immigration & Naturalization
- Orphans
- Passports
- Railroads
- Ships & Passenger Lists
- U.S. - History

Consult Cyndi's List website

1 A good place to begin researching records for other parts of the world is at **cyndislist.com**. It's comprehensive, free to use and has pages for many geographical regions. Each country's homepage follows the same format as this one for the Baltic States, providing links to libraries and archives, mailing lists and information about published sources and local family history centres and societies. The 'how to' sections have articles with research guidelines specific to that region.

Follow your ancestor's trail

2 On the main index, there's a list of topics, too. For example, click on **Cowboys, ranchers and the wild west**. This will bring up the list that offers, among much else, **Migration routes, roads & trails**. Click on it and you're offered links to a list that includes **Wagon trains**, **Orphans**, **Passports**, **People & families**, **Ships & passenger lists** and the **Mormon trail**.

Was your ancestor a missionary?

Fortunately for family historians, 'mission headquarters' expected to be kept updated on their missionaries' progress through regular letters and reports – many of which survive. Missionary work was not a male prerogative: young women were involved, too. If your female ancestor was a missionary, you may be able to discover a lot more about her from missionary records than you would from a census return.

The School of Oriental and African Studies (SOAS) in London has a large archive of documents, photographs and published materials related to missionary work. Find out more at **helpers.shl.lon.ac.uk**. On the homepage click on the link to **Helpers descriptions** and a list appears. Scroll down until you find an entry for the Methodist Missionary Society. Click on that for information about missionary societies.

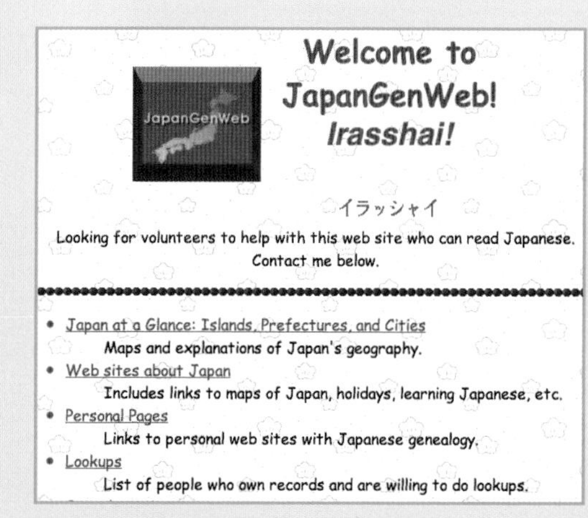

Using the WorldGenWeb Project

The website **worldgenweb.org** differs from Cyndi's List in that it often contains primary information, not just links. It's free of charge, and from links on the homepage you're taken to individual countries' genealogical pages. Each country's page is hosted by a volunteer co-ordinator, so the level of detail varies from one country to another – many of the counties have no host and contain only basic information.

Searching Africa

You can access a country's website from the relevant continent or region's homepage. So if you're interested in Zimbabwe, for example, go to the Africa homepage **africagenweb.org** and select **Zimbabwe**. Only some of the African countries have hosted websites, but all of them provide general information. Some, such as Zimbabwe, offer more detail than others, for example, Somalia.

Did they go East?

If you're looking for ancestors in Japan, you'll be taken via the AsiaGenWeb page to the Japan page, **rootsweb.com/~jpnwgw**, where you can select a language (Japanese, Spanish or English). Choose English and you'll see a Welcome page. Scroll down and you'll find numerous links to relevant websites including family history connections and people who have transcribed lists from immigrant ships.

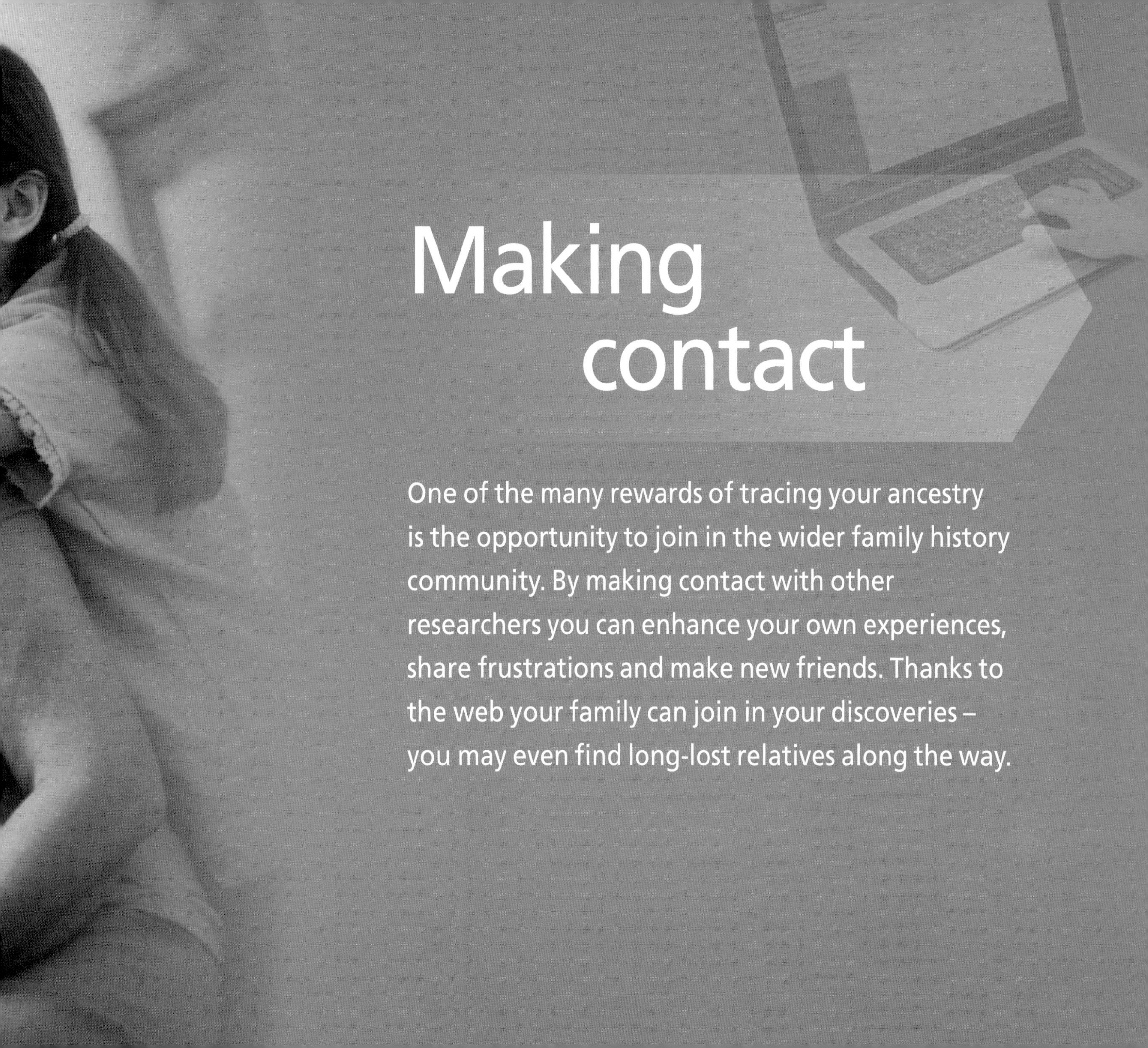

Making contact

One of the many rewards of tracing your ancestry is the opportunity to join in the wider family history community. By making contact with other researchers you can enhance your own experiences, share frustrations and make new friends. Thanks to the web your family can join in your discoveries – you may even find long-lost relatives along the way.

Looking for help online

Tracing your family history is a very personal journey but it doesn't have to be undertaken alone. Your research can be greatly advanced by contact with other researchers who may be able to offer help and advice.

To make faster headway with your search for family members, you can combine the use of traditional research, using birth, marriage and death certificates and census returns with help from the millions of people who make up the online community.

Many of the websites mentioned in this book offer mailing lists, discussion groups and web forums where researchers can meet and discuss areas of common interest and help each other with search problems. For example, **ancestry.co.uk** has an Ancestry Community page where family trees can be shared and message boards used. The American site **genforum.genealogy.com** may be able to assist you in finding relations overseas or help with foreign records. Genes Reunited, at **genesreunited.co.uk**, encourages you to upload your tree to its site and conduct searches of other members' trees.

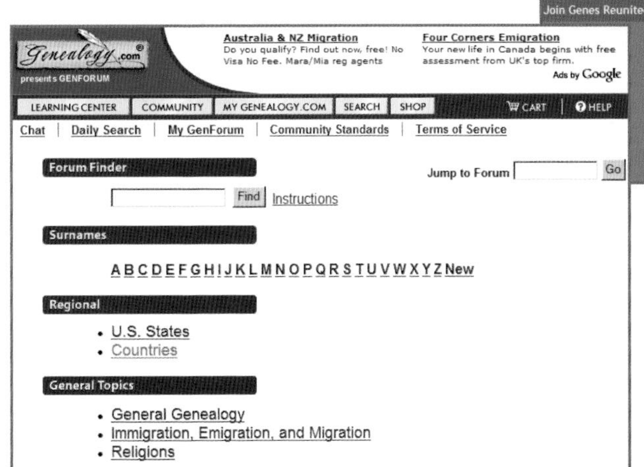

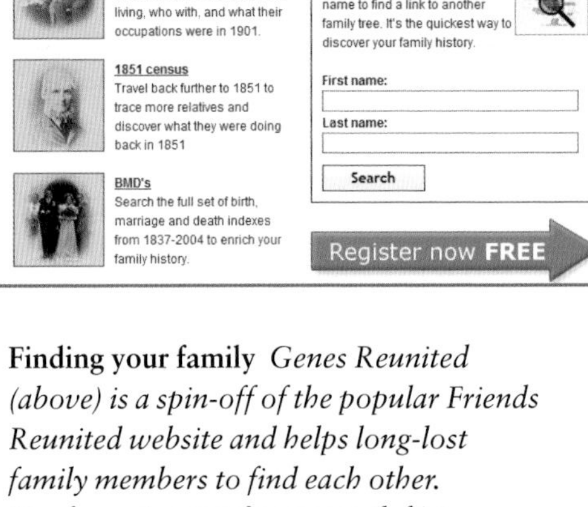

Finding your family *Genes Reunited (above) is a spin-off of the popular Friends Reunited website and helps long-lost family members to find each other. Genforum's* **genealogy.com** *(left) is an American-based sister site to Ancestry and is particularly useful if you suspect your ancestors are spread around the world.*

Joining a networking community

To become part of a mailing list that you think will suit your interests, you'll have to send an email asking to subscribe to that list. Your computer must have the capacity to receive daily emails concerning the subject of your group. See page 280 for more about mailing lists and how they work.

The people you meet online who are researching the same or similar topics to those that interest you will often be able to help you to extend your family tree. They may have information you need, and even be distantly related to you.

Web forums are also helpful, and all you need to do is regularly check the site for updated discussions. If you want to ask or answer a query on a website message board, you'll be prompted to create an online profile so that people can contact you about the message you have left.

Speed up your search

Use sites like **friendsreunited.co.uk** and **facebook.com** and you can quickly see if the people you've identified in your research are listed there. As more people sign up to sites like this, there's a good chance you'll find someone you know. For example, if you sign up to Genes Reunited and upload your family tree for others to view, you'll get email updates when someone shows an interest in your ancestors. This way, you'll link in to other people's family trees, and maybe find a whole new branch of family members.

The online directory **192.com** (see page 192) offers searches of phone directories, electoral rolls, company reports and other sources. If you find the correct person, the site will give you an address, postcode and sometimes a phone number. It's free to search but there's a fee to view full entries. If you're looking for people abroad, **cyndislist.com** has a link to worldwide directories.

Despite all the information you can find by seraching for people on these various online sources, not everyone is listed, so success isn't always guaranteed. A way round this is to put an appeal for information into online message boards or discussion groups. Post a message with the name of the person you're looking for, prominently displayed, and see if anyone replies. If you've an idea of the general area in which the person lives, you can find the local family history society through **ffhs.org.uk** and make an appeal.

Getting help with your search

If you still can't find the person you're looking for, consider trying one of the agencies that specialise in tracing people.

Lookupuk.com

Not only does **lookupuk.com** offer advice, but it also gives access to a huge range of indexes, phone directories, email addresses and newsgroups, as well as offering links to other family research sites such as Ancestry. In addition, you can search the thousands of messages posted on the site – and leave your own messages – making this a really comprehensive site that will help you to contact missing ancestors.

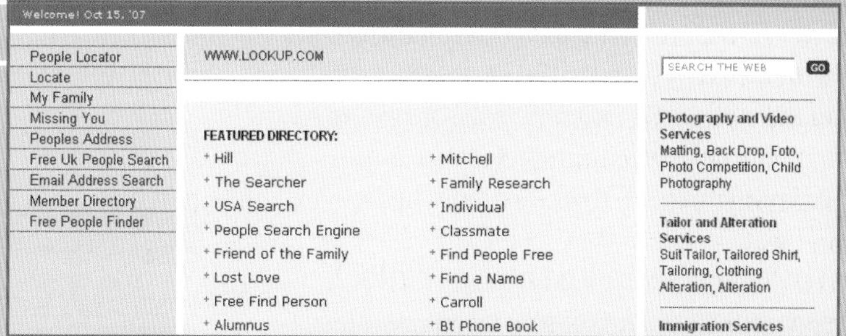

Salvation Army Family Tracing

At **salvationarmy.org.uk/familytracing** you'll find the Salvation Army's Family Tracing Service, which aims to reunite family members. The service is closely linked to colleagues in 100 countries, allowing far-flung families to be reunited more easily. A full-time staff can help you to find relatives, for which a small fee is charged – donations are also accepted. A search can take as little as 5 minutes or a few years, and the success rate is 85 per cent.

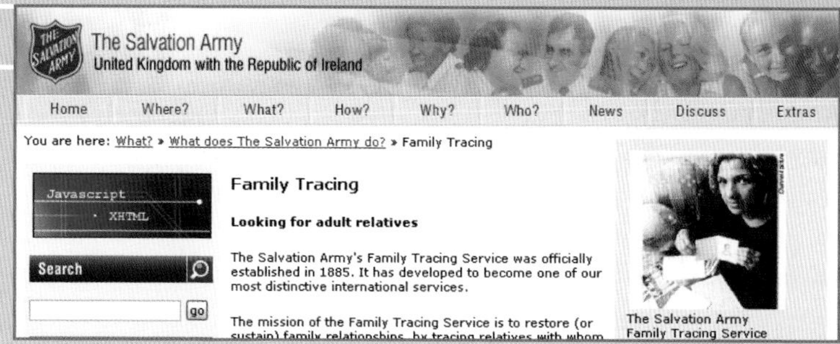

Traceline

This agency specialises in tracing people through its website at **traceline.co.uk**. It carries out searches on people and property, using electoral rolls and civil registration indexes. You can trace property ownership details, which is helpful when you're trying to trace the movements of your ancestors and their descendants. You have to pay for the service you choose, but prices aren't high – the most expensive is about £20.

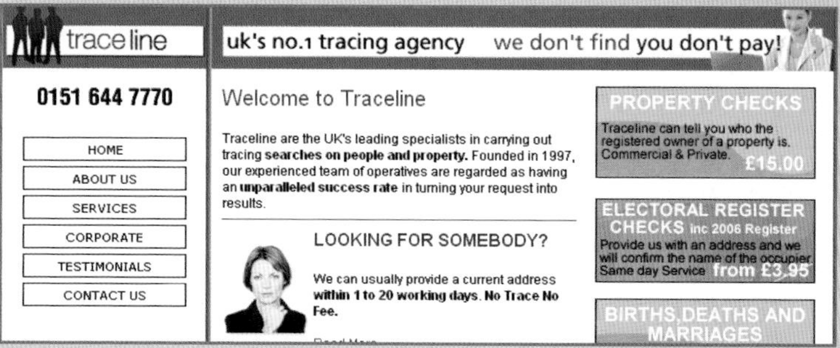

Why make contact?

The internet's a marvellous tool for sharing information. You can put your family history online so that relatives can see what you've achieved, and you may even discover information about your family that's already out there.

Contacting other researchers allows you to correspond with – or even meet – people with common interests, and can help you to discover more about your own family tree in the process. Best of all, a member of the online community may have the answer to one of your problems, or at least be able to point you in the right direction.

How to contact other people

There are a number of ways of contacting people to find answers to your questions. Here are a few of the most popular.

- Mailing lists are an email exchange forum made up of people interested in the same research topic. By subscribing to the list you will receive all the email messages that are posted to that list, in either 'mail mode' or 'digest mode'. Mail mode means that you receive each message as it's posted; digest mode combines a week's worth of messages in one email. When you post a message, it's automatically circulated to all the subscribers on that mailing list.
- Newsgroups work by posting messages on an online message board. You don't need to be a subscriber to use the service.
- Web-based forums are websites that act as message boards. Like newsgroups, they are a place where researchers can post messages for others to read. Both newsgroups and web-based forums have the advantage of not inundating you with emails; their only disadvantage is that you may miss crucial postings if you don't check the message boards regularly for updates.

Family history databases

Another way to join an online community is to sign up with **genesreunited.co.uk** or **ancestry.co.uk/community.** Once you've uploaded your tree, the database will alert you when it detects a match in another member's tree. You can contact that member via the website to see if their match really is part of your tree, or mere coincidence. This can help you to broaden your family tree – as well as open up the possibility of meeting living relatives.

Using Cyndi's List

1 If, for example you are keen to contact the mailing list for an online community, there's a range of subjects to choose from on the Cyndi's list website (see page 46). Go to **cyndislist.com** and from the homepage, click on **'M'**. This will take you to the link for mailing lists.

Choose your topic

2 You can see from the list, that there are many options to chose from. For example, the queries and surnames link will take you to message boards dedicated to that subject, and there is also a link called **Newbies** which will help newcomers and beginners to find mailing lists and forums on the Cyndi's list site.

Establish your boundaries

If you decide to join an online community, you'll find a vast range of topics from which to choose – from surname research sites to those that focus on locations, religions, occupations and countless other subjects. It's important to know what you are trying to achieve so that you can adopt a methodical approach and stick to lists relevant to your search, rather than searching randomly. Here's how to search on two of the most popular websites, Cyndi's List and Genuki.

Present every Sunday *Names of the parishioners from churches all over the world can be viewed on Cyndi's List. You may be able to track down one of your ancestors on this site by searching the appropriate country, year and denomination.*

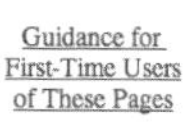

Guidance for First-Time Users of These Pages

UK & Ireland Genealogy

Guidance for Potential Contributors to These Pages

Enter this large collection of genealogical information pages for England, Ireland, Scotland, Wales, the Channel Islands, and the Isle of Man.

Getting started in genealogy	Frequently Asked Questions (FAQs)	Researching UK and Irish genealogy from abroad
World genealogy, newsgroups and bulletin boards, etc.	Recent changes to these pages	Upcoming UK & Ireland Genealogical events (GENEVA)

For the latest GENUKI server status see www.genuki.info which gives news of past, present and (where possible) future incidents that may prevent or hinder your access to parts of GENUKI.

GENUKI Contents

Genealogy Mailing Lists and Usenet Newsgroups

The newsgroups soc.genealogy.britain and soc.genealogy.ireland which the GENUKI Web server has been created to support, are just two of a number of newsgroups devoted to various topics and regions, worldwide. John Fuller provides descriptive listings of these newsgroups, and also of the much larger set of genealogy mailing lists that now exist. (GENUKI's listing of UK&I-related mailing lists is maintained in conjunction with John Fuller's much more general list.)

Additionally, Stephen Woods provides a listing of genealogy newsgroups via which one directly access any of the newsgroups, and can see the FAQ Files that are provided for a number of them.

Find help, report problems, and contribute information.

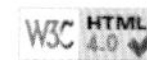

[Last updated Thursday, 06-Jan-2005 13:13:52 GMT - Phil Stringer]

MAILING LISTS

URL: http://www.rootsweb.com/~jfuller/gen_mail.html

Last update: August 21, 2007 by John Fuller, johnf14246@aol.com

Register Resource | Update Resource | Report a Broken Link

Welcome packages are generally provided when you subscribe. Please keep these on file since they c number of lists are included for various countries and areas of the world where the list descriptions do indicated that genealogy is an acceptable, though in some cases unusual, topic for the list.

When subscribing, please make sure that the subscribe command is the only text in the body of the me mailing lists and posting instructions will be contained in the Welcome message you receive when you s

PLEASE NOTE: First, I do not own any of these lists so sending a subscribe message to me will not instructions. Second, I am probably not researching these surnames and geographic areas, so please d

The mailing lists contained in this section are divided into the following categories ... just click on the on

- COUNTRIES OTHER THAN USA
- USA
- SURNAMES
- Adoption
- African-Ancestored (other than Freedmen)
- Cemeteries/Monuments/Obituaries
- Computing/Internet Resources
- DNA Studies/Testing
- Emigration/Migration Ships and Trails
- Family History, Folklore, and Artifacts
- Freedmen (African, Native American, caucasian, etc.)

Using Genuki for your search

1 Genuki, at **genuki.org.uk**, has links to information sites for every region of the British Isles, as well as information on Irish and UK genealogy (see page 44). On the homepage, click on the link to **World genealogy, newsgroups and bulletin boards**. This will take you to a page that links you to these sites.

Search the world

2 Genuki supports a number of newsgroups and mailing lists from around the world, as well as the UK. From this page, if you want to find a list of worldwide mailing lists that are relevant to your research, click on the link to **Mailing lists**.

Join a mailing list

3 You'll then see a page that not only lists newsgroups by subjects, like DNA studies, or Emigration, for example, but it also has a link to USA-based and worldwide message boards. By clicking on the relevant link, you can post messages and get hints and tips from family historians all over the world.

Shared interests

It's encouraging to know you may be only a phone call or web search away from finding someone who is trying to track down the same piece of family history as you – or who may already have found it!

Using family trees online

Finding a family tree that matches and overlaps with yours is exciting, and may open up whole new areas of research. But before you incorporate new family members into your tree, check them against original sources first.

The data uploaded by other researchers into online family trees is what's known as secondary material, and isn't always accurate. It's compiled data, unlike online indexes, and may contain errors of judgment as well as mistakes in reading and typing. Using primary sources – originals – is the only way to ensure the greatest accuracy.

Sorting out your sources

The tendency is to believe what you see on a site, assuming that if it's there, it must be true. Unfortunately this isn't always the case, so it's important to be able to tell a primary source from a secondary one.

PRIMARY SOURCES These are the actual records made by people present at the occasion in question – whether it's in official documents or personal papers. They include parish registers, civil registration certificates, census returns, letters, diaries, newspaper articles and photographs. Usually, the only primary sources that you'll be able to access are photographic images of the original documents, which you can view online.

All in it together *Memories and experiences seem richer and more intense when shared by people with something in common, like these workers on a jaunt in Rhyl, north Wales, in the 1920s.*

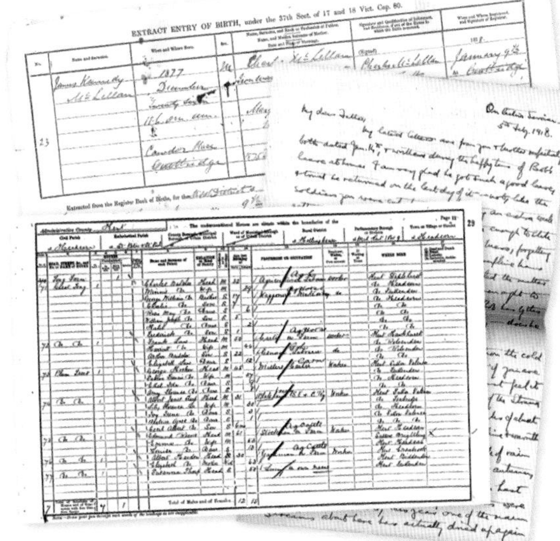

Original documents *If the new information you receive can be confirmed by birth certificates, census records or letters, enter it into your tree.*

You can also request photocopies of original documents from archives and record offices, which they'll send you for a small charge.

SECONDARY SOURCES These are records made about a past event, by people who weren't present. Online genealogy, by its very nature, relies heavily on secondary material. The original, which may be damaged, faded or written in an old-fashioned and often illegible script, has been read by someone and copied out – often several times – before it appears in an online index. The chances for errors to creep in are high, which is why you need to verify any second-hand data.

Confirming the 'facts'

Sometimes the information in other people's online family history can't be backed up, such as when it stems from family stories or memories passed down through the generations. On other occasions, all you need to do is check that the researcher obtained the relevant certificates. It's also worth double-checking spellings, as old handwriting is notoriously hard to read. Here are some useful guidelines to consider before putting other people's research into your own work.

- Ask the original researcher where they found the information and what documents they have.
- Find out if they were unable to find certain primary records.
- Use their names, dates and locations only as a starting point for ordering your own certificates, or for finding parish records, census returns and other primary sources to verify the research and confirm that it ties into your family tree.

Copyright and privacy issues

Online resources are publications and subject to copyright and privacy considerations. When people put material online, they're essentially publishing it. Don't simply copy and paste large amounts of text that don't belong to you. And don't publish online any data you've received without first checking where it comes from and if the person who provided it is happy for you to do so.

Online family trees genesreunited.co.uk

With more than 58 million users, Genes Reunited offers you a great chance of making contact with unknown relatives, once you start searching.

The website lets you search its database of family trees for your ancestors and possible relatives. You need to register before you can make full use of the site, then you can upload your own family tree onto the site for free. It works best when users include as much detail as possible, so try to get your whole family involved – the more information on the site, the greater the chances of finding relatives and discovering shared ancestors. The search engine looks for matches in other people's uploaded trees, and alerts you if it finds any. If you want to contact that someone and view their family tree, you have to upgrade to full membership. This takes only a few moments and costs £9.95 for six months unlimited use. If you choose to share information with other Genes Reunited members, your privacy is protected, as all messages are exchanged via the website.

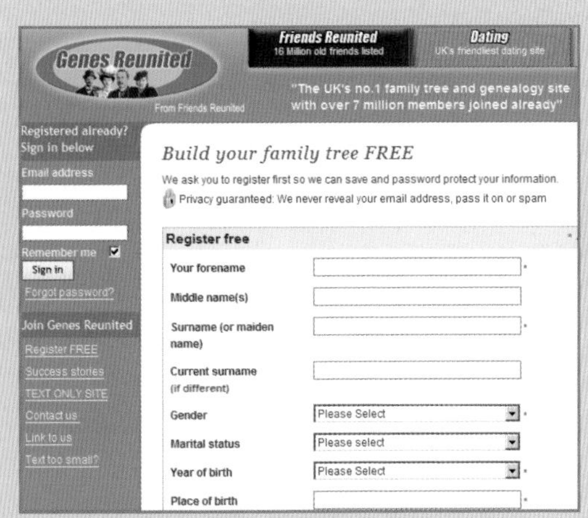

Sign up as a member

1 To become a member of Genes Reunited, go to the homepage, genesreunited.co.uk, and fill in your name, date of birth, place of birth and contact details. You can then begin uploading your family tree (see page 312) and carry out searches of other people's trees.

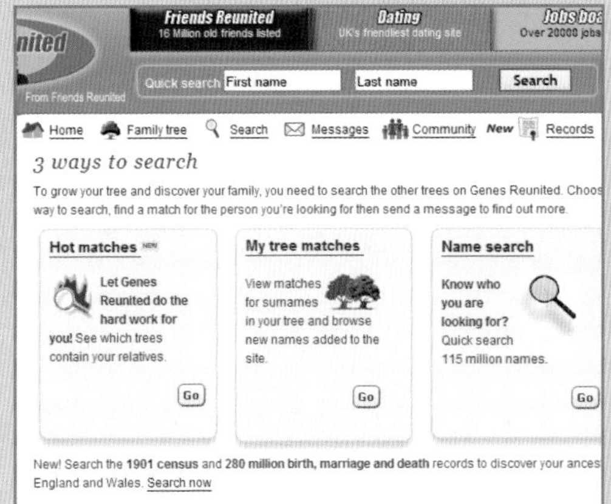

Do a quick name search

2 A quick search can be made by entering a first and last name in the **Quick search** bar. Alternatively, click the **Search** link from the homepage to be taken to the page shown here. Click the **Name search** box, and in the screen that appears you can type the name of the ancestor you are interested in, and their date and place of birth. The search engine then scans its members' trees to see if there's a match.

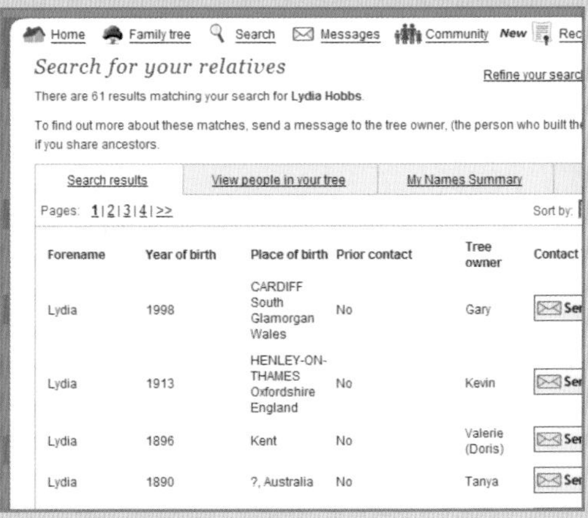

Check the matches

3 This screen shows the results for a quick search for a Lydia Hobbs. There are 66 matches dating back from 1998. Look through the dates and places of birth to see if any of these matches the ancestor you're interested in. If so, you can contact the tree owner by clicking the **Send message** box. If you've not yet paid for full membership, you'll be asked to upgrade.

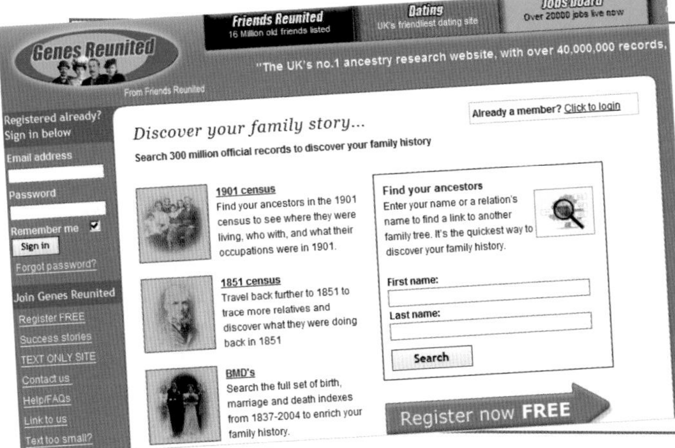

Shared information

Members of Genes Reunited can double-check secondary sources (see page 269) by accessing the census returns from 1841 to 1901, as well as the birth, marriage and death indexes. When you find what you want, you need to buy credits to view the images and details. Fifty credits cost £5 and are valid for seven days.

Writing a 'Trying to find' message

When you put a 'Trying to find' message online, start with the name of the person you're searching for, written in capital letters. This makes it much easier to spot for anyone who may be scanning a long list. Then include as much information as you can to maximise the chances of identifying a match. Wherever possible, give a full name, date and place of birth, and details about the person's parents, along with any other helpful clues you can think of.

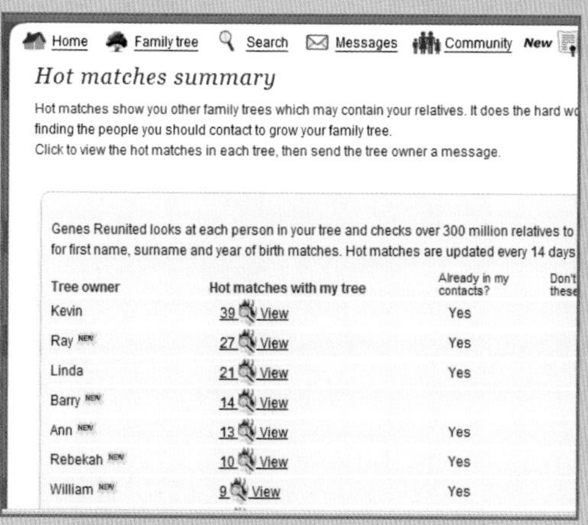

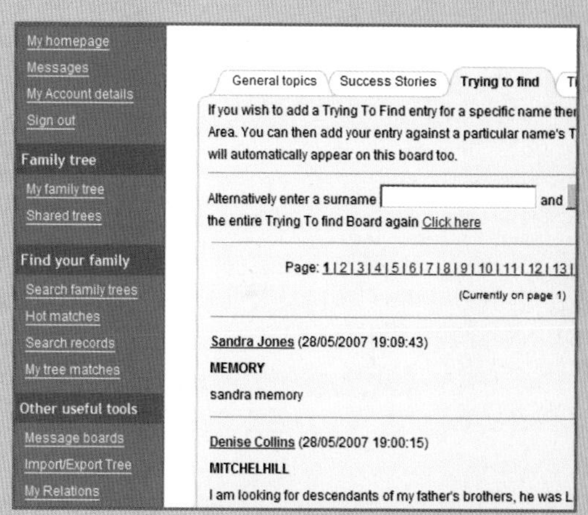

Try 'Hot matches'

4 Alternatively, click the **Hot matches** box on the screen shown at step 2. The search engine will scan other family trees in its database and list other members who have the same names as yours in their family trees. It shows how many names overlap – the more there are, the likelier you are to be related. Click **View** under **Hot matches with my tree** to see a list of the names that you have in common.

Using 'My tree matches'

5 A third option is to click the **My tree matches** box on the screen shown at step 2. The search engine scans other family trees in the database to see how many have the same surnames as your family tree. This is more useful if you're researching unusual surnames. Common names will throw up so many matches, you'll be overwhelmed. But 100 or so matches to an unusual name are worth investigating.

Read and post messages

6 As well as looking for matches in family trees, you can also read and post messages. In the green column to the left of the screen is a heading **Other useful tools**; from there, go to **Message boards**, where you can conduct a surname search. You can read – or perhaps even answer – questions from other Genes Reunited members. And if you can't find a match, you can leave your own 'Trying to find' message. With any luck, you may be contacted by someone with the details you need.

How to develop your family tree online

If you've joined Genes Reunited and found other researchers who might be connected with your family, you'll want to upload your family tree so that you can share information with them. Here's how.

Follow the step-by-step instructions below to upload your family tree to the Genes Reunited website. This can be time-consuming, but it's quite straightforward, so don't be daunted. It doesn't matter if you add only one or two names at a time to your tree, and it's easy to go back in to edit and adapt your entries as you discover new information. Look at the left-hand side of the Genes Reunited homepage. Below the personalised section, you'll find two main headings: **Family tree** and **Find your family**. Each one has a choice of sub-headings, which contain live links to other sections.

Under **Family tree** you'll find links to **My family tree** and **Shared trees. My family tree** lists all the entries in your family tree. Use this option to add and edit your information whenever you want to.

Starting your online family tree

1 On the **genesreunited.co.uk** homepage, click **Family tree** in the top panel and you'll find your registration details – name, year of birth, gender and place of birth. This is your tree's starting point. You can personalise the form by adding other details – such as your nicknames or your job – along with the source of the data. If you are a paid-up member, you can even add your photograph. Click **Add photo** and follow the instructions. Then click **Save changes**.

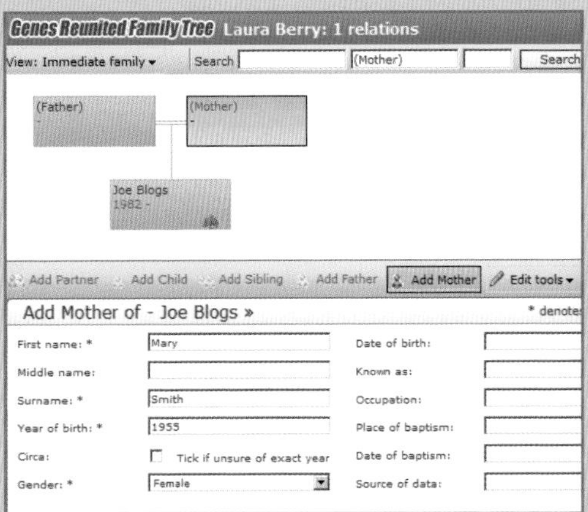

Add your parents

2 Now you can add other members of your family tree. With your entry highlighted, click the **Add mother** link and fill in her details in the form provided. Save the changes and then do the same for your father. Your female relatives appear in pink boxes, and males in blue. Every time you complete a form, click on **Save changes**.

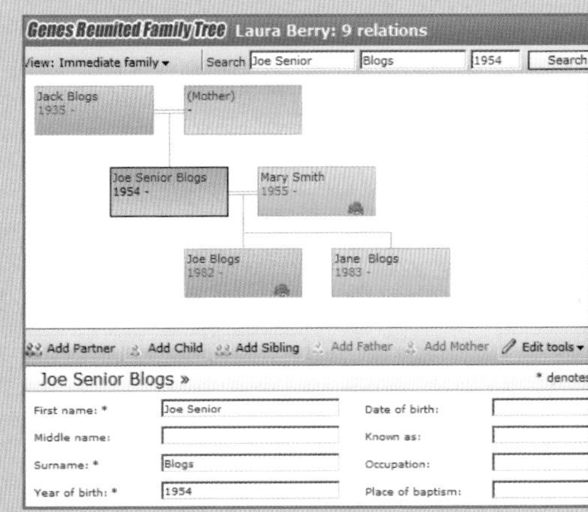

Add more family members

3 To add more names to your tree, such as your paternal grandparents, click on the blue box for your father, then click **Add father** to add his father or **Add mother** to add his mother. The same applies for adding partners, siblings or children. If a flashing-tree symbol appears in one of your boxes, it means someone else's tree includes an ancestor with the same name and year of birth.

If you want to go straight to a particular member of your tree, enter their name and birth details in the search box at the top.

Click on **Shared trees** if you've asked to see someone else's tree, and they've given you permission.

The **Find your family** heading helps you to match up your tree with anyone else showing the same name in their tree (see page 264). It's worth re-doing your searches every few months, because new members may have uploaded their family trees.

Once you're comfortable with the progress of your tree, go back to the homepage and click on **Other useful tools** to find out about importing and exporting your family tree. You can also go to message boards, and do a search on specific ancestors via the **My relations** link.

Faster on your computer *Once you've collected a fair amount of information about your family, it's helpful to upload it onto a family tree on the Genes Reunited website.*

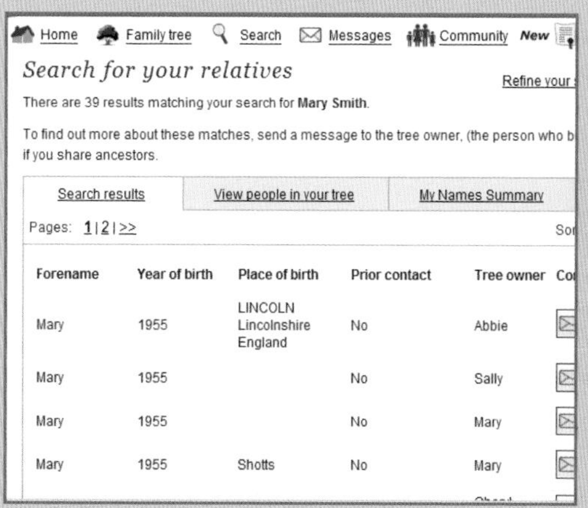

Making connections

4 Move the mouse over the flashing-tree symbol and you'll see a link showing how many matches have been found. Click the link to see the list: if a place of birth matches that of your ancestor, then your family trees may connect somewhere. Click the **Send message** button next to the tree owner's name and type your message in the text box. Explain which member of their tree you are interested in and ask for permission to view their tree.

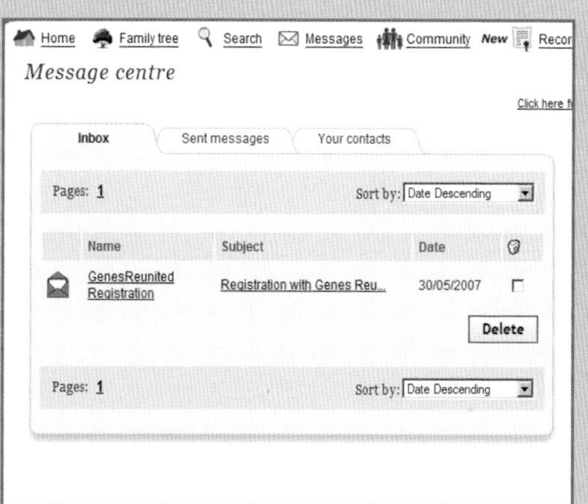

Picking up messages

5 You can check whether any Genes Reunited members have replied to your messages, or whether anyone has sent you a message about your family tree, by clicking the **Messages** link on the top left-hand side of the page. This facility keeps your details safe, as your own email address is never given to anyone else.

Save duplicating work with Gedcom

Gedcom is the term used for the standard file format used by most family historians. For more information about it, see page 278.

If you already have a gedcom file containing your family tree, you don't need to re-enter your family tree details on the Genes Reunited site. You can simply upload the gedcom file. Click on the **Import/export tree** link, choose the gedcom file and click **Import file**.

You can also export your family tree as a gedcom file. From the same page click **Export your family tree to a gedcom file**. Your gedcom file will then be emailed to the address you gave when you first registered with Genes Reunited. You can have it exported to a different email address by changing your sign-in email address – this option is offered before you click the **Export gedcom** button.

Sharing online family trees

Seeing other people's trees online may inspire you to take yours further or give you useful pointers on presentation. You may even be lucky enough to discover one, already compiled, that features some of your own ancestors.

Tracing your family's history is so popular now that it's quite likely that someone, somewhere, is researching a family history that has links with your own. It can be tremendously exciting to link up with distant relatives who share one or more ancestors – and physical quirks – with you. You might find that dad's red hair, granny's lovely voice or George's photographic memory might be replicated elsewhere in your extended family.

When sharing information and finding links between your family tree and someone else's, always be aware that data can be put onto the internet by anyone, and you don't know how just thorough they may have been in their checks.

Double-check everything you find, and use the information only as a starting point for your searches. Mistakes can be made unintentionally, but you don't want to perpetuate them by incorporating them into your own family tree.

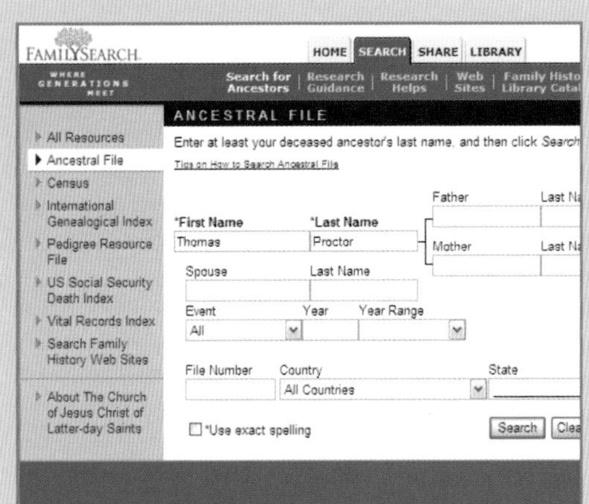

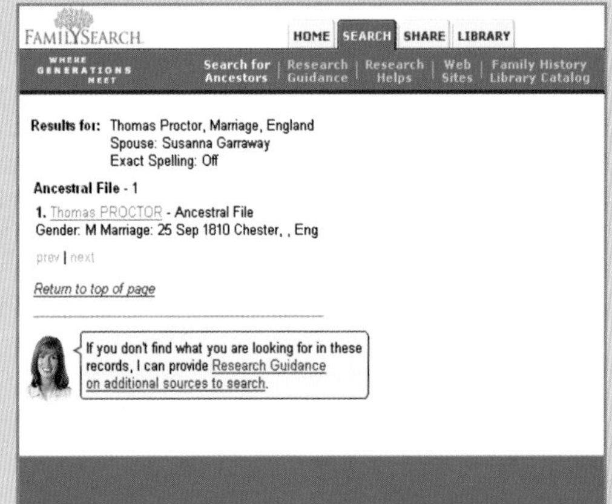

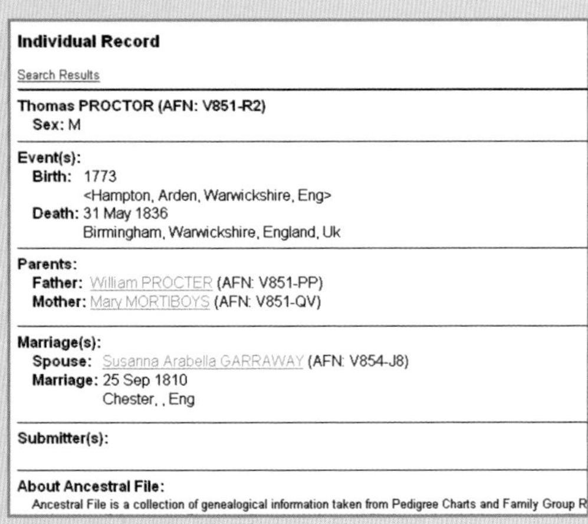

Start an Ancestral File search

1 To search other people's family trees for a Thomas Proctor, who married a Susanna Arabella Garraway early in the 1800s, go to **familysearch.org** and click the **Search** icon at the top of the page. On the next page, click **Ancestral file** on the left. On the search page, enter all the details you have, and click **Search**.

Read the first results

2 You get one search result for Thomas Proctor and it shows that he married in 1810. Click on the name **Thomas Proctor**.

See the details

3 Up come Thomas Proctor's birth and death dates, the names of his parents and date of his marriage to Susanna Arabella Garraway. The data has been submitted by individuals and not checked, so you should verify the information using original parish records – perhaps by visiting the relevant county archive in person – before putting the data into your own family tree.

Familysearch

On **familyseach.org** (see page 138) there's an area devoted to online family trees, known as the **Ancestral File**, which holds thousands of pedigrees put together from submissions by members of the Church of Jesus Christ of Latter-day Saints (the Mormons) and others, since 1978. The search process for this site is similar to that for searching on the International Genealogical Index (IGI), shown on page 138. Below is an example of how to do a search using the Ancestral File.

Rootsweb

This website, **worldconnect.rootsweb.com**, has a vast database of family trees. There are around 500 million names online and the collection continues to expand. It offers mailing lists and message boards, to help you to keep in touch with other family researchers. You can submit your family tree to RootsWeb free of charge, after registering; if you've already registered on Ancestry's website, you can use the same login. On the right, you'll see how to use the website and manage your family tree.

Individual Record FamilySearch™

Search Results

David (AFN: 18JR-Q6F) Pedigree
Sex: M Family

Event(s):
Birth: Abt 974
<, , , Germany>

Parents:
Father: Robert Lord Of INNSBRUCK (AFN: 18JR-Q2L) Family
Mother: Mrs-Robert (AFN: 18JR-Q3S)

Marriage(s):
Spouse: Mrs-David (AFN: 18JR-Q7M) Family
Marriage: Abt 999

Submitter(s): Details

About Ancestral File:
Ancestral File is a collection of genealogical information taken from Pedigree Charts and Family Group R… to the Family History Department since 1978. The information has not been verified against any official r… information in Ancestral File is contributed, it is the responsibility of those who use the file to verify its ac…

Check the further details

4 If you click on a spouse's name or on parents' names, you may find information that has been submitted about these ancestors. Here, one branch of Susanna Arabella Garraway's tree goes back numerous generations to a Robert Lord of Innsbruck in 10th-century Germany, though the information given is rather vague. Click **Details** on the right of the **Submitter** section to find out more about the submitter.

Individual Record

Search Results

Robert Lord Of INNSBRUCK (AFN: 18JR-Q2L)
Sex: M

Submitter(s):
BARBARA PECK - SURNAME
MEDIEVAL FAMILIES PROJECT
15 EAST SOUTH TEMPLE
SALT LAKE CITY UT
USA 84150
Microfilm: NONE
Submission: AF94-103470

Interested Researcher(s):

About Ancestral File:
Ancestral File is a collection of genealogical information taken from Pedigree Charts and Family Group R… against any official records. Since the information in Ancestral File is contributed, it is the responsibility…

Please Note:
Names and address of submitters to Ancestral File and those who have a research interest are provided… commercial use, is strictly prohibited.

Contact the submitter

5 You're shown the address details of the person who submitted the infomation. You can try to contact them, if you're interested in discussing the pedigree. Bear in mind this address may be out of date, but it's worth trying. It's important, whenever you can, to verify the information you find online.

Using worldconnect.rootsweb

To upload your family tree, go to the WorldConnect site. Under the **Submit your family tree to worldconnect** heading, click **Start here**. You'll find instructions on how to convert your family tree to Gedcom (see below) format – don't worry – this won't change your original file. Once reformatted, choose a name for your family tree and follow the steps for uploading it.

You can also change or remove any previously uploaded information by clicking **Update or correct your existing family tree**. This takes you to the **Manage tree** page, which lists all your trees. The editorial options are on the right-hand side of the page, under **Tree settings**. Click on the appropriate option – for example, **Delete tree** to delete the tree from the website.

What is Gedcom?

You'll find the term Gedcom will crop up frequently as you get more involved with online family trees. It comes from Genealogical Data Communications and is the standard file format used by most family history software. Look at page 278 to find out more about it and learn how to use it, if you're not already familiar with it.

Sharing online family trees
Who can see your tree?

There are many sites that allow you to upload your family tree and share data with fellow users. If you've already created a family tree on your home computer using one of the popular brands of software, you can convert it into what's known as a Gedcom file (see page 278) and upload it onto several sites. This will maximise your chances of finding another family member who's working on a branch of your tree.

In all the excitement of getting your tree online and being able to offer it to others to share, it's important to take a little time to decide just who should be able to access it.

How public do you want to go?

If you put your family tree onto Ancestry's website (see below), you can choose who can access it. Go to the **Home** tab and under the **Tools** category choose **Change tree privacy**. If you opt for a **Public Tree**, then other people who are searching Ancestry's OneWorldTree database can see it. But if you want your full tree to be viewable only by invited family members, select **Personal Tree**. This doesn't stop other Ancestry members from finding out if a deceased person's name and date and

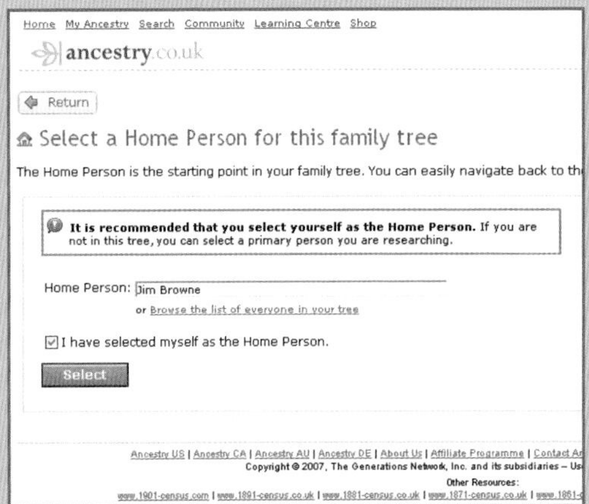

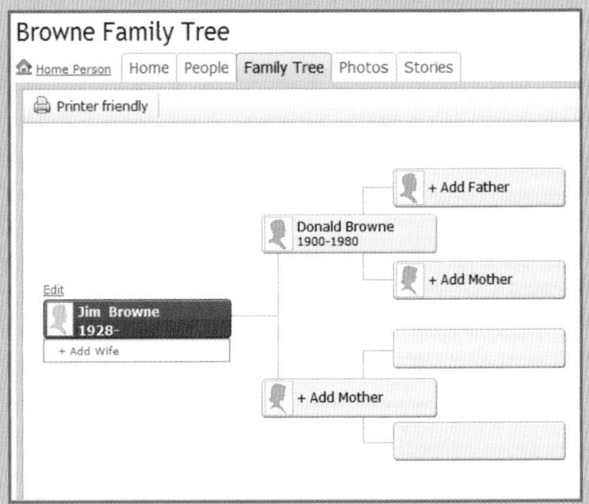

Put your tree on ancestry.co.uk

1 Here, you can build your family tree from scratch or, if you've already created a tree using a program such as Family Tree Maker or Family Historian, you can upload this as a Gedcom file. Go to **My ancestry** and choose either **Create a new family tree** or **Upload an existing family tree**. Then click on **Start your family tree**.

Begin your online family tree

2 If you've selected **Create a new family tree**, click on **Add yourself**. Enter your name, sex, and date and place of birth in the box that comes up. Click on **Save**. Then click on **Add father** and a similar box will appear – but this one gives you the option of adding his date and place of death.

How your tree will look

3 This is what an Ancestry online tree looks like – and it's simple to add new family members. By clicking on + **Add mother** or + **Add wife**, for example, you can quickly and easily develop your tree. There are tabs along the top of the family tree page that take you to pages where you can add photos and stories; if you wish to add a photo, timeline or story to anyone on your tree click on the **People** tab.

place of birth is in your tree, but they'll need to contact you for permission if they want to find out more about an individual.

In the same way, you can search other Ancestry member's trees to see if you've relatives in common. Go to the **My Ancestry** homepage and click on **Find Ancestry members**. A page appears, on which you can enter the name and other details of the ancestor you're interested in. If there's a likely match in someone else's tree, you can contact the tree's author via the site to find out more.

Filling in the detail

4 By clicking on **People**, you can upload one or more photos or fill in some details about yourself. If a green leaf icon appears next to any names on your family tree, it means that the Ancestry database contains a record that may match that person. Click on the icon to be taken to a list of those records.

Using a 'global tree' website

The free-to-use website **gencircles.com** is a 'global tree' site, which means that people from all over the world upload their trees to it, giving you a potential worldwide audience for your findings. You can also post messages on their **Clubs** section. The site is easy to use and you can do basic searches without registering. If you want to upload your family tree and allow others to search it, you'll need to register. Click on the **Register** link on the homepage (see below, right) and follow the prompts. Once you've registered, you can use the Smart Matching facility, which looks for matches by comparing all the people on your tree with all those on other trees already uploaded on the website.

If you want to upload your tree, you'll need to have it in Gedcom format, which your family tree software should be able to do for you (see page 278). From the homepage, you can then navigate to upload your Gedcom file and follow the prompts.

The great thing about this site is that, unlike some other family tree sharing sites, you still 'own' your data, and GenCircles won't pass your details on to any other third party. This also is the case with your email address – which you use to register – so you won't receive any spam email.

If you decide that you don't want your tree on GenCircles any more, you can simply delete it so that it can no longer be seen or searched by any visitors to the site.

Worldwide families *GenCircle's homepage lists the latest family trees to be uploaded. Note how most titles are clear about their content (right).*

Controlling the use of your tree

You can also upload your family tree findings on **genealogy.com**. The site will detect that you're a UK user, and will offer to direct you to **ancestry.co.uk**, its sister site. You have the option, though, to remain on the main site, where you can create your own family tree homepage, upload photos, add links to other sites and edit your page as you would like it.

It's important to bear in mind that the hosts of **genealogy.com** own the rights to your information once you've uploaded it. This means that they can use your information for publicity stories, in articles and on the website if they wish to. If you don't want your family information used by any third party, always check the details of any website to see just who owns the rights to it, and how it will be used once it's posted online.

Using Gedcom files

Each family history software program has its own file format, so you can't just distribute copies of your family tree file and assume every one else will have software that can make sense of it. Fortunately, Gedcom solves this problem.

Gedcom, which stands for Genealogical Data Communication, is a file format designed to make it easier to exchange data between one program and another. All family history databases, whatever their own file format, can import Gedcom files and convert their own data to the Gedcom format.

Sharing a Gedcom file

To create a Gedcom file of information that you want to share with someone else, you'll need to use your family history database's **Export** option.

If the person you're sharing with doesn't already have family history software on their computer, there are several free options, which will let them view your family tree. They could try LegacyFamily Tree, which is available through **legacyfamilytree.com.** Or they could look at Personal Ancestral File on **familysearch.org.** Both of these can be downloaded and installed free of charge. As another option, there are free Gedcom viewers which can be used to view a family tree, although you won't be able to add to it or edit it. You can find Gedcom viewers listed on the Gedcom page on Cyndi's List at **cyndislist.com/gedcom.htm.**

Family Historian software

Unlike other family history databases, Family Historian (see page 38) doesn't need to convert Gedcom files, because it uses Gedcom as its own internal file format – that's why Family Historian files end in **.ged**. If you have Family Historian installed on your computer, then double-clicking on a Gedcom file will automatically start up the Family Historian software with that file loaded.

Receiving a Gedcom file

What do you do if someone sends you a Gedcom file of their family tree? If you have the software called Family Historian installed on your computer (see page 38), you can simply double-click on the file and the program will display it.

With other software, you'll need to use the **Import** option to convert the Gedcom file to your program's own format. Before you do this, it's essential to create a new, blank family tree in your database to take the new data – never import a newly received Gedcom file directly into your existing family tree, as this could overwrite or duplicate information already in your tree with new material that you haven't had a chance to check.

Merging a file

Once you've had a look at a Gedcom file you've received from someone else, you need to combine it with your existing database. You'll have to take into account that each family history database carries out this procedure in its own way. The option is normally called **Merge** or **Match**, so you'll need to look for these words in the index of the online help that goes with your software program. Before you merge any of the new data, make sure to make a back-up of the master file of your family tree, so that if anything goes wrong with the merging, you still have an original, undamaged version of your family tree to use in your next attempt.

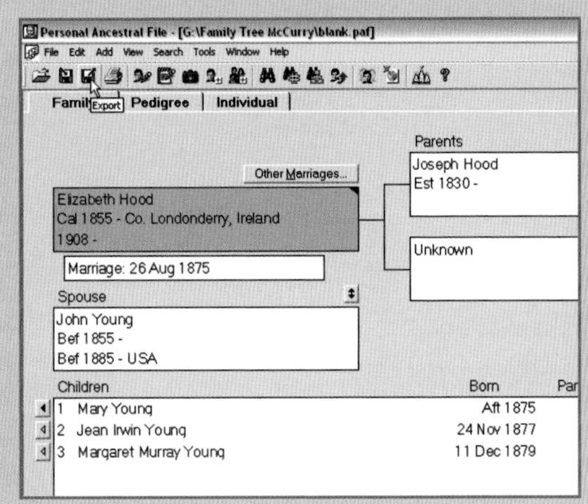

Creating a Gedcom file

1 All family history databases will have an **Export** option, usually on the **File** menu. In Personal Ancestral File (PAF), shown above, there's also an **Export** icon on the toolbar. To create a Gedcom file for exporting, click on the **Export** button.

Protecting privacy

Before you start sharing your Gedcom file with anyone outside your immediate family, you should think carefully about which individuals you include and what information about them is revealed.

Don't forget that once you've given your Gedcom file to someone else, you'll have no control over what they do with it. They could pass it on to other, more distant family members, or they might even submit it to one of the online pedigree databases.

There's no law in the UK against publishing biographical information about individuals without their permission. But even so, many people don't like the idea of their personal details being broadcast, and there's a risk you might fall out with members of your family because you've made public something they feel is private. Certainly, if there's anything in your family that you know is 'not talked about', you should take care to exclude it from a file that may be viewed by complete strangers.

Filtering information

To help you to avoid privacy problems, most family history databases have some kind of 'filtering' facility, which will let you create a Gedcom file containing only individuals who are no longer alive. Some websites will automatically exclude the details of anyone who was born within the past 50 years.

Also, there are separate programs you can use that will do the same thing – such as Gedclean, which can be downloaded free from **raynorshyn.com/gedclean/**.

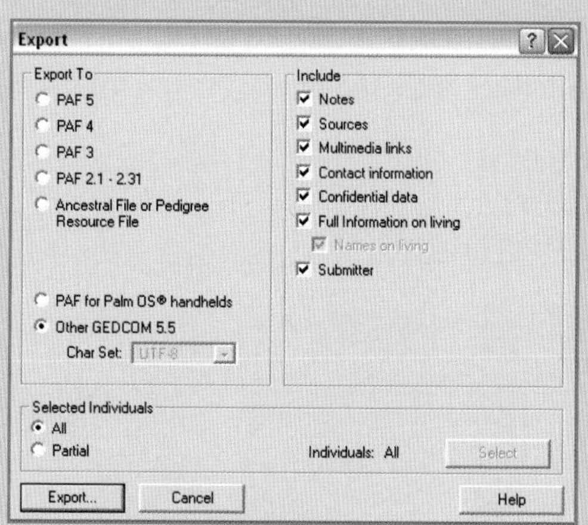

Choosing parameters

2 In the **Export** dialog box, click on the **Other Gedcom 5.5** button. Choose what to include or exclude from the list on the right. You might deactivate **Full information on living** if you're sending your Gedcom to non-family members. You can also choose to include the whole tree or just selected individuals. Once you click on the **Export** button, PAF will prompt you to type in a file name before creating the Gedcom file. Other family history programs should be broadly similar.

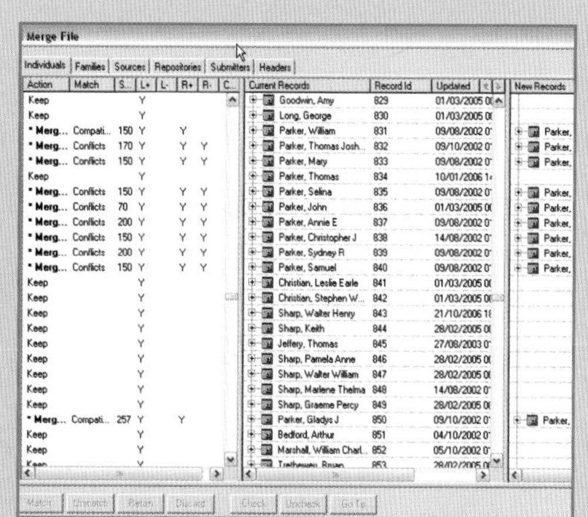

Merging a Gedcom file

1 If you're in Family Historian, make a back-up of your family tree master file, then open your family tree with the program. From the **File** menu click on **Merge/compare file** and select the file you want to match and merge. The software compares all the individuals in the two files and the **Merge file** window shows which are potential matches. It indicates whether they can be merged without difficulty or whether some of the information in the two files conflicts.

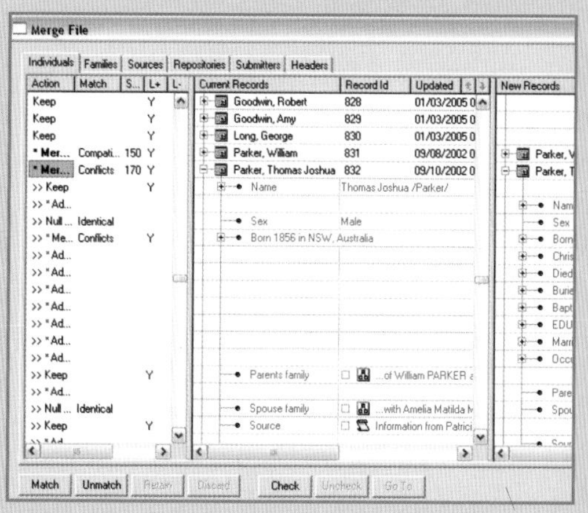

Examining any conflicts

2 Where there's a conflict, you can expand the details of the individual to see where the problem lies, by clicking on the name. In this example, the original file has only an approximate birth date for Thomas Joshua Parker, while the new file has more precise information (and many additional details). Obviously this is a good match, and to add these details into your master file, click on **Merge**.

Making the most of mailing lists

There are thousands of family history mailing lists – any one of them could help you to learn more about your ancestors or share information with other researchers. Getting onto a mailing list is easy to do.

Using a mailing list has many advantages. Most importantly, it can help you to find answers to problems – either by connecting with someone who has already found information on the area you're looking into or, more often, by pointing you in the right direction. And as you gain more experience, you may find that you can help other people. Apart from being excellent tools for family research, mailing lists are also a great place for social networking, as you keep on meeting like-minded people who share your interests.

Finding the right mailing list

The all-embracing nature of family history opens up many avenues of research, including surnames, locations, occupations and ethnic groups. Mailing lists therefore have to cover a vast range of topics, so to begin looking for a suitable list, first decide on the subject that you want your mailing list to be about.

Rootsweb offers a large index of mailing lists that you can search to find the one that suits you. Go to **rootsweb.com** and click on Mailing Lists in the website's tool bar. You then have two search options. The first is to search the mailing list archives. This can provide information that has already been posted to the mailing list. For example, if you're interested in finding out more about an ancestor whose occupation was a cordwainer (a shoemaker), you can use this search box to see what, if any, messages have already been posted. Enter the occupation and press Search and you'll find numerous links to sites that have information about cordwainers.

The second option is to search for a specific mailing list that you wish to join. Here you enter the surname, location or keyword that you want the mailing list to be about, and then click **Search**. Another way to use this search option is to click on **Browse mailing list**. It allows you to browse for a mailing list by surname, location or topic.

Master of his trade *An early 19th-century baker eases a large pie into his oven. You'll be able to find out more about master bakers, and many other occupations, by joining a mailing list. Key in the type of occupation, such as 'Master baker', see left, and begin your search.*

rootsweb Finding our roots together.
AN ancestry.com COMMUNITY
Home | Searches | Family Trees | Mailing Lists | Message Boards

Surnames
Find Your Family Tree In The Worlds Largest Family Tree. Free Trial!
www.OneGreatFamily.com

Family Tree Sites
Free For Life! No Trial Periods:No Software Needed
www.TribalPages.com

Find Your Family Tree
Discover your roots & learn of past family members. Browse online now!

Find a List Search

Keyword | Advanced

Keyword(s): Master Baker

Search | Search tips

Questions? Comments? Suggestions? Email feedback@rootsweb.com

If you don't see what you want straight away, scroll down the page to the box labelled **Other** and browse through the options offered. Click on **Occupations**, for example, and you'll be taken to an alphabetical list. Find the occupation you're interested in, such as **Blacksmithing**. By clicking on this you'll be taken to a page where you can subscribe to the blacksmithing mailing list.

Choosing a 'mode'

The way in which you receive messages from your mailing list is called a 'mode'. There are two options and it's best to decide on your preferred mode before you join the list. The first is to join the mailing list in a **Mail** mode. This means that every time a message is posted on the mailing list it will be forwarded to you as an individual email.

The second is called **Digest** mode, and it groups together several messages and sends them out as one large message. So, instead of receiving lots of individual email messages you'll only receive a couple which contain several messages.

Joining a mailing list

To get onto the blacksmithing mailing list, for example, click on the **Subscribe to Blacksmith-L** link for mail mode, or **Blacksmith-D** for digest mode. An email opens up automatically and you send only the word **Subscribe.**

Once you've sent your email to subscribe to your chosen list, you'll receive a confirmation email welcoming you to the mailing list. This message includes information about how to use the list, and how to unsubscribe.

Mailing list manners

When using mailing lists, news groups and forums, it's important to remember that they have a set of rules. Some of these are set out in their FAQs (Frequently Asked Questions), but others are largely unwritten. These codes of behaviour ensure that online communication is effective and polite. The complete text of Virginia Shea's book on 'Netiquette' can be found and read online at **albion.com/netiquette/book/**. The main points she raises are:

- Make sure that the messages you send are relevant to the list you've joined – if not, the list owner or other members of that list will ask you to discontinue your line of interest.
- Always be polite and clear in the posting of messages, and if you receive an abusive message known as a 'flame' don't retaliate, but try to ignore it.
- Don't include the whole message that you're replying to – just send your reply or, if necessary, include only a small part of the message that you're responding to.
- Don't post messages that are all in upper case because it INDICATES SHOUTING. Only use upper case letters for surnames, so if you're sending a query, enter your surname in upper cases letters – for example, Emma BELL.
- When you respond to an individual, be careful to check that you're sending the response to the desired recipient only, rather than to the whole group. Always check your **To:** line before you click on **Send**.
- Check that your subject heading is appropriate and explains what your message relates to.
- Be careful about the information you're sending. It's unwise to post large portions of written works, as you may be violating copyright laws; similarly don't post messages containing data from other people or from CDs.
- If you've been sent a message personally, don't send that message on to a mailing list unless you have the permission of the person who sent it to you. They may have meant it to be for you only.

Leaving a mailing list

The time may come when you want to leave a mailing list, either because you have all the information you need, or you find that the list isn't what you want.

To unsubscribe from the list, send an email just as you did to subscribe, but this time your message should contain only the word **Unsubscribe.** This will automatically generate your message and all you'll need to do is click **Send.** Within a few moments you'll be sent an email confirming that you have been taken off the mailing list.

Using Genuki for war-related lists

Genuki has a directory of mailing lists which includes war-related lists that will be of interest if you're researching UK and Irish relatives. This site is useful because it contains all the mailing lists that are relevant to British family historians. Go to **genuki.org.uk/indexes/MailingLists.html**. Say you're interested in the area of Birkenhead in Cheshire, scroll down to find that listing and click on it. You'll then be redirected to a mailing list hosted by Rootsweb and you subscribe in the way described, left, in 'Joining a mailing list'.

Using a forum to speed your search

Forums are single-subject areas on the internet where members post messages and files. Whatever your family history query, you're bound to find a forum that can help.

There are all sorts of discussion forums that relate to family history topics. The great advantage of using a forum is that, like a mailing list, it will save you time trying to locate the information that you need, by giving you the opportunity to ask somebody who either already has the information you want, or who knows where to find it.

The main difference between mailing lists and forums is that you use a forum only when you need it, and don't receive a lot of emails, as you do with a mailing list. When you get a reply to your message on a forum, you simply receive an email alerting you to check it.

Discovering family gems

Using forums is a great way of researching family myths or finding elusive information that's difficult to uncover in the archives. There may be a family story that was passed down through several generations but over time the exact details have become hazy and you're unable to find any documented evidence to support it.

If you post a message in a forum related to the surname or subject, explaining what you know and what you'd like to know, you may find that other people who have a similar story to yours or whose ancestors were involved in the same event can shed some light on the facts. Because messages posted in forums are generally not searchable by keyword, it's important to put your message in an appropriate forum category and to explain the key points of your enquiry in its title, so that people who visit the forum and recognise a name, date or place mentioned in the title are attracted to your message.

Using RootsChat

RootsChat is a website dedicated to UK and Irish genealogy, and its primary function is as an easy-to-use message forum. The site allows you to post messages about all aspects of genealogy, which is a great help if you get stuck on any particular area of your family tree. Members are able to answer and offer help and advice. There is an option to hide your email address, so your details will only be displayed if you want them to be.

The message boards are arranged by topics; for example, there are boards specifically dedicated to census problems, surname studies and Welsh, Irish and Scottish ancestry. There's also a section for beginners – which is a great place to start if you're new to family history and messaging boards.

The obvious place to start is on the homepage, so go to **rootschat.com** (see right). You'll be invited to log in or register. Then, if you click on the link to **Enter RootsChat** you'll see, at a glance, some of the topics that are being discussed online. You can start posting and receiving replies straight away, but it's a good idea, before you begin, to go to the **Help** section, where there is information about using the website. If you have any problems, most of them will be covered already in this section.

One of the advanatages of using RootsChat is that you can upload images and Gedcom files to share with other users. This is particularly useful if, for example, you have a picture of an ancestor in uniform that you need help in identifying, or if you'd like to share your findings with someone who shares the same surname with you.

The homepage also contains links to some of the more popular family history websites, such as FindMyPast, so RootsChat is a really handy resource for solving your family history problems, and networking with people who share your interests.

Family history forums that can help

In addition to RootsChat, there are very many websites offering forums for you to use in your research; here are four that are popular and easy to use.

British Genealogy

For the main UK source of family history discussion forums, go to British Genealogy, at **british-genealogy.com/forums**. The site has forums on all sorts of family history topics as well as one for each British county. Search the archive section of the site for an overview of the forums available at British Genealogy.

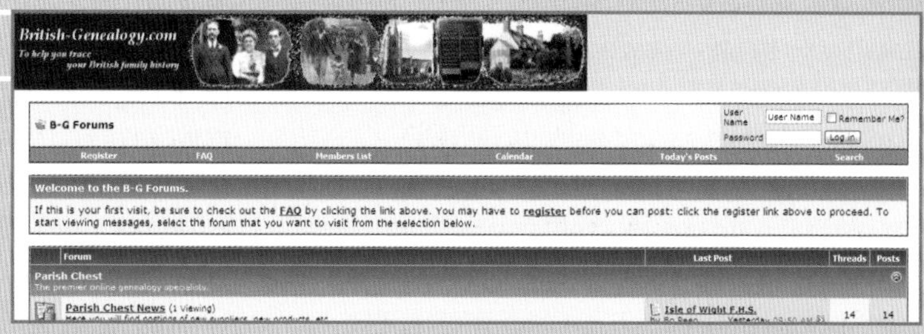

GenForum

There are more than 14,000 online forums devoted to family history on GenForum, at **genforum.genealogy.com**. The topics are not exclusively British and include surnames, religions, US states and migration. To make a search, simply enter the type of forum you want – surname or topic – in the **Forum finder** box.

Ancestry

A large number of family history forums are offered by Ancestry, at **ancestry.com/share/**, in the form of message boards. The boards cover all areas of the British Isles, including individual counties, as well as most other countries. The wide variety of research topics includes the census, the military, occupations and surnames.

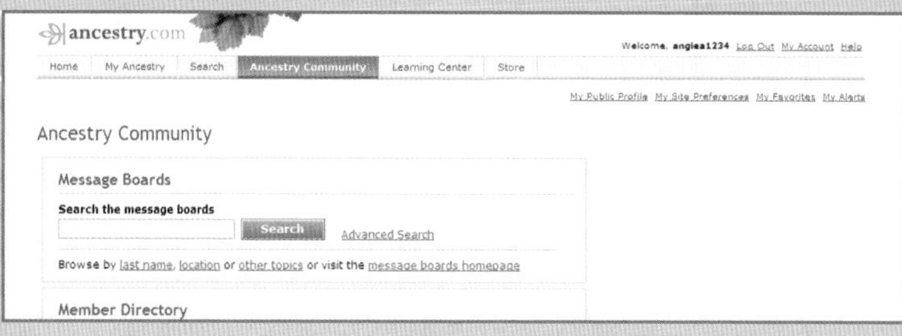

TalkingScot

If you're looking specifically for Scottish ancestry, try **talkingscot.com**. The site has forums on different aspects of Scottish ancestry with links to other sources of information. There's a section for asking questions on any area of family history that you may be stuck on, and one that allows you to upload and share your photos with other researchers.

Setting up your own discussion group

If you find that your particular area of interest isn't being covered by the groups and lists you've looked through, why not launch your own discussion group? If you do it well, you'll attract other like-minded people and further your own research.

When you reach the stage of wanting to pursue a specific aspect of your family's history, forming a discussion group will enable you to make contact with other researchers who can advise and provide information on the topic. It's vital that once you've created a discussion group, interested people can find it, so it makes sense to start your group on a well-known site, such as Yahoo! (see right). In addition, you'll need to advertise your group by posting notes on mailing lists and notice boards.

Making the most of your group

If you set up a family history-based discussion group, you can place it in various subject categories, depending on what you want to discuss. You can choose headings such as occupations, surnames, heritage or geographic origin, and they can be as broad or narrow as you like. You may want the group to be specific, such as one for people who can trace their roots back to ancestors from Dawlish in Devon. But if you'd like to attract as many members as possible by having a broader topic to discuss, you might describe the group as being relevant for all descendants of Devonshire families.

Creating your own discussion group gives you control over the layout of its homepage, and the uploading of photos, documents or images that your group may find interesting. You can invite whoever you choose to join the group, screen applicants before they join and check messages before they're posted on the homepage. Yahoo! allows you to promote your group by including it in their directory of groups, and to customise your group's page, giving you complete control over how it's run. You can also arrange the settings so that message replies posted on the page are

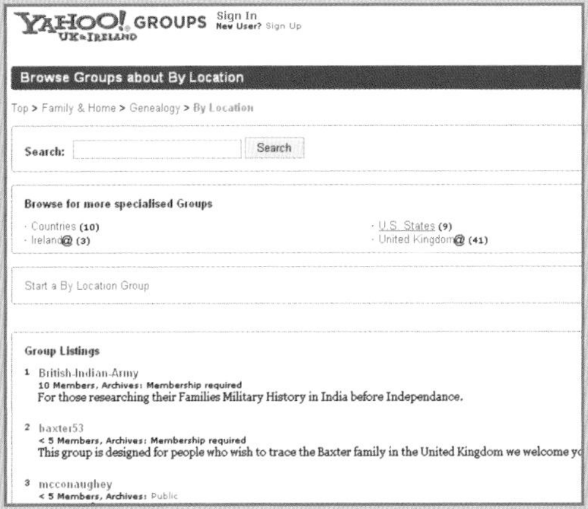

Setting up a discussion group

1 Enter **uk.groups.yahoo.com/** into your web browser, and click on **Sign in**, (new users must Sign Up first). Under the heading 'Browse Groups' click on **Family & home**, and in the next screen click on **Genealogy**. In the following screen under 'Browse for more specialised Groups' click on **By location** then **Start a by location group**. Under 'Select a more specialised subcategory' click on **United Kingdom** and finally, click on the **Place my group here** button.

Describe your group

2 Type in the name of your group as it will appear on your group page and also in search results. You'll also need to enter a group email address. Finally, enter a description of your group. It's important that people who see it will know, at once, what your group is about. Once you're sure you've phrased it well, put this at the top of your group page. Then click on the **Continue** button.

sent out to all members or just to the message sender. A further option allows you to choose between using your group page as a straight forward mailing list, or have it working with web features so that photos and files can be posted and you can even conduct polls. If you decide to use the web features you're then able to select who out of your members can access the photos, files and other features that are posted. It's a good idea to post your own messages and topics from time to time to keep the board fresh and up to date.

Early discussion groups
These pioneers of discussion groups are at the first ever Women's Institute meeting in Anglesey in 1915. Their aims were to educate and campaign. Now the largest women's voluntary organisation in the UK, the W.I. has 211,000 members and a thriving website at **theWI.org.uk**.

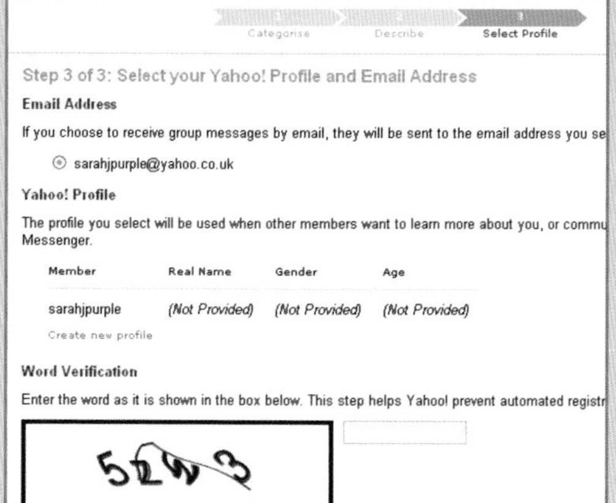

Categorise Describe Select Profile

Step 3 of 3: Select your Yahoo! Profile and Email Address

Email Address

If you choose to receive group messages by email, they will be sent to the email address you se

sarahjpurple@yahoo.co.uk

Yahoo! Profile

The profile you select will be used when other members want to learn more about you, or commu Messenger.

Member	Real Name	Gender	Age
sarahjpurple	(Not Provided)	(Not Provided)	(Not Provided)

Create new profile

Word Verification

Enter the word as it is shown in the box below. This step helps Yahoo! prevent automated registr

Step 1 of 3. Customise sarah_genealogy_UK

Do you want the group to be listed in the Yahoo! Groups directory?

- Yes, list the group. Default
- No, make the group unlisted.

How can people join your group?

- Anyone can join immediately. Default
- People can join only with my approval.

Who can post messages to your group?

- Only group members. (Private discussion group) Default
- Anyone. (Open discussion group)
- Only group owner. (Newsletter)

Invite People to Join sarah_genealogy_UK

The **Invite** feature lets you send email to invite people to join your group. This is one way to extend your online commu and keep connected with other people who are interested in this type of group.

(Please use this feature responsibly and don't spam people you don't know. Invitation abuse can lead to inactivation of your account.)

Enter email addresses or Yahoo! IDs. You may enter up to 50 **email addresses** OR **Yahoo! IDs**.

Please enter one person per line. For example:

jsmith@domain.com
pat2000

sarahjpurple@yahoo.co.uk
laura.berry@yahoo.co.uk
sara.colenso@yahoo.co.uk
james.higgins@yahoo.co.uk
sara.khan@yahoo.co.uk
freya.beales@yahoo.co.uk

Enter an introductory message. Enter a message explaining why you are inviting these people to your group. Your message will be included with the email invitation.

Hello everyone, please accept this invitation to join my genealogy discussion group. I welcome your ideas and suggestions as to how i can carry on my family tree, and what my next steps will be.

Select your profile

3 To receive group messages you'll be asked to provide an email address that the messages can be sent to. The last step is word verification, where you're asked to re-type the word shown into the box on the left. Finally, click on the **Continue** button. The next page will give you a summary of your group, with its name, homepage and the group email address. Then you'll be presented with the next two steps: **Customise your group** and **Invite people to join**.

Customise your group

4 To manage your group now that it's set up, click on **Get started** to use the customise wizard. The first step concerns where you list your group, who can join it and who can post messages. The second step is about the options for messages. The third step is about the archiving of old messages and to whom these messages should be available. These steps are a series of options – you simply click on the button next to an option to select it. At the end of each step click **Next**.

Inviting people to join

5 Having set up and customised your group, you can now invite friends and family to join it. Click on the **Invite people** button and enter their email addresses (the most you can add is 50). Now add a message explaining why you're inviting them to your group; the message will be displayed with your email invitation. Click on the **Submit invite** button to review your invitation and those you invited. Click on **Invite people** once again, to finish.

Should you join a family history society?

Being a member of a family history society links you to a huge network of professionals and enthusiasts who'll be able to help you when necessary. It also gives you access to indexes in the process of being created, which aren't yet available online or to the general public.

Researching your family history in the comfort of your own home has been made easier by the many websites available to family historians. But there are bound to be times when you feel you've reached a dead end, and simply can't find the answers online. That's when being a member of a family history society can help.

What do they do?

Family history societies are a driving force in the world of genealogy, encouraging the indexing and transcribing of important records so that they can be accessed by a wider group of researchers. In fact, it's largely thanks to their hard work and perseverance that many records are online at all.

Most societies publish newsletters, journals and other literature to aid you in your research. Many also produce lists of their members' interests, providing a useful database where you can lodge your own interests, or see if anyone has already done so for that topic. That makes it easier for you to join forces with other members who are researching a similar subject to yourself.

The benefits of joining

It's a good idea to join a family history society near where you live, or one based where your ancestors lived. The social aspect of these societies is as good a reason as any to become a member and you'll meet other novices who are as eager as you are – and probably just as unsure of the next step.

As your research progresses you may find that investigating your family tree becomes almost a passion. In which case, the regular meetings and lectures held by your local family history society will give you the opportunity to learn more about specialised subjects and how to research them.

Although an enormous amount of information is accessible on the internet, a great number of indexes still need setting up and may be available offline only through a family history society. Many societies have libraries that contain unpublished research guides and local histories that are invaluable, but can only be accessed by its members.

Your local family history society may also offer courses in different aspects of genealogical research that can help you to make significant progress.

Choosing a society

We're lucky, in the British Isles, to have such a wide range of family history societies. Most counties and many larger towns have local societies run by dedicated volunteers – both amateurs and experts – who've been working in the field for many years. Then there are those whose interests centre around geographical regions, such as the South West Area Group (SWAG) which takes responsibility for co-ordinating regional projects and providing an influential voice for the family history community in general.

At the other end of the spectrum, you'll find societies created for people interested in specific subjects or social groups, such as the Catholic Family History Society or the Romany and Traveller Family History Society.

If you have a branch of your family who originated abroad, you may find that there's a family history society for that country or region. Contact your local archive or library, where you should be able to find details of family history societies in that region – or check the Genuki website (right), where you'll find one of the best online services for locating a relevant family history society. Another good site to check is the Federation of Family History Societies at **ffhs.org.uk**, although their list is limited to member societies (see page 288). A slightly more random way to find a society is to type 'family history societies' into your search engine and see what comes up.

It's often advisable to join more than one society because your ancestors probably came from more than one area. That way, you can get useful information without having to

Finding a family history society on the Genuki website

There's a detailed list of family history societies on the Genuki website at **genuki.org.uk/Societies**. There are geographically arranged sub-sections for England, Ireland, Scotland, Wales, the Channel Islands and the Isle of Man, within which you can find individual family history societies arranged by county. The largest number of societies is in England, and the Isle of Man has the smallest, with only two.

If you think the ancestor you're searching for moved to Europe or travelled even farther afield, you could try the links to European-based societies, or explore the Asian, American and Canadian family history groups on the website.

There are many societies linked by a common occupation or interest, such as the Railway Ancestors' Family History Society and the Rolls-Royce Family History Society. Some family history societies may be associated with a particular locality and others may have a religious theme – among these you'll find the Catholic, Jewish and Quaker societies.

There's a link to the website of each society listed. You're sure to find a society that will be able to help you to advance your search yourself, or direct you to the most reliable professional help should you need it.

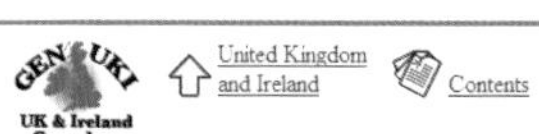

GENUKI UK & Ireland Genealogy

United Kingdom and Ireland | Contents

FAMILY HISTORY AND GENEALOGY SOCIETIES

This page provides means of finding information about societies whose interests relate to the UK & Ireland as pages listing societies that are devoted to smaller geographical areas, such as individual counties.

We provide information about a given society simply by linking to its web pages where these are known to us. Scottish Association of Family History Societies, we provide a link to the postal address listings these provide. commercial) family history societies, i.e. ones that are registered charities.

NOTE: We do not attempt to provide information about the large number of societies that relate just to particu Guild of One-Name Studies (GOONS).

Report errors, request additions.

- **UK AND IRELAND:**
  - Anglo-Austrian FHS
  - Anglo-French FHS
  - Anglo-German FHS *

Steam team *A group of men carry out safety checks on a locomotive in 1930. Railway employees developed a strong sense of 'family' – look on Genuki's list of societies (see above) for the Railway Ancestors' Family History Society if you had railway-worker relatives.*

travel frequently to the relevant archives. You'll also be able to contribute your own research to the local group.

How to join and what it costs

Most societies now have websites so it's a good idea to visit the site of the family history society you're considering joining to find out about the projects they're involved with, and how often and where they hold meetings. You'll want to be sure that it sounds like the sort of group you'd want to be a part of before you subscribe. Many societies give the name of a prominent member of the society, with a contact phone number. Having a talk with them could help you to decide.

Membership fees vary from society to society, but the average cost is about £10 a year. Some societies now allow you to join up online via their websites – it's easy to do, and the site will give you the relevant prompts. If a site doesn't, you'll have to arrange for a membership form to be sent to you and return it, with your subscription, by post.

Using the Federation of Family History Societies

The best place to start looking for information about the huge number of family history societies is through the Federation of Family History Societies (FFHS), a charitable umbrella organisation that represents most British family history societies. It's well worth exploring this site to find out what it offers.

The FFHS was established in 1974 as a charitable, educational organisation with the dual aims of advising and representing family history societies and other genealogical societies on a global basis. This means that individuals can't join it, but their local family history society can – which is a good reason for you to join a family history society.

Staying up to date

The website of the FFHS, **ffhs.org.uk**, is updated regularly with news and information. Its active news section tells you about forthcoming publications, television programmes and new websites which may be of benefit to its member groups and societies.

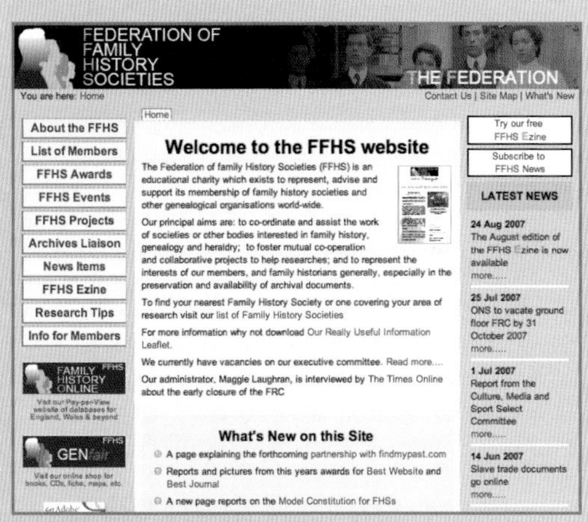

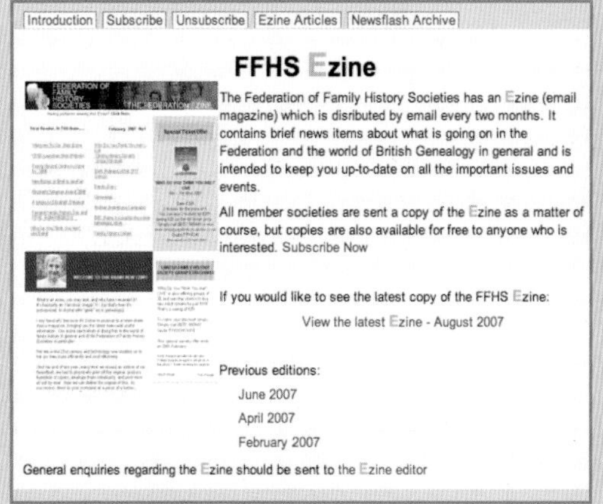

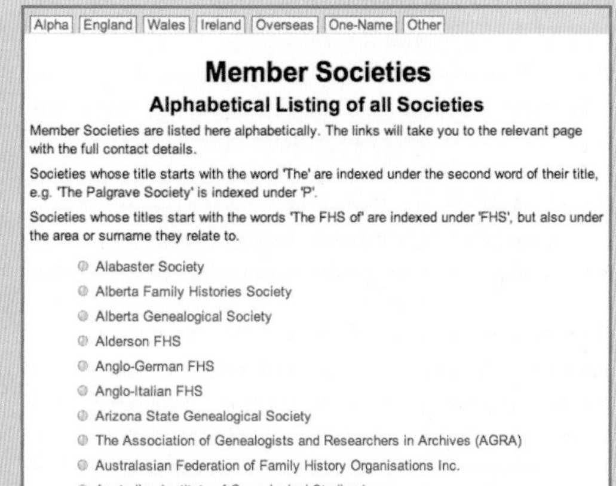

What's on the homepage

The FFHS website, at **ffhs.org.uk**, explains the main functions of the Federation in detail and provides links to a huge amount of information. You'll be able to see a list of its current projects on the website, too. It's worth visiting regularly to keep abreast of the ever-evolving resources available to family historians.

Electronic magazine

The FFHS's electronic magazine, known as the *Ezine*, includes the activities of the large archives and libraries, the latest datasets that have been put online and reports on recent conferences, among many other subjects. It can be viewed online for free, either on the website or by subscribing to the magazine so that it's sent to your email address.

A-Z of the societies

The website has a complete alphabetical listing of all the family history societies that are members of the Federation with links to their websites. You can view separate lists for England and Wales, and there's a directory of one-name-study societies that you could join if you wanted to find others who were researching the same surname as yourself (see page 61).

The FFHS is deeply involved in new projects and passes on information about them to family history societies. It also encourages its member societies to contribute to projects by transcribing records and making information available, which is an ongoing process. The Federation encourages the exchange of ideas between various family history societies on regional projects, and liaises with many major archives on behalf of all family history societies to discuss national projects.

The member societies have been involved in a number of projects such as the indexing of the 1881 census and creating the National Burial Index (see page 59). The FFHS has also embarked on a project, in conjunction with the Imperial War Museum (see pages 194-5), to create a National Inventory of War Memorials. The aim is to bring the names of more than 53,000 memorials to family historians on the internet. In addition to these activities, the Federation also joins forces with other major institutions to undertake further genealogical exercises.

Keeping standards high

In order to encourage the highest possible standards, the Federation presents an annual award to the journal that produces the best contribution to family history and another to the best website hosted by a member society. You can see the winners of these awards online, on the website.

The Federation also helps to educate member societies about good practice in family history by organising meetings and lectures on various subjects, along with regular training courses. Conferences are organised by both the Federation and individual societies and are open to the public. You may want to consider attending one of the conferences as matters relevant to family history are discussed. The scheduled meetings are all listed on the website.

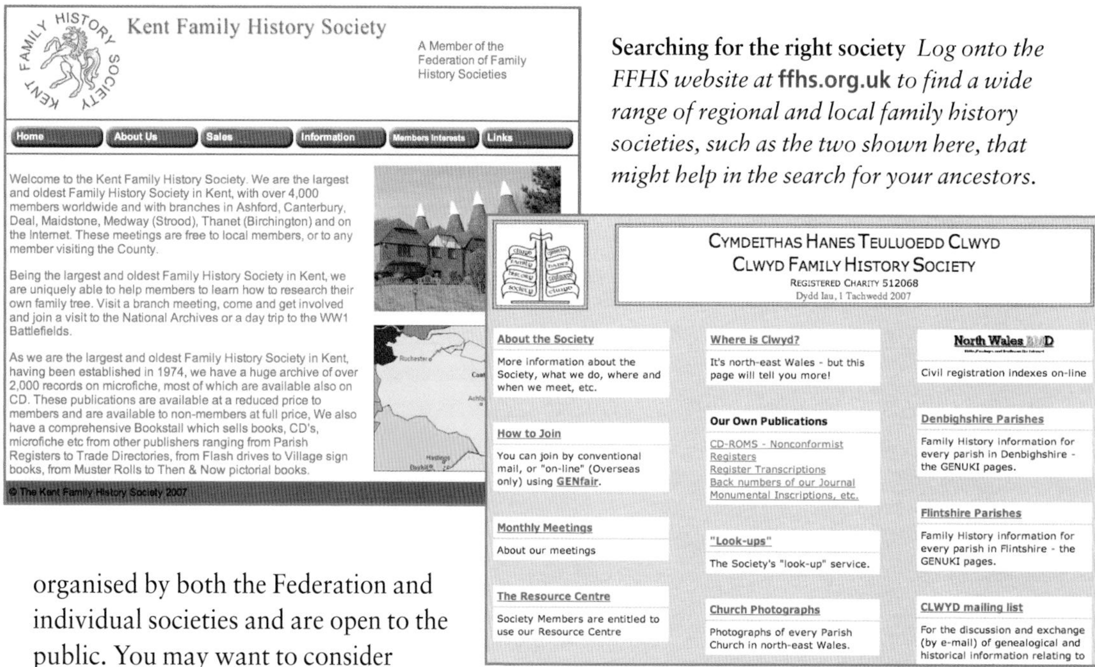

Searching for the right society *Log onto the FFHS website at* **ffhs.org.uk** *to find a wide range of regional and local family history societies, such as the two shown here, that might help in the search for your ancestors.*

Subscribe to the *Ezine*

The FFHS produces a useful online monthly publication known as the *Ezine*. Subscribing to the magazine will keep you up to date with all the latest that's happening in the family history world.

In addition, the FFHS produces leaflets related to various aspects of family history, including guidance on a number of subjects for individual family historians.

Using the website

If you're new to family history research, you'll find the **Research tips** section on the website really helpful. Along with a section on **First steps for novices**, information and links to useful websites are also offered. Guidance is provided on how to make the most of your visits to an archive or record office and the benefits of joining a local family history society. The website links you to family history societies via an A-Z list. In addition, if your research takes you overseas, there are also worldwide links to societies that are farther afield.

The Genfair Shop

The Federation has a wonderful online shop at **genfair.co.uk** that includes historical maps and old books archived on CD. There are links to all the county family history societies in England, Wales, Scotland and Northern Ireland, with details of the books and papers that are on sale.

Tracing your living relatives

Some of your relatives may be complete strangers, yet they share your heritage and genes because you share common ancestors. The exciting thing about looking for your ancestors' descendants is that you'll find and meet new family.

Working forward in time

Most of us know our first cousins and some of us know our second cousins. But very few people can even name their more distant relations, let alone say where they live and what they're doing.

Tracing the living descendants of your direct ancestors' siblings or cousins through several generations can be challenging, but the rewards are great. You might discover, for example, that your recently found distant relatives have family information that's new to you, or they may possess fascinating heirlooms that you knew nothing about.

Journey to find the living

The process of tracing living relatives from distant ancestors is known as 'forward reconstruction'. The best way to do this is to choose one particular relative in your family tree – perhaps your great grandfather's brother – and follow him and his descendants forward through time to the present day. It's best to select someone who was a child in 1901, as they would be of marriageable age after the date that civil registration indexes started to include cross-references. These are likely to lead you to other documents that might provide new information.

If you've chosen someone born some decades before 1901, you'll need to track them through the various census returns, until you reach the1901 census and then follow the path, through subsequent birth, marriage and death certificates, to living descendants in your own generation.

You're fortunate if the surname you're looking for is uncommon, as it'll make searching easier. Also, you can narrow your search if you know the area that the family came from, as many people lived and married close to where they were born.

As you work forward through the generations, you'll find the most useful clues come from marriage certificates, though you may need to order more than one in order to check all the details.You'll know you have the correct marriage when you see the name of the bride or groom's father, which will appear on the certificate. He'll be someone you've already identified.

Then search for the children from that marriage using the spouse's surname or maiden name (listed in the birth indexes after 1911) as the unique identifying factor. Frome here on, it's simply a question of repeating the process until you find living relatives. Depending on how far back you started, it can take a little time, but it's worth it when you find a new branch of your family.

Keep in mind that the descendants of your chosen ancestor may not have married or had children, or may have died in child hood.

Family reunion *Through your research you may discover new relatives. Making contact with them could lead to shared memories and valuable information – even big family get-togethers.*

Contacting new relatives

If you're lucky enough to find a branch of your family that's new to you, and have managed to find contact details, here are a few common sense tips about contacting them.

Never turn up at their home unannounced or even phone out of the blue. They may not have any idea of who you are, or even whether you're genuine. It's best to write a letter with your home address and contact details so they can get in touch. Include a family tree diagram, so they can see at a glance where everyone fits in, and some pictures, so they can see that the tree is genuine.

Generation game *From great grandmother to new-born, four female generations pose for a photo in 1905 – a vital family history find.*

From census to phonebook

As your research progresses beyond the 1901 census towards the present day you'll find that phonebooks and other more recent directories become rewarding resources. Much of the information is online.

Once you have identified a living relative you'll probaby want to get in touch. One way of doing this is by using phone and street directories, following the research that has probably led you to the area where your relative is likely to be living. Birth and marriage certificates, for example, give exact addresses, so it's worth checking a street directory to see if any members of the family still live there. Alternatively, you might be able to find your relative in a local phone book – assuming the family hasn't moved on.

Using online directories

It's possible to check some directories online, and the amount of information available is growing all the time. Here are some suggested routes that may be helpful.

TRY BRITISH PHONE BOOKS The Ancestry website, **ancestry.co.uk**, is expanding its database of family history sources, and this includes putting phone books (1880 to 1984) online. From the Ancestry homepage, click on **Directories and members' lists**, then choose **British phone books**, and it will take you to the search page. The areas of the UK covered

Making connections *Women operators at work in the exchange of the National Telephone Company in 1903. As use of the telephone increased, phone books became essential.*

so far are London, the South East, eastern counties, northwest England, the Midlands, Scotland and Northern Ireland. There are gaps, even in these regions, but this is still a useful source for tracing people's movements after the 1901 census. Looking at older phone books can also give you an indication of people's social status – only the wealthy had telephones in the late 19th and early 20th centuries, and it wan't until the 1950s that most families had a phone.

As the entries go right up to 1984, you may even find the phone number of a living relative. Remember that STD codes have changed a number of times in recent years, so check them, too.

EXPLORE 192.COM The homepage at **192.com** offers a wide range of search services when you're looking for people, businesses or places. Under **Find people**, you can access recent electoral rolls, residential listings, census records, details of births, marriages and deaths, as well as Directory Enquiries (see also page 295). You can test it out by first finding yourself. Under **Find businesses**, there are links to Thomsons' Directory, Dun & Bradstreet business information and a search-by-name index of businesses. **Find places** links you to maps, journey planners and aerial photographs.

SEARCH THE YELLOW PAGES If you discover that your relative is involved in a specific business, you can find the business contact details through **yell.com**, the website version of the *Yellow Pages*. The difference between this and the local printed directories is that **yell.com** allows you to see entries for the whole of the UK. It's essentially a business listing, free to use and you don't need to register to access it.

If you have a specific name for a business you can search for the address and phone number of that business by entering the name in the **Company name** box. If you don't know the company name, enter the type of business in the **Product/service** box. You can also limit the search by entering a geographical area, town or city, or postcode.

Using early directories

Phone directories have been compiled since 1880, and some street directories date back to the early 18th century. Various publishers were responsible for producing directories, the most well known being Kelly's, Pigot's and the Post Office. Depending on the period, directories were issued annually or every two or three years. Most can be consulted at local libraries and record offices. For more about different types of directory, especially old ones, see page 232.

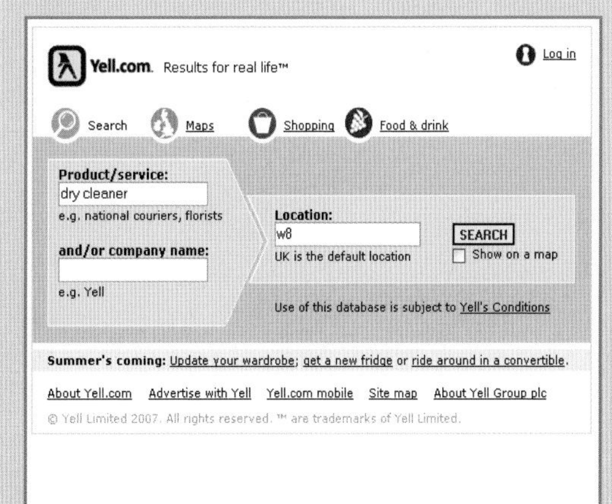

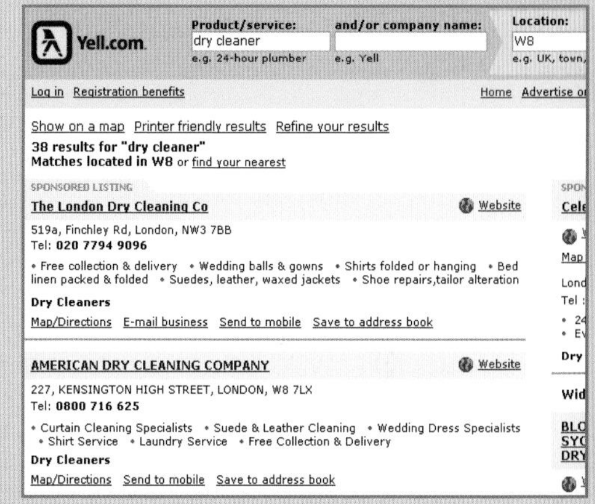

Fill in the details of a business search

1 Say you want to search for a newly discovered relative's dry-cleaning establishment in Kensington, in west London. Go to the **yell.com** homepage. You know that Kensington has the postcode W8. Enter 'dry cleaner' in the **Product/service** box, and 'London w8' in the **Location** box. Then click **Search**.

Examine the results

2 All the relevant matches will appear with links to individual websites of these companies, where they have them. Click on the link to the one you want for further information.

Modern directories and the electoral roll

The phone book is an obvious place to look for living relatives, but some may have chosen not to be in it or traded in their landlines for mobile phones. If this happens, you can turn to the electoral roll.

Electoral rolls have been compiled every year since 1832, when the Great Reform Act was passed, changing the British electoral system. Until then, booming new cities like Manchester had no MPs to represent them, while other tiny, old constituencies – known as rotten boroughs – could return up to two MPs to Parliament. The Act got rid of rotten boroughs and redistributed the seats to the new towns. But as only householders who owned property worth at least £10 could vote, you won't find any of your working class ancestors on these early electoral rolls.

All electoral rolls are available to the public, right up to the present day, and you can use them to locate a living relative. They include everyone of voting age who's registered to vote in a particular area.

Unfortunately, just as a phone subscriber can go ex-directory, so a voter can opt out of the public access version of the electoral roll – but even so, it offers more comprehensive coverage than phone listings.

Votes in secret – and for women *Voting by secret ballot (above) was introduced in Britain in 1872. All women got the vote in 1928, after a violent struggle by the WSPU – the Women's Social and Political Union (right), known as the Suffragettes.*

Examine historic electoral rolls

As well as being able to access modern registers, you can look at past lists – such as the electoral rolls for the neighbourhood where the relative you're tracking was last known to have lived. You can also use historic records to plot your family's movements. If, for example, you want to find out how long your ancestors lived at the address recorded on a census return or a civil registration certificate, you could plot this using successive electoral rolls.

Poll Books keep no secrets

If you're looking for information from before 1832, you'll need to look at land tax returns (see page 214) or browse through Poll Books in local record offices. The books list the names of electors, each voter's parish of register and how he voted (secret balloting was not introduced until 1872).

Votes for women

From 1918, the electoral rolls became much larger, because the right to vote was extended to include soldiers in barracks, policemen, domestic servants – and, most significantly, women over 30 (the vote was not extended to all women until 1928). The data was now organised into 'electoral wards'.

Electoral enquiries online

Electoral records from 1700 onwards can be consulted at local archives and record offices. The British Library also holds a detailed nationwide collection. In addition, there are websites, such as **192.com**, which are now putting electoral roll information online. This website evolved from the old British Telecom Directory Enquiries service and it offers the electoral rolls from 2002 to 2007. Its links include search facilities for the 1861 census and the General Register Office's birth, marriage and death indexes.

It doesn't charge for online directory or local business enquiries, or for general searches of its website, but if you want detailed electoral roll data, you have to pay for it. The site operates a credit scheme; the minimum charge is £9.95 for 5 credits, and it costs 1 credit to view an entry.

Another useful site is **onlinesearches.info.** It offers searches of the electoral roll that will give dates of birth and phone numbers, and also gives UK property ownership details, as well as deaths and marriages.

You can search by forename, surname or full name, as well as by address and post-code. Once you've found the type of search you want, you choose the payment package that suits you and are prompted to make your payment. The search results are emailed to you immediately, or simply shown onscreen.

The modern electoral roll

The UK Electoral Roll includes adults over the age of 18. Despite the fact that it's a legal obligation for every adult to enter their details, a percentage of the population continues to avoid giving their information to the compilers.

People not on the electoral roll include young people under 18, homeless people, travellers and gypsies, active members of the serving forces, certain government personnel, people in prison and non-British citizens.

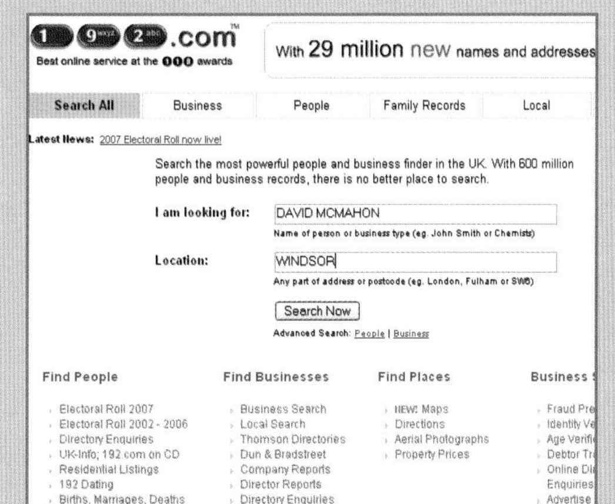

Search the electoral roll

1 If you want to search for a David McMahon, say, who was last known to have been living in Windsor, go to the homepage of the **192.com** website. Enter his name, preferably his full name, in the **I am looking for** box. Enter 'Windsor' in the **Location** box. Click **Search now**.

Read the results

2 A list of all possible entries will be displayed. In this case, one David McMahon appears in the 2007 Electoral Roll and two matches appear in the Historical Roll section. The screen also tells you that searches were conducted in the Free Directory Enquiries, Business Directory and Director Report databases, but there were no matches. If you want to see any of the records, click **Full details**; this will cost you 1 credit (about £2).

Making connections through the internet

The internet has made it easy to track down old friends and relatives through contact sites. If you're trying to find someone who served in the armed forces, they too have dedicated sites for making contact.

Perhaps the most well-known website for providing listings of former school friends is **friendsreunited.co.uk**. Since its launch in 2000 the website has enjoyed huge popularity. It began as a simple site where users could contact old school and work colleagues within the UK, but now has expanded to include other parts of the world, with separate pages for genealogy, job seeking and dating. As well as tracking down old friends, the site can be used to find relatives from all over the world who may be registered on it. When you register on the site, free of charge, you become a Standard member and can post your own information online and look at what other people have posted. If you want to go further and initiate contacts with other users of the site, you have to pay a small fee and become a Full member.

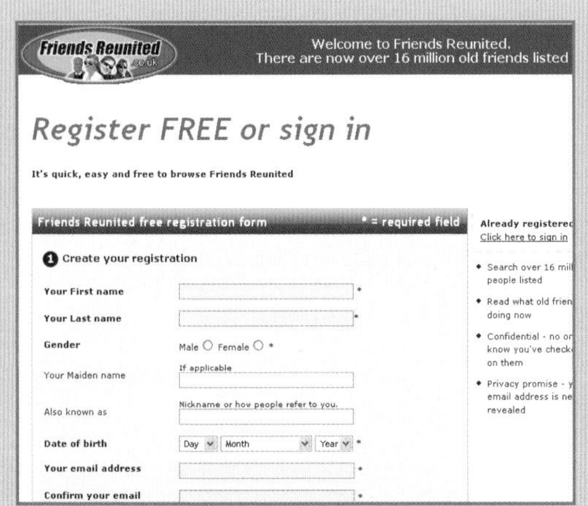

Register with Friends Reunited

1 Go to **friendsreunited.co.uk** and register. This gives you access to the main site so that you can start your search for information about your old school friends, workplace colleagues or relatives. Once registered, you'll be sent to your homepage. You can then access different areas of the site, such as Genes Reunited, Dating, Jobs Board and Connections (which is a way to meet people interested in the same things as you).

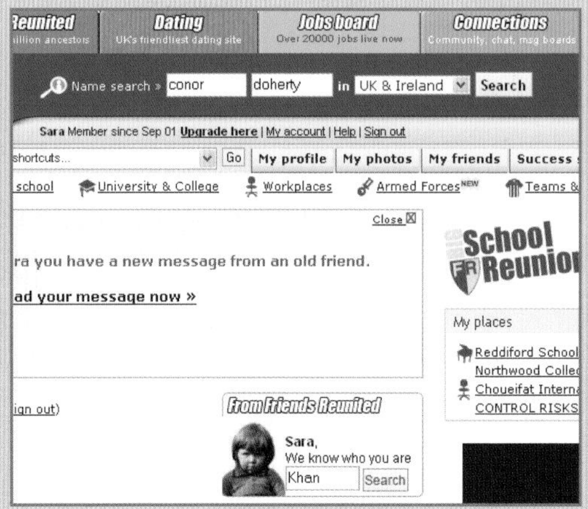

Enter the name you're looking for

2 The simplest way to search the site is by entering the forename and surname of the person you want to find on the **Name search** option at the top of the homepage. If, for example, you're searching for a lost friend, Conor Doherty, who studied at the University of Keele in Staffordshire when you were there, enter his name and click on **Search** to view all the Conor Dohertys listed on the site.

View the person's profile

3 The search produces five possible listings, including the correct entry at the top of the page. Click on **View profile** to see what he's doing now. Profiles are uploaded by each individual, so they'll vary in detail – some people put in photographs and give other personal information. You can send a message to the individual, but first you'll have to subscribe to the website, which costs about £8 for 6 months.

Looking for war veterans

If you know that a relative is or was in the armed forces, it might be worthwhile checking out one of the sites dedicated to military veterans. The Ministry of Defence has a website dedicated to veteran issues at **veterans-uk.info**, run by the Service Personnel and Veterans Agency. It aims to centralise and improve services for current and former employees of the British Armed Forces, but it also includes such groups as the Bevin Boys who worked in the coal mines during the Second World War. Other useful sites include the Royal British Legion, and for locating American friends or relatives in the services, there's the Veterans History Project.

Veterans UK

Down the left-hand side of the homepage at **veterans-uk.info** you'll see a list of topics, including **About SPVA**, describing the work of the Service Personnel and Veterans Agency, and **Service records**, which tells you how to go about obtaining details on servicemen and women. For information dealing exclusively with matters relevant to military veterans, click on **Veterans issues**.

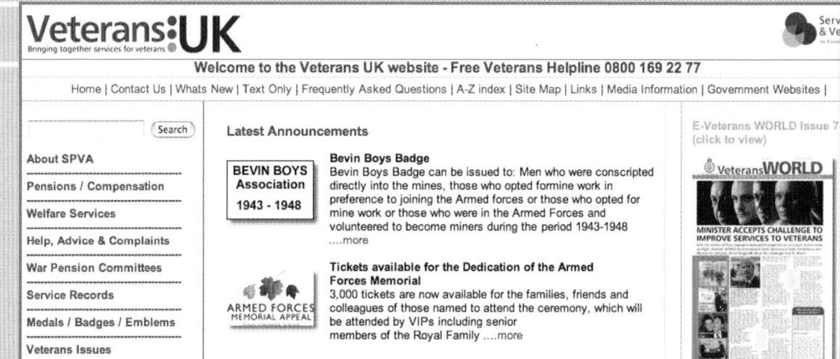

Royal British Legion

The Royal British Legion is dedicated to supporting members and ex-members of the British Armed Forces and was founded in 1921 as a means of giving ex-servicemen a voice, after the horrors of the First World War. Through its website, at **britishlegion.org.uk**, you can contact a network of clubs and branches of the Legion that can put you in touch with lost colleagues or relatives who fought in past wars.

Veterans History Project

Go to **loc.gov/vets** and you'll find a site run by the Library of Congress in the USA. It aims to share the stories of veterans from the First and Second World Wars, the Korean War, the Vietnam War, the Persian Gulf War and ongoing conflicts in Iraq and Afghanistan. Click **Search the veterans collections** and you'll be taken to a screen where you can enter a person's name, and search the records by conflict(s) or branch of service.

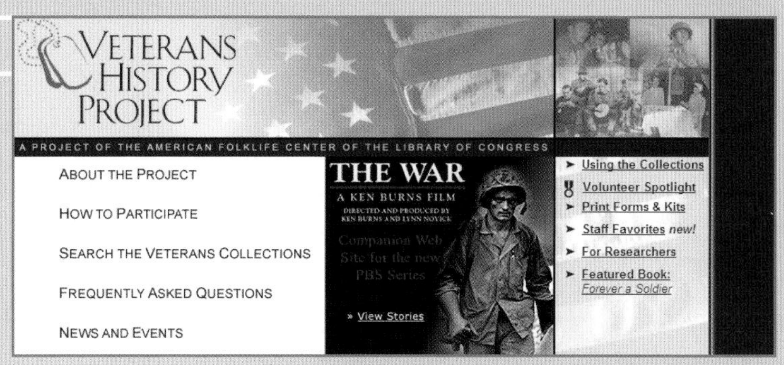

Was your ancestor adopted?

Adoption, with its consequent name changes and shroud of confidentiality, can obscure the trail when you're tracking down some ancestors. Keep persisting, though, and investigations can bear fruit.

Until the 20th century, there was no formal process of adoption, so few paper trails were created when children were given new homes outside the immediate family. Where children were adopted within the extended family, by grandparents, aunts or uncles – perhaps to mask cases of illegitimacy – any surviving information may lie only in letters or documents passed down through the family.

Name-change problems

Searching for a relative who was adopted can be difficult where the name has altered. For example, if you were looking for all six siblings of the novelist Jane Austen, you might miss one. One brother, Edward, was given up for adoption when he was a boy, to his childless uncle and aunt, Mr and Mrs Thomas Knight of Godmersham, in Kent. They made him their heir, and he changed his name to Edward Austen Knight. He would have appeared in subsequent censuses under his adopted name, not under his birth name.

Adoption becomes official

The informal adoption arrangements came to an end in 1926, with the passing of the Adoption of Children Act. From January 1, 1927, a certificate of adoption was issued for each adopted child in England or Wales, with the process formally recorded in the Adopted

A writer's uprooted sibling *Edward Austen, brother of Jane Austen, took his uncle's name when he was adopted and, as Edward Austen Knight, was later recorded as a landowner.*

Help on the internet

Although these websites don't list adopted children, they can help you in starting the difficult task of searching for biological family members.

adoptionsearchreunion.org.uk

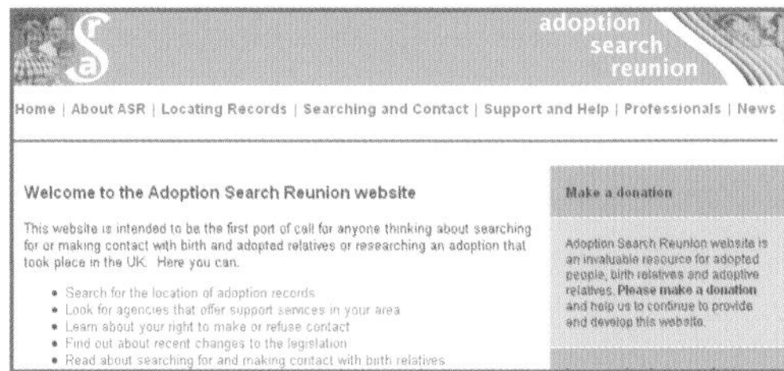

The British Association of Adoption's website provides information about the adoption process, and various ways of contacting relatives. England and Wales are thoroughly covered and information is being expanded to cover Scotland and Northern Ireland. The site also has different sections explaining the adoption system, including one on locating adoption records with a database to help you to do this.

search-line.co.uk

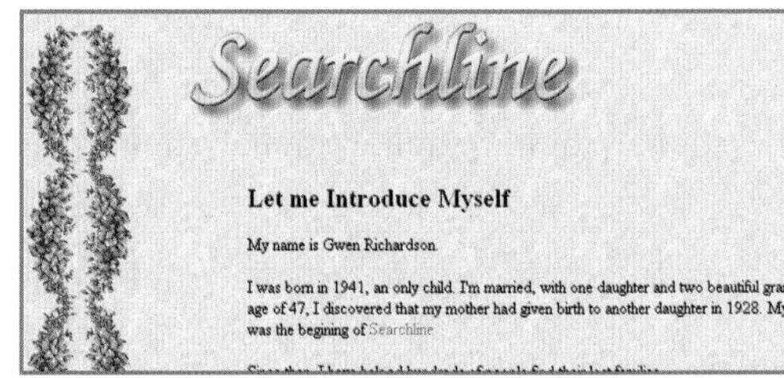

The Searchline website attempts to find long lost relatives – adopted people, in particular. It was started by Gwen Richardson after she tried to find her sister, who was given up for adoption when they were very young. The organisation has a large number of databases that it uses to help to trace missing relatives. There's also a contact register where people can leave their own stories.

Children Register compiled by the General Register Office (GRO). The register is open to the public, indexed by the surname of the adoptive parents, not the birth parents. The certificates include the child's date of birth, the name and address of the adoptive parents, the date of adoption and which court issued it. The child's birth parents aren't recorded.

Scotland has had a separate register since 1930 and it's held at the National Archives of Scotland. Similarly, Northern Ireland has held its own register from 1931 at the General Register Office (Northern Ireland). See pages 96-101 and the Directory for contact details.

Seeing original birth certificates

If you were adopted, and want to see your original birth certificate and details of your biological parents, you can apply to the Adoptions Section of the relevant register office. In England and Wales it's the GRO; in Scotland it's the General Register Office for Scotland (GROS); and in Ireland it's the General Register Office (Northern Ireland). You have to be over 18 in England and Wales, and over 16 in Scotland before you can request this information, and all the countries recommend counselling before you go ahead, particularly if you were adopted before November 11, 1975.

Contacting your birth family

There are rules about contacting your biological family. In England and Wales the GRO's voluntary Adoption Contact Register regulates the process. The Register has two lists: one giving the biological parents (and other close blood relatives) and the other the adopted children. There are also contact details for a mediator between the two parties. Contact is made only if all parties agree to it. The Adoption of Children Registration Act, 2002, though, gave birth parents more rights: since December 30, 2005, birth parents have been able to inform their adopted adult 'child' of their desire for contact. There are details in the Directory for adoption organisations such as Adoption Search, Birthlink (Scotland) and the Irish Adoption Contact Register.

A home for the unwanted

Not all abandoned children in the 18th century were lucky enough to be adopted. Many of London's unwanted children lived wild and rough on the streets. Retired shipbuilder and sailor Thomas Coram became so disturbed by the plight of the destitute and dying children he saw on London's streets that he conceived the idea of a home for them. With the considerable help and influence of his friends – the artist William Hogarth and the musician George Frederick Handel – and a royal charter from King George II, he opened the Foundling Hospital in 1739. It became a refuge for abandoned children where they could be cared for and educated, and it was the first children's charity in England. The charity was renamed the Thomas Coram Foundation for Children, and is known today simply as Coram Family. You can search the site at **coram.org.uk**.

Foundlings *Smiling outside the London Foundling Hospital in the early 20th century, these children were given a second chance at life. Many mothers left tokens of remembrance, as above, for their children.*

Children dispersed around the world

It may seem amazing today, but child labourers were once sent to the farthest reaches of Britain's empire. Others went as a result of the authorities' desire to give them 'a better life' – a misguided promise for many.

From as early as the 17th century, small numbers of children were sent to the new American colonies to provide labour for the settlers. The practice continued until the American War of Independence (1775-81), after which America was no longer an option.

A new life far away

After 1850, when the new Poor Law Unions began to take responsibility for the poor or orphan children in their area, the rate of child migration speeded up. Moving children to new locations was seen as a philanthropic solution to child poverty, although often the parents' consent was not given, particularly if they were in prison or a mental institution. If the children were orphans, they were sent without any real understanding of where they were going and for how long.

There was an underlying political motive to the movement, too, for most of the children were sent to Canada, South Africa, Rhodesia, Australia and New Zealand to provide good 'white stock' for these young or developing countries. The policy continued until 1967 by which time approximately 150,000 children had been affected.

The policy of child migration had a huge emotional impact on the children who were forced to migrate. Many went believing their parents were dead or did not want them; some, as young as three, soon forgot their parents and weren't even sure when or where they had been born. This can make tracing them in their new countries quite difficult, but it's worth persevering.

Evacuation from the danger zones

Migration on a lesser scale took place during the Blitz of the Second World War, when children were evacuated from London and other large cities and towns and placed in safer rural areas.

In some cases entire school classes were sent to the same place, to minimise the disruption in the children's lives. For some, evacuation, with name labels, tightly clutched suitcases and gas masks, was an exciting adventure (right). They found themselves in wonderful rural environments and knew a sense of freedom and closeness to nature they could never have had in the city. For many of them, these temporary refuges became their second homes. But for others it was a traumatic experience, often marked by meanness and cruelty from the people who took them in. There is no national list of child evacuees, but the BBC has a section on the memoirs of evacuees at **bbc.co.uk/ww2peopleswar/categories/c1162/**.

How to trace child migrants

Tracing children who were sent away is an exciting challenge, and there are websites that can help. Here are four of them.

Child Migrants Trust

In 1986 Margaret Humphreys, a social worker, heard from a woman in Australia who'd been sent there at the age of four and now wanted to trace any family she might still have in Britain. Margaret was so appalled that she set up the Child Migrants Trust, **childmigrantstrust.com**, to reunite former child migrants with their long-lost families. The Trust is based in Nottingham, with two offices in Australia.

Child Migrants Trust

About the Child Migrants Trust

The Child Migrants Trust was established in 1987 by its Director, Margaret Humphreys OAM, to address the devastating impact of the child migration schemes. Its origins go back to 1986 when Margaret Humphreys, a Nottinghamshire Social Worker, received a letter from a woman in Australia who claimed that at the age of four she was sent on a boat to a children's home in Australia, and now wanted help to trace her parents or any members of her family in Britain.

Whilst investigating this first plea for help, the enormity of Britain's child migration schemes was exposed. Research uncovered the astonishing fact that over 130,000 children had been deported from Britain and shipped off to a "new life" in distant parts of the Empire. This long history of compulsory migration ended in 1970 when post-war child migration drew to a close. Children as young as three years old had been separated from their Country and all that was familiar, to be brought up in institutions. Many were treated as child slave labour. Most of the children were told that they were orphans whose parents were dead. This was untrue. Many experienced degrading physical, sexual and emotional abuse throughout their childhood.

Barnardo's

The children's charity was founded by Thomas Barnardo in the East End of London in the late 1860s. Barnardo was an enthusiastic proponent of child migration, believing the children would benefit. The Australian branch of Barnado's recognises the role it played in child migration and retains records of the children that passed through its hands. If an ancestor was affected by the scheme, you'll be able to get more information by contacting **barnados.org.au**.

Library and Archives Canada

Canada was one of the main destinations for British child migration. Children sent there were known as 'Home children'. The system began in 1839 and continued into the 1930s, by which time approximately 100,000 children had arrived. The Library and Archives Canada holds a variety of documents relating to this migration on its website, **collectionscanada.ca**. Or you can try **bifhsgo.ca**, which is based in Ottawa and holds digitised lists of children.

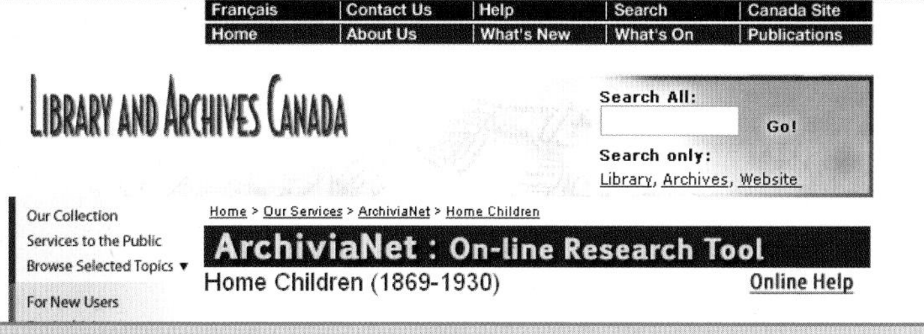

National Archives of Australia

Australia was a hugely important destination for child migration and the National Archives of Australia houses a comprehensive collection of records relating to it. Go to **naa.gov.au** and click on **Publications**, then **Research guides**. Scroll down to the book *Good British Stock* by Barry Coldrey. Click on the **Read online** button. It outlines the history of child migration, and also provides a timeline of the main events.

Cover
Introduction
1. Australian Immigration Policy
2. Child Migration: An Overview and Timeline
3. Guide to the Records
4. Genealogical Sources
Appendixes
1. Abbreviations
2. Who was who in juvenile migration
3. Voluntary and church organisations involved in child migration work
4. Records held by other archives and libraries
5. Organisations helping former child migrants to find family

2. Child Migration: An Overview and Timeline

In the heyday of British imperialism, Father N Waugh, Director of the Archdiocese of Westminster 'Crusade c work of the society:

A double service is rendered to religion, humanity and civilisation, in carrying off the children of distress work with nature, to wrestle with forest, field and stream, to forget the fetid city slums, to think and striv the guardians of the outpost of civilisation, religion and new endeavour… every child a pioneer of the Er

In his rich hyperbole Waugh expressed the commonplace notions surrounding contemporary child migration. H three-hundred-year-old policy of despatching unaccompanied children – abandoned, illegitimate, poverty-stric to cultivate and populate the wide-open spaces of the Empire. Moreover, Waugh and other child migration en the last phase of child migration – the despatch of some 3 200 children from Great Britain and Malta to Austra

Tracing divorce records

A broken marriage can also disperse family members. Before 1858, divorce was almost impossible, then, particularly from the 20th century onwards, it became much easier. This can cause hiccups in your family research.

If you're trying to trace more recent members of your extended family, you may find that someone suddenly disappears from family photos and correspondence. If you're sure that person didn't die or emigrate, it's possible that a marriage broke down and there was a divorce or a legal separation.

The details of a divorce could name a place of residence and living children, as well as the people who were divorcing. From this, you can trace further marriages, offspring of the named children and then their addresses through trade or phone directories.

Family complications *Divorce or separation can create difficulties in finding ancestors. But divorces are recorded so should be traceable, particularly if they took place in the 20th century.*

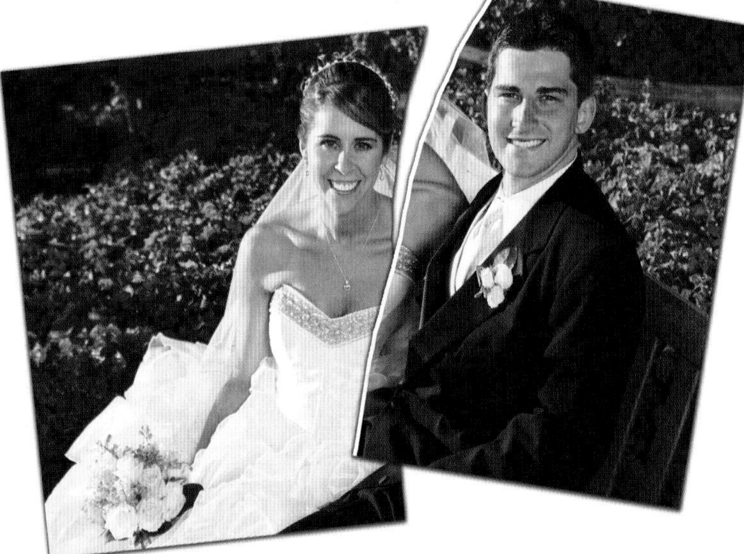

The early story of divorce

Divorce was almost unheard of in the 17th, 18th and early 19th centuries, largely because it was too expensive for all but the richest aristocrat. As marriage was conducted in church, only church courts had the power to approve a legal separation; Henry VIII went so far as to change the law so he could divorce Katherine of Aragon and marry Anne Boleyn, in the hope of having a male heir.

If a couple wanted to remarry, their first marriage had to be declared null and void on the grounds of lack of ability to marry – for example, if they were underage and therefore incapable of giving consent – or there was a legal bar to the first marriage, such as consanguinity (too close a blood relationship).

Divorce after 1858

The Matrimonial Causes Act 1857 allowed husbands in England and Wales to divorce through the civil courts on the grounds of a wife's adultery. A wife couldn't do the same, unless she could prove cruelty as well, and this remained the case until 1925.

From January 1858, the Court for Divorce and Matrimonial Causes heard all divorce cases, and all in London. Lawyers had to be appointed, and the couple had to appear in court, which required time and money – so only the wealthy and very determined could divorce. From 1875, the Probate, Divorce and Admiralty Division of the Supreme Court heard all divorce proceedings.

From 1878, poor women could apply to the local magistrate for a separation and maintenance order if the husband had been convicted of aggravated assault against her. This changed again in 1886, when a wife could apply on the grounds that her husband had deserted her and any children. The husband would then be ordered to pay £2 a week as maintenance.

By 1895, the system had changed to protect all women and children with violent or neglectful husbands. But discrimination was rife. Women who were considered immoral weren't covered and, if the woman had already committed adultery, the husband wasn't obliged to maintain her. Within five years more than 10,000 orders had been applied for. These orders are kept in local record offices, but their survival rate is patchy and few records can be found online.

From 1914, poor people could seek financial aid for divorce under the Poor

Public humiliation *A witness is cross-examined at a London divorce trial in 1900. Until the law changed in 1969, one or other party in a marriage always had to be proved 'guilty'.*

Divorces in Scotland and Ireland

Ordinary people could file for divorce from 1560 in Scotland, making it easier than in England and Wales. The Commissary Court of Edinburgh heard cases up to 1850, and thereafter the Court of Session took over. All these records are held at The National Archives of Scotland (see Directory).

From 1855 to 1984, records of divorce were recorded on Scottish marriage registers – with the words 'Divorce RCE' (Register of Corrected Entries). The General Register Office of Scotland holds an index of divorces from 1984 onwards.

In Ireland, various Acts of Parliament forbade divorce until 1995. But on rare occasions, before 1870, Church Courts granted separations, and after1870, some divorces were agreed by Act of Parliament. After 1995, couples who'd lived apart for five years could divorce, and the records are held in the court where the divorce took place.

Person's rules. This was extended in 1923, when women were allowed to petition for divorce on the sole grounds of their husband's adultery.

The Second World War saw many marriages end, with an increase in rates of divorce as it became easier to obtain. But it wasn't until the Divorce Reform Act of 1969 that irretrievable breakdown of marriage could be used as sole grounds for divorce.

Where the post-1858 records are

If you're looking for legal proof of a divorce from 1858 onwards, the union indexes for the whole of England and Wales are kept at the Principal Registry of the Family Division, London (see Directory). For each divorce case, a file was created and given a unique number. They're arranged in chronological order, and contain the petition, copies of any relevant certificates, detail of the status of the plaintiff, affidavits and the decrees *nisi* and *absolute*. Some are at TNA.

- 1858-1937: the case files are at TNA in class J77 with an index in J78, and have a fairly good survival rate. Surviving decrees are at the Principal Registry.
- 1938 onwards: no case files survive, but surviving decrees are at the Principal Registry.

If there's no surviving case file, check local newspapers of the time, as many divorces were announced in print, especially before 1920. Local records offices may have microfilmed copies of newspapers, with the main repository being at The British Library newspaper archive in London (see Directory).

Records of property disputes

From 1583 onwards, when couples achieved a form of legal separation, disputes often arose about the legal status of any property shared or promised as part of the marriage settlement. Most property disputes were recorded in the Courts of Chancery, and are likely to be held at TNA in series C78. The Privy Council also ensured that separation settlements were honoured: some entries are in the Privy Council Registers in series PC2.

Between 1532 and 1832, appeals from Church Courts were heard by the High Court of Delegates, and from 1832 to 1858, they were heard by the Judicial Committee of the Privy Council. Copies of the proceedings are kept at TNA. If they occurred between 1609 and 1834 they're in series DEL1 (with an index in DEL11/7) and from 1834 to 1858 they're in PCAP1. None of these records is available online; they have to be searched in person at TNA.

Putting your family history online

Creating your own website allows you to share your family tree and other discoveries with family and friends. As you add more to it, and your relatives start to join in, you'll have created a valuable family and social document.

Setting up a website

Your personal website can be as simple as a single page. Or you may want to be more ambitious by adding images, family biographies and links to other sites. It's up to you how much you make of it and what you choose to include.

Creating your own website gives you the freedom to decide how your family history will be told, where images will be displayed, the layout and design of your pages, and what links to other websites are included. A family history website can be built easily and cheaply using the most basic software. Once you've gained a little confidence, you may want to invest in more complex packages, but this section of the book will look at the most straightforward means of going about building your first website and where to get advice in the process (see pages 306-11).

The first decision to make is whether you want your existing internet service provider – or ISP – to host your site for you, or whether you want to establish your own domain.

Your ISP probably includes enough free web space within your monthly subscription package for an online family tree, which you can illustrate with photos and family stories. Your ISP (which could be Orange, Talk Talk, BT or Tiscali, for example) will allocate you a web address that contains the ISP's name. You may be able to change the address, if you want to, as long as the new one is available.

To host your own site with its own domain name you can go to one of the many UK domain-hosting sites, such as **easily.co.uk** and **ukreg.com** (see right), who supply domain names for a small annual fee.

Choosing a name

Each domain name must be unique, so you may find that your first, second or even third choice of name has already been registered by someone else. When you get round to choosing a name, it's a good idea to select one that tells people what your site's about – **higginsfamilyhistory.co.uk**, for example. Calling your website something obscure like **briansbigadventure.co.uk** or quirky like **frankfromthepark.co.uk** might amuse you, but will probably only confuse your friends and family.

The cost of using a domain-hosting site is not excessive – it ranges from about £3 to £30 a year. Domain names cost about £4. Shop around to find one that seems good value.

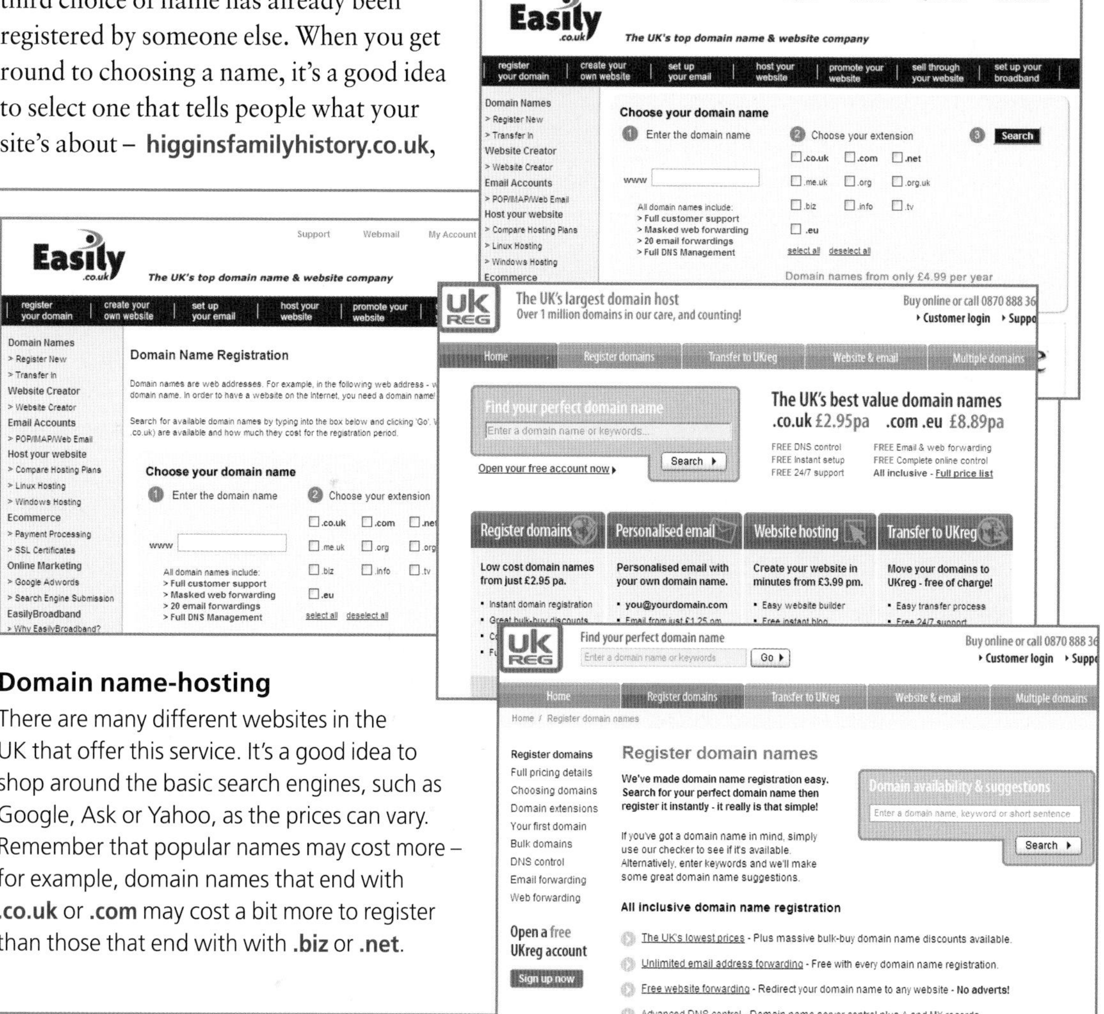

Domain name-hosting

There are many different websites in the UK that offer this service. It's a good idea to shop around the basic search engines, such as Google, Ask or Yahoo, as the prices can vary. Remember that popular names may cost more – for example, domain names that end with **.co.uk** or **.com** may cost a bit more to register than those that end with with **.biz** or **.net**.

Planning the contents of your website

Creating your own family history website is a chance to be as creative as possible with your family tree. But before you launch yourself on a flight of fancy, you need to have a clear idea of what you want the end result to look like and the impression you wish to make on visitors to the site.

It's important to decide on the contents before you get to the really creative part of your website – the layout and look of it. Work out exactly what you want your site to show and the message that you're trying to get across. Ask yourself these questions:

- Which area of your research do you want to focus on? You may want to show the entire family tree, or just focus in on one particular branch of interest, such as a surname, its roots and meaning.
- How much information do you want to include about each ancestor? Do you want to include information on families connected through marriage, or stick to blood relatives?
- How far do you want to go back in time and how much of your family's recent past do you want to cover? Bear in mind that some of your living relatives may not want their information posted on the internet, so be sure to check with them first.

Create a plan

Once you've decided on the content, and how you want to display it, you then need to decide what it will look like. You may want to create what's known as a storyboard (see right). You can display your information in many ways – perhaps as one page of narrative, concentrating on an overview of your research or perhaps a timeline, with links to other ancestors and information, which will make it clear and easy to see.

Having made up your mind about all this, you're ready to decide on the features that you want to display, as this will affect how the website is going to look. Consider the format of the various pages – what colour palette to use, what style of font, how many pages you want, how they'll link together and whether you're going to include any special design features. By keeping the design and formatting relatively simple, you'll create a user-friendly website that others can enjoy.

WRITING THE TEXT Try to make the text interesting, so that you engage your audience. You could perhaps write in a biographical style about some of the fascinating characters in your family tree, or tell some of the stories that were passed down to you by previous generations.

CHOOSING THE PICTURES Images are crucial for bringing your family's story to life and making it as engaging as possible for all those who visit your page. It's quite easy to attach images or stream a video clip onto your website using the software described on pages 36-39. If you have a scanner or digital camera, you can upload images of your documents, such as wills, baptism certificates and personal letters onto your computer, and then transfer them to your website. See page 310 for more advice on using images.

DISPLAYING THE INFORMATION The next step is to work out the detail of how you want to use all your information. For example, you might want to have a photo of each of the people on your tree next to their name, or just have one big gallery with the photos and documents organised in chronological order. Remember that if you're using web space provided by your internet service provider (ISP), it will usually be limited to around 20MB, and the more images and videos you include, the quicker you'll find yourself using up the space.

Be aware of copyright rules

Your website is a publication accessible to the entire online world. This means you can't legally include copyright material which belongs to other people, unless you get their permission first.

So, for example, you can't scan a photo of your ancestor's village from a local history book or postcard and put it on your site. Neither can you include chunks of material you've copied from a CD or from another website, or any of the census images you may have paid for on one of the data services.

Creating a storyboard for your website

Start by drawing up a visual plan, sometimes called a 'storyboard', for each page of your website, so that you can see exactly what information goes where, how it will be presented, and how it will link to each page and ancestor. Putting your thoughts down on paper, deciding how you want your information presented on each page and working out how a user can access it from the homepage will save you time and confusion once you go online and actually start to build your website.

The more familiar you become with your computer and software package (see page 308), the more adventurous you'll be when designing and editing your website.

Plan your website on paper *This storyboard for The Brooker Family Website shows a homepage with links to four other pages – the family tree, family biographies, a family album and a contact page. Drawing it up first helps to make sure your website is packed with information and looks great.*

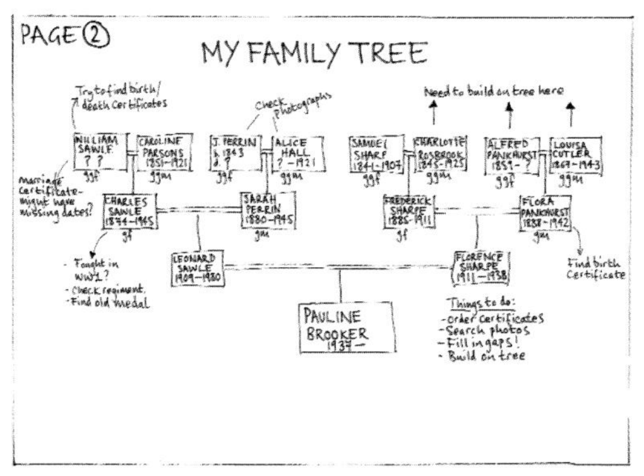

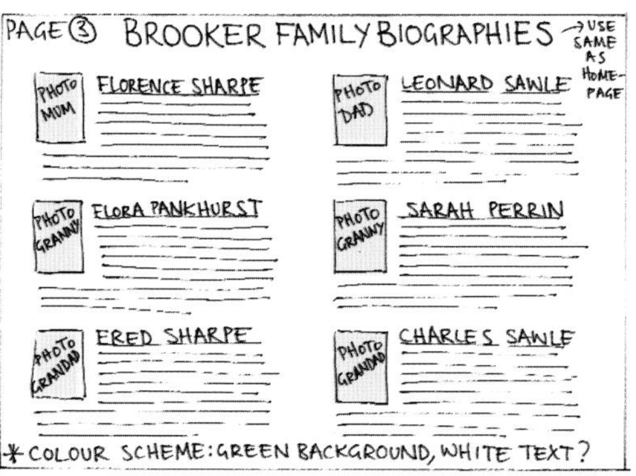

PAGE ⑤ CONTACT PAGE → SAME SIZE + FONT AS BEFORE
MY DETAILS HOME TEL. EMAIL
MY DETAILS WORK TEL. EMAIL
THE CHILDREN'S DETAILS
CAN YOU HELP?
YOUR QUESTIONS:
POST YOUR OWN BROOKER STORY HERE
*EDITABLE / BOX THIS OFF
* COLOUR SCHEME: BACKGROUND - DARK BLUE WITH WHITE TEXT. BOX: WHITE BACKGROUND + BLUE TEXT

Easy ways to create a website

You've planned your website – now you can put it all into action, and it needn't cost you a penny. It's not difficult to create a website, and there's plenty of software available to help you.

You don't have to go out and buy new software to create your website. Your computer may already contain some suitable software, and if not, there are some good free website editors you can download. Since most web pages use a standard file format, it's easy to switch between different editing programs and try them out – you're not locked into the program on which you initially created a page.

Try your existing software

By using most modern word-processing software installed on your PC, you can create and edit pages and then save them in a web-ready format, so that you'll be able to upload them onto your website.

If you don't have word-processing software loaded on your computer, you can download a free software package for Windows at **openoffice.org**. This software contains all the basic office functions, including word processing, spreadsheets and presentations. The word-processing component, Writer, can be used as a simple web editor.

Other types of software can also save information as a web page – if you've got your family data stored in a spreadsheet, this type of file should convert directly into a web-ready format. If you require specific guidance on how to perform these actions, consult your software's help menu, which should give you step-by-step instructions.

Free website programs

There are a number of free programs available online, which are simple to use and can be easily downloaded on to your computer. The following are two good ones to try:

NVU is a free web editor (see right and page 310), which can be downloaded from **nvu.com**. Click on **Enter Nvu site,** then click on **Downloads** at the top of the screen. Scroll down the page to the **Windows download** options, indicated by the Windows symbol on the left. Select the first option, **Windows full installer,** then follow the downloading instructions.

SERIF WEBPLUS is a commercial website creation package, but Serif also has a site which offers website design software for free. Go to **freeserifsoftware.com**, click on the **WebPlus** link under the heading **Websites** and follow the downloading instructions.

Website templates

A quick way to create a website is to use a company like Homestead, **homestead.com**, or Moonfruit, **moonfruit.com**, which offer templates that you simply fill in with your own text and images. You pay a subscription for this service and for your site to be 'hosted' on the web. This does mean the company can make wide use of your material, so you should check any terms and conditions first before committing to such a service.

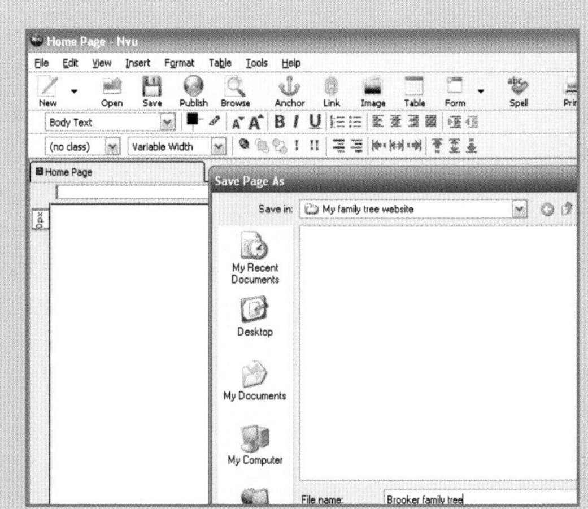

Creating a homepage in Nvu

1 Nvu starts up with a blank page. First of all, save your page by selecting the **Save as** option from the **File** menu located at the top left of the screen. You'll be prompted to enter a title for the page you're starting with. Type **Homepage** into the box on screen and click **OK**. Next, in the **Save as** menu, type in a name for your file. Select **Html files**, in the **Save as type** options, then select the folder you've created for your web page files, and click on **Save**.

Getting help

There are dozens of sites that can help you to get to grips with creating a website. The best place to start is by looking at your program's online help facility – usually accessed by clicking on the **Help** menu at the top of the screen. Two sites specially designed to help family historians to create a website are Cyndi's Home Page Construction Kit at **cyndislist.com/construc.htm** and Web Publishing for Genealogy at **spub.co.uk/wpg/**.

What makes website text work

Behind the scenes, the computer file that makes up a web page consists of the text on the page along with tags, which tell the browser how to display it. The tags and what they do are defined by the HyperText Markup Language (Html) – you'll often see the initials Html mentioned in connection with website creation.

The files for your pages will end in **.htm** or **.html** – which is how the browser knows that the file is a web page. You can see this if you use your browser's **View page source** option (on the **View** menu). For example, near the top of the page, you might see two tags <h1> and </h1> to mark the start and end of the main heading, with the wording of the heading between them.

The page source for a professionally designed website will look complicated, but the good news is you needn't worry about this. Most web creation software allows you to simply key in the text you want and the program does the rest.

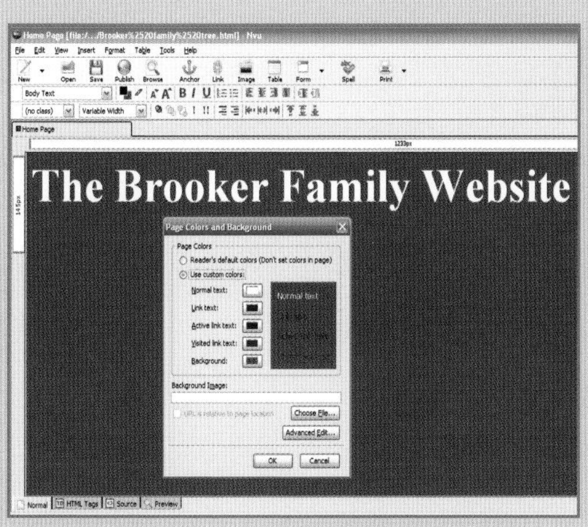

Adding text and colours

2 Choose a title for your homepage and type it into Nvu. Highlight your text and select **Heading 1** from the pre-set sizes in the style box on the toolbar. You could choose **Heading 2** for subheadings and **Body text** for the rest of your text. Click on the **Format** menu, then on the **Font**, **Size** and **Text style** options to style your text. Next, click on the **Page colour and background** option and select **Use custom colours** to choose a colour scheme for your homepage.

Adding images

3 Save the images you want to add in your website folder in jpeg, png or gif format. To add an image to your homepage, first click on the **Image** button on the tool bar. In the **Image properties** dialogue box select **Choose file** and select an image from your folder by double clicking on the file name. Click on the **Alternate text** button and type in a title for your image, which will appear in its place in text-only browsers. Finally, click **OK**.

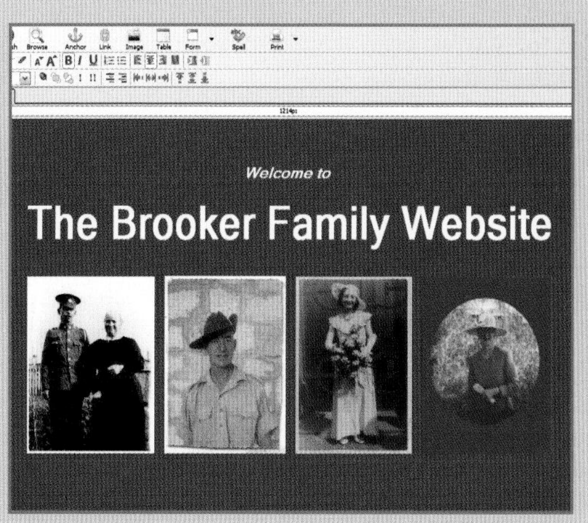

Formatting images

4 Your image will appear on the page. To alter the size of the image click on it, then drag the corner handles. If you're adding more images to your homepage, and you want them all to be the same size, go to the **Image properties** dialogue box, click on the **Dimensions** tab and select **Custom size**. You can then alter the size of the image by **Pixels** or **% of window**. Enter the dimensions into the **Width** and **Height** boxes and click **OK**. See page 310 for more on Nvu.

Getting the most from your website

Once you've set up your first web pages, you can enhance them by adding your family tree and other images, such as photos of ancestors and their memorabilia. This will create a visually exciting family document to impress family and friends, and other family historians.

One of the things you'll probably want to put on your website is your family tree. The best way to produce a tree is by using a family history software package. Some of the most popular packages, such as Family Historian and Legacy Family Tree, are covered on page 38, and on pages 312-15 you'll find information on how to use the software to collate all your ancestral detail and create a family tree. You can then upload the tree to your website.

If you want, you can have more than one tree on your site – say, one for your maternal and one for your paternal ancestors, or perhaps descendant trees for your most important surnames. Just put each in its own separate folder.

Editing and adding pictures

Old family photos are an obvious way to make your website more interesting for visitors. For this you need a scanner to turn the photos into digital images – or a digital camera for up-to-date family shots.

You'll probably want to scan old photos in the best resolution possible, but this will result in huge files, which will be too unwieldy for a website. The answer is to use a program called a graphics editor to make the scanned images smaller – 640x480 pixels is as big as you'd want for a website.

If you have a scanner or digital camera, it will almost certainly have come with a graphics editor free, and this may well be good enough for the basic tasks of resizing photos to a lower resolution or cropping out unwanted areas of a shot. If not, there are plenty of free downloads which can carry out these tasks, such as IrfanView from **irfanview.net**.

If you want to retouch photos – to hide tears or blots, say – you'll need something more sophisticated. Among the commercial graphics editors Adobe Photoshop Elements and Corel Xara are recommended and relatively inexpensive; alternatively, you'll often find older versions of commercial graphics programs given away on computer magazine CDs. The most comprehensive free graphics package is GIMP, available for Windows from **gimp.org/downloads**.

Images are not actually physically part of the page they're displayed on: each one is a separate file and you need to create a link to it on any page where it appears. All website editors can create links to images.

Making it public

Once your website is up and running, it's time to start getting people to visit. First you need to tell everyone in your family about your site, but if you want to make contact with other people who are descended from your ancestors, you'll need to get your site listed in search engines like Google and Yahoo. The most effective way to do this is to submit details to Cyndi's List using the online form at **cyndislist.com/submitnewlink.htm** – this will

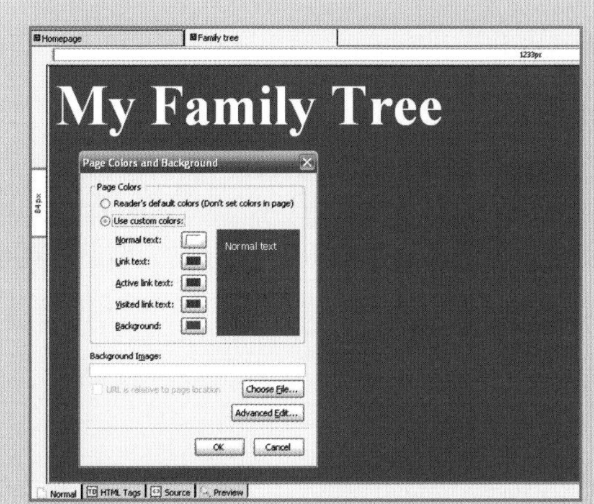

Creating more pages

1 Once you've created your homepage in Nvu, you're ready to add more pages. To create a new blank page click on the **New** button on the tool bar. Your new page will appear in another tab on your screen. Save the page by selecting the **Save as** option from the **File** menu. Give it the title 'Family Tree Page', and remember to select **Html files** in the **Save as type** options. Give it a heading and background colour as you did on your homepage (see page 308).

put your site on the Personal Home Pages section at **cyndislist.com/personal.htm**. Cyndi's List is visited regularly by search engines looking for new links, and within a few weeks any site submitted to it should be displayed by the search engines. Remember to make sure that your contact details are easy to find on your site.

Some family history societies have a page on their website for links to members' sites, so if you belong to a society it will be worth checking whether yours offers this facility.

Fonts tips for websites

Choosing the right font is important if you want people to view your website as you designed it. The program you use to create your website may allow you to choose any fonts it finds on your PC, but someone viewing your site who doesn't have those fonts will see only a rough match. It's best to select one or more of a core set of website fonts (see below) that most people will have on their PC. Use **bold** to pick out key words and for headings, and use *italic* for picture captions. Use colour to differentiate between different pieces of information but take care not to use too much. Don't use font sizes above 16 point, except for headings, as the text won't display correctly on most PCs when your material is uploaded to the web.

Arial Comic Sans Courier Georgia Times Trebuchet Verdana

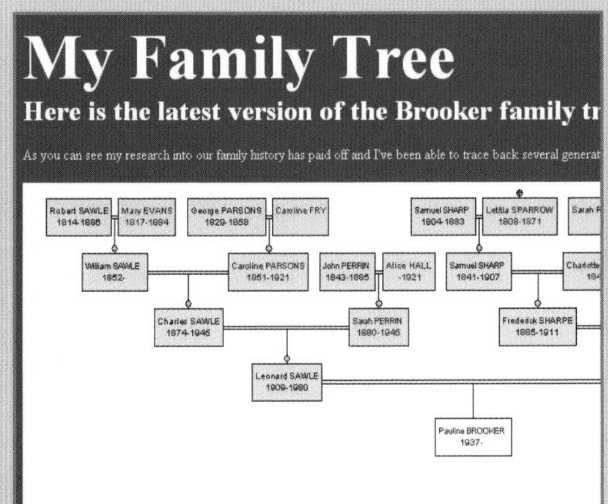

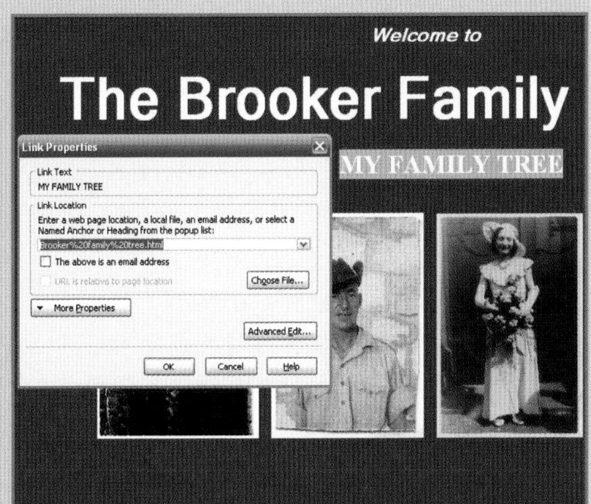

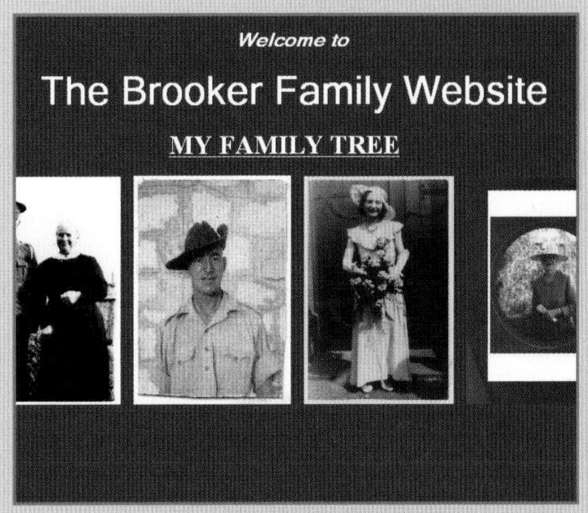

Your family tree

2 Open your family tree in your family tree software (see page 312). Save the diagram as an image file (jpeg, png or gif) into your website folder. You can now insert this image onto your webpage by using the **Image** button on the tool bar (see page 309). To change the size of your family tree, click on the image and drag the corners in or out with the mouse. Or you can double click on the image to bring up the **Image properties** window and alter the size there.

Creating a link on your homepage

3 Once you've completed your family tree page, click on **Save** from the **File menu**. Then go back to your homepage by clicking on the **Homepage** tab. Type the text 'Family Tree' in the space where you want your link to go. Highlight the text, click on the **Link** button on the tool bar. Click on **Choose file**, select your family tree page from your website folder and click **Open**, then click **OK**. The link will now be underlined and active. Click on **Save**.

Putting your website online

4 Click on the **Browse** button on the tool bar. This will display your web page in a web browser with active links. Once you're ready to publish your website, you'll need a domain name (see page 305). When your website is ready, click on the **Publish** button. You'll need to enter a name for your website, its http address and the details of your publishing server. Visit the Nvu website, and click on **Learn how to build your website using Nvu** for further advice.

Using software to create your family tree

Software packages let you create different styles of family tree that you can print out, send to others or put on a website. Most packages work in similar ways, and you'll find using one easy once you start.

There are a number of good software packages that will help you to make a family tree (see page 38). Family Historian, used for the example below, allows you to create a simple pedigree or birth brief family tree (see page 70), as well as the fuller drop-line tree that covers wider family history. You can also add pictures, sounds and videos, and record details of your sources, and so keep track easily of where you found your information – a vital aspect of all research. Family Historian software also lets you see all your information at a glance, displaying it in a different way to most other packages: it gives you a **Records** window that lists all the people you've uploaded with their date and place of birth. When you want to examine and edit each person's full details, you simply view their **Properties** window.

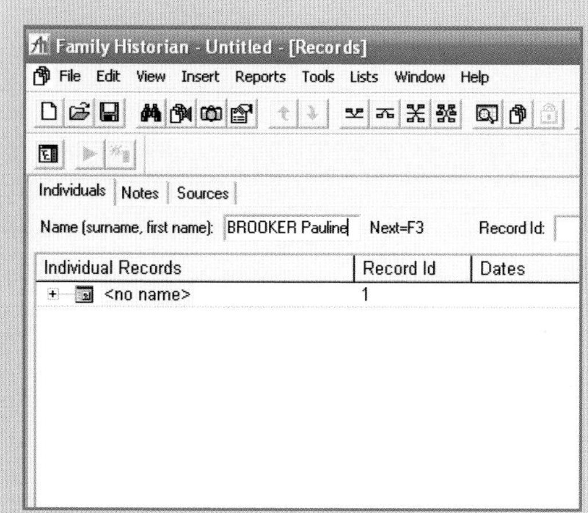

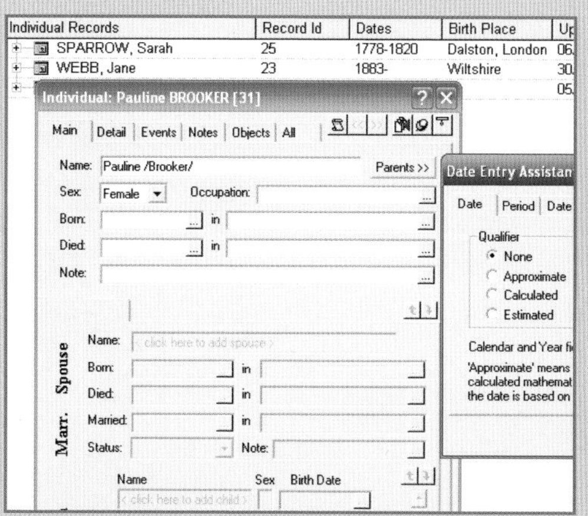

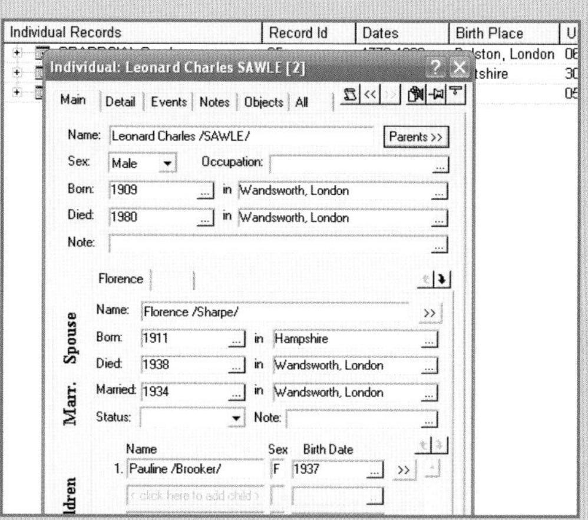

Start loading the family

1 Load the software (in this case, Family Historian) onto your PC, then click on the icon to open it. From the menu, click on **File**, then **New**. You'll see a new file into which you can load your data. The first screen is the **Records** screen (as above). Select **Individuals** and enter the name of the person you wish to record, in this case, Pauline Brooker, starting with her surname. Go to the toolbar menu, and select **Insert**, then **Unrelated individual**.

Add the details

2 This will open another box, which allows you to create a new record for Pauline Brooker. Re-enter her name in the box, then add all the other details you have for her. An **Entry assistant** box will open up to help you to fill in the information. Once you've entered all the details for your starting person, you can begin to build the tree, by entering details of parents. Click on the **Parents >>** button, which you'll find next to the name.

Enter parents' details

3 You'll be asked to select from a drop-down menu that offers **Create new record as parent** or **Link existing record as parent**. At this stage you need to create a new record of a parent, so choose this option and add details, in this case of Pauline's father, Leonard Sawle, and her mother, Florence Sharpe. You can now carry on adding information in the same way.

With all software packages, the best way to learn how to use them is to read through the instructions first. But there's no substitute for experience, so don't hestitate to play around with the software and start uploading branches of your family tree. Once you've gone through the basic steps a few times, you'll quickly gain enough confidence to tackle some of the more advanced features, and soon you'll discover for yourself the full potential of the software, and how you can use it to best suit your needs.

Getting organised

Software packages will let you arrange information in various ways. On Family Historian, for example, material is organised in chronological order – but it also lets you order records alphabetically, by surname, or by place and date of birth. For the latter options, open your family tree in the **Records** window and select the appropriate command. If you haven't entered a date of birth but you know the date of death, the software will estimate the date of birth to 50 years earlier.

Tips to remember

- To find out the name of each button on the tool bar, just hover the mouse cursor over a button and a description of its function will appear.
- When entering names into your tree, it's good practice to enter the surname in capital letters. Then it's easy to see at a glance which names are surnames, especially if your family tree contains names such as Jack James, where the surname isn't obvious. Always use maiden names for women, so you can see where their line starts.

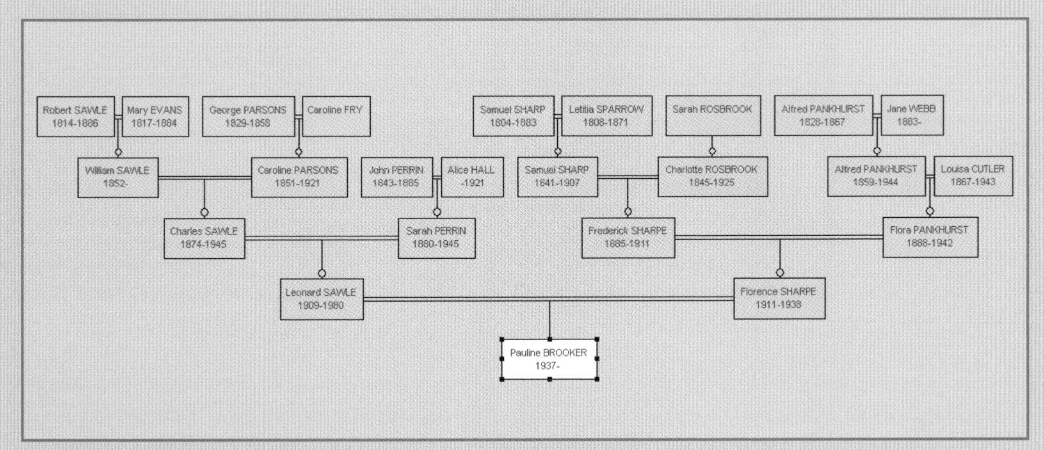

Adding information

If you want to add information about a particular person, for example Florence Sharpe's parents, you need to go to the **Records** window and click once on her name in the **Individual records** list to highlight it. Then click on the **Property dialog** button (shown left), which is on the main tool bar. This will bring up the individual record box, and you can carry on adding information as before.

There are tools to use if your tree contains a great many names and numerous records. If you want to show the chart of a particular person, you can click on any name in the tree, and that will display all the details of ancestors related to that particular individual. By clicking on the buttons in the tool bar, you can display the results either as record sheets or as family tree diagrams, as above. It's a good idea to familiarise yourself with the options.

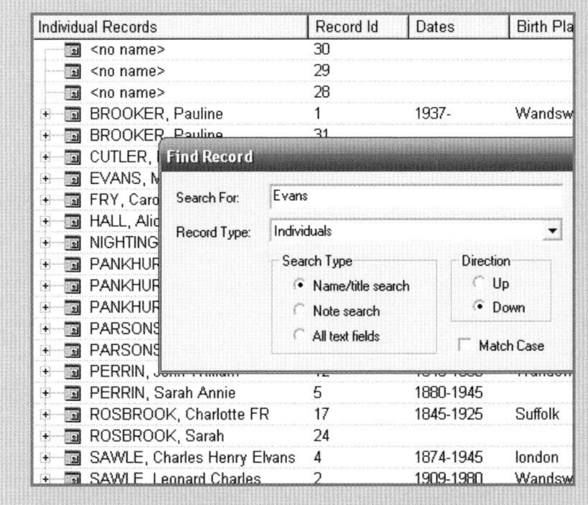

Searching for a record in your tree

You may wish to search for a particular record in order to add information to it. To do this, click on the **Find record** button (shown left) on the tool bar to open a separate search box. Type in the name of the person you're looking for, and this name will then be highlighted in the **Records** window.

Adding images and seeing your trees

Most family tree software allows you to create links between individuals and any number of images – some packages even let you add sound and video clips. You can keep on enhancing your relatives' files and then choose to view all the information in a number of different family tree formats.

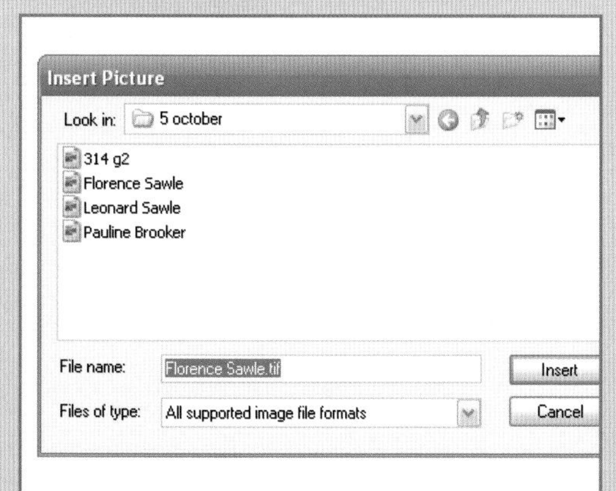

Adding a photo to a record

1 In the **Records** window, highlight the name of the person to whose record you want to add a photo. Now click on the **View multimedia** button located along the tool bar symbolised by a camera (left). This takes you to the **Multimedia records** page. Click on **Insert** from the top panel of options and choose **Pictures** from the drop-down list. The **Insert picture** dialogue box will appear for you to locate your chosen photo from where you saved it on your hard drive. Click on **Open** and the photo will appear in the 'Multimedia' screen.

Linking a photo to other information

2 At the bottom-left of the screen, under **Links and notes**, you'll see the name of the person (or people) that photo has been linked to. If a photo was taken of more than one of your relatives, simply click on the **New link/note** button (left). From the **Create link** box that appears, select whether you want to link the image to an individual, a family, a source record or a note. In the case of a wedding photo showing the bride and groom, you can attach the image to both people in the photo by selecting **An individual** from the list. Then a small version of the **Records** window will appear so that you can find the individual's record.

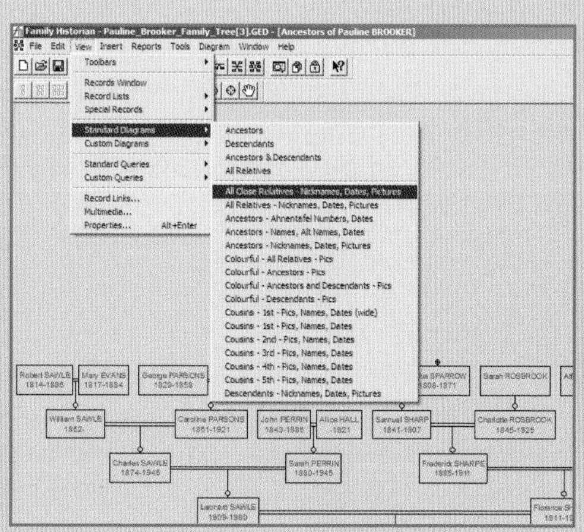

Choose a viewing option

1 You can view the information in your tree in various ways, using the buttons shown here. From left to right, they are **View ancestors**, **View descendants**, **View ancestors and descendants** and **View all relatives**. Select the name of the person you want the tree to be designed around from the **Records** window. Usually, at this point, it will be yourself or the person whose name you started with. In this case, it's Pauline Brooker. Then click on the **View ancestors** icon on the toolbar. The diagram window opens, displaying a diagram of Pauline Brooker's ancestors.

Creating links to people on your family tree can be enhanced by adding old family photos and images of documents. If you have a wedding photo or a family group, add them to your tree to bring it to life and create a fascinating document of facts and images. Some software packages only allow you to upload photos, but Family Historian (see below) also lets you create links between individuals and 'multimedia' (video or audio) files. You can attach as many photos and images as you want to a person's record and, if a photograph includes more than one person on your tree, you can create links between the image and all the individuals. It's a fairly easy process. If you have a digital camera, you can save and upload family pictures to your computer. Documents can be scanned and uploaded in the same way. If you don't have a scanner, taking pictures of documents using a digital camera, then uploading them onto your PC, can work just as well.

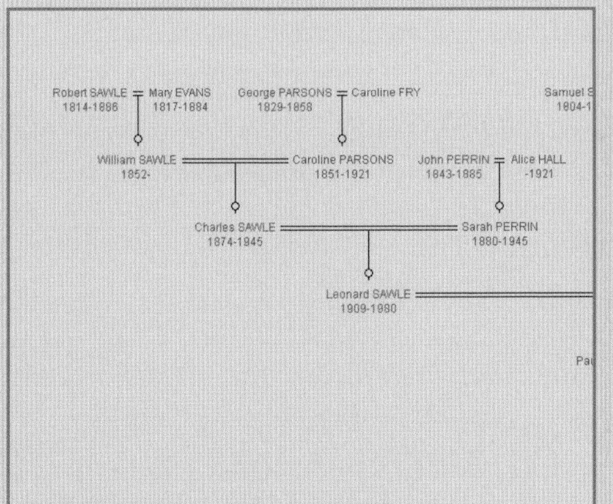

Navigating around your tree

2 You can move around the tree using the following six buttons. From left to right, you can: zoom in, and out, to view the details of a particular ancestor; use the magnifying glass to select areas you want to see close-up; click on the globe to view your complete tree; centre the diagram on the page using the focus symbol; and move the image around using the hand.

You can also change the appearance of the diagram using the following four buttons: the first displays hidden links between relatives; the second adds and removes the text frames, which sometimes makes it easier to read; and the last two buttons display and change the page boundaries.

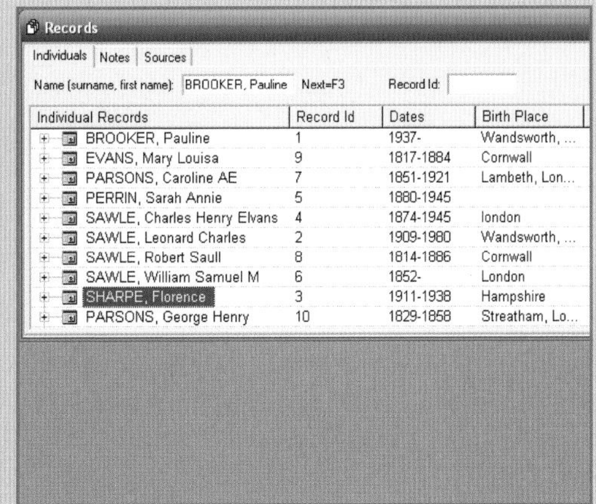

Adding to your tree

3 As you gather more information, you can add to your tree quickly and easily. When you open your file, you'll see that the information you've already added is displayed in the **Records** window. By clicking on the name you wish to view, and by using the options detailed in the previous steps, you can select different views for different ancestors, as well as for the entire tree if you wish.

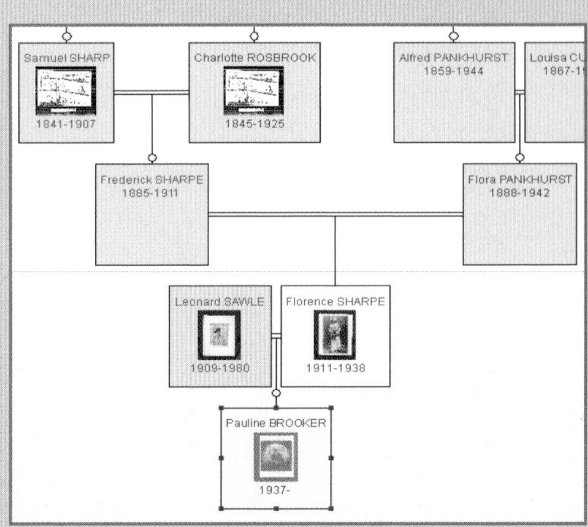

Bringing your tree to life

4 If you choose to view **All close relatives – nicknames, dates, pictures** (see step 1), you'll have a far more animated tree to look at. Any pictures, images or documents that you chose to add will be displayed. This has the advantage of bringing your tree to life, as well as creating a clear, accurate family tree document to share with your friends and family. Save as you go along to make sure you don't lose any data if your PC should crash unexpectedly. Click on the **Save** icon on your toolbar, and you'll be prompted to save your file to your hard drive.

Sharing it all on a blog

One of the biggest bonuses of the internet is the ease and speed with which you can exchange information, and one of the most popular ways of doing this is by 'blogging' – great for family historians who want to share their successes and keep on developing their family trees.

Creating a web log – or 'blog' for short – is a good place to start exchanging information online. A blog is an online journal or newsletter that's frequently updated and intended for public viewing. It's a perfect arena to recount your thoughts and experiences and narrate personal journeys. It also allows anyone who reads it to leave their own comments, stories and perhaps new material that may cast more light on your family's history.

There are two main ways to create blogs: you can use an existing server or website, such as one of those shown on the right, or you can put a blog on your own website (see pages 304-11). This might involve using web space offered by your internet service provider (ISP), buying space from a specialist hosting company or buying your own domain name (the web address for your site) – or even learning a little about HTML (HyperText Markup Language), the language of websites.

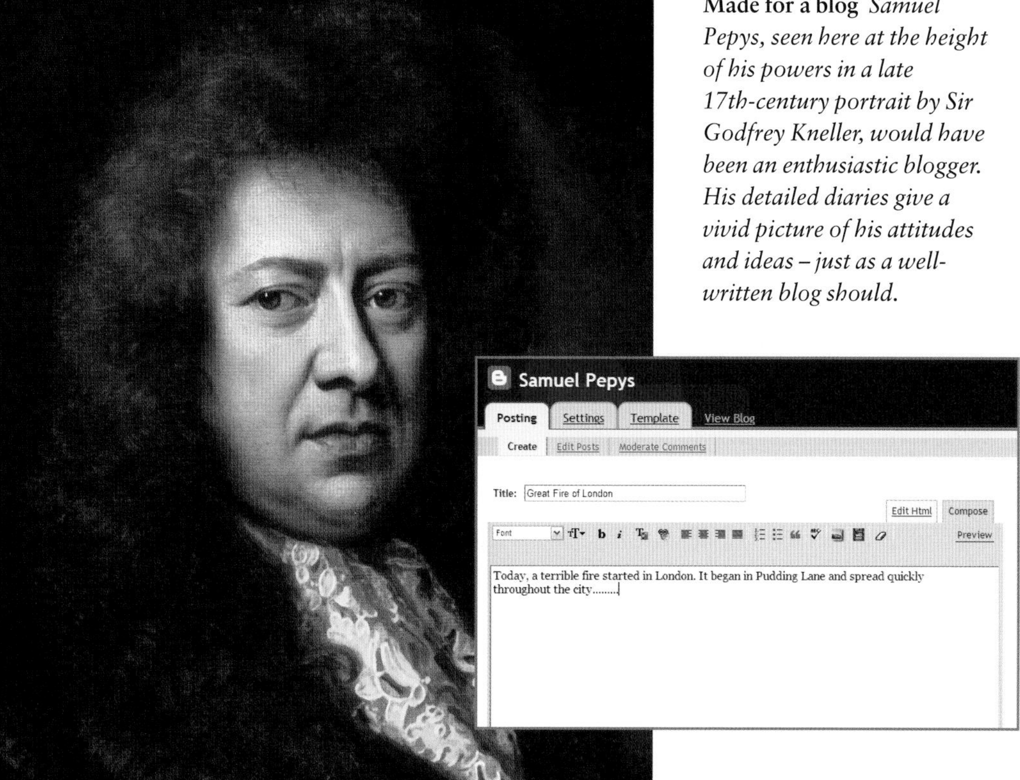

Made for a blog *Samuel Pepys, seen here at the height of his powers in a late 17th-century portrait by Sir Godfrey Kneller, would have been an enthusiastic blogger. His detailed diaries give a vivid picture of his attitudes and ideas – just as a well-written blog should.*

Using space on blogger sites

You'll find it far easier to use an existing site to host your blog than to set up your own website. Blogging is an increasingly popular hobby and the number of hosting sites reflects this. Enter the words 'blog hosts' into a search engine and you'll be offered a choice of sites, some that you pay for, others that are free of charge.

Using free blog sites

Free-to-use blog sites are financed by advertising, so a small advertisement banner will be placed on your blog to help to pay for the cost of hosting it. You won't be asked to pay for anything yourself, but neither will you have any choice as to what is advertised on your blog.

Most blogs allow you to store photos but there are limits to the size of the 'photo album' they will allow you, although they're usually perfectly adequate for normal usage.

Choosing a host for your blog

The first three websites shown below will help you to set up your own blog, and the fourth will prove useful as a source of inspiration: you'll be able to see just how – and how not – to set up and run a blog.

Blogger

Owned by Google, **blogger.com** lets you create your own blog, free of charge, in three easy steps: first, create an account by registering your personal details; then name your blog – which can be anything from your name or interest to something more creative; and finally, choose a design template to personalise your blog. Once you've done this, you can start entering information and images. You'll be prompted along the way.

TypePad

You'll be charged for space on **typepad.com**, which provides a choice of templates and technical support. The site offers a free 30-day trial period, and then you can choose from a range of services and prices, depending on what you want to use it for. The website is targeted mainly at professionals and small businesses.

Blog

There's a mixture of free and chargeable services at **blog.com**. Like **blogger.com** it gives you instructions to follow for creating your own blog. If you want to upgrade from the basic free service, you can choose from one of three 'premium' accounts – which you have to pay for. These accounts offer various extra features, such as letting you disable advertisements or set up a password access to the blog.

Finding family history blogs

If you want to have a look at other people's blogs before designing your own, **cyndislist.com/blogs.htm** has a comprehensive list of the genealogical blogs in circulation. There is also a guide on how to search for and use other people's blogs to help you in your research.

Sharing pictures with your family

Online photo albums and photosharing websites are an excellent way in which to store old photographs and record new memories of your family. The first step is to choose the website that's best for you.

When you look for a photosharing website, you can be spoilt for choice. It's always wise to go with a well-established site that has already attracted many users. Picasa and the other sites covered here are powerful and versatile, offering all kinds of storage and display features. Take a look also at the information about the Nations' Memorybank online archive on pages 322-5.

Picasa

A fast-growing resource for storing photos, **picasa.google.co.uk** is free to use, although you'll need to download the software from the website first. Once you've done this, you can use the site to upload, store and view your pictures. One of the best features of Picasa is that the software automatically searches for every picture you've stored

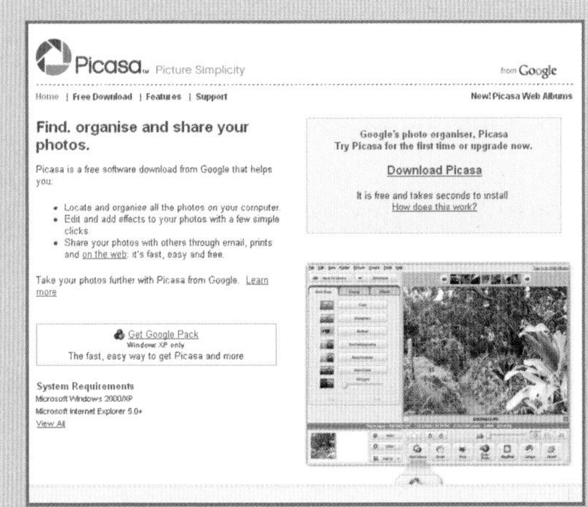

Take the Picasa tour

1 Go to **picasa.google.co.uk** and, on the homepage, download the software. If you want to have a look at the site first, you can then take the Picasa tour. Click on the **Learn more** link.

How to use Picasa

2 The page that comes up shows you all the things that you can do with the Picasa software. It gives instructions about how to organise your findings in an album, edit them and share them with the world.

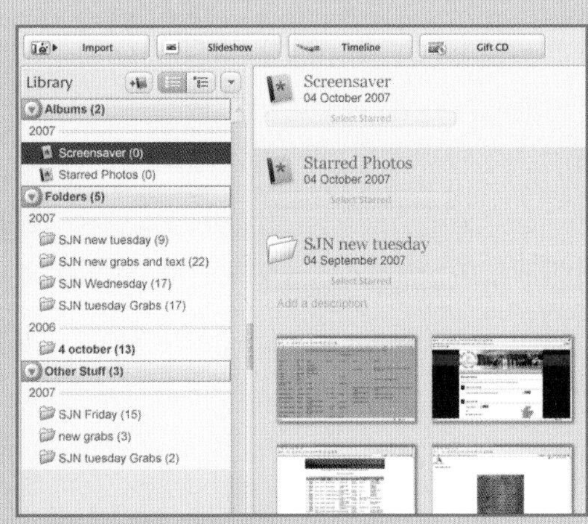

Organise your pictures

3 Once you've downloaded the software, all the images currently stored on your computer will be in one handy place. By clicking on the tabs at the top of the screen, you can import photos, create a slideshow or a timeline, or copy them onto a CD.

on your computer, and instantly puts them all in one place. This is really useful if you tend to store pictures in a number of different files, because it can find pictures and images that you might have feared you'd lost.

Downloading the software is simple: you just click on the link on the homepage. From there, you click on a series of prompt boxes, and once the software is installed, it will automatically put all the photos on your computer into one file. The whole process takes less than 5 minutes.

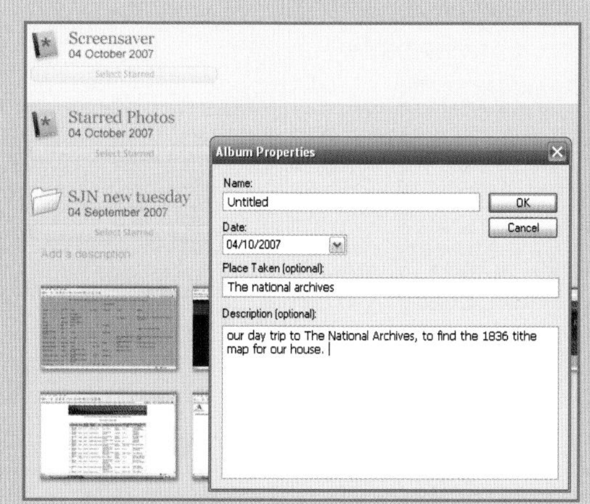

Create an album

4 When you've selected the pictures and images you want to store, you can create an album. This is useful if you want to hold in one handy place a selection of images and documents, that may all relate to one ancestor. Click on **Album**, and you'll be asked to name and describe the contents of the album. You can then share these with friends and family.

Picasa offers the added security of password protection, so only you can see the pictures you've uploaded yourself, if that's what you wish. You can also edit your photos and images, and create slide shows to show to the family. You're allowed up to 1GB of free storage in your online albums, which is around 4,000 standard-size photos.

You can also add captions and comments to any images that you upload, so that you can see at a glance what your image is and what it relates to. If you have friends and family that use Picasa, you'll be able to download their saved images to your own computer.

Picasa constantly works to increase its storage space, so if you're snap-happy, this is a great site for storing all your images.

Flickr

The American website **flickr.com** is one of the largest and most popular photosharing sites. The basic package is free to use, and you can upload 100MB of photos by mobile phone, email or from your own computer. They can then be viewed and shared by you and your family. You can organise the photos using tags, sets, albums or collections, or sort them by subject. The site also enables you to create cards, calendars, prints and DVDs.

Snapfish

Another website where you can upload, share and store photos is **snapfish.co.uk**. Photos can be sent direct to a dedicated email address from a mobile phone or from your own email account. You can customise albums to showcase your pictures and they can all be made into prints or even used to personalise gifts such as mugs and t-shirts. You can store as many low-resolution photos as you like, provided the site is used to order prints, enlargements or high-resolution photos at least once a year, otherwise your photographs will be deleted. (An email reminder is sent after 335 days of inactivity.)

This site is most useful if you regularly order photos or gifts, but not if all you want is free long-term storage.

Photosharing

As well as letting you view and upload photos, the website **photosharing.org.uk** has great photography tips and hints, plus advice on how to get the best out of your digital camera. There are also links to other photosharing sites, and a comprehensive list of websites dealing with different aspects of digital photography. You can even learn how to sell your pictures with the help of the professional gallery section.

Photobucket

The creative, free-to-use **photobucket.com** site links millions of uploaded photos, slideshows, graphics and videos daily to more than 300,000 websites, especially the popular social networking ones (see pages 320-1). You can share your photos by email, mobile phone or an instant messager such as MSN. As well as uploading online you can use the site to create photos, images, videos and music collections, and use different styles of slideshow to play photos back to friends or family members.

Sharing with the family
How to use networking sites

There are many reasons for joining a social networking group. You might want to meet new people who share your interests so that you can exchange stories, photos, videos and other information. Or perhaps you want to stay in touch with other family historians or with family members you've found through your research. You could form a group related to a specific family tree or surname and invite other interested users to join. This group would then have its own homepage, where all the members could write comments, share ideas and developments in their research, and upload photos. In addition, some of the main social networks have extra features that might allow you to create groups sharing common interests or set up forums for discussions on particular subjects.

How a group grows

In recent years, social networking websites and communities have grown massively. Popular sites such as MySpace and Facebook that started with a few thousand users can now claim users in the millions.

Social networking groups grow quickly because each new member can invite non-members to become friends on the website. They receive an email invitation, which they can reply to and use to register their profile on the same site. On most sites, both parties must confirm that they're friends before they're accepted into the group.

Friends you don't know yet

Bear in mind that most users are trying to find new friends and link up with as many other users as possible. So you'll often receive 'friend requests' from people you don't know. This means you need to be careful about the type of information you put on your homepage or personal pages: don't disclose too much, such as your mobile phone number or home address, to other users. These details may be needed to register your profile but they're not in the public domain. A good site will give advice on maximum personal safety and tips on how to stay safe online.

Websites that will help you

Here are some of the most popular social networking sites on the internet. There may be one that can advance your research.

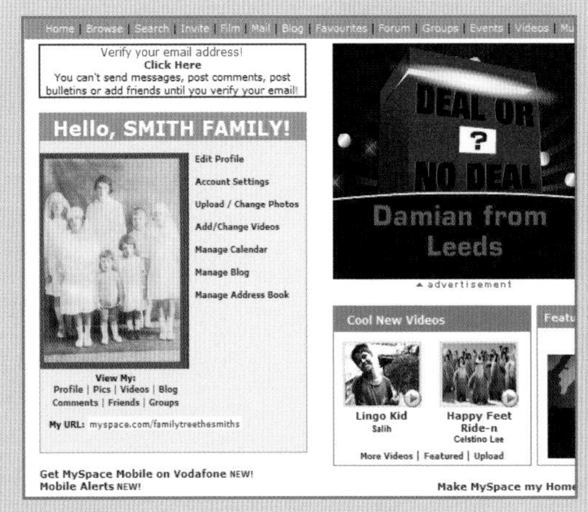

Taking space on MySpace

1 To join, go to **myspace.com** and click on **Sign up**. Once you've registered, you can upload a profile picture, which could be a group photo of your family, or an old photo of a key ancestor you're researching. Then invite friends to your MySpace page by entering their email addresses. Your home page will be displayed with all the information you've provided so far. This page contains some advertising, but isn't the page that people who visit your MySpace will see.

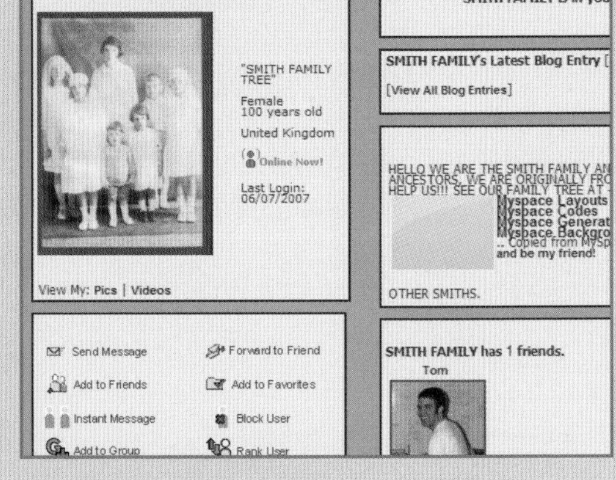

What your MySpace page looks like

2 Click on **View my profile** to see what your MySpace page looks like to other members. You can edit your profile by adding a coloured background, uploading photos and videos, pasting links, creating a website address, and writing about your research and what you're interested in finding out. You can change the name of your page by going back to **Home** and the **Edit profile** page.

• MySpace, at **myspace.com**, is the most popular site in this category. It has more than 175 million registered members worldwide, and is used by a wide variety of people, from friends and family who want to talk online, business people interested in networking, bands and groups passing on information to fans, to people looking for a date. It's quick and easy to create an account and start interacting with new-found family as soon as you've set up your registered profile and created your own homepage (see opposite).

• YouTube's website, **youtube.com**, is great if you want to share, upload and view items such as a family tree. The site contains film and TV clips and music videos, as well as amateur content such as video-blogging and short original videos. Unregistered users can watch most videos on the site, but if you're a registered user (see below), you can upload an unlimited number of videos, creating a storeroom for all your family films, and making them accessible to other people, so that distant relatives can view them online.

• Bebo, at **bebo.com**, bills itself as the next generation in social networking (see below). It has expanded, since it started in 2005, to enable users to upload family photos and videos, post comments and send emails in their search for relatives, as well as offering quizzes, picture slideshows and blogs.

• Other networking sites you might like to visit in your search for relatives are: **facebook.com**, **friendster.com**, **orkut.com**, **dandelife.com**, **webbiographies.com**, **photobucket.com** and **twitter.com**.

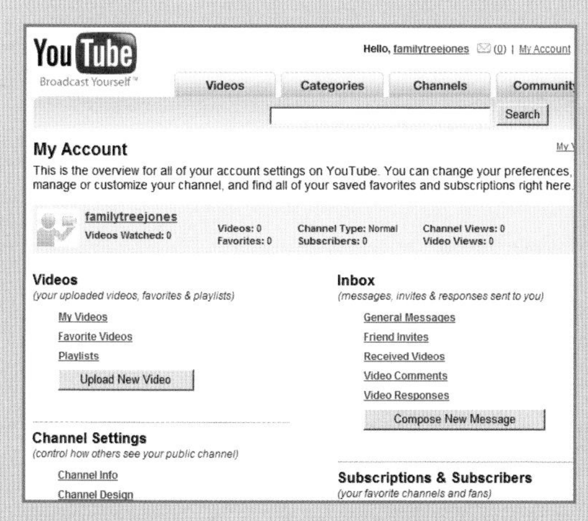

How to join YouTube

1 To create an account on YouTube, go to **youtube.com**, click on **Sign up** and follow the instructions. Navigate to your homepage by clicking on **My account**, where you'll be able to upload videos, invite friends, send videos to other people, search for videos already on the site and save them to your playlists.

Create a group

2 It's easy to create a group from your **My account** page. You can give the group page a website address, such as **youtube.com/group/jonesfamily**. On your group page you can upload videos relevant to the subject of the group, people can comment on the videos, discussions can be held about the subject and other users can ask to join your group.

Put your profile on Bebo

To create a profile page, register first at **bebo.com**, following the prompts. You can keep your homepage private, if you want to. Once you've signed in, un-check the box next to the words **Make my homepage visible to everyone**. Bebo can be used in much the same way as MySpace and YouTube, but as yet doesn't allow you to form groups. You can still use Bebo to interact with people also interested in family history and with other family members.

Sharing with the family
Nations' Memorybank

The online archive Nations' Memorybank (NMB) is a great place to upload your scanned photos, documents and other objects so you can share them with the whole family. At the same time, you can add your memories of some of the people and places that have been important to your family so that your descendants will be able to learn more about those characters in the future. You can make it even more enthralling if you encourage other relatives, especially the older ones, to add their memories and photographs to the database, to help you to create a fascinating insight to your heritage from different angles.

How to register

NMB is free to search, but you need to register and set up an account. Go to **nationsmemorybank.com** and navigate to the **Register** tab along the top of the homepage. Enter your details into the **Log in information** page. You have to choose a username by which you'll be known on the site. Once you've entered a password, your email address, postal address and date of birth, press the **Register** button. You'll receive confirmation of your account, and by

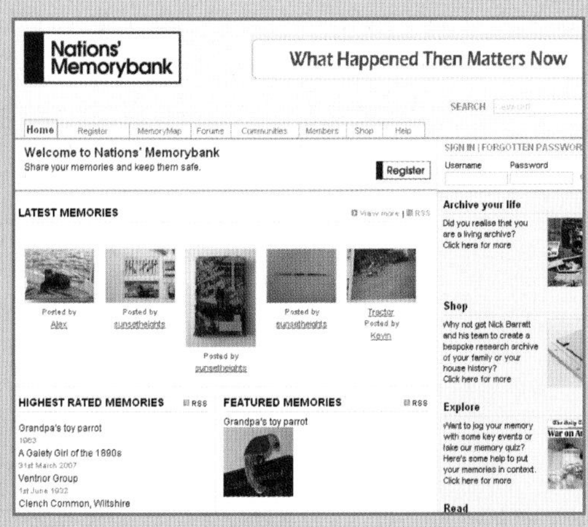

Choose a community

1 Log on to **nationsmemorybank.com** and click on **Communities.** Select the **Family** homepage. The look of this site changes daily, as people add new memories and pictures, but its functions remain the same. NMB has a number of communities that you can join. They come under the headings of **Fashion**, **Military**, **Family**, **House**, **Local**, **National Trust** and **Food**, click on one to start. You'll need to register (see above, right), in order to upload and share memories.

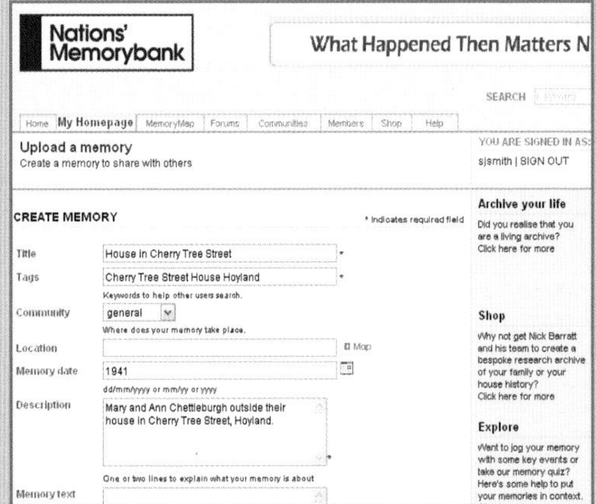

Upload your photograph

2 Click on **Upload a memory**. Enter a title for the picture in the **Tags** box, plus the year and date in the **Memory date** box, and type a few words in the **Description** box, and then enter your **Memory text** (see right). Click on **Browse** and select the image from your computer. When you've added as many photos as you want, click to upload your memory. For more information on location and memory mapping, see page 324.

See your entry

3 The next screen will show your full entry with the images you've selected. This will appear on your homepage where you'll be able to edit the memory. If you go back to the **Family** community page you'll find your memory along with other members' photos and memories from that community.

of research you should be doing. You may find the quiz is a good way of getting information from relatives, who may be slightly reluctant to speak about the past. Ask them questions such as 'What were your parents' occupations?' and 'Did any of your family serve in a war?' and they'll start to open up and let the memories flow.

Some of these subjects may cover areas that you haven't thought about before, and exploring them can often help you to add depth to your family tree research.

Memory map and geotagging

As well as uploading your own memories you can view the memories, photographs and research added by other Nations Memory Bank members. Each memory can be 'geotagged' by entering its location into the interactive UK Memory Map (see below).

The map will reveal any other memories which are located near to your own. If you find anything that's relevant to your research, you can then use the message forums and community page to discuss things further.

Listen and learn

The **Help** page on the site makes four key points to remember when discussing memories with elderly relatives:

1 Prepare your questions carefully – you'll only get what you ask for.
2 Show interest in the answers.
3 Listen carefully to what you're told.
4 Respect feelings and any reservations.

It also suggests recording conversations, then transcribing the details to upload as a memory, categorised by era, subject or event.

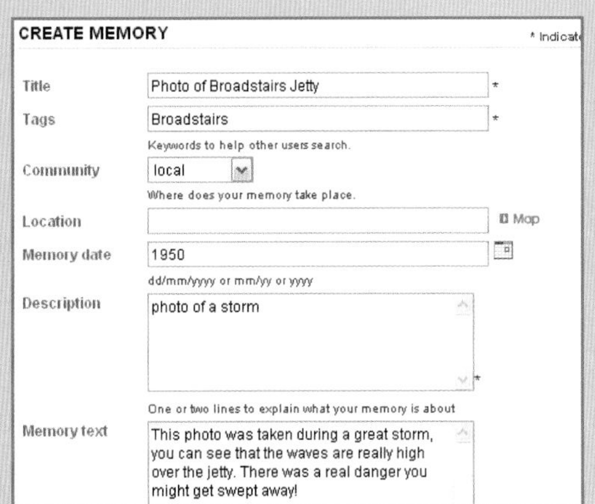

Adding and geotagging a memory

3 You can add to the UK Memory Map by going to your Homepage, clicking on **Upload a memory** and following the instructions on page 322. If you want to 'geotag' your memory so it can be uploaded onto the interactive Memory Map it's important to find the latitude and longitude reference on the map. To do this, click on the **Map** button next to the **Location** box.

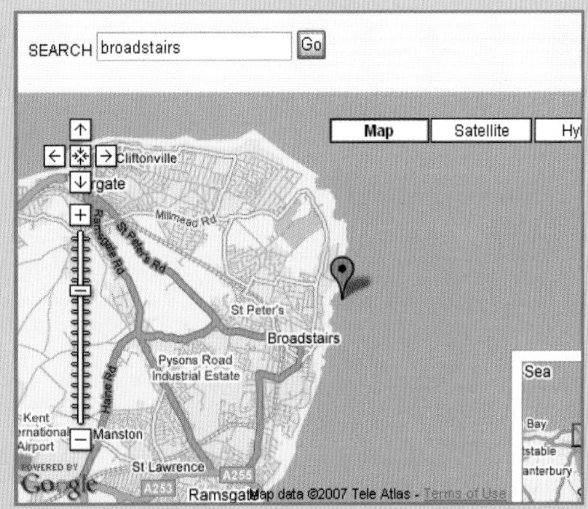

Find the right latitude and longitude

4 A map of the UK appears. Find the location of your memory by zooming in and dragging the mouse to move the picture until you've found the right location. Click the right-hand mouse button and a red balloon will appear to mark the spot of your memory. You can drag this balloon around until it lands on the exact location. Click the **Select** button and the correct co-ordinates will automatically be added to the **Location** box on your **Create memory** form.

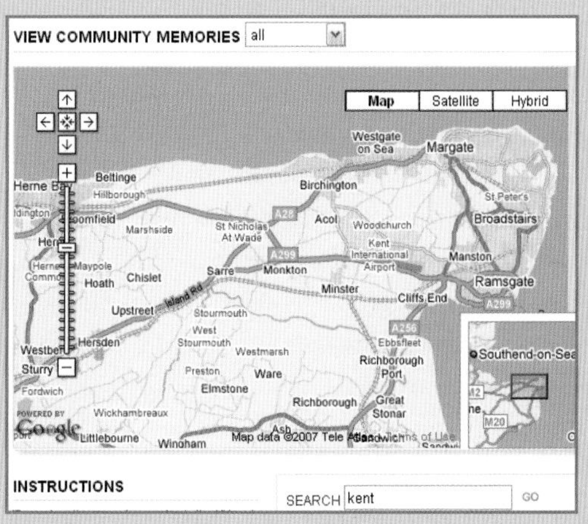

Your memory is on the map

5 If you go back to the **Memory map** pages again, you'll be able to locate your memory on the interactive map of the UK.

Directory of sources

The Directory lists sources of information mentioned in the book, as well as other useful websites and addresses. All websites are shown without the prefixes http:// or www. If you have any difficulty opening a website, try adding one of the prefixes to its address.

192
192.com
Online business and people directory.

1901 Census
1901.censusonline.com
1901census.nationalarchives.gov.uk
Official 1901 census website.

5 Star Shareware
5star-shareware.com
Software packages to download.

Aberdeen City Archives
aberdeencity.gov.uk
Town House, Broad Street
Aberdeen AB10 1AQ
01224 522513
archives@aberdeencity.gov.uk

Access to Archives (A2A)
a2a.org.uk
Database of local history archives.

Adoption Search
adoptionsearchreunion.org.uk
Website for people wishing to trace birth relatives or adopted children.

Albion
albion.com/netiquette/book
Tips on using message boards and forums.

Am Baile
ambaile.org.uk
History and culture of the Scottish Highlands and Islands.

Ancestry
ancestry.co.uk
Website for accessing online records.

Angel fire
angelfire.lycos.com
Site for blogging and photographs.

Angels
fancydress.com
Fancy dress and historical costumiers.

Anglesey County Record Office
anglesey.gov.uk
Archives service
Anglesey County Record Office
Shire Hall, Glanhwfa Road
Llangefni
Anglesey LL77 7TW
01248 752080
archives@anglesey.gov.uk

Antiquus Morbus
antiquusmorbus.com
Glossary of archaic medical terms for diseases and causes of death.

Archon Directory
nationalarchives.gov.uk/archon
Online database of contact details for all record offices and archives around the UK. Plus some overseas repositories.

Army Museums Ogilvy Trust
armymuseums.org.uk
Resource for researching regimental history.
Brigadier C.S. Sibun
58 The Close
Salisbury SP1 2EX
01722 332188
dir@amot.demon.co.uk

Ask.com
ask.com
Search engine.

Avast
avast.com
Anti-virus software to protect your PC.

AVG Free Advisor
free.grisoft.com
Anti-virus software to protect your PC.

AVG Grisoft
grisoft.com
Anti-virus software to protect your PC.

Ayrshire Archives
south-ayrshire.gov.uk
On the homepage, click on Family, *then* Service information, *then* Library Genealogy Resources.
Ayrshire Archives Centre
Craigie Estate
Ayr KA8 0SS
01292 287584
archives@south-ayrshire.gov.uk

Baptist Missionary Society
rpc.ox.ac.uk
Collections offering material relating to missionary work in many parts of the world.
The Librarian/Archivist
Angus Library
Regent's Park College
Pusey Street
Oxford OX1 2LB
01865 288142
andrew.hudson@regents.ox.ac.uk

Barnardo's (UK and Australia)
barnardos.org.uk
barnardos.org.au
Child welfare agency with child adoption records.

Barnardo's (UK Head Office)
Tanners Lane
Barkingside
Ilford, Essex IG6 1QG
020 8550 8822

Bath and North East Somerset Archives and Record Office
batharchives.co.uk
bathnes.gov.uk
Guildhall
High Street
Bath BA1 5AW
01225 477421
archives@bathnes.gov.uk

BBC (Family history section)
bbc.co.uk/familyhistory
Tips and hints, plus record sheets to download.

BeBo
bebo.com
Social networking site.

Bedfordshire and Luton Archives and Record Service
bedfordshire.gov.uk
Select Community and living*, then* Archives and records.
Riverside Building, County Hall
Cauldwell Street
Bedford MK4 9AP
01234 228833
archive@bedscc.gov.uk

Berkshire Record Office
berkshirerecordoffice.org.uk
9 Coley Avenue
Reading RG1 6AF
0118 901 5132
arch@reading.gov.uk

Berwick-upon-Tweed Record Office
berwick-upon-tweed.gov.uk/corp/archives
Council Offices
Wallace Green
Berwick-upon-Tweed TD15 1ED
01289 301865
archives@berwick-upon-tweed.gov.uk

Behind The Name
behindthename.com
History of first names.

Be Safe Online
besafeonline.com
Hints and tips for secure online shopping.

Birmingham City Archives
birmingham.gov.uk/archives
Central Library
Chamberlain Square
Birmingham B3 3HQ
0121 3034217
archives@birmingham.gov.uk

Birthlink
birthlink.org.uk
Services for people with a Scottish connection, separated by adoption.
21 Castle Street, Edinburgh EH2 3DN
0131 225 6441
mail@birthlink.org.uk

Blog
blog.com
Create your own online blog.

Blogger
blogger.com
Create your own online blog.

BMD Index
bmdindex.co.uk
Online registers for civil registration documents.

Bodleian Library
bodley.ox.ac.uk
Main research library for University of Oxford, with many online resources accessible to the public.
Broad Street
Oxford OX1 3BG
01865 277183
admissions@bodley.ox.ac.uk

Bolton Archives and Local Studies
boltonmuseums.org.uk/bolton-archives
Le Mans Crescent
Bolton BL1 1SE
01204 332185
archives.library@bolton.gov.uk

Borthwick Institute
york.ac.uk/inst/bihr
Archives at the University of York.
Borthwick Institute
University of York
Heslington
York YO10 5DD
01904 321166
bihr500@york.ac.uk

Bristol Record Office
bristol.gov.uk/recordoffice
'B' Bond Warehouse
Smeaton Road
Bristol BS1 6XN
0117 922 4224
bro@bristol.gov.uk

British Genealogy
british-genealogy.com
Free site for tracing British genealogy.

British Legion
britishlegion.org.uk
Official website for the British Legion.
The Royal British Legion
48 Pall Mall
London SW1Y 5JY
020 7973 7208/7272

British Library
bl.uk
The UK's national library website contains information on the scope of its collections and how to use its services.
The British Library
96 Euston Road
St Pancras, London NW1 2DB
020 7412 7332
customer-services@bl.uk

British Library India Office
bl.uk/collections/orientaloffice
For contact details see British Library.

British Library Newspaper Library
bl.uk/collections/newspapers
British Library Newspapers
Colindale Avenue
London NW9 5HE
020 7412 7353
newspaper@bl.uk

British Origins
britishorigins.com
English and Welsh records online.

British Postal Museum and Archive
postalheritage.org.uk
Information about 400 years' of postal history.
Freeling House
Phoenix Place
London WC1X 0DL
020 7239 2570
info@postalheritage.org.uk

British Red Cross
redcross.org.uk
British branch of the International Red Cross, that helps to reunite families.
44 Moorfields
London EC2Y 9AL
0870 1707000
enquiry@redcross.org.uk

Build Your Website
build-your-website.co.uk
Online help for building your own web pages.

Bury Archive Service
bury.gov.uk/leisureandculture/libraries/archives
Moss Street
Bury BL9 0DR
0161 253 6782
archives@bury.gov.uk

Business Archives Council
archives.gla.ac.uk
Business archives services, based in the Centre for Business History in Scotland at the University of Glasgow.
Duty Archivist
13 Thurso Street
Glasgow G11 6PE
0141 330 5515

CAD Tutor
cadtutor.net/wb
Website to help you to build your own web pages.

Cambridgeshire County Record Office
cambridgeshire.gov.uk/archives
Shire Hall
Castle Hill
Cambridge CB3 0AP
01223 717281
cal@cambridgeshire.gov.uk

Canada Libraries and Archives
See Libraries and Archives of Canada (LAC).

Catholic history
catholic-history.org.uk/cfhs
catholic-history.org.uk/crs
Websites for the Catholic Family History Society and Catholic Records Society.
Catholic Family History Society
45 Gates Green Road
West Wickham
Kent BR4 9DE
catholicfhs@ntlworld.com

Catholic National Library
catholic-library.org.uk
Comprehensive collection of Catholic family history information and mission registers.
St Michael's Abbey
Farnborough Road
Farnborough
Hampshire GU14 7NG
01252 543 818
library@catholic-library.org.uk

Centre for Kentish Studies/Kent Archives Service
kent.gov.uk/leisure-and-culture/archives-and-local-history
Sessions House
County Hall
Maidstone ME14 1XQ
01622 694363
archives@kent.gov.uk

Ceredigion Archives
archifdy-ceredigion.org.uk
Records of the county formerly known as Cardiganshire.
County Offices
Marine Terrace
Aberystwyth SY23 2DE
01970 633697
archives@ceredigion.gov.uk

Channel 4 – History
channel4.com/history
History section of Channel 4's website.

Cheshire and Chester Archives
cheshire.gov.uk/recoff/home
Cheshire and Chester Archives and Local Studies Service
Duke Street, Chester CH1 1RL
01244 602574
recordoffice@cheshire.gov.uk

Child Migrants Trust
childmigrantstrust.com
Charity reuniting families of child migrants shipped to Australia, Canada and other parts of the Commonwealth.
28A Musters Road
West Bridgford
Nottingham NG2 7PL
0115 982 2811

Church of Ireland Adoption Society (NI)
cofiadopt.org.uk
Assistance for adult adoptees.
Church of Ireland House
61-67 Donegal Street
Belfast BT1 2QH
028 9023 3885
bsr@ireland.anglican.ors

City of Westminster Archives Centre
westminster.gov.uk/archives
10 St Ann's Street
London SW1P 2DE
020 7641 5180
archives@westminster.gov.uk

ClamAV
clamav.net
Anti-virus software to protect your PC.

Collect Britain
collectbritain.co.uk
Showcase of British Library collections.

College of Arms
college-of-arms.gov.uk
Official repository of coats of arms for English, Welsh, Northern Irish and Commonwealth families.
Queen Victoria Street
London EC4B 4VT
020 7248 2762

Commonwealth War Graves Commission
cwgc.org
Database of war memorials and war cemeteries.
2 Marlow Road
Maidenhead
Berkshire SL6 7DX
01628 634221
Use contact form on website for email.

Consumer Direct
consumerdirect.gov.uk
Practical consumer advice.

Convicts to Australia
convictcentral.com
A guide to researching your convict ancestors.

Coram Family
coram.org.uk
Registered children's charity for the care of vulnerable children.

Corel
corel.co.uk
Photo software website.

Cornwall Record Office
cornwall.gov.uk
Old County Hall
Truro TR1 3AY
01872 323127
cro@cornwall.gov.uk

Coventry Archives
theherbert.org/collections/archives/index.htm
John Sinclair House
Canal Basin
Coventry CV1 4LY
024 7678 5158
archives@coventry.gov.uk

Crockford's Clerical Directory
crockford.org.uk
Details of Anglican clergy.

Cumbria Record Office
cumbria.gov.uk/archives
Carlisle Headquarters
The Castle
Carlisle CA3 8UR
01228 607285
carlisle.record.office@cumbriacc.gov.uk

Curious Fox
curiousfox.com
Website for genealogical enquiries.

Cyndi's List
cyndislist.com
Worldwide portal to genealogy sources.

Denbighshire Record Office
denbighshire.gov.uk
Ruthin Gaol, 46 Clwyd Street
Ruthin, Denbighshire LL15 1HP
01824 708250
archives@denbighshire.gov.uk

Derbyshire Record Office
derbyshire.gov.uk/recordoffice
County Hall
New Street
Matlock DE4 3AG
01629 585347
record.office@derbyshire.gov.uk

Devon Record Office
devon.gov.uk/record_office
Great Moor House
Bittern Road
Sowton, Exeter EX2 7NL
01392 384253
devrec@devon.gov.uk

Digital Handsworth
digitalhandsworth.org.uk
A history of the town of Handsworth.

DNA Ancestry Project
dnaancestryproject.com
DNA testing and information.

Dorset Archives
dorsetforyou.com/archives
Dorset History Centre
Bridport Road
Dorchester DT1 1RP
01305 250550
archives@dorsetcc.gov.uk

Dr William's Library
dwlib.co.uk
Research library specialising in English Puritanism and Protestant nonconformity.
14 Gordon Square
London WC1H 0AR
020 7837 3727
enquiries@dwlib.co.uk

Dublin City Archives
dublincity.ie *Enter 'City archives' in* Search *box.*
Records of the civic government of Dublin, from 1171.
138-144 Pearse Street
Dublin 2
00 353 1 6744999
cityarchives@dublincity.ie

Dublin Gazette
irisoifigiuil.ie
Online editions of the Dublin Gazette.

Durham County Record Office
durham.gov.uk/recordoffice
County Hall, Durham DH1 5UL
0191 383 3253
record.office@durham.gov.uk

Easily
easily.co.uk
Website for purchasing and registering domain names.

East Riding of Yorkshire Archives
eastriding.gov.uk *Select* A *from the* A-Z *index and click on* Archives.
Official website for East Riding of Yorkshire Record Office.
The Treasure House
Champney Road
Beverley
Correspondence address:
County Hall
Beverley HU17 9BA
01482 392790
archives.service@eastriding.gov.uk

East Sussex Record Office
eastsussex.gov.uk/useourarchives
The Maltings
Castle Precincts
Lewes
East Sussex BN7 1YT
01273 482349
archives@eastsussex.gov.uk

Edinburgh City Archives
edinburgh.gov.uk
Enter 'City archives' in Search *box.*
Corporate Services
City Chambers
High Street
Edinburgh EH1 1YJ
0131 529 4616

English Handwriting 1500-1700
english.cam.ac.uk/ceres/ehoc
University of Cambridge online tutorial for reading old handwriting.

Essex Record Office
essexcc.gov.uk/ero
Wharf Road
Chelmsford
Essex CM2 6YT
01245 244644
ero.enquiry@essexcc.gov.uk

Explore 192
192.com
Index of businesses, people and properties.

Family Records
familyrecords.gov.uk
Wide-ranging information about family records from official government sources.

Family Search/ Family History Centres
familysearch.org.uk
Worldwide genealogical records collected by The Church of Jesus Christ of Latter-day Saints (LDS). Website lists Family History Centres based in the UK.

Federation of Family History Societies (FFHS)
ffhs.org.uk
An umbrella body for more than 200 family history societies around the UK, whose addresses are on the website.
PO Box 2425
Coventry CV5 6YX
07041 492032
admin@ffhs.org.uk

Find My Past
findmypast.com
Access to indexes held in the GRO and many overseas records.

First Fleet
firstfleet.uow.edu.au/search
A searchable database of 780 First Fleet convicts sent to Australia in 1787.

Flickr
flickr.com
Photo storage and uploading software.

Flintshire Record Office
flintshire.gov.uk/archives
The Old Rectory
Rectory Lane
Hawarden
Flintshire CH5 3NR
01244 532364
archives@flintshire.gov.uk

Francis Frith
francisfrith.com
Old photos, maps and memories of UK and Ireland.

Free BMD
freebmd.org.uk
Online registers for civil registration.

Free CEN
freecen.org.uk
Census returns online.

Free REG
freereg.org.uk
Parish registers online.

Free Serif Software
freeserifsoftware.com
Software downloads for your PC.

Friends Reunited
friendsreunited.co.uk
Website for re-uniting old friends.

Gazettes online
gazettes-online.co.uk
Online editions of the London, Belfast and Edinburgh gazettes, official newspapers.

Gen Circles
gencircles.com
For sharing online family trees.

General Register Office for England and Wales (GRO)
gro.gov.uk
For ordering civil registration certificates online.
PO Box 2, Southport
Merseyside PR8 2JD
0151 471 4800
certificate.services@ons.gsi.gov.uk

General Register Office/ Northern Ireland (GRONI)
groni.gov.uk
For ordering civil registration certificates online.
Oxford House
49-55 Chichester Street
Belfast BT1 4HI
0289 0252021

General Register Office of Republic of Ireland (GROI)
groireland.ie
For ordering civil registration certificates online.
Government Offices
Convent Road
Roscommon
00 353 0 90 6632900

General Register Office for Scotland (GROS)
gro-scotland.gov.uk
For ordering civil registration certificates online.
New Register House
3 West Register Street
Edinburgh EH1 3YT
0131 314 4433
Use contact form on website for email.

Genes Reunited
genesreunited.co.uk
Website with access to online records for finding possible relatives.

Genuki
genuki.org.uk
UK and Ireland genealogical information.

Glamorgan Record Office
glamro.gov.uk
The Glamorgan Building
King Edward VII Avenue
Cathays Park, Cardiff CF10 3NE
029 2078 0282
glamro@cardiff.ac.uk

Glasgow City Archives
glasgow.gov.uk
Enter 'Archives' in Search *box.*
The Mitchell Library, 210 North Street
Glasgow G3 7DN
0141 287 2910
archives@cls.glasgow.gov.uk

Glasgow Museums
glasgowmuseums.com/photolibrary
Glasgow Museums' online photo library.

Gloucestershire Archives and Record Office
gloucestershire.gov.uk/archives
Clarence Row, Alvin Street
Gloucester GL1 3DW
01452 425295
archives@gloucestershire.gov.uk
records@gloucestershire.gov.uk

Google
google.co.uk
Search engine.

Google Earth
earth.google.com
Aerial, satellite images and information from all over the world.

Google Maps
maps.google.co.uk
Modern street directory.

Greater Manchester County Record Office
gmcro.co.uk
56 Marshall Street
New Cross
Manchester M4 5FU
0161 832 5284
archives@gmcro.co.uk

Guernsey Archives Service
user.itl.net/~glen/archgsy
St Barnabas
Cornet Street
St Peter Port GY1 1LF
Channel Islands
01481 724512
archives@gov.gg

Guildhall Library
cityoflondon.gov.uk *Select* Guildhall Library *from* A-Z of Services.
Records ranging from ancient guildsmen to fire insurance.
Aldermanbury
Manuscripts Section
London EC2P 7HH
020 7332 1862
manuscripts.guildhall@cityoflondon.gov.uk

Guild of One-Name Studies
one-name.org
Organisation for surname studies.

Gwent Record Office
llgc.org.uk/cac/cac0004.htm
County Hall, Cwmbran
Gwent NP44 2XH
01633 644886
gwent.records@torfaen.gov.uk

Gwynedd Archives Service
gwynedd.gov.uk/archives
Caernarfon Record Office
Victoria Dock
Caernarfon LL55 1SH
Correspondence address:
County Offices
Swyddfa'r Cyngor
Caernarfon LL55 1SH
01286 679095
archives@gwynedd.gov.uk

Hampshire Record Office
hants.gov.uk/record-office
Sussex Street
Winchester
Hampshire SO23 8TH
01962 846154
enquiries.archives@hants.gov.uk

Herefordshire Record Office
herefordshire.gov.uk/archives
Herefordshire Archive Service
Harold Street
Hereford HR1 2QX
01432 260750
archives@herefordshire.gov.uk

Hertfordshire Archives and Local Studies Centre
hertsdirect.org/heritage
Register Office Block
County Hall, Pegs Lane
Hertford SG13 8EJ
01438 737333 (*or* 01923 471333 *from area codes* 01923 and 020)
hertsdirect@hertscc.gov.uk

Historical Directories
historicaldirectories.org
Digital library of local and trade directories from 1750 to 1919.

Home Office
homeoffice.co.gov.uk
Records of naturalisation since June 1969.
Immigration and Nationality Directorate
Liverpool Customer Contact Centre
Correspondence Team
Department 2
PO Box 306
Liverpool L2 0QN
020 7035 4848
public.enquiries@homeoffice.gsi.gov.uk

Homestead
homestead.com
Online resource for creating your own website.

House Detectives
house-detectives.co.uk
Specialist research service for tracing the history of your house.

Huguenot Society of Great Britain and Ireland
huguenotsociety.org.uk
The Huguenot Library
University College, Gower Street
London WC1 6BT
020 7679 5100
library@huguenotsociety.org.uk

Huntingdonshire County Record Office
cambridgeshire.gov.uk/archives
Grammar School Walk
Huntingdon PE29 3LF
01480 375842
county.records.hunts@cambridgeshire.gov.uk

Ideal Homes
ideal-homes.org.uk
History of south London.

Imperial War Museum (IWM)
iwm.org.uk
Official website for the IWM.
IWM London, Lambeth Road
London SE1 6HZ
020 7416 5320
mail@iwm.org.uk

IWM Duxford, IWM North, HMS *Belfast* and The Cabinet War Rooms
See IWM website for details.

India Office Records
See British Library India Office.

International Committee of the Red Cross (ICRC)
ircrc.org
International organisation dedicated to helping victims of war and disaster.
19 avenue de la Paix
CH 1202 Geneva
Switzerland
00 41 (22) 734 60 01

Institute of Commonwealth Studies (ICS)
commonwealth.sas.ac.uk
Website of the ICS, dedicated to the study of the Commonwealth.
Institute of Commonwealth Studies
University of London
28 Russell Square
London WC1B 5DS
020 7862 8844
ics@sas.ac.uk

Institute of Heraldic and Genealogical Studies (IHGS)
ihgs.ac.uk
79-82 Northgate, Canterbury
Kent CT1 1BA
01227 768664
Use contact form on website for email.

International Ceramic Directory
ceramic-link.de/Seiten/ICD-Historical2.htm
Website for dating old pottery and ceramics.

Irish Adoption Contact Register
adoptionireland.com/register
Mutual consent registry to assist contact between adopted people and their natural parents and families.
The Adopted People's Association
14 Exchequer Street
Dublin 2
Republic of Ireland
info@adoptionireland.com

Irish Manuscripts Commission
irishmanuscripts.ie
irmss.ie
Promotes public awareness of primary source materials and their importance for Irish history, heritage and culture.
45 Merrion Square
Dublin 2
Republic of Ireland
00 353 1 6623832
support@irishmanuscripts.ie

Irish Origins
irishorigins.com
Irish documents online.

Isle of Man Public Record Office
gov.im/registries/publicrecords
Unit 40a, Spring Valley Industrial Estate
Douglas IM2 2QS
Isle of Man
01624 693569
public.records@registry.gov.im

Isle of Wight Record Office
iwight.com/library/record_office
26 Hillside, Newport
Isle of Wight PO30 2EB
01983 823820/1
record.office@iow.gov.uk

Jersey Archives
jerseyheritagetrust.org
Jersey Heritage Trust
The Weighbridge
St Helier JE2 4JY
Jersey
01534 833333
archives@jerseyheritagetrust.org

Jewish Genealogical Society of Great Britain (JGSGB)
jgsgb.org.uk
Official website of the Jewish Genealogical Society. Research enquiries are dealt with by email, not by phone.
33 Seymour Place
London W1H 5AU
020 7724 4232 (*answering machine*)
genealogy@jgsgb.org.uk

Jewish Genealogy
jewishgen.org
Website dedicated to Jewish ancestry.

Kent Archaeological Society
kentarchaeology.org.uk
For gravestones and monuments in and around Kent.

Kent Archives Service
See Centre for Kentish Studies.

Lambeth Palace Library
lambethpalace.org
Principal library and record office for the history of the Church of England. Also a significant resource for local and family history.
Lambeth Palace Road
Lambeth
London SE1 7JU
020 7898 1400
lpl.staff@c-of-e.org.uk

Lancashire Record Office
archives.lancashire.gov.uk
Bow Lane
Preston
Lancashire PR1 2RE
01772 533039
record.office@ed.lancscc.gov.uk

Last Names
last-names.net
Site for locating surname origins.

Learning Curve
learningcurve.gov.uk
Affiliated to The National Archives site, with documents and case studies online.

Leicestershire, Leicester and Rutland Record Office
leics.gov.uk/index/community/museums/record_office
Long Street, Wigston Magna
Leicester LE18 2AH
0116 257 1080
recordoffice@leics.gov.uk

Libraries and Archives of Canada (LAC)
collectionscanada.ca
395 Wellington Street, Ottawa, Ontario KIA 0N4, Canada
Use contact form on website for email.

Lichfield Record Office
staffordshire.gov.uk/archives
The Friary
Lichfield WS13 6QG
01543 510720
lichfield.record.office@staffordshire.gov.uk

Liverpool Record Office and Local History Service
liverpool.gov.uk/archives
Central Library
William Brown Street
Liverpool L3 8EW
0151 233 5817
recoffice.central.library@liverpool.gov.uk

London Library
londonlibrary.co.uk
The world's largest independent library.
14 St James's Square
London SW1 4LG
020 7930 7705
enquiries@londonlibrary.co.uk

London Metropolitan Archives (LMA)
lma.gov.uk
40 Northampton Road
Clerkenwell
London EC1R 0HB
020 7332 3820
ask.lma.cityoflondon.gov.uk

Look Up
lookup.com
Website for tracing missing people.

Lumapix
lumapix.com
Photo storage and upload site.

Manchester City Archives
manchester.gov.uk/libraries/arls
Central Library
St Peter's Square
Manchester M2 5PD
0161 234 1980
archiveslocalstudies@manchester.gov.uk

Manchester City Council Local Image Collection
images.manchester.gov.uk
Images of Manchester, its suburbs and surroundings through the ages.

Manchester County Record Office (Greater)
See Greater Manchester County Record Office.

Manchester University Library (John Rylands University Library)
library.manchester.ac.uk
The University of Manchester
Oxford Road
Manchester M13 9PP
0161 275 2922

Manx National Heritage Library
gov.im/mnh
Promotes history and culture of the Isle of Man.
Douglas IM1 3LY
Isle of Man
01624 648000
enquiries@mnh.gov.im

MapCo
archivemaps.com/mapco
Scanned copies of antique and historical maps.

Mary Evans Picture Library
maryevans.com
Photos, paintings and prints collections online.

Mcafee Store
mcafeestore.com
US-based store for firewall and virus protection for your PC.

Memorial Inscriptions
memorial-inscriptions.org.uk
Database of memorial inscriptions in Cheshire, Staffordshire and Shropshire.

Memories Nostalgia
memories-nostalgia.com
Site for purchasing archival storage boxes.

Microsoft
microsoft.com
Main Microsoft website – for updates, software and information.

Ministry of Defence (MOD)
mod.uk
Website for obtaining service records of Army and Navy personnel whose regular or reserve service ended between 1921 and 1997.
Army Personnel Centre Secretariat
Historical Disclosures
Mail Point 400
Kentigern House
65 Brown Street
Glasgow G2 8EX
0845 600 9663, *choose option 1, then option 3*
disc4.civsec@apc.army.mod.uk

For Navy personnel serving between 1928 and 1938, contact:
Navy Search
TNT Archive Services
Tetron Point
William Nadin Way
Swadlincote
Derbyshire DE11 0BB
01283 227 910
navysearchpgrc@tnt.co.uk

For Navy personnel serving after 1938, write to:
Data Protection Cell (Navy)
Victory View
Building1/52
HM Naval Base
Portsmouth PO1 3PX

Modern Records Centre
modernrecordswarwick.ac.uk
University Library
University of Warwick
Coventry CV4 7AL
024 7652 4219
archives@warwick.ac.uk

MotCo
motco.com
Database of historical maps and plans of London.

Moving Here
movinghere.org.uk
Sources for tracing overseas family history.

Multimap
multimap.com
Modern street directory.

Museum of Childhood
vam.ac.uk/moc
The national childhood collection is held here as part of the Victoria and Albert family of museums.
Cambridge Heath Road
London E2 9PA
020 8983 5200
moc@vam.ac.uk

Museum of English Rural Life, Reading University
merl.org.uk
Dedicated to recording the history of rural life in England.
The University of Reading
22 Redlands Road
Reading RG1 5EX
0118 378 8660
merl@reading.ac.uk

Museum of London
museumoflondon.org.uk
150 London Wall
London EC2Y 5HN
0870 444 3852
info@museumoflondon.org.uk

My Domain
mydomain.com
Website for purchasing and registering domain names.

My Genealogy
mygenealogy.com
Website for uploading family trees; works in conjunction with Ancestry.

My Space
myspace.com
Social networking site.

Name Seekers
nameseekers.co.uk
Site for locating first name and surname origins, and coats of arms.

National Archives of Australia
naa.gov.au
Official website for the National Archives of Australia. Check the website for local contact details.
0061 2 6212 3600
archives@naa.gov.au

National Archives of England and Wales
See The National Archives.

National Archives of New Zealand
archives.govt.nz
10 Mulgrave Street, Thorndon
Wellington
New Zealand
Correspondence address:
PO Box 12-050
Wellington
New Zealand
wellington@archives.govt.nz

National Archives of Scotland (NAS)
nas.gov.uk
H.M. General Register House
2 Princes Street
Edinburgh EH1 3YY
0131 535 1314
enquiries@nas.gov.uk

National Archives of South Africa
national.archives.gov.za
Private Bag X236
Pretoria 0001
South Africa
00 27 12 323 5300
archives@dac.gov.za

National Army Museum
national-army-museum.ac.uk
Museum dedicated to the British Army, its regiments and history. Online collection of records and images.
Royal Hospital Road
Chelsea, London SW3 4HT
020 7730 0717
info@national-army-museum.ac.uk

National Coal Mining Museum for England
ncm.org.uk
History of mining.
Caphouse Colliery
New Road
Overton
Wakefield WF4 4RH
01924 848806
Use contact form on website for email.

National Federation of Women's Institutes
womens-institute.co.uk
nfwi.org.uk
104 New King's Road
London SW6 4LY
020 7371 9300
ha@nfwi.org.uk

National Library of Ireland
nli.ie
Comprehensive collection of information about Ireland.
Kildare Street
Dublin 2
Republic of Ireland
00 353 1 603 0200
info@nli.ie

National Library of Scotland
nls.uk
Main library:
George IV Bridge
Edinburgh EH1 1EW
0131 623 3700
Use contact form on website for email.

National Library of Wales (NLW)
llgc.org.uk
Aberystwyth, Ceredigion SY23 3BU
01970 632 800
Use contact form on website for email.

National Maritime Museum
nmm.ac.uk
British maritime history and related topics.
Greenwich
London SE10 9EF
020 8858 4422

National Monuments Record
english-heritage.org.uk
Archive of England's monuments with photos, drawings and documents.

National Monuments Record Centre (NMRC)
Kemble Drive
Churchward
Swindon SN2 2GZ
01793 414600
nmrinfo@english-heritage.org.uk

National Screen and Sound Archive of Wales
screenandsound.llgc.org.uk
Official site for the National Screen and Sound Archive of Wales.
National Library of Wales
Aberystwyth
Ceredigion SY23 3BU
01970 632828
agssc@llgc.org.uk

Nations' Memory Bank
nationsmemorybank.com
Upload and store memories, images and photographs.

New Zealand
See National Archives of New Zealand.

NORCAP
norcap.org.uk
Help for adopted adults on issues of search and reunion.
112 Church Road
Wheatley
Oxfordshire OX33 1LU
01865 875 000
enquiries@norcap.org.uk

Norfolk Record Office
archives.norfolk.gov.uk
The Archive Centre
Martineau Lane
Norwich NR1 2DQ
01603 222599
norfrec@norfolk.gov.uk

Northamptonshire Record Office
northamptonshire.gov.uk *Enter 'Record office' in the* Search *box.*
Records Office
Wootton Hall Park
Northampton NN4 8BQ
01604 762129
archivist@northamptonshire.gov.uk

North Devon Library and Record Office
devon.gov.uk *Select* Democracy & community, *then* Neighbourhoods & villages, *then* Historical records.
Tuly Street
Barnstaple EX31 1EL
01271 388607
ndevrec@devon.gov.uk

Northumberland Record Office
northumberland.gov.uk/collections
Northumberland Collections Service
Woodhorn
Queen Elizabeth II Country Park
Ashington
Northumberland NE63 9YF
01670 528080
collections@woodhorn.org.uk

North Yorkshire County Record Office
northyorks.gov.uk/archives
Malpas Road
Northallerton DL7 8TB
01609 777585
archives@northyorks.gov.uk

Nottinghamshire Archives
nottinghamshire.gov.uk/archives
Record Office
Castle Meadow Road
Nottingham NG2 1AG
0115 958 1634
archives@nottscc.gov.uk

Old Maps
old-maps.co.uk
Online archive of historic maps.

One Great Family
onegreatfamily.com
Online family tree building.

Ordnance Survey
ordnancesurvey.co.uk
Great Britain's national mapping agency. Maps to view online.

Origins
origins.net
Online records for Britain and Ireland.

Orkney Library and Archives
orkneylibrary.org.uk
The Orkney Library and Archives
44 Junction Road
Kirkwall
Orkney KW15 1AG
01856 873166/87
archives@orkneylibrary.org.uk

Oxfordshire Record Office
oxfordshire.gov.uk/records
St Luke's Church
Temple Road
Cowley
Oxford OX4 2HT
01865 398200
archives@oxfordshire.gov.uk

Parish Register
parishregister.com
Parish registers and local information.

Parliamentary Archives
parliament.uk
Archives and records relating to Parliament, dating from 1497.
Houses of Parliament,
London SW1A 0PW
020 7219 3074
archives@parliament.uk

PC Pro
pcpro.co.uk
Online newspaper about computers, software and technology.

Pembrokeshire Record Office
llgc.org.uk/cac/cac0002.htm
The Castle
Haverfordwest
Pembrokeshire SA61 2EF
01437 763707
record.office@pembrokeshire.gov.uk

People's History Museum
phm.org.uk
Celebrates the working lives of ordinary people.
The Pump House
Left Bank
Bridge Street
Manchester M3 3ER
0161 839 6061
info@phm.org.uk

Photobucket
photobucket.com
Photo sharing site.

Photo London
photolondon.org.uk
Information about London's historic photographic collections, history of photography and other source materials.

PhotoSharing
photosharing.org.uk
Photo sharing site.

Picasa
picasa.google.co.uk
Photo sharing site.

PortCities
portcities.org.uk
Maritime history of UK port cities.

Powys County Archives
powys.gov.uk *From homepage select* Leisure & culture, *then* Archives office.
County Hall, Llandrindod Wells
Powys LD1 5LG
01597 826088
archives@powys.gov.uk

Principal Registry of the Family Division
hmcourts-service.gov.uk
Wills from 1858 to the present day.
First Avenue House
42-49 High Holborn
London WC1 6NP
020 7947 6983

Public Record Office of Northern Ireland (PRONI)
proni.gov.uk
66 Balmoral Avenue
Belfast BT9 6NY
028 9025 5905 (Public Search Room)
proni@dcalni.gov.uk

Ramsdale
ramsdale.org/surname.htm
Origins of English surnames.

Red Cross
See British Red Cross *or* International Committee of the Red Cross.

Religious Society of Friends Library
quaker.org.uk/library
A major collection of material relating to Quakers, started in 1673.
Friends House
173-177 Euston Road
London NW1 2BJ
020 7663 1135
Use contact form on website for email.

Remembrance Travel
remembrancetravel.com
Website for arranging visits to war graves and battle sites.
01622 716729
remembrancetravel@britishlegion.org.uk

Romany and Traveller Family History Society
rtfhs.org.uk
Website for finding out more about gypsy and traveller life.

RootsWeb
rootsweb.com
Sharing genealogical information online.

Royal Air Force Museum
rafmuseum.org.uk/london/collections/archive
Range of archive collections, including personal papers and logbooks.
Department of Research and Information Services
Grahame Park Way, London NW9 5LL
020 8205 2266
Use contact form on website for email.

Royal British Legion Village
rblvillage.legionbranches.net
Community that houses disabled veterans and various Royal British Legion industries.
Aylesford, Kent ME20 7NZ
01732 870102 (*answerphone*)

Royal College of Physicians
rcplondon.ac.uk/heritage
College archives going back to the 16th century.
Heritage Centre
The Royal College of Physicians
11 St Andrews Place
Regent's Park
London NW1 4LE
020 7935 1174
heritage@rcplondon.ac.uk

Royal Commission on the Ancient and Historical Monuments of Scotland (RCAHMS)
rcahms.gov.uk
Independent body responsible for recording, interpreting and promoting Scotland's historic buildings.
John Sinclair House,
16 Bernard Terrace
Edinburgh EH8 9NX
0131 662 1456
info@rcahms.gov.uk

Royal Irish Academy Library
riam.ie/library+catalogue
Resources for genealogical research.
19 Dawson Street,
Dublin 2
Republic of Ireland
00 353 1 676 2570
library@ria.ie

Royal Marines Museum
royalmarinesmuseum.co.uk
The library collection includes Navy and Marine Officer lists.
Archives and Library
Southsea
Hampshire PO4 9PX
023 9281 9385
info@royalmarinesmuseum.co.uk

Royal Naval Museum Library
royalnavalmuseum.org
Resources for studying aspects of naval history.
Information Service
Royal Naval Museum
HM Naval Base (PP66)
Portsmouth PO1 3NH
023 9272 3795
library@royalnavalmuseum.org

Salvation Army's Family Tracing Service
salvationarmy.org.uk/familytracing
For tracing missing relatives.
101 Newington Causeway
London SE1 6BN
0845 634 4747
Use contact form on website for email.

School of Oriental and African Studies (SOAS) Library
helpers.shl.lon.ac.uk/description12.php
Information about missionary societies.
Thornaugh Street, Russell Square
London WC1H 0XG
020 7637 2388
libenquiry@soas.ac.uk

Scotland's People
scotlandspeople.gov.uk
Civil registration and census returns for Scotland online.

Scottish Genealogy Society
scotsgenealogy.com
The Library and Family History Centre holds a wealth of material, including a family history index.
15 Victoria Terrace
Edinburgh EH1 2JL
0131 220 3677
info@scotsgenealogy.com

Scottish Jewish Archives Centre
sjac.org.uk
History of Jewish communities living in Scotland since the 18th century.
129 Hill Street
Glasgow G3 6UB
0141 332 4911
info@sjac.org.uk

Search Line
search-line.co.uk
Website dedicated to reuniting lost friends and relatives, particularly adoptees.

Sheffield Archives
sheffield.gov.uk *Enter 'Archives' in the* Search *box.*
52 Shoreham Street
Sheffield S1 4SP
0114 203 9395
archives@sheffield.gov.uk

Shetland Archives
shetland.gov.uk/archives
Hay's Dock
Lerwick
Shetland ZE1 0WP
01595 741554
info@shetlandmuseumandarchives.org.uk

Shropshire Archives
shropshire.gov.uk/archives.nsf
Castle Gates
Shrewsbury SY1 2AQ
01743 255350
archives@shropshire-cc.gov.uk

Silvermine
freespace.virgin.net/a.data/noframes/index.htm
Website for dating silverware.

Snapfish
snapfish.co.uk
Photo sharing site.

Society of Genealogists
sog.org.uk
Family history library and genealogy centre.
14 Charterhouse Buildings
Goswell Road
London EC1M 7BA
020 7251 8799

Somerset Archives and Record Office
somerset.gov.uk/archives
Obridge Road
Taunton TA2 7PU
01823 337600
archives@somerset.gov.uk

South Africa National Archives
See National Archives of South Africa.

Southampton Archives Service
southampton.gov.uk/leisure/history/archives
South Block
Civic Centre
Southampton SO14 7LY
023 8083 2251
city.archives@southampton.gov.uk

Spatial Literacy
spatial-literacy.org
Useful for geographical surname locating.

Spinning the Web
spinningtheweb.org.uk
History of the Lancashire cotton industry.

Staffordshire Archive Service
staffordshire.gov.uk/archives
Eastgate Street
Stafford ST16 2LZ
01785 278379
staffordshire.record.office@staffordshire.gov.uk

Sticks Research Agency (SRA)
sra-uk.com
Specialist genealogical and historical research organisation.

Streetmap
streetmap.co.uk
Modern online street atlas.

Stoke on Trent Archive Service
staffordshire.gov.uk/archives
City Central Library
Bethesda Street
Hanley
Stoke on Trent ST1 3RS
01782 238420
stoke.archives@stoke.gov.uk

Suffolk Record Office
suffolk.gov.uk
There are three branches:
77 Raingate Street
Bury St Edmunds IP33 2AR
01284 352352
bury.ro@libher.suffolkcc.gov.uk

Gatacre Road
Ipswich IP1 2LQ
01473 584541
ipswich.ro@libher.suffolkcc.gov.uk

The Library
Clapham Road
Lowestoft NR32 1D
01502 405357
lowestoft.ro@libher.suffolkcc. gov.uk

Surname db
surnamedb.com
Site for locating surname origins.

Surrey History Centre
surreycc.gov.uk/surreyhistoryservice
130 Goldsworth Road
Woking GU21 6ND
01483 518 737
shs@surreycc.gov.uk

Sussex Record Office
See East Sussex Record Office *and/or* West Sussex Record Office.

Swansea History
swanseahistoryweb.org.uk
Website dedicated to the history of Swansea.

Symantec
symantec.com
Anti-virus software to protect your PC.

Talking Scot
talkingscot.com
Forum and discussion for Scottish genealogy.

The Clergy of the Church of England database
theclergydatabase.org.uk
Records of all clergy careers.

The Genealogist
thegenealogist.co.uk
Online records.

The National Archives
nationalarchives.gov.uk
The main repository for government records for England and Wales.
Ruskin Avenue, Kew
Surrey TW9 4DU
020 8876 3444
Use contact form on website for email.

***The Scotsman* newspaper**
archive.scotsman.com
Online editions of The Scotsman *newspaper from 1817 to 1950.*

***The Times* online**
timesonline.co.uk
The Times *newspaper online.*

Traceline
gro.gov.uk/gro/content/research/traceline
Section of the main GRO site, dedicated to re-establishing contact between lost family members or friends.

Type Pad
typepad.com
Blog site.

UK BMD
ukbmd.org.uk
List of websites showing transcriptions of civil registration documents.

UKReg
ukreg.com
Website for purchasing and registering domain names.

Ulster Historical Foundation
ancestryireland.com
Northern Irish genealogy site with access to historical trade directories.
Cotton Court, 30 Waring Street
Dublin BT1 2ED
Republic of Ireland
028 90 332288
enquiry@uhf.org.uk

United States of America National Archives
archives.gov/contact
Archives and Records Administration
8601 Adelphi Road
College Park
MD 20740-6001

V&A Museum of Childhood
vam.ac.uk/moc
Cambridge Heath Road
London E2 9PA
020 8983 5200
moc@vam.ac.uk

Veterans' History Project
loc.gov/vets
Library of Congress site for US war veterans.
American Folklife Center
101 Independence Ave, SE
Washington DC 20540-4615
00 1 202 707 4916
vohp@loc.gov

Veterans-UK
veterans-uk.info
Website for tracing war veterans and for putting lost comrades in touch.

Victoria and Albert Museum (V&A)
vam.ac.uk
Cromwell Road
South Kensington
London SW7 2RL
020 7942 2000
vanda@vam.ac.uk

Victoria County History
victoriacountyhistory.ac.uk
An encyclopaedic record of England's places and people.

Vision of Britain
visionofbritain.org.uk
A list of statistics, maps and information for local history.

Warwickshire County Record Office
warwickshire.gov.uk *Enter 'County record office' in* Search *box.*
Cape Road
Warwick CV34 4JS
01926 738959
recordoffice@warwickshire.gov.uk

Wellcome Library
library.wellcome.ac.uk
Books, manuscripts, archives, films and pictures on the history of medicine.
183 Euston Road
London NW1 2BE
020 7611 8348
Use contact form on website for email.

Wesley Historical Society Library
wesleyhistoricalsociety.org.uk/library.htm
Large collection of Methodist information.
Wesley Centre
Oxford Brookes University
Westminster Institute of Education
Harcourt Hill, Oxford OX2 9AT
01865 488319
wco.archives@brookes.ac.uk

West Sussex Record Office
westsussex.gov.uk *Click on* Libraries and archives.
3 Orchard Street, Chichester
West Sussex PO19 1RN
Correspondence address:
County Archivist
West Sussex Record Office
County Hall, Chichester
West Sussex PO19 1RN
01243 753600
records.office@westsussex.gov.uk

West Yorkshire Archive Service
archives.wyjs.org.uk
Registry of Deeds
Newstead Road
Wakefield WF1 2DE
01924 305980
archives@wyjs.org.uk

Wiltshire and Swindon History Centre
heritageadmin@wiltshire.gov.uk
Cocklebury Road
Chippenham
Wiltshire SN15 3QN
01249 705500
wsro@wiltshire.gov.uk

Women's Library
londonnet.ac.uk/thewomenslibrary
Most extensive collection of women's history in the UK.
London Metropolitan University
25 Old Castle Street
London E1 7NT
020 7320 2222
moreinfo@thewomenslibrary.ac.uk

Worcestershire Record Office
worcestershire.gov.uk/records
County Hall
Spetchley Road
Worcester WR5 2NP
01905 766351
RecordOffice@worcestershire.gov.uk

Workhouses
workhouses.org.uk
Site dedicated to the history of workhouses.

Xara
xara.com/products/webstyle
Web graphics website.

Yell
yell.com
Directory of listed businesses.

York City Archives
york.gov.uk *Click on* Leisure, *then* Libraries, *then* York City archives.
Records and documents covering 500 years of life in York.
Art Gallery Building
Exhibition Square
York YO1 7EW
01904 551878
archives@york.gov.uk

Yorkshire Record Offices and Archives
See East Riding of Yorkshire Archives, North Yorkshire County Record Office *or* West Yorkshire Archive Service.

You Tube
youtube.com
Social networking site.

Zone Alarm
zonealarm.com
Online store for PC security packages.

Index

Page numbers displayed in **bold** type indicate main entries.
Numbers in *italic* refer to illustrations and their captions.

BIRTH CERTIFICATES

C

CENSUSES

D

DEATH CERTIFICATES

H

I

INTERNET

N

THE NATIONAL ARCHIVES

U

V

W

Acknowledgments

l = left, **r** = right, **t** = top, **c** = centre, **b** = bottom

10 © Reader's Digest **14** Manchester Jewish Museum **16** The National Archives **18-19** Museum of English Rural Life, University of Reading **20** Betty Loving **21** © Reader's Digest **22** Sarah Snape; Anne Snape/UK Passport Service © Crown copyright material is reproduced with the permission of the Controller of HMSO and Queen's Printer for Scotland; David Halford (medal) **23** Imperial War Museum **24** Anne Snape **25** (l) Museum of English Rural Life, University of Reading (r) Sarah Snape **28** (t) Sarah Snape/Office for National Statistics © Crown copyright material is reproduced with the permission of the Controller of HMSO and Queen's Printer for Scotland (b) The National Archives **29** Anne Snape **30** (t) Felicity Cheetham (b) © Reader's Digest **32** © Reader's Digest **32** (inset) The National Archives **33** (tl) The National Archives (cl) Getty Images (br) The National Archives **34** Getty Images; Digital Vision **35** Jaakko Avikainen/Rex Features **36** (t) Calico Pie (b) ancestry.co.uk **37** Sudeley Castle, Winchcombe, Gloucestershire/Bridgeman Art Library **41** © Reader's Digest **42** (l) © Reader's Digest (r) The National Archives **45** (l) Anne Snape (r) Mary Evans Picture Library **48-49** The National Archives **49** (l) The National Archives (r) Getty Images **51** The National Archives **52** Art Archive **53** Art Archive/ Bradford City Art Gallery/Eileen Tweedy **55** Museum of London **56** Reproduced with the kind permission of the Registrar General for Scotland **57** The National Archives **58** Mary Evans Picture Library **59** Angelo Hornak Photo Library **60** AKG Images/British Library **61** Royal Geographical Society **62** Courtesy of Cardiff Council Libraries and Information Services **64-65** Art Archive/Collegio del Cambio, Perugia/Dagli Orti **65** (b) The National Archives **65** (inset) AKG Images **66** Museum of English Rural Life, University of Reading **69** Pauline Brooker **72** Private Collection © Christopher Wood Gallery, London/Bridgeman Art Library **73** Michael McLellan/Office for National Statistics © Crown copyright material is reproduced with the permission of the Controller of HMSO and Queen's Printer for Scotland **74** Mary Evans Picture Library **75-77** Felicity Cheetham/Office for National Statistics © Crown copyright material is reproduced with the permission of the Controller of HMSO and Queen's Printer for Scotland **78** © Reader's Digest **79** Getty Images **80** Anne Snape **81** Getty Images **82** The National Archives **83** (l) The Times (r) Anne Snape/Office for National Statistics © Crown copyright material is reproduced with the permission of the Controller of HMSO and Queen's Printer for Scotland **85** National Maritime Museum **87** Mary Evans Picture Library **88** Jill Steed **91** Museum of London **93** Anne Snape **95** ©Reader's Digest **96** Popperfoto **97-9** Reproduced with the kind permission of the Registrar General for Scotland **100** www.flyleaf.ie **101** Courtesy of the National Library of Ireland **102** Museum of English Rural Life, University of Reading **103** (r) Art Archive/John Meek (t) Mary Evans Picture Library **104** Museum of English Rural Life, University of Reading **105** The National Archives **108** (c) AKG Images/Archie Miles (b) The National Archives **108-9** Mary Evans Picture Library **110** Museum of English Rural Life, University of Reading **111** The National Archives **113** Museum of English Rural Life, University of Reading **115** Mary Evans Picture Library **116** Museum of London **119** Helen Holmes **121** (t) The National Archives (b) Guildhall Library, City of London **123** (r) Mo Wilson/ Photofusion **125** Mary Evans Picture Library **127** Courtesy of the National Library of Ireland **129** (t) Betty Loving (bl) Felicity Cheetham/Office for National Statistics © Crown copyright material is reproduced with the permission of the Controller of HMSO and Queen's Printer for Scotland (bc & br) The National Archives **130-1** Getty Images **130** British Red Cross Museum and Archives **132** © Croydon Art Collection, Museum of Croydon/Bridgeman Art Library **133** (t) David Halford/by kind permission of the Vicar and Churchwardens of St John the Baptist (Croydon Parish Church) and the Surrey History Centre (b) © Collection of the Earl of Pembroke, Wilton House, Wiltshire/ Bridgeman Art Library **134** Christie's Images **135** The National Archives **136** Private Collection, The Stapleton Collection/Bridgeman Art Library **137** David Halford/by kind permission of the Vicar and Churchwardens of the United Benefice of St Martin's Church, Dorking with St Barnabas, Ranmore, and the Surrey History Centre **139** Mary Evans Picture Library **141** © Manchester Art Gallery/ Bridgeman Art Library **142** © Bonhams, London/Bridgeman Art Library **144** Getty Images **145** Roy Miles Fine Paintings/Bridgeman Art Library **146** NTPL/Andreas von Einsiedel **147-9** Mary Evans Picture Library **152** © Reader's Digest **155** Inventory and Valuation for Probate, 1947 (oil on canvas), Elwell, Frederick William (1870-1958)/© Russell-Cotes Art Gallery and Museum, Bournemouth / The Bridgeman Art Library **156** Private Collection/Bridgeman Art Library **158** Private Collection, Photo © Christies Images/Bridgeman Art Library **162** The National Archives **164** Scottish Viewpoint **166** Istock **169** (t) Ms 313, Manuscripts and Special Collections, The University of Nottingham (inset) Boots "The BOOTS™ word and BOOTS script oval are trade marks of The Boots Company plc" **170** Beamish Photographic Archive, County Durham **173** Lord Montagu of Beaulieu **176** The National Archives **178** Popperfoto **179** The National Archives **180** Mary Evans Picture Library **181** Yale Center for British Art, Paul Mellon Collection, USA/Bridgeman Art Library **182** Anne Snape **184** By courtesy of The Worshipful Company of Gardeners **184** London Stills **185** © 2007 Gerald Sharp Photography **187** Mary Evans Picture Library **188** Popperfoto **191** Museum of English Rural Life, University of Reading **192** © Malcolm Innes Gallery, London/ Bridgeman Art Library **194** Imperial War Museum **194-5** Corbis **196** Mary Evans Picture Library **199** Popperfoto **200** (l) © Reader's Digest Association (r) Imperial War Museum **201** Rex/Paul Webb **202** Lincoln's Inn, London/Bridgeman Art Library **203** Mary Evans Picture Library **204** www.oldbaileyonline.org/Courtesy of Special Collections Department, Harvard Law School Library **204-5** Steve Cotton/artofthestate.co.uk **205** (l) Mary Evans Picture Library (r) Getty Images **206-7** Mary Evans Picture Library **208** (l) The National Archives (r) Mary Evans Picture Library **210** Mary Evans Picture Library **211** The National Archives **213** (t) London Metropolitan Archives (b) Manchester Library and Information Services **214-6** Mary Evans Picture Library **217** Popperfoto **219** Mary Evans Picture Library **220** Popperfoto **222** (t) The National Archives **222-3** AKG Images/Eric Lessing **223** (l) Art Archive/British Library (r) Last Refuge/Adrian Warren **225** Paul Booth Photography **227-32** Mary Evans Picture Library **234** Anne Snape **236-7** Mary Evans Picture Library **242** The National Archives **244-6** Mary Evans Picture Library **247** (t) David Gibson/Photofusion (b) Jewish Museum, London **249** Corbis **250** Getty Images **252** Popperfoto **254** Art Archive/Mitchell Library, Sydney **254-7** Mary Evans Picture Library**258** (l) Angelo Hornak Photo Library (inset) Corbis **259** (l) The Statue of Liberty-Ellis Island Foundation, Inc. and www.ellisisland.org and www.wallofhonor.org (r) Getty Images **261** Mary Evans Picture Library **262** Digital Vision **267-8** Mary Evans Picture Library **269** (t) Michael McLellan/Office for National Statistics © Crown copyright material is reproduced with the permission of the Controller of HMSO and Queen's Printer for Scotland (c) Anne Snape (b) Anne Snape/ The National Archives **273** © Reader's Digest **280** Mary Evans Picture Library **285** WI Archives **287** Mary Evans Picture Library **290** Corbis **291-4** Mary Evans Picture Library **298** Bridgeman Art Library/Jane Austen House, Chawton, Hampshire **299** (t) The Foundling Museum, London/ Bridgeman Art Library (b) © Coram Family in the care of the Foundling Museum **300** Popperfoto **302** iStock **303** Mary Evans Picture Library **304** Shutterstock **311** Mary Evans Picture Library **316** Royal Society of Arts, London/Bridgeman Art Library

How to trace your family history on the internet was published by The Reader's Digest Association Limited, London.

We are committed both to the quality of our products and the service we provide to our customers. We value your comments, so please do contact us on **08705 113366** or via our website at **www.readersdigest.co.uk**

If you have any comments or suggestions about the content of our books, email us at **gbeditorial@readersdigest.co.uk**

Concept Code UK2142/IC
Book Code 400-321 UP0000-1
ISBN 978 0 276 44270 4
Oracle Code 250011344H.00.24

How to trace your family history on the internet was created for Reader's Digest by Amazon Publishing Limited
7 Old Lodge Place, Twickenham TW1 1RQ.

Chief consultant

Nick Barratt
Dr Nick Barratt is one of Britain's best-known experts on family history – a regular face and voice on TV and radio, and a weekly columnist for *The Daily Telegraph*. His broadcasting credits as researcher, adviser and presenter include the Radio 4 series *Tracing Your Roots* and the TV programmes *House Detectives*, *Hidden House History*, *So You Think You're Royal?* and the triple BAFTA-nominated *Who Do You Think You Are?*. Among Nick's publications are *Tracing the History of Your House* and *The Family Detective*.

Contributors
Sarah Newbery, Sara Khan, Laura Berry
James Higgins, Freya Beales

For Amazon Publishing

Editors
Jill Steed, Helen Spence, Celia Coyne
Jackie Matthews

Technical editor
Tony Rilett

Genealogy consultant
Peter Christian

Picture research
Elizabeth Loving, Nicoletta Flessati

Editorial assistant
Kate Overy

Designers
Colin Goody, Murdo Culver, Stuart Perry

Special photography
David Murphy

Proofreader
Barry Gage

Indexer
Hilary Bird

For Reader's Digest

Project editor
John Andrews

Art editor
Julie Bennett

Editorial director
Julian Browne

Art director
Anne-Marie Bulat

Head of book development
Sarah Bloxham

Managing editor
Nina Hathway

Picture resource manager
Sarah Stewart-Richardson

Pre-press account manager
Penny Grose

Product production manager
Claudette Bramble

Senior production controller
Deborah Trott

Origination
Colour Systems Limited, London

Printing and binding
MOHN Media, Germany